GLOBAL
CORPORATE
FINANCE
A Focused Approach

Fourth Edition

GLOBAL CORPORATE FINANCE

A Focused Approach

Fourth Edition

Suk H. Kim
University of Detroit Mercy, USA

World Scientific

NEW JERSEY · LONDON · SINGAPORE · BEIJING · SHANGHAI · HONG KONG · TAIPEI · CHENNAI · TOKYO

Published by

World Scientific Publishing Co. Pte. Ltd.

5 Toh Tuck Link, Singapore 596224

USA office: 27 Warren Street, Suite 401-402, Hackensack, NJ 07601

UK office: 57 Shelton Street, Covent Garden, London WC2H 9HE

Library of Congress Cataloging-in-Publication Data

Names: Kim, Suk H., author.
Title: Global corporate finance : a focused approach / Suk H Kim, University of Detroit Mercy, USA.
Description: Fourth Edition. | New Jersey : World scientific, [2024] |
    Revised edition of Global corporate finance, 2019.
Identifiers: LCCN 2023037527 | ISBN 9789811281952 (hardcover) | ISBN 9789811281969 (ebook) |
    ISBN 9789811281976 (ebook other)
Subjects: LCSH: International business enterprises--Finance. | Corporations--Finance. | International finance.
Classification: LCC HG4027.5 .K555 2024 | DDC 658.15/99--dc23/eng/20230810
LC record available at https://lccn.loc.gov/2023037527

British Library Cataloguing-in-Publication Data
A catalogue record for this book is available from the British Library.

For any available supplementary material, please visit
https://www.worldscientific.com/worldscibooks/10.1142/13559#t=suppl

Desk Editors: Sanjay Varadharajan/Pui Yee Lum

Typeset by Stallion Press
Email: enquiries@stallionpress.com

Printed in Singapore

CURRENCIES OF THE WORLD

Country/Currency	ISO Code	Symbol	in US$	Per US$
Americas				
Argentina peso	ARS		0.00554	180.386
Brazil real	BRL	R$	0.192197	5.20094
Canada dollar	CAD	$	0.744202	1.34377
Chile peso	CLP	$	0.0012	827.06
Colombia peso	COP	Col$	0.0002091	4782.68
Ecuador US dollar		$	1	1
Mexico peso	MXN	$	0.0524735	19.0572
Peru new sol	PEN	S/.	0.2633936	3.7966
Uruguay peso	UYU	$U	0.0251003	39.8393
Venezuela bolivar	VEB	BS	0.538417	18.573
Asia-Pacific				
Australian dollar	AUD	$	0.688991	1.45124
1-mos forward			0.69023	
3-mos forward			0.69182	
6-mos forward			0.69415	
China yuan	CNY	¥	0.147346	6.78675
Hong Kong dollar	HKD	HK$	0.128009	7.81229
India rupee	INR	₹	0.0122416	81.6885
Indonesia rupiah	IDR	Rp	6.426E-05	15561.9
Japan yen	JPY	¥	0.00744343	132.39
1-mos forward				132.411
3-mos forward				132.4
6-mos forward				132.383
Malaysia ringgit	MYR	RM	0.228261	4.37405
New Zealand dollar	NZD	NRs	0.637271	1.56919
Pakistan rupee	PKR	Rs.	0.004376	228.521
Philippines peso	PHP	₱	0.018183	54.9964
Singapore dollar	SGD	S$	0.750634	1.33221
South Korea won			0.0008012	1248.19
Taiwan dollar	TWD	NT$	0.0328556	30.4362
Thailand baht	THB	฿	0.0297624	33.5909
Vietnam dong	VND	đ	4.265E-05	23445.8

(Continued)

(Continued)

Country/Currency	ISO Code	Symbol	in US$	Per US$
Europe				
Czech Rep. koruna	CZK	Kč	0.0447695	22.3366
Denmark krone	DKK	Kr	0.144325	6.92879
Euro area euro			1.07315	0.931836
Hungary forint	HUF	Ft	0.144325	371.344
Norway krone	NOK		0.100104	9.98956
Poland zloty	PLN		0.228726	4.37205
Romania leu	RON	L	0.217542	4.59682
Russia ruble	RUB	R	0.0143526	69.6737
Sweden krona	SEK	kr	0.0959506	10.422
Switzerland franc	CHF	Fr.	1.08315	0.923172
1-mos forward				0.91978
3-mos forward				0.91395
6-mos forward				0.90514
Turkey lira	TRY	YTL	0.0532527	18.7784
UK pound	GBP	£	1.21467	0.823266
1-mos forward			1.21708	
3-mos forward			1.21899	
6-mos forward			1.22088	
Middle East/Africa				
Bahrain dinar	BHD		2.65957	0.376
Egypt pound	EGP	£	0.036136	27.6735
Israel shekel	ILS		0.288596	3.46473
Jordan dinar	JOD		1.41044	0.709
Kenya shilling	KES	KSh	0.0080814	123.741
Kuwait dinar	KWD		3.26777	0.306019
Lebanon pound	LBP		0.0006634	1507.5
Saudi Arabia riyal	SAR	SR	0.266667	3.75
South Africa rand	ZAR	R	0.0587165	17.031
UAE dirham	AED		0.272294	3.6725
				Close
WSJ Dollar Index				96.2

Note: *Obtained exchange rates, currency symbols, currency codes on January 10, 2023.

PREFACE

SOLID FOUNDATION

I taught international finance courses, for the first time in my life, at the University of Detroit Mercy in 1978. Ever since then, my dream has been writing a book with a solid foundation for undergraduate and graduate students in international finance courses offered by both the department of finance and by the department of economics. By the solid foundation, I mean a straightforward textbook with real-world examples from reliable sources of practical information, such as the *Wall Steet Journal* and Investopedia. Investopedia is the world's leading source of financial content on the web. I hope that this 4th edition of *Global Corporate Finance: A Focused Approach (GCF4)* is the kind of book that global-finance watchers have been looking for years.

Tiger Woods, who is called the emperor of golf by people around the world, sometimes, falls into a slump and he does not get a good score. In an interview with a golf journal at one time, he was asked to give "just one piece of advice for people in a slump." His response was "go back to the basics." In order to correct these artificial and wrong habits and get out of the slump, you need to go back to the basics and have a basic framework. He continued, "When I fall into a slump, the first thing I do is to check my fundamental or basic skills." Whether it is golf or study, it is true that the speed of development is accelerated if you have the basic skills.

The GCF4 is suitable for appropriate courses, no matter where in the world it is taught, because it does not adopt any specific national viewpoint. Moreover, it is self-contained, and it combines theory and applications. The earlier editions of the GCF4 have been adopted by many colleges, universities, and management development programs worldwide, particularly because the book stresses practical applications in a user-friendly format.

TO STUDENTS AND NOVI PRACTITIONERS

If you look back on your life 30 or 40 years from now on, you will find that those things you obtained during your college days shaped your entire life and career. College is often described as the best few years of your life. A heady time to learn and grow, to experience and experiment, and to "find yourself" and forge your future. In other words, your knowledge, work ethics, and life-time friends you attained during such a heady time will be with you during good times and bad times throughout your life. Even more importantly, nobody can take them away from you.

In this book, I stressed fundamental concepts and theories with an emphasis on understanding how things work in the real world. I can confidently say that the GCF4 will provide you with a strong foundation you need to jump toward a better tomorrow. In fact, I believe that you will keep this book as a useful reference after you complete the course.

TO PROFESSORS

The 4th edition of *Global Corporate Finance: A Focused Approach* introduces students and practitioners to those principles essential to the understanding of global financial problems and the policies that global business managers contend with. The objective of this book is to equip current and future business leaders with the tools they need to interpret the issues, to make sound global financial decisions, and to manage the wide variety of risks that modern businesses face in a competitive global environment. In line with its objective, the book stresses practical applications in a concise and straightforward manner, without a complex treatment of theoretical concepts.

Instructors who want students to possess practical, job-oriented skills in international finance will find the GCF4 ideal for their needs. Corporate recruiters often criticize business schools for turning out graduates who cannot contribute immediately. At the core of this criticism is the belief that, while students are educated in various theories, little emphasis is placed on developing practical skills. For that reason, I was especially careful that such criticism would not apply to those who adopt this book that aims at developing students' skills in international finance. This book is suitable for both undergraduate- and graduate-level courses in international finance offered by both the department of finance and the department of economics. This book is clearly the "go-to" book on one most important aspect of corporate finance.

PEDAGOGICAL FEATURES

For ease of learning, each chapter of the GCF4 follows a common format:

- At the beginning of each chapter, a mini case is provided to achieve two objectives: (1) to build student interest with regard to the upcoming chapter and (2) to introduce a real-world example that will be explained further by theories and research findings presented in the chapter.
- The introductory mini case is followed by a chapter overview, which describes the chapter themes and the content of the major sections.
- Real-world illustrations, numerical examples, figures, tables, and global finance in practice are integrated throughout the text to clarify discussions of financial concepts and techniques.
- Key terms lists at the end of each chapter contain the essential terms found in the chapter. These terms are presented in bold type the first time they appear in the text.
- A short summary provides students with a handy overview of key concepts for review.
- A number of end-of-chapter problems support text discussions; they reemphasize definitions, concepts, and the application of theory.
- An analytic mini case concludes each chapter. The closing case problems serve a different purpose from the opening ones. They present situations for which students must analyze

possible actions on the basis of what they have learned in the chapter. In other words, the opening cases enhance interest and recall essential facts; the closing case problems enhance the development of critical reasoning skills. Moreover, Internet exercises have been added at the end of each case problem, to explain how the Internet may be used to access international financial data and obtain information on the case concepts.

THE UNDERLYING PHILOSOPHY

Corporate Performance of Foreign Operations: Overall, this book explores two questions, why do companies increase profits as they boost their foreign presence and fare far more successfully than domestic firms? By extending the exploration of these questions into detailed operations and strategies, students learn the successful concepts and techniques of multinational firms. For example, students are introduced to seven key principles of global finance in Chapter 1. Only then can they grasp the platform on which multinational firms build their strategic plans and, at the same time, readers can sharply define the limited outlook of domestic companies that operate without these seven principles. The GCF4 relentlessly pursues the techniques and concepts that boost the performance of global companies until, almost as if second nature, students can pinpoint the formula of growth in foreign markets. Then I conclude this book by discussing how multinational companies can use international accounting, taxation, and transfer pricing to improve their overall performance even further. That is why I am confident that this book will enable students to develop requisite skills in international finance which are essential to improve corporate performance through foreign operations.

Shareholder Value and Corporate Governance: The GCF4 treats shareholder value and effective corporate governance as its foundation. Why? Maximizing shareholder value through effective corporate governance is the best way to strengthen the welfare of all corporate constituents. Stockholders are the owners of the company, and they supply risk capital that protects the welfare of other constituents. Thanks to them, a higher stock price makes it easier for a company to attract additional equity capital. For multinational companies with operations all over the world, effective corporate governance will be especially crucial to their success.

Global Strategy: To be competitive in the new economy, which is characterized by information revolution and global competition, companies need to think globally. Thus, this book emphasizes global strategy to equip readers with fresh ideas and concepts for successful global operations.

Emphasis on the Basics: I believe that students learn most effectively when they first achieve a firm grasp of basics. To stress basics, I initially devoted several chapters to the fundamental concepts of international finance. Once students learn the basics, the advanced material will flow naturally for them. As more advanced topics are developed in later chapters, I tie this material to the fundamentals, stressed earlier in the text, in order to facilitate the learning process and to provide students with the big picture.

User-Friendliness: This book builds on knowledge derived from basic courses in economics and corporate finance. All traditional areas of corporate finance are explored, but from the viewpoint of global financial managers. Tables, figures, and numerical examples clarify discussions of financial concepts and techniques. All end-of-chapter problems are tied or keyed to major topics presented in the chapter. Answers to most end-of-chapter problems are found at the end of the text. In addition to that, I have made extra effort to clearly define all key terms. This book also provides a quick reference glossary with 400 key terms.

Readability: This book is readable and easy to understand because it discusses the basic tools and techniques of global finance without a complex treatment of theoretical concepts. Students become frustrated when they have to study mathematical formulas without corresponding numerical examples. Practically all of the formulas used in this book are accompanied by practical, but straightforward, numerical examples. I emphasize readability because I believe that it will motivate readers to pursue further knowledge in international finance.

A HIGHLY COMPETITIVE SET OF SUPPLEMENTS

A highly completive set of supplements consists of a complete set of ancillary materials which include an Instructor's Manual, a test bank of 700 objective questions, two sets of PowerPoint lecture notes, detailed Word lecture notes and chapter outlines for students. This rich array of support materials for the instructor, prepared by the author, is available online.

Instructor's Manual: The Instructor's Manual includes chapter outlines, chapter objectives, key terms with definitions, and solutions to all end-of-chapter problems.

The Test Bank: The test bank contains 700 objective questions (true or false questions plus multiple choice questions). It includes detailed solutions to all problem multiple choice questions, thereby making it easier for the instructor to check computation results for accuracy and for the instructor to use them as subjective problem questions.

PowerPoint Lecture Notes: Two sets of PowerPoint lecture notes provide lecture outlines and key figures & tables from the text. Detailed PowerPoint slides prepared by the author strictly follow the text; it contains lecture outlines and important figures & tables from the text for each chapter. The other PowerPoint slides do not necessarily follow the text, include some topics not in the text, and are accompanied by separate, detailed Word lecture notes.

Chapter Outlines for Students: Chapter outlines for students include chapter outlines (the list of subtopics), chapter objectives, and key terms with definitions.

AUDIENCE FOR THE BOOK

1. Those college students who want to lay a strong foundation for their future successes.
2. Those novice practitioners who want to build up their knowledge about global finance for a jump toward a better tomorrow.
3. Those managers who want to refresh their knowledge about global finance.
4. College and university libraries.
5. Management/executive training programs.
6. Those who want to become a better-informed citizen about globalization.
7. Those who want to translate the book into any language other than English.

CHANGES TO GCF IN THE 4TH EDITION

All chapters in the 4th Edition have been updated to include new materials, eliminate unnecessary-outdated materials, and include more non-US materials. I have applied what I call a **complete revision** for GCF4; that is, planning anew rather than simply adding on to what we had already written. This approach has undoubtedly helped me to avoid two problems: I have not overlooked important changes in international finance. And, I have not unnecessarily increased the length of the book.

1. Each chapter contains the following four new items: an opening mini case, a "global finance in practice" example (here, examples from the real-world will be used to illustrate chapter concepts), a list of key terms at the end of each chapter, and a closing mini case.
2. Global Finance in Practice 2.2 uses the Hyundai Motor Group (Hyundai-Kia) as a real-world example of the product life cycle theory. The world's top three automakers by sales in 2022 included (1) Toyota, (2) Volkswagen, and (3) Hyundai-Kia. The theory, however, states that Hyundai-Kia is likely to lose its top three position unless it fails to adopt successful market-creating innovations. To find and sustain such innovations, it requires talent acquisition and self-motivation of its employees.
3. The opening case of Chapter 2 discusses Brexit (i.e., Britain's exit from the European Union (EU)), along with its negative consequences. The United Kingdom (UK) had five prime ministers in six years since the UK's 2016 decision to leave the EU, thereby creating a lot of economic and social problems for the UK and for the EU. Chapter 3 discusses the replacement of LIBOR with SOFR on June 20, 2023. Eurobanks and other banks around the world established their lending rates at some fixed percentage above the six-month London Interbank Offered Rate for decades. The London Interbank Offered Rate (LIBOR) is a benchmark interest rate at which major global banks lent to one another in the international interbank market for short-term loans. However, on June 30, 2023, LIBOR was replaced by the Secured Overnight Financing Rate (SOFR), which represented a negative consequence of Brexit. The Secured Overnight Financing Rate is an influential interest rate that banks use to price US dollar denominated derivatives and loans. The SOFR is based on transactions in the US. Treasury repurchase market, where investors offer banks overnight loans backed by their bonds. This and other negative consequences for the UK from the Brexit remind us of an old saying: "If we stick together, we live, if we break, we die."
4. GCF4 discusses more concepts (theories) with practitioner-oriented data. For example, the new edition discusses the balance of payments in Chapter 3 with real data from the three largest economies in the world by GDP (PPP): India, China, and the US.
5. GCF4 discusses economic implications of the Russia-Ukraine War in several chapters. For example, Chapter 9 has the following information. The SWIFT ban against some Russian banks was one of the sanctions against Russia imposed by the European Union and other western countries after Russia invaded Ukraine on February 24, 2022. This ban aimed at weakening the country's economy, to end its invasion of Ukraine by hindering Russian access to the SWIFT financial transaction processing system. According to the Russian National SWIFT Association, around 300 banks used SWIFT in Russia, with more than half of Russian credit institutions represented in SWIFT. Russia used to

have the second highest userbase after the US. Since SWIFT excluded Russia from its use, however, Russian interbank payment transactions have become significantly more complex. In addition, the country's ability to trade goods and exchange currencies have been significantly reduced, making payment only possible in cash, ruble, and Chinese yuan.

6. Many view that US–China relations are poised more for international conflict than for international cooperation because they manifest the west-east divide based on the divergence between market-oriented countries and socialist countries. However, this book questions this widely held view because their growing mutual economic dependence has compelled them to work together for their economic benefits. US–China trade has exploded in the two decades since China joined the WTO in 2001. This trade and other economic cooperation have benefited both US and Chinese consumers and companies. Americans and Chinese will continue to doubt and criticize the intentions and policies of each other's government in a variety of areas, but they will still work quietly together in areas that are mutually beneficial. A number of chapters have discussed such relationships between the US and China.

7. Chapter 9 discusses the failure of the Silicon Valley Bank (SVB) on March 10, 2023 and the reason for the failure. The bank failed because SVB violated the so-called matching principle. This principle says that the firm should match the maturity structure of its assets with its liabilities and equity. SVA almost doubled its assets and deposits during 2021. It got in trouble because it bought long-term, low-yielding bonds with short-term funding from depositors that was repayable upon demand.

8. Chapter 10 lists a number of things that happened to Russia after it invaded Ukraine.

   - Russia turns to the Chinese currency (yuan) amid sanctions.
   - Moscow becomes the number four offshore trading center for yuan.
   - Yuan's share of Russian foreign exchange market jumps from 1 to 45 percent.

9. Chapter 13 discusses the cost of capital with real-world examples. Every industry has its own prevailing average cost of capital. The numbers vary widely. Homebuilding has a relatively high cost of capital, at 6.35 percent, according to data from New York University's Stern School of Business. The cost of capital for retail grocery business is relatively low, at 1.98 percent. The cost of capital is also high among both biotech and pharmaceutical drug companies, steel manufacturers, internet software companies, and integrated oil and gas companies. Those industries tend to require significant capital investment in research and development, equipment, and factories. Among the industries with lower capital costs are money center banks, power companies, real estate investment trusts (REITs), and utilities (both general and water). Such companies may require less equipment or may benefit from very steady cash flows.

10. Chapter 15 lists the US actions of 2022 and 2021 against those firms which violated the Foreign Corrupt Practice Act (FCPA). Enforcement of the FCPA continues to be a high priority area for the Securities and Exchange Commission (SEC). In 2010, the SEC's Enforcement Division created a specialized unit to further enhance its enforcement of the FCPA, which prohibits companies issuing stock in the US from bribing foreign officials for government contracts and other business.

I respectfully request the readers of this fourth edition to email me at stevekim1942@gmail.com if you have any constructive comments for the next edition of the book.

ACKNOWLEDGMENTS

Many colleagues have provided constructure advice critical to the successful development of the GCF4. Our special thanks go to a number of manuscript reviewers for detailed suggestions for this edition in a response to the authors' request for review: Hong Qian (Oakland University) Bahman Mirshab (Lawrence Technological University, John N. Kallianiotis (The University of Scranton), Suk Hun Lee (Loyal University Chicago), Min Xu (The University of Detroit Mercy), and Kenneth Kim (The State University of New York at Buffalo). I am also grateful to Donald Smith (The University of Detroit Mercy) and Kevin Raju (The University of Detroit Mercy) for developing a study guide — Chapter Outlines for Students — to complement this book. Several staff members of World Scientific Publishing deserve special acknowledgement because they have made many valuable contributions to this edition: Pui Yee Lum, Lee Hooi Yean, Juliet Lee, Lixi Dong, Helen K., Sanjay Varadharajan, Nandha Kumar Krishnan, and others.

Both the author and the publisher acknowledge that the following eight articles from *The Wall Street Journal* are used with permission of Dow Jones & Co., Inc and permission was conveyed through Copyright Clearance Centre, Inc.

1. Al Mayadeen English, Stephen Wilmot, "Global Trading Is Shifting, Not Reversing," *The Wall Street Journal*, January 3, 2023, p. A10.
2. Max Colchester and David Luhnow, "Rishi Sunak Becomes U.K. Prime Minister Amid Economic, Political Crisis," *The Wall Street Journal*, October 25, 2022.
3. Chelsey Dulaney and Caitlin McCabe, "How Low Can the Euro Go?" *The Wall Street Journal*, July 8, 2022.
4. Mitchell Pacelle and Daniel Pear, "How Currency Trading Run Amok Crushed a Family," *The Wall Street Journal*, April 8, 1999, pp. C1, C13.
5. The Editorial Board, "A New Financial Threat Emerges in Foreign-Exchange Swaps," *The Wall Street Journal*, December 9, 2022.
6. Nina Trentmann, "CEOs Boost Current Protections, Extend Hedge Contracts as a Strong Dollar Take Toll," *The Wall Street Journal*, November 7, 2022.
7. Jing Yang, "Hong Kong Exchange Seeks to Lure Global Companies," *The Wall Street Journal*, January 5, 2023, p. A11.
8. "Money Rates," *The Wall Street Journal*, January 20, 2023.

The author and the publisher apologize for any errors or omissions in the above list and would be grateful to be notified of any corrections that should be incorporated in the next edition or reprint of this book.

ABOUT THE AUTHOR

 **Suk H. Kim** is an internationally known scholar and author, Dr. Kim has published research monographs, college textbooks, and peer-reviewed journal articles. According to an article by Allen Morrison and Andrew Ipken (*Journal of International Business Studies*, First Quarter, 1991, pp. 143–153), he was among the top 26 international business researchers in the world during the 1980s. His practical-oriented articles have appeared in some top journals such as *The Journal of International Business Studies*, *The Columbia Journal of World Business* (now the *Journal of World Business*), *Management Accounting* (now *Strategic Finance*), the *Journal of Financial Education*, and several others. In addition, Dr. Kim was the founding editor of the two prestigious academic journals: *Multinational Business Review* (*MBR*: 1992–2002) and *North Korean Review* (*NKR*: 2005–2013). For eight years from 2005 to 2013 as the founder-editor of *North Korean Review*, he raised more than $100.000 for NKR and other academic activities about North Korea.

In 1992, Dr. Kim visited Yonsei University in Seoul, South Korea as a Fulbright Scholar and taught international finance for graduate students. He has also held short-term teaching or research appointments at the University of Hawaii at Manoa, the Scott Airforce Base in Illinois, Central Michigan University, Eastern Michigan University, Fort Hays State University (in Hays, Kansas) Yonsei University in South Korea, Fu Jung Catholic University in Taipei, Taiwan, the Bank of Korea in Seoul, South Korea, and other institutions. In addition, he has served on editorial review board members for a considerable number of academic journals here in the United States and abroad.

Dr. Kim received the Distinguished Faculty Award from the University of Detroit Mercy in 2003, the Global Korea Award from Michigan State University in 2008, a 45 years of service award from the University of Detroit Mercy in 2023, and other awards for excellence in teaching and research. He received his Ph.D. in Business Administration from Saint Louis University, his MBA from Pepperdine University, his Master of Arts in Economics from Yonsei University in South Korea, and his Bachelor of Arts in Economics from Soongsil University in South Korea. American missionaries founded Yonsei University on April 10, 1885 and Soongsil University on October 10, 1897.

CONTENTS

PART ONE
THE GLOBAL FINANCIAL ENVIRONMENT

Part One of this book (Chapters 1–3) presents an overview of the global financial environment. Chapter 1 develops the goal of the multinational company to be used in the financial decision-making process and examines the role of global finance in achieving this goal. Chapter 2 examines motives for world trade and foreign investment. Before considering foreign trade and foreign investment separately in the coming chapters, we will discuss key trade and investment theories in this chapter. Chapter 3 describes the balance of payments and the international monetary system.

Chapter 1

GLOBALIZATION AND THE GLOBAL COMPANY

Opening Case 1: How Do Economies of Scale Work with Globalization?

The integration of factors of production and inclusion of consumer groups from different markets around the world — facilitates unprecedented achievements of economies of scale for producers. Access to increased numbers of laborers, investors, markets, resources, technologies, and business models through globalization can theoretically maximize productive efficiency to a level consistent with the size of the world's population.

Economies of Scale ($2 + 2 = 5$): Economies of scale refer to the phenomenon of diminishing marginal costs associated with each additional unit of output. A company experiences economies of scale as it specializes in and is able to produce extra goods with fewer and fewer input costs.

According to economic theory, economies of scale are the natural consequence of specialization and the division of labor. It is one of the chief drivers of economic growth. However, firms do not realize economies of scale in perpetuity; there is a maximum level of efficient output for any given inputs, and operations may sometimes extend too far and cause diseconomies of scale.

Globalization: With access to new inputs and potentially more profitable markets, globalization can increase specialization and operational efficiency. The practical consequences of globalization include lower costs to consumers, access to capital for wealthy countries, access to jobs for poorer countries, increased competition and higher global productivity.

As globalization spreads the division of labor to a global scale, countries are able to export labor and production processes that they are relatively less profitable at and instead specialize in labor that is relatively more profitable. This result can be seen in factory jobs being driven out of the United States, which frees up capital for highly technical, highly productive fields such as IT. Companies are able to pursue higher degrees of efficiency and increase their economies of scale.[1]

---

[1]Sean, R., "How Do Economies of Scale Work with Globalization?" *Investopedia*, June 25, 2019, https://www.investopedia.com/ask/answers/013015/how-do-economies-scale-work-globalization.asp.

Globalization stands for the idea of integrating the world marketplace, creating a so-called "borderless world" for goods and services. In addition, we already have such a world. Consider physical communications (mail, the telephone, the Internet, and airline and ocean shipping networks); entertainment (film and TV, music, news, and sports); economic and business exchange (banking and insurance networks, dependable foreign exchange and stock markets, and reciprocal trade arrangements); and even ideas and competing spiritual values through evangelical Christianity, Islam, and others.[2]

The increasing economic integration of goods, services, and financial markets presents opportunities and challenges for governments, business firms, and individuals. Although business operations in countries across the globe have existed for centuries, the world has recently entered an era of unprecedented worldwide production and distribution. Worldwide production and distribution are critical for the survival of the multinational corporation (MNC) — its ability to produce products and sell them at a profit. International finance is an integral part of total management and cuts across functional boundaries because it expresses inputs, outputs, plants, and results in monetary terms.

This book deals with the financial decisions of an MNC, decisions which both large and small MNCs must make. Thus, the underlying financial principles are basically the same for both types of companies. In this introductory chapter, we lay the foundation for the entire text with seven separate sections. The first section explains reasons to study international finance. The second identifies the primary goal of the MNC and the functions of the financial manager necessary to achieve this primary goal. The third section analyzes MNCs and their performance. The fourth section discusses the major principles of global finance which favor MNCs over domestic companies. The fifth and sixth sections describe two major constraints that impede an MNC's effort to achieve its goal: large agency costs and environmental differences. The last section gives an overview of the book.

1.1. REASONS TO STUDY INTERNATIONAL FINANCE

A college student, such as yourself, should study international finance. "I am not an international finance major," you say. "Why should I have to take a course in international finance?" That is a reasonable question. It is true that most readers of this book will not necessarily work in the international finance department of a large company such as IBM or the foreign exchange department of a large bank such as BBVA Mexico, the largest bank in Mexico. All textbooks on business and economics teach that resources are scarce. We know that your time is one of those scarce resources. Hence, we will give you just a few reasons why you should study international finance.

1.1.1. *To Understand a Global Economy*

The world has recently reached the climax in a drama of economic change. No one can deny the effects of these changes on our hopes for peace and prosperity: political and economic freedom in Eastern Europe; the emergence of market-oriented economies in Asia; the creation

---

[2]Harry, T. R., *Globalization. . .Let's Get It Straight*, MO: O'Fallon, 2001.

of a single European market; trade liberalization through regional trading blocs, such as the European Union, and the world's joint memberships, such as the World Trade Organization. As global integration advances amid intensified international competition, the United States, East Asia, and Europe are expected to lead the world toward a system of free trade and open markets.

In terms of social globalization, the world remains more connected than ever due to the widespread use of digital technologies. In addition, the United Nations identified three mega-trends related to globalization: shifts in production and labor markets, rapid advances in technology, and climate change. Understanding these changes should help you see where the international economy is headed in the future so that you can more effectively respond to these challenges, fulfill your responsibilities, and take advantage of these opportunities.

Most large and many medium-size companies around the world have international business operations. In recent years, it has become clear that international events significantly affect companies which do not have foreign operations. Business school graduates have an advantage in moving their companies forward if they understand the basic elements of international finance. Apart from career interests, people who want to improve their knowledge of the world will be seriously handicapped if they do not understand the economic dynamics and policy issues of finance, trade, and investment flows among nations.

1.1.2. *To Create Value in the MNC*

Every MNC attempts to generate profit and value for its owners and stockholders. Today, the MNC creates value for its stakeholders by combining two critical elements, globalization, and information. Knowledge/information is the driving force for globalization because information/new technology is transforming most local, regional, and national events (economics and business, entertainment, physical communications, and even ideas and competing spiritual values) into global events without borders. Knowledge/information workers are the link to all of the organization's other investments. They provide focus, creativity, and leverage in using those investments to better achieve the organization's objectives. Knowledge/information is an integral part of total management because it teaches us to do a better job in all functional areas, such as production, marketing, financing, and others. Consequently, a typical worker in the information and knowledge age outperforms the counterpart of the industrial age many times over.[3]

1.1.3. *To Make Intelligent Personal Decisions*

When you graduate from college and decide to take a job, you may have the advantage of comparing two job offers: one from JPMorgan Chase (JPM) and another one from Nomura Group. When you decide to buy a car, your choice between the latest models offered by GMC and Hyundai Motor Group may well depend on the exchange rate between the US dollar and the Korean won. When you begin a career and save for your retirement, you may choose between US securities and non-US securities. When you take your next vacation, you may spend it at Tokyo Disneyland or at Euro Disneyland. Although these are not international

---

[3]Covey, S. R., *The 8th Habit: From Effectiveness to Greatness*, New York: Free Press, 2004.

finance jobs, they all require significant knowledge of international finance to make intelligent decisions. In all of these cases, the important point is that you will participate not just in the US economy but in economies around the world.

1.1.4. *To Understand the Fourth Industrial Revolution*

The **fourth industrial revolution** describes a world where individuals move between digital domains and offline reality with the use of connected technology to enable and manage their lives. The first industrial revolution changed our lives and economy from an agrarian and handicraft economy to one dominated by industry and machine manufacturing. Oil and electricity facilitated mass production in the second industrial revolution. In the third industrial revolution, information technology was used to automate production. Although each industrial revolution is often considered a separate event, together they can be better understood as a series of events building upon innovations of the previous revolution and leading to more advanced forms of production.

There are similarities between four industrial revolutions and the five ages of civilization: the hunter and gather age, the agricultural age, the industrial age, the information worker age, and the emerging age of wisdom. Therefore, we may infer the opportunities of the fourth industrial revolution through the characteristics of these five ages of civilization. In both the fourth industrial revolution and the latest two ages of civilization, knowledge workers produce most goods and services with their mind. For the sake of long-term survival, therefore, companies must secure talent acquisition and self-motivate knowledge workers to fully develop their potential. The metaphor of 'a bird flies with both wings' is most appropriately applied to talent acquisition and self-motivation. This is because the production of goods and services in the fourth industrial revolution is basically an activity that creates added value by combining workers' talent and their self-motivation.[4]

Global Finance in Practice 1: To understand that globalization is shifting, not reversing

It is fashionable to talk of deglobalization again. More likely is a continuing reshuffling of trade flows that creates new geopolitical winners — if they are savvy enough to take advantage. Global trade took some big knocks in 2022 because Russia's commodity flows to Europe shrunk to a trickle and lockdowns in China disrupted supply chains. The Biden administration provided massive subsidies for the manufacture of semiconductors and electric-vehicle batteries in the United States, both of which are now dominated by Asia.

Former President Donald Trump unleashed a previous wave of talks about deglobalization in 2018 with his tariffs on Chinese products, that said, US imports boosted from Southeast Asian nations such as Vietnam, Indonesia, and Thailand at China's

---

[4]Xu, M., J. David, and S. H. Kim, "The Fourth Industrial Revolution: Opportunities and Challenges," *International Journal of Financial Research*, 9(2), March 2018, pp. 90–95.

expense, rather than reducing imports overall. On the other hand, the war in Ukraine has redrawn the global energy map, redirecting Russian energy exports to China and India and increasing European imports from the United States and the Middle East without increasing Europe's self-sufficiency.

It stands to reason that globalization cannot be easily reversed. Since the pandemic, the return of inflation has served as a reminder that consumers do not readily accept the cost of increased trade frictions. Subsidies can help in a few politically sensitive industries, such as microchips and batteries. Even so, new trade routes will emerge, or existing ones will expand to replace those under threat. For example, new battery plants in the United States will require massive amounts of input from mining hubs such as Australia, Chile, and Canada.

Mexico has lower wages than China, a well-established manufacturing sector anchored by the automotive industry, and an ideal geographic location for serving the US market. Bank of America analysts see some evidence of this happening, with US imports of Mexican manufactured goods roughly 60 percent higher in October 2022 than before the pandemic. Mexico increased its share of low-tech industrial imports from the United States, while China has decreased its share. The idea behind the rationale is that countries looking to replace China in supplying the US may need to invest a lot.[5]

1.2. COMPANY GOALS AND FUNCTIONS OF FINANCIAL MANAGEMENT

1.2.1. *MNC Goals*

Management is motivated to achieve a number of objectives, some of which conflict with each other. Such conflicts arise because the firm has a number of constituents, such as stockholders, employees, customers, creditors, suppliers, and the local community, whose desires do not necessarily coincide. It is management's responsibility to satisfy such differing desires. Hence, the conflicting objectives confronting management raise the problem of setting priorities. In addition, it is essential for management to set priorities for the most efficient use of a company's scarce resources. Setting priorities by an MNC is particularly important and difficult because it has highly diversified groups of constituents in many countries.

The commonly accepted objective of an MNC is to maximize stockholder wealth on a global basis, as reflected by stock price. The stock price reflects the market's evaluation of the firm's prospective earnings stream over time, the riskiness of this stream, the dividend policy, and quality aspects of the firm's future activities. Quality aspects of future activities include stability, diversification, and growth of sales.

Stockholder wealth maximization is generally accepted as the primary goal of a company in the United States and the United Kingdom. In some other countries such as Germany and Japan, however, the goal of a company is to maximize corporate wealth. "Corporate wealth"

---

[5]Al Mayadeen English, "Global Trading Is Shifting, Not Reversing," *The Wall Street Journal*, January 3, 2023, p. A10.

includes not only the company's stockholder wealth but also its marketing, technical, and human resources. Under this model, a company should treat shareholders on a par with other corporate constituents. In other words, management should strive to increase the corporate wealth for the benefit of all constituents.

There are a number of compelling reasons for management to focus on stockholder wealth maximization. First, because stockholders are the owners of the company, management has a fiduciary obligation to act in their best interests. Second, stockholders provide risk capital that protects the welfare of other constituents. Third, stockholder wealth maximization — a high stock price — provides the best defense against a hostile takeover or a forced corporate restructuring. Fourth, if a company enhances shareholder value, it is easier for the company to attract additional equity capital. For these and other reasons, many financial economists believe that stockholder wealth maximization is the only way to maximize the economic welfare of all constituents.[6]

1.2.2. *Functions of the International Financial Manager*

In order to achieve the firm's primary goal of maximizing stockholder wealth, the financial manager performs three major functions: (1) financial planning and control (supportive tools); (2) the efficient allocation of funds among various assets (investment decisions); and (3) the acquisition of funds on favorable terms (financing decisions).

1.2.2.1. *Financial planning and control*

Financial planning and control must be considered simultaneously. For purposes of control, the financial manager establishes standards, such as budgets for comparing actual performance with planned performance. The preparation of these budgets is a planning function, but their administration is a controlling function.

The foreign exchange market and international accounting play a key role when an MNC attempts to perform its planning and control function. For example, once a company crosses national boundaries, its return on investment depends on not only its trade gains or losses from normal business operations, but also on exchange gains or losses from currency fluctuations.

International reporting and controlling have to do with techniques for controlling the operations of an MNC. Meaningful financial reports are the cornerstone of effective management. Accurate financial data are especially important in international business, where business operations are typically supervised from a distance.

1.2.2.2. *Allocation of funds (investment)*

When the financial manager plans for the allocation of funds, the most urgent task is to invest funds wisely within the firm. Every dollar invested has alternative uses. Thus, funds should be allocated among assets in such a way that they will maximize the wealth of the firm's stockholders.

---

[6]Shapiro, A. C., *Multinational Financial Management*, New York: John Wiley & Sons, 2009, Chapter 1.

There are 200 countries in the world where large MNCs, such as Wal-Mart and Samsung Group can invest their funds. Obviously, there are more investment opportunities in the world than in a single country, but there are also more risks. International financial managers should consider these two simultaneously when they attempt to maximize their firm's value through international investment.

1.2.2.3. *Acquisition of funds (financing)*

The third role of the financial manager is to acquire funds on favorable terms. If projected cash outflow exceeds cash inflow, the financial manager will find it necessary to obtain additional funds from outside the firm. Funds are available from many sources at varying costs, with different maturities, and under various types of agreements. The critical role of the financial manager is to determine the combination of financing that most closely suits the planned needs of the firm. This requires obtaining the optimal balance between low cost and the risk of not being able to pay bills as they become due.

There are still many poor countries in the world. Thus, even Industrial & Commercial Bank of China, the world's largest bank in 2022, cannot acquire its funds from 200 countries. Nevertheless, MNCs can still raise their funds in many countries thanks to recent financial globalization. This financial globalization is driven by advances in data processing and telecommunications, liberalization of restrictions on cross-border capital flows, and deregulation of domestic capital markets. International financial managers use a puzzling array of fund-acquisition strategies. Why? The financial manager of a purely domestic company has just one way to acquire funds — instruments which have varying costs, different maturities, and different types of agreements. The financial manager of an MNC, on the other hand, has three different ways to acquire funds: by picking instruments, picking countries, and picking currencies.

1.3. MNCs AND THEIR PERFORMANCE

1.3.1. *What is a MNC?*

In 1963, the term "multinational corporation" became a household term after a cover story about the institution in *Business Week*. Ever since, international business guided by MNCs has prospered as a result of the need for poor countries to develop, the end of the Cold War, privatization of state-owned businesses and banks, and the growing economic power of the global triad — Asia, the United States, and Europe.[7]

The modern MNC is generally thought to be the Dutch East India Company because they were operating in different countries than the ones where they had their headquarters. This company was a chartered company established in 1602, when the States-General of the Netherlands granted it a 21-year monopoly to carry out colonial activities in Asia. Nowadays many corporations have offices, branches, or manufacturing plants in different countries than where their original and main headquarters is located. This often results in very powerful corporations that have budgets that exceed some national GDPs. MNCs can have a powerful influence in local economies as well as the world economy and play an important role in

---

[7]Baker, J. C., *International Finance*, Upper Saddle River, NJ: Prentice-Hall, 1998, Chapter 1.

international relations and globalization. Most of the largest and most influential companies of the modern age are publicly traded multinational corporations, including Forbes Global 2000 companies.[8]

The World Book Encyclopedia defines an **MNC** as "a business organization that produces a product, sells a product, and provides a service in two or more countries." The US Department of Commerce defines an American MNC as "the US parent and all of its foreign affiliates." A US parent is a person, resident in the United States, who owns or controls a minimum of 10 percent voting equity in a foreign firm. "Person" is broadly defined to include any individual, branch, partnership, associated group, association, estate, trust, corporation, other organization, or any government entity. A **foreign affiliate** is a foreign business enterprise in which a US person owns or controls a minimum of 10 percent voting equity. A **majority-owned foreign affiliate** is a foreign affiliate in which the combined ownership of all US parents exceeds 50 percent.

Donald Lessard, a professor of international finance at MIT, classified all MNCs into three groups in 1991: (1) international opportunists — companies that focus on their domestic markets but engage in some international transactions; (2) multi-domestic competitors — companies that committed to a number of national markets with substantial value added in each country but with little cross-border integration of activities; and (3) global competitors — companies that focus on a series of national and supranational markets with substantial cross-border integration of activities.[9]

1.3.2. *From MNC to Global Company*

What Lessard called "A Global Competitor" has come to be known as a global company. A **global company** is a generic term used to describe an organization that attempts to standardize and integrate operations worldwide in all functional areas. Here are three definitions of a global company — an organization that attempts to:

1. Have a worldwide presence in its market.
2. Integrate its operations worldwide.
3. Standardize operations in one or more of the company's functional areas.

For example, if a company designs a product with a global market segment in mind and/or depends on many countries for the production of a product, it qualifies for a global company. In this type of company, the development of capabilities and the decisions to diffuse them globally are made in the company's home office. Some people believe that a global company must possess all three of these characteristics. Critics of this definition say that there is no global company by that definition.

---

[8]http://en.wikipedia.org/wiki/Multinational_corporation, February 25, 2023.
[9]Lessard, D. R., "Global Competition and Corporate Finance in the 1990s," *Journal of Applied Corporate Finance*, Winter 1991, pp. 59–72.

1.3.3. *Performance of MNCs*

Evidence indicates that US MNCs earn more money as they boost their presence in foreign markets. In 1974, for example, *Business International* reported that 90 percent of 140 Fortune 500 companies surveyed achieved higher profitability on foreign assets. This trend has continued since then. As the world economy has become more integrated, there has been an increase in the number of multinational firms. As of 2017, about half of the publicly traded firms in the US are multinationals. For the average multinational firm, foreign income (sales) represents about 40 percent of aggregate income (sales).[10] MNCs earn more money than purely domestic companies for two major reasons. First, MNCs can raise money at a lower cost than purely domestic companies. Second, MNCs have more investment opportunities than purely domestic companies. All analysts predict that US MNCs will earn more money than US domestic companies for years to come.

Foreign-based companies with a higher degree of international business have also experienced superior performance in recent years. Foreign-owned companies in the world's most developed countries are generally more productive and pay their workers more than comparable locally owned businesses, according to the Organization for Economic Cooperation and Development (OECD). The Paris-based organization also says that the proportion of the manufacturing sector under foreign ownership in European Union countries rose substantially since the 1990s, a sign of increasing economic integration. The finding underlines the increasing importance in the world economy of large companies with bases scattered across the globe. Gross output per employee, a measure of productivity, in most OECD countries, tends to be greater in multinational companies than in locally owned companies.[11] Why do multinational companies perform better than domestic companies do? In the following section, we attempt to answer this important question.

1.4. PRINCIPLES OF GLOBAL FINANCE

The primary objective of this book is to help the reader understand basic principles of global finance. Before we advance too far into the material, perhaps it would be helpful to take a brief look at some of these principles so that you may see where we are heading.

As discussed earlier, the financial manager has three major functions: financial planning and control, the acquisition of funds, and the allocation of funds. However, each of these three functions shares most principles of global finance and their relationships. Seven important principles of global finance are introduced in this section.

1.4.1. *Risk-Return Tradeoff*

The maximization of stockholder wealth depends on the tradeoff between risk and profitability. Generally, the higher the risk of a project, the higher the expected return from

---

[10]Isil, E. *et al.*, "The Corporate Finance of Multinational Firms," November 10, 2019, https://www.brookings.edu/wp-content/uploads/2019/12/Erel-et-al._EJW-Brookings -November-10-2019-final.pdf.
[11]Marsh, P., "Measuring Globalization: The Role of Multinationals in OECD Countries," *The Financial Times*, March 20, 2002, p. 6.

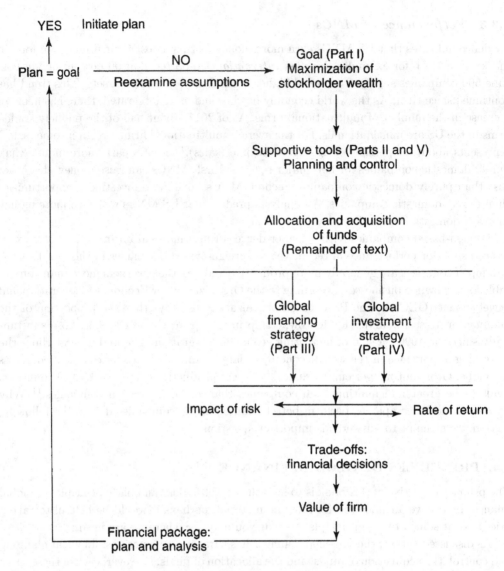

Fig. 1.1 An integrated decision-making model in global finance.

the project. For example, if you are offered a chance to invest in a project which offers an extremely high rate of return, you should immediately suspect that the project is very risky.

The risk-return tradeoff does not apply to 100 percent of all cases, but in a free enterprise system, it probably comes close. Thus, the financial manager must attempt to determine the optimal balance between risk and profitability that will maximize the wealth of the MNC's stockholders. Figure 1.1 shows how the financial manager assesses the various risk-return tradeoffs available and incorporates this into the wealth maximization goal. Given the risk-return tradeoffs, various financial decisions are made to maximize stockholder wealth. All financial decisions involve such tradeoffs. Such decisions include foreign exchange risk management, global reporting and controlling, global financing decision, and global investment decision.

An investor's risk-return tradeoff function is based on the standard economic concepts of utility theory and opportunity sets. An opportunity set shows different combinations of business opportunities, which make the investor equally happy in terms of risk-return tradeoffs.

Companies can benefit from an expanded opportunity set as they venture into global markets. It seems reasonable to assume that international business is riskier than domestic business. However, this is not necessarily true, because returns on foreign investments are not highly positively correlated with returns on domestic investments. In other words, MNCs may be less risky than companies that operate strictly within the boundaries of any one country. Consequently, to minimize risk, companies should diversify not only across domestic projects but also across countries.

Revenue opportunities from international business are also larger than possible revenue opportunities from purely domestic business. MNCs can locate production in any country of the world to maximize their profits and raise funds in any capital market where the cost of capital is the lowest. MNCs may see another advantage from currency gains. These two factors — lower risks and larger profitability for international business — suggest the possibility that an MNC can achieve a better risk-return tradeoff than a domestic company.

Figure 1.2 shows that international business pushes out the opportunity set, thus allowing MNCs to reduce risk, increase return, or attain both. As shown in Fig. 1.2, we can think of three cases where international operations are better than domestic operations. Relative to US project A, international project B has the same return but less risk; international project C has the same risk but higher return; and international project D has higher return but less risk.

1.4.2. *Market Imperfections*

Perfect competition exists when sellers of goods and services have complete freedom of entry into and exit out of any national market. Under such a condition, goods and services would be mobile and freely transferable. The unrestricted mobility of goods and services creates equality in costs and returns across countries. This cost-return uniformity everywhere in the world would remove the incentive for foreign trade and investment.

Factors of production, such as land, capital, and technology, are unequally distributed among nations. Even with such comparative advantages, however, the volume of international business would be limited if all factors of production could be easily transferred among countries. The real world has imperfect market conditions where resources available for the production of goods are somewhat immobile.

The trend toward a global economy through the World Trade Organization, the European Union, and The Southern Common Market — known as Mercosur in Spanish will undoubtedly remove market imperfections that restrict the international flows of goods and services. However, a variety of barriers still impede free movements of goods, services, and financial assets across national boundaries. These barriers include government controls, excessive transportation and transaction costs, lack of information, and discriminatory taxation. Consequently, companies can still benefit from imperfections in national markets for factors of production, products, and financial assets. In other words, imperfect national markets create a variety of incentives for companies to seek out international business.

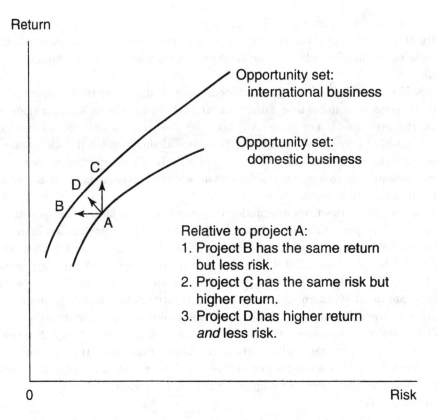

Fig. 1.2 Expanded opportunity set for international business.

For example, Japanese automakers, such as Toyota, established automobile transplants in the United States to avoid US trade restrictions.

1.4.3. *Portfolio Effect (Diversification)*

The **portfolio effect** states that as more assets are added to a portfolio, the risk of the total portfolio decreases. There are some qualifying conditions that we will add to this principle later, but diversification is a very valuable quality.

This principle explains much of the rationale for large MNCs to diversify their operations not only across industries but also across countries and currencies. Some MNCs, such as Nestle of Switzerland, have operations in countries as varied as the United States, Japan, Hong Kong, France, Russia, Mexico, Brazil, Vietnam, Nigeria, and North Korea. Founded in Switzerland in 1866, Nestlé now has operations in about 200 countries around the world. Because it is impossible to predict which countries will outperform other countries in the future, these companies are "hedging their bets."

Domestic investment projects tend to correlate less with foreign investment projects than with other domestic projects. As a result, international diversification is more effective than domestic diversification. The economic cycles of different countries, such as the United States and Europe, do not tend to be totally synchronized. On the other hand, most domestic projects tend to be highly correlated with each other because they depend on the same state of economy. The energy operations of Saudi Aramco in Saudi Arabia, for example, may be hurt if world oil prices unexpectedly take a nosedive. However, this might be offset by its operations in energy-consuming countries such as China and India. Overall, the MNC earns its desired rate of return even if the profitability of its investment in individual countries may not be that predictable.

1.4.4. *Comparative Advantage*

You have perhaps heard on the news that the Japanese and the United States are competitors in the global economy. In some ways, this is true because American and Japanese companies produce many of the same goods. Ford and Toyota compete for the same customers in the market for automobiles. However, trade between the United States and Japan is not like a sports contest, where one team wins, and the other team loses. In fact, the opposite is true. Trade between two countries can make each country better off.

The classical argument for free trade is based on the principle of comparative advantage. Assume that US workers are better at producing computer software than workers in China and that Chinese workers are better at producing shoes than workers in the United States. Comparative advantage states that trade between the two countries — the United States exporting software and China exporting shoes — can boost living standards in both. This is because the United States has comparative advantage in producing software while China has comparative advantage in producing shoes. Trade allows countries to specialize in what they do best and to enjoy a greater variety of goods and services. At the same time, companies earn profits from trade because most trade is carried out by individual companies.

1.4.5. *Internationalization Advantage*

Why do some companies prefer to export while others build overseas manufacturing facilities? When a company expands its operations beyond national borders for the first time, it tends to exploit a foreign market through exports. An export-oriented strategy has served the company well for some time. However, to become part of a global market, a company should have a world presence. Because the world presence cannot be sustained by exports alone, the company should eventually invest.

The advantages of internationalization influence companies to invest directly in foreign countries. These advantages depend on three factors: location, ownership, and internationalization. British Petroleum (BP) has ownership advantages, such as technology, marketing expertise, capital, and brand names. Mexico has location advantages, such as crude oil, abundant labor, and low taxes. Thus, BP has built oil operations in Mexico. These investments magnify both wages of workers in Venezuela and profits of BP from the use of its technology and capital. These magnified portions of location advantages and ownership advantages are called **internationalization advantages**. These internationalization advantages allow MNCs to enjoy superior earnings performance over domestic companies.

1.4.6. *Economies of Scale*

There are economies of scale in the use of many assets. **Economies of scale** take place due to a synergistic effect, which is said to exist when the whole is worth more than the mere sum of its parts $(2 + 2 = 5)$. When companies produce or sell their primary product in new markets, they may increase their earnings and shareholder wealth due to economies of scale. Economies of scale explain why so many Asian companies invested in North America in preparation for the North American Free Trade Agreement of 1994. As the European Union removed trade barriers in 1993 and adopted the euro as its common currency in 1999, they allowed US MNCs to achieve greater economies of scale through their investment in Europe.

Companies can gain from greater economies of scale when their real-capital and monetary assets are deployed on a global basis. The expansion of a company's operations beyond national borders allows it to acquire necessary management skills and spread existing management skills over a larger operation. There are also opportunities to eliminate duplicate facilities and consolidate the functions of production and marketing. In addition, MNCs can raise funds at the lower cost of capital and reduce the pool of money without loss in the level of production. These types of operating and financial economies along with better management can cause an MNC to increase its profit margin and reduce its risks as well.

1.4.7. *Valuation*

The valuation principle states that the value of an asset is equal to the present value of its expected earnings. Because the values of all assets stem from streams of expected earnings, all such assets are valued in the same way. First, the earnings are estimated. Second, the required rate of return for each earning is established. Third, each earning is discounted by its required rate of return, and these present values are then summed to find the value of the asset. Alternatively, the value of an entire firm is determined by dividing the firm's earnings after taxes or net cash flows by its required rate of return.

The value of an MNC is usually higher than the value of a domestic company for two reasons. First, studies show that MNCs earn more profits than domestic companies. Second, earnings of larger companies are capitalized at lower rates. The securities of MNCs have better marketability than those of domestic companies. MNCs are also better known among investors. These factors lead to a lower required rate of return and higher price-earnings ratios. When MNCs attempt to maximize their overall company value, they also face various constraints. Those constraints that hamper an MNC's efforts to maximize its stockholder wealth include large agency costs and environmental differences.

1.5. AGENCY THEORY AND CORPORATE GOVERNANCE

1.5.1. *Agency Theory: Management vs. Stockholders*

Agency theory is a theory that deals with the conflict of interest between managers and shareholders. We may think of managers as agents of the owners. Stockholders delegate decision-making authority to managers on the condition that the agents will act in the stockholders' best interest. However, it has often been argued that the objectives of managers may differ from those of the firm's stockholders. Because the stockholders of most MNCs today are well diversified, the control of these companies is separated from ownership. This situation allows managers to act in their own best interest rather than in the best interest of the stockholders. Thus, some managers may be concerned with their own welfare, such as their own income, power, self-esteem, and prestige. The welfare of managers, therefore, could be increased by management decisions that tend to lower stockholder wealth.

To ensure that managers act in the best interest of the stockholders, the managers must be monitored and rewarded with appropriate incentives. Incentives could include stock options, bonuses, and perquisites. Monitoring can be done by reviewing management perquisites, auditing financial statements, and limiting management decisions. **Agency costs** include incentives and monitoring costs. It is reasonable to assume that managers will undertake actions that are consistent with stockholder wealth maximization. This is because over the long run, their own goals, including survival, will largely depend on the value of the firm.

In this text, we explain the issues and concepts of international finance as though managers act on behalf of the firm's stockholders. Nevertheless, the size of some MNCs can make it difficult to determine whether all managers make decisions on the basis of this single corporate objective — stockholder wealth maximization on a global basis. For example, financial managers of MNCs with many subsidiaries may be tempted to make decisions that would maximize the value of their respective subsidiaries at the expense of their parent company. Consequently, the agency costs of assuring that managers try to maximize stockholder wealth can be larger for MNCs than for purely domestic companies.

1.5.2. *Corporate Governance*

Few issues in the literature and in practice on corporate finance have received as much attention in recent years as corporate governance. In the United States and in other countries, there is new interest in how firms' decision-making structures are organized, the priorities of these structures, and the structures' effect on shareholders. **Corporate governance** refers to the way in which major stakeholders exert control over the operations of a company. The rights of the company's stakeholders in corporate governance are determined by each nation's laws, legal institutions and conventions, and regulations. However, corporate governance is often narrowly defined as the prudent exercise of ownership rights toward the goal of increased shareholder value.[12] In the United States, corporate governance has evolved from a system with a few yet influential individual investors around the turn of the last century to the present environment in which large institutional investors flex their shareholder muscle. Institutional investors include pension funds, mutual funds, university and other nonprofit endowments, and insurance companies.

Today large institutional investors actively encourage effective corporate governance practices to maximize their investment returns. Major corporate governance issues include board independence, executive compensation, and anti-takeover devices. Unlike other stakeholders that have dealings with the corporation — customers, suppliers, lenders, and labor — common shareholders do not have contractual protection of their interests. Thus, shareholder activism is an important part of corporate governance to ensure that managers take actions to mitigate agency problems (conflicts) and thus increase shareholder value. Does good governance matter? Studies by organizations and academics show that good

---

[12]Gillan, S. L. and L. T. Starks, "A Survey of Shareholder Activism: Motivation and Empirical Evidence," *Contemporary Finance Digest*, Autumn 1998, pp. 10–34.

corporate governance tends to lower the cost of capital, to increase returns to shareholders, and to improve profitability.[13]

1.5.2.1. *Shareholder activism*

Shareholder activism is any activity of an investor who tries to change the status quo through voice without the control of the company. The voice reflected in the most common form of shareholder activism covers a broad spectrum of activities, such as a shareholder proposal for proxy fight, direct negotiation with management, and public targeting of a corporation.

Proxy represents the assignment of the voting right to management or a group of outsiders. If earnings are poor and stockholders are dissatisfied, an outside group may solicit the proxies in an effort to overthrow management and take control of the business. This is known as a proxy fight. When performance analysis reveals problems with a company's governance practices, shareholders will directly negotiate with management for needed changes in the company's practices and policies. Public targeting is the use of the media to send information to other investors about the problems and needed changes at a company. The issues addressed by these activism activities span a wide range of topics, but most often pertain to issues of social policy or corporate governance reform.

1.5.2.2. *Changes in corporate governance*

Since 1980, a number of changes have made US managers more responsive to the interests of shareholders. These changes include a more active takeover market, an increased usage of executive incentive plans that increase the link between management performance and corporate performance, and more active institutional shareholders who have demonstrated a growing tendency to vote against management.[14] In addition, as one corporate scandal after another broke in 2002, President George W. Bush signed into law the Sarbanes-Oxley Act on July 30, 2002 to reduce agency problems.

First, the threat of a hostile takeover for inefficiently managed companies tends to encourage managers to make decisions that enhance stockholder wealth. Other companies are more likely to acquire undervalued companies at a low price and might layoff existing managers.

Second, these days many companies partially compensate their executives with stock options which encourage managers to make decisions that maximize their company's stock price. Stock options and other types of incentive plans such as bonuses are designed to increase the link between management performance and corporate performance.

Third, institutions have become more active as shareholders and have compelled managers to act in the stockholders' best interest. Increased shareholder activism by institutions has occurred at the same time as the rapid increase in institutional investor holdings during the last few decades. These holdings grew from approximately one-quarter of US equity markets in 1980 to over two-thirds today. Two rule changes in the early 1990s by the US Securities and Exchange Commission have also sparked the active role of institutional investors.

---

[13]Eietman, D. K., A. I. Stonehill, and M. H. Moffett, *Multinational Business Finance*, New York: Pearson, 2021, Chapter 1.
[14]Hillier, D., M. Grinblatt, and S. Titman, *Financial Markets and Corporate Strategy*, New York: McGraw-Hill/Irwin, 2008, Chapter 17.

The first change, which required complete disclosure of executive compensation packages, put managers under greater pressure to perform up to their level of compensation. The second change made it easier for shareholders to get information about other shareholders and reduced the cost of staging a proxy fight.

Fourth, a series of accounting scandals at companies, such as Enron and WorldCom, compelled the government to introduce a host of new laws and regulations so that managers may not pursue their own private interests at the expense of shareholders. In October 2001, Enron (energy company) declared bankruptcy and its accounting firm, Arthur Andersen — then one of the five largest audit and accountancy partnerships in the world — was effectively dissolved. In addition to being the largest bankruptcy reorganization in the US history at that time, Enron was cited as the biggest audit failure. In 2002, just a year after the Enron scandal, it was discovered that WorldCom (telecommunication company) had inflated its assets by almost $11 billion, making it by far the largest accounting scandal ever.

The Public Company Accounting Reform and Investor Protection Act of 2002, otherwise known as the Sarbanes-Oxley Act, sets up a new oversight body to regulate auditors, creates new laws to increase corporate responsibility, and increases punishments for corporate white-collar criminals. The Act establishes a non-profit organization called the Public Company Accounting Oversight Board to oversee the audit of public companies and to protect the accuracy of audit reports. These and other reforms introduced after recent corporate scandals are expected to strengthen US corporate governance practices.

In the late 2000s, the US government impacted corporate governance in the firms asking for financial help during the 2008 and 2009 economic recession. In formulating a bailout package for the big three American auto companies, Congress first demanded the three CEOs accept compensation of $1. In addition, as the government helped GM navigate through the bankruptcy court process quickly, it demanded CEO Rick Wagoner's resignation.[15]

1.6. ENVIRONMENTAL DIFFERENCES

What are the differences between MNCs and domestic companies from a financial manager's point of view? An efficient allocation of funds among assets (investment) and an acquisition of funds on favorable terms (financing) are conceptually the same for both types of companies. These two types of companies, however, differ because they do business in different environments. International financial managers must understand these differences if they are to succeed in the international environment.

For successful international operations, a manager must have information about environmental factors that affect business operations in foreign countries. Domestic methods should be adjusted to accommodate customs, attitudes, economic factors, and political factors which prevail in the country of operation.

How do management practices in one country differ from those in other countries? In principle, concepts in accounting, economics, finance, management, and marketing are as relevant to business management in one country as they are in another country. However, when a business crosses national boundaries, the environment differs for these functions.

---

[15]Kim, K., J. Nofsinger, and D. Mohr, *Corporate Governance*, 3rd Edition, Upper Saddle River, NJ: Prentice Hall, 2009.

In other words, multinational financial managers are confronted with various environmental constraints when they attempt to maximize their firm's value on a global basis. The three types of environmental constraints described in this section are (1) various risks; (2) conflicts of interest; and (3) multiple environments. These constraints are not mutually exclusive, nor do they exhaust the differences we might find in international business.

1.6.1. *Types of Risk*

Three major risks in international business are political, financial, and regulatory. **Political risks** range from moderate actions, such as exchange controls, to extreme actions, such as confiscation of assets. **Financial risks** involve varying exchange rates, divergent tax laws, different interest and inflation rates, and balance-of-payments considerations. **Regulatory risks** are differences in legal systems, overlapping jurisdictions, and restrictive business practices against foreign companies.

If a company plans to invest heavily in foreign countries, it must consider all of these risks. Business operations which cross national boundaries add dimensions of risk rarely confronted in domestic business operations. Ideally, a company should analyze these risks to understand their underlying causal forces so that the company may develop specific measures to handle them.

1.6.2. *Conflicts of Interest*

Conflicts of interest may occur for a variety of reasons. Owners, employees, suppliers, and customers may have different national identities. The interests of sovereign national states may be divergent. The goals of MNCs and host countries may conflict. Some conflicts of interest may exist within an MNC. Furthermore, the MNC and the external environment may clash.

Companies tend to have home-country nationals in key positions for foreign operations, but they tend to hire local people for no managerial positions. Thus, disparities in salaries and wages are inevitable. Most developing countries require MNCs to hire and train local people for management positions in exchange for local business operations. External conflicts relate to profit-motivated decisions which involve the transfer of funds, production, exports, imports, and employment from one country to another. For instance, an MNC's wishes for foreign exchange remittances frequently conflicts with a local government's restrictions on these remittances.

1.6.3. *Multiple Environments*

In addition to risk and conflict, MNCs can have operational problems because they operate in several international environments. These environmental diversities require different concepts, analytical methods, and information. So, MNCs should identify, evaluate, and predict all environmental variables. Some important environmental variables are the form of business organization, different institutional settings, and cultural differences.

1.7. THE STRUCTURE OF THE BOOK

This book has four major parts. Part One (Chapters 1–3) provides an overview of the global financial environment, such as motives for foreign trade and investment, the balance of payments, and the international monetary system. In other words, this part develops the primary goal of an MNC and the basics of international finance.

Part Two (Chapters 4–8) deals with the forces that affect the relative prices of currencies in international markets. This part is devoted to financial derivatives — currency forwards, futures, options, and swaps — with an emphasis on their relationships to foreign exchange risk management.

Part Three (Chapters 9 and 10) describes sources of global capital. One major facet of corporate finance is to raise funds on favorable terms. In the case of global corporate finance, financing involves the sources of funds for international trade and foreign investment.

Part Four (Chapters 11–15) discusses the management of assets. The second major facet of corporate finance is the efficient allocation of funds among assets. A decision to invest abroad must consider various environmental differences, such as disparities in exchange rates, differences in taxes, and differences in risk factors.

1.8. SUMMARY

The international financial manager has the same objective as every other manager in a multinational firm: to maximize the wealth of the stockholders. If the firm's stock price goes up as a result of the manager's decisions, the decisions were good ones. The stockholders would recognize that the value of the company has been enhanced by the managers' efforts. In order to achieve the firm's primary goal of maximizing stockholder wealth, the financial manager performs three major functions: financial planning and control, the efficient allocation of funds, and the acquisition of funds on favorable terms.

MNCs have superior performance over domestic companies because they enjoy a better risk-return tradeoff, market imperfections, portfolio effect, comparative advantage, internationalization advantage, economies of scale, and a higher valuation. However, when MNCs attempt to maximize their overall company value, they face various constraints, such as large agency costs, a variety of risks, conflicts of interest, and multiple environments.

1.9. KEY TERMS

fourth industrial revolution	globalization
multinational corporation (MNC)	foreign affiliate
majority-owned foreign affiliate	global company
perfect competition	portfolio effect
internationalization advantages	economies of scale
agency theory	agency costs
corporate governance	shareholder activism
proxy	political risks
financial risks	regulatory risks

Closing Case 1: Globalization and the Forth Industrial Revolution

Globalization stands for the idea of integrating the world marketplace, creating a so-called "borderless world" for goods and services. In addition, we already have such a world. Consider physical communications (mail, the telephone, the Internet, and airline and ocean shipping networks); entertainment (film and TV, music, news, and sports); economic and business exchange (banking and insurance networks, dependable foreign exchange and stock markets, and reciprocal trade arrangements); and even ideas and competing spiritual values through evangelical Christianity, Islam, and others.

The fourth industrial revolution describes a world where individuals move between digital domains and offline reality with the use of connected technology to enable and manage their lives. The first industrial revolution changed our lives and economy from an agrarian and handicraft economy to one dominated by industry and machine manufacturing. Oil and electricity facilitated mass production in the second industrial revolution. In the third industrial revolution, information technology was used to automate production. Although each industrial revolution is often considered a separate event, together they can be better understood as a series of events building upon innovations of the previous revolution and leading to more advanced forms of production.

Globalization and technology are intimately intertwined. The movement of people, goods and ideas is accelerated and broadened by new forms of transport and communication. And technological development is, in turn, enhanced by the diversity of ideas and the increased scale that comes from global reach. During each phase of globalization, technology has played a defining role in shaping both opportunities and risks.

As the Fourth Industrial Revolution drives a new phase of globalization — "Globalization 4.0" — here are five things we can learn from looking backwards and forwards, at the impact of technology. (1) Even technology improves, globalization is not inevitable. (2) Global systems and standards matter more than individual technologies. (3) The global village is built on digital foundations. (4) The great game, redux. (5) Positive, shared value should be driving globalization 4.0.

Sources: Nicholas, D. and D. O'Halloran, "The Fourth Industrial Revolution is Driving Globalization 4.0," November *World Economic Forum*, 8, 2018, https://www.weforum.org/agenda/2018/11/the-fourth-industrial-revolution-is-driving-a-new-phase-of-globalization/; Kenneth, A. K. and S. Kim, *Global Corporate Finance: A Focused Approach*, New Jersey: World Scientific Publishing, 2020, Chapter 1; and Xu, M. J. M. David, and S. H. Kim, "The Fourth Industrial Revolution: Opportunities and Challenges," *International Journal of Financial Research*, 9(2), 2018, pp. 88–95.

Case Questions

1. Briefly explain each of the four industrial revolutions.
2. Why is globalization important for business firms?

3. Explain five things we can learn from looking backwards and forwards, at the impact of technology.
4. Visit the website of Velocity Global https://velocityglobal.com/blog/globalization-benefits-and-challenges/ to view benefits and challenges of the globalization. Explain the six benefits of globalization and the eight challenges of globalization in some detail.

BIBLIOGRAPHY

Ball, D. A., M. Geringer, M. S. Minor, and J. M. McNett, *International Business: The Challenge of Global Competition*, New York: McGraw Hill/Irwin, 2019.

Czinkota, M., I. A. Ronkainen, and M. H. Moffett, *International Business*, New York: Wiley, 2015.

Covey, S. R., The *8th Habit: From Effectiveness to Greatness*, New York: Free Press, 2004.

Eiteman, D. K., A. I. Stonehill, and M. H. Moffett, *Multinational Business Finance*, Upper Saddle River, NJ: Pearson, 2021.

Eun, C. S. and G. S. Resnick, *International Financial Management*, Boston: McGraw-Hill/Irwin, 2017.

Glain, S., "Asian Firms, Amid Currency Turmoil, Turn to Hedging Experts to Cut Risk," *The Wall Street Journal*, November 19, 1997, p. A18.

Gillan, S. L. and L. T. Starks, "A Survey of Shareholder Activism: Motivation and Empirical evidence," *Contemporary Finance Digest*, Autumn 1998, pp. 10–34.

Hill, C. and G. Hult, *Loose-Leaf for International Business*, Columbus, Ohio: McGraw-Hill Education, 2018.

Hillier, D., M. Grinblatt, and S. Titman, *Financial Markets and Corporate Strategy*, New York: McGraw-Hill/Irwin, 2011.

Groshen, E. L., "Special Issue: Corporate Governance: What Do We Know and What Is Different about Banks," *Economic Policy Review*, Federal Reserve Bank of New York, April 2003.

Harry, T. R., *Globalization...Let's Get It Straight*, MO: O'Fallon, 2001.

Lessard, D. R, "Global Competition and Corporate Finance in the 1990s," *Journal of Applied Corporate Finance*, Winter 1991, pp. 59–72.

Kim, K., J. Nofsinger, and D. Mohr, *Corporate Governance*, 3rd Edition, Upper Saddle River, NJ: Prentice Hall, 2009.

Madura, J., *Intentional Financial Management*, Boston, MA: Cengage Learning Inc., 2021.

Mankiw, N. G., *Principles of Economics*, Florence, KY: South-Western College Pub., 2017.

Marsh, P., "Measuring Globalization: The Role of Multinationals in OECD Countries," *The Financial Times*, March 20, 2002, p. 6.

Melvin, M. and S. C. Norrbin, *International Financial Management*, London, UK: Elsevier, 2023.

Rugman, A. M., "Multinational Enterprises Are Regional, Not Global," *Multinational Business Review*, Spring 2003, pp. 3–12.

Santomero, A. M., "Corporate Governance and Responsibility," *Business Review*, Federal Reserve Bank of Philadelphia, Second Quarter 2003, pp. 1–5.

Simison, R. L., "Firms Worldwide Should Adopt Ideas of U.S. Management, Panel Tells OECD," *The Wall Street Journal*, April 2, 1998, p. A4.

Scism, L., "Benefiting from Operating Experience, More Finance Chiefs Become Strategists," *The Wall Street Journal*, June 8, 1993, p. B1.

Shapiro, A. C. and P. Hanouna, *Multinational Financial Management*, New York: John Wiley & Sons, 2019.

Xu, M., J. David, and S. H. Kim, "The Fourth Industrial Revolution: Challenges and Opportunities," *International Journal of Financial Research*, April 2018, pp. 96–104.

Chapter 2

MOTIVES FOR WORLD TRADE AND FOREIGN INVESTMENT

Opening Case 2: The Brexit — The UK had Five Prime Ministers in 6 Years Since the 2016 UK's Decision to Leave the EU

The 2016 UK European Union (EU) membership referendum resulted in favor of leaving the EU.

Brexit is the name given to the United Kingdom's departure from the EU. It is a combination of Britain and exit. The UK had five prime ministers in 6 years since the 2016 UK's decision to leave the EU. What has gone wrong? The United Kingdom used to be synonymous with stable, dependable, if sometimes dull, governance. But the resignation of Prime Minister Liz Truss on Thursday, October 20, 2022 — after 6 weeks in office — shows just how chaotic British politics has become in recent years. Truss is the fourth prime minister to resign since the Brexit vote of 2016. That is the fastest turnover in a century. Number 10 Downing Street has effectively become a revolving door.

What is the matter with Britain? Analysts here say it is a story of polarization, populism, a flawed political system, and poor leadership that has at times put party and personal ambition above the good of the country. It begins with former Prime Minister David Cameron who called a referendum on leaving the EU. Cameron hoped the vote in 2016 would end a civil war inside his own Conservative Party on Britain's relationship with Europe and keep the party in power. Prime Minister David Cameron and Chancellor of the Exchequer George Borne delivered a speech on the potential economic impact to the UK of leaving the EU, on May 23, 2016, in Chandler's Ford, England.

It was a miscalculation of historic proportions. The British people voted to leave the EU by a small, but convincing margin. The result not only highlighted Britain's bitter divisions, but also changed the course of the country's foreign, economic and trade policies. Most political scientists and economists predicted that leaving the EU would make this island nation poorer and politically less relevant. It immediately became clear that the architects of the Brexit vote, including its most effective campaigner,

---

Boris Johnson, had no real plan for untangling decades of economic and legal ties with the EU. Political chaos followed. Cameron resigned after the referendum and Theresa May became prime minister. In another major miscalculation, she called a snap election in 2017, only to lose her party's control of the House of Commons. British Prime Minister Theresa May holds a Cabinet meeting to discuss department-by-department Brexit action plans at the prime minister's country retreat Chequeens in Ellenborough, England, on August 31, 2016. May repeatedly tried to drive a Brexit deal through parliament, only to be foiled in part by the anti-European wing of her own party which wanted a clean divorce from Europe. Brexit eventually brought May down as it had her predecessor.

The party then turned to Johnson, the charismatic if deeply flawed show-man who had a track record of winning elections. He campaigned to "get Brexit done." Johnson led the party to a landslide victory in 2019. The next year, he completed the UK's departure from the EU and seemed poised to rule for years.

Then came the coronavirus pandemic, which Johnson underplayed, until he ended up in an intensive care unit with the virus. His government's slow response to COVID led to more than 200,000 deaths — the highest toll in Europe — and drew heavy criticism. But what ended Johnson's premiership was his lying. Family members pay their respects next to the body of a close relative, who died from COVID-19, during the Coronavirus pandemic lockdown at ancestor Central Mosque in Manchester, UK, on February 24, 2021.

Boris Johnson resigns not over policies but deep concerns about his character. While Johnson's government ruled out social gatherings to limit the spread of COVID, government staff held parties. Meanwhile, most Britons stuck to the rules, even if it meant not saying goodbye to dying loved ones. Johnson insisted his govern-ment had adhered to lockdown regulations. In fact, it turned out he had attended two events. He was forced to apologize and pay a fine. Politically, Johnson was finished.

Truss replaced Johnson in September 2022, promising to kick-start the economy with tax cuts for corporations and the rich without reducing public spending. Amid 10 percent inflation here and rising energy prices because of the war in Ukraine, Truss' plan spooked financial markets, crashed the pound, and sent mortgage rates soaring. Tim Bale, a professor of politics at Queen Mary University in London, says one reason Tory prime ministers such as Johnson and Truss have flamed out is because they promised the public things they cannot deliver. In the case of Johnson, it was a cost- and trouble-free Brexit, and with Truss, unfunded tax cuts. "It's a fantasy that many Brits are willing to believe, that because of our supposedly glorious past, we're also entitled to an equally glorious present or future," says Bale, whose new book, *The Conservative Party After Brexit*, comes out in March. "I think politicians continue to feed the myth that we can have Scandinavian levels of welfare on American levels of taxation."

Brexit Timeline

In a referendum held on June 23, 2016, the majority of those who voted chose to leave the EU.

On March 29, 2017, in writing to European Council President Donald Tusk, the Prime Minister formally triggered Article 50 and began the 2-year countdown to the UK formally leaving the EU (commonly known as "Brexit").

The UK had long been expected to leave the EU at 11 pm on March 29, 2019. However, following a House of Commons vote on March 14, 2019, the Government sought permission from the EU to extend Article 50 and agree a later Brexit date.

On March 20, 2019 the Prime Minister wrote to European Council President Donald Tusk, asking to extend Article 50 until June 30, 2019.

Following a European Council meeting the next day, EU27 leaders agreed to grant an extension.

On April 2, 2019, the Prime Minister announced she will seek a further extension to the Article 50 process and offered to meet the Leader of the Opposition to agree a deal that can win the support of MPs.

At a meeting of the European Council on April 10, 2019, the UK and EU27 agreed to extend Article 50 until October 31, 2019.

On October 19, 2019, the Prime Minister's new Brexit deal was lost on amendment in the Commons. In accordance with the European Union (Withdrawal) (No. 2) Act 2019 — commonly known as the "Benn Act" — the Prime Minister wrote to European Council president Donald Tusk, to request an extension to the Brexit process.

On October 28, 2019, EU Ambassadors agreed a further Brexit extension to January 31, 2020.

On December 12, 2019, Boris Johnson won a majority in the UK General Election and reaffirmed his commitment to "get Brexit done" by January 31, 2020.

On January 23, 2020, the EU (Withdrawal Agreement) Act 2020 received Royal Assent. This is the legislation that will implement the withdrawal agreement negotiated by the UK and the EU.

At 11 pm on January 31, 2020, the UK left the EU and entered a transition period.

At 11 pm on December 31, 2020, the transition period ended, and the United Kingdom left the EU single market and customs union.[1]

---

[1]Max, C. and D. Luhnow, "Rishi Sunak Becomes U.K. Prime Minister Amid Economic, Political Crisis," *The Wall Street Journal*, October 25, 2022; https://www.npr.org/2022/10/20/1130184234/liz-truss-prime-minister-resigns-uk-turmoil; and https://commonslibrary.parliament.uk/research-briefings/cbp-7960/.

This book deals with both foreign trade and foreign investment. Because these two types of international transactions are extremely interdependent, Chapter 2 examines motives for foreign trade and foreign investment. Knowledge and understanding of these motives are essential if we are to appreciate the economic dynamics and policy issues of trade and investment flows among nations. Thus, in this important overview, we will discuss key trade and investment theories before we consider them separately in the coming chapters. This chapter also describes global and regional market agreements designed to eliminate trade barriers.

2.1. MOTIVES FOR FOREIGN TRADE

Human desires for goods and services are unlimited, yet our resources are limited. Thus, one of our most important tasks is to seek new knowledge necessary to bridge the gap between desires and resources. The traditional concept of economic man assumed that man allocates his scarce resources between competing uses in the most economical manner. In Robinson Crusoe's world, for example, he would allocate his time for labor between different alternatives. He would use one site on the uncharted island as either the location for a hut (shelter) or as a vegetable garden (food). Of course, the real world consists of many persons and nations that are interdependent for sociological and economic reasons. Most societies face problems similar to those faced by Robinson Crusoe but in more complex forms.

The advantages of economic interdependence between persons and nations center mainly on the efficiency of specialization. Specialization of function or division of labor allows each person or nation to utilize any peculiar differences in skills and resources in the most economical manner. There are a number of reasons why specialization produces a greater amount of goods and services:

1. Natural talents among people are different. If intelligent people specialized only in mental tasks while physically strong people specialized only in physical tasks, the total amount of their output would be greater than if each person tried to do both for herself.
2. Even if the natural abilities of two people are identical, specialization is advantageous because it creates the opportunity for improved skills and techniques through repetition of tasks.
3. The simplification of function through specialization leads to mechanization and the use of large-scale machinery.
4. Personal specialization saves time because one does not have to shift from one task to another.

The theories of comparative advantage, factor endowments, and product life cycle have been suggested as three major motives for foreign trade.

2.1.1. *The Theory of Comparative Advantage*

The classical economic theory of comparative advantage explains why countries exchange their goods and services with each other. Here, the underlying assumption is that some countries can produce some types of goods more efficiently than other countries. Hence, the **theory of comparative advantage** assumes that all countries are better off if each specializes in the production of those goods which it can produce more efficiently and buys those goods which other countries produce more efficiently.

2.1.1.1. *Why comparative advantage occurs*

The theory of comparative advantage depends on two elements:

1. Factors of production, such as land, labor, capital, and technology, are unequally distributed among nations.
2. Efficient production of various goods and services requires combinations of different economic resources and different technologies.

For instance, Canada has vast amounts of fertile land resources and relatively few people. In contrast, Japan has little land and abundant skilled labor. Thus, Canada may produce such land-intensive goods as wheat more economically than Japan, while Japan may produce such labor-intensive goods as cameras more economically than Canada.

However, it is important to recognize that the distribution of economic resources and technology can change over time. This change may alter the relative efficiency of production. In the last 20–30 years, some developing countries have considerably upgraded the quality of their labor forces and have substantially expanded their stock of capital. Therefore, they now produce capital-intensive products such as steel, machinery, and automobiles. Moreover, some newly developed countries such as BRICS now produce high-technology products, such as computers and computer software. BRICS is the acronym for an association of five major emerging national economies: Brazil, Russia, India, China and South Africa. BRICS members are all developing or newly industrialized countries, but they are distinguished by their large, fast-growing economies and significant influence on regional and global affairs; all five are G-20 members. The G20 or Group of Twenty is an intergovernmental forum comprising 19 countries and the EU. It works to address major issues related to the global economy, such as international financial stability, climate change mitigation, and sustainable development.

Example 2.1

Suppose for the time being, that the world has two nations (Canada and Japan) and two commodities (wheat and cameras). For a fixed amount of $1,000 in land, labor, capital, and technology, Canada and Japan can produce either of the two commodities listed in Table 2.1. In other words, if each country were to make one or the other, Canada could produce 180 bushels of wheat or six cameras, while Japan could produce 80 bushels of wheat or eight cameras. If there is no trade, then Canada can produce 90 bushels of wheat and three cameras, while Japan can produce 50 bushels of wheat and three cameras.

It is clear from Table 2.1 that under full employment conditions, Canada's exchange ratio for the two products is one camera (C) for 30 bushels of wheat (W) or 1C = 30W. Japan's

Table 2.1 Production alternatives of wheat and cameras.

Country	Wheat	Cameras
Canada	180	6
Japan	80	8

Table 2.2   Gains to both nations from specialization and trade.

Country	Before Specialization	After Specialization	Exports (−) and Imports (+)	After Trade	Gains from Trade
Canada	90W	180W	−80W	100W	10W
	3C	0C	+4C	4C	1C
Japan	50W	0W	+80W	80W	30W
	3C	8C	−4C	4C	1C

exchange ratio for the two products is one camera for 10 bushels of wheat or 1C = 10W. Thus, Canada has a greater advantage in the production of wheat, whereas Japan has a better advantage in the production of cameras. In other words, these two countries produce both products but at different levels of economic efficiency. If they specialize according to their comparative advantage, Canada must produce only wheat while Japan must produce only cameras. If they trade with each other, larger outputs of both wheat and cameras would be available to both nations because specialization allocates world resources more efficiently.

The exchange ratios for the two products differ in the two countries. This difference becomes the basis for mutually beneficial specialization and trade. Trade requires a new exchange ratio between the two products so that Canada may obtain one camera for less than 30 bushels of wheat and Japan may obtain more than 10 bushels of wheat for one camera. Thus, the terms of trade lie somewhere between 1C = 30W and 1C = 10W or 30W > 1C > 10W. The actual exchange ratio will depend on world conditions of supply and demand. However, assume that the international exchange ratio for the two products is 1C = 20W. The quantities of the two products available to both countries after specialization and trade would be greater than the optimum product mixes before specialization and trade.

Table 2.2 shows the gains of the two nations from specialization and trade. If Canada exports 80 bushels of wheat (out of 180 bushels) for four cameras, it will enjoy 100 bushels of wheat and four cameras. Hence, Canada would have 10 more bushels of wheat and one more camera than the optimum product mix that existed before specialization and trade. If Japan trades four cameras (out of eight cameras) for 80 bushels of wheat, Japan will enjoy four cameras and 80 bushels of wheat. Thus, Japan would enjoy one more camera and 30 more bushels of wheat than its optimum product mix without specialization and trade.

Specialization and trade permit the two countries in our model to obtain a total of 180 bushels of wheat and a total of eight cameras. It is important to note that the two countries had a total of 140 bushels of wheat and a total of six cameras before specialization and trade. Thus, larger outputs of both wheat and cameras are available to the two countries from specialization and trade.

Global Finance in Practice 2.1: Should Tiger Woods Mow His Own Lawn?
Tiger is a great athlete. One of the best golfers to have ever lived. He is better at other activities too. Tiger is probably in better shape than most: He can run faster, lift more, and work quicker. For example, Tiger can probably mow his lawn faster than anyone else. But just because he can mow his lawn fast, does this mean he should?

To answer this question, we can use the concepts of opportunity cost and comparative advantage. Let us say that Tiger can mow his lawn in 2 hours. In the same 2 hours he could film a television commercial for golf clubs and earn $100,000. By contrast, Joe, the kid next door can mow Tiger's lawn in 4 hours. In those same 4 hours he could work at McDonald's and earn $60.

In this example, Tiger's opportunity cost is $100,000 and Joe's is $60. Tiger has an absolute advantage in mowing lawns because he can do the work in less time. Yet Joe has a comparative advantage because he has the lower opportunity cost. The gains in trade from this example are tremendous. Rather than mowing his own lawn, Tiger should make the commercial and hire Joe to mow his lawn. As long as Tiger pays Joe more than $60 and less than $100,000, both of them are better off.[2]

2.1.2. *The Theory of Factor Endowments*

Countries are endowed differently in their economic resources. Thus, Columbia is more efficient in the production of coffee and the United States is more efficient in the production of computers. Columbia has the soil, weather, and abundant supply of unskilled labor necessary to produce coffee more economically than the United States. The United States possesses facilities, key parts, and ample supply of skilled labor necessary to produce computers more efficiently than Columbia.

Differences in these national factor endowments explain differences in comparative factor costs between the two countries. Capital costs are lower in the United States than in India because the United States has more capital than India. Labor costs are lower in India than in the United States because India has more labor than the United States. Simply stated, the more abundant the supply of any factor, the lower the cost of the factor.

The **theory of factor endowments** says that countries are mutually benefited if they specialize in the production of those goods that use a large number of abundant factors and trade those goods among them. This means that a country must specialize in the production and export of any good that uses large amounts of abundant factors. It must import those commodities that use large amounts of production factors scarce at home. On the one hand, most developing countries have a comparative cost advantage in the production of labor-intensive commodities. On the other hand, most industrialized countries enjoy a comparative cost advantage in the production of capital-intensive commodities. Thus, specialization and trade can be mutually beneficial if industrialized countries specialize in the production and export of capital-intensive goods and if developing countries specialize in the production and export of labor-intensive commodities.

---

[2]https://fs.blog/should-tiger-woods-mow-his-own-lawn-the-principles-of-comparative-advantage/, October 31, 2022.

2.1.3. *Product Life Cycle Theory*

All products have a certain length of life. During this life they go through certain stages. A product's life begins with its market introduction; its market grows rather rapidly; its demand reaches maturity; its market declines; and finally, its life ends.

This **product life-cycle theory** attempts to explain both world trade and foreign investment patterns on the basis of stages in a product's life. In the context of international trade, the theory assumes that certain products go through four stages:

1. A large company introduces a new product or a new service in response to some change in the home-country market. After a time lag, this home country establishes itself as an exporter with a monopoly position.
2. Increasing transportation and tariff costs make it less attractive to export the product. Thus, the firm begins to produce its product in some foreign countries. This international production replaces home-country exports in certain foreign markets.
3. Some foreign companies begin to compete in third-country markets. This competition leads to a further reduction in home-country exports.
4. Some foreign companies export the product back to the home country. Many factors such as low labor costs, economies of scale, and government subsidies make it possible for foreign companies to invade the home-country market.

2.1.4. *Other Motives for World Trade*

2.1.4.1. *Economies of scale*

Economies of scale take place due to a synergistic effect which is said to exist when the whole is worth more than the mere sum of its parts. This effect has been frequently defined as "2 + 2 = 5." In other words, another important cause of international trade is that costs may fall as output expand. The economies of mass production can be realized if each country specializes in a limited number of products in which it has a comparative advantage. Mass production and mass marketing improve skills and technologies. Opportunities to eliminate duplicate facilities occur. There are also opportunities to consolidate the functions of production, marketing, and purchasing. These types of operating economies and improved skills can lead to larger outputs of goods and services even if no differences existed in comparative costs among countries.

2.1.4.2. *Differences in tastes*

Even if differences in comparative costs among countries and economies of scale were absent, world trade might take place due to differences in tastes. Suppose that both New Zealand and Korea produce the same amount of fish and meat. If New Zealanders prefer meat and Koreans prefer fish, then a mutually beneficial export of meat from Korea to New Zealand and fish from New Zealand to Korea would take place. Both countries gain from this trade, because the sum total of satisfaction derived from the trade is greater than would be possible under isolated self-sufficiency without trade.

2.1.5. Benefits of Open Trade

Open, competitive trade promotes the economic welfare of all countries that engage in it and does so in four ways. Open trade secures the benefits of national comparative advantage; increases domestic competitive pressures; accelerates the flow of technology and ideas; and broadens the variety of goods and services available to both producers and consumers.

2.1.5.1. Allocation efficiency from comparative advantage

A more traditional approach depicts a world in which markets are competitive and economies of scale do not exist. In these situations, gains stem from comparative advantage. Under the concept of comparative advantage, each country imports those goods produced more efficiently abroad and exports those goods produced more cheaply at home. Such types of trade allow each trading country to devote more of its resources to producing those goods and services that it can produce more efficiently. Because free trade leads to the most efficient use of scarce resources, all countries that engage in free trade would obtain economic gains.

2.1.5.2. Increased competition

Foreign trade strengthens competitive pressures in the domestic economy, stimulating efficiency and growth. An open trade regime effectively increases the number of both actual and potential competitors in the domestic market by including those located beyond a nation's borders. This encourages domestic producers to innovate and become more competitive. Consumers, both at home and abroad, reap the benefits.

2.1.5.3. Increased productivity from production efficiency

Access to international markets through foreign trade stimulates the flow of information across borders. Domestic companies engaged in international competition assimilate new ideas about production methods, product design, organizational structure, and marketing strategy. These new ideas allow domestic companies to employ their resources more efficiently. Thus, open competition through free trade increases productivity.

Open trade also creates opportunities for economies of scale or synergistic effects. The reduction of barriers automatically increases total demand. As economic resources shift to the more efficient producers due to increased competition, companies can expand production to take advantage of the larger market. This dynamic change in market size allows companies to spread fixed costs over more units of production.

2.1.5.4. Expanded menu of goods

Foreign trade expands the menu of goods and services available to both producers and consumers. Companies gain access to a wider variety of inputs. Consumers get to choose from a broader assortment of goods and services. By expanding the choices, foreign trade boosts efficiency and improves living standards.

2.1.6. Free Trade versus Protectionism

The possibility of a foreign embargo on sales of certain products and needs of national defense may cause some countries to seek self-sufficiency in some strategic commodities.

Political and military questions constantly affect international trade and other international business operations. Conflicts have historically taken place between multinational companies (typically exporters) and host countries (typically importers) over political ideology, national sovereignty, control of key industries, balance of payments, and control of export markets.

2.1.6.1. *Reasons for protectionism*

There are a variety of arguments for protectionism: (1) national security, (2) unfair competition, (3) the infant-industry argument, (4) domestic employment, and (5) diversification.

First, if a country wishes to be a world power, it must maintain key sectors, such as steel, for national security. By maintaining strategic commodities, it is assured of supplies in the event of global conflicts and boycotts.

Second, labor-intensive industries in developed countries argue that low wages in foreign countries constitute unfair competition. In addition to low wages, countries with industrial policies enjoy unfair competitive advantage because of their public policies such as special tax incentives, subsidies, and selective protection to overcome the competition.

Third, the logic of the infant industry argument is that protective measures are essential for newly begun domestic industries to establish themselves. They need time and thus protection to realize the economies of mass production.

Fourth, protection maintains domestic employment and living standards. The costs from unemployment may be higher than the costs of inefficient domestic production for certain products.

Fifth, highly specialized economies, such as Kuwait's oil economy, depend on international markets for incomes. These countries need some protection to diversify the economy if they are to reduce their dependence upon world markets for one or two products.

2.1.6.2. *Forms of trade control*

Tariffs, import quotas, and other trade barriers are three primary means of protectionism.

Tariffs are duties or taxes imposed on imported commodities. Tariffs on imported commodities may be imposed for purposes of revenues or protection. Tariffs are usually modest when they are used to increase revenues. However, tariffs are typically high when they are imposed to protect domestic companies from foreign competition. Although protective tariffs do not eliminate the importation of foreign products completely, they clearly put foreign sellers at a comparative disadvantage. Here, consumers must pay more for foreign goods, thereby reducing their consumption of imported commodities.

Import quotas specify maximum amounts of certain products to be imported during a given period of time, usually 1 year. Import quotas may also be used to shield domestic producers from foreign competition. They are sometimes more effective than tariffs in reducing the importation of certain products. Even if tariffs are high, certain commodities may still be imported in relatively large quantities. In contrast, low import quotas totally prohibit imports beyond a quota. Hence, it is no wonder why many countries have recently imposed quotas on the importation of certain goods.

Other trade barriers the general trend around the world since World War II has been to reduce such obvious trade barriers as quotas and tariffs. This trend has compelled governments to replace them with less obvious forms of protection which, according to a survey by Ball and McCulloch, number over 800.[3] Three major classes of such other trade barriers are:

1. Direct government participation in trade.
2. Customs and other administrative procedures.
3. Technical and health regulations or standards.

First, a government's participation in trade covers export subsidies, countervailing duties, and antidumping duties; when engaged in these activities, the government prefers national over foreign bidders. **Countervailing duties** mean additional import duties imposed to offset an export subsidy by another country. **Antidumping duties** are customs duties imposed on an imported product whose price is lower than that of the same product in the home market.

Second, customs and other administrative procedures include customs classification, valuation, and procedures. Import duties imposed on certain products often depend on how they are classified into the tariff schedule and how they are valued by customs authorities. In addition, customs inspectors can discriminate against a good or a country by delaying the importation process.

Finally, technical and health regulations make up the standards which can hinder imports. Governments apply many safety rules and regulations on imports with marking, labeling, packaging, and imposing technical standards. These standards tend to discriminate against imports by imposing greater hardship on foreign than domestic companies.

Other trade barriers can have a significant impact on international trade. For example, Japan is criticized by some countries for its non-tariff barriers, such as extremely stringent product standards on imported products. Some economists argue that these barriers are major causes of the lingering US trade deficit with Japan. Others, however, attribute the deficit to Japan's superior quality and production efficiencies based on teamwork, quality education, and work ethic.

2.2. ECONOMIC INTEGRATION

World leaders have recognized that the reduction or elimination of artificial barriers to trade is necessary for expanding world trade. The worldwide postwar efforts to expand foreign trade included the elimination of tariff barriers through the World Trade Organization and the stabilization of currencies through the International Monetary Fund. At the same time these efforts went forward on the international level, many countries around the world also pursued economic cooperation at the regional level. Regional economic cooperation is based on the premise that countries in a region connected by historical, geographic, cultural, economic, and political similarities may be able to strike more intensive cooperative agreements for mutually beneficial economic advantages.

2.2.1. *From GATT to WTO*

In 1947, 23 countries signed the General Agreement on Tariffs and Trade (GATT) in Geneva. To join GATT, countries must adhere to the **most favored nation** (MFN) clause, which

---

[3]Ball, D. A. and W. H. McCulloch, *International Business*, Homewood, IL: Irwin, 2007, Chapter 3.

requires that if a country grants a tariff reduction to one country, it must grant the same concession to all other countries. For example, if the United States cuts its tariff from 20 to 10 percent on wool sweaters from Australia, it must grant the same concession on wool sweaters from all other countries. The MFN clause also applies to quotas and licenses.

GATT members had held many talks since 1947 to expand and promote world trade. First, GATT members held periodic meetings from 1947 to 1952 to cut specific tariffs. Second, the Kennedy Round (1964–1967) covered across-the-board tariff reductions on industrial products. Perhaps the most important part of the Kennedy Round was to reduce trade barriers between the United States and the European Community. Third, the Tokyo Round (1973–1979) of multilateral trade negotiations discussed the reduction of non-tariff barriers. The most important part of these agreements is a series of detailed codes spelling out permissible and non-permissible "good" behavior by governments in almost all non-tariff measures. Fourth, the Uruguay Round (1986–1993) discussed the expansion of trade liberalization to include services, intellectual property rights, and agricultural products.

The new organization, known as the World Trade Organization (WTO), has replaced the GATT since the Uruguay Round Accord became effective on January 1, 1995. Today WTO's 164 members and 23 observer governments account for more than 99 percent of world trade. WTO has five major functions: (1) administrating its trade agreements, (2) forum for trade negotiations, (3) monitoring national trade policies, (4) technical assistance and training for developing countries, and (5) cooperation with other international organizations. China joined the WTO in 2001. China's WTO membership has further legitimized the idea of free trade.

On January 23, 2017, the amendment to the WTO Trade Related Aspects of Intellectual Property Rights (TRIPS) Agreement marks the first time since the organization opened in 1995 that WTO accords have been amended, and this change should secure for developing countries a legal pathway to access affordable remedies under WTO rules.[4]

The WTO has more power to enforce the rules of international trade than the GATT. Under the WTO there is a powerful dispute-resolution system, with three-person arbitration panels. Countries may bring charges against their trading partners to a WTO panel. WTO members cannot veto the panel's rulings, as was the case under GATT. If an offending country fails to comply with panel recommendations, its trading partners are guaranteed the right to compensation. As a final resort, the trading partners are given the right to impose countervailing sanctions against the offending country. The WTO launched the current round of negotiations, known as the Doha Round, at the fourth ministerial conference in Doha, Qatar in November 2001, to liberalize global commerce further. Major issues include moratorium on tariffs for electronic commerce, easier access to foreign markets for high tech, banking, and insurance exports, elimination of agricultural subsidies, tougher labor standards around the world, revision of US anti-dumping laws, and more time for developing countries to liberalize trade. The negotiations have been highly contentious, and agreement has not been reached as of the end of 2022, despite the intense negotiations at several ministerial conferences and at other sessions.

---

[4]WTO | 2017 News items — WTO IP rules amended to ease poor countries' access to affordable medicines.

2.2.2. *Trading Blocs: Types of Economic Cooperation*

A **trading bloc** is a preferential economic arrangement between a group of countries that reduces intraregional barriers to trade in goods, services, investment, and capital. There are more than 50 such arrangements at the present time. There are five major forms of economic cooperation among countries: free trade area, customs union, common market, economic union, and political union.

The **free trade-area** type of cooperation requires member countries to remove all tariffs among themselves. However, the member nations are allowed to have their own tariff arrangements with non-member countries. The United States–Mexico–Canada Agreement (USMCA) of 2020 illustrates the free trade-area type of corporations.

Under the **customs-union** arrangement, member nations not only abolish internal tariffs among themselves but also establish common external tariffs. The trading bloc, called Mercosur in Spanish, constitutes a customs union. Mercosur is made up of four member countries: Argentina, Brazil, Paraguay, and Uruguay. The group encompasses 295 million people and has a combined GDP of nearly $2 trillion. Mercosur also counts Bolivia, Chile, Colombia, Ecuador, Guyana, Peru, and Suriname as associate members.

In a **common market** type of agreement, member countries abolish internal tariffs among themselves and levy common external tariffs. Moreover, they allow the free flow of all factors of production, such as capital, labor, and technology. The Central American Common Market exemplifies a common-market type of agreement among Costa Rica, El Salvador, Guatemala, Honduras, and Nicaragua. This common market wishes to permit the free flow of production factors among its member countries, but its goal is hampered by the non-uniformity of economic conditions among them.

The **economic union** combines common-market characteristics with harmonization of economic policy. Member nations are required to pursue common monetary and fiscal policies. This means that economic-union members have to synchronize taxes, money supply, interest rates, and regulation of capital markets. The current version of the EU represents an economic union. The name of the European Economic Community (EEC) was officially changed to the EU on November 1, 1993, when the Maastricht Treaty of the EEC went into effect.

The **political union** combines economic-union characteristics with political harmony among the member countries. Essentially, countries merge with each other to create a new nation. Thus, it is the ultimate market agreement among nations. In the 1950s, Egypt, Syria, and Yemen formed a political union, but it did not last long. Thus, in its pure form, an example of the political union does not exist.

2.2.3. *Regional Economic Agreements*

The world has been swiftly moving toward trading blocs in recent years. Economists divide trading nations into three groups based on Europe, North America, and Asia. The world's future economic landscape will see that companies will compete within the boundaries of trading blocs — whether in Europe, North America, or Asia. Each of these trading blocs is expected to pose its own challenges. If countries continue to compete with one another as single nations, they could lose their competitiveness in the world marketplace. Many world leaders loudly assail regional trading blocs that serve as protectionist trade umbrellas. However, they also concede that trading blocs may be an unfortunate but emerging trend.

2.2.3.1. *The European Union*

The EU is an economic union of 27 member states, located primarily in Europe. The membership of the EU declined by one under the Brexit because the UK formally left the EU on January 31, 2020. Committed to regional integration, the EU was established by the Treaty of Maastricht on November 1, 1993 upon the foundations of the European Communities. According to the May 2020 report by the Global Office of the International Comparison Program (ICP) at the World Bank, China, US, and EU are the largest economies in the world. The Gross Domestic Product (GDP) of the EU with 27 Member States represented 16.0 percent of world GDP, expressed in Purchasing Power Standards (PPS). China and the United States were the two largest economies, with shares of 16.4 and 16.3 percent, respectively. The EU has developed a single market through a standardized system of laws which apply in all member states, ensuring the free movement of people, goods, services, and capital. It maintains common policies on trade, agriculture, fisheries and regional development. Seventeen member states have adopted a common currency, the euro, constituting the Eurozone.[5]

2.2.3.2. *United States–Mexico–Canada Agreement*

The USMCA entered into force on July 1, 2020. The **USMCA** substituted the North America Free Trade Agreement (NAFTA). The North American Free Trade Agreement or NAFTA was an agreement signed by the governments of the United States, Canada, and Mexico creating a trilateral trade bloc in North America. The agreement came into force on January 1, 1994. It superseded the Canada–United States Free Trade Agreement between the United States and Canada. Business leaders, government officials, and scholars viewed the NAFTA as a natural trading bloc because of American technology, Canadian resources, and Mexican labor.[6]

The UGMCA is a mutually beneficial win for North American workers, farmers, ranchers, and businesses. The Agreement creates more balanced, reciprocal trade supporting high-paying jobs for Americans and grow the North American economy.

Agreement highlights include:

- Creating a more level playing field for American workers, including improved rules of origin for automobiles, trucks, other products, and disciplines on currency manipulation.
- Benefiting American farmers, ranchers, and agribusinesses by modernizing and strengthening food and agriculture trade in North America.
- Supporting a 21st century economy through new protections for US intellectual property and ensuring opportunities for trade in US services.
- New chapters covering digital trade, anticorruption, and good regulatory practices, as well as a chapter devoted to ensuring that small and medium-sized enterprises benefit from the Agreement.

---

[5]http://en.wikipedia.org/wiki/European_Union, March 8, 2010.
[6]http://en.wikipedia.org/wiki/North_American_Free_Trade_Agreement, Marcy 8, 2010.

2.2.3.3. *Asian integration efforts*

Asia represents the third major region of the world economy, although it is difficult to clearly delineate its boundaries. Hence, the development in Asia has been quite different from that in Europe and in the Americas. While European and North American agreements have been driven by political will, market forces may force more formal integration on the politicians in Asia. If Asian countries continue to compete in the world marketplace as single nations, they could lose their competitiveness in the world marketplace. While Japan and China are the dominant forces in the area to take leadership in such an endeavor, neither these two countries nor other countries want Japan and China to do it.

As a result, Asia does not have a strong trading bloc such as USMCA or EU, but it has two loose affiliations: the Association of Southeast Asian Nations (ASEAN) and the Asian Pacific Economic Cooperation (APEC). Created in 1967, ASEAN consists of Brunei, Burma (currently Myanmar), Indonesia, Malaysia, the Philippines, Singapore, Thailand, and Vietnam; since then, ASEAN has added Cambodia and Laos. In recent years, ASEAN and three other countries (China, Korea, and Japan), known as ASEAN Plus Three, agreed to create a free trade area. APEC was formed in 1989 to promote multilateral economic cooperation on issues of trade and investment. APEC consists of 21 Pacific Rim countries that account for half of world output and includes the world's four largest economies: the United States, Japan, Russia, and China.

2.2.4. *Corporate Response to Trading Blocs*

Corporations' investments are an important consideration in the proliferation of trading blocs. On the one hand, investments are made in various blocs to ensure continued access to the markets should protectionist barriers be erected. In a sense this necessity may foster inefficiency because investments would not be made with the objective of optimization in mind. However, if trading blocs attract nations with similar consumer profiles, these investments do make sense from an overall business-development and customer-service point of view. Regional strategies may, in turn, accelerate the concentration of the different markets that comprise the trading blocs.

Many companies may not have the resources nor the time to invest in all of the emerging trading blocs. To ensure future competitive capability, many strategic alliances have been forged across national and regional borders in recent years. These alliances involve arrangements ranging from contract manufacturing to joint research and development. Corporate mergers have occurred across regional borders to guarantee access to blocs as local entities.

What impact will these corporate investments and alliances have on both blocs and the argument that blocs are indeed basically protectionists? The "stateless" corporation may be able to move production and investment wherever it gets its best return without concern for a particular country or a region. Technology has made such transfer relatively swift and quite painless.

First, corporations and their assets can no longer be held hostage by a dismayed government or even a supranational organization. Second, it is becoming increasingly difficult to establish a product's national/regional origin which makes protectionist moves correspondingly difficult. Finally, the interdependence that is being formed by companies may also spill over in a major way to the national and regional levels as well.

2.3. MOTIVES FOR FOREIGN INVESTMENT

In recent years, many companies have been induced to enter into new and profitable markets abroad. Economic and political forces in the host countries, along with their desire to sell more abroad, are largely responsible for the expansion of direct foreign investment. Companies find it increasingly easier to reach foreign markets through direct investment. The product life-cycle theory, the portfolio theory, and the oligopoly model have been suggested as bases for explaining and justifying foreign investment.

2.3.1. *Product Life-Cycle Theory*

The theory of product life cycle explains changes in the location of production. When new products are introduced in their home country markets, their sales and profits tend to increase sharply until they reach maturity. Competition increases rapidly as these products approach their maturity point; this competition narrows profit margins. At this stage, companies may utilize foreign manufacturing locations to lower production costs and sustain profit margins.

This theory assumes that larger companies in highly advanced countries have a comparative advantage in new products over the companies in developing nations. Companies in developing countries, however, have a comparative advantage in fabricating mature products. Highly advanced technologies, highly educated labor resources, and abundant capital are essential to develop new products. They are readily available to larger firms in advanced countries. Larger markets and necessary alteration requirements in early production stages are additional reasons why larger companies in the developed areas of the world first introduce new products in the home country markets.

As products become mature, product defects and technological imperfections inherent in new products are ironed out so that the method of production becomes standardized. Competition begins to appear during the stage of market growth and becomes highly intensive during the stage of market maturity. At this point, some companies will shift their standardized manufacturing methods to developing countries for a number of good reasons:

1. Standard production methods require many unskilled workers.
2. Most developing countries have an abundant supply of unskilled labor.
3. Labor costs are lower in developing countries than in advanced countries.

2.3.2. *Portfolio Theory*

Portfolio theory indicates that a company is often able to improve its risk-return performance by holding a diversified portfolio of assets. This theory represents another rationale for foreign investment. This theory rests on two variables: risk and return. Risk is the variability of returns associated with an investment project. Two projects may have the same long-term average rate of return. But one project may fluctuate widely in annual return while the other may have a stable return. A project whose returns fluctuate widely is said to be riskier than the other whose returns are stable.

Typically, only a few financial variables are known in advance. Business executives and investors are, basically, risk averse. Thus, they desire to minimize the overall degree of risk for their investment projects. Fortunately, there are many business situations in which the risks of individual projects tend to offset each other. As a consequence, successful diversification makes it possible for investors to have a portfolio with risk less than the sum of the risks of the individual projects in the portfolio.

A study by Levy and Sarnat indicated that a company is often able to improve its risk-return performance by holding an internationally diversified portfolio.[7] The key element in portfolio theory is the correlation coefficient between projects in the portfolio. When projects with low degrees of correlation are combined with each other, a company is able to reduce its risk of expected return. The Levy–Sarnat model assumes that foreign investment projects tend to be less correlated with each other than domestic investment projects. The economic cycles of different countries, France and Saudi Arabia, for example, do not tend to be totally synchronized. On the other hand, most domestic projects tend to be highly correlated with each other because they depend on the same state of economy.

2.3.3. *Oligopoly Model*

If you have ever purchased a can of tennis balls in the United Sates, there is a high likelihood it is from one of the top manufacturers Penn, Wilson, Dunlop, or Prince. These four companies make most of the tennis balls sold in the United States. Together these four firms determine the quantity of tennis balls and the price at which tennis balls are sold. Analysts say that only a small number of giant multinational companies in each major industry also dominate the world market of that segment.

An **oligopoly** exists where there are only a few firms whose products are usually close substitutes for one another. Because a few firms dominate a market, each of these firms has a large share of the market. Thus, the policies of one firm have repercussions on the other firms.

The oligopoly model offers a way of explaining why multinational companies (MNCs) invest in foreign countries. The **oligopoly model** assumes that business firms make foreign investments to exploit their quasi-monopoly advantages. The advantages of an MNC over a local company may include technology, access to capital, differentiated products built on advertising, superior management, and organizational scale.

Horizontal investments for foreign production of the same goods as made in a home market are made to produce operational economies of scale. A horizontal investment may reduce the number of competitors, eliminate duplicate facilities, and expand a firm's operation in an existing product line. Vertical investments for foreign production of raw materials are usually made to control input sources. The control of input sources may make it possible for companies in an oligopolistic industry to raise barriers to the entry of new competitors and to protect their oligopoly position. Some companies make defensive investments to prevent others from getting an unanticipated advantage.

2.3.4. *Other Studies of Motives for Foreign Investment*

Many foreign investors are motivated by strategic decisions. Although there are numerous sorts of strategic considerations, we can group them into two categories: those from the standpoint of investors and those from the standpoint of host countries.

---

[7]Levy, H. and M. Sarnat, "International Diversification of Investment Portfolios," *American Economic Review*, September 1970, pp. 668–675.

2.3.4.1. *Considerations from the standpoint of investors*

Nehrt and Hogue suggested that companies invest abroad for several purposes[8]:

1. New markets
2. Raw materials
3. Production efficiency
4. New knowledge

   (i) First, many companies attempt to satisfy local demand or expand their markets through foreign manufacturing locations. For example, Japanese and Korean automobile manufacturers have built their assembly plants in the United States to satisfy local demand and to expand their market.

  (ii) Second, oil companies, mining companies, and lumber companies find it difficult or costly to obtain raw materials at home. Hence, they invest their money abroad to obtain these raw materials.

 (iii) Third, some production efficiency-oriented companies look for low costs of production, such as low labor costs. This is one of the most important reasons why MNCs choose countries in Africa, Asia, and South America for their overseas investment.

 (iv) Fourth, some companies invest abroad to seek new knowledge and managerial expertise. For example, German, Japanese, and Korean companies have acquired US located electronic firms for their technology.

2.3.4.2. *Considerations from the standpoint of host countries*

The National Industrial Conference Board surveyed a sample of 60 nations and found that many developing countries have various incentive programs for private foreign investments. They include tax incentives, tariff exemptions, financial assistance, remittance guarantees, administrative assistance, protection against competitive investments and imports, and protection against nationalization and political risk. These and other incentive programs would undoubtedly motivate MNCs to invest in those nations offering them.[9]

2.3.4.3. *Mixed considerations*

Aharoni studied the process for foreign investment decisions. After surveying 38 American companies which had invested in Israel, he found the following investment motives[10]:

1. Outside proposals such as those from foreign governments.
2. Fear of losing market.
3. The bandwagon effect, which means that successful foreign operations reported by a company induce competitors to go abroad.
4. Strong competition from abroad in the home market.

---

[8]Nehrt, L. and D. W. Hogue, "The Foreign Investment Decision Process," *Quarterly Journal of AISEC International*, February–April 1968, pp. 43–48.

[9]Industrial Conference Board, *Obstacles and Incentives to Private Foreign Investment*, New York: Conference Board, 1969.

[10]Aharoni, Y., The *Foreign Investment Decision Process*, Boston: Harvard University Press, 1966.

In addition to these four motives, the survey also detected a number of auxiliary motives for foreign investment:

1. Utilization of old machinery.
2. Capitalization of know-how; spreading of research, development, and other fixed costs.
3. Creation of a market for components and other products.
4. Indirect return to a lost market through investment in a country that has commercial agreements with these lost territories.

Global Finance in Practice 2.2: An Example of the Life Cycle Theory with Hyundai Motor Group (Hyundai-Kia)

Hyundai among the Top Three Auto Maker: The World's top three automakers by sales in 2022 include the following: (1) Toyota, (2) Volkswagen, and (3) Hyundai. Their 2022 sales were 10.48 million units for Toyota, 8.3 million units for Volkswagen, and 6.848 million units for Hyundai. Using the product life cycle theory, we can see how Hyundai, a relative newcomer in the auto industry, quickly became the world's third largest auto maker in 2022. However, to understand Hyundai's product life cycle, it is important to also understand the product life cycle of automobiles in general.

Product Life Cycle of Automobiles in General

- **First stage:** Cars were invented in the 19th century, but only the extremely wealthy could afford them.
- **Second stage:** In 1903, Henry Ford founded the Ford Motor Company. Their main innovation in the automobile industry was two-fold. First, they were the first to mass produce cars. The primary way that they were able to achieve production efficiency was through economies of scale and the use of assembly lines. This led to cost efficiency. Therefore, this led to their second innovation: they were the first to make cars affordable to many people.
- **Third stage:** Eventually, almost everyone in the United States that wanted a car eventually owned a car, and for Ford to continue to grow, they needed to export. By becoming an exporter, they could further exploit their near-monopoly-like power to the global marketplace.
- **Fourth stage:** Eventually, Ford Motors faced domestic competition from abroad. When exporters have domestic competition, they must then figure out how to survive. Normally, it is not easy for exporters to compete with domestic rivals. Therefore, some exporters may choose to collaborate with their domestic competitors to survive. It is here where Hyundai's product life cycle begins.

Product Life Cycle of Hyundai Automobiles

- **First stage:** In 1968, Hyundai Motor Company was officially born, with the introduction of its very first model "the Cortina." This car was a result of a collaboration with Ford. Together, they took advantage of the location and know-how of Korean manufacturing to lower production costs in order to sustain profit margins.

- **Second stage:** In the 1970s, Hyundai became an exporter. In fact, they even competed with Ford in some third-country markets in South America and Europe.
- **Third stage:** In 1980s, Hyundai began to export to the US, where Ford Motors was founded. In February 1986, Hyundai launched its subcompact Excel model in the US market. The customer response was immediate. In 1986, total numbered 168,882 — an industry record for an import car distributor in its first year.
- **Fourth stage:** Eventually, for Hyundai to continue to grow, they needed to lower their production costs. To grow in the US markets, Hyundai undertook a direct investment in the United States. Today, Hyundai automobiles that are sold in the US car market are no longer exports. They are assembled in the United States. In 2022, Hyundai is the fourth largest car company in the United States, behind GM, Toyota, and Ford, and the third largest car company in the world. Hyundai acquired Kia in 1998, thus making it possible for the company to become the world's third largest automaker in 2022.[11]

How Can Hyundai-Kia Maintain its Top Position?

According to the product life cycle theory, Hyundai-Kia is likely to lose its top position unless the company handles the following two issues better than its competitors. In the fourth industrial revolution, knowledge workers produce most goods and services with their mind. For the sake of a long-term survival, therefore, companies must secure talent acquisition and self-motivate knowledge workers to fully develop their potential.[12]

The main assets and primary drivers of the industrial age were machines and capital. People were necessary but replaceable. This is because machines controlled the labor speed of workers through the assembly line and management controlled the labor speed of workers through the quota system. Management focused on motivating employees to perform the physical labor needed to produce the products and services. In the fourth industrial age, however, the challenge is how companies can secure talent acquisition and self-motive their knowledge workers to release their human potential.

Innovation accompanied by new technology comes in several varieties. For the sake of a long-term survival with prosperity, however, companies should place a primary emphasis on the market-creating innovations because only such innovations bring

---

[11]Top 15 Automakers in the World, https://www.factorywarrantylist.com/car-sales-by-manufacturer.html.

[12]Min, X., J. M. David, and S. H. Kim, "The Fourth Industrial Revolution: Opportunities and Challenges," *International Journal of Financial Research*, Vol. 9, No. 2, 2018, pp. 88–95; World Car Sales by Manufacture: Top 15 Automakers in the World, https://www.factorywarrantylist.com/car-sales-by-manufacturer.html; and Bryan, C. M., C. M. Christensen, and D. van Bever, "The Power of Market Creation: How Innovation Can Spur Development," in A. D. Reader, *Foreign Affairs: Fourth Industrial Revolution*, January/February 2015, pp. 198–209.

Table 2.3 How to motivate employees.

The Past (Industrial Age)	The Future (Digital Age)
My paycheck	Purpose
My satisfaction	Development
My boss	A caring manager
My annual review	Ongoing conversations
My weaknesses	A focus on strengths

Source: Gallup, "What Is Employee Engagement and How Do You Improve You Improve it?" https://www.gallup.com/workplace/285674/improve-employee-engagement-workplace.aspx#ite-357473.

permanent jobs that ultimately create prosperity. Talent acquisition tends to focus on long-term human resources planning and finding appropriate candidates for positions that require a very specific new skill set. Consequently, companies must secure the talent acquisition to make their market-creating innovations successful.

Once companies secure talent acquisition, they should make their employees self-motivate their human potential. Remember, anything lasting and worthwhile in life takes effort, sacrifice, commitment, and perseverance. Employees need more than a fleeting warm-fuzzy feeling and a good paycheck to invest in their work and achieve more for their company. People want purpose and meaning from their work. They want to be known for what makes them unique. This is what drives employees to work harder for their company. And they want relationships, particularly with a manager who can coach them to the next level. Table 2.3 shows the differences between the traditional approaches to motivate employees and the new approaches to motivate employees.

2.4. A SYNTHESIS OF FOREIGN TRADE AND INVESTMENT THEORIES

Traditionally, economists concentrated on trade only at the national level, while management scholars focused almost exclusively on the behavior of MNCs. Both groups of scholars thus failed to incorporate trade and investment theories into a single theory of international involvement. This was not a serious problem when foreign trade was largely carried on by intermediaries while producers remained at home. However, MNCs have recently crossed the confines of individual nation-states to carry on their operations throughout the world. Consequently, motives for foreign trade and investment are too closely interrelated with each other to consider them separately.

2.4.1. *Eclectic Theory*

The **eclectic theory**, associated with Dunning, attempts to explain a logical link between the international allocation of resources and the exchange of goods between countries. In other words, this theory makes the case for an integrated approach to international economic

involvement based on the advantages of both a country's location and a company's ownership. Location-specific advantages, such as natural resources and low labor costs, are advantages that are available only or primarily in a single location. Ownership-specific advantages,
such as capital funds and technology, are advantages that favor MNCs over local companies.
The eclectic theory implies that location-specific advantages favor a host foreign country
while ownership-specific advantages favor an investing firm. Thus, the eclectic theory helps
explain cross-country differences in patterns of MNCs' international involvement.

When a company expands its operations beyond national borders for the first time, it
tends to exploit a foreign country's markets through exports. A company favors investment
in a foreign country only if it is most profitable for the company to internationalize its
advantages in that country. Dunning argues that a company is willing to invest in overseas
production facilities if the company has the following three kinds of advantages[13]:

1. **Ownership-specific advantages:** This is the extent to which a company has tangible
   and intangible assets unavailable to other firms.
2. **Internalization advantages:** It is in the company's best interest to use its ownership-
   specific advantages rather than license them to foreign owners.
3. **Location-specific advantages:** The company will profit by locating part of its production facilities overseas.

It is important to note that empirical tests of the eclectic theory show that a major part
of foreign direct investment is made by large, research-intensive companies in oligopolistic
industries. These companies find it profitable to invest overseas because they enjoy both
location and ownership advantages.

2.5. SUMMARY

Several theories explain the motives for world trade and foreign investment. The theory of
comparative advantage and the theory of factor endowments explain why countries exchange
their goods and services with each other. The theory of comparative advantage depends
on two assumptions. First, economic resources are unequally distributed among nations.
Second, efficient production of various products requires combinations of different economic
resources and different technologies.

Both the product life-cycle theory and the portfolio theory provide a conceptual rationale
for foreign investment. The product life-cycle theory assumes that a country uses foreign
manufacturing locations when products approach their maturity point. The portfolio theory
maintains that a company invests overseas because internationally diversified portfolios of
assets improve risk-return performance.

A synthesis of foreign trade and investment theories is needed to form a single theory of
international economic involvement. We can integrate trade and investment theories into a
model which demonstrates how these theories influence a firm's choice of entry mode best

---

[13]Dunning, J. H., *International Production and the Multinational Enterprise*, London: George Allen and
Unwin, 1981.

suited to a particular country. The eclectic theory postulates that specific factors of both firm and country are necessary for a firm's foreign investment. When it is most profitable for a multinational firm to internationalize its oligopolistic advantages in a given foreign country, it will invest in that country; otherwise, it will exploit the country through exports.

2.6. KEY TERMS

theory of comparative advantage	theory of factor endowments
product life-cycle theory	economies of scale
tariffs	import quotas
countervailing duties	antidumping duties
most favored nation	trading bloc
free trade-area	customs-union
common market	economic union
political union	portfolio theory
oligopoly	oligopoly model
eclectic theory	Brexit
US–Mexico–Canada Agreement (USMCA)	

2.7. PROBLEMS

Assume that production possibilities data for the United States and Taiwan are as follows:

		Production Alternatives		
Country	Product	A	B	C
USA	Clothing	0	30	90
	Food	30	20	0
Taiwan	Clothing	0	20	60
	Food	15	10	0

1. What is the comparative cost of clothing and food in the United States?
2. What is the comparative cost of clothing and food in Taiwan?
3. Identify the product that each country should specialize in according to comparative advantage.
4. Assume that both countries decided to specialize in a product according to the comparative advantage. With 1 food = 3 clothing terms of trade, the United States exchanges 10 tons of its food for 35 units of Taiwanese clothing. With the assumption that B is the optimum-product mix, prepare a table such as Table 2.2.
5. With a fixed investment of $10,000, the United States produces more in both clothing and food than Taiwan. Does this mean that specialization and trade do not provide any benefits for the United States?

Closing Case 2: The Fruits of Free Trade Under the World Trade Organization

> The essential difference between free trade and protection is this: Under a system of free trade excellence of the product is the only means by which it can secure a market, while under protection an inferior article can dominate the market through the aid of legislation. The necessary effect of free trade is, therefore, to encourage efficiency in production, while the necessary effect of protection is to encourage skill in corruption. Prosperity is an abundance of commodities. The merit of any policy or system can be evaluated by its effect on the volume of commodities available for the use of the people. (William Bourke Cochran, in the Name of Liberty, 1925)

In 1947, 23 countries signed the GATT in Geneva, a voluntary association of countries designed to promote free trade. GATT members have held many talks since 1947 to expand and promote world trade. Such talks resulted in vast tariff reductions for industrialized countries. Many developing countries have implemented similar tariff reductions. These tariff reductions have caused world trade to increase two times faster than world output since 1950, thereby boosting the standard of living for millions of people around the world.

The general trend around the world since the World War II has been to reduce obvious trade barriers, such as tariffs. Tariff reductions through several rounds of trade negotiations are an indication not only that countries are committed to work jointly toward freer trade but also that tariffs are the easiest trade barrier to tackle. In addition, negotiating rounds have dealt with the increasingly important and complex non-tariff issues.

The biggest change from the Uruguay Round of trade negotiations (1986–1993) was the agreement to replace the GATT with the WTO. Under the WTO, there is a clearly defined dispute settlement mechanism. This dispute-settlement system allows small and developing countries to have influence for the first time in dealing with trade practices in other countries. Further, by bringing cases to the panel, accused countries may agree to settle before a ruling is made. Consequently, the WTO's settlement body has had a much heavier caseload than existed under the old GATT system. China joined the WTO in 2001, thereby further legitimizing the idea of free trade. As of March 2021, the WTO consisted of 164 countries and 25 observer countries, all of whom are in the process of applying for its membership. Based in Geneva, Switzerland, the WTO has a staff of about 600 individuals from 70 different countries and a budget of 197 million Swiss francs. Today WTO members account for 97 percent of world trade.

The WTO is a consensus-based organization. Decisions are made by the entire membership, typically by consensus. A majority vote is also possible, but it has never been used in the WTO and was extremely rare under the WTO's predecessor, GATT. The WTO's agreements have been ratified in all of the members' legislative bodies. As shown in Fig. 2.1, the WTO's top-level decision-making body is the Ministerial Conference, which meets at least once every 2 years. There have been 12 WTO Ministerial Conferences so far in Geneva, Switzerland (June 2022), in Buenos Aires, Argentina (December 2017), Nairobi, Kenya (December 2015), Ballie,

Indonesia (December 2013), Geneva, Switzerland (December 2011), Geneva, Switzerland (December 2009), Hong Kong (December 2005), Cancun, Mexico (November 2003), Doha, Qatar (November 2001), Seattle, Washington (November 1999), Geneva, Switzerland (May 1998), and Singapore (December 1996).

Below the Ministerial Conference is the General Council, which meets several times a year in the Geneva headquarters. The General Council also meets as the Trade Policy Review Body and the Dispute Settlement Body. At the next level, the Goods Council, Services Council, and Intellectual Property Council report to the General Council and meet frequently. At the last level, numerous specialized committees, working groups, and working parties deal with the individual agreements and other areas such as the environment, development, membership applications, and regional trade agreements.

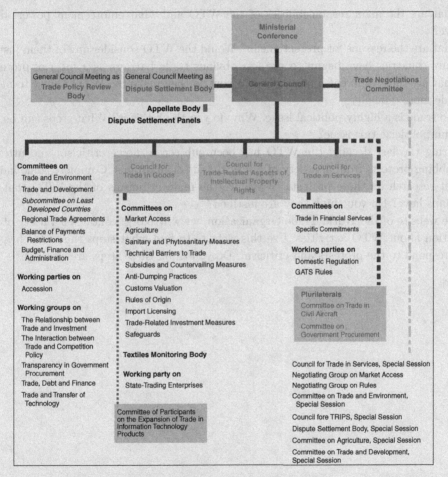

Fig. 2.1 Organizational chart of the World Trade Organization.

Sources: www.wto.org, accessed August 30, 2022; Cletus C. Coughlin, "The Controversy Over Free Trade: The Gap Between Economists and the General Public," *Review*, Federal Reserve Bank of St. Louis, January/February 2002, pp. 1–21; John D. Daniels and Lee H. Radebaugh, *International Business*, New York, Addison-Wesley, 2017, Chapter 6; and Robert D. McTeer, Jr., *The Fruits of Free Trade: 2002 Annual Report*, Federal Reserve Bank of Dallas, 2002.

The WTO Secretariat, with offices only in Geneva, is headed by a Director-General. Because decisions are made by members only, the Secretariat has no decision-making powers. Its main duties are to supply technical and professional support for the various councils and committees, to provide technical assistance for developing countries, to monitor and analyze developments in world trade, to provide information to the public and the media, and to organize the ministerial conferences. The Secretariat also provides some forms of legal assistance in the dispute settlement process and advises governments wishing to become Members of the WTO.

Case Questions

1. What are the main responsibilities of the WTO and what enforcement powers does it have?
2. What are the reasons for protectionism? Would the WTO consider any of them justified?
3. Many countries have begun to use less obvious trade barriers as a form of protection. What are these different approaches and how do they make the WTO ability to monitor trade more difficult?
4. Free trade is a highly political issue. Why do you think this is? What steps can be taken to un politicize this issue?
5. During the last decade, the WTO has been subject to fierce criticism and attention-grabbing protests from a variety of political and social groups. Complete some independent research on these protests. What are the main criticisms of the WTO that these groups have? Do you think they are justified?
6. The website of the World Trade Organization, www.wto.org, contains a variety of information about WTO activities. Use this website to find what steps the WTO has taken to respond to the protests and criticism. Do you think these steps are effective?

Chapter 3

BALANCE OF PAYMENTS AND INTERNATIONAL MONETARY SYSTEM

Opening Case 3: The Relationship between FDI and Exports[1]

Foreign direct investment (FDI) and international trade are both drivers of the global economy, facilitating the cross-border transfer of goods, services, and capital around the world. Research shows that the relationship between FDI and international trade is often complementary rather than competitive, although they represent different types of transaction and play different economic roles. However, neither has escaped criticism and both have faced growing opposition from protectionist governments, despite the positive impacts they can have on recipient countries.

FDI can be measured in stocks or flows. FDI stock measures all direct investments held by non-residents in a country during a specific reporting period. Inward stock is the value of investments owned by foreign companies in a host nation, while outward stock is the value of investment held by domestic companies overseas. These investments are typically in foreign business operations or assets, rather than buying and selling securities that are considered portfolio investments. Countries around the world track the levels of FDI they attract as an indicator of economic performance, with high inbound FDI seen as both a sign of economic growth and a creator of it.

International trade is the buying and selling of products and services on international markets. This activity increases consumer choice, creating competitive markets that should result in reduced end prices and increased quality of products and services. International trade is widely seen as positive for the global economy. Trade and FDI contribute to a country's gross domestic product (GDP) in different ways that are often linked. Trends in FDI and international trade are not always correlated, however, particularly when viewed from a global perspective.

Many studies have shown how FDI and trade can be complementary to each other and it is widely held that inward FDI has a net positive impact on a country's exports. This is due to the transfer of technology and new products for export, facilitating

---

[1]Whiteaker, J., "The Relationship Between FDI and International Trade," *Investment Monitor*, August 30, 2022, https://www.investmentmonitor.ai/analysis/the-relationship-between-fdi-and-international-trade.

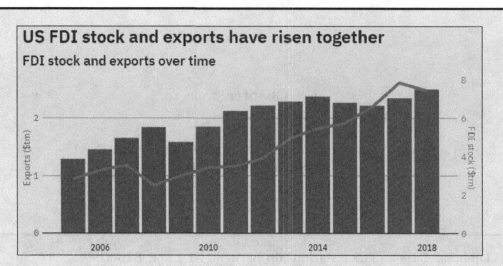

Fig. 3.1 The relationship between the US FDI and the US exports.
Source: Investment Monitor analysis of UNCTADStat.

access to international markets, increasing domestic capital, and providing training to the local workforce. FDI can facilitate the transfer of intangible assets such as skills and technological knowledge that trade cannot. As shown in Fig. 3.1, analysis by Investment Monitor shows a positive relationship between inward FDI stock and exports have risen together.

In general, FDI stock in the US has increased, as has its volumes of exports. Although there are other contributing factors, we can deduce there is a positive correlation between FDI and trade in this case. The US is by far the largest recipient country of FDI globally, but this trend has also been observed in countries that attract comparatively lower volumes of inbound FDI and whose outward FDI flows are greater than their inward flows.

This chapter discusses two closely related topics in international finance: the balance of payments and the international monetary system. A country's **balance of payments** is commonly defined as the record of transactions between its residents and foreign residents over a specified period. These transactions include exports and imports of goods and services, cash receipts and payments, gifts, loans, and investments. Residents may include business firms, individuals, and government agencies. The balance of payments helps business managers and government officials to analyze a country's competitive position and to forecast the direction of pressure on exchange rates. The ability of multinational companies (MNCs) to move money across national boundaries is critical. MNCs depend on this ability for exports, imports, payment of foreign debts, and dividend remittances. Many factors affect a firm's ability to move funds from one country to another. In particular, a country's balance of payments affects the value of its currency, its ability to obtain currencies of other countries, and its policy toward foreign investment.

The **international monetary system** consists of laws, rules, institutions, instruments, and procedures, which involve international transfers of money. These elements affect foreign exchange rates, international trade and capital flows, and balance-of-payments adjustments. Foreign exchange rates determine the prices of goods and services across national boundaries. These exchange rates also affect international loans and foreign investments. Hence, the international monetary system plays a critical role in the financial management of multinational business and economic policies of individual countries.

3.1. AN OVERVIEW OF THE BALANCE OF PAYMENTS

3.1.1. *Sources and Uses of Funds*

The balance of payments is a sources-and-uses-of-funds statement reflecting changes in assets, liabilities, and net worth during a specified period. Transactions between domestic and foreign residents are entered in the balance of payments either as debits or credits. In other words, balance-of-payments statistics are gathered on a single-entry basis.

In dealing with the rest of the world, a country earns foreign exchange on some transactions and expends foreign exchange on others. Transactions that earn foreign exchange are often called credit transactions and represent sources of funds. These transactions are recorded in the balance of payments as credits and are marked by plus signs (+). The following transactions represent credit transactions:

1. Exports of goods and services.
2. Investment and interest earnings.
3. Transfer receipts from foreign residents.
4. Investments and loans from foreign residents.

Transactions that expend foreign exchange are sometimes called debit transactions and represent the uses of funds. These transactions are recorded in the balance of payments as debits and are marked by minus signs (−). The following transactions represent debit transactions:

1. Imports of goods and services.
2. Dividends and interest paid to foreign residents.
3. Transfer payments abroad.
4. Investments and loans to foreigners.

We can apply these elementary principles to the recording of transactions in the balance of payments. Some hypothetical transactions may illustrate this single-entry approach.

Example 3.1

(a) An American company sells $30,000 worth of machinery to a British company (earn foreign exchange); (b) an American woman visits her husband in Japan and she cashes $5,000 worth of US traveler's checks at a Japanese hotel and spends the $5,000 in Japan before returning to the United States (expend foreign exchange); (c) the US Red Cross sends $20,000 worth of flood-relief goods to Chile (expend foreign exchange); (d) an American purchases $5,000 worth of French bonds (expend foreign exchange); and (e) a US bank lends $10,000 to a Canadian firm for 90 days (expend foreign exchange).

3.1.2. *The Balance of Payments as a Whole*

A country incurs a "surplus" in its balance of payments if credit transactions exceed debit transactions or if it earns more abroad than it spends. On the other hand, a country incurs a "deficit" in its balance of payments if debit transactions are greater than credit transactions or if it spends more abroad than it earns.

Essentially, analysts focus on those transactions that occur because of self-interest. These transactions include exports, imports, unilateral transfers, and investments. The arithmetic sum of these transactions represents the balance-of-payments surplus or deficit. A balance-of-payments surplus occurs when receipts exceed payments. By the same token, a balance-of-payments deficit takes place when payments exceed receipts. Changes in reserves and related items occur to account for the differences between international payments and receipts. These items are used to eliminate international disequilibrium.

Surpluses and deficits in the balance of payments are of considerable interest to banks, companies, portfolio managers, and governments. They are used to do the following:

1. Predict pressures on foreign exchange rates.
2. Anticipate government policy actions.
3. Assess a country's credit and political risks.
4. Evaluate a country's economic health.

The transactions of (a) through (e) in Example 3.1 represent autonomous transactions. In Example 3.1(a), the export of US machinery earns a foreign exchange of $30,000 and, thus, is a credit. The transactions of Examples 3.1(b) through 3.1(e) cause the United States to expend a foreign exchange of $40,000 and, therefore, are debits. Consequently, the United States has an overall deficit of $10,000 in its balance of payments and must undertake $10,000 worth of transactions to make up the difference. In this case, the transactions of the United States involve sales of its gold, reductions in its balance of convertible foreign currencies, or increases in the balance of the US dollars held by other nations.

Now, for a moment, suppose that the United States has a surplus in its balance of payments rather than a deficit. To account for this surplus in the US balance of payments, US reserves, such as gold and convertible foreign currencies, would increase by $10,000, or the balance of the US dollars held by other nations would decrease by $10,000. These transactions are designed to account for the surplus in the balance of payments.

3.1.3. *Balance-of-Payments Accounts*

The balance of payments identifies transactions along functional lines. The International Monetary Fund (IMF) classifies balance-of-payments transactions into five major groups:

1. **Current Account:** merchandise, services, income, and current transfers.
2. **Capital Account:** capital transfers, nonproduced assets, and nonfinancial assets.
3. **Financial Account:** direct investments, portfolio investments, and other investments.
4. **Net Errors and Omissions**.
5. **Reserves and Related Items**.

We can classify balance-of-payments transactions into several different groups. However, it is important to note that a country interacts with other countries in two ways. First, it

Table 3.1   Generic balance-of-payments analytic presentation.

1. **Current Account**
   1.1   Net exports and imports
   1.2   Net exports and imports of services
   1.3   Net investment income (i.e., interest, dividend, and employee compensation)
   1.4   Net current transfers (i.e., gifts and grants)
2. **Capital Account**
   2.1   Capital transfers related to the purchase and sale of fixed assets
3. **Financial Account**
   2.2   Net foreign direct investment
   2.3   Net portfolio investment
   2.4   Net financial derivatives (swaps, options, futures)
   2.5   Net other investments (i.e., trade credit, loans, currency, and deposits)
   Total (Groups 1 through 3): balance on current, capital, and financial account
4. **Net Errors and Omissions**
   2.6   Missing data such as unreported foreign funds
5. **Reserves and Related Items**
   2.7   Changes in official reserve assets
   2.8   Net credits and loans from the International Monetary Fund
   2.9   Exceptional financing

buys and sells goods and services in world product markets. Second, it buys and sells financial assets in world financial markets. You could use your $3,000 to buy a personal computer from Toshiba, or instead, you could use that money to buy stock in the Toshiba Corporation. The first transaction would represent a flow of goods, while the second would represent a flow of financial assets. Here, we discuss these two activities and the close relationship between them.

The IMF format in Table 3.1, usually known as analytic presentation, is regarded as useful for analyzing balance of payments developments in a uniform manner. In other words, the format facilitates a variety of analytical perspectives. Each of the five major data categories has a name and particular analytical use.[2] Table 3.2 shows India's balance-of-payments analytic presentation for 4 years from 2018 to 2021.

3.1.3.1. *The current account — Group 1*

The **current account** includes merchandise exports and imports (balance on goods), earnings and expenditures for invisible trade items (services), income on investments (income), and current transfers. Entries in this account are "current" in nature because they do not give rise to future claims. The balance of payments on the current account is the broadest measure of a country's international trade because it includes investment income as well as trade in goods and services. A surplus on the current account represents an inflow of funds, while a deficit represents an outflow of funds.

---

[2]For a detailed discussion about the balance of payments, see Jacque, L. L., *International Corporate Finance*, Hoboken, NJ: Wiley and Sons, 2020, Chapter 4; Eiteman, D. K., A. L. Stonehill, and M. H. Moffett, *Multinational Business Finance*, New York: Pearson, 2021, Chapter 3; Melvin, M. and S. C. Norrbin, *International Money and Finance*, London, UK: Elsevier, 2023, Chapter 3; and the International Monetary Fund's Balance of Payments Statistics Yearbook.

Table 3.2   India: Balance of payments (millions of US dollars).

Year	2018	2019	2020	2021
Current account (excludes reserves and related items)	**−65,599.4**	**−29,762.9**	**32,730.0**	**−33,422.4**
Goods, credit (exports)	332,086.9	331,271.6	281,545.5	402,424.4
Goods, debit (imports)	518,778.5	488,949.6	376,995.3	579,145.2
Balance on goods	−186,691.6	−157,678.0	−95,449.9	−176,720.8
Services, credit (exports)	204,955.6	214,761.5	203,145.2	240,655.5
Services, debit (imports)	124,181.6	130,535.2	116,037.5	137,974.0
Balance on goods and services	−105,917.7	−73,451.7	−8,342.2	−74,039.4
Primary income, credit	21,380.8	23,347.6	22,598.6	23,711.9
Primary income, debit	51,137.5	52,725.5	54,643.4	61,332.0
Balance on goods, services, and primary income	−135,674.3	−102,829.5	−40,387.0	−111,659.5
Secondary income, credit	76,763.0	80,741.9	79,973.0	86,512.4
Secondary income, debit	6,688.2	7,675.2	6,855.9	8,275.3
Capital account (excludes reserves and related items)	**−123.1**	**−1,155.6**	**−1,056.3**	**−307.6**
Capital account, credit	319.0	368.1	440.3	723.6
Capital account, debit	442.1	1,523.7	1,496.7	1,031.2
Balance on current and capital account	−65,722.5	−30,918.5	31,673.7	−33,730.0
Financial account (excludes reserves and related items)	**−60,232.6**	**−86,127.8**	**−69,767.7**	**−100,010.6**
Direct investment, assets	11,417.8	13,140.7	11,122.7	17,238.7
Equity and investment fund shares	7,374.8	7,287.8	5,326.6	8,414.7
Debt instruments	4,043.0	5,852.9	5,796.1	8,824.0
Direct investment, liabilities	42,117.5	50,610.6	64,362.4	44,727.3
Equity and investment fund shares	39,234.1	43,135.7	59,495.8	41,121.4
Debt instruments	2,883.4	7,475.0	4,866.5	3,605.9
Portfolio investment, assets	−1,719.7	2,179.5	681.4	2,689.4
Equity and investment fund shares	−1,719.7	2,179.5	681.4	2,689.4
Debt instruments	—	—	—	—
Portfolio investment, liabilities	−11,317.6	26,763.6	15,793.1	8,407.6
Equity and investment fund shares	−4,361.0	13,768.5	24,854.1	5,223.3
Debt instruments	−6,956.6	12,995.1	−9,061.0	3,184.2
Financial derivatives (other than reserves) and employee stock options	−189.3	−2,651.8	347.5	5,904.6
Fin. derivatives and employee stock options, assets	19,933.4	25,199.7	20,846.3	22,328.0
Fin. derivatives and employee stock options, liabilities	20,122.7	27,851.4	20,498.7	16,423.4
Other investment, assets	62,790.7	59,932.5	61,548.8	63,640.6
Other equity	0.0	—	—	—
Debt instruments	62,790.7	59,932.5	61,548.8	63,640.6
Other investment, liabilities	101,732.2	81,354.4	63,312.6	136,349.0
Other equity	1,820.0	—	—	—
Debt instruments	99,912.2	81,354.4	63,312.6	136,349.0
Balance on current, capital, and financial account	−5,489.9	55,209.4	101,441.4	66,280.6
Net errors and omissions	**1,711.4**	**558.4**	**2,411.8**	**783.2**
Reserves and related items	**−3,778.5**	**55,767.7**	**103,853.3**	**67,063.8**
Reserve assets	−3,778.5	55,767.7	103,853.3	67,063.8
Net credit and loans from the IMF (excluding reserve position)	0.0	0.0	0.0	0.0
Exceptional financing	—	—	—	—

Source: International Monetary Fund, https://data.imf.org/regular.aspx?key=62805740&fbclid=IwAR11O AUs00CC86FynD4rWxKYdi1DZxfmP3RvxdJnAmXHUkWfnZ-jPGP42xM.

Balance on goods refers to the balance between exports and imports of physical goods such as automobiles, machinery, and farm products. Merchandise exports and imports are the largest single components of total international payments for most countries.

Services include invisible items such as insurance and financial services, travel and transportation, computer, and information services, plus fees and royalties. A country's purchases of services represent imports with debits recorded. A country's sales of these services to foreigners represent exports with credits recorded. The balance between the exports and imports of goods and services is called the **balance on goods and services**.

Income on investments includes interest, dividends, and compensation of employees. Investment income represents the flow of earnings from foreign direct and portfolio investments made in prior years. For example, the income that Mexican investors currently earn from their previous foreign investments falls into the income balance. The initial foreign investment of capital, however, was a capital outflow recorded in either the capital account or the financial account during the year when it was originally made.

Current transfers consist of all transfers that are not transfers of capital; they directly affect the level of disposable income and should influence the current consumption of goods and services. Current transfers include gifts and grants from both private parties and governments. Private gifts and grants include personal gifts of all kinds, philanthropic activities, and shipments by relief organizations. For example, money sent by immigrants to their families in their native countries represents private transfers. Government transfers include money, goods, and services given as aid to other countries. For instance, goods and services provided by the US government to other countries as part of a drought relief program represent government transfers.

Table 3.2 shows that India enjoyed a current account surplus of about $33 billion in 2020, but it had incurred a current account deficit of $66 billion in 2018, $30 billion in 2019, and $33 billion in 2021. In fact, India has had a current account deficit for years. Economists argue that a rare current account surplus of $33 billion in 2020 reflected "a lower trade deficit and a sharp rise in exports of software services as well as stronger inbound remittances from Indians working abroad." The Indian lower trade deficit of 2020 more or less had to do with the lockdown of the Indian economy designed to prevent the spread of COVID-19.

3.1.3.2. *The capital account — Group 2*

The **capital account** consists of capital transfers and the acquisition or disposal of nonproduced, nonfinancial assets. The major types of capital transfers include the transfer of title to fixed assets, the transfer of funds linked to the sale or acquisition of fixed assets, debt forgiveness by creditors, and migrants' transfers of goods and financial assets as they leave or enter the country. Nonproduced, nonfinancial assets include the sale or purchases of nonproduced assets (i.e., the rights to natural resources) and the sale or purchases of intangible assets (i.e., patents, copyrights, trademarks, and leases). Although conceptually important, capital-account transactions are generally small in most countries.

3.1.3.3. *The financial account — Group 3*

The **financial account** consists of foreign direct investments, foreign portfolio investments, and other investments. **Foreign direct investments (FDI)** are equity investments, such as purchases of stocks, the acquisition of entire firms, or the establishment of new subsidiaries. The US Department of Commerce defines FDI as investments in either real capital assets or financial assets with a minimum of 10 percent ownership in a foreign firm. If McDonald's opens up a fast-food outlet in Vietnam, that is an example of foreign direct investment.

Foreign portfolio investments are purchases of foreign bonds, stocks, financial derivatives, or other financial assets without a significant degree of management control. The desire for return, safety, and liquidity in investments is the same for international and domestic portfolio investors. However, international portfolio investments have additional risks, such as changes in exchange rates, wars and revolutions, and expropriations. Portfolio investments in utilities, governments, and government agencies are active because the risk of loss in these fields is lower than in other fields. If a South African buys bonds in the Volkswagen Corporation of Germany, this is an example of foreign portfolio investment.

Financial derivatives are instruments whose value is derived from the value of one or more underlying assets such as commodities, precious metals, currency, bonds, stocks, and stocks indices. The four most common examples of derivative instruments are forwards, futures, options, and swaps.

Other investments include changes in trade credit, loans, currency, and deposits. Both portfolio investment and other investments consist of short-term capital flows and long-term capital flows. Some short-term capital flows occur due to changes in the current account or changes in long-term investment. More specifically, these changes may take place because of merchandise trade, service trade, current transfers, and investments. Short-term capital movements, induced by such transactions, are sometimes called compensating or accommodating adjustments. These compensating accounts change only for one reason-to finance other items in the balance of payments. In contrast, other short-term flows can be attributed to the differences in interest rates among nations and to the expected changes in foreign exchange rates. Short-term capital movements caused by such changes are frequently called autonomous adjustments. These autonomous accounts change for purely economic reasons.

Large current account (Group 1) deficits imply large financial account (Group 3) surpluses, while large current account surpluses imply large financial account deficits. However, there are rare cases where a country has had large twin surpluses or large twin deficits. For example, China has enjoyed large twin surplus for years. On the other hand, Table 3.2 shows that India has had a considerable amount of twin deficits for at least 3 years — 2018, 2019 and 2021.

3.1.3.4. *Net errors and omissions — Group 4*

The balance of payments should always be balanced in theory because all debits are offset by credits and vice versa. However, it rarely does balance in practice for a number of reasons. Balance-of-payments data gathered from many different sources are incomplete and may be interpreted differently by individuals and agencies. Many transactions are not recorded but are known to have occurred because other components of the balance of payments reveal an imbalance. Thus, the debits and credits may not be balanced at the end of a year. This is why the net errors and omissions are treated as a "plug" item to keep the balance-of-payments accounts in balance.

Net errors and omissions occur for several reasons. First, they may be due to unreported foreign funds coming to a country for investment in some form of asset. Second, increased trading in foreign currencies, in combination with the flexible exchange system, undoubtedly produces large errors in payments figures. Third, because most data on the balance of payments depends on personnel in banks and other business offices to complete federal forms, these persons sometimes make multimillion-dollar mistakes.

3.1.3.5. *Total, Groups 1–4*

Usually known as the overall balance of payments, this balance is the net result of trading, capital, and financial activities. It constitutes the sum of all transactions (Groups 1 through 4) that must be financed by the use of official reserves. The overall balance of payments is often used to evaluate a country's competitive position in terms of all private transactions with the rest of the world.

3.1.3.6. *Reserves and related items — Group 5*

Group 5 consists of official reserve assets, use of IMF credit and loans, exceptional financing, and gold. They represent only purchases and sales by official monetary authorities, such as the Reserve Bank of India or the European Central Bank. Changes in reserves and related items are necessary to account for the deficit or surplus in the balance of payments.

Reserve assets are government-owned assets. They include monetary gold, convertible foreign currencies, deposits, and securities. The principle convertible currencies for most countries are the US dollar, the British pound, the euro, and the Japanese yen. Credit and loans from the IMF are usually denominated in special drawing rights. **Special drawing rights (SDRs)**, sometimes called "paper gold," are rights to draw on the IMF. SDRs can be used as means of international payment. Exceptional financing is financing mobilized by a country's monetary authorities that are not regarded as official reserves. Examples of this account include postponing the repayment of foreign currency debt and drawing on private bank loans to finance transactions that would otherwise deplete the country's reserve assets.

The reserve account of a country also includes its liabilities to foreign official holders, which constitute foreign authorities' reserves. A country's liabilities to foreign official holders are sometimes called foreign reserve assets. For example, Indian liabilities to foreign official holders, such as the Central Bank of the Russian Federation or the Bank of Thailand, refer to foreign official deposits with US banks and official holdings of US Treasury securities. Foreign governments frequently wish to hold such assets in the United States because of their interest earnings.

The net result of all activities in Groups 1 through 4 in Table 3.1 must be financed by changes in reserves and related items. Thus, these two items — Total, Groups 1 through 4 and Group 5 — are identical except that the sign is reversed. In other words, the net result of all actives in Groups 1 through 4 was financed by various accounts in Group 5. Any transaction which finances the balance-of-payments surplus should be recorded as a debit (increase in reserve assets and decrease in official liability); any transaction which finances the balance-of-payments deficit should be recorded as a credit (decrease in reserve assets and increase in official liability).

3.1.3.7. *International investment position*

Trade balance is a flow concept because it measures the economic activities of a country over a 1-year period. The **international investment position** is a stock concept because it summarizes a country's assets and liabilities on a given date. Tables 3.3 and 3.4 show the international investment position of the US and of China from 2012 to 2021.

These two tables reveal striking differences in the international investment positions between the two countries. First, the US is the largest net debtor nation in the world, while China is the largest net creditor nation. For the US and China over the same period, a largely reciprocal relationship is evident. Rapid growth of the US foreign debt (negative net position) coincided with the rapid increase of China's foreign credit (net position) during the 2010s.

Table 3.3 The international investment position of the USA (billions of US dollars).

Types of Investment	2012	2013	2014	2015	2016	2020	2021
US Assets	**22,562**	**24,145**	**24,883**	**23,431**	**24,061**	**32,041**	**35,065**
Direct Investment	5,970	7,121	7,242	7,057	7,422	9,316	10,970
Portfolio Investment	11,603	9,206	9,704	9,570	10,011	14,399	16,309
Other Investment*	4,417	7,370	7,503	7,710	6,399	7,699	7,074
Reserve Assets	572	448	434	384	407	627	712
US Liabilities	**27,080**	**29,513**	**31,828**	**30,892**	**32,242**	**46,969**	**53,189**
Direct Investment	4,662	5,815	6,379	6,729	7,596	11,897	14,813
Portfolio Investment	15,541	15,541	16,922	16,646	17,360	25,170	28,480
Other Investment*	6,877	8,157	8,527	10,367	10,074	9,902	9,896
Net Position	**−4,518**	**−5,369**	**6,945**	**7,461**	**8,181**	**−14,707**	**−18,124**

Note: Data obtained by the author from International Monetary Fund, Balance of Payment Statistics Yearbook, 2018 and 2022. * is used as a plug item to make the difference between assets and liabilities will be equal to the net position.

Table 3.4 The international investment position of China (billions of US dollars).

Types of Investment	2012	2013	2014	2015	2016	2020	2021
Chinese Assets	**5,213**	**5,986**	**6,438**	**6,156**	**6,507**	**8,879**	**9,324**
Direct Investment	532	660	882	1,095	1,358	2,580	2,581
Portfolio Investment	241	259	263	261	367	902	980
Other Investment*	1,054	1,187	1,394	1,389	1,684	2,046	2,336
Reserve Assets	3,388	3,880	3,899	3,406	3,098	3,351	3,427
Chinese Liabilities	**3,347**	**3,990**	**4,836**	**4,483**	**4,557**	**6,592**	**7,341**
Direct Investment	2,068	2,331	2,599	2,696	2,755	3,231	3,624
Portfolio Investment	336	386	796	817	811	1,995	2,155
Other Investment*	943	1,274	1,441	970	991	1,726	1,562
Net Position	**1,866**	**1,996**	**1,602**	**1,673**	**1,950**	**2,287**	**1,983**

Note: Data obtained by the author from International Monetary Fund, Balance of Payment Statistics Yearbook, 2018 and 2022. * is used as a plug item to make the difference between assets and liabilities will be equal to the net position.

As shown in Table 3.3, the US foreign debt has grown at such a breathtaking pace that few were aware of the consequence of rising national debt. Budget experts normally identify four main consequences of rising national debt: lower living standards, policy constraints, less revenue available for other public expenditure, and reduced international influence. What are the major causes of the US foreign debt? Mounting budgets and trade deficits are primarily responsible for such a hedge US foreign debt.

China's foreign credit has increased, but its growth rate has been relatively slow in recent years for a variety of reasons. Nevertheless, some Americans have expressed their concern about China's potential influence on the US economy. China's holdings of Treasury securities reached about $1 trillion in 2021. This is about 25 percent of the total foreign holdings of Treasury securities. In other words, a growing US debt to China can make the US more vulnerable to pressure from China that influences the US interest rate and the value of the dollar.

However, some economists insist that net international investment positions themselves may not be particularly meaningful. This is why many economists look at three broad categories of international investment positions: direct investment, portfolio investment, and other investment. In other words, analysts break down international investment holdings into several categories so that they can draw policy implications from each category about the liquidity status of a country.

Short-term foreign assets in the US, such as bank deposits and government securities, are meaningful because foreigners can withdraw these holdings on very short notice. For example, if they fear capital losses from further depreciation of the dollar, or if interest rates decline, foreign investors may turn away from dollar-denominated short-term assets. These actions by foreign investors may endanger the stability of the US financial system. Foreign official assets in the USA are also significant. If foreign monetary authorities decide to liquidate their holdings of US government securities, the financial strength of the dollar will fall. Long term investments, such as long-term corporate securities and direct investment, are less important because they respond to basic economic trends and are not subject to erratic withdrawals.

3.1.4. *How to Reduce a Trade Deficit*

Some countries have had trade deficits for many years. However, compensating transactions cannot be maintained indefinitely. Therefore, some adjustments must be made to correct trade deficits. A trade deficit may be reduced in several ways: deflate the economy, devalue the currency, and establish public control.

3.1.4.1. *Deflate the economy*

If a country adopts tight monetary and fiscal policies, its inflation and income decrease. Lower inflation and income are expected to increase exports and reduce imports, thus improving the trade balance. To reduce its trade deficit, therefore, a country should control government budget deficits, reduce the growth of money supply, and institute price and wage controls. On the other hand, these policies may slow the economy.

3.1.4.2. *Devalue the currency*

A country may reduce its trade deficit by devaluating its currency against the currencies of major trading partners. A currency devaluation may improve the trade balance because weak currency makes imported goods more expensive and exported goods less expensive. Currency devaluation might not correct a trade deficit, however, (1) if foreign markets do not buy more goods in response to lower prices; (2) if domestic companies do not have the capacity to produce more goods for exports; (3) if domestic residents continued to import foreign goods, regardless of their higher prices; and (4) if middlemen do not pass on changes in prices to their customers.

3.1.4.3. *Establish public control*

In general, there are two types of public controls: foreign exchange controls and trade controls. Think, for a moment, of a case in which increased Mexican imports create a shortage in its foreign exchange. Under exchange controls, the Mexican government would force its exporters and other recipients to sell their foreign exchange to the government or to designated banks. Then, the government would allocate this foreign exchange among the various users of foreign exchange. In this way, the Mexican government restricts Mexican imports to a certain amount of foreign exchange earned by Mexican exports. Thus, imports under exchange control are less than they would be under free market conditions.

When governments are faced with a serious payment deficit, they may manipulate exports and imports through tariffs, quotas, and subsidies. High tariffs on imported goods and import quotas by Mexico would reduce Mexican imports. On the other hand, the Mexican government may subsidize certain Mexican exports to make them competitive in world markets and to increase the volume of Mexican exports. Special taxes on foreign direct investments by Mexican firms tend to reduce Mexican capital outflows. However, these protectionist policies may increase inflation, erode purchasing power, and lower the standard of living.

Global Finance in Practice 3: How Low Can the Euro Go?

The euro is hurtling toward parity with the US dollar for the first time since its early years of existence. Investors are betting it could get a lot worse for the common currency.

The descent adds to the eurozone's inflation woes and complicates the European Central Bank's plans for unwinding its pandemic stimulus. It also carries big implications for US investors and businesses with operations on the continent, as the value of their overseas earnings slides in dollar terms.

In the morning of July 8, 2022, the euro traded at $1.0099, putting it within striking faces an distance of parity, or equal value with the dollar. It recovered later to finish the day at $1.0188. A day earlier it settled at $1.0162, its lowest closing level since December 2002. James Athey, investment director at Abrdn, said he thinks the euro will fall to around 97 US cents, and sees even steeper declines as possible in the short term.

Europe's common currency has fallen more than 10 percent for first 6 months of 2022 as the European economy energy crisis brought on by Russia's war in Ukraine that threatens to drive the bloc into recession.

The euro's slide will have ripple effects on global economies, corporate earnings, and consumers' wallets. For Americans traveling abroad, a weak euro means their dollars can go further. But for US companies, a weak euro can be a headache, making it harder to compete in export markets. Companies in the S&P 500 generate about 14 percent of their revenue from Europe.

For the eurozone, the effects are particularly acute. A weaker euro compounds Europe's inflation pressure by making imports — particularly of key commodities — more expensive. And unlike in the past, the weaker euro is not expected to provide much of a boost to the bloc's manufacturers by making exports more attractive abroad.

"Theoretically it helps the exporter side of the equation, like in Germany, but they are having supply chain issues and gas supply issues," said Brad Bechtel, global head of foreign exchange at Jefferies. A weaker euro can make euro-denominated assets — such as stocks — less attractive. The benchmark Stoxx Europe 600 index has fallen 14 percent as of July 2022, less than the 18 percent fall in the S&P 500. But in dollar terms, it has fallen further than the US index.

"At the margin it just makes European investments less desirable," Mr. Athey said. "As a vote of confidence, if there was an international price for an economy, it would be its currency. This does tend to be a flashing warning sign for foreign investors. "Not all investors and strategists are convinced the euro may plunge below parity. Viraj Patel, a global macro strategist for Vanda Research, said he sees parity as the bottom of the euro's slide.[3]"

3.1.5. *The J Curve*

There are a variety of reasons why currency depreciation will not necessarily improve the balance of trade. One possible reason why a weak currency will not always reduce the trade deficit has to do with the J-curve effect. The **J-curve** is the term most commonly used by economists to describe the relationship between the trade balance and currency devaluation. As illustrated in Fig. 3.2, the J-curve effect holds that a country's currency depreciation causes its trade balance to deteriorate for a short time, followed by a flatting out period, and a significant improvement occurs for an extended period. When a country's currency depreciates against the currencies of major trading partners, the country's exports tend to rise and imports fall, which improves the trade balance. In the short run, however, a country's trade deficit may deteriorate just after its currency depreciates because the higher cost of imports will more than offset the reduced volume of imports.

This J-curve effect received wide attention in the mid-1980s when the US dollar plunged in the foreign exchange market, while the US trade deficit hit new peaks.[4] Specifically, the US dollar began to decline after reaching its peak in March 1985, but the US trade deficit hit a new record each year from 1985 through 1987. The US trade deficit began to fall with the rapid expansion of American exports in 1988. Economists estimate that trade patterns typically lag currency changes by at least 18 months. A number of researchers examined various cases of devaluations carried out by developing countries in the 1960s through

---

[3]Dulaney, C. and C. McCabe, "How Low Can the Euro Go?" *The Wall Street Journal*, Jul8 8, 2022, https://www.wsj.com/articles/how-low-can-the-euro-go-11657267448.
[4]Forsyth, R. W., "No Overnight Cure: The Trade Deficit Follows the J Curve," *Barron's*, February 10, 1986, p. 28.

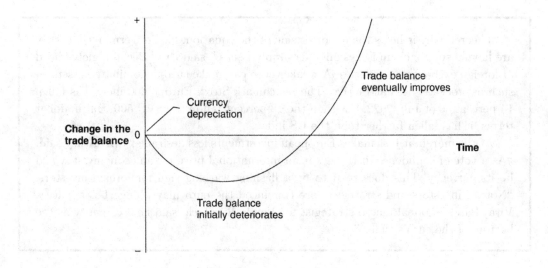

Fig. 3.2 The J-curve effect.

the 1980s. Their studies confirmed the existence of the J-curve effect in about 40 percent of the cases.[5]

3.2. A SUCCESSFUL FOREIGN EXCHANGE SYSTEM

A multinational company's access to international capital markets and its freedom to move funds across national boundaries are subject to a variety of national constraints. These constraints are frequently imposed to meet international monetary agreements when it comes to determining the exchange rates. Constraints may also be imposed to correct the balance-of-payments deficit or to promote national economic goals. Today, about 50 countries use a fixed exchange rate system, while the rest of the countries in the world use some type of floating exchange rate system.

A successful exchange system is necessary to stabilize the international payment system. To be successful, an exchange system should meet the following three conditions:

1. Balance-of-payments deficits or surpluses by individual countries should not be too large or extended.
2. Such deficits or surpluses should be corrected in ways that do not cause unacceptable inflation or physical restrictions on trade and payments for either individual countries or the world.
3. The maximum sustainable expansion of trade and other international economic activities should be facilitated.

Theoretically, continuous balance-of-payments deficits and surpluses cannot exist around the world. Under a system of freely flexible exchange rates, a foreign exchange market clears

---

[5]Edwards, S., *Real Exchange Rates, Devaluation, and Adjustment: Exchange Rate Policy in Developing Countries*, Cambridge, MA: MIT Press, 1989, and Will, K., "J Curve: Definition and Uses in Economics and Private Equity," *Lincoln Financial*, Investopedia, December 23, 2020.

itself in the same way a competitive market for goods does. Just like every commodity price, each exchange rate moves to a level where demand and supply are equal. Under a system of fixed exchange rates, central banks or other designated agencies buy and sell on the open market to absorb surpluses and to eliminate deficiencies of foreign currencies at the fixed exchange rates.

3.2.1. *Currency Values and Terminology*

A **foreign exchange rate** is the price of one currency expressed in terms of another currency. A **fixed exchange rate** is an exchange rate which does not fluctuate or which changes within a predetermined band. The rate at which the currency is fixed or pegged is called **par value**. A floating or **flexible exchange rate** is an exchange rate, which fluctuates according to market forces.

Although governments do not attempt to prevent fundamental changes in the exchange rate between their own currency and other currencies, they typically attempt to maintain orderly trading conditions in the market. A flexible exchange system has a number of advantages.

1. Countries can maintain independent monetary and fiscal policies.
2. Flexible exchange rates permit a smooth adjustment to external shocks.
3. Central banks do not need to maintain large international reserves to defend a fixed exchange rate.

However, a flexible exchange system has several disadvantages. First, the exchange rates under a pure version of this system are highly unstable, thereby discouraging the flow of world trade and investment. Second, flexible exchange rates are inherently inflationary because they remove the external discipline of government economic policy.

A system of fixed exchange rates provides stability of exchange rates, but it has some disadvantages.

1. The stability of exchange rates may be too rigid to address major upheavals such as wars, revolutions, and widespread disasters.
2. Central banks need to maintain large international reserves to defend themselves against a fixed exchange rate.
3. Fixed exchange rates may result in destabilizing speculation that causes the exchange rate to "overshoot" its natural equilibrium level. Overshoot (beyond fair value) is natural after devaluation. For example, all three developing-country financial crises since 1980-the Latin American crisis of the 1980s, the Mexican peso crisis of 1994, and the Asian crisis of 1997-occurred under a fixed exchange rate regime.

Four concepts-appreciation, depreciation, revaluation (upvaluation), and devaluation-are all related to changing the value of a currency. An **appreciation** is a rise in the value of a currency against other currencies under a floating rate system. A **depreciation** is a decrease in the value of a currency against other currencies under a floating rate system. Under a system of floating rates, a country's exchange rate will appreciate if it raises interest rates to attract capital. Similarly, its exchange rate will "depreciate" if it reduces interest rates.

A **revaluation** is an official increase in the value of a currency by the government of that currency under a fixed rate system. A **devaluation** is an official reduction in the par value of a currency by the government of that currency under a fixed rate system. Under a system of fixed rates, a country may "devalue" its exchange rate by setting a lower intervention price at which it will intervene in the foreign exchange market. It may "revalue" or "upvalue" its exchange rate by setting a higher intervention price.

3.3. THE INTERNATIONAL MONETARY FUND

The **International Monetary Fund** (IMF) was created as a weak kind of central banks' central bank at the Bretton Woods conference in 1944 to make the new monetary system feasible and workable. Its major purpose was to assist members who would have structural trade problems or currencies with highly unstable values. The IMF permitted its deficit members to buy with their local currencies some of its own holdings of convertible currencies. These deficit countries were expected to buy back, with gold or other convertible currencies, the local currencies they had sold to the IMF after they had improved their balance of payments. Thus, the IMF's major weapon is the power to declare its members ineligible to utilize its holdings of international reserves.

The IMF was created in 1944 by 29 countries, but today, it consists of 190 countries. Article I of the IMF Articles of Agreement clearly sets forth its objectives as follows:

1. To promote international monetary cooperation.
2. To facilitate the balanced growth of international trade.
3. To promote exchange stability.
4. To eliminate exchange restrictions.
5. To create standby reserves.

The IMF established rules and procedures to keep participating countries from going too deeply into balance-of-payments deficits. Those countries with short-term payments difficulties could draw upon their reserves. The amount of such reserves is defined in relation to each member's quota. This quota is determined based on factors such as trade, national income, and international payments. Each member is required to contribute 75 percent of its quota in its own currency and 25 percent in special drawing rights or convertible currencies.

These quotas for IMF members are reviewed at least every 5 years to determine whether quotas should be increased to accommodate the growth of the world economy. The voting power of the members is determined by 250 "basic votes", plus one vote for each SDR 100,000 of quota. Because of its large quota, the United States holds 20 percent of the total votes, followed by Japan (6.14 percent), China (6.04 percent), and Germany (5.31 percent).

IMF members borrow by exchanging their own currencies for the convertible currencies of other member countries. A member country may draw, virtually at will, 100 percent of its quota from the IMF at any time; the 100 percent of its quota is called the reserve tranche. A country could borrow beyond this amount up to an additional 100 percent of its quota; this 100 percent is called the credit tranche. Thus, a member country could conceivably borrow 200 percent of its quota in convertible currencies. However, to borrow more than 100 percent of its quota, a member must accept restrictions imposed by the IMF to ensure that steps are being taken to correct the borrower's currency problems.

3.3.1. *International Monetary System*

The world experienced international monetary disorder from 1914 to 1945. World War I ended the stability of exchange rates for the currencies of major trading partners. The Great Depression of 1929–1932 and the international financial crisis afterwards resulted in international monetary chaos. To summarize the international monetary system from 1914 to 1945, we find a mixture of widely fluctuating exchange rates and controlled exchange rates.

The Bretton Woods Agreement of 1944 marked a new era for the operation of the international monetary system, which was a system of fixed exchange rates based on a revised gold standard, called the gold exchange standard. Each currency was fixed within a narrow range of values in relation to gold or the US dollar. Many member countries were unable or unwilling to abide by the Bretton Woods Agreement because its provisions were complex and because their interests conflicted. Nevertheless, the Bretton Woods Agreement and the activity of the IMF were the main features of the international monetary system from 1945 to 1973.

Two problems raised serious questions about the function of the Bretton Woods Agreement as the international monetary system. First, the growth of monetary reserves was inadequate. Second, effective balance-of-payments adjustments could not be achieved under the Agreement. Attempts to save the Bretton Woods Agreement through the introduction of SDRs and the Smithsonian Agreement failed when the whole system collapsed in 1973. Since 1973, the international monetary system has been characterized by a confusing mixture of freely floating, managed floating, joint floating, and fixed rates. Table 3.5 shows a brief history of the international monetary system.

3.3.2. *Special Drawing Rights*

The IMF had been concerned about the lack of growth in gold holdings and about the consequent lack of growth in international reserves, which was slower than a growth in world trade. To solve these problems, the IMF created **special drawing rights** (SDRs) as an artificial international reserve in 1970.

3.3.2.1. *Definition*

The IMF uses a simplified basket of several major currencies to determine its daily valuation. The weight for each currency is changed periodically. As shown in Table 3.6, the current percentage weights for these currencies are 43.38 percent for the US dollar, 29.31 percent for the euro, 12.28 for the Chinese yuan, 7.59 percent for the Japanese yen, and 7.44 percent for the British pound. The weight reflects the relative importance of each country in world trade and the amount of the currency held as reserves by members of the IMF.

3.3.2.2. *Interest rate*

Like any national currency, SDRs carry a weekly determined interest rate. The rate is based on a weighted average of the representative short-term rates in the money markets of the base currencies. The SDR interest rate is paid by the IMF members on any shortfall of SDR subscriptions (below their cost-free allocation), and on non-concessional IMF loans.

Table 3.5 History of international monetary system.

1914	Breakdown of gold standard and monetary disorder began.
1934	The US dollar pegged at $35 per ounce of gold.
1944	Conference of Bretton Woods, New Hampshire, established a fixed exchange system based on the US dollar. IMF and World Bank created.
1958	European Economic Community was established.
1963	The US levied "Interest Equalization Tax" on foreign borrowings in US capital markets.
1963	The US imposed voluntary controls on capital outflows from US banks and companies.
1968	The US imposed mandatory controls on foreign investment by US companies.
1970	Special drawing rights created.
1971	On August 15, the US dollar floated; the convertibility of the US dollar was eliminated; an import surcharge was imposed.
	On December 17, the Smithsonian Agreement reached; the US dollar was devalued from $35 per ounce of gold to $38.
1972	A snake (2.25%) within a tunnel (4.5%) was established.
1973	The US dollar was devalued from $38 per ounce of gold to $42.22 in March.
1973	Organization for Petroleum Exporting Countries imposed an oil embargo, eventually quadrupling world prices of oil.
1976	IMF meeting in Jamaica, known as the "Jamaica Agreement", legalized the existing floating system.
1978	The EEC established the European Monetary System, which officially replaced a snake within a tunnel. This is a joint floating system.
1982	Latin American debt crisis began.
1985	Group of Five countries reached the "Plaza Agreement" to reduce the value of the US dollar.
1987	Major industrialized countries reached the "Louvre Accord" to support stability and exchange rates around their current levels.
1992	High German interest rates caused "the September 1992 currency crisis in Europe." Italy and the United Kingdom withdrew from the European Monetary System.
1993	The July 1993 currency crisis in Europe forced the EEC to widen the allowable deviation band to +15 percent.
1993	A Single European Community was created. The name of the EEC was changed to the European Union (EU).
1994	Mexican peso suffered major devaluation (40%) and began to float.
1997	In July, currency turmoil erupted in Thailand and spread to Indonesia, South Korea, and other South Asian countries.
1999	On January 1, 11 European countries launched a single European currency called the euro, with a common monetary policy established by an independent European Central Bank.
2001	On January 1, Greece adopted the euro.
2001	On January 8, the Argentine peso, whose value was fixed to the US dollar at parity since 1991 through a currency board was first devalued to Ps1.4 per dollar and then floated.
2002	On January 1, the euro began public circulation and traded alongside the national currencies. On March 1, the euro replaced the national currencies of euro-zone countries.
	On February 13, the Venezuelan boliva, fixed to the dollar since 1996, was floated as a result of the increasing economic crisis.
2004	On May 1, 10 more countries joined the EU, thereby increasing it to 25 members.
2005	On July 21, China abandoned the peg of its currency yuan (renminbi) to the US dollar, revalued its currency from yuan 8.28 per dollar to yuan 8.11 per dollar, and adopted a managed float as its exchange regime.
2007	On December 1, the US great recession started as a result of its financial crisis. On January 1, Romania and Bulgaria joined the EU, thereby increasing it to 27 members.
2008	In April, the euro peaked in strength against the US dollar at $1.60 per euro and went down to $1.25 per euro by late October.
2010	In December, the US dollar, on an index basis across multiple currencies, hit a record low.

Table 3.5 (*Continued*)

2013	On January 7, Croatia joined the EU, thereby increasing it to 28 members.
2014	At the end of March 2014, the IMF secured an $18 billion bailout fund for the provisional government of Ukraine in the aftermath of the 2014 Ukrainian revolution.
2016	On April 24, the Republic of Nauru becomes the 189th member of IMF
2016	On June 23, 51.9 percent of British voters chose to leave the EU in the referendum.
2018	In November 2018, the US, Canada, and Mexico reached a new trade agreement to update the North American Trade Agreement. The new deal will be known as the United States-Mexico–Canada Agreement, or USMCA.
2020	On January 31, the UK formerly ceased to be a member of the EU state, thereby reducing it to 27 members.
	On July 1, the USMCA entered into force. The USMCA substituted the North America Free Trade Agreement (NAFTA).
	On October 16, Principality of Andorra became the 190th member of IMF.
2022	Since Russia invaded Ukraine on February 24, the IMF has provided Ukraine with one or two billion dollars in emergency financing disbursement a few times.

Table 3.6 SDR currency basket.

Currency	Weights Determined in the 2022 Review	Fixed Number of Units of Currency for a 5-year Period Starting August 1, 2022
US Dollar	43.38	0.57813
Euro	29.31	0.37379
Chinese Yuan	12.28	1.0993
Japanese Yen	7.59	13.452
Pound Sterling	7.44	0.080870

The IMF pays its members the interest rate on the fraction of their SDR subscriptions that is above their allocation quota.

3.3.2.3. *Allocations*

SDR allocations by the IMF are officially authorized by the G-20 conferences and published by the International Monetary Fund. Allocations began in 1970 in yearly installments, creating an initial pool of SDR 9.3 billion by 1972. A second series of installments brought the total to SDR21.4 billion by 1981. Since then, up to the 2008 banking crisis, no new allocations have taken place. On April 2, 2009, the G-20 authorized the issuance of $250 billion in new SDRs to augment the foreign reserves of IMF members and quickly channel resources into emerging economies. There have been four general allocations, most recently in 2021, when the IMF's Board of Governors approved a general allocation of about SDR 456 billion, equivalent to US$650 billion, to boost global liquidity.

3.3.2.4. *Use of SDRs*

The IMF has the authority to extend the range of official holders of SDRs beyond its member countries and the IMF's General Resources Account. It has designated about

20 organizations as prescribed holders. Each of these institutions can acquire and use SDRs in transactions and operations with other prescribed holders and with any of the IMF's member countries. Prescribed holders have the same degree of freedom as IMF members to use SDRs for a variety of international transactions.

IMF members may also use SDRs in a variety of voluntary transactions and operations by agreement among themselves and with prescribed holders. More specifically, IMF members and prescribed holders buy and sell SDRs both spot and forward; to borrow, lend, or pledge SDRs; to use SDRs in swaps and in settlement of financial obligations; or to make donations (grants) with SDRs.

The SDR is an international reserve asset created by the IMF in 1970 and allocated to its members to supplement existing reserve assets. All member countries of the IMF are eligible to receive an allocation of SDRs and may use SDRs in transactions and operations among themselves, with prescribed holders, and with the IMF itself.

The SDR is used as a unit of account or as a basis for the unit of account by a number of international and regional organizations. The SDR has also been used to denominate private financial instruments. The use of the SDR as a unit of account is explained, in part, by the fact that the value of the SDR tends to be more stable than that of any single currency in the basket, since it is a weighted average of the exchange rates of the four major currencies in which the prices of goods and services in international trade are denominated.

3.4. SUMMARY

The balance of payments summarizes all international transactions between the residents of a country and residents of foreign countries during a specified period. The systematic record of these international transactions requires pre-established principles. These principles include rules or procedures, such as debits and credits, and definitions of terminology, such as the current account. The balance of payments is neither an income statement nor a balance sheet. The balance of payments is a sources-and-uses-of-funds statement reflecting changes in assets, liabilities, and net worth during a specified period. Some countries have had deficits for many years. These deficits cannot be indefinitely financed by compensating transactions. The balance-of-payments deficit can be corrected by deflating the economy, devaluing the currency, and establishing public control. The first two methods are supposed to correct international disequilibrium through changes in prices, income, and interest rates. Government controls, such as exchange and trade controls, can be used to alleviate or correct the balance-of-payments deficit.

Financial managers must understand the international monetary system if they are to manage multinational businesses efficiently. Foreign exchange rates determine prices of goods and services that multinational companies buy and sell across national boundaries. These exchange rates also have an impact on foreign investments.

3.5. KEY TERMS

balance of payments   the international monetary system
current account   balance on goods

services   balance on goods and services
income   current transfers.
capital account   a financial account
foreign direct investments (FDI) foreign portfolio investments
financial derivatives   other investments
special drawings rights (SDRs)   J curve
the foreign exchange rate   a fixed exchange rate
par value   a flexible exchange rate
appreciation   depreciation
revaluation   devaluation
International Monetary Fund   special drawing rights (SDRs)

3.6. PROBLEMS

1. Answer Questions 1a through 1c using Example 3.1.

   a. Prepare the balance of payments in a good form.
   b. Does the country have a balance-of-payments deficit or surplus?
   c. How can the country account for this payment's imbalance?

2. Assume that a country has a current-account deficit of $10,000 and a financial-account surplus of $12,000.
   Assume: that capital account and net errors & omissions are negligible.

   a. Does the country have a balance-of-payments deficit or surplus?
   b. What will happen to the country's official reserve account?

3. A country has a merchandise trade surplus of $5,000, an income balance of zero, a current transfer surplus of $3,000, and a current account deficit of $4,000. What is the service trade balance?

4. Assume: (1) a country has a current account surplus of $10,000; (2) its financial account has a deficit of $15,000; and (3) its other two accounts-capital account and net errors and omissions are negligible. What is the balance of the country's reserve account? How can the country eliminate the $5,000 imbalance in its balance-of-payments?

Closing Case 3: US–China Trade Relations

The history of Chinese trade is long and distinct with the 20th century being marked by large shifts in policy. A focus on the history of trade between the US and China helps to reveal some of the fundamental moments in the history of Chinese trade. In 1936, the US accounted for 22 percent of China's exports and 20 percent of its imports. In 1949, the Chinese Communist Party seized control of China and founded the People's Republic of China after decades of struggle. Under this new regime, the economy was completely state controlled. These changes, the Korean War from 1950 to 1953, and the subsequent embargo toward China, caused a sharp decline in the US–China trade relations. In 1972, the American share of China's total trade accounted for only 1.6 percent.

In 1978, under the new leadership of Deng Xiaoping, China began the long process of economic reform. Initially focused on just agricultural reform, these economic reforms eventually became a transition to a capitalist and globally integrated economy. Focused on the four modernizations — the modernization of industry, agriculture, science and technology, and national defense — these reforms represented a deep-seated shift in policy and helped to spur a steady growth of the US–China trade. Between 1990 and 2013, China's total trade (both imports and exports) rose from $20 million to $2.5 trillion.

The government-directed capitalism of China for 3.5 decades from 1978 to 1913 had lifted over 400 million people out of poverty, made China the second-largest economy in the world, and caused China to become the third-largest trading nation in the world. In 2013, China was the second-largest US trading partner, its third-largest export market, and its biggest source of imports. However, some of the policies of China's tightly managed capitalism, such as its currency manipulation, had created considerable friction with its trading partners, raising serious international concerns about growing current account imbalances, most notably with the US.

For 13 years, China had applied for WTO membership, but this effort had not been successful mainly due to US opposition. This opposition was based on a laundry list of economic and political issues, including concerns with human rights, tension between Taiwan and China, China's nuclear arsenal, objections from labor unions in the US, and the use of protectionist policies by China. "As bad as our trade deficit with China is today, it will grow even worse if we approve a permanent trade deal," said House Minority Whip David Bonior (D. Mich) back in October 1999. Even with this opposition, on November 15, 1999, an historic agreement was reached between Chinese and American trade negotiators, which set the stage for China's formal entry into the WTO.

One of the major worries by opponents of normalizing trade relations with China was a concern of a growing trade imbalance between the two countries. The US trade deficit with China increased from $69 billion in 1999 to about $300 billion in 2013. Many believed that this growing deficit was due to China's high tariffs and numerous restrictions on American exports. In joining the WTO on December 11, 2001, China agreed to lower its average tariff from 16.7 percent in 2000 to 10 percent in 2005 and reduce the number of items under import license and quota from approximately 300 to zero in the next 5 years. In addition, China agreed to liberalize foreign investment in banking, insurance, financial services, wholesale/retail trade, and telecommunications. All these industries had been under tight government control until China joined the WTO.

In return, the US granted China permanent normalized trade relations status. Without this legislation, China's trade status would be open to yearly debate, as it had been in the past. Additionally, China, as a member of the WTO, has enjoyed open markets with all other WTO members, including the US. One area where this had provided a great advantage for China's exports was in its textile industry.

In 2009, China overtook Germany as the largest exporting nation worldwide. Since 2014, China has been not only the world's largest exporter but also the largest trading nation in terms of the sum of its exports and imports. Despite the ongoing coronavirus pandemic, 2021 was another remarkable year in terms of international trade. China's exports of goods totaled a record high of 3.36 trillion US dollars, 30 percent more than the previous year. That year, China's export of goods and services constituted 19 percent of the GDP. A country's economy is considered relatively open if its exports made up around 15 percent or more of its GDP.

As far as merchandise and service exports are concerned, China is known as "the world's factory" for being the largest supplier of manufactured goods. In 2021, China exported over 3.2 trillion US dollars of manufactured goods, the highest of all time. That year, China's major exports were automatic data processing machines and components, followed by clothes and clothing accessories, integrated circuits, and mobile phones. As a consequence of the ongoing coronavirus pandemic, an increasing number of exporting enterprises shifted their businesses online.

Is China the US largest trading partner? Yes, China is currently the US's largest goods trading partner with $559.2 billion in total (two way) goods trade during 2020. Goods exports totaled $124.5 billion; goods imports totaled $434.7 billion. The US goods trade deficit with China was $310.3 billion in 2020.

Case Questions

1. What are some of the sources of trade friction between China and the United States? Why do some scholars view this friction as a positive sign?
2. What is managed trade, and how does it apply to China and the United States?
3. Discuss what steps the United State can take to reduce its trade deficit with China. Mention the deflation of economies, devaluation of currency, and establishment of public control.
4. Suppose that the value of the US dollar sharply depreciates. Under these conditions, how would the J-curve discussed in this chapter apply to the trade relationship between China and the United States?
5. Discuss in broad terms the major changes since WWII in the trade relations between China and the United States in terms of actual balance of payments and foreign direct investment.
6. The website of the US Central Intelligence Agency www.cia.gov and the website of the US Census Bureau www.census.gov both contain economic data and statistics on trade. Use specific numbers from these two sites to support some of your claims in the answer to question 5.

Sources: The World Factbook, https://www.cia.gov/library/publications/the-world-factbook/ (Central Intelligence Agency, Washington, DC), accessed April 15, 204; Anonymous, "American Firms Rushing to Build in China," *USA Today*, August, 2002; Anonymous, "Competing with China," *Business Mexico*; July 2002; Aeppel, T., "US–China

Trade Becomes a Delicate Issue of Turf," *Wall Street Journal*, July 23, 2003; Armbrecht, F. M. Jr., "WTO Entry, Government's Welcome Could Spur Foreign R&D in China," *Research Technology Management*, September/October, 2002; Brown, S. and P. Caputo, "China's Growing Economic Influence in East Asia After WTO," *Southwest Economy*, Federal Reserve Bank of Dallas, May/June 2002, pp. 13–15; Cheng, C. Y., "The future prospects of US–China economic relations," *USA Today*; September, 2002; H. Cooper, "Trade Gap Sets Record For March — Oil's Rise Is Cited; Debate Now Focuses On Status of China," *Wall Street Journal*, May 22, 2000; Wonacott, P. and G. Winestock, "A Global Journal Report: China and US Make Progress On Trade Rifts," *Wall Street Journal*, September 26, 2002; "Economy of China," Wikipedia; and https://en.wikipedia.org/wiki/Economy_of_China, March 1, 2023; and Areddy, J. T., "US Trails China in Key Research, Report Says," *The Wall Street Journal*, March 2, 2023, p. A1.

PART TWO
CORPORATE FOREIGN EXCHANGE RISK MANAGEMENT

In 1997, two American finance professors — Robert Merton of Harvard University and Myron Scholes of Stanford University — received the Nobel Prize in economics for their groundbreaking work on option pricing that helped spawn the present $1 quadrillion derivatives industry. In the early 1970s, Professor Scholes invented an insightful method of pricing options and warrants at a time when investors and traders still relied on educated guesses to determine the value of various stock-market products. Professor Merton later demonstrated the broad applicability of this options-pricing formula that led to the incredible growth in the derivatives market.

Part Two (Chapters 4–8) explains relationships between exchange rates and economic variables with an emphasis on foreign exchange risk management. This part covers not only the spot market but also the derivatives market. Currency derivatives — forwards, futures, options, futures options, and swaps — are contracts whose values are derived from the prices of underlying currencies. They are offered through two channels: organized exchanges and over-the-counter markets. Organized exchanges such as the Chicago Mercantile Exchange and similar exchanges around the world have expanded their menu of products. Over-the-counter (OTC) markets, such as banks and some other financial institutions, also offer and are willing to tailor make these products for their customers. Before we consider currency derivatives separately in coming chapters, we will describe key derivative terminologies below.

DERIVATIVES AND TERMINOLOGY

Cap: An option that protects the buyer from a rise in a particular interest rate above a certain level.

Collar: The simultaneous purchase of a cap and sale of a floor with the objective of maintaining interest rates within a defined range.

Credit-default swap: A swap contract in which the *buyer* of the CDS makes a series of payments to the *seller* and, in exchange, receives a payoff if a credit instrument, such as a bond or loan undergoes a default. Some financial institutions, such as AIG incurred massive losses from their credit default swaps during the 2007–2009 recession.

Dealer: A counterparty who enters into a swap in order to earn fees or trading profits, serving customers as an intermediary.

Derivative: A contract whose value depends on, or is derived from, the value of an underlying asset.

End-user: A counterparty who engages in a swap to manage its interest rate or currency exposure.

Exercise (strike) price: The price at which some currency underlying a derivative instrument can be purchased or sold on or before the contract's maturity date.

Floor: An option that protects the buyer from a decline in a particular interest rate below a certain level.

Forward: An OTC contract obligating a buyer and a seller to trade a fixed amount of a particular asset at a set price on a future date.

Future: A highly standardized forward contract traded on an exchange.

Futures option: A contract giving the holder the right, but not the obligation, to buy or sell a futures contract at a set price during a specified period.

Hedging: The reduction of risk by eliminating the possibilities of foreign exchange gains or losses.

Notional value: The principal value upon which interest and other payments in a transaction are based.

Option: A contract giving the holder the right, but not the obligation, to buy or sell a fixed amount of an asset at a set price during a specified period.

OTC market: The market in which currency transactions are conducted through a telephone and computer network connecting currency dealers, rather than on the floor of an organized exchange.

Swap: A forward-type contract in which two parties agree to exchange a series of cash flows in the future according to a predetermined rule.

Swaption: An option giving the holder the right to enter or cancel a swap transaction.

Underlying: The asset, reference rate, or index whose price movement determines the value of the derivative.

Chapter 4

THE FOREIGN EXCHANGE MARKET AND PARITY CONDITIONS

Opening Case 4: How Much Is the Forex Market Worth In 2022?

The worldwide 2022 foreign exchange market is worth $2,409,000,000 ($2.409 quadrillion). More than $6.6 trillion on average every day is traded on foreign exchange markets. This is significantly higher than the previous analysis done by the Bank for International Settlements (BIS) in 2016 when it was valued at $1.934 quadrillion dollars.

The foreign exchange market is the largest financial market in the world in terms of trading volume, liquidity, and value. Unlike other markets such as equities, the forex industry is the only financial market with 24/7 availability. Not surprisingly, spot forex is the most popular asset class with $2 trillion worth of spot transactions traded daily in foreign exchange markets. After spot foreign exchange, the instruments with the largest daily turnover are:

- Forwards $1 trillion;
- Foreign exchange swaps $3.2 trillion;
- Currency swaps $108 billion;
- Options and others $294 billion.

As the largest financial market in the world, forex market participants are mainly financial institutions such as hedge funds, investment managers, multinational corporations, as well as commercial, investment and central banks. Retail foreign exchange trading only accounts for a mere 5.5 percent of the entire forex market globally.

The majority of foreign exchange trading is facilitated in five major financial hubs around the world, with 79 percent of forex trading occurring in the United Kingdom, United States, Hong Kong, Singapore, and Japan. The UK is by far the largest foreign exchange trading center, contributing 43.1 percent of the world's foreign exchange turnover. With the recent rise in the popularity of foreign exchange trading in Asia, China has increased from the 13th to the 8th largest forex trading center in the world.

The global foreign exchange market is comprised of over 170 different major, minor and exotic currencies. Although traders have a diverse range of currency pair options to choose from, seven major foreign exchange pairs make up 68 percent of global foreign exchange transactions. In 2019, the seven most frequently traded currency pairs and their share of the OTC forex turnover were the:

1. United States Dollar vs. Euro 24 percent;
2. United States Dollar vs. Japanese Yen 17.8 percent;
3. United States Dollar vs. Great British Pound 9.3 percent;
4. United States Dollar vs. Australian Dollar 5.2 percent;
5. United States Dollar vs. Canadian Dollar 4.3 percent
6. United States Dollar vs. Chinese Yuan 3.8 percent;
7. United States Dollar vs. Swiss Franc 3.6 percent.

The World's Most Popular Currencies

The United States Dollar (USD) plays a key role in financial markets and international economics due to pegged currencies, dollarization, as well as most Central Banks holding their reserves in USD. Although 43.1 percent of foreign exchange transactions take place in the UK, 88 percent of global foreign exchange transactions include the USD on one side of the transaction, showing the dominance of the USD currency in international foreign exchange trading. The second most likely currency to be included in a foreign exchange transaction is the Euro. A boost in turnover for the Euro during the past 3 years can be linked to increased turnover for the EUR/CHF and EUR/JPY currency pairs. While the third most likely currency to be included in foreign exchange transactions is the Japanese Yen, turnover has declined since 2016. Unlike the EUR and JPY, the volume of GBP, AUD, CAD, and CHF being traded has remained unchanged over the last 3 years.[1]

The efficient operation of the international monetary system has necessitated the creation of an institutional structure, usually called the foreign exchange market. This is a market where one country's currency can be exchanged for another country's. Contrary to what the term might suggest, the foreign exchange market actually is not a geographic location. It is an informal network of telephone, telex, satellite, facsimile, and computer communications between banks, foreign exchange dealers, arbitrageurs, and speculators. The market operates simultaneously at three tiers:

1. Individuals and corporations buy and sell foreign exchange through their commercial banks.
2. Commercial banks trade in foreign exchange with other commercial banks in the same financial center.
3. Commercial banks trade in foreign exchange with commercial banks in other financial centers.

The first type of foreign exchange market is called the retail market, and the last two are known as the interbank market.

---

[1] https://www.compareforexbrokers.com/forex-trading/statistics/.

We must first understand the organization and dynamics of the foreign exchange market in order to understand the complex functions of global finance. This chapter explains the roles of the major participants in the exchange market, describes the spot and forward markets, discusses theories of exchange rate determination (parity conditions), and examines the roles of arbitrageurs.

4.1. PARTICIPANTS IN THE EXCHANGE MARKET

The foreign exchange market consists of a spot market and a forward market. In the spot market, foreign currencies are sold and bought for delivery within two business days after the day of a trade. In the forward market, foreign currencies are sold and bought for future delivery.

There are many types of participants in the foreign exchange market: exporters, governments, importers, multinational companies (MNCs), tourists, commercial banks, and central banks. But large commercial banks and central banks are the two major participants in the foreign exchange market. Most foreign exchange transactions take place in the commercial banking sector.

4.1.1. *Commercial Banks*

Commercial banks participate in the foreign exchange market as intermediaries for customers such as MNCs and exporters. These commercial banks also maintain an interbank market. In other words, they accept deposits of foreign banks and maintain deposits in banks abroad. Commercial banks play three key roles in international transactions:

1. They operate the payment mechanism.
2. They extend credit.
3. They help to reduce risk.

4.1.1.1. *Operating the payment mechanism*

The commercial banking system provides the mechanism by which international payments can be efficiently made. This mechanism is a collection system through which transfers of money by drafts, notes, and other means are made internationally. In order to operate an international payments mechanism, banks maintain deposits in banks abroad and accept deposits of foreign banks. These accounts are debited and credited when payments are made. Banks can make international money transfers very quickly and efficiently by using telegraph, telephones, and computer services.

4.1.1.2. *Extending credit*

Commercial banks also provide credit for international transactions and for business activity within foreign countries. They make loans to those engaged in international trade and foreign investments on either an unsecured or a secured basis.

4.1.1.3. *Reducing risk*

The letter of credit is used as a major means of reducing risk in international transactions. It is a document issued by a bank at the request of an importer. In the document, the bank agrees to honor a draft drawn on the importer if the draft accompanies specified documents. The letter of credit is advantageous to exporters. Exporters sell their goods abroad against the promise of a bank rather than a commercial firm. Banks are usually larger, better known, and have better credit risks than most business firms. Thus, exporters are almost completely assured of payment if they meet specific conditions under letters of credit.

4.1.1.4. *Exchange trading by commercial banks*

Most commercial banks provide foreign exchange services for their customers. For most US banks, however, currency trading is not an important activity and exchange transactions are infrequent. These banks look to correspondents in US money centers to execute their orders.

A relatively small number of money center banks conduct the bulk of the foreign exchange transactions in the United States. Virtually all the big New York banks have active currency trading operations. Major banks in Chicago, San Francisco, Los Angeles, Boston, Detroit, and Philadelphia also are active through head office operations as well as affiliates in New York and elsewhere. Thus, all commercial banks in the United States are prepared to buy or sell foreign currency balances for their commercial customers as well as for the international banking activities of their own institutions.

Bank trading rooms share common physical characteristics. All are equipped with modern communications equipment to keep in touch with other banks, foreign exchange brokers, and corporate customers around the world. About 25 US banks, also known as primary dealers, have direct telephone lines with the Federal Reserve Bank of New York. Traders subscribe to the major news services to keep current on financial and political developments that might influence exchange trading. In addition, the banks maintain extensive "back office" support staff to handle routine operations such as confirming exchange contracts, paying, and receiving dollars and foreign currencies, and keeping general ledgers. These operations generally are kept separate from the trading room itself to assure proper management and control.

In other important respects, however, no two trading rooms are alike. They differ widely according to the scale of their operations, the roster of their corporate customers, and their overall style of trading. The basic objectives of a bank's foreign exchange trading policy are set by senior management. That policy depends upon factors such as the size of the bank, the scope of its international banking commitments, the nature of trading activities at its foreign branches, and the availability of resources.

4.1.1.5. *Global market and national markets*

Banks throughout the world serve as market makers in foreign exchange. They comprise a global market in the sense that a bank in one country can trade with another bank almost anywhere. Banks are linked by telecommunications equipment which allows instantaneous communication and puts this "over the counter" market as close as the telephone or the telex machine.

Because foreign exchange is an integral part of the payment mechanism, local banks may benefit from closer access to domestic money markets. They usually have an advantage in trading their local currency. For instance, buying and selling pound sterling for dollars is most active among the banks in London. Similarly, the major market for Swiss francs is in Zurich, for Japanese yen, in Tokyo. But the local advantage is by no means absolute. Hence, dollar-euro trading is active in London and dollar-sterling trading is active in Zurich. Furthermore, New York banks trade just as frequently with London, German, or Swiss banks in all major currencies as they do with other New York banks.

Foreign exchange is traded in a 24-hour market. Somewhere in the world, banks are buying and selling dollars for, say, euros at any time during the day. Figure 4.1 shows a map of major foreign-exchange markets around the globe with time zones included for each major market. This map should help readers understand the 24-hour operation of major foreign-exchange markets around the world. Banks in Australia and the Far East begin trading in Hong Kong, Singapore, Tokyo, and Sydney at about the time most traders in San Francisco go home for supper. As the Far East closes, trading in Middle Eastern financial centers has been going on for a couple of hours, and the trading day in Europe just begins. Some of the large New York banks have an early shift to minimize the time difference of 5–6 hours with Europe. By the time New York trading gets going in full force around 8 a.m., it is lunch time in London and Frankfurt. To complete the circle, West Coast banks also extend "normal banking hours" so they can trade with New York or Europe, on one side, and with Hong Kong, Singapore, or Tokyo, on the other.

One implication of a 24-hour currency market is that exchange rates may change at any time. Bank traders must be light sleepers so that they can be ready to respond to a telephone call in the middle of the night which may alert them to an unusually sharp exchange rate

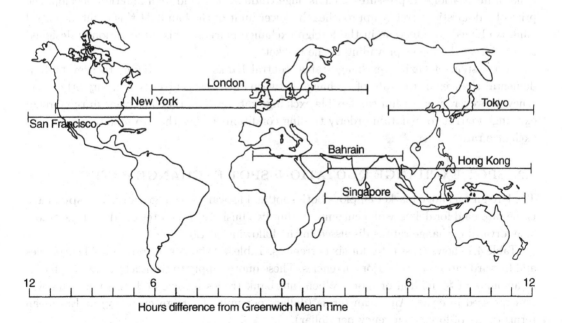

Fig. 4.1 A map of major foreign exchange markets with time zones.

movement on another continent. Many banks permit limited dealing from home by senior traders to contend with just such a circumstance.

4.1.2. *Central Banks*

Central banks, such as the South African Reserve Bank and the Uruguay's central bank attempt to control the growth of the money supply within their jurisdictions. They also strive to maintain the value of their own currency against any foreign currency. In other words, central bank operations reflect government transactions, transactions with other central banks and various international organizations, and intervention to influence exchange rate movements.

Central banks serve as their governments' banker for domestic and international payments. They handle most or all foreign exchange transactions for the government as well as for important public-sector enterprises. They may also pay or receive a foreign currency not usually held in official reserves. For example, the Central Bank of the European Union handles a substantial volume of foreign exchange transactions for its correspondents who wish to buy or sell euros for other currencies. Moreover, most central banks frequently enter into exchange transactions with international and regional organizations which need to buy or sell the local currency. The most important role of central banks in exchange-market operations is their intervention in the exchange market to influence market conditions or the exchange rate. They carry out intervention operations either on behalf of the country's treasury department or for their own account.

In a system of fixed exchange rates, central banks usually absorb the difference between supply of and demand for foreign exchange in order to maintain the par value system. Under this system, the central banks agree to maintain the value of their currencies within a narrow band of fluctuations. If pressures such as huge trade deficits and high inflation develop, the price of a domestic currency approaches the lower limit of the band. At this point, a central bank is obliged to intervene in the foreign exchange market. This intervention is designed to counteract the forces prevailing in the market.

In a system of flexible exchange rates, central banks do not attempt to prevent fundamental changes in the rate of exchange between their own currency and any other currency. However, even within the flexible exchange-rate system, they intervene in the foreign exchange market to maintain orderly trading conditions rather than to maintain a specific exchange rate.

4.2. SPOT EXCHANGE QUOTATION: SPOT EXCHANGE RATE

The foreign exchange market employs both spot and forward exchange rates. The **spot rate** is the rate paid for delivery of a currency within two business days after the day of the trade. The forward exchange rate is discussed in the following section.

Table 4.1 shows cross rates for six currencies. Table 4.2 shows spot rates for 45 currencies and forward rates for five major currencies. These quotes apply to transactions among banks in amounts of $1 million or more. When interbank trades involve dollars, these rates will be expressed in either American terms (dollars per unit of foreign currency) or European terms (units of foreign currency per dollar).

Table 4.1 Cross rates.

	Dollar	CdnDlr	Euro	Pound	Yen	Franc
US$	1	1.34377	0.931836	0.823266	132.39	0.923172
Ca$	0.744202	1	0.69349	0.612641	98.5493	0.686998
Euro	1.07315	1.44198	1	0.883369	142.094	0.990662
UK£	1.21467	1.63223	1.13204	1	160.8	1.12141
Japan¥	0.0074434	0.0101471	0.0070372	0.0062159	1	0.006971
SwissFr	1.08315	1.45537	1.00942	0.891734	143.451	1

Source: https://www.barchart.com/forex/major-rates accessed on January 10, 2023.

Table 4.2 Exchange rates.

Country/Currency	ISO Code	Symbol	In US$	Per US$
Americas				
Argentina peso	ARS		0.00554	180.386
Brazil real	BRL	R$	0.192197	5.20094
Canada dollar	CAD	$	0.744202	1.34377
Chile peso	CLP	$	0.0012	827.06
Colombia peso	COP	COL$	0.0002091	4,782.68
Ecuador US dollar		$	1	1
Mexico peso	MXN	$	0.0524735	19.0572
Peru new sol	PEN	S/.	0.2633936	3.7966
Uruguay peso	UYU	$U	0.0251003	39.8393
Venezuela bolivar	VES	BS	0.538417	18.573
Asia-Pacific				
Australian dollar	AUD	$	0.688991	1.45124
1-mos forward			0.69023	
3-mos forward			0.69182	
6-mos forward			0.69415	
China yuan	CNY	¥	0.147346	6.78675
Hong Kong dollar	HKD	HK$	0.128009	7.81229
India rupee	INR	₹	0.0122416	81.6885
Indonesia rupiah	IDR	Rp	6.426E-05	15,561.9
Japan yen	JPY	¥	0.00744343	132.39
1-mos forward				132.411
3-mos forward				132.4
6-mos forward				132.383
Malaysia ringgit	MYR	RM	0.228621	4.37405
New Zealand dollar	NZD	NRs	0.637271	1.56919
Pakistan rupee	PKR	Rs.	0.004376	228.521
Philippines peso	PHP	₱	0.018183	54.9964
Singapore dollar	SGD	S$	0.750634	1.33221
South Korea won			0.0008012	1,248.19
Taiwan dollar	TWD	NT$	0.0328556	30.4362
Thailand baht	THB	฿	0.0297624	33.5909
Vietnam dong	VND	₫	4.265E-05	23,445.8
Europe				
Czech Rep. Koruna	CZK	Kč	0.0447695	22.3366
Denmark Krone	DKK	Kr	0.144325	6.92879
Euro area euro			1.07315	0.931836

(*Continued*)

Table 4.2   (*Continued*)

Country/Currency	ISO code	Symbol	In US$	Per US$
Hungary forint	HUF	Ft	0.144325	371.344
Norway Krone	NOK		0.100104	9.98956
Poland zloty	PLN		0.228726	4.37205
Romania leu	RON	L	0.217542	4.59682
Russia ruble	RUB	R	0.0143526	69.6737
Sweden Krona	SEK	Kr	0.0959506	10.422
Switzerland franc	CHF	Fr.	1.08315	0.923172
1-mos forward				0.91978
3-mos forward				0.91395
6-mos forward				0.90514
Turkey lira	TRY	YTL	0.0532527	18.7784
UK pound	GBP	£	1.21467	0.823266
1-mos forward			1.21708	
3-mos forward			1.21899	
6-mos forward			1.22088	
Middle East/Africa				
Bahrain dinar	BHD		2.65957	0.376
Egypt pound	EGP	£	0.036136	27.6735
Israel shekel	ILS		0.288596	3.46473
Jordan dinar	JOD		1.41044	0.709
Kenya shilling	KES	KSh	0.0080814	123.741
Kuwait dinar	KWD		3.26777	0.306019
Lebanon pound	LBP		0.0006634	1507.5
Saudi Arabia riyal	SAR	SR	0.266667	3.75
South Africa rand	ZAR	R	0.0587165	17.031
UAE dirham	AED		0.272294	3.6725
				Close
WSJ Dollar Index				96.2

Sources:
1. Exchange rates: https://www.x-rates.com/
2. Currency symbols: https://www.xe.com/symbols.php
3. Currency codes: https://www.iban.com/currency-codes
4. Accessed all sites on January 10, 2023.

As shown in Table 4.2, currency quotes in both American (direct quote from the US perspective) and European terms (indirect quote from the US perspective) are listed side by side. Column 4 of Table 4.2 shows the number of US dollars required to buy one unit of foreign currency. Given this amount, one can determine the number of foreign currency units required to buy one US dollar (Column 5). This conversion can be achieved by simply taking the reciprocal of the given quotation. In other words, the relationship between US dollars and British pounds can be expressed in two different ways, but they have the same meaning. Column 4 presents the reciprocals of the exchange rates in Column 5. Column 4 equals 1.0 divided by Column 5.

For some major currencies, such as the British pound and the Swiss franc, rates also are given for future delivery. Foreign exchange risk can be minimized by purchasing or selling foreign currency for future delivery at a specified exchange rate. For large amounts, this can be accomplished through banks in what is called the forward market; the 30-, 90-, and 180-day rates in Table 4.2 reflect this. The Euro Area Euro of Table 4.2 is the euro, a

European common currency which replaced the national currencies of euro zone countries on March 1, 2002.

WSJ Dollar Index at the bottom of Table 4.2 is an index (or measure) of the value of the US dollar relative to the world's 16 most heavily traded currencies. The index is weighted using data provided by the BIS on total foreign exchange (FX) trading volume. The BIS is a supranational organization of central banks that provides triennial data, allowing for a continually updated index. The index rises when the US dollar gains value against the other currencies and falls when the US dollar loses value against the currencies.

4.2.1. *Direct and Indirect Quotes for Foreign Exchange*

Foreign exchange quotes are frequently given as a direct quote or as an indirect quote. In this pair of definitions, the home or reference currency is critical. A **direct quote** is a home currency price per unit of a foreign currency, such as $0.2300 per Saudi Arabian riyal (SR) for a US resident. An **indirect quote** is a foreign currency price per unit of a home currency, such as SR4.3478 per US dollar for a US resident. In Saudi Arabia, the foreign exchange quote, "$0.2300," is an indirect quotation, while the foreign exchange quote, "SR4.3478", is a direct quotation. In the United States, both quotes are reported daily in *The Wall Street Journal* and other financial press.

4.2.2. *Cross Rates*

A **cross rate** is an exchange rate between two non-home currencies. In just about every country, foreign currencies are quoted against the home currency, but there are instances where MNCs should know the exchange rate between two non-home currencies. For example, a US company may want to know the exchange rate between the Mexican peso and the British pound. Because foreign currencies are quoted against the dollar in the United States, their exchange rate is determined through their relationship to the US dollar. The type of exchange rate desired here is known as the cross rate because it reflects the value of one foreign currency against another foreign currency.

Once we understand how two currencies in an exchange quote can be converted into each other, we can learn how the relationships among three or more currencies are reflected in exchange quotes. For example, if the Australian dollar ($A) is selling for $0.60 and the buying rate for the South African rand (R) is $0.15, then the $A and R cross rate is R4 per $A, and the R and $A cross rate is $A0.25 per rand.

Example 4.1

A somewhat more complicated cross-rate calculation may be necessary for some foreign-exchange users. Let us assume that the dollar price of the British pound is $1.6000 per pound and that the Mexican peso price of the dollar is Mex$4 per dollar.

To determine the price of pounds in terms of Mexican pesos or the price of Mexican pesos in terms of pounds, one must convert both quotations to a common denominator, i.e., the US dollar:

$$£0.6250/\$ = \$1.6000/£ : £1/\$1.6000$$

$$Mex\$4.0000/\$ \text{ (as initially given)}$$

Because the prices of dollars are now quoted in terms of both pounds and pesos, we can obtain the price of pounds in terms of pesos:

$$\text{Mex\$/£} = \frac{4.0000}{0.6250} = \text{Mex\$6.4000/£}.$$

Similarly, we can determine the price of pesos in terms of pounds:

$$\text{£/Mex\$} = \frac{0.6250}{4.0000} = \text{£0.1563/Mex\$}$$

The exchange rate between two currencies is called the cross rate if it is obtained from the rates of these two currencies in terms of a third currency. Table 4.1 shows cross rates for six major currencies.

4.2.3. *Measuring a Percentage Change in Spot Rates*

MNCs frequently measure the percentage change in the exchange rate between two specific points in time, e.g., the current spot rate and the forecasted spot rate 1 year ahead. For example, if the Australian dollar appreciates from $0.6400 to $0.6800 over a 1-year period, US MNCs are likely to raise questions like: What is the percent increase in the dollar value of the Australian dollar? What is the percent increase in the dollar value of Australian dollar-denominated accounts receivable or accounts payable held by Americans?

4.2.3.1. *Direct quotations*

When the home currency price for a foreign currency (direct quote) is used, the percentage change in the value of the foreign currency is computed by the following formula:

$$\text{Percentage Change} = \frac{\text{ending rate} - \text{beginning rate}}{\text{beginning rate}} \tag{4.1}$$

Example 4.2

Assume that the spot rate changes from $0.6400 per $A (Australian dollar) to $0.6800 per $A over a 1-year period. The percentage change in the Australian dollar spot rate using direct quotes for a US company is calculated as follows:

$$\text{Percentage Change} = \frac{\$0.6800 - \$0.6400}{\$0.6400} = 0.0625$$

In this case, the Australian dollar has become 6.25 percent stronger than the US dollar over the 1-year period.

4.2.3.2. *Indirect quotations*

When the foreign currency price of a home currency (indirect quote) is used, the formula to compute the percentage change in the spot rate for a foreign currency becomes:

$$\text{Percentage Change} = \frac{\text{beginning rate} - \text{ending rate}}{\text{ending rate}} \tag{4.2}$$

Example 4.3

Converting Example 4.2 into indirect quotations, we can assume that the Australian dollar appreciates from $A1.5625 per dollar to $A1.4706 per dollar. The percentage change in the Australian dollar spot rate using indirect quotes for a US company is computed as follows:

$$\text{Percentage Change} = \frac{\$A1.5625 - \$A1.4706}{\$A1.4706} = 0.0625$$

In both methods of computation, the Australian dollar appreciated by 6.25 percent against the US dollar over the 1-year period.

4.2.4. *The Bid–Ask Spread*

Up to this point, we have ignored bid-ask spreads in our discussion of foreign exchange transactions. International banks serve as foreign exchange dealers who stand ready to quote bid and ask prices on major currencies for their customers. A bank's **bid price** is the price at which the bank is ready to buy a foreign currency. A bank's **ask price** is the price at which the bank is ready to sell a foreign currency. The **bid-ask spread** is the spread between bid and ask rates for a currency; this spread is the bank's fee for executing the foreign exchange transaction.

$$\text{Bid–ask spread} = \frac{\text{ask price} - \text{bid price}}{\text{ask price}} \tag{4.3}$$

Example 4.4

The bid price is $1.5000 for the British pound and $0.0130 for the Japanese yen. The ask price is $1.6000 for the pound and $0.0140 for the yen.

Applying Eq. (4.3) to the bid-ask spread for the pound, we obtain:

$$\text{Bid–ask spread} = \frac{\$1.6000 - \$1.5000}{\$1.6000} = 0.0625 \quad \text{or} \quad 6.25\%$$

Applying Eq. (4.3) to the bid-ask spread for the yen, we obtain:

$$\text{Bid–ask spread} = \frac{\$0.0140 - \$0.0130}{\$0.0140} = 0.0714 \quad \text{or} \quad 7.14\%$$

4.3. FORWARD EXCHANGE QUOTATION: FORWARD EXCHANGE RATE

The **forward rate** is the rate to be paid for delivery of a currency at some future date. The exchange rate is established at the time the contract is made, but payment and delivery are not required until maturity. Forward rates are usually quoted for fixed periods of 30, 90, or 180 days from the day of the contract. In some instances, actual contracts in major currencies can be arranged for delivery at any specified date up to 1 year.

Table 4.2 shows the forward rates for only four major currencies: British pounds, Canadian dollars, Japanese yen, and Swiss francs. The current spot rate and the forward rate may be the same during a period of foreign exchange stability. However, there usually is a difference between the spot rate and the forward rate; this difference is known as the spread.

Example 4.5

Forward quotations are made either "outright" or in terms of the spread on the spot rate. Suppose that the 90-day outright forward quotation is $0.7900 per Can$ for Canadian dollars and $0.6000 per SFr for Swiss francs and that the spot rate is $0.8000 per Can$ and $0.5800 per SFr. The spread between the forward rate and the spot rate is stated in terms of points; one point equals 0.01 percent or $0.0001. Point quotations for the two 90-day forward rates are determined as follows:

Spot or Forward Rate	Canadian Dollars	Swiss Francs
90-day forward rate	$0.7900	$0.6000
Less: spot rate	0.8000	0.5800
90-day forward quote in points	−100	+200

In giving a forward quote for the Canadian dollar, a trader might say "minus 100" or "a discount of 100." For the Swiss franc, the trader would say "plus 200" or "a premium of 200." Thus, when the forward rate is less than the spot rate, it is said to be at a discount. When the forward rate is greater than the spot rate, it is said to be at a premium. Outright quotations are normally used for retail customers of the bank, while point quotations are usually employed for traders.

A forward premium or discount is sometimes expressed in terms of the annualized percentage deviation from the spot rate. The premium or discount is computed by the following formula:

$$\text{Premium (discount)} = \frac{n\text{-day forward rate} - \text{spot rate}}{\text{spot rate}} \times \frac{360}{n} \qquad (4.4)$$

Applying Eq. (4.4) to the 90-day forward quote for Canadian dollars given in Example 4.5, we obtain:

$$\text{Forward discount} = \frac{\$0.7900 - \$0.8000}{\$0.8000} \times \frac{360}{90}$$

$$= -0.05 \quad \text{or} \quad -5.00\%$$

Applying Eq. (4.4) to the 90-day forward quote for Swiss francs given in Example 4.5, we obtain:

$$\text{Forward premium} = \frac{\$0.6000 - \$0.5800}{\$0.5800} \times \frac{360}{90}$$

$$= +0.1379 \quad \text{or} \quad +13.79\%$$

4.3.1. *Key Reasons for Forward Exchange Transactions*

Actual exchange market participants are banks, companies, individuals, governments, and other financial institutions. However, these participants are called arbitrageurs, traders, hedgers, or speculators, depending on the purpose of their participation in the exchange market. Arbitrageurs seek to earn riskless profits by taking advantage of differences in interest rates among countries. Traders use forward contracts to eliminate possible exchange losses on export or import orders denominated in foreign currencies. Hedgers, mostly MNCs, engage in forward contracts to protect the home-currency value of foreign-currency denominated assets and liabilities. Speculators deliberately expose themselves to exchange risk by engaging in forward contracts in order to make a profit from exchange rate fluctuations.

Individuals and corporations buy and sell forward currencies to provide protection against future changes in exchange rates. So long as we do not have a single world currency, some degree of exchange risk exists in any system. We cannot eliminate some possibility of foreign exchange losses in either the fixed exchange-rate system or the flexible exchange-rate system.

Example 4.6

Assume that an American firm purchases machinery through its UK branch for £10,000 with terms of 90 days. Let us also assume that the spot rate for pounds is $1.70 per pound and the 90-day forward rate for pounds is $1.80 per pound. Payment should be made in British pounds 90 days from the day of the shipment.

Actually, there are two alternative ways of payment available to the American firm. First, the firm could buy pounds in the spot market 90 days from the day of the shipment to pay the credit. If the spot rate for pounds rises to $2.00 during this time, the American firm should spend $20,000 to buy the sum of £10,000. Second, it could also buy £10,000 in the forward market for $18,000 to pay the credit on the due date. By so doing, the American firm would avoid the risk of a $2,000 loss ($20,000 − $18,000). However, if the spot rate for pounds declines to $1.50 during this period, the American firm would lose $3,000 ($15,000 − $18,000) under the forward contract.

4.3.2. *Speculation in the Foreign Exchange Market*

Foreign exchange markets facilitate both commercial and private transactions such as foreign trade, loans, and investments. In addition, they give rise to exchange speculation. The purpose of speculation in the foreign exchange market is to make a profit from exchange-rate fluctuations by deliberately taking an uncovered position. Speculation can be undertaken in both the spot market and the forward market.

4.3.2.1. *Speculating in the spot market*

Suppose a speculator anticipates that the spot rate of the Swiss franc will appreciate in 90 days. The speculator will purchase francs at today's spot rate, will hold them for 90 days, and will resell them at a higher rate.

Example 4.7

The present spot rate for francs is $0.4000 per SFr. A speculator's expectation of the spot rate for francs in 90 days is $0.4500. If the speculator's expectation proves correct, what would be his dollar profit from speculating $10,000 in the spot market?

With $10,000, the speculator could buy SFr25,000 ($10,000/$0.4000) in the spot market, hold them for 90 days, and resell them at $0.4500 per SFr for a gross of $11,250 (SFr25,000 × $0.4500). As a result, the speculator would earn a net profit of $1,250 or 12.50 percent on the original $10,000 of capital. But spot speculation is risky. If the spot rate declines to $0.3500 during this period, the SFr25,000 would have an ending value of $8,750 (SFr25,000 × $0.3500) for a net loss of $1,250. Theoretically speaking, no limit exists to the potential profit, but the maximum loss would be $10,000.

A speculator is not locked into an absolute 90-day terminal date but may simply hold the currency until a date that seems to be most profitable. This is possible because the speculator could close out the position before 90 days or hold it longer than 90 days if his expectation changes after the spot purchase.

4.3.2.2. *Speculating in the forward market*

Suppose a speculator anticipates that the Swiss franc's spot rate in 90 days will exceed its 90-day forward rate as quoted today. The speculator buys francs for 90-day future delivery at today's forward rate, waits for 90 days, and then sells the francs spot to close the position.

Example 4.8

The present 90-day forward rate for francs is $0.4300. A speculator's expectation of the spot rate for francs in 90 days is $0.4500. If the speculator's expectation proves correct, what would be his dollar profit from speculating $10,000 in the forward market?

The speculator could buy SFr23,256 forward for $10,000 at the forward quotation of $0.4300, receive them in 90 days, and then sell them at the spot rate of $0.4500 for a gross of $10,465. Profit would be $465. The profit of $465 in this case cannot be related to any investment base to determine a rate of return because no capital was invested at the time the contract was entered.

Clearly, there is greater risk for a speculator in forward transaction than in spot transaction. Forward market speculation involves a more remote payment date and a greater chance of unfavorable fluctuations. There are two types of risk here. The first risk is the possibility that foreign exchange rates will fluctuate. The second risk is the possibility that the forward contract will not be carried out. The first risk will affect the speculator only if he carries an open position in the forward contract. The speculator can eliminate this risk by purchasing an offsetting forward contract. Although the speculator has a net position of zero, he still carries the second risk because he stands in the middle.

4.4. INTERNATIONAL PARITY CONDITIONS

In this section, specific attention is given to the theory of foreign exchange-rate determination. This theory is based on a relationship between the money market and the foreign exchange market; this relationship prevails without restrictions imposed by government policy on the extent to which rates can move. Such a free-market situation will establish the nature of interrelationships among the money markets and the foreign exchange markets. In other words, we can postulate a simple set of parity conditions that should hold among inflation rates, interest rates, spot rates, and forward rates. This idea, commonly known as the law of one price, is enforced by arbitrageurs who, by following the famous dictum of "buy low, sell high," prevents all but minor deviations from equality.

There are five major theories of exchange-rate determination:

1. The Theory of Purchasing Power Parity;
2. The Fisher Effect;
3. The International Fisher Effect;
4. The Theory of Interest-Rate Parity;
5. The Forward Rate as an Unbiased Predictor of the Future Spot Rate.

It is important to remember that the economic relationships of these five theories result from arbitrage activities.

4.4.1. *Efficient Exchange Markets*

Investors make risk-return decisions in the framework of available exchange markets. We base our discussion of the theories of exchange-rate determination on the assumption of efficient exchange markets. **Efficient exchange markets** exist when exchange rates reflect all available information and adjust quickly to new information. Because exchange markets are highly competitive in such a situation, the market participants buy and sell foreign exchange in a way that eliminates all profits in excess of the minimum required to sustain their continued participation. In other words, the concept of efficient exchange markets depends on three hypotheses:

1. Market prices such as product prices, interest rates, spot rates, and forward rates should reflect the market's consensus estimate of the future spot rate.
2. Investors should not earn unusually large profits in forward speculation. Because exchange-rate forecasts based on market prices are accurate, publicly available forecasts of the future spot rate do not lead to unusual profits in forward speculation.
3. It is impossible for any market analyst to beat the market consistently.

Certainly, these conditions are not completely met in practice. Thus, exchange markets are assumed efficient if the conditions are only reasonably met. There are many indications that support the efficient market assumption for international money and exchange markets. First, foreign currencies and other financial assets are traded by companies and individuals who have broad market contacts, sophisticated analytical capabilities, and modern communications. Because new information is widely, quickly, and cheaply disseminated to investors, market prices are rapidly adjusted to reflect significant developments. Second, since 1973 the major trading countries of the world have adopted the system of freely floating rates, and their governmental interference in exchange markets has been minimal.

4.4.2. *The Theory of Purchasing Power Parity*

The **theory of purchasing power parity** (PPP) explains why the parity relationship exists between inflation rates and exchange rates. The PPP theory has an absolute version and a relative version. The absolute version of the PPP theory maintains that the equilibrium exchange rate between domestic and foreign currencies equals the ratio between domestic and foreign prices. For example, if one American dollar can buy one bushel of wheat and one British pound can buy two bushels of wheat, the exchange rate between the two currencies is $0.50 per pound.

Specifically, the PPP theory in its simplest form holds that the exchange rate must change in terms of a single currency to equate the prices of goods in both countries. For example, if the prices of British goods rise relative to the prices of US goods, the British pound should depreciate to keep the dollar price of goods in Britain the same as the dollar prices of identical goods in the United States. Otherwise, arbitrageurs would have an incentive to purchase goods in the United States and sell them in Britain until these prices were again equalized.

Unfortunately for this analysis, the world is more complex than this simple example. The real world is characterized by transportation costs, tariffs, quotas, and all sorts of impediments to the equalization of prices for identical goods worldwide. Thus, it is not difficult to understand why the absolute PPP relationship does not hold very well for any pair of countries.

The relative version of the PPP doctrine states that in the long run, the exchange rate between the home currency and the foreign currency will adjust to reflect changes in the price levels of the two countries. In other words, it relates equilibrium changes in the exchange rate to changes in the ratio of domestic and foreign prices.

$$\frac{e_t}{e_0} = \frac{(1 + I_\mathrm{d})^t}{(1 + I_\mathrm{f})^t} \tag{4.5}$$

where e_t = the dollar price of one unit of foreign currency in period t; e_0 = the dollar price of one unit of foreign currency in period 0; I_d = domestic inflation rate; and I_f = foreign inflation rate. If we solve Eq. (4.5) for the new exchange rate (e_t), we obtain:

$$e_t = e_0 \times \frac{(1 + I_\mathrm{d})^t}{(1 + I_\mathrm{f})^t} \tag{4.6}$$

Example 4.9

This time, let us assume that the exchange rate between US dollars and British pounds is $2 per pound. Let us further accept the fact that the United States will have an inflation rate of 10 percent for the coming year and that England will have an inflation rate of 20 percent over the same period.

The new exchange rate of $1.83 per pound is obtained in this way:

$$e_1 = \$2 \times \frac{(1 + 0.10)}{(1 + 0.20)} = \$1.83/\pounds$$

Example 4.9 indicates that the US dollar price of the pound should decrease in value by about 10 percent from $2 per pound to $1.83 per pound to equalize the dollar price of goods in two countries. If the exchange rate does not fall by the amount suggested by the PPP theory, then we could say that the US dollar is undervalued or the British pound is overvalued.

The main justification for the PPP theory is that if the exchange rate stays the same at $2 per pound, British exports of goods and services will become less competitive with comparable products produced in the United States. British imports from the United States will also become more price-competitive with higher-priced British products.

4.4.2.1. *Appraisal of the PPP theory*

The PPP theory not only explains how relative inflation rates between two countries can influence their exchange rate, but it can also be used to forecast exchange rates. It is important to remember that the PPP doctrine is supposed to work well under a freely floating exchange-rate system. With the termination of the fixed exchange-rate system in 1973, the relative price levels and exchange rates in most industrial countries fluctuated widely. The experience of recent years indicates that, while movements in dollar exchange rates for some major currencies reflected differences in inflation rates that was not the case for sharp short-period fluctuations in these rates. In addition, the PPP theory did not work that well for some other currencies.

There are some obvious weaknesses of the PPP theory. First, it assumes that goods are easily traded. This is not the case for such goods as housing and medical services. The PPP theory, moreover, relies on an index of prices such as the consumer price index. Such an index may be misleading because only traded goods directly affect the balance on goods and services. However, even non-traded goods indirectly affect the price of traded goods through their impact on the overall cost of living and on wage demands.

Second, the PPP theory assumes that tradable goods are identical across countries. However, even tradable goods are not always identical when they are produced in different countries. For example, some Americans prefer Japanese cars, and others prefer American cars. Moreover, customer preferences for automobiles change over time. If Japanese cars suddenly become more popular, the increase in demand will drive up the price of Japanese cars. But despite the price differential between the two markets, there might be no opportunity for profitable arbitrage because customers do not view the Japanese and American cars as equivalent.

Third, we must compare a similar basket of goods in each country with its trading partners in order to test the PPP theory. If we try to compare the prices of dissimilar goods, we have to rely on price indexes. It then becomes a question of which index is most reflective of goods traded between countries.

Fourth, many other factors influence exchange rates besides relative prices. These include relative interest rates, relative income levels, and government interference in the foreign exchange market. Thus, it is difficult to measure the precise magnitude of exchange-rate movements attributable to differences in inflation rates.

In spite of these limitations, the PPP theory is quite useful and seems to be valid over the long run. If a country's inflation rate remains higher than that of its trading partners for a long period, that country's currency will tend to depreciate in order to prevent the country from being forced out of the export market. According to many empirical studies, this fact exists whether it is caused by the PPP theory alone or by a combination of factors.

4.4.3. *The Fisher Effect*

The **Fisher Effect**, named after economist Irving Fisher, assumes that the nominal interest rate in each country is equal to a real interest rate plus an expected rate of inflation:

$$\text{Nominal rate} = \text{Real rate} + \text{Inflation} \tag{4.7}$$

The real interest rate is determined by the productivity in an economy and a risk premium commensurate with the risk of a borrower. The nominal interest rate embodies an inflation premium sufficient to compensate lenders or investors for an expected loss of purchasing power. Consequently, nominal interest rates are higher when people expect higher rates of inflation and are lower when people expect lower rates of inflation.

The real interest rate is thought to be relatively stable over time. Moreover, in a free market where investors can buy any interest-bearing securities, real interest rates are identical everywhere, but nominal interest rates will vary by the difference in expected rates of inflation. The Fisher Effect asserts that real interest rates are equalized across countries through arbitrage. For example, if expected real rates of interest were higher in Switzerland than in the United States, capital would flow from the United States to Switzerland. On the other hand, if real rates of interest were higher in the United States than in Switzerland, capital would flow from Switzerland to the United States. This process of arbitrage would continue, in the absence of government intervention, until the expected real rates of interest are equalized in both countries.

4.4.3.1. *Appraisal of the Fisher Effect*

Empirical studies have found that most of the variation in nominal interest rates, particularly for short-term government securities, can be attributed to changing inflationary expectations. The hypothesis of the Fisher Effect, based on long-term securities, suffers from an increased financial risk inherent in fluctuations of a bond market value prior to maturity. Comparisons of corporate securities are influenced by unequal creditworthiness of the issuers. In addition, changes in long-term interest rates and changes in inflation rates are not concurrent because long-term rates relative to short-term rates are not that sensitive to changes in prices. However, the Fisher Effect based on long-term maturities has worked fairly well in recent years. First, long-term interest rates, adjusted for inflation, have been relatively stable in most industrial countries in recent years. Second, long-term real rates of interest in most countries have been relatively close together in recent years.

4.4.4. *The International Fisher Effect*

The **International Fisher Effect** states that the future spot rate should move in an amount equal to, but in the opposite direction from, the difference in interest rates between two countries. A future spot rate of a currency with a higher interest rate would depreciate in the long run; a future spot rate of a currency with a lower interest rate would appreciate in the long run. For example, if the interest rate over the next year is 4 percent in the United States and 10 percent in Switzerland, the franc would depreciate against the dollar by 6 percent.

When investors purchase the currency of a country to take advantage of higher interest rates abroad, they must also consider any possible losses due to fluctuations in the value of the foreign currency prior to maturity of their investment. To clarify this point, assume that interest rates are higher in Switzerland than in the United States. In this case, US investors in Swiss securities must be rewarded with a higher interest rate to offset the expected depreciation of a spot rate for the franc when they convert the principal and interest into dollars. Swiss investors in US securities must be rewarded with a higher future spot rate for the dollar to offset the lower interest rate in the United States. In other words, the International Fisher Effect holds that the interest differential between two countries should be an unbiased predictor of the future change in the spot rate.

4.4.4.1. *Short-run behavior*

The relationship between interest rates and exchange rates is a complex one which incorporates numerous behavioral parameters. The short-run behavior of interest and exchange rates, quite contrary to their long-run behavior, shows that a rise in interest rates in a given country is expected to raise the value of that country's currency, and vice versa. In other words, currencies of countries with higher interest rates than the United States tend to appreciate in value against the dollar. Higher interest rates in a given country would raise the value of its currency because higher interest rates could attract capital from investors in other countries. By the same token, currencies of countries with lower interest rates than the United States tend to depreciate in value against the dollar because investors in other countries would sell their currencies in exchange for the dollar. Hence, the exchange rate moves in the same direction as the difference in interest rates between two countries.

4.4.5. *The Theory of Interest-Rate Parity*

The movement of short-term funds between two countries to take advantage of interest differentials is a major determinant of the spread between forward and spot rates. According to the interest parity theory, the spread between a forward rate and a spot rate should be equal but opposite in sign to the difference in interest rates between two countries. In a free market, the currency with the higher interest rate would sell at a discount in the forward market; the currency with the lower interest rate would sell at a premium in the forward market. In fact, the forward discount or premium is closely related to the interest differential between the two currencies.

The interest-rate parity theory holds that the difference between a forward rate and a spot rate equals the difference between a domestic interest rate and a foreign interest rate:

$$\frac{n\text{-day } F - S}{S} \times \frac{360}{n} = i_\text{d} - i_\text{f} \tag{4.8}$$

where n-day $F = n$-day forward rate, S = spot rate, i_d = domestic interest rate, and $i_\text{f} =$ foreign interest rate.

Example 4.10

Let us assume four things: (1) the Swiss interest rate = 9 percent; (2) the US interest rate = 7 percent; (3) the spot rate for the Swiss franc = \$0.4000; and (4) the 180-day forward rate for the Swiss franc = \$0.3960.

In this case, the percentage discount on the 180-day forward rate is equal to the interest rate differential:

$$\frac{\$0.3960 - \$0.4000}{\$0.4000} \times \frac{360}{180} = 0.07 - 0.09$$
$$-0.02 = -0.02$$

Swiss securities would earn 2 percent more than American securities, but Swiss francs sell in the forward market at a 2 percent discount.

This outcome is brought about by arbitrageurs who enter into forward contracts to avoid the exchange-rate risk. If interest rates are higher in Switzerland than in the United States, arbitrageurs in search of a higher yield could move their funds from the United States to Switzerland. In order to avoid the exchange-rate risk at maturity, the arbitrageurs would sell the francs in exchange for dollars in the forward market. Consequently, the forward rate for the Swiss franc with the higher interest rate would depreciate; the forward rate for the US dollar with the lower interest rate would appreciate. Such transactions will continue until the interest differential in favor of Switzerland is equal to the forward discount for the Swiss franc. Under this condition, there is no incentive for capital to move in either direction because the interest differential is offset by the forward discount.

4.4.6. *The Forward Rate and the Future Spot Rate*

If speculators think that a forward rate is higher than their prediction of a future spot rate, they will sell the foreign currency forward. This speculative transaction will bid down the forward rate until it equals the expected future spot rate. By the same token, if speculators believe that a forward rate is lower than an expected future spot rate, they will buy a foreign currency forward. This speculative transaction will bid up the forward rate until it reaches the expected future spot rate. Under this condition, there is no longer any incentive to buy or sell a foreign currency forward, because forward rates are unbiased predictors of future spot rates.

4.4.7. *Synthesis of International Parity Conditions*

In the absence of predictable exchange-market intervention by central banks, an expected rate of change in a spot rate, differential rates of national inflation and interest, and forward premiums or discounts are all directly proportional to each other. Because money, capital, and exchange markets are efficient, these variables adjust very quickly to changes in any one of them. Consequently, the forward rate is the best possible forecaster of the future spot rate. Example 4.11 and Fig. 4.3 illustrate all of the fundamental parity relations simultaneously with the aid of a two-currency model: the US dollar and the Swiss franc.

Example 4.11

Let us assume the following:

1. The current spot rate for the Swiss franc: SFr1 = $0.5000.
2. The 1-year forward rate for the Swiss franc: SFr1 = $0.4750.
3. The expected spot rate in 1 year for the Swiss franc: SFr1 = $0.4750.
4. The expected rate of inflation for 1 year: Switzerland = 10 percent; US = 5 percent.
5. Interest rates on 1-year government securities: Switzerland = 12 percent; US = 7 percent.

We will now discuss international parity relationships among spot rates, forward rates, inflation rates, and interest rates, using these five assumptions.

First, the PPP theory holds that any change in the differential rate of inflation between two countries tends to be offset by an equal but opposite change in the spot rate. A 5 percent higher rate of inflation in Switzerland is offset by a 5 percent depreciation in the spot rate for the franc. This 5 percent depreciation in the spot rate for the franc is computed by

Eq. (4.1):

$$\text{Percentage change} = \frac{\text{ending rate} - \text{beginning rate}}{\text{beginning rate}}$$

$$\text{Percentage change} = \frac{0.4750 - 0.5000}{0.5000} = -0.05 \quad \text{or} \quad -5\%$$

Second, the Fisher Effect suggests that real interest rates are identical everywhere and that nominal interest rates will vary by the difference in expected rates of inflation. The real inflation-adjusted interest rate in both countries is computed by Eq. (4.7): nominal rate = real rate + inflation.

The US: 7% = real rate + 5%; real rate = 2%

Switzerland: 12% = real rate + 10%; real rate = 2%

The nominal interest rate in Switzerland (12 percent) is 5 percent higher than the nominal interest rate in the United States (7 percent). This difference is identical to the 5 percent difference in expected rates of inflation between Switzerland (10 percent) and the United States (5 percent).

Third, the International Fisher Effect states that a future spot rate should move in an amount equal to, but in the opposite direction from, the difference in interest rates between two countries. The 5 percent interest differential in favor of Switzerland is equal to the 5 percent depreciation in the future spot rate for the franc (remember that the 5 percent franc depreciation was computed in relation to the PPP theory).

Fourth, the Interest Parity Theory assumes that the spread between the forward rate and the spot rate should be equal but opposite in sign to the difference in interest rates between the two countries. The 5 percent higher rate of interest in Switzerland is consistent with the 5 percent forward discount for the Swiss franc. The 5-percent forward discount for the franc is computed by Eq. (4.4):

$$\text{Premium (discount)} = \frac{n\text{-day forward rate} - \text{spot rate}}{\text{spot rate}} \times \frac{360}{n}$$

$$\text{Forward discount} = \frac{0.4750 - 0.5000}{0.5000} \times \frac{360}{360} = -0.05 \quad \text{or} \quad -5\%$$

Finally, under a freely floating exchange system, the forward rate is an unbiased predictor of the future spot rate. The 1-year forward rate of $0.4750 for the franc is identical with the expected spot rate in 1 year of $0.4750 for the franc. This means that the 5 percent 1-year forward discount for the franc is an unbiased predictor that the franc will depreciate by 5 percent over the next year.

Figure 4.2 illustrates these five key theories of exchange-rate determination and their relationships on the basis of Example 4.11: the theory of purchasing power parity (Relationship A), the Fisher Effect (Relationship B), the International Fisher Effect (Relationship C), the theory of interest rate parity (Relationship D), and the forward rate as an unbiased predictor of the future spot rate (Relationship E). Relationship F does not represent any particular theory, but it has to be true by definition if Relationships A-E are all true. This framework emphasizes the links that exist among spot exchange rates, forward rates, interest rates, and inflation rates.

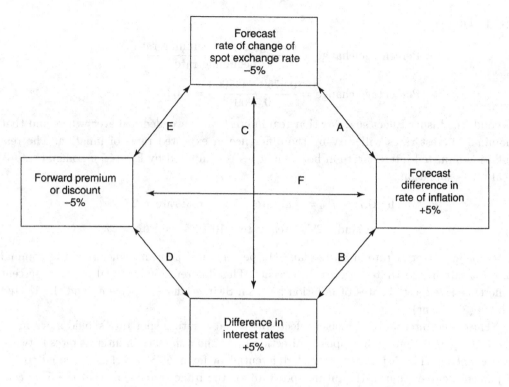

Fig. 4.2   Relationships among various financial rates.

Global Finance in Practice 4: Major Determinants of Exchange Rates

The following five Factors are the principal determinants of the exchange rate between two countries. Note that these factors are in no particular order; like many aspects of economics, the relative importance of these factors is subject to much debate.

Differentials in Inflation

Typically, a country with a consistently lower inflation rate exhibits a rising currency value, as its purchasing power increases relative to other currencies. Those countries with higher inflation typically see depreciation in their currency compared with the currencies of their trading partners.

Differentials in Interest Rates

Higher interest rates offer lenders in an economy a higher return relative to other countries. Therefore, higher interest rates attract foreign capital and cause the exchange rate to rise. The impact of higher interest rates is mitigated, however, if inflation in the country is much higher than in others, or if additional factors serve to drive the currency down. The opposite relationship exists for decreasing interest rates — that is, lower interest rates tend to decrease exchange rates.

Current Account Deficits

A deficit in the current account shows the country is spending more on foreign trade than it is earning, and that it is borrowing capital from foreign sources to make up the deficit. In other words, the country requires more foreign currency than it receives through sales of exports, and it supplies more of its own currency than foreigners demand for its products. The excess demand for foreign currency lowers the country's exchange rate until domestic goods and services are cheap enough for foreigners, and foreign assets are too expensive to generate sales for domestic interests.

Terms of Trade

The terms of trade is related to current accounts and the balance of payments. If the price of a country's exports rises by a greater rate than that of its imports, its terms of trade have favorably improved. Increasing terms of trade shows greater demand for the country's exports. This, in turn, results in rising revenues from exports, which provides increased demand for the country's currency (and an increase in the currency's value). If the price of exports rises by a smaller rate than that of its imports, the currency's value will decrease in relation to its trading partners.

Strong Economic Performance

Foreign investors inevitably seek out stable countries with strong economic performance in which to invest their capital. A country with such positive attributes will draw investment funds away from other countries perceived to have more political and economic risk. Political turmoil, for example, can cause a loss of confidence in a currency and a movement of capital to the currencies of more stable countries.[2]

4.5. ARBITRAGES

Arbitrage is the purchase of something in one market and its sale in another market to take advantage of a price differential. Professional arbitrageurs quickly transfer funds from one currency to another in order to profit from discrepancies between exchange rates in different markets. The process of arbitrage also works through the foreign exchange market to bring interest rates in national markets closer together. Even small discrepancies between the exchange rates and interest rates in different markets would motivate enough arbitrage to eliminate these discrepancies quickly.

4.5.1. Geographic Arbitrage

In principle, the exchange rate for a given currency should be the same in every geographic market. However, geographic arbitrage could arise when local demand-and-supply conditions

---

[2]Alexandra Twin, "5 Factors That Influence Exchange Rates, *Investopedia*, July 2, 2022, https://www.investopedia.com/trading/factors-influence-exchange-rates/.

might create temporary discrepancies among various markets. Arbitrage specialists would buy the currency in a market where its price is lower and then sell the currency where its price is higher. If the exchange rate differential is larger than the transaction cost, an arbitrage profit would be made.

4.5.1.1. *Two-point arbitrage*

A **two-point arbitrage** is the arbitrage transaction between two currencies. Suppose, for example, that the quotes of the South African rand against the US dollar are $0.20 in New York and $0.25 in Johannesburg. The price of rands in terms of dollars is higher in Johannesburg than in New York. An arbitrageur could benefit by buying rands with dollars in New York and then selling the rands in exchange for dollars in Johannesburg. Arbitrage tends to wipe out the exchange rate differential that originally triggered it. The purchase of rands in New York would drive the price of rands against the dollar up toward the Johannesburg rate. The sale of rands in Johannesburg would drive the price of rands against the dollar down toward the New York rate. This arbitrage process would continue until the price of rands in terms of the dollar is the same in both markets.

The basic economic principle of "buy low, sell high" dominates the arbitrage transaction of buying and selling currencies in two national money markets. Exchange rates in two different locations must be stated in a given currency if this principle is to be applied in foreign exchange. Thus, the arbitrage process becomes slightly more difficult to understand if exchange rates are quoted in different currencies. Let us restate our previous example in a slightly different way. The price of rands against the dollar is $0.20 in New York. The price of dollars against the rand is R4 in Johannesburg. The quotes in both locations in terms of $/R are as follows:

New York	Johannesburg
$0.20/R (as initially given)	$0.25/R (1 ÷ 4)

The rand enjoys a higher price against the dollar in Johannesburg than in New York. This price differential leads to the following transactions in each market.

1. In New York, investors would buy rands and sell dollars.
2. In Johannesburg, investors would sell rands and buy dollars.

4.5.1.2. *A three-point arbitrage*

A **three-point arbitrage**, commonly known as a triangle arbitrage, is an arbitrage transaction among three currencies. This type of arbitrage can occur if any of the three cross rates is out of line. Consider the possibility that the cross rates of exchange are Rs60/$, Rs10/HK$, and HK$3/$. An arbitrageur could make a profit of $1. She would buy 60 Indian rupees for $1, then purchase six Hong Kong dollars for 60 Indian rupees, and finally buy $2 for the six Hong Kong dollars. A large volume of such transactions would strengthen the rupee against the dollar, strengthen the Hong Kong dollar against the rupee, and strengthen the dollar against the Hong Kong dollar. This arbitrage process causes some consistent patterns of rates to emerge at which no further arbitrage would be profitable. In other words, the arbitrage will continue until dollars can no longer be bought more cheaply in one market than the price at which they are sold in another market. Currency cross rates such as those given in Table 4.1 can be prepared to ensure that the exchange rates are consistent with each other in all markets.

4.5.2. *Covered-Interest Arbitrage*

Covered interest arbitrage is the movement of short-term funds between countries to take advantage of interest differentials with exchange risk covered by forward contracts. When investors purchase the currency of a foreign country to take advantage of higher interest rates abroad, they must also consider any losses or gains. Such losses or gains might occur due to fluctuations in the value of the foreign currency prior to the maturity of their investment. Generally, investors cover against such potential losses by contracting for the future sale or purchase of a foreign currency in the forward market.

Their actions, aimed at profits from interest rate differentials between countries, lead, in equilibrium, to the condition of so-called interest parity. The interest rate parity theory says that any exchange gains or losses incurred by a simultaneous purchase and sale in the spot and forward markets are offset by the interest rate differential on similar assets. Under these conditions, there is no incentive for capital to move in either direction because the effective returns on foreign and domestic assets have been equalized.

Figure 4.3 presents a graphic representation of the theoretical relationship between the forward premium or discount and the interest rate differential. The vertical axis represents the interest differential in favor of the foreign currency and the horizontal axis shows the forward premium or discount on that currency. The interest parity line shows the equilibrium state. This chapter ignores transaction costs for simplicity. However, it is important to recognize the fact that transaction costs cause the interest parity line to be a band rather than a thin line. Transaction costs include the foreign exchange brokerage costs on spot and forward contracts as well as the investment brokerage cost for buying and selling securities.

Point A of Fig. 4.3 shows that the forward discount for foreign exchange is 1 percent and that the foreign interest rate is 2 percent higher than the domestic interest rate. In this case, the arbitrageur could employ the so-called covered interest arbitrage to make a profit. Specifically, the arbitrageur would earn 2 percent more on her investment in foreign securities and lose 1 percent on the repurchase of the domestic currency in the forward market by taking the following actions: (1) she buys spot foreign currency with domestic currency, (2) invests the foreign currency in foreign securities, and (3) sell the foreign currency in the forward market, The net result is that the arbitrageur would make a profit of 1 percent from this covered interest arbitrage transaction.

The arbitrageur would have to convert the foreign currency to domestic currency at the end of maturity. The exchange rate may fall before the arbitrageur has returned her funds to her home country. For that reason, the arbitrage transaction involves foreign exchange risks. To avoid these risks, she will cover the transaction by selling forward the same amount of the foreign currency at 1 percent discount. The investment protected by forward sales is called covered interest arbitrage.

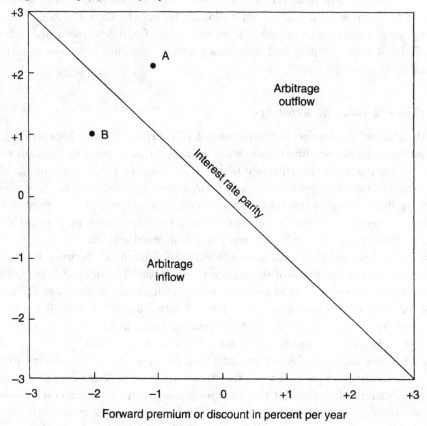

Fig. 4.3   Covered interest arbitrage.

Example 4.12

Suppose: (1) the Swiss interest rate = 10 percent; (2) the US interest rate = 8 percent; (3) the spot rate for Swiss francs = $0.5000; and (4) the 180-day forward rate for Swiss francs = $0.4975.

The forward discount for the franc is obtained by using Eq. (5.4):

$$\text{Forward discount} = \frac{\$0.4975 - \$0.5000}{\$0.5000} \times \frac{360}{180} = -0.01 \quad \text{or} \quad -1\%$$

The interest differential is 2 percent (10 − 8 percent) in favor of the Swiss franc. The covered-interest arbitrage would work as follows:

1. Borrow dollars in the United States   −8%
    Buy francs spot with the dollars
2. Invest the francs in Swiss securities   +10%
3. Sell francs forward against dollars at a discount   −1%
    Net profit   +1%

These transactions would cause four tendencies in foreign exchange markets and money markets:

1. The spot rate of the franc against the dollar will tend to appreciate as investors buy francs against dollars.
2. The forward rate of the franc against the dollar will tend to depreciate as investors sell francs against dollars.
3. The US interest rate will tend to rise as investors borrow dollars.
4. The Swiss interest rate will tend to fall as investors lend francs.

The first two tendencies would increase the original forward discount of 1 percent toward the initial interest differential of 2 percent. The last two tendencies would reduce the initial interest differential of 2 percent toward the original forward discount of 1 percent. These four tendencies would continue until the forward discount for the franc equals the interest rate differential in favor of the franc.

At Point B of Fig. 4.3, the foreign interest rate is 1 percent higher than the domestic interest rate. The cost of forward cover (forward discount) is 2 percent. In this case, the arbitrageur would sell the foreign currency for the domestic currency, invest this domestic currency in home-country securities, and repurchase the foreign currency in the forward market at a discount. She loses 1 percent on this investment in home-country securities, but she earns 2 percent on the repurchase of the foreign currency. Hence, the arbitrageur would make a profit of 1 percent.

Example 4.13

Suppose: (1) the Canadian interest rate = 10 percent; (2) the US interest rate = 9 percent; (3) the spot rate for Canadian dollars = $0.8500; and (4) the 180-day forward rate for Canadian dollars = $0.8415.

The forward discount for the Canadian dollar is obtained by using Eq. (4.4):

$$\text{Forward discount} = \frac{\$0.8415 - \$0.8500}{\$0.8500} \times \frac{360}{180} = -0.02 \quad \text{or} \quad -2\%$$

The interest differential is 1 percent (10 − 9 percent) in favor of the Canadian dollar. The covered-interest arbitrage would work as follows:

1. Borrow Canadian dollars in Canada   −10%
   Buy US dollars with the Canadian dollars
2. Invest the US dollars in US securities   +9%
3. Sell US dollars forward at a premium   +2%
   Net profit   +1%

These transactions would cause four tendencies in foreign exchange and money markets:

1. The spot rate of the Canadian dollar against the US dollar will tend to depreciate as investors sell Canadian dollars against US dollars.
2. The forward rate of the Canadian dollar against the US dollar will tend to appreciate as investors buy Canadian dollars against US dollars.
3. The US interest rate will tend to fall as investors lend US dollars.
4. The Canadian interest rate will tend to rise as investors borrow Canadian dollars.

The first two tendencies would reduce the original forward discount of 2 percent toward the initial interest differential of 1 percent. The last two tendencies would increase the initial interest differential by 1 percent toward the original forward discount of 2 percent. These forces will work until the interest rate differential equals the forward discount.

Any point above the interest parity line, such as Point A, has the following two features: (1) the first step of the arbitrage process is to borrow money in the home country, and (2) funds would move from the home country to the foreign country (arbitrage outflow). Any point below the interest parity line, such as Point B, has the following two features: (1) the first step of the arbitrage process is to borrow money in the foreign country, and (2) funds would move from the foreign country to the home country (arbitrage inflow).

The interest parity line of Fig. 4.3 identifies the equilibrium position for the relationship between interest rate differentials and forward premiums or discounts. Every point on this line represents a situation in which the interest rate differential equals the forward premium or discount. In this case, arbitrageurs would have no incentive to transfer funds from one country to the other. However, at any point off the line, there should be an incentive to move funds from one country to another. Such transfers of funds would cause interest differentials or forward premiums (discounts) to move toward the interest parity line.

The theoretical equilibrium position exists only under a free market system. Because there are a variety of artificial barriers and intervention by government authorities in both foreign exchange and money markets, this equilibrium condition hardly ever exists in practice.

4.6. SUMMARY

Exchange rates represent the prices of one currency in terms of another currency. They are determined by the forces of supply and demand under a free market system. The primary function of the foreign exchange market is to transfer purchasing power denominated in one currency to another, thereby facilitating foreign trade and investment. The foreign exchange market consists of two tiers: the interbank market, in which banks trade with each other, and the retail market, in which banks deal with their non-bank customers.

A major problem of multinational corporations is the fact that cash flows must cross national boundaries. These flows are subject to various constraints imposed by government authorities and exchange-rate fluctuations. Trades in currencies take place in the foreign exchange markets for immediate delivery (spot market) and future delivery (forward market). The foreign exchange market is a worldwide network of telephone and computer communications between banks.

The five major theories of exchange-rate determination are (1) the theory of purchasing power parity, (2) the Fisher Effect, (3) the International Fisher Effect, (4) the interest rate parity theory, and (5) the forward rate as an unbiased predictor of the future spot rate. These five theories illustrate the links that exist among spot rates, interest rates, inflation rates, and forward rates. In efficient exchange markets, spot exchange rates are theoretically determined by the interplay of differential national rates of inflation and interest, and the forward premium or discount.

Essentially, the PPP doctrine and the interest parity theory explain why exchange rates, in the long run, move toward positions of equilibrium in which prices in different countries and their interest rates are the same. This is because arbitrageurs buy currencies in one market and sell them in another market in order to take advantage of price or interest differentials prevailing at differential national markets. Thus, the process of arbitrage works through the foreign exchange market to bring inflation and interest rates in different markets closer together.

4.7. KEY TERMS

cap	collar
credit-default swap	dealer
derivative	floor
forward	future
futures option	hedging
notional value	option
over-the-counter (OTC) market	swap
swaption	underlying
spot rate	direct quote
indirect quote	cross rate
bid price	ask price
bid-ask spread	forward rate
efficient exchange markets	theory of purchasing power parity (PPP)
fisher Effect	international Fisher Effect
arbitrage	two-point arbitrage
three-point arbitrage	

4.8. PROBLEMS

1. If the Swiss franc is selling for $0.5618 and the Japanese yen is selling for $0.0077, what is the cross rate between these two currencies.

2. a. If the spot rate changes from $0.11 per peso to $0.10 per peso over a 1-year period, what is the percentage change in the value of the Mexican peso?

   b. If the spot rate changes from Mex$10.00 per dollar to Mex$9.00, what is the percentage change in the value of the Mexican peso?

3. If a bank's bid price is $1.60 for the British pound and it's ask price is $1.65, what is the bid-ask spread for the pound?

4. Assume: (1) spot rate for Canadian dollars = $0.8089; (2) 180-day forward rate for Canadian dollars = $0.8048; (3) spot rate for Swiss francs = $0.4285; and (4) 180-day forward rate for Swiss francs = $0.4407. Determine the 180-day forward discount or premium on both the Canadian dollar and the Swiss franc.

5. Fill in the following blank spaces:

	British Pounds	Swiss Francs
Direct (Outright)		
Spot	$2.0787	$0.4108
30-day forward		0.4120
90-day forward		0.4144
Points (Spread)		
30-day forward	−13	
90-day forward	−60	
Percentage Discount or Premium a Year		
30-day forward		
90-day forward		

6. Assume that the current exchange rate is $2.00 per pound, the US inflation rate is 10 percent for the coming year, and the British inflation rate is 5 percent over the same period. What is the best estimate of the pound future spot rate 1 year from now?

7. Assume that you can buy a particular basket of goods for $108 in the United States and ¥14,000 in Japan.

   a. What should the ¥/$ exchange rate be according to the absolute purchasing power parity?

   b. If the actual exchange rate were ¥120 per dollar, would the dollar be considered undervalued or overvalued?

8. The following quotations and expectations exist for the Swiss franc:
   Present spot rate $0.5000
   90-day forward rate $0.5200
   Your expectation of the spot rate in 90 days $0.5500

   a. What is the premium or discount on the forward Swiss franc?

   b. If your expectation proves correct, what would be your dollar profit or loss from investing $4,000 in the spot market? How much capital do you need now to carry out this operation? What are the major risks associated with this speculation?

   c. If your expectation proves correct, what would be your dollar profit or loss from investing $4,000 in the forward market? How much capital do you need now to speculate in the forward market? What are the major risks associated with the speculation?

9. An American firm purchases $4,000 worth of perfume (Mex$20,000) from a Mexican firm. The American distributor must make the payment in 90 days in Mexican pesos. The following quotations and expectations exist for the Mexican peso:

Present spot rate	$0.2000
90-day forward rate	$0.2200
Your expectation of the spot rate in 90 days	$0.2500
US interest rate	15%
Mexican interest rate	10%

a. What is the premium or discount on the forward Mexican peso? What is the interest differential between the United States and Mexico? Is there an incentive for covered interest arbitrage?

b. If there is an incentive for covered interest arbitrage, how can an arbitrageur take advantage of the situation? Assume: (1) the arbitrageur is willing to borrow $4,000 or Mex$20,000 and (2) there are no transaction costs.

c. If transaction costs are $100, would an opportunity still exist for covered interest arbitrage?

d. What alternatives are open to the importer if she wants to cover her transaction against the foreign exchange risk?

e. Assume that your expectation proves correct and that the importer decides to cover this transaction. What would be the opportunity cost of each alternative? Which alternative is more attractive and why?

f. Would you advise the American firm to cover its foreign transaction? Why or why not?

10. You must make a $100,000 domestic payment in Los Angeles in 90 days. You have $100,000 now and decide to invest it for 90 days either in the United States or in the United Kingdom. Assume that the following quotations and expectations exist:

Present spot rate per pound	$1.8000
90-day forward rate per pound	$1.7800
US interest rate	8%
UK interest rate	10%

a. Where should you invest your $100,000 to maximize your yield with no risk?

b. Given the US interest rate, the UK interest rate, and the spot rate, what would be an equilibrium forward exchange quotation? This equilibrium situation should provide you with no advantage or disadvantage associated with investing in one country or the other.

c. Given the spot rate, the forward rate, and the US interest rate, what is the equilibrium UK interest rate?

11. Assume that ¥1 = $0.0077 in New York, $1 = Skr2.00 in London, and Skr1 = ¥65 in Tokyo.

   a. If you have 10,000 yen on hand, how could you use a triangle arbitrage to earn a profit?
   b. If you ignore transaction costs, what is the arbitrage profit per yen initially traded?

Closing Case 4: The Big Mac Hamburger Standard

The theory of purchasing power parity (PPP) is one of the oldest theories in international economics. The theory states that, in the long run, the exchange rates between two currencies should move toward the rate that would equalize the prices of an identical basket of goods and services in the two countries. As a theoretical proposition, it serves as a solid foundation for thinking about the conditions under which prices in international markets adjust to attain long-term equilibrium. As a practical matter, however, PPP has been a more puzzling concept.

The Economist, a monthly business publication, has established another, yet somewhat more recent, tradition: the Big Mac PPP. Since 1986, *The Economist* has evaluated prevailing exchange rates on the basis of Big Mac price differentials in various countries around the world. A similar index has also been developed by the Union Bank of Switzerland in its annual comparison of prices and incomes around the globe. These light-hearted studies of international burger prices have predictably stimulated the passion of the popular media and the financial press. The Big Mac index was devised as an enjoyable guide to whether currencies are at their "correct" level. As *The Economist* puts it, "the index is not intended to be a predictor of exchange rates, but a tool to make economic theory more digestible." An identical basket of goods and services in this particular case is a McDonald's Big Mac, which is made to roughly the same recipe in more than 100 countries. The Big Mac PPP is the exchange rate that would make a burger cost the same in America as it does abroad. Comparing Big-Mac PPPs with actual exchange rates is one test of whether a currency is undervalued or overvalued.

The second column of Table 4.3 shows the local-currency prices of a Big Mac: the third converts them into dollar. The fourth column shows Big Mac PPPs. For example, dividing the Swiss price by the American gives a dollar PPP of SFr2.48. The actual rate on February 11, 2003 was SFr 1.37, implying that the Swiss franc is 81 percent overvalued against the dollar. The average American price is $2.54. Argentina is a place for bargain hunters: a Buenos Aries Big Mac costs only $0.80. At the other extreme, the Swiss price of $4.61 is enough to make Big Mac fans choke on their all beef patties. This implies that the Argentinean peso is the most undervalued currency (by 69 percent), and the Swiss franc is the most overvalued (by 81 percent). In general, the dollar is undervalued against the currencies of most big industrial countries, but overvalued against the currencies of developing countries.

Country	In Local Currency	In Dollars	Implied PPP of Dollar	Actual Exchange Rate	Local Currency Under(−)/Over(+) Valuation
USA	2.54	2.54	—	—	—
Switzerland	6.30	4.61	2.48	1.37	+81
Denmark	24.75	3.57	9.74	6.92	+40
Britain	1.99	3.24	1.28	1.63	+27
Sweden	24.0	2.81	9.45	9.45	+11
Euro Area	2.57	2.76	0.99	0.93	+6
South Korea	3,000	2.51	1,181	1196.70	−1
Japan	294	2.42	116	121.30	−4
Taiwan	70.0	2.01	27.6	34.90	−21
Hong Kong	10.2	1.31	4.02	7.80	−48
China	9.9	1.19	3.90	8.29	−53
South Africa	9.70	1.13	3.82	8.57	−55
Russia	35.00	1.10	13.80	31.82	−57
Brazil	3.30	1.00	1.52	3.59	−58
Argentina	2.50	0.80	0.98	3.13	−69

Table 4.3 The Hamburger standard.

Case Questions

1. Name currencies of the 15 countries listed in Table 4.3 and write down their traditional symbols.
2. Calculate the dollar price of a Big Mac (column 3), the implied PPP of the dollar (column 4), and the local currency under(−)/over(+) valuation (column 6) for Denmark and Hong Kong.
3. In 2003, it cost $0.80 to buy a Big Mac in Argentina, $2.54 to buy a Big Mac in the United States, and $4.61 to buy a Big Mac in Switzerland. How do we explain these deviations from PPP?
4. A web page of *The Economist*: https://www.economist.com/big-mac-index provides the Big Mag Index. Use this web page to obtain the latest version of the hamburger standard shown in Table 4.3.

Sources: http://www.oanda.com/products/bigmac/bigmac.shtml as of February 11, 2003; Cumby, R. E., "Forecasting Exchange Rates and Relative Prices with the Hamburger Standard: Is What You Want What You Get With McParity?" Manuscript, Georgetown University, 1995; Pakko, M. R. and P. S. Pollard, "For Here or To Go? Purchasing Power Parity and the Big Mac," *Review*, Federal Reserve Bank of St. Louis, January/February 1996, pp. 3–21; and https://www.economist.com/big-mac-index, accessed September 1, 2022.

Chapter 5

CURRENCY FUTURES AND OPTIONS

Opening Case 5: Derivative Risks

Although derivatives (futures, options, swaps, and others) are legitimate and valuable tools for hedging risks, like all financial instruments they create risks that must be managed. Warren Buffett, one of the world's most wise investors, states that "derivatives are financial weapons of mass destruction, carrying dangers that, while now latent, are potentially lethal."

On one hand derivatives neutralize risks while on the other hand they create risks. In fact, there are certain risks inherent in derivatives. Derivatives can be dangerous if not managed properly. In the 1990s, Procter & Gamble lost $157 million in a currency speculation involving dollars and German Marks, Gibson Greetings lost $20 million and Long-Term Capital Management, a hedge fund, lost $4 billion with currency and interest-rate derivatives.

The source of a lot of the risk associated with derivative contracts arises from the fact that they are leveraged contracts. Derivative products are "leveraged" because only a proportion of their total market exposure needs to be paid to open and maintain a position. Thus, the market exposure with derivative contracts can be several times the cash placed on deposit as margin for the trade or paid in the form of a premium. The following example will support Warren Buffet's assertion that "derivatives are financial weapons of mass destruction."

"Do you know how many days it took for a son to lose $150 million in foreign-exchange trading that it had taken his father decades to accumulate? The answer is just 60 days. The following story illustrates how volatile the currency derivatives market was in the 1990s. "Dad, I lost a lot of money," Zahid Ashraf, a 44-year-old from the United Arab Emirates, confessed to his ailing father, Mohammad. "Maybe no matter," the father said, recalling the conversation in court testimony. Mohammad Ashraf, who had built one of the largest gold and silver trading businesses in the Persian Gulf, then asked, "How much have you lost?" The answer — about $150 million — mattered plenty to the stunned 69-year-old family patriarch.

In 2 months of foreign-currency trading in 1996, Zahid wasted much of a fortune ($250 million) that it had taken his father decades to build. The tight-knit Ashraf family estimates that Chicago-based commodities giant Refco Inc. collected about $11 million in commissions for the trades. So, they sued Refco for $75 million of their losses. The Ashrafs contended that "Refco brokers conspired Zahid Ashraf to execute massive unauthorized speculative trading in currency futures and options" and "to conceal these trades from other family members." However, after a seven-day trial in February 1999, the jury ruled against the Ashrafs, not only rejecting their claim, but also finding that the family's Eastern Trading Co. still owed Refco $14 million to Zahid's uncovered losses. Because it involved a family business whose home turf is far from the world's financial capitals, such as New York or London, the debacle transpired virtually unnoticed. But it serves as yet another reminder of hazards posted by the volatile derivates markets of the 1990s.[1]

This chapter is divided into three closely related sections. The first section discusses currency futures. With a **currency futures contract**, one buys or sells a specific foreign currency for delivery at a designated price in the future. The second section describes currency options. A **currency option** is the right to buy or sell a foreign currency at a specified price by a specified date. The third section examines currency futures options. A **currency futures option** is the right to buy or sell a futures contract of a foreign currency at any time for a specified period.

5.1. THE CURRENCY FUTURES MARKET

The Chicago Mercantile Exchange (CME), known as "The Merc", was founded in 1919 as a nonprofit organization to trade spot and futures commodity contracts. In 1972, the CME introduced futures trading in foreign currencies through the International Monetary Market (IMM) as an alternative to regular forward contracts offered by commercial banks. Today, CME is the largest options and futures contracts open interest (number of contracts outstanding) exchange of any futures exchange in the world. The Merc trades several types of financial instruments: interest rates, equities, currencies, and commodities. Most major exchanges around the world have added currency futures in recent years.

5.1.1. *Futures Market Participants*

Futures contracts are deals made now to take place in the future. In a futures contract, the buyer and the seller agree on:

1. A future delivery date;
2. The price to be paid on that future date;

---

[1] "How Currency Trading Run Amok Crushed a Family," *The Wall Street Journal*, Apr. 8, 1999, pp. C1, C13; and Moffett, M. H., A. I. Stonehill, and D. K. Eiteman, *Fundamentals of Multinational Finance*, Boston, MA: Addison-Wesley, 2003, p. 157; and https://www.mbaknol.com/investment-management/risks-associated-with-derivatives/, March 10, 2023.

3. The quantity of the currency.

The currency futures market was created for those who use foreign exchange in business. Businesses which deal with international transactions routinely buy and sell foreign exchange in the spot market. They enter the futures market only to protect themselves against risks from volatile exchange rates. The currency futures contract is like an insurance policy against changes in exchange rates. In practice, most currency futures contracts are nullified by opposing trades, so futures traders rarely take delivery of a foreign currency; in fact, 95 percent of them are terminated before the delivery.

There are two distinct classes of traders in the currency futures market: hedgers and speculators. **Hedgers** buy and sell currency futures contracts to protect the home currency value of foreign-currency denominated assets and liabilities. They include MNCs, importers, exporters, bankers, and brokers, who require protection against adverse exchange rate movements. They expect their profits to come from managerial skills in conducting their business activities, not from incidental fluctuations in exchange rates. **Speculators**, on the other hand, buy and sell currency futures contracts for profit from exchange rate movements. They trade futures strictly for profit; they can make or lose fortunes. A speculator trades currency futures but never uses the currency.

A hedger may place a contract with another hedger who wishes to cover currency needs in the opposite direction, but the other party to the contract typically is a speculator. Though criticized for greed, speculators play a vital role in futures markets by assuming the risk of the hedger. Their presence not only gives the market liquidity and continuity but also eases entry and exit.

Currency futures trading can take place for hedging or speculation, as well as for arbitrage. In particular, some traders quickly take advantage of any profitable differential, for the same currency, between rates quoted in different markets, such as the spot market, the futures market, and the forward market.

5.1.2. *The Futures Market and the Forward Market*

Futures contracts are normally available in a predetermined amount and for one of several specified maturity dates. CME offers a fully global product suite of many futures and options contracts in a number of currencies. These products are available for trading electronically virtually around-the-clock on the CME Globex platform and on its trading floor. The CME also lists a number of cross-rate foreign exchange products that are non-US dollar pairs you need. Table 5.1 shows futures contracts currently available for seven currencies and three cross rates along with contract sizes specified by the CME. Futures contracts mature on only four days of the year; the maturity dates occur on the third Wednesday of March, June, September, and December.

While the principle of protection against currency price fluctuations is the same in the futures and forward markets, there are two major differences. First, the forward market offers contracts for specific amounts of currencies tailored to particular needs, while the futures market offers only standardized contracts in predetermined amounts. Take, for example, an importer who wishes to cover accounts payable of $A140,000. He could cover only a portion of the risk in the futures market but could arrange for full coverage with a single contract in the forward market. Second, a forward contract can cover the exact date the foreign currency is needed, but the futures contract has a standardized delivery date. Suppose an MNC wishes

Table 5.1   Currencies traded on the CME.

Currency	Contract Size
Australian dollar	$A100,000
British pound	£62,500
Canadian dollar	Can$100,000
Euro	€125,000
Japanese yen	¥12,500,000
Mexican peso	MX$500,000
New Zealand dollar	$NZ100,000
Cross-Rate Futures	
(Underlying Currency/Price Currency)	
Euro/British pound	€125,000
Euro/Japanese yen	€125,000
Euro/Swiss franc	€125,000

to lift its hedge before the expiration date of the futures contract. It must assume some risk of a currency price fluctuation between the settlement date of the transaction and the delivery date of the contract.

Because MNCs have specialized needs, they normally prefer the forward contract. Consider IBM, which on April 20 realizes it will need $A240,000 on May 20 (30 days later). If IBM tries to lock in the future purchase price of Canadian dollars with a futures contract, the closest contract settlement date is the third Wednesday of June. Also, the amount of Australian dollars needed ($A240,000) is more than the standardized amount ($A100,000) specified in the contract. The best IBM can do is to buy two futures contracts ($A200,000), but the forward market can be tailored to meet the individual needs of MNCs. IBM can buy a forward contract of $A240,000 with a maturity date of 30 days from Bank of America.

Currency futures contracts and forward contracts are acquired for hedging, speculation, or arbitrage. Yet, the futures market is more centralized, standardized, and less customer-oriented than the forward market. The futures market and the forward market differ in notable ways:

1. **Price Range:** Because the CME specifies a maximum daily price range for each day, a futures market participant is not exposed to more than a limited amount of daily price change. But forward contracts have no daily limits on price fluctuations.
2. **Maturity:** CME futures contracts are available for delivery on one of only four maturity dates per year, but banks offer forward contracts for delivery on any date.
3. **Size of Contract:** The futures market offers only standardized contracts in predetermined amounts, but the forward market offers contracts for specific amounts of currencies tailored to specific needs.
4. **Regulation:** The futures market is regulated by the Commodity Futures Commission, but the forward market is self-regulating.
5. **Settlement:** Less than 5 percent of the CME futures contracts are settled by actual delivery, but more than 90 percent of forward contracts are settled by delivery.
6. **Location:** Futures trading takes place on organized exchanges, but forward trading is negotiated directly between banks and their clients.

7. **Credit Risk:** The CME guarantees to deliver the currency on schedule if the seller defaults or to acquire it if the buyer defaults. On the other hand, a bank dealing in the forward market must satisfy itself that the party with whom it has a contract is creditworthy.

8. **Speculation:** CME brokers accommodate speculative transactions, whereas banks generally discourage speculation by individuals.

9. **Collateral:** A security deposit (margin) must back every futures contract, but forward contracts do not require any margin payment. Compensating balances are required in most forward contracts.

10. **Commission:** In the futures market, commissions of intermediaries depend on published brokerage fees and negotiated rates on block trades. In the forward market, a "spread" between the bank's buy and sell prices sets the commissions of intermediaries.

11. **Trading:** Futures contracts are traded in a competitive arena, but forward contracts are traded by telephone or telex.

5.1.3. *How to Read Currency Futures Quotes*

Bloomberg and other websites show currency future quotations, though they do not list the newest or least active contracts. To explain how to read currency futures quotes, we will focus on the Australian dollar futures traded on the CME. Table 5.2 presents the Australian dollar futures prices reported in the *Wall Street Journal* on one recent day.

The top, bold-faced line for each currency gives the name of the currency, such as Australian dollar (AUD); the exchange on which it is traded according to a key in the table, such as the CME; the size of a single contract, such as AUD100,000 per contract; and the way in which prices are quoted, such as dollars ($) per AUD. The first column gives the months for which delivery of the currency may be obtained. Currency delivery takes place in March, June, September, and December. The second column gives the opening price of the day. The next three columns tell us the contract's highest, lowest, and closing (settlement) prices for the day. These figures, viewed together, show how volatile the market was during the trading day. A broker uses settlement prices to evaluate portfolios or for deciding whether to call for more margin. Currency futures losses must be settled every day, and profits are credited daily to customer accounts.

The sixth column from the left of the quotation, labeled "change", shows the difference between the latest settlement price and the one for the previous day. A plus (+) sign indicates prices ended higher; a minus (−) sign indicates prices ended lower. The right-hand column, labeled "open interest", refers to the total number of outstanding contracts; that is, those that have not been canceled by offsetting trades. This column allows us to see how much interest there is in trading a particular contract. The closest months usually attract the most activity, as we can see from the difference between the June contracts and the September contracts.

Table 5.2 Currency futures quotations in the CME: Australian dollar.

	Open	High	Low	Settle	Change	Open Interest
Australian Dollar (CME) — AUD 100,000; $ per AUD						
Sept	0.8604	0.8768	0.8598	0.8725	0.0090	93,262
Dec	0.8575	0.8682	0.8518	0.8641	0.0088	5,187

5.1.4. *Market Operations*

An agreement to buy a futures contract is a **long position** and an agreement to sell a futures contract is a **short position**. To trade futures, people give their broker an order to enter them into a contract as either a buyer (the long position) or as a seller (the short position), depending on which way they think the market is heading. In other words, those investors with a long position assume that actual exchange rates or stock prices will go up in the future. On the other hand, those investors with a short position assume that actual exchange rates or stock prices will go down.

Global Finance in Practice 5: Short Sellers Feel the Pain

The market's comeback in 2023 has been very bad news for one group: short sellers. Short seller's profit from stock declines by borrowing shares of companies that they believe are overvalued, selling them, and then buying them back at a lower price later. They made huge gains in 2022, when markets around the world tumbled.

But their fortunes have reversed in January 2023 as the stock market has clawed back some of its losses. A Goldman Sachs index tracking the 50 most shorted stocks in the Russell 3000 has returned 15 percent so far this year through Thursday, January 26 substantially outperforming the S&P 500, which is up 6 percent. Other stocks that got crushed in 2022 have also raced higher. Tesla Inc., TSLA –4.59 percent decrease; red down pointing triangle coming off its worst year on record, has staged a 44 percent January rally. Meanwhile, money-losing cryptocurrency exchange Coinbase Global Inc. COIN –5.61 percent decrease; red down pointing triangle is up 73 percent. Short sellers who have incurred hefty losses are actively trimming their positions, said Ihor Danowski, managing director of predictive analytics at S3 Partners. Investors betting against stocks have racked up $81 billion of mark-to-market losses on short positions this month (January) through Thursday, January 26 after accumulating $300 billion in gains in 2022, Mr. Danowski said.

Investors and analysts say the rally appears to be driven by a few things. Signs that inflation is cooling have stoked bets among investors that the Federal Reserve will pivot from raising interest rates to cutting them as soon as the second half of the year. That has helped risky assets across the board rise. Especially risky corners of the market, such as stocks with high short interest, have rallied even more. Analysts say that has likely forced short sellers to close out bearish positions to cut their losses — resulting in what is known on Wall Street as a short squeeze.[2]

5.1.4.1. *Margin requirements*

Some form of deposit ensures that each party fulfills its commitment; this type of deposit is called the margin. The exchanges set a minimum margin for each contract, but brokers often require larger margins from clients. The amount of a futures margin depends on the volatility of the contract value and hence on the risk. Margin levels also vary for hedging and

---

[2]Pitcher, J. and A. Otani, "Short Sellers Feel the Pain," The *Wall Street Journal*, January 30, 2023, p. A1.

speculating accounts. For example, exchanges and brokerage firms normally require lower margins for hedging accounts because they carry less risk than speculating accounts.

The two basic types of margins are required: the initial margin and the maintenance margin. The **initial margin** is the amount market participants must deposit into their margin account at the time they enter into a futures contract. Then, on a daily basis, the margin account is debited or credited to protect buyers and sellers against the possibility of contract default. Initial margins for futures contracts typically range between 1 and 4 percent of a contract's face value and are set by the exchanges where the contracts are traded.

The **maintenance margin** is a set minimum margin customers must always maintain in their account. On any day that market losses reduce funds in the account below the maintenance margin, the broker calls on his customer for an additional deposit to restore the account to the initial margin level. Requests for additional money are known as **margin calls**. The maintenance margin is usually 75 percent of the initial margin.

In addition to these two basic types of margins, market participants are required to post performance bond margins. **Performance bond margins** are financial guarantees imposed on both buyers and sellers to ensure that they fulfill the obligation of the futures contract. In other words, they are required to make or take delivery of the futures contract unless their position is offset before the expiration of the contract. The purpose of a performance bond margin is to provide integrity.

Example 5.1

Lisa George buys Australian-dollar futures contracts to cover possible exchange losses on her import orders denominated in Australian dollars. She has to put up an initial margin of $3,000. The maintenance margin imposed by the exchange is 75 percent of the initial margin, or $2,250. When would she get a margin call from her broker?

If the spot rate for Australian dollars declines, the value of Ms. George's position declines. As long as the decline is less than $750, Lisa George does not need to put up any additional margin. Yet, if the cumulative decline in value comes to $751, her margin account would stand at $2,249. She would get a margin call from her brokerage firm and must restore the account to the initial level of $3,000. Otherwise, the exchange will sell out her position and return any remaining balance in her account.

5.1.4.2. *Speculation in the futures market*

Speculation offers potentially large profits or losses due to the highly leveraged nature of futures trading. Because margin requirements average less than 4 percent of the contract's full value, it is possible to control large amounts of currencies with little capital. Speculators deliberately expose themselves to exchange risk by engaging in futures contracts in order to make profits from exchange rate movements.

Example 5.2

Kenneth Lee, a speculator, enters into a futures contract for March delivery of 125,000 Swiss francs on February 1. The futures exchange rate of the Swiss franc for March delivery (March 15) is $0.5939 per franc. The margin requirement is 2 percent. His expectation of the spot rate for francs on March 15 is $0.6117. If his expectation proves correct, what would be his rate of return on investment?

Because the margin requirement is 2 percent, Mr. Lee may control this delivery of SFr125,000 for $1,484.75 (SFr125,000 × $0.5939 × 0.02). He could buy SFr125,000 futures for $74,237.50 at the futures quotation of $0.5939, receive them on March 15, and then sell them at the spot rate of $0.6117 for a gross of $76,462.50. Profit would be $2,225. So, he would earn a net profit of $2,225, or 150 percent on the original investment of $1,484.75. Here, the exchange rate would rise by only 3 percent [(0.6117 − 0.5939)/0.5939], but the rate of return on investment is 150 percent. Yet, the same leverage could lead to equally substantial losses. If the spot rate declines by 3 percent during this period, Mr. Lee would lose about 150 percent of his investment.

5.1.4.3. *Hedging in the futures market*

A single forward contract can arrange for the precise amount and maturity that the bank's customer desires. A single futures contract is available only in a predetermined amount for one of the four maturity dates each year. These two features of the futures market may force MNCs to assume some risks of coverage and of currency fluctuation because they usually need a specified amount of a currency on a specified date. Still, these risks can be minimized in a properly structured hedge. Prices in the spot and futures markets move in the same direction by similar amounts due to arbitrage transactions between these two markets.

Example 5.3

On February 1, an American firm imports 5,000 Swiss watches at a cost of 250,000 francs with payment and delivery due on March 1. The Swiss firm, being a tough negotiator, has demanded that the payment be made in Swiss francs upon the delivery of the watches. The exchange rates are $0.6667 per franc in the spot market and $0.6655 per franc in the futures market for delivery on March 15.

Given the costs of marketing the watches, the importer decides that the futures exchange rate is low enough for the company to purchase them and make a profit on the transaction. However, the importer must pay for the watches on March 1, though the expiration date of the futures contract is March 15. The importer can hedge most of its exposure by buying March Swiss franc contracts on February 1 with the intention of lifting the hedge on March 1. Because franc contracts are available from the CME in units of 125,000, the importer would purchase two March contracts, as given in Table 5.3.

The importer could trade out of the contracts by selling them before receiving a delivery notice on March 15. The only risk that the company still faces comes from the difference in

Table 5.3   Buying two franc futures contracts on February 1.

	Spot Market	Futures Market for March 15 Delivery
Exchange rate	$0.6667/SFr	$0.6655/SFr
Cost of SFr250,000	$166,675	$166,375
Action taken	None	Buy two March 15 contracts

the value of the contract on March 1 and its value on March 15. Assume that by March 1 the following two things would happen: (1) the spot rate appreciates to $0.7658 and (2) the futures rate rises to $0.7650. The importer could close out the franc futures contracts by selling them on March 1, as shown in Table 5.4.

On March 1, the importer purchases 250,000 francs in the spot market for $191,450 and settles its import bill. But this $191,450 is higher ($24,775) than its original value on February 1 ($166,675); in other words, the exchange loss from the spot transaction is $24,775. The futures contract the company sold on March 1 ($191,250) is higher ($24,875) than the $166,375 the company anticipated in the futures contract it purchased on February 1; in other words, the exchange gain from the futures transaction is $24,875. The $24,875 gain from the futures transaction exceeds the $24,775 loss from the spot transaction. The risk that the importer assumed on February 1 by purchasing two contracts whose maturity did not coincide with the March 1 usage date of the currency resulted in a windfall exchange gain of $100 ($24,875 – $24,775). This $100 gain arose from the difference between the spot rate and the futures rate prevailing on the day the contracts were liquidated. This difference is the "basis."

The basis, unlike the spot rate itself, is relatively stable and narrows toward zero as the contract moves toward maturity. For example, the basis on February 1 was $0.0012 per franc ($0.6667 – $0.6655), while by March 1 it had shrunk to $0.0008 ($0.7658 – $0.7650). The degree of uncertainty about the futures price diminishes further as the contract approaches its March 15 expiration date. On March 15, the futures rate, in effect, becomes the spot rate.

In Example 5.3, the difference of $0.0004/SFr on the basis between February 1 and March 1 accounted for the windfall exchange gain of $100. This gain might easily have been an exchange loss of a similar amount if the exchange rate of the Swiss franc had depreciated during the same period. The important point is that the importer was protected from any major loss regardless of exchange rate movements. For example, if the importer had not purchased the futures contract and bought 250,000 francs in the spot market on March 1, the watches would have cost an additional $24,775.

Frequent futures traders may try to coordinate trading between two different markets or two different currencies through a strategy called spread trading. **Spread trading** means buying one contract and simultaneously selling another contract. They will always make money on one contract and lose money on the other contract. Thus, they may make or lose more money on one contract than they lose or make on the other, but they are protected from major loss regardless of exchange rate movements.

Table 5.4 Reversing the earlier futures contracts on March 1.

	Spot Market	Futures Market for March 15 Delivery
Exchange rate	$0.7658/SFr	$0.7650/SFr
Cost of SF250,000	$191,450	$191,250
Action taken	Buy SF250,000	Sell two March 15 contracts

5.2. THE CURRENCY OPTIONS MARKET

Founded in 1790, the Philadelphia Stock Exchange, the oldest securities market in the United States, started currency options trading in 1983; since then, the Chicago Mercantile Exchange and the Chicago Board Options Exchange added currency options trading. Currency options are now traded on exchanges throughout the world, including those in the United States, London, Amsterdam, Hong Kong, Singapore, Sydney, Vancouver, and Montreal. However, the volume of over-the-counter (OTC) currency options trading is much larger than that of organized-exchange options trading.

Currency options are currently available in six currencies at the Philadelphia Exchange: Australian dollar, British pound, Canadian dollar, European euro, Japanese yen, and Swiss franc. Table 5.5 shows the three-letter currency codes, trading symbols, and contract sizes for the first six currencies. In addition, a significant number of currency options are traded outside the organized exchanges. Many banks and other financial institutions have just begun to offer currency options that have exercise prices and exercise dates to meet the specific needs of their corporate clients.

Currency code, usually known as ISO 4217, is the international standard describing three-letter codes to define the names of currencies established by the International Organization for Standardization (ISO). The ISO 4217 code list is the established norm in banking and business all over the world for defining different currencies, and in many countries the codes for the more common currencies are so well known publicly, that exchange rates published in newspapers or posted in banks use only these to define the different currencies, instead of translated currency names or ambiguous currency symbols. ISO 4217 codes are used on airline tickets and international train tickets to remove any ambiguity about the price. A **ticker (trading) symbol** is a three-letter abbreviation used to uniquely identify a publicly traded currency on a particular stock market.

5.2.1. *Basic Terms*

Currency options give the holder the right to buy or sell a foreign currency at a set price on or before a specified date. There are two types of options: calls and puts. A **currency call option** gives the buyer the right, but not the obligation, to buy a particular foreign currency at a specified price anytime during the life of the option. A **currency put option** gives the buyer the right, but not the obligation, to sell a particular foreign currency at a specified price anytime during the life of the option. The grantor of an option (otherwise

Table 5.5 Currency options contract size traded on the Philadelphia exchange.

Currency	Currency	Ticker	Contract Size
Australian dollar	AUD	XDA	A$50,000
British pound	GBP	XDB	£31,250
Canadian dollar	CAD	XDC	Can$50.000
European euro	EUR	XDE	€62,500
Japanese yen	JPY	XDN	¥6,250,000
Swiss franc	CHF	XDS	SFr62,500

known as the writer) must deliver the currency if a holder calls, or he must buy it if it is put to him by a put holder. For this obligation, the writer receives a fee or premium.

The holder of a call option will benefit if the underlying currency's price rises, while the holder of a put option will benefit if it falls. If the currency's price does not change much during the life of the option, the holder of the option loses his entire investment. For this reason, options are risky, but there is a potential for large profits in options. To buy a foreign currency outright on the spot market, an investor must pay the entire purchase price of the currency, but the price of an option is a small fraction of the price of the underlying currency.

The **strike price** or the exercise price is the price at which the buyer of an option has the right to buy or sell an underlying currency. Option buyers can decide whether or not to go through with the deal any time up until the expiration date. Options pay no interest and become worthless at expiration unless the price of the underlying currency changes. Only certain expiration dates are available; the exchange, which lists the option, chooses these expiration dates.

Options differ from all other types of financial instruments in the patterns of profit-loss they produce. The beauty of options is that the holder of an option has the possibility of unlimited profit, but his maximum loss would be limited to the amount of premium paid. The holder has the choice of exercising the option or allowing it to expire unused. The holder will exercise the option only when it becomes profitable. On the downside, the holder can let the option expire and walk away with a loss no more than the premium paid for it. On the other hand, the possibility of unlimited profit or loss exists in the spot market, the forward market, and the futures market. The profit structures for long and short positions in both the forward market and the futures market exactly mirror each other. In other words, the long or short position on an underlying currency produces a one-to-one gain or loss depending on where the spot rate ends up relative to the contracted futures rate. The buyer of a futures contract earns one dollar for every dollar the seller of the futures contract loses, and vice versa.

5.2.2. *How to Read Currency Option Quotes*

To explain how to read currency option quotes, we will focus on the Swiss franc option traded on the Philadelphia Stock Exchange. Table 5.6 reflects typical quotes in Bloomberg and other websites for options on the Swiss franc. Although the table does not show them, there are two sets of figures for each of most currencies. One set consists of quotes for European-style options and another set of quotes for American-style options. A European-style option can be exercised only at the time of expiration. An American-style option can be exercised at any time between the date the option is written and its maturity date. Because American-style options are more flexible than European-style options, American-style options are typically more valuable than European-style options for a given strike price, exchange rate volatility, and period to maturity. There are also a number of cross-rate options contracts available for several sets of two currencies, such as Euro-Japanese yen.

The first column shows the spot rate of the underlying currency. In Table 5.6, "Option & Underlying" means that 58.51 cents or $0.5851 was the spot dollar price of one Swiss franc at the close of trading on the preceding day. The second column shows various strike prices,

Table 5.6 Swiss franc option quotations traded on Philadelphia exchange.

Option & Underlying	Strike Price	Calls — Last			Puts — Last		
		Aug	Sep	Dec	Aug	Sep	Dec
58.51	56.5	—	—	—	0.00	0.03	1.16
58.51	58	0.71	1.05	1.28	0.27	0.81	1.18
58.51	59.5	0.15	0.40	—	2.32	—	—

Table 5.7 Option: In the money, out of the money, or at the money?

	Call Option	Put Option
In-the-money	Spot > Strike	Spot < Strike
At-the-money	Spot = Strike	Spot = Strike
Out-of-the money	Spot < Strike	Spot > Strike

prices of the underlying currency at which options confer the right to buy or sell. There are several different strike prices listed for the Swiss franc, which means that there were several options available for the Swiss franc.

Then follow two groups of three figures. The first group gives the closing prices or premiums for call options at a given strike price valid until each maturity date (Aug, Sep, and Dec). The second group gives the closing prices or premiums for put options at a given strike price valid until each maturity date (Aug, Sep, and Dec). Options mature on the Saturday before the third Wednesday of the expiration month.

Generally, prices are highest for call options whose strike price is below the spot rate and for put options whose strike price is above the spot rate. The volume of options trading is frequently large relative to trading in the underlying currency. This reflects trading by professionals who make their money on numerous but short-term transactions and by holders of foreign exchange who hedge large blocks with options. Such hedging provides price protection similar to that offered by currency futures.

5.2.3. *Currency Option Premiums*

An option that would be profitable to exercise at the current spot rate is said to be **in the money**. An option that would not be profitable to exercise at the current spot rate is said to be **out of the money**. When the strike price of any call or put option equals the current spot rate, the option is said to be "**at-the-money**." Table 5.7 should help you determine whether any call option or put option is in the money, out of the money, or at the money.

A **currency option premium** is the price of either a call or a put that the option buyer must pay the option seller (option writer). This premium depends on market conditions, such as supply, demand, and other economic variables. Regardless of how much the market swings, the most an option buyer can lose is the option premium. He deposits the premium with his broker, and the money goes to the option seller. Option buyers are not required to maintain margin (deposit) accounts because of this limited and known risk.

Option sellers, on the other hand, face risks similar to participants in the spot or futures markets. For example, because the seller of a call option is assigned a short position, the risk is the same as for someone who initially bought a foreign currency. The option seller posts margin to demonstrate her ability to meet any potential contractual obligations.

Even though the marketplace is the ultimate determinant of an option premium, there are some basic guidelines traders use to calculate option premiums. In general, an option premium is the sum of intrinsic value and time value (sometimes referred to as speculative value):

$$\text{Total Value (Premium)} = \text{Intrinsic Value} + \text{Time Value} \qquad (5.1)$$

However, it is important to note that both intrinsic value and time value are influenced by volatility of the difference between a strike price and the price of the underlying currency.

5.2.3.1. *Intrinsic value*

Intrinsic value is the difference between the current exchange rate of the underlying currency and the strike price of a currency option. In other words, intrinsic value equals the immediate exercise value of the option, but it cannot be lower than zero because investors can let their option expire unexercised in case of a possible loss. As a result, any option with an intrinsic value is said to be "in-the-money." As an example, consider a put option with a strike price of $1.70 per pound and a current spot rate of $1.50 per pound. The intrinsic value of this put is $0.20 ($1.70 – $1.50) in the money because the immediate exercise of the put would give a $0.20 cash inflow.

5.2.3.2. *Time value*

The second major component of an option premium is time value. **Time value** is the amount of money that options buyers are willing to pay for an option in the anticipation that over time a change in the underlying spot rate will cause the option to increase in value. In general, the longer the length of time before the settlement date, the higher the option premium. This is because the right to buy or sell something is more valuable to a market participant if you have 4 months to decide what to do with the option rather than just 1 month. For example, an expiration date in June has four additional months beyond February for the spot rate to change above or below the strike price. As the option approaches its maturity, the time value declines to zero.

5.2.3.3. *Value of exchange-rate volatility*

Volatility of the underlying spot rate is one of the most important factors which influences the value of the option premium. Volatility measures the fluctuation in price over a given period of time. The greater the variability of the currency, the higher the probability that the spot rate will be below or above the strike price. Thus, more volatile currencies tend to have higher option premiums.

5.2.3.4. *Summary*

Typically, options have positive values even if they are out-of-the money (i.e., zero intrinsic value). Investors will usually pay something today for out-of-the-money options on the chance of profit before maturity. They are also likely to pay some additional premium today for in-the-money options on the chance of an increase in intrinsic value before maturity. Thus, the price of an option is always somewhat greater than its intrinsic value.

5.2.4. *Currency Call Options*

A currency call option is a contract that gives the buyer the right to buy a foreign currency at a specified price during the prescribed period. People buy currency call options because they anticipate that the spot rate of the underlying currency will appreciate. Currency option trading can take place for hedging or speculation.

5.2.4.1. *Hedging in the call options market*

MNCs with open positions in foreign currencies can utilize currency call options. Suppose that an American firm orders industrial equipment from a German company, and its payment is to be made in euros upon delivery. A euro call option locks in the rate at which the US company can purchase euros for dollars. Such an exchange between these two currencies at the specified strike price can take place before the settlement date. Thus, the call option specifies the maximum price, which the US company must pay to obtain euros. If the spot rate falls below the strike price by the delivery date, the American firm can buy euros at the prevailing spot rate to pay for its equipment and can simply let its call option expire.

Example 5.4

Let's see how call options may be used to cover possible exchange losses on import orders denominated in foreign currencies. Assume that on February 1 an American firm has purchased a mainframe computer from a Swiss firm for 625,000 francs; its payment must be made in Swiss francs on June 1. Let us further assume that the premium for a franc call option with a strike price of $0.5000 and a June expiration date is 0.03 cents per franc. Because there are 62,500 units per franc option, the US firm will need 10 call options to buy 625,000 francs. The spot rate for francs is $0.4900; the US company's bank believes that the spot rate by June 1 will rise to $0.6000.

There are two alternatives available to the US company: do not hedge, or hedge in the options market. If the US company does not want to cover its open position, it would wait for 4 months, buy francs at the prevailing exchange rate in the spot market, and use these francs to pay for its imports. If the bank's forecast is accurate, the US company would spend $375,000 to purchase 625,000 francs at the spot rate of $0.6000.

The price of 10-franc call options is $187.50 (0.03 cents × 10 options 62,500 units per contract). If the US company decides to hedge its position in the options market, on June 1 it would exercise its right to buy 625,000 francs for $312,500 ($0.500 × 625,000 francs). Consequently, the US firm would spend a total of $312,687.50 ($187.50 + $312,500) to purchase 625,000 francs. By doing so, the American firm would avoid the risk of a $62,312.50 loss ($375,000 – $312,687.50). Still, if the future spot rate for francs remains below the strike price of $0.5000, the US company can let its options expire and buy Swiss francs at the prevailing spot rate when it must pay for its imports. Here the US firm would lose its option premium of $187.50.

5.2.4.2. *Speculating in the call options market*

Individuals may speculate about currency call options based on their expectations of exchange rate fluctuations for a particular currency. The purpose of speculation in the call options market is to make a profit from exchange-rate movements by deliberately taking an uncovered position. If a speculator expects that the future spot rate of a currency will increase, he makes the following transactions: The speculator will (1) buy call options of the currency; (2) wait for a few months until the spot rate of the currency appreciates high enough; (3) exercise his option by buying the currency at the strike price; and (4) then sell the currency at the prevailing spot rate. When a speculator buys and then exercises a call option, his profit (loss) is determined as follows:

$$\text{Profit (Loss)} = \text{Spot Rate} - (\text{Strike Price} + \text{Premium}) \qquad (5.2)$$

Example 5.5

Suppose that the call premium per British pound on February 1 is 1.10 cents, the expiration date is June, and the strike price is $1.60. Richard Smith anticipates that the spot rate of the pound will increase to $1.70 by May 1. If Mr. Smith's expectation proves correct, what would be his dollar profit from speculating one pound call option (31,250 units per contract) in the call options market?

Richard Smith could make a profit of $2,781.25 by making the following trades:

1. Buy call options on February 1   −$0.0110 per pound
2. Exercise the option on May 1   −$1.6000 per pound
3. Sell the pound on May 1   +$1.7000 per pound
4. Net profit as of May 1   +$0.0890 per pound
5. Net profit per contract: £31,250 × $0.0890 = $2,781.25

Richard's profit of $0.0890 per pound can also be obtained by Eq. (5.2):

$$\text{Profit} = \$1.700 - (\$1.6000 + \$0.0110) = \$0.0890$$

Richard Smith does not need to exercise his call options in order to make a profit. Currency call option premiums rise and fall as exchange rates of their underlying currency rise and fall. If call options become profitable, their premiums will rise. They can be sold on an exchange just like any foreign currency itself. So, a call-option holder such as Mr. Smith can save the expense and bother of taking possession of the currency and selling it.

5.2.4.3. *Graphic analysis of a call-option price*

Figure 5.1 shows the typical relationship between the market value of a call option and its intrinsic value. Up to the point where the strike price equals the spot rate, time value increases as the spot rate increases, but the market value exceeds the intrinsic value for all spot rates. Call options have positive values even if they are out of the money because they have time value. It is also important to note that the intrinsic value of a call option becomes zero whenever the strike price exceeds the spot rate. In other words, the intrinsic value is zero until the spot rate reaches the strike price, then rises linearly (one cent for one-cent increase in the spot rate).

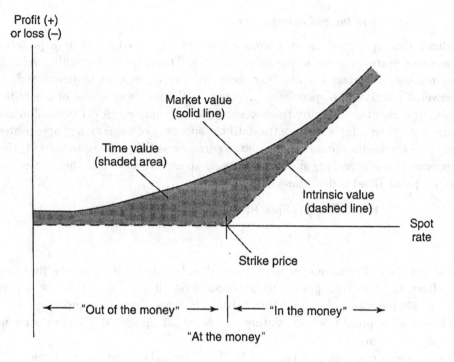

Fig. 5.1 The market value of a call option.

5.2.5. *Currency Put Options*

A currency put option is simply a contract that gives the holder the right to sell a foreign currency at a specified price during a prescribed period. People buy currency put options because they anticipate that the spot rate of the underlying currency will depreciate.

MNCs with open positions in foreign currencies can employ currency put options to cover such positions. Consider an American company, which has sold an airplane to a Japanese firm and has agreed to receive its payment in Japanese yen. The exporter may be concerned about the possibility that the yen will depreciate by the time it is scheduled to receive its payment from the importer. To protect itself against such a yen depreciation, the exporter could buy yen put options, which would enable it to sell yen at the specified strike price. In fact, the exporter would lock in the minimum exchange rate at which it could sell Japanese yen in exchange for US dollars over a specified period of time. On the other hand, if the yen appreciates over this time period, the exporter could let the put options expire and sell the yen at the prevailing spot rate.

Individuals may speculate with currency put options based on their expectations of exchange rate fluctuations for a particular currency. For example, if speculators believe that the Swiss franc will depreciate in the future, they can buy franc put options, which will entitle them to sell francs at the specified strike price. If the franc's spot rate depreciates as expected, they can buy francs at the spot rate and exercise their put options by selling these francs at the strike price. If a speculator buys and then exercises a put option, his profit (loss) is determined as follows:

$$\text{Profit (Loss)} = \text{Strike Price} - (\text{Spot Rate} + \text{Premium}) \qquad (5.3)$$

For example, the profit for the holder of a put option with a strike price of $0.585/SFr, a premium of $0.005/SFr, and a spot rate of $0.575/SFr is:

$$\text{Profit} = \$0.585 - (\$0.575 + \$0.005) = \$0.005/\text{SFr}$$

Speculators do not need to exercise their put options in order to make a profit. They could also make a profit from selling put options because put option premiums fall and rise as exchange rates of the underlying currency rise and fall. The seller of put options has the obligation to purchase the specified currency at the strike price from the owner who exercises the put option. If speculators anticipate that the currency will appreciate, they might sell their put options. But if the currency indeed appreciates over the entire period, the put options will not be exercised. On the other hand, if speculators expect that the currency will depreciate, they will keep their put options. Then they will sell their put options when the put option premiums go up.

5.2.5.1. *Graphic analysis of a put-option price*

Figure 5.2 shows the typical relationship between the market value of a put option and its intrinsic value. Up to the point where the strike price equals the spot rate, time value declines as the spot rate increases, but the market value exceeds the intrinsic value for all spot rates. Put options have positive values even if they are out of the money because they

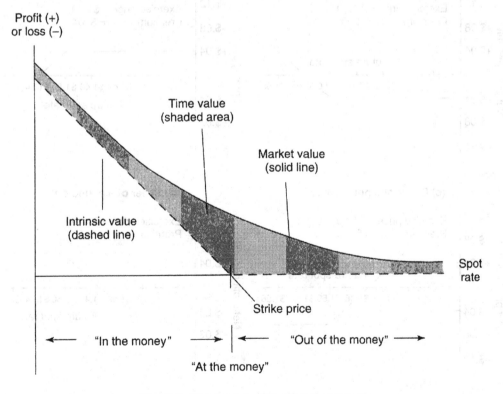

Fig. 5.2 The market value of a put option.

have time value. It is also important to note that the intrinsic value of a put option becomes zero whenever the spot rate exceeds the strike price.

5.2.6. *Profit–Loss Profiles of Options*

Figure 5.3 presents "profit–loss profiles" which trace the relationship between the exchange rate at expiration of the contract and the net gain (loss) to the trader.

Assume that the call premium per British pound is $0.04, the strike price is $1.50, and the contract matures in 2 months. The vertical axes of Figs. 5.3(a) and 5.3(b) measure profit or loss for the call-option trader at different spot rates (horizontal axes) for the pound at the time of maturity. For the buyer of a call option on the pound, the loss is limited to the price originally paid for the option. The entire price ($0.04) would be lost if the spot rate is $1.50 or less. The call-option holder would earn $0.04 at $1.54, but this gain is offset by the $0.04 premium. Thus, this point ($1.54) is called the break-even point. The call-option holder would realize a one-to-one gain (unlimited profit) at any spot rate above $1.54.

For the seller of a call option, the gain is limited to the premium originally charged for the option. The entire premium ($0.04) would be earned if the spot rate is $1.50 or less. The call-option seller would suffer a one-to-one loss at any spot rate above $1.54.

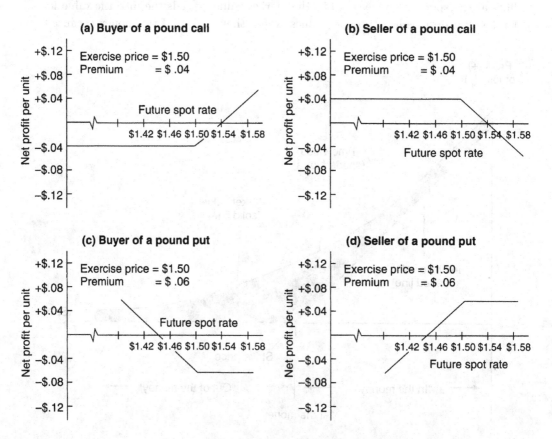

Fig. 5.3   Profit-loss profiles for an option holder.

Assume that the put premium per British pound is $0.06, the strike price is $1.50, and the contract matures in 2 months. Figures 5.3(c) and 5.3(d) show profit–loss profiles of a put-option trader. The buyer of a put option would obtain a one-to-one gain at any rate below $1.44 but only up to the point where the profit–loss profile of the put-option holder intercepts the vertical axis. The break-even spot rate of $1.44 is the price at which the holder neither gains nor loses on exercise of the option: this is the point where the gain of $0.06 is offset by the premium of $0.06. The holder would lose money at spot rates above $1.44, but the loss is limited to the premium originally paid for the option.

The seller of a put option would suffer a one-to-one loss at any spot rate below $1.44 but only up to the point where the profit-loss intercepts the vertical axis. For the seller of a put option, the gain is limited to the premium originally charged for the option. The entire premium ($0.06) would be earned if the spot rate is $1.50 or higher.

5.3. FUTURES OPTIONS

The Chicago Mercantile Exchange introduced currency futures options, or currency options on futures, in January 1984. Currency futures options do not reflect the options on the underlying currency itself, but they reflect the options on futures contracts of that currency. They were originally established for the German mark, but they are now available for the British pound, Canadian dollar, Japanese yen, Mexican peso, and Swiss franc. Futures options trade in an expiration cycle of March, June, September, and December, just like their underlying futures contracts.

Currency futures options give the holder the right to buy or sell a foreign currency at a designated price in the future. There are two types of currency futures options: currency-futures calls and currency-futures puts. A currency-futures call option gives the buyer the right, but not the obligation, to buy a particular currency-futures contract at a specified price anytime during the life of the option. A currency-futures put option gives the buyer the right, but not the obligation, to sell a particular currency-futures contract at a specified price anytime during the life of the option. Table 5.8 shows futures positions after options have been exercised.

MNCs with open positions in foreign currencies can use currency futures options to cover such positions. Individuals may speculate about currency futures options based on their expectation of exchange rate movements for a particular currency. Those who believe the futures prices are too low could buy call options on futures. Those who believe the futures prices are too high could buy put options on futures.

If a call futures option is exercised, the holder gets a long position in the underlying futures contract plus a cash amount equal to the current futures price minus the exercise price. If a put futures option is exercised, the holder gets a short position in the underlying

Table 5.8 Futures positions after option exercise.

	Call Option	Put Option
Buyer assumes	Long futures position	Short futures position
Seller assumes	Short futures position	Long futures position

futures contract plus a cash amount equal to the exercise price minus the current futures price.

Example 5.6

Consider an investor who has June futures call option on one contract of the British pound (62,500) with a strike price of $1.580. The current futures price of the pound for delivery in June is $1.630. If the investor exercises her option, she will receive $3,125 (62,500 × 0.05) plus a long position in a futures contract to buy £62,500 in June. If desired, she can immediately close out her long position at no cost; this would leave the investor with the $3,125 cash payoff.

Example 5.7

Consider an investor who has June futures put option on one contract of the Swiss franc (125,000) with a strike price of $0.65. The current futures price of the franc for delivery in June is $0.55. If the investor exercises her option, she receives $12,500 (125,000 × 0.10) plus a short position in a futures contract to sell SFr125,000. If desired, she can immediately close out her short position at no cost; this would leave the investor with the $12,500 cash payoff.

5.4. SUMMARY

Three major instruments of the foreign exchange market are currency futures, currency options, and currency futures options. The three types of contracts are similar because they are all used by those who have specific expectations about future exchange-rate movements. Yet, they differ because: (1) holders of currency futures must buy or sell the currency on the settlement date; (2) owners of currency options have the right to buy or sell the currency at a specified price; and (3) holders of currency futures options have the right to buy or sell the futures on the currency.

These three types of currency contracts are acquired for hedging, speculation, or arbitrage. They appeal to individuals and small companies because they offer standard contracts in predetermined amounts and their purchase prices are small. MNCs with open positions in foreign currencies can use these three markets to cover such positions as an alternative to the forward market offered by commercial banks.

The trading of futures and options involves six major classes of risk: credit, market, liquidity, legal, settlement, and operations. Credit risk derives from the extension of credit to counterparties who may be unwilling or unable to fulfill their contractual obligations. Market risk refers to the effect of changes in the price of the underlying instrument on the value of an open derivative position. Liquidity risk is the risk that a securities firm or bank is unable to liquidate or offset a position because of a lack of counterparties in the market. Legal risk arises when contracts are unenforceable or inadequately documented. Settlement risk happens when a counterparty fails to provide funds or instruments at the agreed time. Operations risk is a loss that results from human error or deficiencies in systems or controls.

5.5. KEY TERMS

currency futures contract	currency option
currency futures option	hedger
speculator	long position
short position	initial margin
maintenance margin	margin calls
performance bond margins	spread trading
currency code	ticker (trading) symbol
currency call option	currency put option
strike price	in the money
out of the money	at-the-money
currency option premium	intrinsic value
time value	

5.6. PROBLEMS

1. An American company sells yen futures contracts to cover possible exchange losses on its export orders denominated in Japanese yen. The amount of the initial margin is $20,000, and the maintenance margin is 75 percent of the initial margin. The value of the company's position declines by $6,000 because the spot rate for yen has increased.

   a. What is the dollar amount of the maintenance margin?
   b. Should the broker issue margin calls to the company?
   c. What is the amount of additional deposit to restore the account to the initial margin level?

2. A speculator enters into a futures contract for September delivery (September 19) of £62,500 on February 2. The futures exchange rate is $1.650 per pound. He believes that the spot rate for pounds on September 19 will be $1.700 per pound. The margin requirement is 2 percent.

   a. If his expectations are correct, what would be his rate of return on the investment?
   b. If the spot rate for pounds on September 19 is 5 percent lower than the futures exchange rate, how much would he lose on the futures speculation?
   c. If there is a 65 percent chance that the spot rate for pounds will increase to $1.700 by September 19, would you speculate in the futures market?

3. On March 20, a Detroit investor decides to invest $1 million in a British 3-month certificate of deposit (CD) with an annual yield of 20 percent. He expects that this 20 percent rate of return on the British CD is more than he could have realized by investing in the domestic market. The investor buys British pounds in the spot market and purchases the CD from a British bank. The exchange rates are $2.0000 per pound on the spot market and $2.0050 per pound in the futures market for June delivery (June 20).

   a. The investor buys enough British pounds in the futures market to cover the principal and accrued interest at the time of maturity. Summarize the transaction.
   b. By June 20, the British pound has depreciated to $1.8500 per pound. Remember that the spot rate and the futures rate become the same by the delivery date. On

June 20, the investor decides to close the position by selling British pounds in the spot market and reversing the futures contracts. Summarize the transaction.

c. Compare the exchange gain (loss) from the futures transaction with the exchange loss (gain) from the spot transaction. What is the windfall profit (net exchange gain)?

d. If the investor had not hedged his investment, how much exchange loss would he have suffered on the transaction? Remember that the British pound has depreciated to $1.8500 on June 20.

4. The call premium per British pound on March 1 is $0.04, the expiration date is September 19, and the strike price is $1.80. A speculator believes that the spot rate for the pound will rise to $1.92 by September 19.

a. If the speculator's expectations are correct, what would be her dollar profit from speculating two-pound call options (£62,500)?

b. If the spot rate were $1.76 per pound when the option expired, would the speculator exercise the options? What would be her loss from this speculation?

5. The put premium per British pound on March 1 is $0.04, the settlement date is September 19, and the strike price is $1.80. A speculator anticipates that the spot rate for the pound will fall to $1.72 by September 19. If the speculator's expectations are correct, what would be his dollar profit from speculating two put options (62,500 pounds)?

6. A US company has bought 30 personal computers from a British company for 62,500 pounds. Its payment must be made in British pounds 90 days from now. The premium for a pound call option with a strike price of $1.60 and a 90-day expiration date is $0.04 per pound. The current spot rate for pounds is $1.58; the US company expects that the spot rate in 90 days will rise to $1.66. The US company has two alternatives: do not hedge and hedge in the options market. Should the US company choose the call option hedge or the no hedge?

7. A US exporter is scheduled to receive 125,000 francs in 60 days. The premium for a franc put option with a strike price of $0.50 and a 90-day settlement date is $0.03 per franc. The company anticipates that the spot rate in 90 days will be $0.46. Should the company hedge its accounts receivable in the options market? If the spot rate were $0.51 in 90 days, how would it affect the company's decision?

8. The exchange rate for Japanese yen is $0.0069 per yen, and a call option has a strike price of $0.0065. An investor has two yen call options. If the investor exercises the call options, how much profit would he realize? (*Hint*: See Table 5.5 for the size of a contract for yen call options and ignore option premiums.)

9. The exchange rate for Japanese yen is $0.0069 per yen, and a put option has a strike price of $0.0070. An investor has two yen put options. If the holder exercises the put option, how much profit would he realize? (*Hint*: See Table 5.5 for the size of a contract for yen put options and ignore option premium.)

10. On October 23, the closing exchange rate of British pounds was $1.70. Calls which would mature the following January with a strike price of $1.75 were traded at $0.10.

a. Were the call options in the money, at the money, or out of the money?

b. Compute the intrinsic value of the call.

c. If the exchange rate of British pounds rises to $1.90 prior to the January option expiration date, what is the percentage return on investment for an investor who purchased a call on October 23?

11. With reference to Problem 5.10, put options with the same strike price and a January maturity for British pounds were traded at $0.05 on October 23.

a. Were the put options in the money, at the money, or out of the money?
b. Compute the intrinsic value of the put.
c. If the exchange rate of British pounds falls to $1.65 just prior to expiration, what is the percentage return on investment for an investor who purchased a put-on October 23?

Closing Case 5: Merck's Use of Currency Options

The effect of foreign currency fluctuations on a company depends on a company's business structure, its industry profile, and its competitive environment. This case recounts how Merck assessed its foreign exchange exposure and decided to hedge those exposures.

The Company

Merck celebrated its 120th anniversary in 2021 in discovering, developing, producing, and distributing human and animal health pharmaceutical products. Today the company does business in more than 100 countries around the world, with 68,000 employees as of December 31, 2021. Thus, it is part of an industry which makes its products available for prevention, relief, and cure of disease throughout the world.

Approximately 54 percent of worldwide sales for Merck come from foreign operations. International earnings assets for the company account for 40 percent of its total earnings assets. The pharmaceutical industry is highly competitive, with no company holding more than 5 percent of the worldwide market. Merck ranks first in pharmaceutical sales in the world but has slightly less than 5 percent of the market share worldwide.

As Merck became increasingly global, it continued to establish and enhance strategic alliances here in the US and abroad in order to discover, develop, and market innovative products. Moreover, Merck understands that future competition will be more global in nature. To prepare its managers for this broader challenge, Merck continues to expand the international nature of its management training. Programs focus increasingly on international issues such as foreign exchange risk management, and training program participants reflect the worldwide nature of the company's businesses. For example, the senior-level managers who attended its Executive Development Programs in recent years came from 30 countries.

US pharmaceutical companies have expanded significantly into foreign markets more than their counterparts in other industries because they have to fund high risk and growing research expenditures. These companies also differ in their method of doing business overseas. Although many US exporters bill their customers in US dollars, most pharmaceutical companies bill their customers in local currencies. Consequently, the impact of exchange rate volatility tends to be more immediate and direct.

Foreign subsidiaries of pharmaceutical companies are typically importers of products at some stage of production. And these subsidiaries are responsible for completing, marketing, and distributing the product within the country of incorporation. Sales are denominated in local currency, but costs are denominated in a combination of the local currency and the parent country currency.

Identification and Measurement of Exchange Exposure

Every company faces exposure to foreign exchange risk as soon as it chooses to maintain a physical presence in a foreign country. Foreign exchange fluctuations can affect a US multinational company in three ways. First, the dollar value of net assets held in foreign currencies may be changed. This type of exposure is called translation or accounting exposure; it measures the effect of an exchange rate change on published financial statements of a firm. Second, the expected results of outstanding transactions, such as accounts receivable and/or accounts payable, may be changed. This sort of exposure is known as transaction exposure; it measures the effect of an exchange rate change on outstanding obligations which existed before exchange rates changed but were settled after the exchange rates change. The third type of exposure is referred to as economic exposure; it involves the potential effects of exchange rate changes on all facets of a firm's operations: product market, factor market, and capital market. Economic exposure consists of future revenue exposure and competitive exposure. Future revenue exposure is the possibility that the dollar value of future revenues expected to be earned overseas in foreign currencies may be changed. Competitive exposure is the possibility that a company's competitive position may be changed — for example, a competitor whose costs are denominated in a weak currency will have greater pricing flexibility and thus a potential competitive advantage.

Competitive exposure has been the subject of recent academic study on exchange risk management. Such exposures are best exemplified by the adverse effect of the strong dollar on the competitive position of US industry in the early 1980s. This was true not only in export markets but also in the US domestic market, where the strengthening US dollar gave Japanese and European based manufacturers a large competitive advantage in dollar terms over domestic US producers.

With its significant presence worldwide, Merck has exposures in approximately 40 currencies. As a first step in assessing the effect of exchange rate movements on revenues and net income, Merck constructed a sales index that measures the relative strength of the dollar against a basket of currencies weighted by the size of sale in those countries. The company used 1978 as the base year of its sales index. When the index is above 100 percent, foreign currencies have strengthened against the dollar, thereby indicating a positive exchange effect on dollar revenues (exchange gains).

When the index is below 100 percent, the dollar has strengthened against the foreign currencies, thereby resulting in a negative exchange impact on dollar revenues (exchange losses). Merck evaluated its sales index from 1972 to 1988 and found that it had significant exchange exposure of its net overseas revenues.

Given the significant exchange exposure of its overseas revenues, Merck then decided to review its global allocation of resources across currencies; the main purpose of this review was to determine the extent to which revenues and costs were matched in individual currencies. The review revealed that the distribution of the company's assets differs somewhat from the sales mix, primarily because of the concentration of research, manufacturing, and headquarters operations in the United States.

Hedging Exposures with Financial Instruments

Having concluded that a diversified strategy (resource deployment) was not an appropriate way for Merck to address exchange risk, it considered the alternative of financial hedging. Thinking through this alternative involved the following five steps: (1) projecting exchange rate volatility; (2) assessing the impact of the 5-year strategic plan; (3) deciding on hedging the exposure; (4) selecting the appropriate financial instruments; and (5) constructing a hedging program. Based on this five-step process, Merck decided to choose currency options as its risk management tool.

Identifying a company's exchange risk and deciding what action should be taken require extensive analysis. Merck management felt that, as a result of this analysis of its currency exposures, it developed an appropriate financial hedging plan — one that insures against the potentially damaging effects of currency volatility on the company's strategic plan.

Apparently, this hedging strategy has worked well for Merck since 1989 (Schlesinger, 2000). Because Merck does about half its business overseas, the dollar surge in the 1980s "really put a crimp in the performance of the company" as the dollar value of foreign revenue fell, recalls Chief Financial Officer Judy Lewent. In response, the company was repeatedly forced into sudden cutbacks in planned research and development spending and capital investments. Beginning in 1989, Merck started hedging against foreign-exchange movements, a practice honed throughout the decade. Thus, even as the dollar surged against the euro in any year, Ms. Lewent says, "we were able to go through the year and continue our budget commitments to our operating people."

Case Questions

1. Why do you think Merck did not neutralize the impact of unexpected exchange rate changes on its future revenues through a diversification strategy?
2. Describe each of Merck's five-step processes of its foreign exchange risk management: exchange forecasts, strategic plan impact, hedging rationale, financial instruments, and hedging program.
3. Why did Merck select "options" as its major hedging instrument?

4. The web site of the Chicago Mercantile Exchange — https://www.cmegroup.com/ — and the web site of the Philadelphia Stock Exchange — https://www.nasdaq.com/solutions/nasdaq-phlx/— show a variety of information about currency futures and options. Use these web sites to depict the prices of British pound futures and options.

Sources: Lewent, J. C. and A. John Kearney, "Identifying, Measuring, and Hedging Currency Risk at Merck," *Journal of Applied Corporate Finance* (Winter 1990), pp. 19–28; and https://www.cmegroup.com/, September 1, 2022.

Chapter 6

FINANCIAL SWAPS

Opening Case 6: Central Bank Currency Swap Tracker

Since the Great US Recession of the late 2000s, Central banks around the world have entered into a multitude of bilateral currency swap agreements with one another. These agreements allow a central bank in one country to exchange currency, usually its domestic currency, for a certain amount of foreign currency. The recipient central bank can then lend this foreign currency to its domestic banks, on its own terms and at its own risk. Swaps involving the US Federal Reserve System (Fed) were the most important of all the cross-border policy responses to the financial crisis, helping to alleviate potentially devastating dollar funding problems among non-US banks. Fed swaps again helped to prevent global dollar shortages in early 2020, when the spread of the COVID-19 pandemic plunged the world into deep recession.

While the terms of swap agreements are designed to protect both central banks involved in the swap from losses owing to fluctuations in currency values, there is some risk that a central bank will refuse, or be unable, to honor the terms of the agreement. For this reason, lending through currency swaps is a meaningful sign of trust between governments.

In October 2008, the Fed extended swap lines to Brazil, Mexico, South Korea, and Singapore. In 2020, during the COVID-19 crisis, both the Fed and The European Central Bank (ECB) again extended swap lines to select developing-country central banks. The Fed approved emergency lines on March 19, 2020, for Brazil, Mexico, South Korea, and Singapore — the same developing nations that had received them in 2008. How were these four same countries chosen in both 2008 and 2021, out of the many that requested them? This was because the Fed trusted these four countries.

Here is how bilateral currency swap agreement works. At the start of a swap, central bank 1 (i.e., the Bank of Korea) sells a specified amount of currency A (Korean won) to central bank 2 (The US Federal Reserve System) in exchange for currency B

(US dollar) at the prevailing market exchange rate. Central bank 1 agrees to buy back its currency at the same exchange rate on a specified future date. Central bank 1 then uses the currency B it has obtained through the swap to lend to local banks or corporations. On the specified future date that the swap unwinds, and the funds are returned, central bank 1, which requested activation of the swap, pays interest to central bank 2.[1]

A **swap** is an agreement between two parties, called **counterparties,** who exchange sets of cash flows over a period of time in the future. When exchange rates and interest rates fluctuate, the risks of forward and money market positions are so great that the forward market and the money market may not function properly. Currency futures and options are inflexible and available only for selected currencies. In such cases, multinational companies (MNCs) and governments may use swap arrangements to protect the value of export sales, import orders, and outstanding loans denominated in foreign currencies.

Financial swaps are now used by MNCs, commercial banks, world organizations, and sovereign governments to minimize currency and interest rate risks. These swaps compete with other exchange risk management tools, such as currency forwards, futures, and options, but they also complement these other instruments.

Chapter 6 consists of three major sections. The first section describes the emergence of the swap market. The second section discusses two major types of financial swaps — interest rate swaps and currency swaps. The third section evaluates motivations for swaps.

6.1. THE EMERGENCE OF THE SWAP MARKET

The origins of the swap market can be traced back to the late 1970s, when currency traders developed currency swaps to evade British controls on the movement of foreign currency. The market has grown rapidly since then. In this section, we consider the origins of the swap market, drawbacks of parallel and back-to-back loans, and the growth of the swap market.

6.1.1. *The Origins of the Swap Market*

Financial swaps are usually regarded as an outgrowth of parallel and back-to-back loans. Parallel and back-to-back loans work similarly except in one respect. Parallel loans involve four firms, while back-to-back loans involve only two firms. These two instruments attained prominence in the 1970s when the British government-imposed taxes on foreign currency transactions to prevent capital outflows. The parallel loan became a widely accepted vehicle by which these taxes could be avoided. The back-to-back loan was a simple modification of the parallel loan, and the currency swap was a natural extension of the back-to-back loan.

---

[1]Steil, B., B. D. Rocca, and D. Walker, "Central Bank Currency Swaps Tracker," December 1, 2021, https://www.cfr.org/article/central-bank-currency-swaps-tracker.

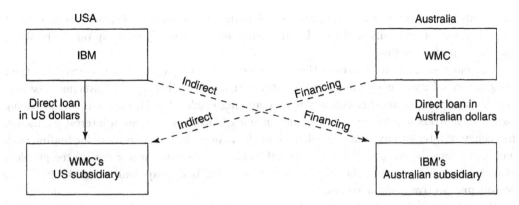

Fig. 6.1 The structure of a parallel loan.

6.1.1.1. *Parallel loans*

A **parallel loan** refers to a loan which involves an exchange of currencies between four parties, with a promise to re-exchange the currencies at a predetermined exchange rate on a specified future date. Typically, though not always, the parties consist of two pairs of affiliated companies. Parallel loans are commonly arranged by two multinational parent companies in two different countries.

The structure of a typical parallel loan is illustrated in Fig. 6.1. Assume that: (1) a parent corporation (IBM) in the United States with a subsidiary in Australia wants to obtain a 1-year Australian dollar loan and (2) a parent corporation (Western Mining Company, WMC) in Australia with a subsidiary in the United States wishes to obtain a 1-year US dollar loan. In other words, each parent wants to lend to its subsidiary in the subsidiary's currency. These loans can be arranged without using the foreign exchange market. IBM lends the agreed amount in US dollars to the American subsidiary of WMC. In return for this loan, WMC lends the same amount of money in Australian dollars to the Australian subsidiary of IBM. Parallel loan agreements involve the same loan amount and the same loan maturity. Of course, each loan is repaid in the subsidiary's currency. The parallel loan arrangement avoids foreign exchange risk because each loan is made and repaid in one currency.

6.1.1.2. *Back-to-back loans*

A **back-to-back loan** refers to a loan which involves an exchange of currencies between two parties, with a promise to re-exchange the currencies at a specified exchange rate on a specified future date. Back-to-back loans involve two companies domiciled in two different countries. For example, AT&T agrees to borrow funds in the United States and then to lend those borrowed funds to Toyota in Japan, which, in return, borrows funds in Japan and then lends those funds to AT&T in the United States. By this simple arrangement, each firm has access to the capital markets in the foreign country without any actual across-border flows of capital. Consequently, both companies avoid exchange rate risk in a back-to-back loan.

6.1.2. *Drawbacks of Parallel and Back-to-Back Loans*

While parallel and back-to-back loans offer definite benefits to participating companies, three problems limit their usefulness as financing tools. First, it is difficult to find counterparties with matching needs. Second, one party is still obligated to comply with such an agreement even if another party fails to do so. Third, such loans customarily show up on the books of the participating parties.

Currency swaps can overcome these problems fully or partly, and this explains their rapid growth. First, a company in one country with a use for this type of financing must find another company in another country with matching needs, that is, mirror-image financing requirements. These requirements include currencies, principals, types of interest payments, frequency of interest payments, and length of the loan period. Search costs for finding such a company may be considerable if it is possible. Currency swaps largely resolve the problem of matching needs because they are arranged by specialized swap dealers and brokers who recruit prospective counterparties.

Second, parallel and back-to-back loans are actually two loans with two separate agreements which exist independently of each other. If the first company defaults on its obligations to the second company, the second company is not legally relieved of its obligations to the first company. To avoid this problem, a separate agreement, defining the right of offset, must be drafted. If this agreement is not registered, the situation and outcome described above may still arise. On the other hand, registration itself may cause problems. With currency swaps, however, the right of offset is usually embodied in the agreement.

Third, parallel and back-to-back loans are carried on the books of the participating parties. In other words, the exchange of principals under these two instruments involves net increases in both assets and liabilities; these amounts are customarily recorded in full in the counterparties' books. With currency swaps, however, the principal amounts usually do not show up in the participants' books. Many commercial banks prefer currency swaps to parallel and back-to-back loans to keep the transactions off their books. These off-book transactions of currency swaps and other derivatives may enable banks to avoid increases in their capital requirements under applicable regulations. However, such off-book transactions may be disallowed in the near future as accounting-standard setters in the United States and other countries require MNCs to include derivative transactions in their financial statements. For example, the Dodd–Frank Act of 2010 provides US regulators with authority to regulate swaps and other derivatives.

6.1.3. *The Growth of the Swap Market*

Salomon Brothers arranged the first currency swap in August 1981 with the World Bank and IBM as counterparties. The World Bank wanted to obtain Swiss francs and German marks to finance its operations in Switzerland and West Germany without having to tap the capital markets of these two countries directly. On the other hand, IBM, which had previously acquired fixed-rate obligations in francs and marks, obtained an unrealized capital gain in terms of dollars when the dollar appreciated. Because IBM's management believed that the dollar's appreciation would not continue, it wanted to realize the capital gain and remove itself from its mark-franc exposure.

It was a short step from currency swaps to interest rate swaps. If swaps could be used to convert one type of currency obligation to another at the applicable interest rate on each currency, a similar type of contract could be used to convert one type of borrowing (fixed rate) to another (floating rate). The first interest rate swap was put together in London

Table 6.1 Notional value of derivatives (US$ billions).

Year	2021	2022
Over-the-counter derivatives	609,996	632,238
Exchange traded derivatives	5,863	38,241
Total	615,859	670,479

Source: The Exchange Traded Derivatives Outstanding, the BIS Statistics Explorer, Table D1 and Over-the-Counter Derivatives Outstanding, the BIS Statistics Explorer, D5.1, https://www.bis.org/statistics/index.htm?m=6, January 23, 2023.

in 1981, and their use spread to the United States the next year. The swap concept was extended in 1986 when the Chase Manhattan Bank introduced the commodity swap. In 1989, Bankers Trust introduced the first reported equity swap. Since then, the swap market has grown at an unimaginable rate.

Table 6.1 shows the notional value of derivatives in 2021 and 2022. Exchange-traded derivatives consist of interest rate futures, currency futures, equity futures, interest rate options, currency options, and equity options. Over-the-counter (OTC) derivatives include currency contracts, interest rate contracts, equity contracts, commodity contracts, and credit-default swaps.

One noteworthy item in this table is the credit default swap that received a lot of attention during the recent US financial crisis. This swap is the newest type of swap and is a subset of a new class of instruments known as synthetic equity. The **credit default swap** (CDS) is a kind of insurance in which the investor of the CDS makes a series of payments to the seller and receives payoff if its bond or loan undergoes a default. By doing so, the risk of default is transferred from the holder of the fixed income security to the seller of the swap. The CDS was once widely acclaimed as an example of financial innovation. However, the subprime mortgage crisis in the United States during 2007–2009 triggered massive losses in many financial institutions with CDS contracts. A prominent example is the world's largest insurer AIG which was bankrupted and forced to see government assistance mainly due to massive losses from its credit default swaps. The famous investor Warren Buffett called the CDS as weapons of mass destruction.

Table 6.2 shows the amount of outstanding swaps from 1987 to 2022. By 2022, the total swap market had reached $472 trillion. And interest swaps account for about 94 percent of the total swap market, while currency swaps account for about 6 percent of the total swap market. US dollars account for about 30 percent of these swaps, while other major currencies such as the Japanese yen, the euro, the British pound, and the Swiss franc account for most of the remaining 70 percent.

6.2. PLAIN VANILLA SWAPS

The basic form of a swap — the simplest kind — is called a **plain vanilla swap**. Though many variants of the plain vanilla swap exist, all swaps have the same basic structure. Two counterparties agree to make payments to each other on the basis of some quantity of underlying assets. These payments include interest payments, commissions, and other service payments. The swap agreement contains a specification of the assets to be exchanged, the

Table 6.2 The value of outstanding swaps (billions of US dollars).

Year	Interest Rate Swaps	Currency Swaps	Total Swaps
1987	683	183	866
1990	2,311	578	2,889
1993	6,178	900	7,078
1996	12,811	1,197	14,008
1999	38,372	2,444	40,816
2002	68,274	4,560	72,834
2005	169,106	8,504	177,610
2008	309,760	13,322	323,082
2011	402,611	22,791	425,402
2012	369,999	25,420	395,419
2016	289,103	22,971	312,074
2017	318,870	25,535	344,405
2018	349,761	26,012	375,773
2021	372,376	28,748	401,124
2022	442,223	30,280	472,503

Source: The International Monetary Fund, International Financial Markets and the BIS Statistics Explorer, the BIS Statistics Explorer, https://www. bis.org/statistics/index.htm?m=6, January 23, 2023.

rate of interest applicable to each, the timetable by which the payments are to be made, and other provisions. The two parties may or may not exchange the underlying assets, which are called notional principals, in order to distinguish them from physical exchanges in the cash markets. In the sections that follow, we discuss the two forms of a plain vanilla swap: interest rate swaps and currency swaps.

6.2.1. *Swap Banks*

It is difficult and time-consuming for two end users to arrange a swap directly. A more efficient structure for them is to obtain a financial intermediary who serves as counterparty to both end users. This counterparty is called a swap bank. A **swap bank** is a generic term used to describe a financial institution which assists in the completion of a swap. The swap bank profits from the bid-ask spread it imposes on the swap coupon.

The swap bank serves as either a broker or a dealer. A **swap broker** is a swap bank who acts strictly as an agent without taking any financial position in the swap transaction. In other words, the swap broker matches counterparties but does not assume any risk of the swap. The broker receives a commission for this service. A **swap dealer** is a swap bank who actually transacts for its own account to help complete the swap. In this capacity, the swap dealer assumes a position in the swap and thus assumes certain risks.

6.2.2. *Interest Rate Swaps*

An **interest rate swap** is a swap in which counterparties exchange cash flows of a floating rate for cash flows of a fixed rate, or exchange cash flows of a fixed rate for cash flows of a floating rate. No **notional principal** changes hands, but it is a reference amount against which the interest is calculated. Maturities range from under 1 year to over 15 years, but most transactions fall within a 2-year to 10-year period. While swaps are inherently international

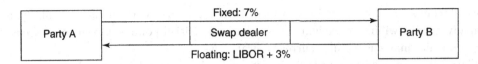

Fig. 6.2 An interest rate swap.

in nature, interest rate swaps can be purely domestic. However, when they are arranged in the Eurocurrency market, interest rate swaps have counterparties from different countries or foreign arranging banks.

In a typical interest rate swap, one company has an initial position in a fixed rate debt instrument, while another company has an initial position in a floating rate obligation. In this initial position, the company with the floating rate obligation is exposed to changes in interest rates. By swapping this floating rate obligation with the fixed rate obligation, this company eliminates exposure to changing interest rates.

Borrowers may want to arrange an interest rate swap for a number of reasons. First, changes in financial markets may cause interest rates to change. Second, borrowers may have different credit ratings in different countries. Third, some borrowers have different preferences for debt service payment schedules. Because market imperfections exist in different international financial markets with diversified borrowers and lenders, the objectives of interest rate swaps can be achieved easily and readily. Interest rate swaps are normally arranged by an international bank which serves a swap broker or a swap dealer. Through interest rate swaps, borrowers obtain a lower cost of debt service payments and lenders obtain profit guarantees.

Example 6.1

Assume that a swap agreement covers a 5-year period and involves annual interest payments on a $10 million principal amount. Party A agrees to pay a fixed rate of 7 percent to Party B. In return, Party B agrees to pay a floating rate of SOFR + 3 percent to Party A. **SOFR** (the Secured Overnight Financing Rate) is a benchmark.

Interest rate for dollar-denominated derivatives and loans that replaced the London Interbank Offered Rate (LIBOR) on June 30, 2023.

Figure 6.2 shows the basic features of this transaction. Party A pays 7 percent interest on $10 million or $700,000 each year to Party B. Party B makes an interest payment on $10 million each year to Party A in return, but the actual amount of the interest payments depends on the prevailing SOFR.

If the SOFR is 5 percent at the time of the first payment, Party B will have to pay $800,000 to Party A. Party A still owes $700,000 to Party B because its interest is fixed at 7 percent on a $10 million loan. If these mutual interest obligations offset each other, Party B owes only $100,000 to Party A. Typically, only payment of the net amount, the difference between the two interest obligations, actually takes place. This practice avoids unnecessary payments.

6.2.3. *Currency Swaps*

A **currency swap** is a swap in which one party provides a certain principal in one currency to its counterparty in exchange for an equivalent amount in a different currency. For example, a British company may be anxious to swap British pounds for US dollars. Similarly, a US company may be willing to exchange US dollars for British pounds. Given these needs, the two companies may engage in a currency swap.

Currency swaps achieve an economic purpose similar to parallel loans. However, currency swaps have effectively displaced parallel loans because companies seeking parallel loans have difficulty matching needs, have no right of offset, and must place such loans in the counterparties' books.

A typical currency swap involves three sets of cash flows. First, at the initiation of the swap, the two parties actually exchange the currencies in which the principals are denominated. This differs from the interest rate swap in which both parties may deal in the same currency and can pay the net interest amount. Second, the parties make periodic interest payments to each other during the life of the swap agreement. Third, at the termination of the swap, the parties again exchange the currencies in which the principals are denominated.

Example 6.2

Assume that the current spot rate for British pounds is 0.5 pounds per dollar ($2 per pound), the US interest rate is 10 percent, and the British interest rate is 8 percent. BT (British Telecommunications) wishes to exchange 5 million pounds for dollars. In return for these pounds, GM would pay $10 million to BT at the initiation of the swap. The term of the swap is 5 years, and the two firms will make annual interest payments.

With the interest rates in Example 6.2, GM will pay 8 percent on the 5 million pounds it received; so, the annual payment from GM to BT will be 400,000 pounds. BT received $10 million and will pay interest at 10 percent; so, BP will pay $1 million each year to GM. In actual practice, the counterparties will make only net payments. For example, if the spot rate for pounds changes to 0.45 pounds per dollar at year 1, one pound is worth $2.22. Valuing the interest obligations in dollars at this exchange rate, BT owes $1 million and GM owes $888,000 (400,000 pounds ×$2.22). Hence, BT will pay the $112,000 difference. At other times, the exchange rate could be different, thereby making the net payment reflect the different exchange rate.

At the end of 5 years, the two counterparties again exchange principal. In Example 6.2, BT would pay $10 million, and GM would pay 5 million pounds. This final payment terminates the currency swap. Figure 6.3(a) shows the initial exchange of principal; Figure 6.3(b) represents the annual interest payment; and Figure 6.3(c) shows the second exchange of principal that completes the swap.

6.2.4. *Swaptions, Caps, Floors, and Collars*

In this section, we consider several related instruments before we complete our survey of financial swaps. These instruments are swaptions, caps, floors, and collars.

A **swaption** is an option to enter into a plain vanilla interest-rate swap. A **call swaption** gives the holder the right to receive fixed-interest payments. A **put swaption** gives the holder the right to make fixed interest payments. Call swaptions are attractive when interest rates are expected to fall. Put swaptions are attractive when interest rates are expected to rise. Banks and investment firms usually act as dealers rather than as brokers. In other words, these banks and investment firms stand ready to enter into swaptions on either the buying or selling side.

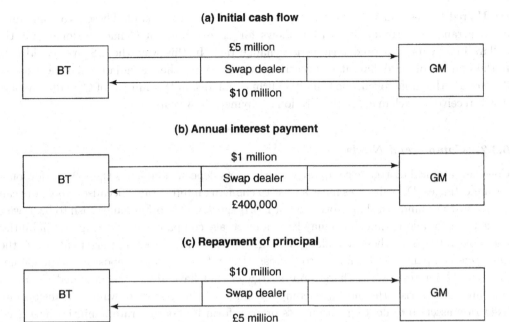

(a) Initial cash flow

£5 million

BT → Swap dealer → GM

$10 million

(b) Annual interest payment

$1 million

BT → Swap dealer → GM

£400,000

(c) Repayment of principal

$10 million

BT → Swap dealer → GM

£5 million

Fig. 6.3 A currency swap.

Swaptions are an alternative to caps, floors, and collars, all of which are traded by the same bank personnel who trade swaptions. An **interest rate cap** sets a maximum rate on floating rate interest payments; an **interest rate floor** sets a minimum rate on floating rate interest payments; and an **interest rate collar** combines a cap with a floor. A buyer of one of these instruments pays to the seller a one-time premium, which is a small percentage of the notional principal. The buyer of a cap receives a cash payment from the seller when the floating reference rate for the cap is higher than the cap's strike rate when the two rates are matched against each other on a given date. The buyer of a floor receives a cash payment from the seller when the floating reference rate for the floor is lower on a given date than the floor's strike rate.

6.3. MOTIVATIONS FOR SWAPS

There are three basic motivations for swaps. First, companies use swaps to provide protection against future changes in exchange rates. Second, companies use swaps to eliminate interest rate risks arising from normal commercial operations. Third, companies use swaps to reduce financing costs.

6.3.1. *Currency Risk Management*

Companies use currency swaps to eliminate currency risks arising from overseas commercial operations. A currency swap can take many forms. One type of currency swap accommodates two companies that have long-term needs in two different currencies. Assume the following two things: First, a US firm, hired to build several power plants in Canada, expects to receive payment in Canadian dollars in 3 years. Second, a Canadian firm has bought machinery from the United States and will make payment in US dollars in 3 years. These two companies could arrange a currency swap that allows for an exchange of Canadian dollars for US dollars in 3 years at a predetermined exchange rate. In this way, the US firm could lock in the number of US dollars it will receive in exchange for the Canadian dollar payment in 3 years. By the same token, the Canadian firm could lock in the number of Canadian dollars it will receive in exchange for the US dollar payment in 3 years.

6.3.2. *Commercial Needs*

Consider a typical mortgage company which accepts deposits and lends these funds for long-term mortgages. Deposit rates must adjust to changing interest rates because depositors can withdraw their funds on short notice. Most mortgagors, on the other hand, wish to borrow at a fixed rate for a long time. This may leave a mortgage company with floating rate liabilities and fixed rate assets, thereby making it vulnerable to rising rates. If interest rates rise, the mortgage company will be forced to increase the rate it pays on deposits, but it cannot increase the interest rate it charges on mortgages that have already been issued. To avoid this interest rate risk, the mortgage company might use interest rate swaps to transform its fixed rate assets into floating rate assets or transform its floating rate liabilities into fixed rate liabilities.

Example 6.3

Let's extend Example 6.1 to make the discussions on motivations for swaps concrete. A mortgage company (Party A) has just lent $10 million for 5 years at 7 percent with annual payments, and it pays a deposit rate that equals SOFR + 1 percent. With these rates, the company would lose money if SOFR exceeds 6 percent. This vulnerability might prompt the mortgage company to consider an interest rate swap. In other words, in exchange for the fixed rate mortgages that it holds, the company might want to pay a fixed rate of interest and receive a floating rate of interest.

Figure 6.4 shows Example 6.1 (Fig. 6.2) with additional information about the mortgage company (Party A). The company receives payments at a fixed rate of 7 percent on the mortgage. After it enters the swap, the company also pays 7 percent on a notional principal of $10 million to Party B. In effect, it receives mortgage payments and passes them through to Party B under the swap agreement. In return, Party A receives a floating rate of SOFR + 3 percent from Party B. From this cash flow, the company pays its depositors SOFR + 1 percent and thus this leaves a periodic inflow of 2 percent to the company.

In Example 6.3, the mortgage company now has a fixed rate inflow of 2 percent, and it has succeeded in escaping its exposure to interest rate risk. No matter what happens to the level of interest rates, the company will enjoy a net cash flow of 2 percent on $10 million. This example clarifies why a company has a strong motivation to enter the swap market. The mortgage company faces exposure to changing interest rates because of the very nature of the mortgage industry. The company, however, secures a fixed rate position by engaging in an interest rate swap.

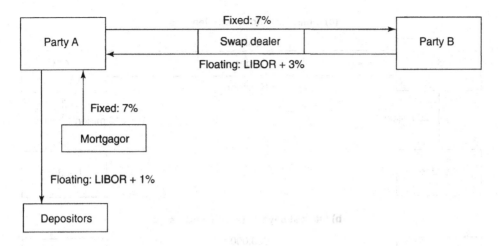

Fig. 6.4 Motivation for the interest rate swap.

6.3.3. *Comparative Advantage*

In many instances, one company may borrow money at a lower rate of interest in the capital market than another firm. For example, a US company (GM) may borrow money at a favorable rate in the United States, but it might not have favorable access to the capital market in the United Kingdom. Similarly, a British company (BT) may have good borrowing opportunities domestically but poor opportunities in the United States.

These comparative advantages usually exist because of market imperfections or differences in risk. US banks may not have the same information as British banks have, or they may evaluate information differently. Tax considerations or some kind of government-sanctioned discrimination might cause foreign borrowers to be treated differently from domestic borrowers. Borrowers' risks might also vary from country to country so that domestic firms might be considered to be less risky than foreign firms. Companies can frequently use swaps not only to save money but also to diversify their funding sources.

Example 6.4

In Example 6.2, we assumed that two companies (GM and BT) faced the same rate for each currency. Let's now assume that BT has access to pounds at a rate of 7 percent, while GM must pay 8 percent to borrow pounds. On the other hand, GM can borrow dollars at 9 percent, while BT must pay 10 percent for its dollar borrowings. As a result, BT enjoys a comparative advantage in borrowing pounds and GM has a comparative advantage in borrowing dollars. These rate differentials raise the possibility that each firm can exploit its comparative advantage and share the gains by reducing overall borrowing costs. This possibility is shown in Figs. 6.5(a)–6.5(c), which resemble Figs. 6.3(a)–6.3(c).

In Fig. 6.5(a), BT borrows 5 million pounds from a British lender at 7 percent, while GM borrows $10 million from a US lender at 9 percent. After these borrowings, both companies have the funds to engage in a currency swap that we have already analyzed in Example 6.2. To initiate the swap, BT forwards the 5 million pounds it has just borrowed to GM, which

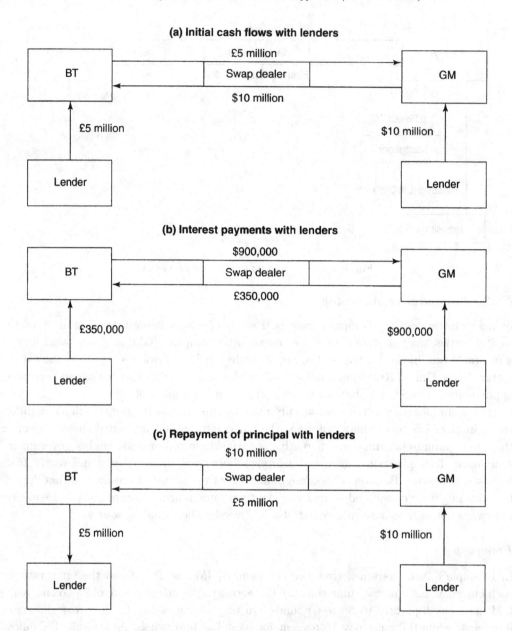

(a) Initial cash flows with lenders

(b) Interest payments with lenders

(c) Repayment of principal with lenders

Fig. 6.5 Motivation for the currency swap.

reciprocates with the $10 million it has borrowed. In effect, the two companies have made independent borrowings and then exchanged the proceeds.

Figure 6.5(b) shows that the swap terms are identical with these two loan terms. BT pays interest payments of 9 percent ($900,000) on the $10 million it received from GM, and GM pays interest payments at 7 percent (350,000 pounds) on the 5 million pounds it received from BT. Notice that these rates are the same ones that the two firms must pay their lenders. Now we can clearly see how the swap benefits both parties. Had each party borrowed the other currency on its own, BT would have paid a full 10 percent and GM would have paid a full 8 percent. By using the swap, both parties achieve an effective borrowing rate that is 1 percent lower than what they could have obtained by borrowing the currency they needed directly. By engaging in the swap, both firms use the comparative advantage of the other to reduce borrowing costs. Figure 6.5(c) shows the termination of cash flows for the swap when both parties repay the principal.

Global Finance in Practice 6: A New Financial Treat Emerges in Foreign Exchange Swap.

The global financial system is bloated with some \$65 trillion in hidden dollar debts, a recent report (2021) from the Bank for International Settlements warns. This takes the form of foreign-exchange swaps that entail a currency trade made today with a commitment to reverse it in the future. Those future commitments constitute a form of debt, but they often are not recognized as such by accounting rules for banks or other companies. This level of off-balance-sheet forex-swap debt dwarfs the \$28 trillion in on-balance-sheet swap liabilities that BIS tabulates.

The BIS notes that this form of credit has exploded in recent years, rising from \$37 trillion in off-balance-sheet obligations on the eve of the 2008 panic. A variety of factors explain the increase, most traced to the consequences of 15 years of unnaturally low interest rates around the world.

Asset managers such as pension funds and insurers in developing economies have expanded investments in dollar-denominated assets as part of a search for yield amid lower interest rates globally. The fund managers then must enter into foreign-exchange swaps to hedge currency mismatches between their assets and liabilities. These swaps are a form of liability that entails liquidity and counterparty risks but are not recorded as credit or debt on the balance sheet.

Abracadabra, a new financial risk is born. This off-balance-sheet debt poses several threats to financial stability. No one knows for sure where all of this debt is lurking. And many events could trigger a cascading crisis.

One vulnerability is exchange-rate volatility. Sudden swings up or down in the value of the dollar relative to other currencies can trigger short-term collateral calls and liquidity crunches. This appears to have been part of the panic that struck British pension funds in September, as a sharp decline in the pound led to margin calls on forex hedges on top of the collateral calls pension managers faced related to their interest-rate derivatives.

Interest-rate risk is another danger. One reason the forex-swap market grew so fast in recent years is that a steeper US yield curve compared to other major economies — relatively lower short-term interest rates and relatively higher long-term rates — essentially allowed banks and other firms to borrow short and lend long in dollars. As the US yield curve has inverted, investors must roll over their short-term swap arrangements at much higher rates.

Meanwhile, dollar-denominated foreign-exchange-swap debts are overwhelmingly held outside the US — American banks and companies tend to be creditors in these arrangements — and this exacerbates the liquidity risk. The Federal Reserve is not able to act as a lender of last resort to foreign banks or other institutions that face dollar liquidity squeezes arising from their swap positions. This leaves foreigners dependent on their local central banks' currency swap arrangements with the Fed to provide dollar liquidity.

Because the Fed cannot and should not put itself and American taxpayers on the hook to bail out a market of this size, the world can only hope that these swap positions unwind smoothly as central banks return to less abnormal monetary policy. But the BIS report on these hidden debts serves as a warning for the future.

The Fed has become so focused on managing inflation (which it does badly) and domestic employment (which it may not be able to do at all) that officials tend to ignore asset prices and other evidence of financial risks — which they would not even be able to measure in this case were it not for the BIS. Perhaps we will all get lucky and this forex-swap bomb will not detonate. But it is dangerous for the Fed to keep counting on luck when its easy money policies create new financial risks.[2]

6.4. SUMMARY

The swap market has emerged largely because financial swaps escape many of the limitations inherent in currency futures and options markets. First, because swaps are custom tailored to the needs of two parties, swap agreements are more likely to meet the specific needs of the counterparties than currency futures and options. Second, major financial institutions are readily identifiable on futures and options exchanges, but only the counterparties know that the swap takes place. Hence, the swap market affords a privacy that cannot be obtained in foreign exchange trading. Finally, currency futures and options trading are subject to considerable government regulation, but the swap market has virtually no government regulation.

Nevertheless, financial swaps have limitations of their own. First, to have a swap transaction, one potential counterparty must find another counterparty which is willing to take the opposite side of the transaction. Second, a swap agreement cannot be altered without the agreement of both parties because the swap agreement is a contract between two counterparties. Third, the exchanges effectively guarantee currency futures and options contracts for all parties, but the swap market has no such guarantor.

6.5. KEY TERMS

swap	counterparties
parallel loan	back-to-back loan
credit default swap (CDs)	plain vanilla swap
swap bank	swap broker

---

[2]The Editorial Board, "A New Financial Threat Emerges in Foreign-Exchange Swaps," *The Wall Street Journal*, December 9, 2022, https://www.wsj.com/articles/a-new-financial-threat-emerges-foreign-exchange-swaps-debt-bank-for-international-settlements-11670429317.

swap dealer   interest rate swap
notional principal   SOFR
currency swap   swaption
call swaption   put swaption
interest rate cap   interest rate floor
interest rate collar

6.6. PROBLEMS

1. A swap agreement covers a 5-year period and involves annual interest payments on a $1 million principal amount. Party A agrees to pay a fixed rate of 12 percent to Party B. In return, Party B agrees to pay a floating rate of SOFR + 3 percent to Party A. The SOFR is 10 percent at the time of the first payment. What is the difference (the net payment) between the two interest obligations?

2. Assume that the current spot rate for the Polish zloty is 2.5 zlotys per dollar ($0.40 per zloty), the US interest rate is 10 percent, and the Polish interest rate is 8 percent. Party C wishes to exchange 25 million zlotys for dollars. In return for these zlotys, Party D would pay $10 million to Party C at the initiation of the swap. The term of the swap is 5 years and the two firms will make annual interest payments. The spot rate for the zloty changes to 2.2222 zlotys per dollar or $0.45 per zloty in year 1. What is the net payment for year 1?

3. A mortgage company (Party E) has just lent $1 million for 5 years at 12 percent with annual payments, and it pays a deposit rate that equals SOFR + 1 percent. With these rates, the company will lose money if LIBOR exceeds 11 percent. This vulnerability prompts the mortgage company to enter an interest rate swap with Party F. This swap agreement covers a 5-year period and involves annual interest payments on a $1 million principal amount. Party E agrees to pay a fixed rate of 12 percent to Party F. In return, Party F agrees to pay a floating rate of SOFR + 3 percent to Party E. Determine an annual net cash flow available for the mortgage company.

4. The current spot rate for the Polish zloty is 2.5 zlotys per dollar or $0.40 per zloty. Party G has access to zlotys at a rate of 7 percent, while Party H must pay 8 percent to borrow zlotys. On the other hand, Party H can borrow dollars at 9 percent, while Party G must pay 10 percent for its dollar borrowings. Party G wishes to obtain $10 million in exchange for 25 million zlotys, while Party H wants to obtain 25 million zlotys in exchange for $10 million. How can these two parties achieve a lower borrowing rate?

Closing Case 6: Regulations of Derivative Markets

Financial derivatives — forwards, futures, options, and swaps — are contracts whose values are linked to or derived from values of underlying assets, such as securities, commodities, and currencies. There are two types of markets for financial derivatives: organized exchanges and OTC markets. Organized exchanges such as the Chicago Mercantile Exchange are regulated by governments, while OTC markets such as banks are unregulated. Derivatives are used by corporations, banks, and investors to reduce a variety of risks such as exposure to currency movements (hedging) or to make leveraged bets on the market direction of these instruments (speculation).

Derivative markets have shown extraordinary growth over the past few years. For example, the size of the global OTC derivative markets increased from $21 trillion of contracts in 1992 to $700 trillion of contracts in 2013; the amount of outstanding exchange-traded derivatives exceeded $26 trillion in 2013. In addition, recent years have witnessed numerous accounts of derivative-related losses on the part of established and reputable firms. The recent rapid growth of derivative markets and large derivative-related losses have triggered concern and even alarm over the dangers posed by the widespread use of derivatives.

What lessons do these losses and growth hold for policymakers? Do they indicate the need for more strict government supervision of derivative markets or for new laws and regulations to limit the use of these instruments? Apparently, US regulatory authorities think that derivatives pose inherent dangers. In the first half of 1997, Congress had introduced some half-dozen bills designed to ban or limit derivatives. In January 1997, the Securities and Exchange Commission (SEC) adopted a regulation requiring companies to present estimates of losses they could suffer from financial instruments. The Financial Accounting Standard Board (FASB) adopted its Statement No. 133, *Accounting for Derivative Instruments and Hedging Activities* in 1998. FASB No. 133 requires companies to report the fair market value of their derivatives in their balance sheets and to include some derivative gains or losses in their income statements. The legal status of derivatives was further cast into doubt in 1998 when the Commodity Futures Trading Commission (CFTC) suggested it had the right to regulate trading in these instruments under the Commodity Futures Trading Commission Act of 1974. Especially, big targets of these reforms are privately negotiated contracts through OTC markets.

Gillette did a strange thing in January 1999. To finance its European operations, it raised money through a Eurobond deal denominated in euros, even though it would have been cheaper to issue in US dollars and then swap the proceeds to euros. Gillette's decision not to execute the currency swap on the 5-year deal cost the company about 10 basis points or 300,000 euros per year. In fact, Gillette was not the only US borrower to forfeit a lower cost of funding. General Electric issued 250 million euros in Eurobonds rather than offering bonds in dollars and then swapping for euros. Lynn Seymour, Gillette's controller, explains that currency swaps have formed an integral part of the company's borrowing strategy in the past. "We have borrowed in US dollars, swapped to floating, foreign-denominated debt, like Deutsche marks, because it was cheaper," she said. However, under the new accounting rules, this procedure becomes more troublesome.

Gillette's action exemplifies that companies will frequently choose a costlier option to avoid government regulations. When the FASB issued its FASB 133 in 1998, some US companies, such as Gillette Corp., decided to undertake the costlier transaction rather than face problems under FASB 133. FASB 133 requires companies to report the fair market value of their derivatives in their balance sheets and to include derivative gains and losses in their income statements. Business executives argue that such accounting treatments of derivatives will distort their company earnings.

According to Ira Kawaller of Kawaller & Associates, a New York management consulting firm, currency swaps and interest-rate swaps must be marked to market as the present value of cash flows and recorded in current income, subjecting the company to earnings volatility. "This is going to be a big problem for multinational companies," he noted. Bob Sullivan, managing partner of PricewaterhouseCoopers, agreed: "For the top Fortune 100 companies, this is a major issue," adding that, as far as debt markets are concerned, this is the "biggest topic" raised by FASB 133. Although it is too early to tell exactly how the FASB will interpret the new rules, it is already clear that FASB 133 is a major headache for American issuers in international debt markets. Thus, some companies such as Gillette and General Electric would rather pay greater funding costs than face balance sheet and income volatilities.

In developing the standard, the FASB reached six decisions that became the cornerstones of FASB 133. First, derivative instruments represent rights or obligations that meet the definitions of assets or liabilities. Second, fair value is the only relevant measure for derivative instruments. Third, only items that are assets or liabilities should be reported as such on the balance sheet. Fourth, therefore, all derivatives are reported at fair value on the balance sheet. Fifth, special hedge accounting is appropriate for derivatives designed and effective in offsetting changes in fair values or cash flows for the risk being hedged. Six, changes in fair value for derivatives not designated and qualifying as hedges are currently recorded in earnings. FASB 133 permits an entity to use the fair-value accounting model and the cash flow hedge accounting model. Under these two accounting models, the entity must recognize gains or losses on derivative hedging instruments as earnings.

Since 1997, several hundred letters from big companies, accountants, and even Federal Reserve Chairman Alan Greenspan have laid out the potential damage of these derivative regulations. In February 2000, a White House panel on OTC derivatives urged the Congress to exempt the $700 trillion derivative market from government regulation. Nevertheless, standard-setters around the world — the United States, the United Kingdom, Canada, other industrial countries, and the International Accounting Standards Committee — have recently proposed and/or issued their standards to increase disclosure of off-balance sheet derivative transactions.

As mandated by Title VII of *the Dodd-Frank Act of 2010*, sufficiently liquid and standardized derivatives transactions are now subject to central clearing requirements, and many of those will be required to be executed on new electronic trading platforms (known as "Swap Execution Facilities" or SEFs). However, some derivatives will still fall into the category of OTC, which means that their terms are privately negotiated between two parties, and some will also remain unclear.

Examples of derivatives which are subject to new swap regulation under Title VII include interest rate swaps, credit default swaps, non-deliverable FX forwards, swaptions and equity total return swaps. Regulators such as the SEC, CFTC have proposed, and in many cases, finalized numerous rankings in order to meet G20 objectives aimed at increasing transparency and reducing system risks in the derivative market.

Case Questions

1. Why have currency swaps replaced parallel loans?
2. Explain both interest rate swaps and currency swaps. Which instrument has a greater credit risk: an interest rate swap or a currency swap?
3. What are major classes of risk in derivative trading?
4. What is the potential damage of government derivative rules on derivative users?
5. List and discuss the major features of the Dodd-Frank Act of 2010.
6. The website of the SEC www.sec.gov and the website of the FASB) www.fasb.org describe standard practices for financial reporting by companies in the United States. Contact the above websites to learn proposed accounting standards and the status regarding reactions to these proposed standards.

Sources: Kroszner, R. S. and R. J. Shiller, eds., "The Repurchase Agreement Market *Reforming U.S. Financial Markets: Reflections before and after Dodd–Frank,* Cambridge, MA: The MIT Press, 2011; Boughey, S., "US Issuers in Euromarket Are Snakebit by FAS 133," *Investment Dealers Digest,* February 22, 1999, p. 13; and Ronner, A. and M. Blok, "Hedging Foreign Currency Exposure: Consequences of FAS 133," *Journal of Applied Finance,* 11(1), 2001, 25–34; Simon Boughey, "US Issuers in Euromarket Are Snakebit by FAS 133," *Investment Dealers Digest,* February 22, 1999, p. 13; Kolb, B. *Futures, Options, and Swaps,* 3rd Edition, Malden, MA.: Blackwell Publishers, 2000, pp. 779–783; McGee, S. and E. MacDonald, "Pre-emptive Strike by Derivatives Players," *The Wall Street Journal,* February 21, 1997, pp. C1 and C13; and Kuprianov, A., "Derivatives Debacles: Case Studies of Large Losses in Derivatives Markets," *Economic Quarterly,* Federal Reserve Bank of Richmond, Fall 1995, pp. 1–39.

Chapter 7

MANAGING TRANSACTION EXPOSURE
AND ECONOMIC EXPOSURE

Opening Case 7: How CFOs Can Boost Currency Protections

Finance executives at large US companies, including beverage giant Coca-Cola Co. and materials-science company Dow Inc., have increased their foreign currency hedges and covering longer time periods as the strong dollar continues to take a toll on earnings. The dollar in recent quarters has surged against major international currencies as the Federal Reserve's rate increases outpace those of other central banks, making higher-yielding dollar assets more attractive for investors.

The Wall Street Journal Dollar Index, which measures the performance of the US currency against a basket of others, has increased about 15 percent from the beginning of 2022 by the end of October 2022. A strong dollar crimps income from abroad as it gets converted into fewer dollars. Finance chiefs and treasurers have responded by looking for additional protection, as they try to ensure that their overseas earnings are worth a certain amount when translated into US dollars. Changes to companies' hedge contracts include covering larger amounts of earnings as well as longer durations beyond the usual 18 to 24 months.

Here is how Avon Products overcame the Asian Financial Crisis of 1977. Avon Products, Inc. is a global manufacturer and marketer of beauty and related products. In 1996, the Asian market accounted for 16 percent of Avon's total revenues ($4.8 billion). This case recounts how Avon minimized its currency exposure to the Asian financial crisis of 1997–1998 through the use of three hedging techniques: the balance-sheet hedge, leads and lags, and forward contracts.

First, Avon produces and sells all its own products in 10 Asian countries. This strategy, known as the balance-sheet hedge, has enabled Avon to maintain the same amount of exposed assets and exposed liabilities in Asian currencies. Avon suffered neither a gain nor a loss from the Asian crisis because devaluations of the Asian currencies affected both the company's assets and liabilities equally.

Second, when the crisis began in Thailand in July 1997, Avon had its Asian unit remit its earnings weekly rather than monthly (leads) and had, moreover, delayed its dollar payments to some Asian suppliers (lags).

Third, just before other Asian countries allowed their currencies to depreciate, Avon sold about $50 million worth of five Asian currencies forward against the dollar for periods of up to 15 months.[1]

Foreign exchange risk is the risk of loss due to changes in the international exchange value of national currencies. So long as we do not have a single world currency, some degree of exchange risk will exist, no matter what the system. Fluctuations in the value of the currency had been quite frequently pronounced even under the fixed exchange-rate system. A study by DeVries, for example, shows that during the 20-year period from 1948 to 1968, 96 countries devalued their currencies by more than 40 percent, and 24 countries devalued their currencies by more than 75 percent.[2] This problem has become more complicated in the last four decades because most countries have permitted their currencies to float since 1973. Daily currency fluctuations and frequent currency crises have become a way of life since then. Daily currency fluctuations and the increasing integration of the world economy are two major reasons why multinational companies (MNCs) consider exchange-rate risk as the most important one among many risks.

This chapter has three major sections. The first section describes the basic nature of foreign exchange exposure. The second section explains how transaction exposure can be measured and hedged. The third section explains how economic exposure can be measured and hedged.

7.1. BASIC NATURE OF FOREIGN EXCHANGE EXPOSURES

Foreign exchange exposure refers to the possibility that a firm will gain or lose because of changes in exchange rates. Every company faces exposure to foreign exchange risk as soon as it chooses to maintain a physical presence in a foreign country. Likewise, a firm faces exposure to exchange risk when it chooses to finance its operations in foreign currencies. Both exchange risks are analyzed in the context of investing and financing decisions. In addition, foreign trade and loans may involve foreign exchange risk. An important task of the international financial manager is to compare potential losses with the cost of avoiding these losses.

Three basic types of exchange exposures are translation exposure, transaction exposure, and economic exposure. Translation exposure is the accounting-based changes in consolidated financial statements caused by exchange rate changes. Transaction exposure occurs when exchange rates change between the time that an obligation is incurred and the time that it is settled, thereby affecting actual cash flows. Economic exposure reflects the change

---

[1]Trentmann, N., "CFOs Boost Currency Protections, Extend Hedge Contracts as Strong Dollar Takes Toll," *The Wall Street Journal*, November 7, 2022, https://www.wsj.com/articles/cfos-boost-currency-protections-extend-hedge-contracts-as-strong-dollar-takes-toll-11667815634; and Bleakly, "F. R., How US Firm Copes with Asian Crisis: Avon Moves to Protect against Volatile Currencies," *The Wall Street Journal*, December 26, 1997, pp. A2, A4.

[2]DeVries, M. G., "The Magnitude of Exchange Devaluation," *Finance and Development*, No. 2, 1968, pp. 8–16.

in the present value of the firm's future cash flows because of an unexpected change in exchange rates.

7.1.1. *Exposure Management Strategy*

A survey by the Wharton School of the University of Pennsylvania found that an increasing number of US firms hedge against currency risks. The study found that 83 percent of large firms used some form of hedging methods and 45 percent of medium-size firms used a variety of hedging techniques.[3] Most large MNCs manage their foreign exchange risk by using a pre-established exposure management strategy. For example, Merck uses the following five steps for currency exposure management: (1) projecting exchange rate volatility, (2) assessing the impact of the 5-year strategic plan, (3) deciding on hedging the exposure, (4) selecting the appropriate financial instruments, and (5) constructing a hedging program.[4] To protect assets adequately against risks from exchange rate fluctuations, MNCs must (1) forecast the degree of exposure, (2) develop a reporting system to monitor exposure and exchange rate movements, (3) assign responsibility for hedging exposure, and (4) select appropriate hedging tools.

7.1.1.1. *Forecast the degree of exposure*

To develop a viable hedging program, an MNC must forecast the degree of exposure in each major currency in which it operates. Approaches range from gut feelings to sophisticated economic models, each of which has had varying degrees of success. Whatever the approach, the MNC should estimate and use ranges within which it expects a currency to vary over the forecasting period. Some companies develop in-house capabilities to monitor exchange rates, using economists who also try to obtain a consensus of exchange rate movements from the banks with which they deal. Their concern is to forecast the direction, magnitude, and timing of an exchange rate change. Other companies contract out their forecasting needs.

7.1.1.2. *Develop a reporting system to monitor exposure and exchange rate movements*

Once the MNC has decided how to forecast the degree of exposure, it should develop a reporting system that will assist in protecting it against risk. To achieve this goal, substantial participation from foreign operations must be combined with effective central control. Because exchange rates change frequently, MNCs should obtain input from those who are attuned to the foreign country's economy. Central control of exposure protects resources more efficiently than letting each subsidiary monitor its own exposure. The management of the MNC should devise a uniform reporting system for all of its subsidiaries. The report should identify the exposed accounts it wants to monitor, the amount of exposure by currency of each account, and the different times under consideration.

---

[3]Robin, J. A., *International Corporate Finance*, New York: McGraw-Hill/Irwin, 2010, p. 175.
[4]Lewent, J. C. and A. John Kearney, "Identifying, Measuring, and Hedging Currency Risk at Merck," *Journal of Applied Corporate Finance*, Winter 1990, pp. 19–28.

7.1.1.3. *Assign responsibility for hedging exposure*

It is important for management to decide at what level hedging strategies will be determined and implemented. Most MNCs today continue to centralize exchange exposure management because it is impossible for regional or country managers to know how their foreign exchange exposure relates to other affiliates. A three-country study of exchange risk management by Belk found that 66 percent of the sample companies highly centralized their exposure management, 19 percent lowly centralized their exposure management, and only 15 percent decentralized their exposure management.[5] However, a centralized policy may miss opportunities to detect the possibility of currency fluctuations in certain regions or countries. Thus, some MNCs decentralize some exposure management decisions so that it can react quickly to a more rapidly changing international environment.

7.1.1.4. *Select appropriate hedging tools*

Once an MNC has identified its level of exposure and determined which exposure is critical, it can hedge its position by adopting operational techniques and financial instruments. **Operational techniques** are operational approaches to hedging exchange exposure that include diversification of a company's operations, the balance sheet hedge, and exposure netting. **Financial instruments** are financial contracts to hedging exchange exposure that include currency forward and futures contracts, currency options, and swap agreements. This chapter and Chapter 8 will discuss these and other hedging devices in detail.

Coca-Cola is a good example of how MNCs use operational techniques and financial instruments for their foreign exchange exposure management. Because Coca-Cola earns about 80 percent of its operating income from foreign operations, foreign currency changes can have a major impact on reported earnings. The company manages its currency exposures on a consolidated basis, which allows it to net exposures from different operations around the world and takes advantage of natural offsets — for example, cases in which Japanese yen receivables offset Japanese yen payables. It also uses financial contracts to further reduce its net exposure to currency fluctuations. Coca-Cola enters into currency forward contracts and purchases currency options in several countries, most notably the euro and Japanese yen, to hedge firm sales commitments. It also buys currency options to hedge certain anticipated sales.[6]

7.1.2. *Transaction Exposure*

Gains or losses may result from the settlement of transactions whose payment terms are stated in a foreign currency. **Transaction exposure** refers to the potential change in the value of outstanding obligations due to changes in the exchange rate between the inception of a contract and the settlement of the contract. Transactions, which are subject to transaction exposure, include credit purchases and credit sales whose prices are stated in foreign

---

[5]Belk, P. A., "The Organization of Foreign Exchange Risk Management: A Three-Country Study," *Managerial Finance*, 28(11), 2002, pp. 43–52.

[6]Daniels, L. H. R. and D. P. Sullivan, *International Business*, Upper Saddle River, NJ: Prentice-Hall, 2004, p. 620.

currencies, borrowed and loaned funds denominated in foreign currencies, and uncovered forward contracts.

Receipts and payments denominated in foreign currencies are considered to be exposed. If exposed receipts are greater than exposed payments, foreign currency depreciations will cause exchange losses, and foreign currency appreciations will cause exchange gains. On the other hand, if exposed receipts are smaller than exposed payments, foreign currency depreciations will create exchange gains, and foreign currency appreciations will create exchange losses.

Example 7.1

An American firm has sold machinery to a British firm through its UK subsidiary for 10,000 pounds with terms of 180 days. The payments must be received in pounds. The spot rate for pounds is $1.70 and the US seller expects to exchange 10,000 pounds for $17,000 when payment is received.

Transaction exposure arises because of the risk that the US exporter will receive something other than $17,000 when the British pound receipts are exchanged for dollars. If the spot rate declines to $1.40 180 days from today, the US exporter would receive only $14,000, $3,000 less than the expected $17,000. However, if the spot rate rises to $1.90 during the same period, the exporter would receive $19,000, an increase of $2,000 over the amount expected. If the US exporter had invoiced in dollars, the transaction exposure would have shifted to the British importer. Unlike translation gains and losses, transaction gains and losses have a direct impact on actual cash flows.

7.1.3. *Economic Exposure*

Economic exposure, also called operating exposure, competitive exposure, or revenue exposure, measures the impact of an exchange-rate change on the net present value of expected future cash flows from a foreign investment project. Future effects of changes in exchange rates occur under the general category of economic risk. An MNC may have established its subsidiary in a country with price stability, readily available funds, favorable balance of payments, and low rates of taxation. These positive features may disappear over time if the economic situation of the country deteriorates. Eventually, the local currency will devalue or depreciate. The subsidiary is likely to face immediate operational problems if it has to pay for its imports in hard currencies or if it has borrowed from abroad. Exchange rate changes may also affect such economic factors as inflationary forces, price controls, the supply of loanable funds, and local labor availability.

Economic exposure is a broader and more subjective concept of exposure than either translation or transaction exposure because it involves the potential effects of exchange rate changes on all facets of a firm's operations. Economic exposure is difficult to measure but may be more significant than the others because it relates to the long-term profit performance and hence the value of the firm.

Example 7.2

For the coming year, a Malaysian subsidiary of an American firm is expected to earn 35 million ringgits after taxes, and its depreciation charge is estimated at 5 million ringgits.

The exchange rate is expected to decrease from M$4 per dollar at present to M$5 per dollar for the next year.

The difference between the first-year cash flows with and without devaluation is computed as follows:

Profit after taxes   M$35 million
Depreciation   +5 million
Cash flows from operation   M$40 million

Predevaluation rate (M$4 = $1)   M$40 million = $10 million
Postdevaluation rate (M$5 = $1)   M$40 million = −$ 8 million
Potential exchange loss $ 2 million

The subsidiary's economic loss is a decline in Malaysian-ringgit cash flows equal to $2 million over the next 12 months. The translation loss or the transaction loss is a one-time loss, but the economic loss is an open-ended event. If the anticipated business activity were to stay the same for the next 5 years, cash flows would decrease by $2 million per year for 5 years.

7.1.4. *Comparison of the Three Exposures*

The management of foreign-exchange risk based on translation exposure is basically static and historically oriented. By definition, translation exposure does not look to the future impact of an exchange-rate change that has occurred or may occur. In addition, it does not involve actual cash flows. In contrast, both transaction and economic exposures look to the future impact of an exchange-rate change which has occurred or may occur. These exposures also involve actual or potential cash-flow changes.

Transaction risk and economic risk are the same in kind, but they differ in degree. For example, economic risk is essentially subjective because it depends on estimated future cash flows for an arbitrary time horizon. Transaction risk, on the other hand, is essentially objective because it depends on outstanding obligations which existed before changes in exchange rates but were settled after changes in exchange rates. Table 7.1 illustrates the major differences among these three exposures.

7.2. TRANSACTION EXPOSURE MANAGEMENT

An action which removes transaction risk is said to "cover" that risk. A cover involves the use of forward contracts, a combination of spot market and money market transactions, and other techniques to protect against a foreign exchange loss in the conversion from one currency to another. The term, "conversion", relates to transaction exposure because the transaction exposure involves the actual conversion of exposed assets and liabilities from one currency to another. If MNCs decide to cover their transaction exposure, they may select from a variety of financial instruments and operational techniques. Operational techniques, such as exposure netting, leading and lagging, and price adjustments through transfer prices will be discussed in the next chapter. This chapter will focus on the following four financial instruments.

1. Forward market hedge;
2. Money market hedge;

Table 7.1 Major differences among three exposures.

Variables	Translation Exposure	Transaction Exposure	Economic Exposure
Contract	Specific	Specific	General
Duration	A point in time	Period of contract	Project life
Gains (losses)	Easy to compute	Intermediate to compute	Difficult to compute
Measurement	Depends on accounting rules	Depends on actual changes in spot rates	Depends on actual changes in spot rates
Hedging	Easy	Intermediate	Difficult
Extent of Exposure	Determined by accounting rules	Determined by the nature of the contract	Determined by product and market factors
Value	Book value of assets and liabilities	Contract value of assets and liabilities	Market value of assets
Management of exposure	By treasury department	By treasury department	By all departments

3. Options market hedge;
4. Swap agreements.

7.2.1. *Forward Market Hedge*

A **forward exchange-market hedge** involves the exchange of one currency for another at a fixed rate on some future date to hedge transaction exposure. The purchase of a forward contract substitutes a known cost for the uncertain cost due to foreign exchange risk caused by the possible devaluation of one currency in terms of another. Although the cost of a forward contract is usually smaller than the uncertain cost, the forward contract does not always assure the lowest cost due to foreign exchange-rate change. The forward contract simply fixes this cost in advance, thus eliminating the uncertainty caused by foreign exchange-rate changes. For example, an American company may have a euro import payable in nine months. The American company can cover this risk by purchasing euros at a certain price for the same date forward as the payment maturity.

7.2.2. *Money-Market Hedge*

A **money-market hedge** involves a loan contract and a source of funds to carry out that contract in order to hedge transaction exposure. In this case, the contract represents a loan agreement. Assume that an American company has a British pound import payable in 90 days. To hedge transaction exposure from this import payable, the American company may borrow in dollars (loan contract), convert the proceeds into British pounds, buy a 90-day British Treasury bill, and pay the import bill with the funds derived from the sale of the Treasury bill (source of funds). Of course, it can buy British pounds in the foreign exchange spot market when the import bill becomes due, but this approach involves transaction risk.

A money-market hedge is similar to a forward-market hedge. The difference is that the cost of the money-market hedge is determined by differential interest rates while the cost of the forward market approach is determined by the forward premium or discount. If foreign exchange markets and money markets are in equilibrium, the forward market approach and the money market approach incur the same cost.

7.2.3. *Options-Market Hedge*

If a company has a foreign currency receivable or a foreign currency payable, the options-market hedge can protect the company from exchange rate fluctuations. By buying a call option on the foreign currency, a US company can lock in a maximum dollar price for its foreign-currency accounts payable. By purchasing a put option on the foreign currency, the company can lock in a minimum dollar price for its foreign-currency accounts receivable.

Companies understand that hedging techniques such as the forward market hedge and the money-market hedge can backfire or may even be costly when an accounts-payable currency depreciates or an accounts-receivable currency appreciates over the hedged period. Under these circumstances, an uncovered strategy might outperform the forward market hedge or the money-market hedge. The ideal type of hedge should protect the company from adverse exchange rate movements but allow the company to benefit from favorable exchange rate movements. The options-market hedge contains these attributes.

To see how currency options provide such a flexible optional hedge against transaction exposure, assume that Boeing exported a DC10 to British Airways and billed £10 million in 1 year. If Boeing purchases a put option on £10 million, this transaction provides Boeing with the right, but not the obligation, to sell up to £10 million at a fixed exchange rate, regardless of the future spot rate. With its pound receivable, Boeing would protect itself by exercising its put option if the pound weakens, but benefit by letting its put option expire unexercised if the pound strengthens.

7.2.4. *Swap-Market Hedge*

When exchange rates and interest rates fluctuate too widely, the risks of forward market and money market positions are so great that the forward market and the money market may not function properly. Currency options are available only for a selected number of currencies and are inflexible. In such cases, MNCs may use swap arrangements to protect the value of export sales, import orders, and outstanding loans denominated in foreign currencies.

The **swap market hedge** involves an exchange of cash flows in two different currencies between two companies. Swaps take many forms, but one type of swap — currency swap — accommodates an MNC's needs to cover its transaction risk. In a currency swap, one company provides a certain principal in one currency to another company in exchange for an equivalent amount in a different currency. For example, a Swiss company may be anxious to swap Swiss francs for US dollars. Similarly, a US company may be willing to exchange US dollars for Swiss francs. Given these needs, the two companies engage in a currency swap.

Example 7.3

To see how forward exchange-market, money-market, options-market, and swap-market hedges may be utilized to protect against transaction exposure, assume that an American firm has sold an airplane to a Swiss firm for 100,000 francs with terms of 90 days. Let us further assume that the spot rate for francs is $0.5233, the 90-day forward rate for francs is $0.5335, the Swiss 90-day interest rate is 10 percent, and the US 90-day interest rate is 17.8 percent. The interest rates are in equilibrium with forward exchange quotations, and this is confirmed by the following computation using Eq. (4.8):

$$\frac{n\text{-day } F - S}{S} \times \frac{360}{90} = \text{domestic rate} - \text{foreign rate}$$

$$\frac{\$0.5335 - \$0.5233}{\$0.5233} \times \frac{360}{90} = 17.8\% - 10.0\%$$

$$7.8\% = 7.8\%$$

The US company's bank believes that the spot rate in 90 days will rise to $0.6000, which is higher than the implicit unbiased forecast of $0.5335 that exists in the currency forward quotation. In addition, assume that put options with a three-month settlement date have a strike price of $0.5369 per franc and a premium of $0.01 per franc. Finally, a swap dealer says that she will find a Swiss company which is willing to swap Swiss francs for US dollars at an exchange rate of $0.5400 per franc.

Five alternatives are available to the US company: do not hedge (take the transaction risk), hedge in the forward market, hedge in the money market, hedge in the options market, or use swap agreements.

If the US company decides to accept the transaction risk, it would receive 100,000 francs in 90 days and sell them in the foreign exchange market for dollars. If the bank's forecast is accurate, the US company would receive $60,000 ($0.6000 × 100,000 francs) in 90 days. However, that receipt is subject to foreign exchange risk. If the franc should decline to $0.4000, the US company would receive only $40,000, which is $20,000 less than expected. The $40,000 could in fact be insufficient to cover the manufacturing cost of the airplane. On the other hand, if the franc should increase in value even more than the bank's forecast, the US company would receive substantially more than $60,000.

If the US company wishes to hedge its transaction exposure in the forward market, it would sell 100,000 francs in the forward market for $53,350. This is known as a covered transaction in which the US firm no longer has foreign exchange risk. In 90 days, the US firm would receive 100,000 francs from the Swiss importer, deliver the proceeds to the bank against its forward sale, and receive $53,350. It should be recognized that the certain $53,350 is less than the uncertain $60,000 expected from the unhedged position because the forward market quotation is not identical to the bank's forecast.

In addition to the forward market approach, the US company can also cover its transaction against foreign exchange risk through the money-market approach. The money-market approach works as follows: (1) borrow 97,561 francs from a Swiss bank at 10 percent per annum (2.5 percent per quarter) in exchange for a promise to pay 100,000 francs (97,561 francs × 1.025); (2) receive $51,054 (97,561 francs × $0.5233) by exchanging the 97,561 francs for dollars at the current spot rate of $0.5233; (3) invest this sum in the US money market at 17.8 percent per annum (4.45 percent per quarter) and receive $53,326 ($51,054 × 1.0445) at the end of three months. This sum should be equal to the sum received in the forward market hedge described earlier. The small difference between these two sums is due to a compounding error.

The US firm can cover its franc receivables with the put option. The US firm buys put options for a total premium of $1,000 (100,000 francs × $0.01), exercises its options in 90 days, and sells 100,000 francs at a strike price of $0.5369 for $53,690. Thus, the US firm would obtain a net amount of \$52,690 (\$53,690 − \$1,000) in exchange for 100,000 francs at the end of three months. If the spot rate of the Swiss franc should exceed \$0.5369 in 90 days, the US firm would let the option contract expire unexercised and convert the 100,000 francs at the prevailing spot rate.

Finally, the US firm can cover its transaction risk with currency swaps. The US firm is anxious to swap its 100,000 francs for US dollars. Through a swap dealer, it may be able to find a Swiss company which may be willing to exchange US dollars for 100,000 francs. Given these needs, the two companies could arrange a currency swap that allows for an exchange of 100,000 francs for US dollars at a predetermined exchange rate of \$0.5400. In this way, the US company could lock in the number of US dollars at \$54,000 it will receive in exchange for 100,000 francs in 90 days.

7.2.4.1. *Options vs. forward contracts*

A forward contract is often an imperfect hedging instrument because it is a fixed agreement to buy or sell a foreign currency at a specified price in the future. However, in many practical situations, companies are not sure whether their hedged foreign-currency cash flows will materialize. Consider the situations where: (1) an overseas deal may fall through; (2) a bid on a foreign-currency contract may be rejected; and (3) a foreign subsidiary's dividend payments may exceed the expected amount. In such cases, companies may not need the obligation, but the right, to buy or sell a foreign currency at a specified price in order to reduce their exchange-rate risk. Giddy suggested that companies should use the following rules to choose between forward contracts and currency options for hedging purposes[7]:

1. When the quantity of a foreign-currency cash outflow is known, buy the currency forward; when the quantity is unknown, buy a call option on the currency.
2. When the quantity of a foreign-currency cash inflow is known, sell the currency forward; when the quantity is unknown, buy a put option on the currency.
3. When the quantity of a foreign-currency flow is partially known and partially uncertain, use a forward contract to hedge the known portion and an option to hedge the maximum value of the uncertain remainder.

7.2.4.2. *Cross hedging*

A **cross hedge** is a technique designed to hedge exposure in one currency by the use of futures or other contracts on another currency that is correlated with the first currency. Frequently, futures or forward markets are not available for some currencies. In these situations, MNCs may be able to use a substitute or proxy for the underlying currency that is available. The idea behind cross hedging is this. If MNCs cannot find a forward contract on a particular currency in which they have an exposure, they may wish to hedge their exposure through a forward contract on a related currency.

Assume the following four things: (1) a US company has accounts payable in Hong Kong dollars 90 days from now; (2) the Hong Kong dollar expects to appreciate against

---

[7]Giddy, I. H., "The Foreign Exchange Option as a Hedging Tool," *Midland Corporate Finance*, Fall 1983, pp. 32–43.

the US dollar; (3) forward contracts or other hedging techniques are not available for the Hong Kong dollar; and (4) the British pound and the Hong Kong dollar tend to move in a similar direction against the US dollar. In this case, the US firm could effectively hedge this position by using the pound as a proxy forward. In other words, the US firm can eliminate its exchange risk by purchasing the British pound in the forward market.

7.2.5. *Swap Agreements*

Swaps take many forms, but they can be divided into four general categories: currency swaps, credit swaps, interest-rate swaps, and back-to-back loans.

7.2.5.1. *Currency swaps*

A **currency swap** is an agreement between two parties to exchange local currency for hard currency at a specified future date. In other words, a company purchases the specified amount of local currency in the foreign exchange market and simultaneously buys a forward contract to sell this amount of local currency for hard currency at a future date. The former transaction is a spot transaction, and the latter transaction is a forward transaction. Thus, the currency swap is a simultaneous spot and forward transaction. This arrangement allows the company to recover the foreign exchange at a predetermined exchange rate.

To see how a currency swap works, assume that a US parent company wants to lend British pounds to its British subsidiary and to avoid foreign exchange risk. The parent company would buy pounds in the spot market and lend them to the subsidiary. At the same time, the parent firm would sell the same amount of pounds in exchange for dollars in the forward market for the period of the loan. The parent company would receive the loan repayment in terms of pounds from the subsidiary at maturity and exchange the pounds with the dollars to close the forward contract. Alternatively, the US parent could enter into a swap agreement with a foreign exchange dealer where they trade dollars for pounds now and pounds for dollars at maturity.

7.2.5.2. *Credit swaps*

A **credit swap** is a hedging device similar to the foreign currency swap. This arrangement is a simultaneous spot and forward loan transaction between a private company and a bank of a foreign country. Suppose that an American company deposits a given amount of dollars in the New York office of a Colombian bank. In return for this deposit, the bank lends a given amount of pesos to the company's subsidiary in Colombia. The same contract provides that the bank could return the initial amount of dollars to the company on a specified date and that the subsidiary could return the original amount of pesos to the bank on the same day. By so doing, the American company recovers the original dollar amount of its deposit, and the Colombian bank obtains a free hard-currency loan in the United States.

Example 7.4

A subsidiary in Israel requires the Israel shekel equivalent of $1 million at the current exchange rate of NIS4 per dollar, or NIS4 million. To obtain NIS4 million for the subsidiary in Israel, the parent must open a $1 million credit in favor of an Israeli bank. The Israeli bank charges the parent 10 percent per annum on the NIS4 million made available to the subsidiary and pays no interest on the $1 million that the parent has deposited in favor of the bank. The parent's opportunity cost on the $1 million deposit is 20 percent.

The total cost of this swap consists of the parent's opportunity cost and the interest charge on the local currency loan. The opportunity cost at 20 percent on the $1 million is $200,000 and the 10 percent interest on the NIS4 million (NIS400,000) is $100,000 at the prevailing rate of NIS4 per dollar. Thus, the total swap cost is $300,000 on a loan equivalent of $1 million or 30 percent. This example suggests that a direct loan costs the parent 20 percent while the credit swap costs it 30 percent. The parent cannot choose between these two alternatives solely on the basis of comparative costs because the direct loan is unhedged while the credit swap is hedged. The meaningful comparison of the two lending alternatives requires the parent to explicitly consider foreign exchange fluctuations. The direct loan is 10 percent cheaper only if the exchange rate stays the same.

If the MNC is unable to predict future exchange rate changes with a fair degree of accuracy, it may attempt to identify the future exchange rate that equates the cost of the credit swap with the cost of the direct loan. That is to say, the exchange rate where the MNC would be indifferent between the two financing alternatives. Assume that this exchange rate is denoted by y. The cost of the direct loan from the parent consists of $200{,}000y$ = the Israeli shekel cost equivalent of the direct loan ($1 million × 20 percent) plus $(1{,}000{,}000y - 4{,}000{,}000)$ = the potential foreign exchange loss from the repayment of the loan principal ($1 million). The cost of the credit swap consists of $200{,}000y$ = the Israeli shekel cost equivalent of the $1 million deposited in favor of the Israeli bank plus $400{,}000$ = the interest paid on the NIS4 million loan extended by the Israeli bank at 10 percent per annum. Because the cost of the direct loan and the cost of the credit swap are the same at the exchange rate of y, we obtain:

$$\frac{\text{Direct Loan Cost}}{200{,}000y + (1{,}000{,}000y - 4{,}000{,}000)} = \frac{\text{Credit Swap Cost}}{200{,}000y + 400{,}000}$$

$$y = 4.4$$

If the MNC company believes that the foreign exchange rate will not deteriorate to the equilibrium exchange rate of NIS4.4 per dollar, it should choose the unhedged alternative which will be less costly. It should select the hedged alternative whenever its subjective assessment indicates that there is a significant chance for the foreign exchange rate to deteriorate beyond NIS4.4 per dollar.

7.2.5.3. *Interest rate swaps*

Interest rate swaps can be used to alter the exposure of a portfolio of assets or liabilities to interest rate movements. An **interest rate swap** is a technique where companies exchange cash flows of a floating rate for cash flows of a fixed rate, or exchange cash flows of a fixed rate for cash flows of a floating rate. Interest rate swaps are actively used when companies have costs of debt that are fixed but revenues that vary with the level of interest rates.

Take the example of a French company that borrowed $100 million from the Bank of America a year ago at 9.5 percent. The long-term interest rate in the United States has started to fall and the French company believes that it will continue to fall. To take advantage of this drop in interest rates, the French company decides to enter an interest rate swap in dollars. It swaps $100 million with a fixed rate of 9.5 percent for $100 million with a floating rate equal to a six-month SDR rate. In effect, the French company is now protected against a downward movement in interest rates. Conversely, a reverse swap is arranged if the French company believes that the US interest rate will increase.

7.2.5.4. *Back-to-back loans*

Back-to-back loans or parallel loans are arranged by two parent companies in two different countries. Suppose that a US parent has a subsidiary in Japan and that a Japanese parent has a subsidiary in the United States. Let us further assume that each parent wants to lend to its subsidiary in the subsidiary's currency. These loans can be arranged without using the foreign exchange market. The US parent lends the agreed amount in dollars to the American subsidiary of the Japanese parent. In return for this loan, the Japanese parent lends the same amount of money in yen to the Japanese subsidiary of the American parent. Parallel loan agreements involve the same amount of loan and the same loan maturity. Of course, each loan is repaid in the subsidiary's currency. The parallel loan arrangement avoids foreign exchange risk because each loan is made and repaid in one currency.

There are a number of variations on this basic swap scheme. A variation may involve blocked funds. Assume that GM and IBM have their subsidiaries in Colombia. The Colombian subsidiary of GM has idle pesos but can not remit to the United States because of Colombian restrictions on the remittance of funds. On the other hand, the Colombian subsidiary of IBM needs peso loans for expansion. In this case, in Colombia the GM subsidiary lends pesos to the IBM subsidiary, while in the United States IBM lends dollars to GM.

Global Finance in Practice 7: What Risk Management Techniques Do Companies Use?

Andrew Marshall asked 180 multinational firms headquartered in the UK, the USA, and Asia to indicate the currency derivatives contracts they used as foreign exchange risk management techniques. As Table 7.2 indicates, the respondents of all three regions strongly preferred forward contracts as their financial hedging instrument. The most frequently used forward contracts were followed by options and swaps. This same survey showed that the respondents of all regions also used operational techniques, such as netting, leading and lagging, and balance sheet hedge to manage transaction exposure. The survey indicates that many multinational companies employ both financial contracts and operational techniques to deal with transaction exposure.

Table 7.2 Currency derivatives contracts usage by Asian, UK, and US multinational firms.

Type of Product	Percentage of Firms Used		
	Asia	UK	USA
Forward contracts (percent)	88	92	98
Futures contract	24	4	4
Futures options	10	8	9
Options	58	46	43
Swaps	52	36	54

Source: Marshall, A. P., "Foreign exchange risk management in UK, USA and Asia Pacific multinational companies," *Journal of Multinational Financial Management*, June 2000, pp. 185–211.

According to the 2009 survey by the International Swaps and Derivatives Association (ISDA), over 94 percent of the world's 500 largest companies used derivatives to help manage their risks. These 500 companies with their headquarters in 32 different countries represented a broad range of industries from basic materials to office equipment to retail and even health care. All companies in Canada, France, Great Britain, Japan, and the Netherlands reported the use of derivatives to alleviate their risks. The survey found that foreign exchange derivatives were the most widely used instruments (88 percent of the sample), followed by interest rate derivatives (83 percent) and commodity derivatives.[8]

7.3. ECONOMIC EXPOSURE MANAGEMENT

Companies can easily hedge translation and transaction exposures because these risks are based on projected foreign-currency cash flows. However, it is exceedingly difficult, if not impossible, for companies to hedge economic exposure for several reasons. The scope of economic exposure is broad because it can change a company's competitiveness across many markets and products. A company always faces economic risks from competition. When based in foreign currencies, the risks are long-term, hard to quantify, and cannot be dealt with solely through financial hedging techniques.

As a result, international financial managers should assess economic exposure comprehensively. Their analysis should account for how variations in exchange rates influence: (1) a company's sales prospects in foreign markets (product market); (2) the costs of labor and other inputs to be used in overseas production (factor market); and (3) the home-currency value of financial assets and liabilities denominated in foreign currencies (capital market). Consequently, those techniques used to eliminate translation and transaction risks — forwards, money markets, options, swaps, leads and lags of inter-subsidiary accounts, and transfer pricing adjustments are not feasible for hedging economic exposure.

Economic exposure management is designed to neutralize the impact of unexpected exchange-rate changes on net cash flows. Diversified operations and financing can reduce economic exposure. They permit the MNC to react to those opportunities which disequilibrium conditions in the foreign exchange, capital, and product markets present. Moreover, diversification strategies do not require that management predict disequilibrium conditions. Still, they require that it recognizes them when they occur. In other words, the primary technique to minimize economic risk is strategic management in choosing product markets, pricing policies, promotion, and investment and financing alternatives.

---

[8]Schieffer, J., "Over 94% of the World's Largest Companies Use Derivatives to Help Manage Their Risks, According to ISDA Survey," The International Swaps and Derivatives Association (ISDA), April 23, 2009, https://derivsource.com/2009/04/23/over-94-of-the-worlds-largest-companies-use-derivatives-to-help-manage-their-risks-according-to-isda-survey/#:~:text=(ISDA)%20today%20announced%20the%20results, their%20business%20and%20financial%20risks.

When managing economic exposure, MNCs resort to maneuvers across functional areas of operations. The functional areas of business operations for MNCs are production, marketing, and finance. Production and marketing are clearly critical because they determine a company's existence — its ability to produce products and to sell them at a profit. But finance is an integral part of total management and cuts across functional boundaries.

Economic exposure management depends on the assumption that disequilibrium conditions exist in national markets for factors of production, products, and financial assets. For example, consider the cases where there are temporary deviations from purchasing power parity and the International Fisher Effect. Companies could observe changes in comparative costs, profit margins, and sales volume in one country compared to another.

7.3.1. *Diversified Production*

Several production strategies can deal with economic exposure when disequilibrium conditions exist: (1) plant location, (2) input mix, (3) product sourcing, and (4) productivity increase.

First, companies with manufacturing facilities in many countries can quickly lengthen their production runs in one country and shorten them in another in line with the changing currency costs of production. Second, well-managed companies can substitute their input mix between domestic and imported inputs, depending on the relative prices of inputs and the degree of possible substitution. Third, well diversified companies can make shifts in sourcing raw materials, components, and products in accordance with currency value fluctuations. Fourth, companies assaulted by wide swings in currency values can improve productivity by closing inefficient plants, automating production processes, and negotiating concessions from unions.

7.3.2. *Diversified Marketing*

Marketing programs are normally adjusted only after changes in exchange rates. Yet, marketing initiatives under conditions of exchange-rate changes can obtain competitive leverage: (1) product strategy, (2) pricing strategy, (3) promotional options, and (4) market selection.

First, product differentiation, diversification, and deletions reduce the impact of exchange-rate fluctuations on worldwide corporate earnings. Second, prices may be adjusted to cope with the consequences of currency-value changes. A pricing strategy is affected by a variety of factors such as market share, profit margin, competition, and price elasticity. Third, the size of promotional budgets for advertising, personal selling, and merchandising could be adjusted to reflect changes in currency values. For example, a devaluation of the Japanese yen may well be the time to increase a US company's advertising budget in Japan. Fourth, a worldwide distribution system enables companies to neutralize the impact of unexpected exchange-rate changes on overall company revenues.

7.3.3. *Diversified Financing*

On the financial side, additional tools to protect against economic risk are the currency denomination of long-term debt, place of issue, maturity structure, capital structure, and leasing versus buying. For example, LSI Corporation, a manufacturer of custom-made microchips based in California, uses four financial instruments: (1) equity markets in London and other European markets; (2) Japanese equity through institutional investors such as Nomura Securities; (3) local Japanese credit markets through its joint venture partners; and (4) Eurobond issues through Swiss and US securities firms.

Diversified financing sources allow a company to improve its overall financial performance because interest-rate differentials do not always equal expected changes in exchange rates. In addition to taking advantage of unexpected differentials in diversified markets, companies reduce economic risk by matching the mix of currencies in loan portfolios or operating expenses to the mix of currencies in expected revenues.

7.3.4. *Summary of Economic Exposure Management*

Purely domestic companies do not have as many options for reacting to international disequilibrium conditions as MNCs. International diversification neutralizes the impact of unexpected exchange-rate changes on corporate cash flows. Exchange rate changes under conditions of disequilibrium are likely to increase competitiveness in some markets and to reduce it in others. However, at least one serious constraint may limit the feasibility of a diversification strategy: companies with worldwide production systems may have to relinquish large economies of scale. However, these companies could still diversify sales functions and financing sources.

7.4. SUMMARY

This chapter has discussed two foreign exchange exposures and their management. Every single company faces an exposure to gain or loss from changes in exchange rates because globalization is totally re-shaping the way we live and do business. Transaction exposure refers to possible gains or losses which may result from the settlement of transactions whose payment terms are stated in a foreign currency. Economic exposure measures the total impact of exchange rate changes on a firm's profitability.

In essence, a hedge or a cover is a type of insurance that provides security against the risk of loss from a change in exchange rates. When devaluation seems likely, the MNC must determine whether it has any unwanted net exposure to foreign exchange risk. When the company finds that it has an unwanted net exposure to exchange risk, it can use a variety of operational techniques and financial instruments to reduce this net exposure. They include forward market hedge, money-market hedge, options-market hedge, swaps, and others. These financial instruments are primarily used to minimize transaction exposures. Economic exposure can be managed by balancing the sensitivity of revenues and expenses of changes to exchange rates through diversification and strategic planning.

7.5. KEY TERMS

foreign exchange exposure	operational techniques
financial instruments	transactional exposure
economic exposure	forward exchange-market hedge
money-market hedge	swap-market hedge
cross hedge	currency swap

credit swap	interest rate swap
back-to-back loans	translation exposure
current-noncurrent method	monetary-nonmonetary method
temporal method	current-rate method
parent currency	functional currency
hedge	balance-sheet hedge
exposure netting	lagging
leading	transfer prices

7.6. PROBLEMS

1. A US company negotiated a forward contract to buy 100,000 British pounds in 90 days. The company was supposed to use the 100,000 pounds to buy British supplies. The 90-day forward rate was $1.40 per pound. On the day the pounds were delivered in accordance with the forward contract, the spot rate of the pound was $1.44. What was the real cost of hedging the pound payables in this example?

2. Boeing sold an airplane to Korean Airlines for 840 million won with terms of 1 year. Boeing will receive its payment in Korean won. The spot rate for the Korean currency is 700 won per dollar and Boeing expects to exchange 840 million won for $1.2 million (840 million ÷ 700) when payment is received.

   a. If the spot rate for won rises to 600 won per dollar 1 year from today, what is the potential transaction gain or loss?

   b. If the spot rate for won declines to 1,000 won per dollar at maturity, what is the potential transaction gain or loss?

3. For the coming year, a Singapore subsidiary of an American company is expected to earn an after-tax profit of S$25 million and its depreciation charge is estimated at S$5 million. The exchange rate is expected to rise from S$2.00 per dollar to S$1.5 per dollar for the next year.

   a. What is the potential economic gain or loss?

   b. If the anticipated business activity were to stay the same for the next 3 years, what would be the total economic gain or loss for 3 years?

4. A US company purchased several boxes of watches from a Swiss company for 300,000 francs. This payment must be made in Swiss francs 90 days from today. The following quotations and expectations exist:

90-day US interest rate	4.00 percent
90-day Swiss interest rare	3.00 percent
90-day forward rate for francs	$0.400
Spot rate for francs	$0.404

   Would the company be better off using the forward market hedge or the money market hedge?

5. For the coming year, a British subsidiary of an American company is expected to incur an after-tax loss of £50 million and its depreciation charge is estimated at £10 million. The exchange rate is expected to rise from $1.5 per pound to $1.7 per pound for the next year. What is the potential economic gain or loss?

6. A US company has bought a number of TV sets from a Japanese company for 100,000 yen. This payment must be made in Japanese yen 180 days from today. The following quotations and expectations exist:

Present spot rate	$0.0050
180-day forward rate	$0.0051
Japanese interest rate	7.00 percent
US interest rate	11.00 percent
Highest expected spot rate 180 days hence	$0.0052
Lowest expected spot rate 180 days hence	$0.0046

The US company does not have any idle dollar balances at present, but it expects to have adequate cash in 180 days. Identify the alternatives available for making payment.

7. An American firm has just sold merchandise to a British customer for 100,000 pounds, with payment in British pounds three months from now. The US company has purchased from its bank a three-month put option on 100,000 pounds at a strike price of $1.6660 per pound and a premium cost of $0.01 per pound. On the day the option matures, the spot exchange rate is $1.7100 per pound. Should the US company exercise the option at that time or sell British pounds in the spot market?

8. Assume that a subsidiary in New Zealand needs $NZ500,000 and that a credit swap has been proven the least costly-hedged alternative. Further assume that the best unhedged alternative is the direct loan from the parent and the cost of the direct loan is 20 percent. The current exchange rate is $0.5000 per New Zealand dollar. To obtain $NZ500,000 for the subsidiary in New Zealand, the parent must open a $250,000 credit ($0.5000 × $NZ500,000) in favor of a New Zealand bank. The New Zealand bank charges 10 percent per year on the $NZ500,000 made available to the subsidiary and pays no interest on the $250,000 deposit that the parent has deposited in the bank.

   a. What is the exchange rate which would make the direct loan and the credit swap equally attractive?

   b. If most market analysts predict that the exchange rate will be $NZ2 per dollar in 180 days, which alternative would you recommend?

   c. If most market analysts predict that the exchange rate will be $NZ3 per dollar in 180 days, which alternative would you recommend?

   d. If the New Zealand bank should pay 5 percent interest on the $250,000 credit, what is the exchange rate that would make the direct loan and the credit swap equally attractive?

Closing Case 7: Foreign Exchange Risk Management

Foreign exchange risk is a currency risk that exists when a financial transaction is denominated in a currency other than the domestic currency of the company. The exchange risk arises when there is a risk of an unfavorable change in exchange rate between the domestic currency and the denominated currency before the date when the transaction is completed.

Foreign exchange risk also exists when the foreign subsidiary of a firm maintains financial statements in a currency other than the domestic currency of the consolidated entity.

Investors and businesses exporting or importing goods and services, or making foreign investments, have an exchange-rate risk but can take steps to manage (i.e., reduce) the risk.

Many businesses were unconcerned with, and did not manage, foreign exchange risk under the international Bretton Woods system. It was not until the switch to floating exchange rates, following the collapse of the Bretton Woods system, that firms became exposed to an increased risk from exchange rate fluctuations and began trading an increasing volume of financial derivatives in an effort to hedge their exposure. The currency crises of the 1990s and early 2000s, such as the Mexican peso crisis, Asian currency crisis, 1998 Russian financial crisis, and the Argentine peso crisis, led to substantial losses from foreign exchange and led firms to pay closer attention to their foreign exchange risk.

Case Questions

1. Evaluate pros and cons of various exchange-hedging instruments and techniques.
2. What are the different types of foreign exchange risk major multinational companies such as GM will encounter?
3. Explain why many multinational companies such as Hyundai Motor Co. of Korea borrows in a basket of currencies rather than exclusively in a single foreign currency or Korean currency called "won."
4. What are two ways to hedge economic exposure?
5. Explain why many multinational companies do not hedge their economic exposure (i.e., future foreign-currency revenues).
6. The websites for various multinational companies disclose exchange-rate hedging activities and their exchange gains or losses. (*Hint*: see footnotes of annual reports.) Based on the website of IBM www.ibm.com and the website of British Petroleum https://www.bp.com/, describe the management of foreign exchange risk for either company.

Source: https://en.wikipedia.org/wiki/Foreign_exchange_risk, accessed August 30, 2022.

Chapter 8

TRANSLATION EXPOSURE MANAGEMENT

Opening Case 8: Main Features of Accounting Exposure

Translation exposure has these main features:

1. Because accounting exposure, commonly known as translation exposure, is based on book values only, it does not reflect the true economic value a company has at risk. By the same token, the gains and losses of foreign-exchange trading as measured by this concept bear no relationship to the real impact exchange rate changes have on the value of the firm itself. They are purely of a paper nature.
2. In connection with the above feature, accounting exposure is incapable of encompassing the various and complex ways in which exchange rate changes will really affect a company.
3. Accounting exposure is a function of the method used in translating foreign-currency financial statements. The application of different translation methods may lead to very different account exposures and to different bases for corporate decision-making.
4. Accounting exposure is a concept that is static and historically oriented rather than dynamic and geared toward the future; in other words, it measures assets and liabilities for given past dates instead of flows of currencies over future periods of time. Under this accounting concept, the exposure of two companies may show exactly the same values although they can be in different economic situations and would be affected differently by exchange rate changes.[1]

Translation exposure, sometimes called accounting exposure, measures the effect of an exchange rate change on published financial statements of a firm. Foreign-currency assets and liabilities that are translated at the current exchange rate are considered to be exposed. In accounting terms, the difference between exposed assets and exposed liabilities is frequently called net exposure. If exposed assets are greater than exposed liabilities, foreign currency depreciations will result in exchange losses and foreign currency appreciations will produce

---

[1]Glau, M., "Strategic Management of Exchange Rate Risks," *Long Range Planning*, August 1990, pp. 65–75.

exchange gains. On the other hand, if exposed assets are smaller than exposed liabilities, foreign currency depreciations will lead to exchange gains and foreign currency appreciations will lead to exchange losses.

This chapter has three major sections. The first section discusses four translation rules commonly used by multinational companies (MNCs) to consolidate their worldwide operations into home currency. The second section analyzes major differences between two major translation rules: FASB no. 8 and FASB no. 52. The third section considers some techniques designed to reduce translation risk.

8.1. TRANSLATION RULES

Before we discuss translation rules, we will look at a numerical example to see how net exchange gains or losses occur.

Example 8.1

A US parent company has a single wholly-owned subsidiary in Malaysia. This subsidiary has exposed assets of 100 million ringgits and exposed liabilities of 50 million ringgits. The exchange rate declines from M$4 per dollar to M$5 per dollar.

The potential-foreign-exchange loss on the company's exposed net assets of 50 million ringgits would be $2.5 million:

Exposed assets	M$100 million
Exposed liabilities	−M$50 million
Net exposure	M$50 million

Predevaluation rate (M$4 = $1)	M$50 million =	$12.5 million
Postdevaluation rate (M$5 = $1)	M$50 million =	−$10.0 million
Potential exchange loss		$2.5 million

These translation gains and losses do not involve actual cash flows because they are only translated into dollars, not converted into dollars. In other words, they are purely of a paper nature. Some companies are concerned about this risk because it affects their ability to raise capital, cost of capital, earnings per share, stock price, and key financial ratios.

Financial statements are intended to present information about the performance, financial position, and cash flows of a company. To meet this purpose, the financial statements of separate entities within a business enterprise are consolidated and presented as though they were the financial statements of a single economic entity. Financial statements are frequently restated or translated from one currency into another to assist the users of the financial statements such as investors and creditors.

Accounting for foreign currency translation is undoubtedly one of the most controversial technical issues facing MNCs. Many of the problems associated with currency translation come from the fact that foreign exchange rates, used to carry out the translation process, are seldom fixed. Consequently, actual operating results can vary, often markedly, from reported results because of differences in the translation rates employed. This is why foreign currency translation has become even more controversial and important since 1973 when the flexible exchange-rate system was established. This flexible exchange system abolished the old fixed exchange-rate system that was established in 1944 based on the Bretton Woods Agreement.

If exchange rates have changed since the previous accounting period, the translation of financial statement items denominated in foreign currencies will result in foreign exchange gains or losses. The possible extent of these gains or losses often depends on the rules that govern translation. The four translation methods most widely used by MNCs are current-noncurrent, monetary–nonmonetary, temporal, and current rate.

8.1.1. *Current/Noncurrent Method*

In using this, one assumes that financial-statement accounts should be grouped according to maturity. Under the **current–noncurrent method**, all current assets and current liabilities of foreign affiliates are translated into the parent currency at current exchange rates. All noncurrent assets, noncurrent liabilities, and owners' equity are translated at historical exchange rates.

8.1.2. *Monetary/Nonmonetary Method*

Under the **monetary–nonmonetary method**, monetary assets and monetary liabilities are translated at current exchange rates. Nonmonetary assets, nonmonetary liabilities, and owners' equity are translated at historical rates. Monetary assets include cash, accounts receivable, and notes receivable. Nonmonetary assets include inventory and fixed assets. In general, all liabilities are monetary liabilities.

8.1.3. *Temporal Method*

The **temporal method** produces essentially the same results as the monetary-nonmonetary method under generally accepted accounting principles of historical accounting in the United States. The only difference is that under the monetary–nonmonetary method, inventory is always translated at the historical rate. Under the temporal method, inventory is usually translated at the historical rate, but it could be translated at the current rate if inventory is carried at market prices or at replacement costs.

8.1.4. *Current Rate Method*

The **current-rate method** is the simplest; all assets and liabilities are translated at the current rate. Existing equity accounts such as common stock and paid-in capital are translated at the historical rate.

8.1.5. *Comparison of the Four Translation Methods*

All financial-statement items restated in terms of the parent currency are the foreign currency amount multiplied by the appropriate exchange rate. Table 8.1 compares the four-translation methods — current–noncurrent, monetary–nonmonetary, temporal, and current rate — in terms of the exchange rate for each balance-sheet item.

Table 8.1   Exchange rates used to translate balance-sheet items.

Balance-Sheet Accounts	Current/ Noncurrent	Monetary/ Nonmonetary	Temporal	Current Rate
Cash	C	C	C	C
Receivables	C	C	C	C
Payables	C	C	C	C
Inventory	C	H	H or C	C
Fixed assets	H	H	H	C
Long-term debt	H	C	C	C
Net worth	H	H	H	H

Note: C represents the current rate and H represents the historical rate.

Table 8.2   Comparison of four translation methods.

Accounts	Foreign Currency	Current/ Noncurrent		Monetary/ Nonmonetary		Temporal		Current Rate	
Cash	FC100	1	$100	1	$100	1	$100	1	$100
Receivables	150	1	150	1	150	1	150	1	150
Inventory	200	1	200	2	400	1	200	1	200
Fixed assets	250	2	500	2	500	2	500	1	250
Total	FC700		$950		$1,150		$950		$700
Current debts	FC100	1	$100	1	$100	1	$100	1	$100
Long-term debt	300	2	600	1	300	1	300	1	300
Net worth	300	2	600	2	600	2	600	2	600
Gains (losses)			(350)		150		(50)		(300)
Total	FC700		$950		$1,150		$950		$700

Example 8.2

Assume that a foreign subsidiary of a US MNC has the following: (1) cash = FC100; (2) accounts receivable = FC150; (3) inventory = FC200; (4) fixed assets = FC250; (5) current liabilities = FC100; (6) long-term debt = FC300; and (7) net worth = FC300. Let us further assume that the historical exchange rate is $2 = FC1, the current exchange rate is $1 = FC1, and inventory is carried at market prices. Remember that the functional currency (FC) depreciates from $2 per FC to $1 per FC.

Table 8.2 illustrates the effect of each translation method on the balance sheet. Exchange gains or losses are shown here as a separate plug (balancing) account to show how they would be derived. However, in actual practice net worth would be used as a plug figure, or exchange gains and losses would be closed out to retained earnings.

Under the current–noncurrent method, an exchange loss of $350 is recorded because current assets are greater than current liabilities. On the other hand, under the monetary–nonmonetary method, an exchange gain of $150 is recorded because monetary liabilities exceed monetary assets. Under the current rate method, the exchange loss is $300 for two reasons: (1) all accounts except net worth are translated at the current exchange rate and (2) exposed assets are greater than exposed liabilities.

8.2. FASB NO. 8 AND FASB NO. 52

The accounting profession has recognized the growing importance of foreign currency transactions and/or foreign operations. In October 1975, the Financial Accounting Standards Board (FASB) issued its Statement No. 8, *Accounting for the Translation of Foreign Currency Transactions and Foreign Currency Financial Statements*. FASB No. 8 formerly required US companies to translate their foreign-currency financial statements into dollars by applying the appropriate exchange rate to the measurement basis of each account; the appropriate exchange rate may be the historical rate, the current rate, or the average rate. This statement also requires companies to show all foreign exchange gains or losses in their quarterly and annual income statements, regardless of whether these gains or losses were realized or unrealized.

FASB No. 8 was a product of considerable effort, including extensive exposure drafts and discussion memoranda, by the FASB to resolve the translation issue. However, from its inception in Autumn 1975, FASB No. 8 was the subject of extensive debate; most of the criticism centered on recognizing foreign exchange gains or losses. Companies claimed that FASB No. 8 grossly distorted their earnings because of the sharp fluctuations in foreign exchange rates. The FASB issued its Statement No. 52, *Foreign Currency Translation*, on December 7, 1981. FASB No. 52 supersedes FASB No. 8. In 1982, US companies were allowed to utilize either FASB No. 8 or FASB No. 52. Ford used FASB No. 52 in 1982 to exclude its translation loss of about $220 million from the income statement. In the same year, General Motors employed FASB No. 8 to include its translation gain of about $384 million in the income statement.

FASB No. 52 requires the use of the current exchange rate in translating foreign-currency financial statements into US dollars. Such translation adjustments are placed directly in stockholders' equity rather than income. Thus, FASB No. 52 has substantially reduced fluctuations in many companies' reported earnings caused by gyrations in foreign exchange rates under FASB No. 8.

8.2.1. *Functional Currency*

In this section, two terms are extensively used: parent currency and functional currency. **Parent currency**, sometimes called reporting currency, is the currency of the country where the parent company is located. For example, the parent currency of US-based MNCs is the dollar. The **functional currency**, usually called foreign currency or local currency, is the currency of the country where the foreign operation of an MNC is located. The functional currency of an entity, as defined in FASB No. 52 (paragraph 39), is "the currency of the primary economic environment in which the entity operates; normally, that is the currency of the environment in which an entity primarily generates and expends cash."

The term, "functional currency", was first used in the translation literature in conjunction with FASB No. 52. Functional currency is, in fact, a key feature of FASB No. 52 because it determines the choice of translation method. This feature is very important because the translation method employed determines the translation rate and the disposition of exchange gains and losses. If the foreign currency is determined to be the functional currency, FASB No. 52 is used to carry out the translation process. On the other hand, if the US dollar is deemed to be the functional currency, FASB No. 8 is used to remeasure foreign currency operations in dollars.

Normally, a foreign subsidiary's functional currency is the currency of the foreign country in which it operates and generates net cash flows. For example, a French subsidiary with relatively contained and integrated operations in France would have the euro as its functional currency. Such translation adjustments do not affect cash flows and are not included in net income. Consequently, translation adjustments are placed directly in stockholders' equity. However, if the French subsidiary has some transactions and open account balances denominated in Swiss francs from a Swiss customer, those balances must be restated into euros and gains or losses must be included in the subsidiary's net income before the statements are translated into US dollars during the consolidation process.

The functional currency of an entity is not always identical with the currency of the country in which the foreign operation is located or the currency of the country in which the records are maintained. The dollar is the functional currency and exchange gains or losses must be included in the net income for those foreign operations whose cash flows directly affect the parent's US dollar cash flows on a current basis. Such a situation may occur when the foreign entity is merely an extension of the parent company. In this case, the functional currency is the reporting currency of the parent company. For example, if the Mexican subsidiary of a US parent company received all of its raw materials from the United States and resold all of its output back to the United States, the US dollar should be the functional currency.

Foreign subsidiaries in countries with runaway inflation are another case in which the reporting currency is used as the functional currency. FASB No. 52 (paragraph 11) states that "the financial statements of a foreign entity in a highly inflationary economy shall be remeasured as if the functional currency were the reporting currency." A highly inflationary economy is defined as one that has cumulative inflation of approximately 100 percent or more over a 3-year period. The cumulative inflation for 3 years is a compounded rate; as a result, an annual inflation rate of about 26 percent produces a cumulative inflation of 100 percent over 3 years.

8.2.2. *Differences Between FASB Nos. 8 and 52*

The underlying assumption of FASB No. 8 was that consolidated financial statements should reflect the transactions of the consolidated group as though all operations, including foreign operations, were extensions of the parent's domestic operations. This premise failed to recognize the fact that in many cases the operations of foreign subsidiaries exist in other environments and involve foreign-currency cash flows in those other environments. Thus, the results of accounting after translation did not correctly portray the foreign-currency cash flows.

FASB No. 52 is intended to portray foreign-currency cash flows. Companies using the functional currency approach and the current rate method can maintain compatible income and cash flows before and after translation. Financial summary indicators, such as profit margin, gross profit, and debt-to-equity ratio, are almost the same after translation into the reporting currency as they are in the functional currency. In addition, the volatility of a company's reported earnings should be reduced under FASB No. 52 because its foreign exchange gains or losses are placed directly in stockholders' equity rather than in income.

8.2.3. *Translation of Foreign Currency Financial Statements*

FASB No. 8 had formally required US firms to use the temporal method from 1976 until the FASB replaced it with FASB No. 52 in December 1981. According to the temporal method, balance-sheet items carried at current or future prices should be translated at the current exchange rate, while balance-sheet items carried at historical prices should be translated at the applicable historical rate. Under this method, sales revenue and operating expenses are translated at the average exchange rate, while cost of goods sold and depreciation are translated at the applicable historical rate. Exchange gains or losses from the translation of the balance sheet should be included in the income statement.

Under FASB No. 52, the current exchange-rate method is used to translate foreign currency balance sheets from their functional currency into the reporting currency. The current exchange-rate method is the easiest to apply because under this method, all assets and liabilities are translated at the current exchange rate. Only owners' equity is translated at the historical exchange rate. Unlike the controversial FASB No. 8, FASB No. 52 does not require companies to include translation adjustments in net income. Instead, a company will report these translation adjustments separately and accumulate them in a separate component of equity until it sells or substantially liquidates the foreign net investment.

Under FASB No. 52, all income-statement elements are translated in a manner that produces approximately the same result as using the exchange rate in effect on the dates on which these elements are recognized. However, paragraph 12 of FASB No. 52 provides that "because translation at the exchange rates on the dates the numerous revenues, expenses, gains, and losses are recognized is generally impractical, an appropriately weighted average exchange rate for the period may be used to translate those elements."

Example 8.3

The Canadian subsidiary of a US multinational corporation with a Canadian dollar functional currency started business and acquired fixed assets on January 1, 2014, when the Canadian dollar/US dollar exchange rate was 0.85. Table 8.3 applies the temporal method and the current exchange-rate method to hypothetical financial statements which are affected by an 11.8 percent devaluation of the Canadian dollar. For this devaluation, the exchange rate on December 31, 2014 was 0.75 and the weighted average rate for the period was 0.80.

Table 8.3 shows that fluctuations in reported earnings in this example are reduced significantly under FASB No. 52 because we used a single rate in translating balance-sheet items and reported translation adjustments in equity. Under the New standard, moreover, net income of the US parent company is the same as what is expected based on the level of earnings in Canadian dollars.

Under FASB No. 52, a translation loss of $11 is the expected economic effect of the Canadian dollar whose value declined against the US dollar. This translation loss of $11 is reported in the balance sheet as "equity adjustments from translation." On the other hand,

Table 8.3   Translation of foreign currency operations under FASB Nos. 8 and 52.

	Canadian Dollars	FASB No. 8		FASB No. 52	
		Rates Used	US Dollars	Rates Used	US Dollars
Balance Sheet					
Cash and receivables	100	0.75	75	0.75	75
Inventory	300	0.81*	243	0.75	225
Fixed assets, net	600	0.85	510	0.75	450
Total	1,000		828		750
Current Liabilities	180	0.75	135	0.75	135
Long-term debt	700	0.75	525	0.75	525
Common Stock	100	0.85	85	0.85	85
Retained Earnings	20		83		16
Equity Adjustments from translation					−11
Total	1,000		828		750
Income Statement					
Revenue	130	0.80	104	0.80	104
Cost of goods sold	−60	0.83*	−50	0.80	−48
Depreciation	−20	0.85*	−17	0.80	−16
Other expenses	−10	0.80	−8	0.80	−8
Exchange gain (loss)			70		
Income before tax	40		99		32
Income tax	−20	0.80	−16	0.80	−16
Net income	20		83		16
Ratios					
Net income to revenue	0.15	0.80		0.15	
Gross profit margin	0.54	0.52		0.54	
Long-term debt to equity	5.83	3.13		5.83	

Note: *Historical rates for inventory, cost of goods sold, and depreciation of fixed assets.

FASB No. 8 required the US parent company to report a translation gain of $70 in the income statement.

Under FASB No. 52, key Canadian-dollar ratios, such as net income to revenue, gross profit, and long-term debt to equity, are maintained after translation from the Canadian dollar to the US dollar. However, these ratios in the Canadian dollar are significantly different from those in the US dollar under FASB No. 8.

8.3. HEDGING TRANSLATION EXPOSURE

When a devaluation or upvaluation seems likely, a company must determine whether it has an unwanted net exposure to exchange risk. Management's basic objective with any exposure is to minimize the amount of probable exchange losses and the cost of protection. **Hedge** is an approach designed to reduce or offset a possible loss. An arrangement that eliminates translation risk is said to hedge that risk. A hedge is designed to substitute a known cost of buying protection against foreign exchange risk for an unknown translation loss. One can use a variety of techniques to deal with translation exposure. These techniques consist of one major group of hedging devices: a balance-sheet hedge.

8.3.1. *Balance-Sheet Hedge*

Balance-sheet hedges are generally employed to minimize translation exposure. A **balance-sheet hedge** involves the selection of the currency in which exposed assets and liabilities are denominated so that an exchange-rate change would make exposed assets equal to exposed liabilities. To attain this objective, a company must maintain the same amount of exposed assets and exposed liabilities in a particular currency. A devaluation would affect both types of balance-sheet accounts equally; thus, the company would suffer neither a gain nor a loss.

When an MNC has several subsidiaries, a variety of funds adjustment techniques can be used to reduce its translation loss. These techniques require the company to adopt the following two basic strategies:

1. The company must decrease soft-currency assets and increase soft-currency liabilities.
2. The company must increase hard-currency assets and decrease hard-currency liabilities.

Hard currencies are those currencies which are likely to appreciate; soft currencies are those currencies which are likely to depreciate.

Most techniques for hedging an impending local currency (soft currency) devaluation reduce local-currency assets and/or increase local-currency liabilities to generate local-currency cash. In order to reduce translation exposure, these local-currency funds must be converted into hard-currency assets. This conversion can be accomplished, either directly or indirectly, by a variety of funds adjustment techniques. Direct funds-adjustment techniques include pricing exports in hard currencies and imports in the local currency, investing in hard-currency securities, and replacing hard-currency loans with local-currency loans.

8.3.2. *Indirect Fund-Adjustment Methods*

A variety of indirect fund-adjustment methods can be used to reduce foreign currency exposure.

8.3.2.1. *Exposure netting*

MNCs can net certain exposures from different operations around the world so that they may hedge only their net exposure. For example, when an MNC has both receivables and payables in a given foreign currency, these receivables and payables can be offset through netting, which will reduce the amount of foreign exchange exposure. **Exposure netting** is a method of offsetting exposures in one currency with exposures in the same or another currency in such a way that gains or losses on the first exposure will be offset by losses or gains on the second exposure. Unlike the simple case we discussed exposure netting on a currency-by-currency basis above, MNCs have a portfolio of currency positions. If MNCs want to apply exposure netting aggressively, it helps to centralize their exposure management function in one location.

8.3.2.2. *Leading and lagging*

Leading and lagging is another operational technique that MNCs can use to reduce foreign exchange exposure. **Leading** means to pay or collect early, whereas **lagging** means to pay or collect late. MNCs should lead soft currency receivables and lag hard currency receivables to avoid the loss from the depreciation of the soft currency and to obtain the gain from the appreciation of the hard currency. For the same reason, MNCs will try to lead hard currency payables and to lag soft currency payables.

8.3.2.3. *Transfer pricing*

Transfer prices are prices of goods and services sold between related parties, such as a parent and its subsidiary. Transfer prices are frequently different from arm's length prices (fair market prices) so that they can be used to avoid foreign currency exposure. For example, an MNC can remove funds from soft-currency countries by charging higher transfer prices on goods sold to its subsidiaries in those countries. For the same reason, an MNC can keep funds at those subsidiaries in hard-currency countries by charging lower prices on goods sold to its subsidiaries in those countries. Governments usually assume that MNCs manipulate their transfer prices to avoid financial problems or to improve financial conditions. Thus, most governments set up policing mechanisms to review the transfer pricing policies of MNCs.

Global Finance in Practice 8: Translation Risk Management by McDonald's

There are various financial products that companies can use to mitigate or reduce translation risk. One of the most popular products is called a forward contract, which locks in an exchange rate for a period of time. The rate lock allows companies to fix the value of their foreign assets based on the forward contract's exchange rate.

Companies that sell products overseas and earn foreign revenue can request that their foreign clients pay for goods and services in the company's home currency. As a result, the risk associated with local currency fluctuations would not be borne by the company but instead by the client who is responsible for making the currency exchange prior to conducting business with the company. However, the policy of shifting the exchange rate risk onto a foreign customer can backfire, if the customer doesn't want to take on the exchange rate risk, and as a result, finds a local company to do business with instead.

McDonald's Corporation (MCD) is the largest restaurant chain in the world and generates a significant portion of its earnings from international business. McDonald's reported $4.7 billion in revenue for the first quarter of 2020, of which 60 percent was generated internationally.

As a result, the restaurant chain must contend with translation risk on a quarterly basis considering the size and scope of the restaurants, assets, and revenue generated overseas. Below is a portion of the quarterly report which shows the impact of currency translation exposure on the company's financial performance.

- Revenue declined by 6 percent for the first quarter of 2020, but with currency translation factored in, the decline was only 5 percent.
- Net income or profit was $1.1 billion for Q1 2020 — a 17 percent decline from 1 year earlier, but after factoring in currency translation, it declined by 16 percent.

KEY FINANCIAL METRICS — CONSOLIDATED
Dollars in Millions, Except Per Share Data

Quarters Ended March 31,	2020	2019	Inc./ (Dec.)	Inc./(Dec.) Excluding Currency Translation
Revenues	$4,714.4	$5,024.1	(6)%	(5)%
Operating income	1,693.6	2,094.0	(19)	(17)
Net income	1,106.9	1,328.4	(17)	(16)
Earnings per share-diluted	$1.47	$1.72	(15)%	(13)%

Notes: Results for the quarter reflected sales performance declines due to restaurant closures, limited operations and dramatic changes in consumer behavior as a result of COVID-19. Foreign currency translation had a negative impact of $0.02 on diluted earnings per share for the quarter.

Although a 1 percent impact on net income from currency translation doesn't appear to be material, it boosted net income by approximately $11 million for the quarter 1. McDonald's has various types of hedges in place to help mitigate the risk of exchange rate losses and translation risk.[2]

8.4. SUMMARY

Translation exposure occurs when companies translate financial statement accounts from a foreign currency to their home currency. The possible extent of translation gains and losses often depends on the rules that govern translation. The four translation methods most widely used by MNCs are current-noncurrent, monetary-nonmonetary, temporal, and current. This chapter presented a numerical example to compare these four recognized methods.

US companies were required to use FASB 8 (the temporal method) from 1975 until the FASB issued its Statement No. 52 (the current rate method) in 1981. The FASB issued its Statement No. 52 because accountants and executives raised two major complaints about FASB 8. First, FASB 8 required US companies to show gains and losses in their current income statement, thereby distorting their earnings. Second, FASB 8 required US companies to use different rates for different balance sheet items. Under FASB 52, all gains and losses are treated as net worth, and all balance sheet items are translated at current exchange rate except net worth.

MNCs can use a variety of methods to deal with translation exposure. These methods consist of one major group of hedging devices: a balance-sheet hedge. Balance-sheet hedges are generally employed to minimize translation exposure. A balance-sheet hedge involves the selection of the currency in which exposed assets and liabilities are denominated so that an exchange-rate change would make exposed assets equal to exposed liabilities. Because

---

[2]Kenton, W., "What Is Translation Risk," *Investopedia*, May 7, 2022, https://www.investopedia.com/terms/t/translationrisk.asp.

translation gains and losses are purely of paper nature, most MNCs do not employ financial instruments, such as currency forwards, futures, and options.

8.5. KEY TERMS

translation exposure	current-noncurrent method
monetary-nonmonetary method	temporal method
current-rate method	parent currency
functional currency	hedge
balance-sheet hedge	exposure netting
lagging	leading
transfer prices	

8.6. PROBLEMS

1. A US company has a single, wholly-owned affiliate in Japan. This affiliate has exposed assets of 500 million yen and exposed liabilities of 800 million yen. The exchange rate appreciates from 150 yen per dollar to 100 yen per dollar.

   a. What is the amount of net exposure?
   b. What is the amount of the translation gain or loss?
   c. If the Japanese yen declines from 150 yen per dollar to 200 yen per dollar, what would be the amount of the translation gain or loss?

2. The British subsidiary of a US company had current assets of £1 million, fixed assets of £2 million, and current liabilities of £1 million at both the beginning and the end of the year. There are no long-term liabilities. The pound depreciated during the year from $1.50 per pound to $1.30 per pound.

   a. What is the amount of net exposure?
   b. What is the amount of the translation gain or loss?

3. Assume that a Malaysian subsidiary of a US company has the following: (1) cash = M$1,000; (2) accounts receivable = M$1,500; (3) inventory = M$2,000; (4) fixed assets = M$2,500; (5) current liabilities = M$1,000; (6) long-term debt = M$3,000; (7) net worth = M$3,000 and net income before translation gain or loss = M$225. Let us further assume that the historical exchange rate is $0.25 per ringgit, the current exchange rate is $0.20 per ringgit, the average exchange rate is $0.225 per ringgit, and inventory is carried at cost.

   a. Prepare the balance sheet of the US subsidiary in Malaysia.
   b. Determine the dollar net income without the translation gain or loss.
   c. Determine the translation gain or loss under FASB No. 8 and FASB No. 52.
   d. If the functional currency is determined to be the US dollar, which translation method should be used? What kind of impact would it have on the company's net income?
   e. Compute Malaysian-ringgit debt ratio, return on investment, and long-term debt to equity ratio. Compare these ratios with the ratios in dollars under FASB No. 8 and FASB No. 52.

4. In 1982, Ford incurred an after-tax loss of $658 million, adopted FASB No. 52, and had a translation loss of $220 million. In the same year, General Motors earned an after-tax profit of $963 million, used FASB No. 8, and had a translation gain of $348 million.

   a. Why do you think that in 1982, Ford adopted a new accounting rule FASB No. 52, while GM used an old accounting rule FASB No. 8?
   b. What would have been Ford's reported net loss if it used FASB No. 8 instead of FASB No. 52?
   c. What would have been GM's reported net income if it adopted FASB No. 52 instead of FASB No. 8?

5. Assume that a subsidiary in New Zealand needs $NZ500,000 and that a credit swap has been proven to be the least costly-hedged alternative. Further assume that the best unhedged alternative is the direct loan from the parent and the cost of the direct loan is 20 percent. The current exchange rate is $0.5000 per New Zealand dollar. To obtain $NZ500,000 for the subsidiary in New Zealand, the parent must open a $250,000 credit ($0.5000 × $NZ500,000) in favor of a New Zealand bank. The New Zealand bank charges 10 percent per year on the $NZ500,000 made available to the subsidiary and pays no interest on the $250,000 deposit that the parent has deposited in the bank.

   a. What is the exchange rate which would make the direct loan and the credit swap equally attractive?
   b. If most market analysts predict that the exchange rate will be $NZ2 per dollar in 180 days, which alternative would you recommend?
   c. If most market analysts predict that the exchange rate will be $NZ3 per dollar in 180 days, which alternative would you recommend?
   d. If the New Zealand bank should pay five percent interest on the $250,000 credit, what is the exchange rate that would make the direct loan and the credit swap equally attractive?

6. The current exchange rate of Saudi Arabian riyal is SR4 per $1. The Exton Company, the Saudi Arabian subsidiary of a US multinational company, has the following balance sheet:

Assets		Claims on Assets	
Cash	SR 500		
Accounts receivable	SR 600	Accounts payable	SR 100
Inventory (cost)	SR 400	Notes payable	SR 200
Inventory (market price)	SR 800	Other payables	SR 1,000
Total current assets	SR 2,300	Total current Liab.	SR 1,300
		Long-term debt	SR 800
Plant and equipment	SR 2,400	Common stock	SR 1,000
Accumulated depreciation	SR (1,400)	Retained earnings	SR 200
Net plant and equipment	SR 1,000	Exchange loss or gain	—
Total assets	SR 3,300	Total claims	SR 3,300

If the Saudi Arabian riyal devalues from SR4 per $1 to SR5 per $1, what would be the translation loss (gain) under each of the following methods: current/noncurrent, monetary/nonmonetary, temporal, and current rate?

Closing Case 8: FASB No. 52 vs. FASB No. 8

FASB No. 52, which replaced FASB No. 8 in 1981 revises the existing accounting and reporting requirements for translation of foreign currency transactions and foreign currency financial statements. It presents standards for foreign currency translation that are designed to (1) provide information that is generally compatible with the expected economic effects of a rate change on an enterprise's cash flows and equity and (2) reflect in consolidated statements the financial results and relationships as measured in the primary currency in which each entity conducts its business (referred to as its "functional currency."

An entity's functional currency is the currency of the primary economic environment in which that entity operates. The functional currency can be the dollar or a foreign currency depending on the facts. Normally, it will be the currency of the economic environment in which cash is generated and expended by the entity. An entity can be any form of operation, including a subsidiary, division, branch, or joint venture. The statement provides guidance for this key determination in which management's judgment is essential in assessing the facts. A currency in a highly inflationary environment (3-year inflation rate of approximately 100 percent or more) is not considered stable enough to serve as a functional currency and the more stable currency of the reporting parent is to be used instead.

The functional currency translation approach adopted in this Statement encompasses:

a. Identifying the functional currency of the entity's economic environment.
b. Measuring all elements of the financial statements in the functional currency.
c. Using the current exchange rate for translation from the functional currency to the reporting currency if they are different.
d. Distinguishing the economic impact of changes in exchange rates on a net investment from the impact of such changes on individual assets and liabilities that are receivable or payable in currencies other than the functional currency.

Translation adjustments are an inherent result of the process of translating a foreign entity's financial statements from the functional currency to US dollars. Translation adjustments are *not* included in determining net income for the period but are disclosed and accumulated in a separate component of consolidated equity until sale or until complete or substantially complete liquidation of the net investment in the foreign entity takes place.

Transaction gains and losses are a result of the effect of exchange rate changes on transactions denominated in currencies other than the functional currency (for example, a US company may borrow Swiss francs or a French subsidiary may have a receivable denominated in kroner from a Danish customer). Gains and losses on those foreign currency transactions are generally included in determining net income for the period in which exchange rates change unless the transaction hedges a foreign currency commitment or a net investment in a foreign entity. Intercompany transactions of a long-term investment nature are considered part of a parent's net investment and hence do not give rise to gains or losses.

In 1982, Ford incurred an after-tax loss of $658 million, adopted FASB No. 52, and had a translation loss of $220 million. In the same year, General Motors earned an after-tax profit of $963 million, used FASB No. 8, and had a translation gain of $348 million. When new rules are issued, companies are allowed to use either old rules or new rules for a number of years. In 1982, US companies were allowed to use either FASB No. 52 or FASB No. 8.[3]

Case Questions

1. What are the main features of translation exposure?
2. Three basic types of exchange exposure are translation exposure, transaction exposure, and economic exposure. Briefly explain each of these three types of exposure.
3. What is the basic translation hedging strategy?
4. How does FASB No. 8 differ from FASB No. 52?
5a. Why do you think that in 1982, Ford adopted a new accounting rule FASB No. 52, while GM used an old accounting rule FASB No. 8?
5b. What would have been Ford's reported net loss if it used FASB No. 8 instead of FASB No. 52?
5c. What would have been GM's reported net income if it adopted FASB No. 52 instead of FASB No. 8.
6. The mission of the Financial Accounting Standard Board (FASB) is to establish and improve standards of financial accounting and reporting for the guidance and education of the public, including issuers, auditors, and users of financial information. Use the FASB's home page — www.fasb.org — to see current accounting standards and comment letters to proposed standards.

[3] *Source*: Kim, K., *Global Corporate Finance: A Focused Approach*, New Jersey: World Scientific, 2011, Chapter 8.

PART THREE
THE GLOBAL FINANCING STRATEGY

Part Three (Chapters 9 and 10) describes sources of global finance. One major facet of financial management is to raise funds on favorable terms. In the case of global financial management, this involves those sources of funds necessary to finance world trade and foreign investment. These funds can come from either internal or external sources. Internal sources of funds, such as earnings and depreciation, are the major sources of funds for most multinational companies (MNCs). But external sources of funds, such as bank loans and Eurodollars, are important as well.

A dramatic expansion in international capital flows has emerged in recent years for several reasons. First, revolutionary advances in information and communications technology, together with significantly lower transportation and transaction costs have accelerated the growth of cross-border financial flows. Second, financial innovations in the United States and other industrial countries, such as mutual funds, hedge funds, and derivatives, have made cross-border investments more accessible to institutional and individual investors. Third, the removal of capital controls and broader liberalization of financial markets in most countries around the world have stimulated competition and resulted in a growing integration of domestic and offshore markets. MNCs should take into account these three factors in financing their international transactions. This is because the factors increased not only the efficiency of global capital markets, but also created new systematic risks associated with increased asset-price variability.

Chapter 9

INTERNATIONAL FINANCIAL MARKETS

Opening Case 9: The World's 10 Largest Financial Companies and the World's 10 Largest Economies

Table 9.1 lists the world's 10 largest financial companies and the world's 10 largest economies as of December 31, 2021. China claimed the top four of the world's 10 largest financial companies in terms of assets. The remaining six companies on the top 10 list were from the United States (two: JP Morgan Chase and Bank of America, France (two: BNP Paribas and Credit Agricole), Canada (one: HBC) and Japan (one: Mitsubishi UFJ Financial Group). The so-called G-5 group (the USA, Japan, German, the UK, and France) were among the world's 10 largest economies. It is important to note, however, that newly advanced countries, such as India and South Korea were among the world's top 10 largest economies.

China appears to be on its way to becoming the new center of global economic power. As of 2021, China has the second-largest economy in the world with a GDP of $17.7 trillion, behind the United States GDP of $22.9 trillion. If the economy were represented in purchasing power parity (PPP), China edges out America ($23 trillion) as the largest economy with a purchasing power of more than $27.3 trillion.

How did China go from a poor society, devastated by World War Two and its own civil war by the mid-20th century, to the number two economy today? After decades of economic stagnation and setbacks under Communist rule, China began to open itself to international trade and liberalize the economy when it established diplomatic and trade relations with the US in 1979. As China's subsequent export growth fueled the growth of manufacturing and urbanization, China rose to be a major global economic power over the next four decades. All of these trends together point to the emergence of China as a dominant economic power for the coming century.

Leaders of developing countries understand that international banks perform vital tasks for their governments and local companies. Despite this understanding, some critics argue, using a few selected statistics, that host governments are powerless over large international financial institutions. For example, in 2021 only two countries

---

Table 9.1   The world's 10 largest financial companies and the world's 10 largest economies (trillion of US dollars as of 2021).

Financial Companies			Countries		
Ranking	Name	Assets	Ranking	Name	GDP
1	Indus and Comm Bank of China	$5.9	1	USA	$23.0
2	China Construction Bank	4.5	2	China	17.7
3	Agricultural Bank of China	4.3	3	Japan	4.9
4	Bank of China	4.1	4	Germany	4.2
5	JP Morgan Chase	4.0	5	UK	3.2
6	Mitsubishi UFJ Financial Group	3.7	6	India	3.2
7	HBC	3.0	7	France	2.9
8	Bank of America	2.4	8	Italy	2.1
9	BNP Paribas	2.4	9	Canada	2.0
10	Credit Agricole	2.3	10	S. Korea	1.8

Sources: https://en.wikipedia.org/wiki/List_of_largest_banks and https://www.investopedia.com/insights/worlds-top-economies/.

(the US and China) had gross domestic products (GDP) greater than the total assets of Indus and Comm Bank of China. Table 9.1 indicates that this statement must be true. In fact, when we compare these two (banks and economies), the grand total assets of the world's 10 largest financial companies are greater than the combined GDP of the eight largest economies, excluding the USA and China. However, a nation's GDP is a measure of value-added, while a company's assets are the total book value of all outstanding assets.

International financial markets are a major source of funds for international transactions. Most countries have recently internationalized their financial markets to attract foreign business.

Recent financial globalization is being driven by advances in data processing and telecommunications, liberalization of restrictions on cross-border capital flows, deregulation of domestic capital markets, and greater competition among these markets for a share of the world's trading volume. This globalization involves both a harmonization of rules and a reduction of barriers that will allow for the free flow of capital and permit all firms to compete in all markets. In other words, financial market imperfections declined because of this global integration of money and capital markets. Yet, there are still excellent opportunities for companies to lower their cost of capital and for investors to increase their return through international financial markets. This chapter examines the three financial markets — Eurocurrency, international bond, and international equity — that allow companies to serve customers around the world. In addition, this chapter also discusses developing countries' debt problems and financial crises of industrialized countries.[1]

---

[1] https://en.wikipedia.org/wiki/List_of_largest_banks and https://www.investopedia.com/insights/worlds-top-economies/.

9.1. EUROCURRENCY MARKETS

The **Eurocurrency market** consists of banks that accept deposits and make loans in foreign currencies outside the country of issue. These deposits are commonly known as Eurocurrencies. Thus, US dollars deposited in London are called Eurodollars; British pounds deposited in New York are called Eurosterling; and Japanese yen deposited in London are called Euroyen.

Because Eurodollars are the major form of Eurocurrency, the term "Eurodollar" frequently refers to the entire Eurocurrency market. **Eurodollars** could be broadly defined as dollar-denominated deposits in banks all over the world except the United States. These banks may be foreign banks or foreign branches of US banks. However, many experts narrowly define Eurodollars as dollar-denominated deposits in Western European banks or foreign branches of US banks in Western Europe. Hence, they distinguish between Eurodollars and petrodollars in the Middle East or between Eurodollars and Asian dollars in Hong Kong or Singapore. The dominant Eurocurrency remains the US dollar. More recently, however, the euro (€) has become an important currency for denominating Eurocurrency loans and Eurobonds as the US dollar weakened.

Eurocurrency markets are very large, well-organized, and efficient. They serve a number of valuable purposes for multinational business operations. Eurocurrencies are a convenient money market device for MNCs to hold their excess liquidity. They also are a major source of short-term loans to finance corporate working capital needs and foreign trade. In recent years, the so-called "Eurobond markets" have developed as a major source of long-term investment capital for MNCs.

9.1.1. *Creation of Eurodollars*

Many MNCs and governments have learned to use the Eurodollar market as readily as they use the domestic banking system. Major sources of Eurodollars are the dollar reserves of oil-exporting countries, foreign governments or business executives preferring to hold dollars outside the US, foreign banks with dollars in excess of current needs, and MNCs with excess cash balances. Once Eurodollars come into existence, they can create themselves through the lending and investing activities of commercial banks.

Because there are usually no legal reserves against Eurodollar deposits, we may argue that Eurodollar deposits could expand indefinitely. Who creates this infinite expansion of Eurodollars? Three parties do so jointly: (1) public and private depositors by always keeping their money in non-US banks on deposit, (2) banks by keeping none of their Eurodollar deposits in the form of cash, and (3) public and private borrowers who make it possible for the banks to find Eurodollar loans. However, there are a number of checks to this expansion. First, public and private depositors may hold a portion of their money in the form of non-deposit cash. Second, banks may retain a part of their Eurodollar deposits as a liquid reserve. Third, borrowers may convert the dollars borrowed into local currency. This conversion will not only stop the further expansion of Eurodollar deposits, but it may actually reduce the volume of outstanding Eurodollar deposits.

9.1.1.1. *Uses of Eurodollars*

European banks with Eurodollars may use these funds in a number of ways. First, they may redeposit their Eurodollars in other European banks or European branches of a US bank.

Second, they may make loans to non-bank users such as MNCs. These MNCs use the dollars to meet their dollar obligations or to buy local currencies. Third, they may transfer their dollars to Eurodollars in European branches of a US bank which in turn would lend these funds to the US home office.

Heavy borrowers in the Eurodollar market are governments and commercial banks. Many countries have recently been suffering foreign-loan-related problems. Hence, they want Eurodollars to improve their international reserves. Many commercial banks rely on Eurodollars to grant credit to exporters and importers. Eurobanks frequently swap Eurodollars with local currencies in order to make loans to domestic companies. In addition, international development banks have been regular borrowers in the market. European countries outside the Group of Ten, Latin America, and Asia are the three largest users of Eurodollars.

Many of the private non-bank borrowers continue to be companies engaged in international operations, such as exporters, importers, and investors. They are attracted by the size of the market and the importance of the US dollar as an international reserve. A second advantage of Eurodollar loans is that the funds raised in the external market have no restrictions about their deployment. In contrast, funds raised in national money markets have some restrictions in almost all cases. Finally, international money markets provide MNCs with flexibility in many ways such as terms, conditions, and covenants.

9.1.2. *Eurodollar Instruments*

The two major types of instruments used in the Eurodollar market are Eurodollar deposits and Eurodollar loans.

9.1.2.1. *Eurodollar deposits*

Eurodollar deposits are either fixed time deposits or negotiable certificates of deposit. Most Eurodollar deposits are in the form of time deposits.

Time deposits are funds being placed in a bank for a fixed maturity at a specified interest rate. In contrast to the US practice, Eurobanks do not maintain checking accounts (demand deposits) for their customers. While maturities of these time deposits range from one day to a few years, most of them have a maturity of less than 1 year. Time deposits are for fixed periods, but Eurobanks are frequently flexible if the depositor desires to withdraw his deposits early.

A **certificate of deposit** (CD) is a negotiable instrument issued by a bank. In other words, negotiable CDs are formal negotiable receipts for funds left with a bank for a specified period of time at a fixed or floating rate of interest. The important advantage of a CD over a time deposit is its liquidity because the holder of a CD can sell it on the secondary market at any time before the maturity date. Eurobanks issue negotiable CDs to attract idle funds from MNCs, oil exporting countries, and wealthy individuals.

Negotiable CDs for Eurodollars were first introduced in 1966 by the London branch of First National City Bank of New York (now Citicorp). Currently, most major Eurobanks issue negotiable CDs whose safety and liquidity are assured by an active secondary market. The secondary market consists of broker/dealer firms which are members of the International CD Market Association. This association was established in London in 1968 to provide customers with the highest quality of services.

9.1.2.2. *Eurodollar loans*

Eurodollar loans range from a minimum of $500,000 to $100 million, typically in multiples of $1 million. Their maturities range from 30 days to a few years. Short-term Eurodollar financings represent the major part of the Eurodollar lending business. Short-term Eurodollar loans are usually conducted under pre-arranged lines of credit. Under such an arrangement, the Eurobank establishes a maximum loan balance (line of credit) after investigation of its client's credit standing. Although the commitment period is typically 1 year, advances under a line of credit are normally made against notes with maturities of 90 or 180 days. Lines of credit are renewable after a thorough review process. These short-term Eurodollar loans are usually made on an unsecured basis and repaid at the maturity date.

Eurobanks also provide international concerns with medium-term loans. Two major forms of medium-term Eurodollar loans are revolving Eurodollar credits and Eurodollar term loans. A **revolving credit** is a confirmed line of credit beyond 1 year. Maturities of Eurodollar term loans range from 3 to 7 years. These terms loans are a less popular form of medium-term Eurodollar loans than revolving Eurodollar credits.

9.1.2.3. *Interest rates*

Two sets of interest rates are Eurodollar-deposit interest rates and Eurodollar-loan interest rates. Eurodollar deposit and loan rates are determined by forces of supply and demand. More specifically, these rates depend on the rates in a corresponding home currency, spot and forward exchange rates, domestic and Eurocurrency rates in other currencies, and the inflation rate in various countries. Many economists have assumed that Eurodollar-deposit rates depend on US money market rates. In other words, US CD rates provide an effective floor for Eurodollar deposit rates.

Interest rates on Eurodollar deposits are usually higher than those on deposits in the United States. Interest rates on Eurodollar loans are generally lower than similar loan rates in the United States. With deposit rates higher and lending rates lower in the Eurodollar market than in the US market, Eurobanks must operate on a narrower margin. A number of factors enable Eurobanks to operate profitably on narrower margins than domestic markets.

1. Eurobanks, being free of reserve requirements, can lend a larger percentage of their deposits.
2. Eurobanks have very little or no regulatory expenses, such as deposit insurance fees.
3. Eurodollar loans are characterized by high volumes and well-known borrowers; these two features reduce the costs of information gathering and credit analysis.
4. Many Eurodollar loans take place out of tax-haven countries.
5. Eurobanks are not forced to lend money to borrowers at concessionary rates, usually. lower than prevailing market rates.

Eurobanks used to establish their lending rate at some fixed percentage above the 6-month London Interbank Offered Rate. **London Interbank Offered Rate** (LIBOR) is a benchmark interest rate at which major global banks lend to one another in the international interbank market for short-term loans. However, on June 30, 2023, LIBOR was replaced by the Secured Overnight Financing Rate (SOFR). **The Secured Overnight Financing**

Rate is an influential interest rate that banks use to price US dollar denominated derivatives and loans. The SOFR is based on transactions in the US Treasury repurchase market, where investors offer banks overnight loans backed by their bond assets.[2]

In the absence of tight controls on international financial transactions, arbitrage and risk differences affect the relationship between rates in the internal market (the US market) and in the external market (the Eurodollar market). An absence of government controls on international capital flows results in arbitrage between internal and external segments of the market for dollar credit. The arbitrage keeps the spread between internal and external rates within a narrow margin. In general, risks on external dollar deposits are somewhat greater than those on internal dollar deposits.

9.1.3. *Euronote Issue Facilities*

Euronote issue facilities (EIFs), a recent innovation in non-bank short-term credits, are notes issued outside the country in whose currency they are denominated. EIFs consist of Euronotes, Euro-commercial paper, and Euro-medium-term notes. These facilities are popular because they allow borrowers to go directly to the market rather than relying on financial intermediaries such as banks.

Euronotes are short-term debt instruments underwritten by a group of international banks called a "facility." An MNC makes an agreement with a facility to issue Euronotes in its own name for a number of years. Euronotes typically have maturities from 1 to 6 months. But many MNCs continually roll them over as a source of medium-term financing. Euronotes are sold at a discount from face value and pay back the full value at maturity. **Eurocommercial paper** (ECP), like domestic commercial paper, is unsecured short-term promissory notes sold by finance companies and certain industrial companies. These notes are issued only by the most credit-worthy companies because they are not secured. Their maturities range from 1 to 6 months. Like Euronotes, Eurocommercial paper is sold at a discount from face value.

Euro-medium-term notes (EMTNs) are medium-term funds guaranteed by financial institutions with short-term commitments by investors. The main advantage of the EMTN is that banks underwrite or guarantee the funds for a period of 5–7 years. If the borrower cannot sell all or part of their notes, the banks will then buy all or part of the notes. At the same time, the borrower does not have to issue new notes every time their old notes mature. Consequently, the EMTN provides a medium source of funds, without the obligation to pay the interest on the debt when the funds are not needed. In this type of arrangement, the borrower raises funds in the form of short-term notes with maturities of 30 days, 3 months, or even longer. These short-term notes are distributed to investors by financial institutions. At the maturity of these notes, the borrower reissues the notes. At this point, the investors may buy the new notes or take their funds back. This process is repeated at every maturity of the notes.

---

[2]Kurt, D., "Secured Overnight Financing Rate (SOFR) Definition and History," *Investopedia*, March 22, 2022, https://www.investopedia.com/secured-overnight-financing-rate-sofr04683954.

9.2. EUROCURRENCY INTERBANK MARKET

The Eurocurrency interbank market plays a major role in channeling funds from banks in one country to banks in another country. The interbank market has over 1,000 banks from 50 different countries, but about 20 major banks dominate the entire interbank market. Although transactions in US dollars still dominate the interbank market, there are flourishing interbank markets in euros, Swiss francs, Japanese yen, and British pounds.

9.2.1. *An Overview of Eurocurrency Interbank Market*

9.2.1.1. *Interbank clearing house systems*

This section describes three key clearing house systems of interbank transfers: Clearing House Interbank Payment System (CHIPS), The Clearing House Automated Payments System (CHAPS), and The Society for World Interbank Financial Telecommunications (SWIFT). These three systems transfer funds between banks through wire rather than checks. **CHIPS** is the largest private sector USD (US dollar) clearing system in the world, clearing and settling $1.8 trillion in domestic and international payments per day. Its patented algorithm matches and nets payments resulting in an extremely efficient clearing process.

CHAPS is a company that facilitates large money transfers denominated in British pounds (GBP). CHAPS is administered by the Bank of England (BoE) and is used by 30 participating financial institutions. Over 5,000 additional institutions also engage with the system by way of partnership agreements with the 30 primary institutions.

SWIFT is an interbank communication network that carries messages for financial transactions worldwide. The SWIFT represents a common denominator in international payments and uses the latest communication technology. Consequently, banks can execute international payments more cheaply and efficiently than ever before. More than half of all high-value cross-border payments worldwide use the SWIFT network. Swift is a cooperative company under Belgian law and is owned and controlled by its shareholders (financial institutions) representing approximately 2,400 shareholders from across the world. More than 11,000 global SWIFT member institutions in over 200 countries and territories sent an average of 42 million messages per day through the network in 2021, marking an increase of 11.4 percent over 2020.

The SWIFT ban against some Russian banks is one of the sanctions against Russia imposed by the European Union and other Western countries after Russia invaded Ukraine on February 24, 2022. This ban aimed at weakening the country's economy to end its invasion of Ukraine by hindering Russian access to the SWIFT financial transaction processing system. According to the Russian National SWIFT Association, around 300 banks used SWIFT in Russia, with more than half of Russian credit institutions represented in SWIFT. Russia used to have the second highest userbase after the United States. Since the Swift excluded Russia from its use, however, Russian interbank payment transactions have become significantly more complex. In addition, the country's ability to trade goods and exchange currencies has been significantly reduced, making payment be only possible in cash.

9.2.1.2. *Functions of the interbank market*

The Eurocurrency interbank market has at least four related functions. First, the interbank market is an efficient market system through which funds move from banks in one country to banks in other countries. Second, the interbank market gives banks an efficient mechanism to buy or sell foreign-currency assets and liabilities of different maturities in order to hedge their exposure to interest-rate and foreign-exchange risks. Third, the interbank market is a convenient source of additional loans when banks need to adjust their balance sheets either domestically or internationally. Fourth, because of this market, banks sidestep regulations on capital adequacy and interest rates prevalent in many domestic banking markets.

9.2.1.3. *Risks of participating banks*

Participating banks in the Eurocurrency interbank market face at least five different risks: (1) credit or default risk, (2) liquidity risk, (3) sovereign risk, (4) foreign exchange risk, and (5) settlement risk. First, credit risk is the risk that a borrowing bank may default on its interbank loan. This risk is a concern because interbank loans and deposits are not secured. Second, liquidity risk is the risk that other banks may withdraw their interbank deposits suddenly. Here, the bank may have to sell off illiquid assets for less than their face value to meet its deposit drain. Third, sovereign risk is the risk that a foreign country may prevent its banks from repaying interbank loans or deposits received from banks in other countries. Fourth, foreign exchange risk is the risk that a bank participant in this market will gain or lose due to changes in exchange rates. Fifth, settlement risk is the risk of a breakdown or non-settlement on the major wire-transfer systems.

Regulators and analysts have expressed some concern about the stability of this market for two major reasons. First, interbank funds have no collateral. Second, central bank regulations are inadequate. These two factors expose the market to potential "**contagion**"; problems at one bank affect other banks in the market. This kind of contagion ultimately threatens the market's stability and its functions.

9.2.1.4. *Minimum standards of international banks*

With the global crisis created by the collapse of several international banks in the 1980s, bank regulators throughout the world agreed that something had to be done to protect against future massive failures. The Basle Committee under the auspices of the Bank for International Settlements and the central-bank governors of the Group of Ten countries reached an agreement on minimum standards in 1988 for international banks and their cross-border activities. The **Bank for International Settlements** is a bank in Switzerland that facilitates transactions among central banks. This agreement established an international bank capital standard by recommending that globally active banks had to maintain capital equal to at least 8 percent of their assets by the end of 1992. The accord distinguishes between more and less risky assets so that more capital would be held against investments with greater risk. As a result, the 8 percent standard called for in the accord applies not to a bank's total assets but to its risk-weighted assets. Safe government bonds or cash, for example, receive a zero weight in calculating aggregate risk exposure, whereas long-term lending to banks and industrial companies in emerging markets receives a 100 percent weight.

Such minimum capital standards are meant to work in conjunction with direct supervision of banks and basic market discipline to restrain excessive risk taking by banks that have access to the safety net.

In June 2004, the Basel Committee on Banking Supervision released for public comment the new Basel Capital Accord, which would replace the 1988 Capital Accord. On July 8–9, 2009 The Basel Committee announced a final package of measures to enhance the three pillars of the Basel II framework: Basel II uses a **three pillars** concept — (1) minimum capital requirements (addressing risk), (2) supervisory review and (3) market discipline — to promote greater stability in the financial system. The first pillar requires banks to maintain the 8 percent equity capital as the minimum standard, but it changes the way the capital standard is computed in order to consider certain risks.

Basel III (or the Third Basel Accord) is a global, voluntary regulatory standard on bank capital adequacy, stress testing and market liquidity risk. Basel III was published by the Basel Committee on Banking Supervision in **November 2010**, and was scheduled to be introduced from 2013 until 2015; however, implementation was extended repeatedly to January 1, 2022 and then again until January 1, 2023, in the wake of the COVID-19 pandemic. The third installment of the Basel Accords (*see Basel I, Basel II*) was developed in response to the deficiencies in financial regulation revealed by the late-2000s financial crisis. Basel III was supposed to strengthen bank capital requirements by increasing bank liquidity and decreasing bank leverage. In summary, these regulations should result in a somewhat safer financial system, while perhaps restraining future economic growth to a small degree.

9.2.1.5. *"Three Cs" of central banking*

Recent movement toward a highly integrated global financial system has caused bankers to develop "three Cs" of central banking: consultation, cooperation, and coordination. Central banks are important participants in the consultation, cooperation, and coordination process due to their key role in monetary and exchange rate policies.

Consultation involves not only an exchange of information, but also an explanation of current economic conditions and policies. By reducing information uncertainty, this process enhances the understanding of what is going on in the world at-large and it can successfully contribute to the policy-making process.

In cooperation, countries retain full national sovereignty, but decide voluntarily to allow the actions of the other countries to influence their own decisions. While the central banks make sovereign decisions, they may agree to certain mutually advantageous courses of action and even engage in certain joint efforts agreeable to all parties.

Finally, central bank coordination requires individual central banks to relinquish some or all decision-making powers to other countries or international institutions. Some loss of national sovereignty is inevitably involved.

9.2.2. *The Role of Banks in Corporate Governance*

Market-based and bank-based systems of corporate governance reflect the relative importance of public and private capital markets to a nation's economy. In the United States, increasing restrictions on commercial banking has coincided with the growth of public capital markets. However, banks have been the main source of capital in Japan for several reasons. First, the Bank of Japan provides major industries with long-term loans at favorable rates through commercial banks. Second, Japanese banks have ample funds for loans because of the country's high savings rates and huge trade surpluses. Third, there are a few restrictions on commercial banking in Japan.

9.2.2.1. *The United States: A market-based system of corporate governance*

Several pieces of legislation enacted in the wake of the Depression (1929–1933) fundamentally altered the role of financial institutions in corporate governance. The legislation caused the fragmentation of financial institutions and institutional portfolios, thereby preventing the emergence of powerful large-block shareholders who might exert pressure on management. In contrast, countries such as Germany and Japan, which do not operate under the same constraints, developed systems that allowed banks to play a larger role in firms' affairs.

Traditionally, US banks have faced the following prohibitions on equity-related activities. First, banks cannot own stock for their own account. Second, banks cannot actively vote on shares held in trust for their banking clients. Third, banks cannot make a market in equity securities. Fourth, banks cannot engage in investment banking activities.[3]

However, US Congress and regulatory agencies have recently started to relax some constraints. For example, interstate banking was legalized in 1994; full interstate branch banking has been permitted since 1997. In addition, US banks, securities firms, insurance companies, and asset managers have been allowed to freely enter each other's business or merge since early 2000. These recent changes generated fierce competition among financial institutions and reduced the number of commercial and investment banks. Consequently, surviving banks are bigger, better capitalized, and better prepared to serve companies in creative ways.

Most financial experts predicted that these changes would eventually create universal banks in the United Kingdom and the United States. A **universal bank** participates in many kinds of banking activities and is both a commercial bank and an investment bank as well as providing other financial services such as insurance. These are also called full-service financial firms, although there can also be full-service investment banks which provide asset management, trading, and underwriting. The concept is most relevant in the United Kingdom and the United States, where historically there was a distinction drawn between pure investment banks and commercial banks. However, the global financial crisis of 2008 enabled US and UK financial institutions to create universal banks. Notable examples of such universal banks include BNP Paribas and Société Générale of France; HSBC, Standard Chartered and RBS of the United Kingdom; Deutsche Bank of Germany; ING Bank of the Netherlands; Bank of America, Citigroup, JPMorgan Chase and Wells Fargo of the United States; and UBS and Credit Suisse of Switzerland. Although it originated in Europe, universal banking is similar to the Japanese keiretsu.

---

[3]Buttler, K. C., *Multinational Finance*, Cincinnati, OH: South-Western College Publishing, 1997, Chapter 17.

9.2.2.2. *Japan: A bank-based system of corporate governance*

The national difference in corporate governance results in dissimilar financial structures for corporate control. The bank-based system in Japan and Germany, for example, rely on a concentrated ownership in the hands of a main bank and/or the business partners for both debt and equity capital. Large Japanese companies use a higher degree of leverage than US companies. The ability to take on such large amounts of debt stems in part from the vast mutual-aid networks — keiretsu — that most Japanese companies can tap. **Keiretsu** is a Japanese word that stands for a financially linked group of companies that play a significant role in the country's economy.

Keiretsu, usually with the main bank at the center, forms the backbone of corporate Japan. Keiretsu ties constitute a complex web of tradition, cross-shareholdings, trading relationships, management, cooperative projects, and information swapping. The keiretsu provides financial support, management advice, and favorable contracts to their members. A key mission of the keiretsu is to provide a safety net when corporate relatives get into trouble. Moreover, Japanese banks, unlike their US counterparts, can hold the borrowing company's common stock. Thus, the main bank has access to information about the company and has a say in its management. In most countries, this sort of bank influence on corporate affairs would be unacceptable.

However, recent economic problems and deregulations in Japan have changed the country's financial structures. These changes include reduced bank borrowing, more capital market financing, the erosion of the main bank power in corporate affairs, the reduction of cross-shareholdings, and the weaker keiretsu system. These changes are likely to reduce the role of banks in corporate governance in Japan.

9.2.2.3. *Political dynamics*

There is a growing consensus that corporate governance reform should be a matter of global concern. Although some countries face more serious problems than others, existing governance mechanisms have failed to effectively protect investors in many countries. For example, executives and politicians faced public uproar after the US corporate scandals of 2001 and 2002. Other countries, such as the United Kingdom, have also experienced a spate of corporate scandals in recent years. The Sarbanes–Oxley Act of the US, passed in 2002, is designed to reform three areas: (1) accounting regulation, (2) audit committee, and (3) executive responsibility.

The US government was not the only organization that proposed changes in the corporate governance system. Indeed, groups like the Business Roundtable (made up of corporate executives), the US Chamber of Commerce, the Securities Industry Association, and the New York Stock Exchange (NYSE) made their own proposals for change. One particularly influential group is the NYSE, which can enact standards for firms that choose to list on the exchange. As the NYSE is generally considered the most prestigious exchange in the world in which to be listed, it has the power to influence the corporate system not only in the United States but also around the world. Nevertheless, the US financial crisis of the late 2000s revealed corporate governance failures in the US mortgage industry.

Consumers had reaped the benefits of such deregulation for many years, but some experts blame the US deregulation of its financial institutions for the US - originated global credit crisis of 2007–2009. The financial market has become increasingly competitive as a number of deregulation efforts in recent years opened these markets to more financial organizations and institutions. For example, the Gramm–Leach–Bliley Financial Services Modernization Act of 1999 repealed the last vestiges of the Glass–Seagull Act of 1933, thereby eliminating the last barrier between commercial and investment banks. Such deregulations and extra pressure on banking regulators for lax policies enabled financial institutions to engage in each other's businesses more aggressively. These new opportunities, which led to such innovations as structured investment vehicles that borrowed short and invested long, had initially made US financial institutions highly profitable, but they had eventually caused many banks to lose most of their value on highly leverage assets. Such reckless and unsustainable lending practices resulted from the deregulation and securitization of real estate mortgages in the United States The result has been a large decline in the capital of many banks and US government sponsored enterprises, tightening credit around the world, which resulted in the worst recession (2007–2009) since the Great Depression of the 1930s.

Figure 9.1 shows recessions since the great depression. Many law makers and regulators in the United States and other countries around the world adopted and/or recommended the regulation of financial markets along with stronger corporate governance structures to prevent another financial crisis. For example, the United States adopted much tighter

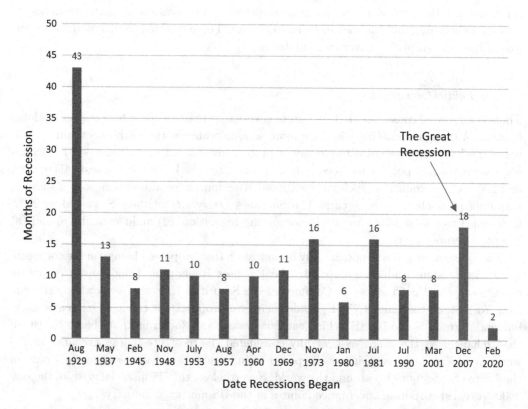

Fig. 9.1 US recessions since the great depression of the 1930s.

rules of finance in 2010 through the Dodd-Franc Act to prevent future financial crises and costly bailouts. Among other things, the Act prohibits banks from making risky investments with their own money, which may reduce the core capital of banks. Furthermore, a new independent Consumer Financial Protection Bureau was established to protect consumers from predatory lending. In addition, a new Financial Stability Oversight Council of regulators would be responsible for monitoring the **systematic risk** affecting the entire financial market.

9.3. THE INTERNATIONAL CAPITAL MARKET

The **international capital market** consists of the international bond market and the international equity market.

9.3.1. *The International Bond Market*

International bonds are those bonds which are initially sold outside the country of the borrower. International bonds consist of foreign bonds, Eurobonds, and global bonds. An important issue with bond financing has to do with the currency issue. The currency of issue is not necessarily the same as the country of issue, although the two may coincide. For example, if a US company sells a yen-denominated bond in Japan, the currency of issue is that of the country of issue. However, if a US company sells a dollar-denominated bond in Japan, the currency of issue is not that of the country of issue. In the former of these situations, the bond is called a foreign bond; in the latter, the bond is called a Eurobond. A global bond is hybrid in nature because it can be sold inside as well as outside the country in whose currency it is denominated. For example, a dollar-denominated bond tradable in New York (domestic market) and Tokyo (Eurobond market) is called a global bond. Let us provide a more general description of these three international bonds: foreign bonds, Eurobonds, and global bonds.

9.3.1.1. *Foreign bonds*

Foreign bonds are bonds sold in a particular national market by a foreign borrower, underwritten by a syndicate of brokers from that country, and denominated in the currency of that country. Foreign bonds, of course, fall under the regulatory jurisdiction of national or domestic authorities. Dollar-denominated bonds sold in New York by a Mexican firm are foreign bonds; these bonds should be registered with the US Securities and Exchange Commission (SEC). Foreign bonds are similar in many respects to the public debt sold in domestic capital markets, but their issuer is a foreigner.

The first foreign bond was issued in 1958. Most large foreign-bond issues had been floated in the United States, Great Britain, and Switzerland. The weakening British pound in the late 1950s reduced the importance of the domestic British capital market for foreign firms. The Interest Equalization Tax (1963–1974) of the United States effectively stopped New York's usefulness as a capital market for new foreign bonds. Thus, international borrowers and investors shifted their activities from the United States to Europe. This shift caused the Eurobond market to develop.

9.3.1.2. *Eurobonds*

Eurobonds are bonds underwritten by an international syndicate of brokers and sold simultaneously in many countries other than the country of the issuing entity. In other words, foreign bonds refer to the bonds issued in the external sectors of financial markets — sectors that fall outside the regulatory environment of national authorities. Eurobonds, therefore, are issued outside the country in whose currency they are denominated. The Eurobond market is almost entirely free of official regulation but is self-regulated by the Association of International Bond Dealers. For example, dollar-denominated bonds sold outside the United States are Eurobonds; these bonds are not registered under the US Securities Act and may not be offered or sold to Americans as part of the distribution.

The first Eurobond issue was launched in 1963. Eurobonds are direct claims on leading MNCs, governments, or governmental enterprises. They are sold simultaneously in many countries through multinational syndicates of underwriting brokers. The Eurobond market is similar to the Eurodollar market in one respect. Both markets are "external" because obligations available in these markets are denominated in foreign currencies outside the country of issue.

There are a number of important differences between the Eurodollar market and the Eurobond market. First, the Eurodollar market is an international money market, but the Eurobond market is an international capital market. Second, the Eurodollar market is a financial intermediation market; major world banks operate as intermediaries between depositors and borrowers of Eurodollars. By contrast, the Eurobond market is a direct market in which investors hold the securities issued by the final borrowers; in other words, Eurobonds are issued directly by the final borrowers.

The Eurobond market has a number of attractive factors. First, interest income earned on Eurobonds is usually not subject to a withholding tax. The absence of this tax makes Eurobonds attractive to those investors who either want to evade taxes or who cannot recover taxes withheld. Second, the Eurobond market is often described as a market free from national regulations. Many countries, including the United States, tend to strictly regulate the access of foreign borrowers to their domestic capital markets. But these countries are often more flexible about securities denominated in foreign currencies and sold to their residents who already possess those foreign currencies. Moreover, disclosure requirements in the international bond market are less stringent than those of the United States.

9.3.1.3. *Global bonds*

As noted above, there is some separation between the Eurobond market and the domestic bond market. An issue normally must choose on which bond market to sell. Demand for the bond is thus constrained by the barriers between the markets. In the last few years, an instrument known as the global bond has been developed to overcome this segmentation.

Global bonds are bonds sold inside as well as outside the country in whose currency they are denominated. For example, dollar-denominated bonds sold in New York (domestic bond market) and Tokyo (Eurobond market) are called dollar global bonds. Similarly, pound-denominated bonds sold in London and Los Angeles are pound global bonds. While global bonds follow the domestic market practice of registration of bonds, they follow the

Eurobond market practice regarding their distribution. Dollar global bonds combine SEC registration and US clearing arrangements with separate clearing on the Eurobond market.

The World Bank issued the first such bonds in September 1989 and still remains the leading issuer of global bonds. The Bank raised $1.5 billion through a dollar global-bond issue that was offered in the US as well as in Eurobond markets. Since then, the World Bank has issued global bonds in US dollars, euros, Japanese yen, and British pounds. On July 15, 1992, Japan's Matsushita Electric Industrial issued the first global bond by a corporate borrower. These days multinational firms, industrial countries, and even some developing countries issue global bonds. By allowing issuers to solicit demand for a variety of markets and to offer greater liquidity to investors, global bonds have potential to reduce borrowing costs. Such cost savings might be, however, offset by the fixed costs of borrowing through the global format, such as registration and clearing arrangements. These costs for global bonds are presumably higher than for comparable Eurobond issues.

Global Finance in Practice 9: Sovereign-Government Bond Ratings

There are several ways to analyze or compare the quality of bonds. Two financial service firms — **Standard & Poor's (S&P) and Moody's Investor Service** — assign letter ratings to indicate the quality of bonds. Table 9.2 shows bond rating by these two firms.

Triple A and double A are extremely safe. Single A and triple B bonds are strong enough to be called "investment grade": these bonds are the lowest-rated bonds that many banks and other institutional investors are allowed by law to hold. Double B and lower bonds are speculative; they are **junk bonds**, with a fairly high probability of default. Many financial institutions are prohibited from buying these junk bonds. During the peak of Asian currency crisis in December 1997, S&P and Moody's downgraded the credit ratings on Thailand, Indonesia, and South Korea to junk-bond status. This move sparked widespread sales of Asian bonds by portfolio managers because they are restricted to holding only investment-grade debt securities. Bond ratings are important to both investors and issuers because they have a direct, measurable influence on the bond's interest rate and the borrower's cost of debt.

Since the early 1990s, US domestic bonds have been assigned quality ratings by S&P and Moody's that reflect their probability of default. These two rating agencies now provide credit ratings on many international bond issues. Sovereign governments issue a sizable portion of all international bonds. In rating a country's credit risk, their analysis centers on an examination of economic risk and political risk.

Economic risk is assessed on the basis of a country's external financial position, balance of payments, economic structure and growth, economic management, and economic prospects. Political risk is assessed on the basis of the country's political system, social environment, and international relations.

Country credit ratings usually represent the ceiling for ratings that S&P and Moody's will assign obligations of all entities domiciled within that country.

For example, 20 Korean banks lost investment-grade status of their bonds in late December 1997 as S&P and Moody's cut Korea's rating to junk-bond status. Table 9.3 shows sovereign ratings by these two rating agencies for selected countries: five countries with the highest credit rating and five countries with junk-bond status.

Table 9.2   Bond ratings by Moody's and Standard & Poor's.

Moody's	S&P	Description
Aaa	AAA	Highest quality
Aa	AA	High quality
A	A	Upper medium grade
Baa	BBB	Medium grade
Ba	BB	Lower medium grade/some speculative elements
B	B	Speculative
Caa	CCC	
Ca	CC	More speculative; higher risk of default
C	C	
–	D	In default

Table 9.3   Sovereign ratings by Moody's and Standard & Poor's.

Moody's		S&P	
Canada	Aaa	Canada	AAA
Luxemburg	Aaa	Luxemburg	AAA
Norway	Aaa	Norway	AAA
Singapore	Aaa	Singapore	AAA
Sweden	Aaa	Sweden	AAA
Congo	B3	Congo	B–
Ecuador	Caa3	Ecuador	B–
Georgia	Ba2	Georgia	BB
Jordan	B1	Jordan	B+–
Mongolia	B3	Mongolia	B

Source: https://tradingeconomics.com/country-list/rating, January 12, 2023.

9.3.2.   *Types of International Bonds*

Five types of international bonds are straight (fixed-rate) bonds, floating-rate notes, convertible bonds, bonds with warrants, and other bonds. However, straight bonds and floating rate bonds account for about 95 percent of the total bond market.

9.3.2.1.   *Straight bonds*

These bonds have fixed maturities and carry a fixed rate of interest. Straight bonds are repaid by amortization or in a lump sum at the maturity date. The **amortization method** refers to the retirement of a long-term debt by making a set of equal periodic payments. These periodic payments include both interest and principal. Alternatively, a borrower may retire his or her bonds by redeeming the face value of the bonds at maturity. Under this method, a fixed interest on the face value of the bonds is paid at regular intervals.

Fixed-rate bonds are technically unsecured, debenture bonds because almost all of them are not secured by any specific property of the borrower. Because of this, debenture bond-holders become general creditors in the event of default; they look to the nature of the borrower's assets, its earning power, and its general credit strength.

Perhaps the greatest advantage of all types of international bonds for individual investors is that interest income on them is exempt from withholding taxes at the source. Investors must report their interest income to their national authorities, but both tax avoidance and tax evasion are extremely widespread. Official institutions hold a large portion of investment in international bonds and are not liable for tax. Another large class of investors in international bonds consists of private institutions. These private institutions legally avoid tax by being in tax haven countries.

9.3.2.2. *Floating-rate notes*

These notes are frequently called floating-rate bonds. The rate of return on these notes is adjusted at regular intervals, usually every 6 months, to reflect changes in short-term market rates. Because one of their main objectives is to provide dollar capital for non-US banks, most floating-rate notes are issued in dollars.

Like other international bonds, floating-rate notes are issued in denominations of $1,000 each. They usually carry a margin of 1/4 percent above the LIBOR, and this margin is normally adjusted every 6 months. The link between the rate of return on floating-rate notes and LIBOR rates is intended to protect the investor against capital loss.

9.3.2.3. *Convertible bonds*

These convertible bonds are convertible into parent common stock. The conversion price is usually fixed at a certain premium above the market price of the common stock on the date of the bond issue. Investors are free to convert their fixed-income securities into common stock at any time before the conversion privilege expires; the borrowing company is obliged to issue new stock for that purpose.

The convertible provision is designed to increase the marketability of fixed-rate Eurobonds. Convertible bonds provide investors with a steady income and an opportunity to participate in rising stock prices. Thus, their interest rates have been 1.5 to 2 percent below those on fixed-rate bonds. Because international investors are inflation-conscious, they prefer convertible bonds which maintain the purchasing power of money.

9.3.2.4. *Bonds with warrants*

Some international bonds are issued with warrants. A **warrant** is an option to buy a stated number of common shares at a stated price during a prescribed period. Warrants pay no dividends, have no voting rights, and become worthless at expiration unless the price of the common stock exceeds the exercise price. Convertible Eurobonds do not bring in additional funds. When they are converted, common stock increases, and the convertible securities are retired. When warrants are exercised, common stock and cash increase simultaneously.

9.3.2.5. *Other bonds*

A major portion of other bonds is zero-coupon bonds. **Zero-coupon bonds** provide all of the cash payment (interest and principal) when they mature. The bond does not pay periodic interest but is sold at a deep discount from its face value.

9.3.3. *The International Equity Market*

Besides debt instruments like the Eurodollar and bond markets, the equity capital market is another important source of financing. Evidence indicates that the 20th century's final decade (1990s) went down in history as the period when much of the world discovered the stock market as a major source of funds for their global expansion. Companies will increasingly turn to the stock market to raise money. This section focuses on how ownership in publicly owned corporations is traded throughout the world. The stock market consists of the primary market and secondary market. The **primary market** is a market where the sale of new common stock by corporations to initial investors occurs. The **secondary market** is a market where the previously issued common stock is traded between investors.

In recent years, a number of new trends began to emerge in the stock markets around the world: (1) alliance, (2) crosslisting, and concentration.

9.3.3.1. *Stock market alliance*

There are some 150 stock exchanges in the world. Within the past 10 years, these stock exchanges scrambled to align with each other. There is a variety of reasons for this consolidation of stock exchanges: the growing speed and power of telecommunication links, big and small investors' keen interest in stocks from all parts of the world, and the fear of being left behind. Moreover, if national exchanges do not take the initiative, they could be bypassed by new electronic trading systems. These same forces caused the burgeoning of online trading and pushed national securities firms to expand their business overseas. In addition, these same factors have caused another wave for stock markets to become publicly traded on the different stock exchanges.

9.3.3.2. *Crosslisting*

With the rise of cross-border mergers during the 1990s and the 2000s, there arises a need for companies to crosslist their stocks on different exchanges around the world. By crosslisting its shares on foreign exchanges, an MNC hopes to:

1. Allow foreign investors to buy their shares in their home market.
2. Increase the share price by taking advantage of the home country's rules and regulations.
3. Provide another market to support a new issuance.
4. Establish a presence in that country in the instance that it wishes to conduct business in that country.
5. Increase its visibility to its customers, creditors, suppliers, and host government.
6. Compensate local management and employees in the foreign affiliates.

Companies are obligated to adhere to the securities regulations of all countries where their shares are listed. A decision to crosslist in the US means any company, domestic or foreign, must meet the accounting and disclosure requirements of the US Securities and Exchange Commission. Rules for listing requirements differ markedly from country to country, but analysts regard US requirements as the most restrictive in the world. Reconciliation of a company's financial statements to US standards can be a laborious process. Some foreign companies are reluctant to disclose hidden reserves and other pieces of company information. It might not appear too difficult for US companies to cross list certain foreign exchanges because their listing requirements are not that restrictive, but certain barriers still exist, such as a foreign country's specific rules and reporting costs.

9.3.3.3. *Stock market concentration*

European stock markets have become more integrated since the European Union's decision to switch their monetary union from the European Currency Unit to the euro beginning in 1999. Increasing integration, as reflected in converging price dynamics across markets, results from various structural changes in European stock markets. There is already a large amount of crosslisting and trading among exchanges. Competition among exchanges for listing and order flow has long characterized European securities markets. In addition, exchanges have become subject to competition for order flow from alternative trading systems. Because there are benefits from achieving large size and attracting liquidity, another important response to competitive pressures has consisted of mergers among exchanges. Concentration of the stock market capitalization is not an "EU-phenomenon," but reflects a worldwide trend toward a single global market for certain instruments.

9.4. INTERNATIONAL LOANS

Large international loans to developing countries have become extremely important for European, Japanese, and US banks. For some banks, international loans have become as important as their domestic banking operations. On the other hand, global debt problems have raised serious questions about large loans to developing and East-bloc countries.

9.4.1. *The Latin American Debt Crisis of the 1980s*

Developing countries dramatically increased their borrowing from lenders in the Western industrial countries from 1973 to 1982. The total external debt of the non-oil developing countries increased from $130 billion in 1973 to $840 billion in 1982, a 6.5-fold increase. Over this 10-year period, the debt grew at an average compound rate of 20 percent per year. At the outset, few people worried as the external debts of these countries mounted in the 1970s. Several poor countries in Africa experienced difficult servicing problems. Yet, by the early 1980s, more developed borrowers such as Poland, Mexico, Brazil, and Argentina had difficulty in servicing their huge external debts.

The first major blow to the international banking system came in August 1982, when Mexico announced that it could not meet its regularly scheduled payments to international creditors. Shortly thereafter, Brazil and Argentina were in the same situation. By spring 1983, about 25 developing countries could not make regularly scheduled payments and negotiated rescheduling with creditor banks. These countries accounted for two-thirds of the total debt owed by non-oil developing countries to private banks.

A worldwide recession compounded the lending crisis. It put downward pressure on oil prices and on OPEC's revenues. OPEC — Organization of Petroleum Exporting Countries — is an organization established by a number of oil exporting countries to formulate uniform policies such as selling prices on their oil-export sales. In 1980, OPEC contributed almost $42 billion to the loanable funds of the international banks, but by 1982, OPEC nations withdrew $26 billion from these loanable funds.

Observers feared that the debt crisis would provoke an international banking crisis and a global depression. Thus, lenders, borrowers, the International Monetary Fund (IMF), and the World Bank worked together to overcome this crisis through rescheduling, refinancing, additional loans, and restrictive economic policies. These original measures were not sufficient to solve the 7-year-old debt crisis completely. In 1989, US Treasury Secretary Nicholas Brady put forth a set of principles, known as the Brady Plan, to resolve the problem. The Brady Plan offered three options to the creditor banks: (1) convert their loans to marketable bonds with a face value equal to 65 percent of the original loan amount; (2) convert their loans into new guaranteed bonds with a reduced interest rate of 6.5 percent; or (3) keep their old loans but provide additional funds equal to 25 percent of their original loan amount. As you might imagine, most banks chose either the first or the second option, while only few banks took the third option. Those bonds that originated from the second option under the Brady Plan have come to be called Brady bonds. This option included the following provisions: (1) extend the debt maturities by 25 to 30 years; (2) compel the debtor countries to purchase zero-coupon US Treasury bonds to guarantee the bonds; and (3) make these bonds marketable. In 1992, 20 debtor nations, including Argentina, Brazil, Bulgaria, Mexico, Nigeria, Poland, and the Philippines, had issued Brady bonds. These debtor countries had converted approximately $100 billion in bank debt into Brady bonds. These Brady bonds are largely credited with solving the decade-long global debt crisis of the 1980s.

9.4.2. *The Mexican Peso Crisis of 1994*

Before the December 1994 devaluation, the Mexican government had essentially pegged the peso to the US dollar through its exchange-rate stabilization program. Mexico permitted its exchange rate to fluctuate within a band of 2 percent. However, in December 1994 Mexico faced a balance of payments crisis. Investors lost confidence in Mexico's ability to maintain the exchange rate of the peso within its trading band, in part because of Mexico's large current account deficit, which had reached almost $28 billion in 1994. Intense pressure on the peso in foreign exchange markets threatened to exhaust Mexico's international reserves. This pressure eventually compelled the Mexican government to float the peso and led to the now-famous peso crisis between December 1994 and early 1995.

Mexico decided to devalue, widening the band on the exchange rate on December 20 and going to a freely floating rate on December 22. The latter decision was actually forced because the earlier one collapsed as investor confidence in the peso disappeared. Widening the band clearly presaged devaluation and led to a massive capital flight from the peso, and loss of $6 billion or half of the remaining reserves in one day. Judging by their public economic plans, the Mexican authorities had in mind an exchange rate of 4.07 pesos to the dollar, a 14 percent devaluation from the earlier 3.50 floor. But with confidence imploding, the peso dropped immediately to 5.80, a 40 percent devaluation. A rash of speculative attacks against other Latin American currencies — Argentina (peso), Brazil (real), Peru (new sol), and Venezuela (bolivar) — broke out immediately through what became known as the "tequila" effect. Several non-Latin American countries — Thailand, Hong Kong, the Philippines, and Hungary — also suffered brief speculative attacks. However, only few countries actually devalued their currencies. Argentina was the only other country that suffered a sharp recession as a result of the Mexican peso crisis.

The United States and the International Monetary Fund arranged the Mexican rescue package of $50 billion to avert a broader financial crisis. The Mexican rescue plan unveiled on January 31, 1995 by President Clinton included $20 billion in US loans, $17.8 billion of IMF credit, $10 billion from the Bank for International Settlements, $1 billion from Canada, and $1 billion from several Latin American countries. President Clinton used his authority to tap the Treasury's exchange stabilization fund. This fund, primarily used to stabilize the dollar on the world market, had not been used for anything but short-term lending and had never been used on this scale to help another country.

9.4.3. *The Asian Financial Crisis of 1997*

Thailand's economy surged until early 1997 partly because the Thais found they could borrow dollars at low-interest rates overseas more cheaply than they could the baht at home. By late 1996, foreign investors began to move their money out of Thailand because they worried about Thais' ability to repay. In February 1997, foreign investors and Thai companies rushed to convert their baht to dollars. The Thai central bank responded by buying baht with its dollar reserves and raising interest rates.

The rise in interest rates drove prices for stocks and land downward. This dynamic situation drew attention to serious problems in the Thai economy: a huge foreign debt, trade deficits, and a banking system weakened by the heavy burden of unpaid loans. The Thai central bank ran out of dollars to support the baht. On July 2, 1997, the central bank stopped the baht's fixed value against the dollar. And then the currency lost 16 percent of its value in one day.

Investors and companies in the Philippines, Malaysia, Indonesia, and Korea realized that these economies shared all of Thailand's problems. So, investors and companies rushed to convert local currencies into dollars. And then, the peso, ringgit, rupiah, and won toppled in value like dominos in a row. In the fourth quarter of 1997, the IMF arranged emergency rescue packages of $18 billion for Thailand, $43 billion for Indonesia, and $58 billion for Korea. By the end of 1998, the Asian crisis of 1997 spread to Russia, Brazil, and many other countries. Again, the IMF arranged bail-out packages of $23 billion for Russia in July 1998 and $42 billion for Brazil in November 1998. This means that from Fall 1997 to Fall 1998, IMF-led rescue packages for Asia, Russia, and Brazil racked up some $184 billion to keep world markets safe.

9.4.3.1. *Causes of the crisis*

Although many explanations have been offered on the causes of the Asian crisis most views fall into one of two theories: the "fundamentalist" view and the "panic" view.[4]

---

[4]Neely, M. C., "Paper Tigers? How the Asian Economies Lost Their Bite," *The Regional Economist*, Federal Reserve Bank of St. Louis, January 1999, pp. 5–9.

The fundamentalist view focuses on how borrowing countries' policies and practices fed the crisis, whereas the panic view focuses on the role lenders played.

The Fundamentalist View holds that flawed financial systems were at the root of the crisis and its spread. The maturity mismatch and the currency mismatch — the use of short-term debt for fixed assets and unhedged external debt — made banks and firms vulnerable to sudden swings in international investors' confidence. Many economists believe that these two types of mismatch were caused by moral hazard because most East-Asian companies and financial institutions operated with implicit or explicit government guarantees.

The Panic View holds that problems in Thailand were turned into an Asian crisis because of international investors' irrational behavior and because of overly harsh fiscal and monetary policies prescribed by the IMF once the crisis broke. The panic view is consistent with the concept of **financial contagion**, which occurs when: (1) events in one financial market trigger events in other markets and (2) the magnitude of the response in the other markets appears unfounded in economic fundamentals.

9.4.3.2. *Policy responses*

Just like the previous developing-country crises, lenders, borrowers, and international financial institutions worked together to overcome the crisis. External payments were stabilized through IMF-led aid programs, the rescheduling of short-term foreign debts, and reductions in foreign borrowings through painful reversals of current account deficits. The IMF has established new financing packages to encourage the adoption of policies that could prevent crises in selected developing countries.

9.4.4. *Summary of Currency Crises*

All three crises' episodes occurred under fixed exchange rate regimes. Economic theory suggests that a pegged exchange rate regime can become vulnerable when cross-border capital flows are highly mobile. A central bank that pegs its exchange rate to a hard currency implicitly guarantees that any investors can exchange their local currency assets for that hard currency at the prevailing exchange rate. If investors suspect that the government will not or cannot maintain the peg, they may flee the currency; this capital flight, in turn, deletes hard currency reserves and forces the devaluation they fear.

9.5. FINANCIAL CRISES OF INDUSTRIALIZED COUNTRIES

When communism collapsed in 1990, some Western economists and policymakers declared that the triumph of capitalism over socialism has solved the central problem of depression prevention for all practical purposes.[5] However, this conclusion turned out to be premature because major industrialized countries — Japan, European Union, and the US have faced their own severe economic problems since 1990.

---

[5]Krugman, P., *The Return of Depression Economics and the Crisis of 2008,* New York: W.W. Norton & Company, 2009, Chapter 1.

9.5.1. *Europe's Eurosclerosis of 1980s and Beyond*

Eurosclerosis is a term coined in the 1970s and the early 1980s to describe a European economic pattern of high unemployment and slow job creation in spite of overall economic growth. This was in contrast to what the United States experienced in the same period when economic expansion was accompanied by high job growth. Later, the term tended to be used more broadly to refer to overall economic stagnation for the European Union and other countries.

European currency crises in early 1990s and the collapse of the Soviet Union in 1991 actually improved the possibility of the European monetary union (the euro) on January 1999. Today, the European Union (EU) consists of 28 countries, 27 countries of which use the euro as their common currency. The integration of European economies through the EU and the adoption of the euro as their common currency resulted in market-opening liberalization and avoided currency crisis since the early 1990s. However, their promised economic prosperity through the expansion of the EU is yet to be realized. Economic performance varies from state to state, but the EU's overall high unemployment rate has existed throughout the last two decades.

Furthermore, Greece, Italy, Portugal, Spain, and Ireland — known now as the PIIGS — the weak sisters of Europe with high structural deficits, has created the so-called "Euro Debt Crisis" in the late 2000s. Anxiety about the health of the euro was not simply a crisis of debts for these five countries but also a crisis for the entire EU. The issue has at its heart elements of a political crisis, because it goes to the central dilemma of the European Union: the continuing grip of individual states over economic and fiscal policy, which makes it difficult for the union as a whole to exercise the political leadership needed to deal effectively with a crisis. Thus, this debt crisis has become the most severe test of the 16-nation eurozone in its 11-year history because default for a member of the eurozone is simply unacceptable.[6]

9.5.2. *Japan's Economic Trap of 1990s and Beyond*

In the beginning of 1990 the market capitalization of Japan — the total value of all the stocks of all the nation's companies was larger than that of the United Stages with twice Japan's population and more than twice its GDP.[7] However, the stock market went into reverse in 1989, land prices collapsed in 1992, credit cooperatives and regional banks came under attack in 1994, large banks teetered on the edge of bankruptcy in 1997 and a major credit crunch occurred in 1998.

The Japanese recession was triggered by a build-up of bad debt in the country's banking system. Money had been borrowed using inflated property values as security. The world was assured that safeguards were in place and that any failing bank would be helped out by others, through what was known as the 'convoy system'. But neither the convoy system nor securitized debt could withstand a fall in property prices combined with a growing rate of default by borrowers. The Financial Times reported in 2008, "Japan's 1990s banking crisis has gone down as one of the worst in history, generating a staggering $700 billion of credit

---

[6]http://en.wikipedia.org/wiki/PIIGS, March 10, 2010.
[7]Krugman, P., *The Return of Depression Economics and the Crisis of 2008,* New York: W.W. Norton & Company, 2009, Chapter 3.

losses. As of October 2008, Japanese share prices were 70 percent lower than at their 1989 peak, while property values were about 40 percent lower than they were in 1990. Economic (GDP) growth in the 1990s averaged less than 1 percent a year, leading economists to talk of the "lost decade" or "an economic trap."[8]

9.5.3. *US Recessions of 2000 and 2020*

The collapse of the Soviet Union in 1991, along with the unusually strong performance of both the US economy and its stock market from the mid-1980s to the mid-2000s elevated the United States to an unsurpassed level of economic, military, and cultural power. However, in the late 2000s, the United States faced the first wave of decline since the 1950s, a phenomenon largely triggered by its external economic problems, Iraq and Afghanistan wars, and budget deficits. The US financial crisis has hit the global economy hard and terrified many people around the world. Uncertainty seems the most appropriate term to describe today's circumstances.

The sub-prime mortgage crisis, investment bank failures, falling home prices, and tight credit pushed the US into a great recession by mid-2008. GDP contracted until the third quarter of 2009, making this the deepest and longest downturn since the Great Depression (see Fig. 9.1). To help stabilize financial markets, the US Congress established a $700 billion Troubled Asset Relief Program (TARP) in October 2008. The government used some of these funds to purchase equity in US banks and other industrial corporations. In January 2009, the $787 billion economic stimulus signed by President Obama, which had grown to $862 billion, is supposed to be used over 10 years — two-thirds on additional spending and one-third on tax cuts — to create jobs and to help the economy recover. Approximately two-thirds of these funds have been injected into the economy by the end of 2010.[9] In addition, the Federal Reserve System reduced the interest rate under its control, known as the federal fund rate, to the lowest level since 1933 (see Fig. 9.2).

Almost all past US recessions had happened mainly due to economic reasons. Causes of some specific recessions are the boom bust — easy money (the Great Depression), the Arab oil embargo against the US and other Western countries (1973 recession), tight monetary policy in an effort to fight mounting inflation (1980–1981 recession), and the subprime mortgage crisis (the 2008 great recession). Between 1980 and 1982 the US economy experienced a deep recession (usually known as a double dip), the primary cause of which was the disinflationary monetary policy adopted by the Federal Reserve System. One noteworthy recession is the 1981–1982 recession that received a lot of attention. This is because just everybody called "inflation was a public enemy number one" at the time and the government adopted a tight monetary policy to make the recession even worse on purpose.[10]

Unlike past US recessions caused by economic reasons, the United States entered into a recession in February 2020, a result of the Coronavirus Disease 2019 (COVID-19) pandemic.

---

[8] "Lessons of the 1990s recession in Japan," *Socialist*, October 8, 2008, http://www.socialistparty.org.uk/articles/6468, February 25, 2010.
[9] The US Central Intelligence Agency, *The World Factbook*, https://www.cia.gov/library/publications/the-world-factbook/geos/us.html, March 10, 2010.
[10] "Early 1980s recession," *Wikipedia*, https://en.wikipedia.org/wiki/Early_1980s_recession.

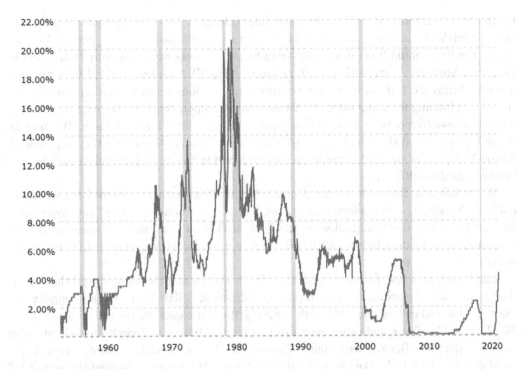

Fig. 9.2   Federal funds rate — 62 year historical chart.

Notes: Shaded bars show recessions. The width of each shaded bar represents the length of the recession.

Source: https://www.macrotrends.net/2015/fed-funds-rate-historical-chart, January 30, 2023.

The **COVID-19 recession**, also referred to as the Great Lockdown, is a global economic recession caused by the government responses to the COVID-19 pandemic. To prevent the spread of COVID-19, lockdown orders were issued in many parts of the country and travel restrictions were put in place. This recession lasted only 2 months (see Fig. 9.1), but tough measures, along with general fears of the coronavirus, caused swift and large aggregate demand and supply shocks that resulted in the deepest economic downturn since the Great Depression.[11]

9.5.4. *The Collapse of the SVB and the Matching Principle*

The collapse of the Silicon Valley Bank (SVB) — the US's 16th largest bank — on March 10, 2023, created fear of a worldwide banking crisis. The SVB happened to be the biggest to fail since the 2008 financial meltdown. "SVB's failure was not related to regulator changes. Rather, it was a textbook case of mismanagement," as Michael Barr, the Federal Reserve Vice Chairman for supervision, said on March 27, 2023.[12] Indeed, this crisis happened

---

[11]Kim, S., M. Xu, and J. David, "Highly Unusual Features of the 2020 US Recession," *Journal of Public Administration, Finance and Law*, Issue 23, 2022, pp. 190–198, https://www.jopafl.com/uploads/issue23/HIGHLY_UNUSUAL_FEATURES_OF_THE_2020_US_RECESSION.pdf.

[12]Quarles, R. K., "What Congress Should Ask Congress in SVB's Aftermath," *The Wall Street Journal*, March 28, 2023, p. A15.

because the SVB violated the so-called matching principle. This principle says that the firm should match the maturity structure of its assets with its liabilities and equity. In other words, the firm should finance its short-term financial assets with short-term funds and its long-term financial assets with long-term funds. "The SVA almost doubled its assets and deposits during 2021. It got in trouble because it bought long-term, low-yielding bonds with short-term funding from depositors that was repayable upon demand. Accounting rules said it did not have to recognize losses on the assets as long as it did not sell them. When rising interest rates caused the bonds' value to drop, it got stuck in them, and they kept falling. Silicon Valley Bank still had to maintain enough liquidity to pay withdrawals, which became increasingly difficult."[13]

When Lehman Brothers collapsed in 2008, the US government rescued banks, shareholders, depositors, automakers, and others. This time around, however, the government decided to do just one thing, allowing the Federal Deposit Insurance Corporation (FDIC) to guarantee depositors beyond $250,000. This decision failed to restore confidence in the world financial system.

The investors' fears of contagion, such as credit crunch and recession, forced the US and the EU to take extraordinary steps to prop up billions of dollars of the bank's deposits. For example, the collapse of the SVB with a $200 billion in assets on December 31, 2022 led JP Morgan, Citi Bank and other giants to provide $30 billion in deposits to help show up the First Republic Bank. Credit Suisse Group AG, the Swiss banking giant, struck a deal on March 19, 2023, to be bought by rival UBS Group AG, thereby marking the end of 167 years as an independent institution. KPMG has been in a hot seat because the SVB failed just 14 days after the accounting firm gave a clean bill of health. Signature Bank went down 11 days after the firm signed off on its audit.

9.6. SUMMARY

The international financial market consists of the Eurodollar market, the international bond market, and the international equity market. Eurodollars are dollar-denominated deposits in banks all over the world except the United States. The Eurodollar market is the truly international money market undisturbed by the rules and restrictions of any national authority. Eurodollars have become a major source of short-term loans for MNCs to finance their working capital needs and foreign trade. With the growth in availability of Eurodollars, Eurobanks have begun to extend medium-term Eurodollar loans for MNCs to finance their medium-term needs. Although the international bond and equity markets are of a more recent vintage, they parallel the importance of multinational financial management and mainly facilitate expansion involving fixed asset commitment.

Recent events in many debtor countries have brought analysts and investors to question international bankers about loans to economically risky countries. For some banks, international lending can be as important as their domestic operations. Thus, international banks must reduce the impact of country risk through systematic assessment and management. When communism collapsed in 1990, some Western economists and policymakers declared

---

[13]Weil, J. and J. Eaglesham, "KPMG Gave Banks Clean Bill of Health," *The Wall Street Journal*, March 14, p. A8.

that the triumph of capitalism over socialism has solved the central problem of depression prevention for all practical purposes. However, this conclusion turned out to be premature because major industrialized countries — Japan, European Union, and the US have faced their own severe economic problems since 1990.

9.7. KEY TERMS

eurocurrency market	Eurodollars
certificate of deposit (CD)	revolving credit
London Interbank Offered Rate (LIBOR)	secured overnight financing rate (SOFR)
euronote issue facilities (EIFs)	euro note
euro commercial paper (ECP)	euro-medium-term notes (EMTNs)
clearing house interbank payment system	clearing house automated payments system
SWIFT	contagion
Bank for International Settlements	three pillars
universal bank	keiretsu
international capital market	eurosclerosis
international bonds	foreign bonds
Eurobonds	global bonds
junk bonds	straight bonds
amortization	method warrants
zero-coupon bonds	primary market
secondary market	the fundamentalist view
the panic view	financial contagion

9.8. PROBLEMS

1. Fill in the following blank spaces with a reserve ratio of 20 percent.

	Acquired Reserves	Required Reserves	Excess Reserves	Amount Bank Can Lend
Bank 1	$100.00	$20.00	$80.00	$80.00
Bank 2				
Bank 3				
Bank 4				
Bank 5				
Bank 6				
Bank 7				
Bank 8				
Bank 9				
Bank 10				
Bank 11				
Bank 12				
Bank 13				
Total amount loaned				

2. Assume that an international bank has the following simplified balance sheet. The reserve ratio is 20 percent.

Assets		1	2	Liabilities & Net Worth	1	2
Reserves	$4,400	—	—	Demand Deposits $20,000		
Securities	$7,600					
Loans	$8,000					

  a. Determine the maximum amount which this bank can safely lend. Show in Column 1 how the bank's balance sheet will appear after the bank has loaned this amount.

  b. By how much has the supply of money changed?

  c. Show the new balance sheet in column 2 after checks drawn for the entire amount of the new loans have been cleared against this bank.

  d. To what extent will this lending alter the supply of money?

  e. Aside from the leakage of required reserves at each stage of the lending process, there are some other leakages of money from the lending process. List and discuss them.

  f. Assume: (1) an American citizen transfers $2,000 of his deposits from a US bank to a Eurobank, and (2) Eurobanks as a whole keep 5 percent of their Eurodollar deposits in vault cash. Determine the maximum amount of Eurodollar supply that Eurobanks can create on the basis of $2,000.

3. A multinational company holds a $1,000 zero-coupon bond with a maturity of 15 years and a yield rate of 16 percent. What is the market value of the zero-coupon bond?

4. A multinational company has issued a 10-year, $1,000 zero coupon bond to yield 10 percent.

  a. What is the initial price of the bond?

  b. If interest rates dropped to 8 percent immediately upon issue, what would be the price of the bond?

  c. If interest rate rose to 12 percent immediately upon issue, what would be the price of the bond?

5. A multinational company has common stock outstanding. Each share of the common stock pays $3.60 dividends per year, and the stockholder requires a 12-percent rate of return. What is the price of the common stock?

Closing Case 9: The Collapse of a Prominent Hedge Fund

In late September 1998, a group of large financial institutions urgently invested $3.5 billion in Long-Term Capital Management (LTCM), a prominent hedge fund, to prevent its imminent collapse. These firms — Goldman Sachs, Merrill Lynch, Morgan Stanley Dean Witter, J.P. Morgan, Chase Manhattan, United Bank of Switzerland, and several others — had been encouraged to undertake the rescue by the Federal Reserve Bank of New York, which feared that a sudden failure of the fund could significantly disrupt world financial markets. The label "hedge fund" refers to investment companies that are unregulated because they restrict participation to a relatively small number of wealthy investors. The amount invested in hedge funds reached $300 billion in 1998.

The LTCM was formed in 1994, by a former Salmon Vice Chairman John Meirwellen, two Nobel laureates Robert Merton and Myron Schols, former students of Professors Merton and Schols, and several other prominent investors. The fund posted profits of 43 percent in 1995 and 41 percent in 1996. However, in August 1998 alone, LTCM's positions dropped 40 percent as a result of financial crisis in Russia and several other countries. These bad outcomes were compounded by the huge amount of debt that LTCM had used to finance its transactions. Like other hedge funds, LTCM used derivative instruments to structure its investment transactions. Before its final crisis, LTCM had only $4 billion of equity capital, but over $100 billion in its futures contracts, forward contracts, options, swaps, and other assets.

How could some of the world's best-known investors, some of the best economists, and some of the smartest mathematicians get crushed so quickly? LTCM had made a variety of investments all over the world, focused primarily on the expectation that various financial markets spread and volatility would converge to their historical norms. LTCM's leverage and its trading strategies made it vulnerable to the extraordinary financial market conditions that emerged after Russia's devaluation of the ruble and declaration of a debt moratorium on August 17, 1998.

Russia's actions sparked "a flight to quality" in which investors avoided risk and sought out quality. As a result, volatility, risk, and liquidity spreads rose sharply in markets around the world. For example, LTCM had made heavy bets that interest rates throughout Europe would move closer together as many of its nations moved toward monetary union. But with investors suddenly more eager to buy deutsche mark bonds, the spread between German and other European-government bonds widened rapidly — precisely what LTCM had bet against and thus causing the fund's bet to lose money. In another instance, the yield spread between US Treasuries and private securities also sharply widened — again what the fund had bet against.

"A hedge fund (LTCM) borrowed billions of dollars to make big bets on esoteric securities. Markets turned and the bets went sour. Overnight, the firm lost most of its money, and Wall Street suddenly shunned it. Fearing that its collapse could set off a full-scale market meltdown, the US government intervened and encouraged private interests to bail it out." This history almost repeated in 2008, except there was no bail out for the fund. It was Long-Term Capital Management (LTCM), the hedge fund based in Greenwich, Connecticut, and the rescue occurred in 1998, 10 years before the latest crisis peaked in 2008.

The LTCM fiasco momentarily shocked Wall Street out of its complacent trust in financial models, and was replete with lessons, for Washington as well as for Wall Street. But the lessons were ignored, and in the next decade they were repeated, with far more harmful consequences. Instead of learning from the past, Wall Street re-enacted it in larger form, in the mortgage debacle cum credit crisis.

Case Questions

1. What are the causes of the great recession of 2007–2009?
2. What are hedge funds? What is the market size of hedge funds?
3. Why has the financial press criticized hedge funds in recent years?
4. How can Mexican investors beat the competition?
5. Visit the Web site http://en.wikipedia.org/wiki/ to review the strategies used by hedge funds. Visit the Web site <http://biz.yahoo.com/funds/>, click on top performers to review the performance of top mutual funds, and then conduct a comparative analysis of performance for international mutual funds and purely domestic portfolios.

Sources: Roe, M. J., "The Derivatives Market's Payment and Priorities as Financial Crisis Accelerator," *Stanford Law Review*, March 2011, pp. 539–548; *Economic Report of the President to Congress*, 1999, pp. 63–67; Lowenstein, R., "Long-Term Capital Management: It's a Short-Term Memory," *New York Times*, September 7, 2008; and Kim, K., *Global Corporate Finance: A Focused Approach*, New Jersey: World Scientific, 2011, Chapter 12.

Chapter 10

FINANCING INTERNATIONAL TRANSACTIONS

Opening Case 10: The Yuan's the New Dollar as Russia Rides to the Redback

Chinese entrepreneur Wang Min is delighted about Russia's embrace of the yuan. His LED lights company can price contracts to Russian customers in yuan rather than dollars or euros, and they can pay him in yuan. It is "win-win", he says. Wang's plans have been transformed by the conflict in Ukraine and the subsequent Western sanctions on Moscow that have shut Russia's banks and many of its companies out of the dollar and euro payment systems.

His contract manufacturing business with Russia has been small in the past, but now he is preparing to invest in warehousing there. "We hope that next year sales in Russia can account for 10–15 percent of our total sales," said the businessman from China's southern coastal province of Guangdong, whose annual revenue of about $20 million mainly comes from Africa and South America.

Wang is seeking to capitalize on a rapid "humanization" of Russia's economy this year as the isolated country seeks financial security from Asian powerhouse China. He sees a win-win situation in Chinese exporters reducing their currency risks and payment becoming more convenient for Russian buyers.

While the yuan, or renminbi, has been making gradual inroads into Russia for years, the crawl has turned into a sprint in the past nine months as the currency has swept into the country's markets and trade flows, according to a Reuters review of data and interviews with 10 business and finance players. Russia's financial shift eastwards could boost cross-border commerce, present a growing economic counterweight to the dollar, and limit Western efforts to pressure Moscow by economic means.

Summaries

- Russia turns to the Chinese currency amid sanctions.
- Moscow becomes the No. 4 offshore trading center for yuan.
- Yuan's share of Russian foreign exchange market jumps from 1 to 45 percent.

- Russian central bank supports the trend but warns of risks.
- This content was produced in Russia where the law restricts coverage of Russian military operations in Ukraine.[1]

This book emphasizes financial problems that arise when managing multinational operations. However, the financial manager of a multinational company (MNC) must be familiar with certain mechanics of financing foreign trade and foreign investment because most MNCs are frequently engaged in foreign trade and investment activities.

The first three sections cover the sources of financing foreign trade, while the last three sections discuss the sources of financing foreign investment. The first section discusses three basic documents involved in foreign trade: draft, bill of lading, and letter of credit. The second section analyzes the various payment terms of foreign trade. The third section describes the major sources of financing foreign trade. The three major sources of funds for foreign investment are internal sources of funds, external sources of funds, and sources of funds from development banks. MNCs may use internally generated funds such as profits and depreciation charges. If internal sources of funds are insufficient, they may obtain their capital from sources within their home country and/or in foreign countries. In addition to these internal and external sources of funds, development banks provide MNCs with a variety of financing sources.

10.1. BASIC DOCUMENTS IN FOREIGN TRADE

Three important documents involved in foreign trade are:

1. A draft, which is an order to pay.
2. A bill of lading, which is a document involved in the physical movement of the merchandise by a common carrier.
3. A letter of credit, which is a third-party guarantee of the importer's creditworthiness.

10.1.1. *Basic Objectives of Documentation*

Documentation in foreign trade is supposed to assure that the exporter will receive the payment and the importer will receive the merchandise. More specifically, a number of documents in foreign trade are used to eliminate noncompletion risk, to reduce foreign exchange risk, and to finance trade transactions.

10.1.1.1. *Noncompletion risk*

The risk of noncompletion is greater in foreign trade than in domestic trade. This is why exporters want to keep title to the goods until they are paid and importers are reluctant to pay until they receive the goods. Foreign trade and domestic trade use different instruments and documents. Most domestic sales are on open-account credit. Under this credit, a buyer

---

[1]Fabrichnaya, E. and S. Shen, "The Yuan's the New Dollar as Russia Rides to the Redback," *Reuters*, November 29, 2022.

does not need to sign a formal debt instrument because credit sales are made on the basis of a seller's credit investigation of the buyer. Buyers and sellers are typically farther apart in foreign trade than in domestic trade. Thus, the sellers are seldom able to ascertain the credit standing of their overseas customers. The buyers may also find it difficult to determine the integrity and reputation of the foreign sellers from whom they wish to buy. Much of this noncompletion risk is reduced through the use of three key documents: the draft, the bill of lading, and the letter of credit.

10.1.1.2. *Foreign exchange risk*

Foreign exchange risk arises when export sales are denominated in a foreign currency and are paid at a delayed date. In international trade, the basic foreign exchange risk is a transaction risk. Transaction risk is the potential exchange loss from outstanding obligations as a result of exchange-rate fluctuations. Forward contracts, futures contracts, currency options, and currency denomination practices can be used to reduce foreign exchange risk associated with foreign trade.

10.1.1.3. *Trade financing*

Because all foreign trade involves a time lag, funds are tied up in the shipment of goods for some period of time. Most trade transactions are free of noncompletion and foreign exchange risks due to well-drawn trade documents and forward contracts. Banks are thus willing to finance goods in transit or even prior to shipment. Financial institutions at both ends of the cycle offer a variety of financing alternatives that reduce or eliminate either party's (exporter or importer) working capital needs.

10.1.2. **Drafts**

A **draft** or a **bill of exchange** is an order written by an exporter that requires an importer to pay a specified amount of money at a specified time. Through the use of drafts, the exporter may use its bank as the collection agent on accounts that the exporter finances. The bank forwards the exporter's drafts to the importer directly or indirectly (through a branch or a correspondent bank) and then remits the proceeds of the collection back to the exporter.

A draft involves three parties: the drawer or maker, the drawee, and the payee. The **drawer** is a person or business issuing a draft. This person is ordinarily the exporter who sells and ships the merchandise. The **drawee** is a person or business against whom the draft is drawn. This person is usually an importer who must pay the draft at maturity. The **payee** is a person or business to whom the drawee will eventually pay the funds. A draft designates a person or bank to whom payment is to be made if the draft is not a negotiable instrument. Such a person, known as the payee, may be the drawer himself or a third party such as the drawer's bank. However, this is generally not the case because most drafts are a bearer instrument. Drafts are negotiable if they meet a number of conditions:

1. They must be in writing and signed by the drawer–exporter.
2. They must contain an unconditional promise or order to pay an exact amount of money.
3. They must be payable on sight or at a specified time.
4. They must be made out to order or to bearer.

If a draft is made to order, the funds involved should be paid to the person specified. If it is made to bearer, the funds should be paid to the person who presents it for payment.

When a draft is presented to a drawee, the drawee or his bank accepts it. This acceptance acknowledges in writing the drawee's obligation to pay a sum indicated on the face of the draft. When drafts are accepted by banks, they become bankers' acceptances. Because bankers' acceptances are highly marketable, the exporter can sell them in the market or discount them at his bank. Whenever they are sold or discounted, the seller adds his endorsement on the back of the draft. In the event an importer fails to pay at maturity, the holder of the draft will have recourse for the full amount of the draft from the last endorser.

Drafts are used in foreign trade for a number of reasons:

1. They provide written evidence of obligations in a comprehensive form.
2. They allow both the exporter and the importer to reduce the cost of financing and to divide the remaining cost equitably.
3. They are negotiable and unconditional; that is, drafts are not subject to disputes which may occur between the parties involved.

10.1.2.1. *Types of drafts*

Drafts can be either sight (demand) drafts or time (usance) drafts. A sight draft is payable upon demand to the drawee-importer. Here the drawee must pay the draft immediately or dishonor it. A time draft is payable a specified number of days after presentation to the drawee. When a time draft is presented to the drawee, she may have her bank accept it by writing or stamping a notice of acceptance on its face. When a draft is drawn on and accepted by a bank, it becomes a bankers' acceptance.

Drafts may also be documentary drafts or clean drafts. Documentary drafts require various shipping documents such as bills of lading, insurance certificates, and commercial invoices. Most drafts are documentary because all these shipping documents are necessary to obtain the goods shipped. The documents attached to a documentary draft are passed on to an importer either upon payment (for sight drafts) or upon acceptance (for time drafts). If documents are to be delivered to an importer upon payment of the draft, it is known as a D/P (documents against payment) draft. If the documents are passed on to an importer upon acceptance, the draft is called a D/A (documents against acceptance) draft.

When a time draft is accepted by an importer, it becomes a trade acceptance or a clean draft. When clean drafts are used in foreign trade, the exporter usually sends all shipping documents directly to the importer and only the draft to the collecting bank. In this case, the goods shipped are surrendered to the importer regardless of payment or acceptance of the draft. The clean draft, therefore, involves a considerable amount of risk. This is why clean drafts are generally used in cases in which there is a considerable amount of faith between the exporter and the importer or in cases in which multinational firms send goods to their foreign subsidiaries.

10.1.3. *Bills of Lading*

A **bill of lading** is a shipping document issued to an exporting firm or its bank by a common carrier which transports the goods. It is simultaneously a receipt, a contract, and a document of title. As a receipt, the bill of lading indicates that specified goods have been received by the carrier. As a contract, it is evidence that the carrier is obliged to deliver the goods to the importer in exchange for certain charges. As a document of title, it establishes ownership of the goods. Thus, the bill of lading can be used to insure payment before the goods are delivered. For example, the importer cannot take title to the goods until she obtains the bill of lading from the carrier.

10.1.3.1. *Types of bills of lading*

Bills of lading are either straight bills of lading or order bills of lading. A straight bill of lading requires that the carrier deliver the goods to the designated party, usually the importer. It is used when the goods have been paid for in advance; thus, it is not a title to the goods. An order bill of lading provides that the carrier delivers the goods to the order of a designated party, usually the exporter. The exporting firm retains title to the goods until it receives payment. Once payment has been made, the exporting firm endorses the order bill of lading in blank or to its bank. The endorsed document can be used as collateral against loans. It accompanies a documentary draft which requires such other documents as the bill of lading, commercial invoices, and insurance certificates. The procedures to handle these two types of bills of lading are well established. Commercial banks and other financial institutions in almost every country handle these documents efficiently.

Bills of lading can also be either on-board bills of lading or received-for-shipment bills of lading. An on-board bill of lading indicates that the goods have actually been placed on board the vessel. On-board bills of lading are important because some insurance coverage such as war risk are effective only if goods are on board. By contrast, a received-for-shipment bill of lading merely acknowledges that the carrier has received the goods for shipment but does not guarantee that the goods have been loaded on the vessel. The cargo could sit on the dock for some time before it is shipped. This bill of lading is thus unsatisfactory when seasonal or perishable goods are involved. A received-for-shipment bill of lading can easily be converted into an on-board bill of lading by an appropriate stamp which shows the name of the vessel, the date, and the signature of an official of the vessel.

Finally, bills of lading may be either clean bills of lading or foul bills of lading. A clean bill of lading suggests that the carrier has received the goods in apparently good condition. The carrier does not have any obligation to check the condition of the cargo beyond external visual appearance. On the other hand, a foul bill of lading bears a notation from the carrier that the goods appeared to have suffered some damage before the carrier received them for shipment. Because a foul bill of lading is generally not acceptable under a letter of credit, it is important that the exporter obtains a clean bill of lading.

10.1.4. *Letters of Credit*

A **letter of credit** is a document issued by a bank at the request of an importer. In the document, the bank agrees to honor a draft drawn on the importer if the draft accompanies specified documents such as the bill of lading. In a typical use, the importer asks that his local bank write a letter of credit. In exchange for the bank's agreement to honor the demand for payment that results from the import transaction, the importer promises to pay the bank the amount of the transaction and a specified fee.

10.1.4.1. *Advantages of letters of credit*

The letter of credit is advantageous to both exporters and importers because it facilitates foreign trade. It gives a number of benefits to exporters. First, they sell their goods abroad against the promise of a bank rather than a commercial firm. Because banks are usually larger and have better credit risks than most business firms, exporters are almost completely assured of payment if they meet specific conditions. Second, they can obtain funds as soon as they have such necessary documents as the letter of credit and the bill of lading. When shipment is made, the exporter prepares a draft on the importer in accordance with the letter of credit and presents it to his local bank. If the bank finds that all papers are in order, it advances the funds — the face value of the draft less fees and interest.

Although its major beneficiaries are exporters, the letter of credit also gives a number of benefits to importers. First, it assures them that the exporter will be paid only if he provides certain documents, all of which are carefully examined by the bank. If the exporter is unable or unwilling to make proper shipment, recovery of the deposit is easier from the bank than from the exporter. Second, the letter of credit enables the importer to remove commercial risk to the exporter in exchange for other considerations. Thus, the importer can bargain for better terms, such as a lower price. Moreover, it is less expensive to finance the goods under a letter of credit than by borrowing.

10.1.4.2. *Types of letters of credit*

Letters of credit can be irrevocable or revocable. Most credits between unrelated parties are irrevocable. An irrevocable letter of credit can be neither canceled nor modified by the importer's bank without the consent of all parties. A revocable letter of credit can be revoked or modified by the importer's bank at any time before payment. This letter of credit is used as a method of arranging payment, but it does not carry a guarantee of payment. Most banks do not favor revocable letters of credit; some banks refuse to issue them because they may become involved in resulting litigation.

Letters of credit may also be confirmed or unconfirmed. A confirmed letter of credit is a letter of credit confirmed by a bank other than the issuing bank. An exporter might want a foreign bank's letter of credit confirmed by a domestic bank when the exporter has some doubt about the foreign bank's ability to pay. In this case, both banks are obligated to honor drafts drawn in accordance with the letter of credit. An unconfirmed letter of credit is a guarantee of only the opening bank. Thus, the strongest letter of credit is a confirmed, irrevocable letter of credit. Such a letter of credit cannot be canceled by the opening bank, and it requires both the opening and confirming banks to guarantee payment on drafts issued in connection with an export transaction.

Finally, letters of credit are either revolving or non-revolving. A revolving letter of credit is a letter of credit whose duration may revolve weekly or monthly. A $50,000 revolving credit, for example, might authorize an exporter to draw drafts up to $50,000 each week until the credit expires. The revolving letter of credit is often used when an importer must make frequent and known purchases. However, most letters of credit are non-revolving. In other words, letters of credit are typically issued and valid for a single transaction — one letter for one transaction.

10.1.5. *Additional Documents*

In addition to the three documents described here — the draft, the bill of lading, and the letter of credit — other documents must generally accompany the draft as specified in the letter of credit. Some additional documents commonly required in international trade are commercial invoices, insurance documents, and consular invoices. These and some other documents are required to obtain the goods shipped; they are also essential to clear the merchandise through customs and ports of entry and departure.

10.1.5.1. *Commercial invoice*

A **commercial invoice** is issued by the exporter; it contains a precise description of the merchandise, such as unit prices, quality, total value, financial terms of sale, and shipping features. Some shipping features are free on board (FOB), free alongside (FAS), cost and freight (C&F), and cost, insurance, freight (CIF). The commercial invoice may also include some other information such as the names and addresses of exporter and importer, the number of packages, transportation and insurance charges, the name of the vessel, the ports of departure and destination, and any export or import permit numbers.

10.1.5.2. *Insurance documents*

All shipments in international trade are insured. Most insurance contracts used today automatically cover all shipments made by the exporter. The risks of transportation range from slight damage to total loss of merchandise. In most cases, insurance coverage, provided by the carrier up to the port of destination, is sufficient. But most ocean carriers do not have any responsibility for losses during the actual transportation except those directly attributed to their negligence. Therefore, some form of marine insurance should be arranged to protect both the exporter and the importer. Additional coverage ranges from such limited coverage as collision, fire, and sinking, to the broad coverage of all risks.

10.1.5.3. *Consular invoices*

Exports to many countries require a **consular invoice** issued by the consulate of the importing country. The consular invoice provides customs officials with information and statistics for the importing nation. More specifically, a consular invoice is necessary to obtain customs clearance; it also provides customs officials with information necessary to assess import duties. The consular invoice does not carry any title to the goods, and it is not negotiable.

10.1.5.4. *Other documents*

Other documents might be required by the importer or might be necessary in clearing the goods through ports of entry or exit. These documents include certificates of origin, weight lists, packing lists, and inspection certificates. A certificate of origin certifies the country where the goods are grown or manufactured. A weight list itemizes the weight of each item. A packing list identifies the contents of individual packages. An inspection certificate is a document issued by an independent inspection company to verify the contents or quality of the shipment.

10.1.6. *A Typical Foreign Trade Transaction*

As shown in Fig. 10.1, there are many steps and documents in the entire process of completing a foreign trade transaction. Each step or document is a sub-system of the entire transaction process which itself is closely connected by a variety of other subsystems. Thus, the successful completion of a trade transaction may be viewed as an integral unit of many parts which are directly or indirectly interrelated. A typical trade transaction might require the following 14 steps:

1. Importer places an order for a $1 million worth of machines with an inquiry if Exporter is willing to ship under a letter of credit.
2. Exporter agrees to ship under a letter of credit and thus Importer arranges to have its bank open a letter of credit in favor of Exporter.
3. Importer's bank issues the letter of credit (L/C) in favor of Exporter and sends it to Exporter's bank.
4. Once Exporter's bank receives the L/C, it will notify Exporter.
5. Exporter ships the machines to Importer through a common carrier that issues an order bill of lading.

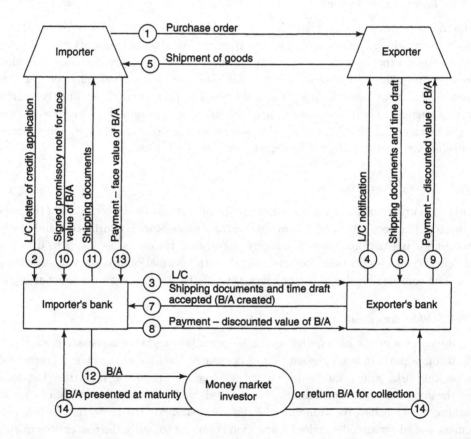

Fig. 10.1 The process of a typical trade transaction.

6. Exporter prepares a 60-day draft on Importer in accordance with the L/C and presents it to Exporter's bank along with such other documents as the bill of lading. At the same time, Exporter endorses the order bill of lading so that a title to the machines goes with the holder of the documents.

7. Exporter's bank forwards the draft and other documents to Importer's bank for acceptance. When the draft is accepted by Importer's bank, it becomes a banker's acceptance (B/A). This means that Importer's bank has promised to pay the draft in 60 days.

8. Exporter instructs its bank to have the B/A discounted by Importer's bank. Alternatively, Exporter's bank receives the B/A from Importer's bank and then it may sell the B/A to an investor at a discount. Another alternative is that Exporter's bank may hold the B/A for 60 days and present it to Importer's bank for payment.

9. If Exporter's bank has discounted the B/A with Importer's bank, it transfers the proceeds less any fees and discount to Exporter.

10. Importer's bank notifies the arrival of the documents to Importer. Importer signs a promissory note to pay its bank for the machines in 60 days.

11. Then Importer's bank releases the shipping documents so that Importer can claim the shipment.

12. Importer's bank may sell the B/A in the money market to an investor.

13. In 60 days, Importer's bank receives the funds from Importer to cover the maturing B/A.

14. On the same day, the holder of the B/A presents it to Importer's bank for payment. Or, the holder of the B/A may return it to Exporter's bank for collection through normal banking channels.

10.2. THE PAYMENT TERMS OF EXPORT TRANSACTIONS

Because trade competition has become increasingly severe, MNCs must know how best to finance their foreign trade. The terms and conditions under which foreign trade takes place vary significantly. They range from cash before delivery to sales in a foreign currency with credit terms over one year. Supply and demand conditions at the time of sale determine the actual terms and conditions of any particular transaction. But most foreign transactions involve longer credit terms than domestic transactions.

10.2.1. *Countertrade*

Countertrade refers to world trade arrangements that are variations on the idea of a barter. Modern countertrade covers various international trade arrangements in which the sale of goods and services by an exporter is linked to an import purchase of other goods and services. It became popular in the 1960s and 1970s as a way for communist countries to finance their international trade without money. In recent years, countertrade has gained new stature in international trade.

World trade continues to grow faster than world production because of increased countertrade. Unfortunately, no reliable figures on the volume of countertrade are available because there is so much secrecy involved. In the 1980s and 1990s, countertrade activities increased. In 1972, there were just 14 countries engaged in countertrade. By 1979, the list had increased to 27 countries, by 1984, 88, by 1989, 94, and by 1995, over 140 countries.[2] The countries engaged in countertrade today range from developing nations, such as China and India to industrialized nations, such as the United Kingdom and Japan.[3] There is no way to determine the actual magnitude of countertrade, but some analysts estimate that it accounts for a third of world trade.[4] In fact, more than 80 countries nowadays regularly use or require countertrade exchanges. The Annual Report 2017 of FCI — Facilitating Open Account-Receivable Finance — reported that the global factoring volumes reached 2,375.967 in 2016. **FCI** is the Global Representative Body for Factoring and Financing of Open Account Domestic and International Trade Receivables. With close to 400-member companies in approximately 90 countries FCI offers a unique network for cooperation in cross-border factoring.[5]

According to an official US statement, "The US Government generally views countertrade, including barter, as contrary to an open, free trading system and, in the long run, not in the interest of the US business community. However, as a matter of policy the US Government will not oppose US companies' participation in countertrade arrangements unless such action could have a negative impact on national security." A large part of countertrade has involved military sales.

We discuss several forms of countertrade below: simple barter, clearing arrangement, switch trade, counterpurchase, compensation agreement, and offset agreement.

10.2.1.1. *Simple barter*

Foreign trade, like domestic trade, is conducted in terms of money. However, foreign trade without money is possible through a barter system. **Simple barter** is a direct exchange of goods between two parties without the use of any currency as a medium of exchange. Most barter arrangements are one-time transactions carried under a single contract. Barter terms are usually arranged between two countries on a bilateral trading agreement. For example, in one recent year General Electric traded its turbine generator to Romania in exchange for Romanian products.

Of course, individual transactions are made within the framework of intergovernmental trade agreements. Such barter deals are popular among nonmarket countries. Barter deals allow countries with a shortage of foreign exchange to obtain their deficit goods in return for their surplus goods. They also allow companies in countries that are short on foreign currency to obtain goods they would not be able to obtain otherwise.

10.2.1.2. *Clearing arrangement*

A **clearing arrangement** is a form of barter in which any two countries agree to buy a certain amount of goods and services from one another within a given period of time. Both

---

[2]Stevens, J., "Global Purchasing and the Rise of Countertrade," *Purchasing and Supply Management,* September 1995, pp. 28–31.

[3]Anyane. N. K. and S. C. Harvey, "A Countertrade Primer," *Management Accounting,* April 1995, pp. 47–50; and Choudry, Y. A., M. McGeady, and R. Stiff, "An Analysis of Attitudes of US Firms Toward Countertrade," *Columbia Journal of World Business,* Summer 1989, pp. 31–38.

[4]http://en.wikipedia.org/wiki/Counter_trade, March 10, 2010.

[5]https://fci.nl/downloads/Annual%20Review%20%202017.pdf, February 25, 2019.

parties set up clearing accounts with each other that are debited whenever one country imports from the other. At the end of an agreed-upon period of time, any account imbalances are cleared by a hard currency payment or by the transfer of additional goods.

Payments for exports to nonmarket countries are often made through clearing arrangements whereby sales are balanced with purchases from importing countries. This clearing arrangement has led to many bilateral trading agreements which try to identify the goods each country will trade and to set overall trade limits.

10.2.1.3. *Switch trade*

A **switch trade** is a trading arrangement under which a third party purchases any account imbalance between the two countries. In other words, the third party will purchase the imbalance from the surplus country on behalf of the deficit country, which is then resold. Thus, switch trading is not really a separate form of countertrade but rather the inclusion of a middleman who serves to multilateralize the barter arrangement. The basic purpose of switch trading is to eliminate the imbalance in barter trade between two countries. Unfortunately, one of the countries frequently fails to sell sufficient goods to its trading partner. In this case, a shortage in clearing funds will be incurred for the deficit country. Hence, one country becomes a creditor, and the other becomes a debtor. When this occurs, the bilateral trading agreement tends to break down.

A breakdown is harmful to both countries, but there are two practical methods to avoid this breakdown. First, the bilateral trading agreement may specify that the debtor country pay amounts in excess of the allowable variations in the form of gold or convertible currency to the creditor country. This type of solution is known as a clearing arrangement. Second, to reconcile the imbalance in barter transactions between the two countries, they may agree to utilize a switch trade broker.

10.2.1.4. *Counterpurchase*

This form of countertrade typically takes place between a Western industrial country and a Third World country. A **counterpurchase**, also known as an "indirect offset," involves a standard hard-currency export, but the seller agrees to a return purchase of goods and services that are not directly related to the goods that the seller sold.

10.2.1.5. *Compensation (buy-back) agreement*

A **compensation agreement** is an agreement by an exporter of plant and/or equipment to receive compensation in the form of future output from that plant. Examples of buy-back transactions include Japan's recent agreements with Taiwan, Singapore, and Korea to exchange its computer chip production equipment for computer chips produced by the plant as full or partial payment.

A typical buy-back transaction involves very large expenditures and a long-term time frame for fulfillment. Thus, such an arrangement has attributes that make it an alternative form of direct investment. The value of the buy-back agreement normally exceeds the value of the original sale.

10.2.1.6. *Offset agreement*

An **offset agreement**, frequently called "direct offset", is an arrangement similar to the counterpurchase, but the seller is required to use goods and services from the buyer country in the final product. In other words, under an offset agreement the seller is required to offset the purchase price of the buyer in some way.

For decades, foreign buyers of US arms mostly wanted to help the US seller build the planes, missiles, or other weapons being sold to reduce the purchase price. Since the mid-1980s, buyers have increasingly wanted commercial and military technology to broaden the purchaser's economy. In fact, such contracts and technology transfers now occur in aerospace, transportation equipment, and electrical equipment. The terms of the offset on individual contracts may vary substantially. The most common categories of offsets are: coproduction, licensed production, subcontractor production, overseas investment, and technology transfer.

10.2.2. *Cash Terms*

Cash terms may be either COD or CBD. COD terms mean cash on delivery of the goods, and CBD terms mean cash before delivery of the goods. Under either COD or CBD terms, an exporter does not extend credit. Although credit risk does not exist under either terms, COD terms are accompanied by a risk that an importer may refuse a shipment, while CBD terms avoid all risk. Under CBD terms, an exporter may insist on cash at the time of order or he may specify the time of cash payment prior to shipment. Another possible arrangement is that a part of the payment is made at the time of order, that progress payments are made between the time of order and the time of shipment, and that the final payment is made just before the release of goods to a common carrier.

Cash terms are the exception in these days of severe international competition. An importer does not like cash-type transactions though such transactions are ideal from the exporter's point of view. One reason for this dislike is that an importer is forced to accept all risks in transit, in foreign exchange fluctuations, and in the quality of the goods received. Consequently, the exporter will insist on cash terms only in instances of the importer's poor credit standing or extreme political risks in the importing country. If the sale involves products specially manufactured for the importer, the exporter may demand some kind of advance-payment arrangement.

10.2.3. *Consignments*

Goods for export may be consigned to a subsidiary, the exporter's own agent, an independent agent, or an import house. Assume that an exporter in New York ships to an importer in London 100 cases of quart bottles on a consignment basis. A **consignment** is the delivery of goods into the possession of another for the purpose of sale. Because the exporter pays all the expenses connected with the shipment, the importer incurs no expenses at the time this shipment is delivered to her warehouse. Actually, the 100 cases of bottles are still on the exporter's inventory. Thus, if the importer should fail, the exporter can demand that all the unsold bottles be returned to him.

10.2.4. *Credit Terms*

Most importers are not required to pay for goods before or on delivery, but they are allowed a short postponement period before payment is made. During this period, the exporter extends one of three types of credit to the importer: (1) open account, (2) notes payable, and (3) trade or bankers' acceptances.

10.2.4.1. *Open accounts*

Open account credit does not require the importer to sign a formal debt instrument as evidence to the amount that she owes the exporter. The importer simply charges her purchases, much in the same fashion that domestic retail stores extend credit to their customers. Then the importer's account is carried on the books of the exporter like other receivables. This arrangement places the entire financial burden upon the exporter. Because banks usually refuse to advance against accounts receivable, it ties up large amounts of the exporter's capital. In addition, with this arrangement the exporter assumes the risks of foreign exchange blockage and buyer default. Therefore, open account terms are extended only to trusted customers in countries that have no foreign exchange or political problems.

10.2.4.2. *Promissory notes*

In some export transactions, promissory notes are given instead of open account credit. In this case, the importer is requested to sign a **promissory note** that evidences her debt to the exporter. Thus, this arrangement makes the importer recognize her debt formally. The note calls for the payment of the obligation at some future date.

10.2.4.3. *Trade acceptances*

A trade acceptance is a form of short-term financing common in almost all foreign trade activities. In fact, it is the largest source of short-term funds for importers. Under this method of financing, the exporter draws a draft on the importer ordering her to pay the draft at some specified future date. The exporter will not release the goods until the importer accepts the draft. When the importer accepts the draft, it becomes a **trade acceptance**. When a bank accepts the draft, it becomes the bankers' acceptance.

10.2.4.4. *The cost of the cash discount foregone*

Most credit terms include a net period which refers to the period of time allowed for payment. Terms "net 30" mean that the invoice price must be paid within 30 days. The terms "2/10, net 30" indicate that a 2 percent discount is offered if payment is made within 10 days; otherwise, the full amount of the bill must be paid within 30 days. The annual interest cost of the cash discount not taken may be computed as follows:

$$\frac{\text{Percent Cash Discount}}{100 - \text{Percent Cash Discount}} \times \frac{360}{\text{Net Credit Period}} \qquad (10.1)$$

Thus, the annual interest cost of forgoing the terms "2/10, net 30" is

$$\frac{2}{100 - 2} \times \frac{360}{20} = 36.73\%$$

Here we used 360 days rather than 365 as the number of days in the year for ease of calculation. If 365 days are used, the cost of the cash discount foregone increases to 37.24 percent. It is also important to note that the cost of the cash discount foregone is not an explicit cost associated with trade credit but an implied cost.

10.3. SOURCES OF FINANCING FOREIGN TRADE

Banks, private nonbank financial institutions, and governments pool their resources to finance foreign trade. Banks finance foreign trade through a variety of methods. Export trading companies, factoring, and forfaiting are also used to finance foreign trade. The Export–Import Bank and the Private Export Funding Corporation are major forces in helping US exporters sell their goods and services to foreign buyers.

10.3.1. *Bank Financing*

Banks are important lenders to those engaged in international trade. They provide several forms of credit which are convenient to exporters and importers, including trust receipts, bankers' acceptances, loans to exporters, and loans to importers.

10.3.1.1. *Trust receipts*

A **trust receipt** establishes that borrowers hold certain goods in trust for the lender. When goods are shipped under a time draft, the importer generally signs a trust receipt that collateralizes the draft by the goods. The document provides that the importer will be the agent of her bank in the sale of the goods. The bank retains title to the goods until the importer has made full settlement. The importer is allowed to sell the goods but must turn the proceeds of the sale over to the bank in payment of the loan. The bank assumes any losses that occur under a trust receipt.

10.3.1.2. *Bankers' acceptances*

We can best explain how this method of financing operates with the following illustration: Assume that a Detroit firm desires to import a $10,000 shipment of perfumes from a French firm. The French firm is willing to grant a 60-day credit. The Detroit firm may arrange to have its Detroit bank open a letter of credit in favor of the French firm. The letter of credit states that the Detroit bank will honor drafts drawn on the Detroit firm if they are drawn in accordance with detailed terms in the letter of credit. When shipment is made, the French firm prepares a 60-day draft on the Detroit firm and presents it to its French bank. The French bank will advance the euro equivalent of $10,000, less interest and fees, to the French firm. Then the French bank will forward the draft, along with such shipping documents as the bill of lading, to its Detroit correspondent bank which, in turn, will present it to the Detroit firm's bank for acceptance. If all papers are found to be in order, the Detroit bank accepts the draft and it becomes a bankers' acceptance. Thus, **bankers' acceptances** are drafts accepted by banks.

Because bankers' acceptances are of very high quality, the French bank can easily arrange its sale and thus recover the funds it advanced. If the French firm did not discount the draft at its French bank, it could sell the draft to an investor at a discount. The Detroit firm obtains the credit it wants, and the risks with the exception of the accepting bank are minimal. The credit transaction is completed when, in 60 days, the Detroit bank, which looks for repayment, pays the bankers' acceptance by the Detroit firm.

Example 10.1

An exporter has a $10,000 bankers' acceptance for six months, the acceptance fee is 1 percent per year, and the discount rate on this bankers' acceptance is 12 percent per year. If the exporter chooses to hold the bankers' acceptance until maturity and then collect, it will receive the face amount less the acceptance fee:

Face amount of the bankers' acceptance	$10,000
Less: 0.5 percent acceptance fee for 6 months	50
Amount received by exporter in 6 months	$9,950

Alternatively, the exporter can sell the bankers' acceptance at a 6 percent discount rate (12 percent/2) and receive $9,350 immediately:

Face amount of the bankers' acceptance	$10,000
Less: 0.5 percent acceptance fee for six months	50
6 percent discount rate for 6 months	600
Amount received by exporter immediately	$9,350

10.3.1.3. *Loans to exporters and importers*

Bankers' acceptances are a form of bank loan to exporters. Banks can also make loans to exporters by cashing, purchasing, discounting, and collecting drafts. Banks cash drafts if the drafts are denominated in local currency and are drawn on time. They purchase drafts if the drafts are denominated in foreign currencies. In this case, drafts are generally exchanged for local currency at an appropriate exchange rate. They discount drafts if the drafts are denominated in local currency and if the terms of the sales involve time drafts. When banks collect drafts, they simply act as agents for exporters. However, they may lend against either the total or a percentage of the drafts outstanding.

10.3.2. *Other Private Financing*

Some popular forms of other private financing consist of export trading companies, factoring, and forfaiting.

10.3.2.1. *Export trading companies*

In October 1982, President Reagan signed into law the **Export Trading Company Act** to help small and medium-size firms sell their goods overseas. Originally, the Export Trading Company Act was conceived as the US answer to highly successful Japanese trading companies, which handle most of the country's exports.

The Export Trading Company Act of 1982 removed two major barriers that had long put US exporters at a disadvantage. First, this act allows bank holding companies, previously barred by Federal regulations from investing in commercial enterprises, to invest in export trading companies. Second, it permits competing companies to join for export purposes without fear of antitrust ramifications. An export trading company (ETC) must obtain certification from the Secretary of Commerce that it will not restrain domestic or export trade of the United States. When the Secretary of Commerce notifies the Attorney General of certification, the ETC is exempted from both criminal antitrust prosecution and the Bank Holding Company Act, so long as its activities conform to those described in the certification.

Export trading companies engage primarily in two forms of activity: trade intermediation and export outlets for US manufacturing companies. In their role as trade intermediaries, export trading companies can provide small and medium-size firms with comprehensive "one-stop" services, such as market analysis, distribution services, documentation, financing, foreign exchange transactions, transportation, and legal assistance. They can buy products from other US companies and export these products either through their own outlets or to outside distributors.

10.3.2.2. *Factoring*

Factors buy a company's accounts receivable largely on a nonrecourse basis and thus accelerate the conversion of the company's claims against its customers. "Nonrecourse" means that the factor has no right to claim reimbursement from the seller of accounts receivable if the seller's customers fail to pay their bills. Factors perform a number of additional functions such as credit checking, bookkeeping, collecting accounts, and risk bearing. The factor reviews the credit of the borrower's customers and establishes credit limits in advance. The maximum amount of advance against uncollected accounts receivable is established as a percentage of the invoice value. The factor receives an interest charge on the daily balance of advances plus a commission for credit analysis, bookkeeping, collecting accounts, and risk taking.

Exporters may turn to a factor when they have difficulty collecting on open account sales or when their bank is unwilling to collect notes receivable. Factors' rates on foreign accounts are usually higher than those of banks. Thus, factors are frequently used as a last resort by exporters who need funds badly and/or who have almost no hope for collecting.

The factor's credit investigation of the exporter's customers is relatively quick and inexpensive. For this reason, even if the exporter does not discount his accounts receivable, he can still use the factor's facilities to estimate his prospective accounts' credit worthiness. If the exporter discounts his accounts receivable on a nonrecourse basis, the factor will assume all commercial and political risks of nonpayment. For these services, factors charge a commitment fee of 1 to 2 percent and a rate of interest in excess of the prime lending rate. The Factors Chain International (FCI), the world's largest network of factoring companies, reported that 400 members from 90 countries financed 84 percent of the worldwide cross-border factoring services in 2016.[6] An exporter's use of factors depends on two considerations. The first consideration is whether the exporter can perform credit evaluation functions as well as the factor. Because large international factors evaluate the

---

[6]https://fci.nl/downloads/Annual%20Review%20%202017.pdf, April 22, 2019.

same customer for many companies, they build credit files and expertise, allowing them to evaluate credit at a lower cost than the exporter. The second consideration is whether the availability of funds and the interest charged by alternative sources are more attractive than those offered by the factor.

Example 10.2

An exporter has recently sold its accounts receivable of $10,000 to a factor. The factor advances 80 percent of the receivables, charges 1 percent interest per month, and charges a 2 percent factoring commission (one-time charge). Both the interest and the commission are paid on a discount basis.

The exporter's net proceeds are computed as follows:

Face value	$10,000
Less: 20 percent reserve due from factor	$2,000
2 percent factoring fee	$200
Funds available for advance	$7,800
Less: 1 percent interest on advance	$78
Net proceeds from advance	$7,722

Hence, the exporter receives a cash advance of $7,722 now and expects to recover the $2,000 reserve later. The annualized cost of factoring the accounts receivable is 14.71 percent $[(\$200 + \$78 \times 12)/(\$7,722)]$.

10.3.2.3. *Forfaiting*

Because capital goods such as plants and airplanes are quite expensive, the importer may not be able to make payment on the goods within a short period of time. Thus, long-term financing may be required on some international trade of capital goods. The exporter could finance such a sale but may not desire to do so because its credit may extend over several years.

A forfaiting transaction involves an importer that issues a promissory note to pay for the imported goods over a period of three to five years. The notes are extended to the exporter who sells them at a discount to a forfaiting bank. The importer will make semiannual payments during the period to the forfaiting bank. In other words, a **forfaiting** transaction refers to the purchase of financial obligations such as promissory notes without recourse to the exporter. The forfaiting markets, centered in London and Zurich, are largely free of government support, supervision, or regulation.

A typical forfaiting transaction involves four parties: the importer, the exporter, a bank, and the forfaiter. The importer pays the exporter with promissory notes that will mature at set intervals over a several-year period. A bank in the importer's country then guarantees these promissory notes; those notes guaranteed by a bank are usually irrevocable, unconditional, and transferable. The exporter in turn sells the guaranteed paper to the forfaiter at a discount from the face value; the amount of discount depends on the importer's credit rating, the guaranteeing bank's credibility, and interest costs over the paper's lifetime. As the paper matures, the forfaiter or the holder of the paper presents it to the guaranteeing bank for payment.

Table 10.1 Differences between factoring and forfaiting.

Factoring	Forfaiting
Occasionally with recourse	Always without recourse
Maturity of 6 months or less	Maturity of 6 months to 10 years
On-going, revolving deals	One-time deals
Works with consumer goods	Works with capital goods
Avoids developing countries	Works well in developing countries
Less expensive	More expensive

Source: Hill and Tanju, "Forfaiting: What Finance and Account-ing Managers Should Know," *Financial Practice and Education*, Fall/ Winter 1998, pp. 53–58.

The forfaiting arrangement allows the exporter to avoid most risks involved in his export sales. However, this financing method has a number of drawbacks. First, the amount of the discount can be quite large. Second, the guaranteeing bank normally charges a substantial fee and places a freeze of equal value on the importer's account. Third, the exporter still faces some risk if the bank guarantor and/or the importer refuses to pay on the ground that the notes have some hidden legal defect. Conceptually, forfaiting is a form of factoring. Factoring is normally used for short-term, relatively small deals with repeat customers. Forfaiting, on the other hand, is typically used for medium-term, one-time major deals up to $100 million in size. Table 10.1 shows major differences between these two forms of export financing.

10.3.3. *Government Financing*

The United States has several government sources of export financing: Export–Import Bank (Exim Bank), Private Export Funding Corporation, and Foreign Credit Insurance Association.

10.3.3.1. *Export–import bank*

The **Export–Import Bank** (Exim Bank) was founded in 1934 as an independent agency of the US government. The bank is a financially self-sustaining US government agency set up to promote US exports through a variety of export financing and loan guarantees. The creation of the Foreign Credit Insurance Association (FCIA) in 1963 completed the triad of official loan, guarantee, and insurance offerings demanded by US exporters. Exim Bank officials have fully managed these three basic export-finance programs since the bank took over the FCIA in 1983. Exim Bank operations must conform to the two general guidelines. First, loans must be used exclusively to finance the export of goods and services of US origin. Second, loans should have reasonable assurance of repayment and related transactions should not adversely affect the US economy.

The Exim Bank was originally created to facilitate trade with the former Soviet Union, but its purpose has been expanded over the years. It now finances US exports to Russia and many other countries through a variety of loan and guarantee programs, such as direct loans, discount loans, cooperative financing facility, and guarantees.

10.3.3.2. *Private Export Funding Corporation*

The **Private Export Funding Corporation** (PEFCO) was created in 1970 at the initiation of the Bankers' Association for Foreign Trade with the support of the US Treasury Department and the US Exim Bank. The basic purpose of the PEFCO was to mobilize private capital in order to finance US exports of big-ticket items such as aircraft and power plants. PEFCO's stockholders consist of 54 commercial banks, seven large manufacturers, and one investment banker. All of PEFCO's loans are guaranteed by the Exim Bank and are general obligations to the United States. Thus, the PEFCO itself does not evaluate credit risks of foreign borrowers, economic conditions in foreign countries, and other factors that might affect the collection of its loans. Most PEFCO loans have medium-term maturities of seven years, but some have maturities over 15 years.

10.3.3.3. *Foreign Credit Insurance Association (FCIA)*

Most exporters sell under letters of credit, as described in the earlier part of this chapter. In this type of sale, banks assume all risks in export transactions except for transactions under revocable letters of credit. However, importers frequently do not want to open letters of credit because of the cost or difficulty of securing them. At other times, under severe competition, exporters must sell on open account or on draft terms without letters of credit. Under these circumstances an exporter could suffer heavy losses even after carefully examining an importer's creditworthiness. These losses may develop from such situations as expropriation and riots beyond the control of the exporter or the importer.

Global Finance in Practice 10: Here is How Foreign Firms Can Raise Money and Sell their Products in China

Hong Kong is making a pitch to multinational companies to list on its stock market, despite heightened tensions between China and the West. The city's stock exchange hopes a new initiative that allows mainland Chinese investors to trade shares of international companies will present a compelling case for some of the world's largest businesses to raise funds in the Asian financial hub.

"Hong Kong will become the only market in the world where companies have the ability to capture the demand from two gigantic pools of investors that are uncorrelated," said Nicolas Agurin, chief executive of Hong Kong Exchanges and Clearing Ltd., in an interview. "You could have the best of both worlds," he added.

In December 2022, securities regulators said foreign companies with primary listings in Hong Kong could — for the first time — be eligible for inclusion in the 8-year-old Stock Connect trading link with mainland China. The plan will give these companies direct access to China's active individual investor base if their stocks meet market-capitalization criteria and other requirements.

Mr. Agurin is also pitching international companies on the value of making their shares available in China — a huge consumer market for multinationals. "If they are companies that have some sales revenues, manufacturing or whatever from the mainland, that would be a plus," he said. It is important to know that China is the largest creditor nation in the world and the largest consumer market in the world.[7]

10.4. INTERNAL SOURCES OF FUNDS FOR FOREIGN INVESTMENT

Internal sources of funds are those funds generated within a parent-affiliate network. They include capital contributions from the parent, loans with parent-company guarantees, funds provided by operations from retained earnings and depreciation, and intersubsidiary funds transfers.

10.4.1. *Funds from the Parent*

Three major types of funds supplied by the parent are equity contributions, direct loans, and indirect loans under parent company guarantees.

10.4.1.1. *Equity contributions*

Every new foreign subsidiary must receive some funds in the form of equity to satisfy both authorities in the host country and outside creditors about its solvency. Occasionally, MNCs decide on expansion funds in the form of an equity investment for their own foreign subsidiary. This part of recapitalization gives the foreign subsidiary an increased capital base to support additional loans. More specifically, equity contributions of cash are used to acquire going concerns, to buy out local minority interests, to set up new foreign subsidiaries, or to expand existing subsidiaries. Although they are a normal way of direct investments, in some developing countries direct equity investments take the form of machinery or technology instead of cash. Some MNCs have acquired a percentage of common stock equity of foreign businesses in exchange for supplying machinery, equipment, tools, and intangibles (patents, engineering, etc.) necessary for manufacturing certain products.

Common stockholders have residual claims on earnings and assets in the event of liquidation. Hence, an equity investment is not very flexible for the investor, but it is most acceptable to the host country and outside creditors. Dividends — the profit remittances derived from equity investments — are heavily taxed when we compare equity contributions with investments derived from other funding alternatives. Normally, dividends from countries to foreign shareholders are subject to local income taxes as well as to withholding taxes. Withholding taxes are incurred when local earnings are distributed abroad as dividends. This explains why many MNCs are reluctant to make large equity investments in their foreign subsidiaries.

10.4.1.2. *Direct loans*

MNCs may elect to provide investment funds to their foreign operations in the form of intracompany loans instead of increasing their equity contributions. However, the parent company lends money as an owner to its subsidiaries. The intracompany loan usually contains a specified repayment period for the loan principal and earns interest income which is taxed relatively lightly. These two features of intracompany loans compare favorably with an open-ended equity investment which produces profits in the form of heavily taxed dividends.

Parent loans to foreign subsidiaries are usually more popular than equity contributions for a number of reasons. First, parent loans give a parent company greater flexibility in repatriating funds from its foreign subsidiary. In nearly every part of the world, laws make it more difficult to return funds to the parent through dividend payments or equity reductions than through interest and principal payments. Moreover, a reduction in equity is often construed as a plan to leave the country.

Second, tax considerations are another reason for favoring parent loans over equity contributions. In most cases, interest payments on internal loans are tax deductible in the host country, while dividends are not. Moreover, principal payments, unlike dividend payments, do not generally constitute taxable income. Thus, it is possible that both a parent and its subsidiaries will save taxes by using loans instead of equity contributions.

MNCs can also provide credit to their subsidiaries not only by making loans but also by delaying the collection of accounts receivable. The amount of credit available through these intracompany accounts is limited to the amount of goods exchanged. Moreover, governments frequently limit the length of the credit term. However, because intracompany accounts involve no formal documents, they are easier to use. In addition, most governments interfere less with payments on intracompany accounts than on loans.

10.4.1.3. *Parent guarantees*

When foreign subsidiaries have difficulty in borrowing money, a parent may affix its own guarantees. While MNCs have been traditionally reluctant to guarantee the debts of their subsidiaries, indications are these guarantees will increase. There are a variety of parent guarantees:

1. The parent may sign a purchase agreement under which it commits itself to buy its subsidiary's note from the lender in the event of the subsidiary's default.
2. The lender may be protected on only a part of the specific loan agreement.
3. Another type of guarantee is limited to a single loan agreement between a lender and the subsidiary.
4. The strongest type requires that the lender be protected on all loans to the subsidiary without limits on amount or time.

The types of loans with parent guarantees and the availability of such loans depend largely upon the parent's prestige and credit standing.

10.4.2. *Funds Provided by Operations*

Once a newly formed subsidiary gets on its feet, **internal fund flows** — retained earnings and depreciation — are the major sources of funds. These internal fund flows, coupled with local credits, leave relatively little need for fresh funds from the parent.

Foreign subsidiaries are not always free to remit their earnings in hard currency elsewhere. Many developing countries have problems with their balance of payments and do not have sufficient international reserves. Thus, they restrict repatriation of funds for a specified number of years or to a certain percentage of the net income. These factors frequently force foreign subsidiaries to reinvest their internally generated funds in the host country. An initial project may have to be smaller than actual demand requirements if a company wishes to use these internal fund flows for the expansion of an initial project in later years. If the anticipated expansion is necessary to meet current demand and the normal demand growth, MNCs would have no difficulty in profitably using the internal fund flows in the host country.

10.4.3. *Loans from Sister Subsidiaries*

Availability of intersubsidiary credit, in addition to funds from the parent, vastly expands the number of possibilities for internal financing. For example, if a subsidiary in Austria has funds which it does not need immediately, it may lend these funds to a sister subsidiary in Norway, and vice versa. However, many countries impose exchange restrictions on capital movements to limit the range of possibilities for intersubsidiary loans. Moreover, the extensive use of intersubsidiary financial links makes it extremely difficult for a parent company to control its subsidiaries effectively.

Nevertheless, many subsidiaries borrow cash from their sister subsidiaries. When there are only a few subsidiaries within a company's family, it is straightforward to arrange intersubsidiary loans. One subsidiary treasurer may negotiate directly with another sister subsidiary treasurer to obtain or give credit. However, an MNC with many subsidiaries in many countries may prefer to have its central staff handle all excess funds or to establish a central pool of these funds on a worldwide basis under two conditions: (1) if the number of financial relationships does not exceed the capability of the main office to manage them effectively; and (2) if a parent company does not want to lose control over its subsidiaries.

10.5. EXTERNAL SOURCES OF FUNDS FOR FOREIGN INVESTMENT

If an MNC needs more funds than the amount that can be reasonably generated within a corporate family, the parent or its foreign subsidiaries may seek outside sources of funds. Such external sources of funds include joint business ventures with local owners and/or borrowings from financial institutions in the parent country, the host country, or any third country.

Although subsidiaries can borrow directly from outside the host country, most of them borrow locally for a number of reasons:

1. Local debts represent automatic protection against losses from a devaluation of local currency.
2. Subsidiary debts frequently do not appear on the consolidated financial statement issued by a parent as part of its annual report.
3. Some host countries limit the amount of funds that foreign companies can import from outside the host country.
4. Foreign subsidiaries often borrow locally to maintain good relations with local banks.

10.5.1. *Commercial Banks*

As noted earlier, commercial banks are a major financial intermediary in trade credit. They are also the most important external source of financing non-trade international operations. The types of loans and services provided by banks vary from country to country, but all countries have some funds available at local banks.

Most of the local loans obtained by subsidiaries are short-term credits from commercial banks. These short-term credits are used largely to finance inventory and accounts receivable. They are self-liquidating loans to the extent that sufficient cash flows are produced to repay the credits as inventories are sold on credit and receivables are collected over the business cycle. The principal instruments used by banks to service an MNC's request for a loan are (1) overdrafts, (2) unsecured short-term loans, (3) bridge loans, (4) currency swaps, and (5) link financing.

10.5.1.1. *Overdrafts*

An **overdraft** is a line of credit which permits the customer to write checks beyond deposits. The bank establishes the maximum amount of such credit based on its analysis of the customer's request, needs, and potential cash flows. The borrower agrees to pay the amount overdrawn and interest on the credit. Although some banks waive service charges for their credit-worthy customers, others frequently require service charges and other fees.

10.5.1.2. *Unsecured short-term loans*

Most short-term bank loans for MNCs to cover seasonal increases in current assets are made on an unsecured basis. The percentages of such loans vary from country to country and reflect variations in individual bank policy and central government regulations. Most MNCs prefer to borrow on an unsecured basis because bookkeeping costs of secured loans are high and because these loans have a number of highly restrictive provisions. However, some foreign subsidiaries cannot obtain loans on an unsecured basis because they are either financially weak or have not established a satisfactory performance record.

10.5.1.3. *Bridge loans*

Bridge loans are short-term bank loans used while a borrower obtains long-term fixed rate loans from capital markets. These bridge loans are repaid when the permanent financing arrangement is completed. During the peak of its currency crisis in early December 1997, Korea obtained a bridge loan of $1.3 billion from the Bank of Japan. This bridge loan was aimed at tiding Korea over until a $58 billion rescue package arranged by the International Monetary Fund began to kick in.

10.5.1.4. *Currency swaps*

Currency swaps are agreements to exchange one currency with another for a specified period after which the two currencies are re-exchanged. Arbi loans are the best-known example of such swaps. An arbi loan is arranged in a country where money is readily available at reasonable rates. It is converted to the desired local currency, but the borrower arranges a forward exchange contract to insure converting the local currency into the foreign currency of original denomination at a specified future date. Thus, arbi loans allow MNCs to borrow in one market for use in another market and to avoid foreign exchange risks. The cost of arbi loans includes the interest on the loans and the charges associated with the forward exchange contract.

10.5.1.5. *Link financing*

Link financing is an arrangement that banks in strong-currency countries help subsidiaries in weak-currency countries obtain loans by guaranteeing repayment on the loans. These subsidiaries borrow money from local banks or firms with an excess of weak money. Certainly, banks in strong-currency countries require some sort of deposits from a borrower's parent company and the borrower must pay local interest rates. To protect itself against foreign exchange risk, the lender usually hedges its position in the forward exchange market.

10.5.2. *Interest Rates on Bank Loans*

Interest rates on most business loans are determined through direct negotiations between the borrower and the bank. The prevailing prime lending rate and the credit worthiness of the borrower are the two major factors of the interest rate charged. The prime rate is the rate of interest charged on short-term business loans to the most credit-worthy customers.

Interest rates may be paid on either a collect basis or on a discount basis. On a collect basis, interest is paid at the maturity of the loan, which makes the effective rate of interest equal to the satiated rate of interest. On a discount basis, interest is paid in advance, which increases the effective rate of interest. Most short-term securities, such as Treasury bills, euro commercial papers, and bankers' acceptances, are sold on a discount basis.

Example 10.3

Assume that a company borrows $10,000 at 10 percent. Compute the effective rate of interest for the loan on a collect basis as well as on a discount basis.

The effective rate of interest on a collect basis is

$$\frac{\$1,000}{\$10,000} = 10\%$$

The effective rate of interest on a discount basis is

$$\frac{\$1,000}{10,000 - \$1,000} = 11.11\%$$

10.5.2.1. *Compensating balances*

Compensating balances are those that borrowers are required by their bank to keep in their account. Banks typically require their customers to hold from 10 to 20 percent of their outstanding loan balance on deposit in a non-interest-bearing account. Required compensating balances are used to: (1) cover the cost of accounts; (2) increase the liquidity position of the borrower that can be used to pay off the loan in case of default; and (3) increase the effective cost of borrowing.

Example 10.4

Assume that a company borrows $20,000 at 10 percent. Calculate the effective interest cost if the loan requires a minimum compensating balance of 20 percent ($4,000) and it is on a discount basis.

The effective interest cost of the loan is:

$$\frac{\$2,000}{\$20,000 - \$4,000 - \$2,000} = 14.29\%$$

10.5.2.2. *Currency movement and interest rates*

In reality, the value of the currency borrowed will change with respect to the borrower's local currency over time. The actual cost of a bank credit by the borrower depends on the interest rate charged by the bank and the movement in the borrowed currency's value over the life of the loan. Thus, the effective interest rate may differ from the interest rate we computed in Examples 14.1 and 14.2. In this case, the effective interest rate is computed as follows:

$$r = (1 + i_f)(1 + i_e) - 1 \tag{10.2}$$

where r = the effective interest rate in US dollar terms; i_f = the interest rate of the foreign currency; and i_e = the percentage change in the foreign currency against the US dollar.

Example 10.5

A US company borrows Swiss francs for one year at 10 percent. The franc appreciates from $0.50 to $0.60 or 20 percent over the life of the loan. Interest on this loan is paid at maturity. The effective interest rate of the loan in US dollar terms is

$$r = (1 + 0.10)(1 + 0.20) - 1$$

$$= 32\%$$

Example 10.6

A US company borrows British pounds for 1 year at 10 percent. The pound depreciates from $1.50 to $1.20 or 20 percent over the life of the loan. Interest on this loan is paid at maturity. The effective interest rate of the loan in US dollar terms is

$$r = (1 + 0.10)(1 - 0.20) - 1$$

$$= -12\%$$

A negative effective interest rate implies that the US borrower actually paid fewer dollars in total loan repayment than the number of dollars borrowed. Such a result can arise if the British pound depreciates substantially over the life of the loan. As shown in Example 14.5, however, the effective interest rate in dollar terms can be much higher than the quoted interest rate if the British pound appreciates substantially over the life of the loan.

10.5.3. *Edge Act and Agreement Corporations*

Edge Act and Agreement corporations are subsidiaries of American banks which are physically located in the United States, but they engage in international banking operations. The Edge Act of 1919 allows American banks to perform as holding companies and to own stock of foreign banks. Thus, these banks can provide loans and other banking services for American-owned companies in most countries around the world. **Edge Act corporations** are domestic subsidiaries of banking organizations chartered by the Federal Reserve Board; **Agreement corporations** are Edge equivalents chartered by individual states. Both types of subsidiaries may perform not only international banking operations, but they may also finance foreign industrial projects through long-term loans or equity participation.

10.5.3.1. *Types of activities*

Edge Act and Agreement corporations typically engage in three types of activities: international banking, international financing, and holding companies. In their capacity as international banking corporations, Edge Act and Agreement corporations may hold demand and time deposits of foreign parties. They can make loans, but these loans to any single borrower cannot exceed 10 percent of their capital and surplus. They can also open or confirm letters of credit, make loans or advances to finance foreign trade, create bankers' acceptances, receive items for collection, remit funds abroad, buy or sell securities, issue certain guarantees, and engage in foreign exchange transactions.

In their capacity as international financing corporations, Edge Act and Agreement corporations invest in the stock of nonbank financial concerns, development corporations, or commercial and industrial companies. Certainly, such investments require prior specific consent of the Federal Reserve Board or state banking authorities under certain circumstances. Edge Act subsidiaries have financed some foreign finance companies and official development corporations. In most cases, however, they finance commercial and industrial companies directly through loans and equity contributions. The major purpose of such financing activities is to provide promising foreign companies with capital at an early or important stage.

In their capacity as holding companies, Edge Act and Agreement corporations can own shares of foreign banking subsidiaries and affiliates. Member banks of the Federal Reserve System are not permitted to own shares of foreign banking subsidiaries. A foreign banking subsidiary may be more advantageous than a branch for two reasons. First, foreign branches are allowed to carry on only the activities allowed to their parent banks in the United States. Second, certain countries do not permit non-domestic banks to open branches in their territory. In other instances, Edge Act and Agreement corporations have been the instrument through which US banks have acquired equity interests in well-known foreign banks.

10.5.4. *International Banking Facilities*

Since December 3, 1981, banks in the United States have been allowed to establish international banking facilities at their offices in the United States. **International banking facilities** (IBFs) are vehicles that enable bank offices in the United States to accept time deposits in either dollars or foreign currency from foreign customers, free of reserve requirements and of other limitations. Foreigners can also borrow funds from IBFs to finance their foreign investment projects. IBFs have been further strengthened by legislation in New York, California, and other states which exempt them from state and local income taxes. IBFs are located in the United States, but in many respects, they function like foreign branch offices of US banks. In other words, the creation of IBFs means the establishment of offshore banking facilities in the United States similar to other Eurocurrency market centers.

In order to qualify for IBFs, institutions must be depository institutions, Edge or Agreement corporations, or US branch offices of foreign banks which are legally authorized to do business in the United States. These institutions do not require the approval of the Federal Reserve Board to establish IBFs; a simple notification is sufficient. In addition, they are not required to establish a separate organizational structure for IBFs, but they must maintain separate books which would distinguish their offshore business from their domestic business.

IBFs have a number of advantages over bank operations through foreign locations. First, small banks can enter into the Eurocurrency market easily, because they no longer need to establish a foreign office or a domestic subsidiary exclusively for international banking operations. Second, US banks can reduce operating costs because they have more direct control and use existing support services such as personnel and facilities.

IBFs also have several disadvantages when we compare them to offshore banking centers, caused mostly by regulations that IBFs serve only nonresidents. First, IBFs must receive written acknowledgement from their customers that deposits do not support activities within the United States and that IBF loans finance only operations outside the United States. Second, IBFs are prohibited from offering demand deposits or transaction accounts that could possibly substitute for such accounts now held by nonresidents in US banks. Third, IBFs are also prevented from issuing negotiable certificates of deposits or bankers' acceptances though they can issue letters of credit and undertake repurchase agreements. Fourth, time deposits offered to nonbank foreign residents require minimum deposits and withdrawal of $100,000 to preserve the wholesale nature of the business; they also require a minimum maturity or two business days' notification prior to withdrawal.

10.5.5. *Strategic Alliances*

In a trend that accelerated during the 1980s, companies have begun to link up with former competitors in a vast array of strategic alliances. A **strategic alliance** is any collaborative agreement between two companies that is designed to attain some strategic goal. International licensing agreements, marketing arrangements or management contracts, and joint ventures are some examples of strategic alliances. Most strategic alliances, however, are equity alliances or joint ventures.

Partners of strategic alliances might gain economies of scale or a variety of other commercial advantages. However, financial synergy, where a financially strong company helps a financially weak company, represents a key advantage of strategic alliances. Starbucks partnered with Barnes and Nobles bookstores in 1993 to provide in-house coffee shops, benefiting both retailers. In 1996, Starbucks partnered with PepsiCo to bottle, distribute, and sell the popular coffee-based drink, Frappacino. A Starbucks-United Airlines alliance has resulted in their coffee being offered on flights with the Starbucks logo on the cups and a partnership with Kraft foods has resulted in Starbucks coffee being marketed in grocery stores. In 2006, Starbucks formed an alliance with the NAACP, the sole purpose of which was to advance the company's and the NAACP's goals of social and economic justice.

An international **licensing agreement** is an agreement whereby an MNC (the licensor) allows a local firm (the licensee) to produce the licensor's products in the firm's local markets in return for royalties, fees, and other forms of compensation. The licensor's products are intangible assets such as patents, trademarks, intellectual property, and technological expertise. The local licensee assumes the responsibility to produce, market, or distribute the licensor's products in the local market.

10.5.5.1. *Joint ventures*

A joint venture is a corporate entity in which two or more parties, for example, an MNC and host-country companies, have equity interest. In the past, use of a wholly owned subsidiary was the most common approach to overseas investment because worldwide strategy depended on complete control over all foreign operations. However, more and more host countries require that MNCs have some local participation. In some situations, MNCs will seek local partners even when there are no local requirements to do so.

There are four types of international joint ventures. First, two companies from the same country form a joint venture to conduct a business in a third country. Second, an MNC forms a joint venture with host-country companies. Third, an MNC and a local government form a joint venture. Fourth, companies from two or more countries establish a venture in a third country.

Many factors may induce MNCs to enter into joint ventures with local partners, other MNCs, and local governments. These factors include tax benefits, local marketing expertise, more capital, less political risk, and quick acquisition of new technologies.

On the other hand, MNCs want tight control of their foreign subsidiaries to efficiently allocate investments and to maintain a coordinated marketing plan on a global basis. Dividend policy, financial disclosure, transfer pricing, establishment of royalty and other fees, and allocation of production and marketing costs among plants are just some areas in which each owner has an incentive to engage in activities that could hurt its partners. This is why most MNCs resist local participation. In fact, there are many cases in which MNCs have chosen to pull out of foreign countries rather than to comply with government regulations that require joint ventures with local partners.

10.5.5.2. *Motives for strategic alliances*

Motives for strategic alliances may consist of two broad types: general and specific to international business. General motives for strategic alliances are to: (1) spread and reduce costs, (2) avoid or counter competition, (3) secure horizontal and vertical links, (4) specialize in a number of selected products, assets, or technologies, and (5) learn from other companies.

MNCs may collaborate with other companies to: (1) gain location-specific assets, (2) overcome legal constraints, (3) diversify geographically, and (4) minimize exposure in risky environments. First, MNCs may seek to form a strategic alliance with local companies that will help them manage location-specific problems, such as cultural, political, and economic differences. Second, strategic alliances may help MNCs overcome governmental constraints. Many countries limit foreign ownership. Government procurement, particularly military procurement, is another reason that may force MNCs to collaborate. Third, geographic diversification through strategic alliances enables MNCs to smooth their sales and earnings because business cycles occur at different times within different countries. Finally, one way for MNCs to minimize loss from foreign political occurrences is to minimize the base of assets located abroad or share them with local companies.

10.5.6. *Project Finance*

Project finance refers to an arrangement whereby a project sponsor finances a long-term capital project on a non-recourse basis. "Non-recourse" is used here to mean that the project sponsor has legal and financial responsibilities for the project. Three characteristics distinguish project finance from other forms of financing[8]:

1. The project is established as an individual legal entity and relies heavily on debt financing.
2. The debt repayment is contractually tied to the cash flow generated by the project.
3. Government participation comes in the form of infrastructure support, operating or financing guarantees, or assurances against political risk.

Project finance offers several benefits over conventional debt financing. Project finance normally restricts the usage of the project's cash flows. The lenders, rather than the managers, can decide whether to reinvest excess cash flows or to use them to reduce the loan balance by more than the minimum required. Second, project finance increases the number and type of investment opportunities, thereby making capital markets more "complete." Third, project finance permits companies whose earnings are below the minimum requirements, specified in their existing bond indentures, to obtain additional debt financing.

In recent years, many large projects, such as the Alaska oil pipeline, the Channel Tunnel between England and France, and the EuroDisney theme park outside Paris have been funded by project finance. Project finance is either a build-operate-own contract (BOO) or a build-operate-transfer (BOT) project. In a BOO contract, the sponsor assumes ownership of the project at the end of the contract life. In a BOT project, ownership of the project is transferred to the host government. Project finance is widely used today in China, India, Turkey, and many other emerging markets.

International capital markets, such as bank loans, bonds, and equity offerings, contribute a substantial amount to infrastructure project finance — about $30 billion a year. The World Bank predicts that the fast growth of the market for infrastructure finance in the 1990s and beyond is likely to continue for many years to come. First, governments want to give their clients efficient, high-grade services without using tax money. Developing countries have the potential for increased access to international capital markets.

10.6. DEVELOPMENT BANKS

Development banks provide MNCs with a broad range of financing resources. They are banking organizations established to support the economic development of underdeveloped areas

---

[8]Butler, K. C., *Multinational Finance*, Cincinnati: South-West Publishing Company, 2000, pp. 428–430.

through intermediate and long-term loans. There are three broad groups of development banks: worldwide, regional, and national.

10.6.1. *World Bank Group*

The **World Bank Group** is a group of worldwide financial institutions organized after the devastation of World War II to aid economic reconstruction. Since 1947, the World Bank has funded over 12,000 development projects, via traditional loans, interest-free credits, and grants. Today, with 189 member countries, staff from more than 170 countries, and offices in over 130 locations, the World Bank Group is a unique global partnership: five institutions working for sustainable solutions that reduce poverty and build shared prosperity in developing countries. These five institutions include the International Bank for Reconstruction and Development (IBRD), the international Center for Settlement of Investment Disputes (ICSID) the International Development Association (IDA), the International Finance Corporation (IFC), the Multilateral Investment Guarantee Agency (MIGA).

10.6.1.1. *International Bank for Reconstruction and Development*

The **International Bank for Reconstruction and Development** (IBRD), commonly known as the World Bank, was established at the Bretton Woods conference in 1944 as a companion institution to the International Monetary Fund. Because the major objective of the World Bank was to finance reconstruction and development after World War II, it made certain loans in Europe for reconstruction. It found its resources completely inadequate for this purpose and thus stopped reconstruction loans. However, the World Bank was able to concentrate on lending for economic development because the Marshall Plan provided funds for reconstruction in Europe. The Marshall Plan was the European economic recovery program established by the United States in 1948. The overriding objective of the Plan was to restore the productive capacity of European industry destroyed during World War II. The Plan existed slightly less than four years and channeled more than $10 billion in American aid to Europe.

ICSID is the world's leading institution devoted to international investment dispute settlement. Established in 1960, IDA aims to reduce poverty by providing low-zero interest loans (called credits) and grants for programs that boost economic growth, and reduce inequalities, and improve people's living conditions. IFC is the largest global development institution focused on the private sector in developing countries. MIGA provide political risk insurance and credit enhancement for cross-border private sectors and lenders.

10.6.2. *Regional Development Banks*

Regional groups of countries have established regional development banks to promote effective economic development within the member countries. Leading regional development banks are the Inter-American Development Bank, the European Investment Bank, the European Bank for Reconstruction and Development, the Asian Development Bank, and the African Development Bank.

10.6.2.1. *Inter-American Development Bank*

The **Inter-American Development Bank** (IDB) was founded in 1959 by the United States and 19 Latin American countries to further the economic development of its member countries. Twenty-six Latin American countries and 15 other countries now own the Bank, which is headquartered in Washington, D.C. IDB loans are available only when private sources are not available on reasonable terms. The IDB usually finances no more than 50 percent of total project cost.

The IDB has three types of activity:

1. With its Ordinary Capital Resources Fund, the Bank makes development loans to both public and private institutions. These loans are earmarked for projects that promote Latin America's economic development.
2. With its US-created Social Progress Trust Fund, the Bank makes loans to finance projects with high social value.
3. With its Fund for Special Operations, the Bank makes loans whose terms are much more lenient than those available in the regular money and capital markets. Maturities may be extremely long, repayment may be made in the borrower's currency, or interest rates may be arbitrarily low.

10.6.2.2. *European bank for reconstruction and development*

The **European Bank for Reconstruction and Development** (EBRD) was established in 1990 by 42 countries as a development bank for emerging democracies in Eastern Europe. These 42-member countries include the United States, Japan, Russia, and European countries. The London-based EBRD encourages reconstruction and development in the eastern and central European countries through loans, guarantees, and equity investments in private and public companies.

10.6.2.3. *European Investment Bank*

The **European Investment Bank** (EIB) was established in 1958 by members of the European Community. Its resources are used to support the socio-economic infrastructure of the member nations or their basic industries. Most of these loans have maturities from 12 to 20 years. Ordinarily, 3 or 4-year intervals are established before loan repayments begin.

The EIB has three types of responsibilities:

1. It assists in financing projects which involve two or more member governments. In this case, it plays an important role in coordinating the activities of different national financial agencies.
2. It promotes the potential of economies of scale. It helps specialize or expand the operations of plants or firms in countries with a comparative advantage in certain lines of business.
3. It helps achieve a more uniform and high level of economic maturity within the European Union.

10.6.2.4. *Asian Development Bank*

The **Asian Development Bank** (ADB) was formed in 1966 by 17 Asian countries in partnership with the United States, Canada, Britain, Germany, and other European countries. The ADB has its headquarters in Manila and 47 members; 17 are from outside the region. Bank founders created the ADB to promote the economic growth and development of its member countries. The ADB accomplishes its goals by offering loans, grants, and technical assistance. The ADB makes long-term loans to private companies without government guarantees. Some ADB loans go to Asian national banks that reloan to private enterprises through their respective development agencies. Some other ADB loans are used to supply risk capital. Only member countries, and occasionally, private enterprises, can borrow from the Bank.

10.6.2.5. *African Development Bank*

The African Development Bank (ADB) Group is a regional multilateral development finance institution established to contribute to the economic development and social progress of African countries that are the institution's Regional Member Countries (RMCs). The AfDB was founded following an agreement signed by member states on August 14, 1963, in Khartoum, Sudan, which became effective on September 10, 1964. The AfDB comprises three entities: the African Development Bank (ADB), the African Development Fund (ADF) and the Nigeria Trust Fund (NTF). As the premier development finance institution on the continent, the AfDB's mission is to help reduce poverty and to improve living conditions for Africans and mobilize resources for the continent's economic and social development. The AfDB headquarters is officially in Abidjan, Côte d'Ivoire.[9]

10.7. SUMMARY

This chapter has discussed various documents and operations essential to finance foreign trade. The extension of credit on foreign trade is of critical importance to both exporters and importers in a transaction. For exporters, their willingness and ability to extend credit are crucial determinants of sales volume across national boundaries. For importers, their ability to continue operations relies on the lag between payments by their customers and remittances to their foreign suppliers. The three basic documents used in normal export-import transactions are the draft, the bill of lading, and the letter of credit. Some forms of countertrade such as barter and switch trading make international transactions possible without money. However, most transactions across national boundaries are conducted in terms of money. In addition, this chapter has examined a number of private and government sources to finance foreign trade.

For purposes of expansion, new investment, and day-to-day operations, the international financial manager must be familiar with various sources of internal or external funds. This chapter has discussed three types of internally generated funds: (1) retained earnings and

---

[9] African Development Bank Group, "What Is the African Development Bank?" https://www.afdb.org/en/about-us/frequently-asked-questions, January 30, 2023.

depreciation provided by operations, (2) equity contributions, loans, and credits from the parent company, and (3) loans from sister subsidiaries. External sources of funds include borrowing from financial institutions in a parent country or abroad, joint ventures with local partners, project finance, and development banks. Finally, development banks provide MNCs with a variety of financing sources. They are banks established to aid in economic development through equity participation, loans, or some intermediate form of investment. They may be worldwide, regional, or national.

10.8. KEY TERMS

draft	bill of exchange
drawer	drawee
payee	bill of lading
letter of credit	commercial invoice
consular invoice	countertrade
simple barter	clearing arrangement
switch trade	counter purchase
compensation agreement	offset agreement
consignment	open account
promissory note	trade acceptance
trust receipt	bankers' acceptances
Export Trading Company Act	factors
forfaiting	export–import bank
Private Export Funding COrporation (PEFCO)	internal fund flows
overdraft	bridge loan
currency swap	link financing
compensating balances	edge act corporations
agreement corporations	international banking facilities (IBFs)
strategic alliance	licensing agreement
joint venture	project finance
World Bank Group	International Bank for Reconstruction and Development
European Investment Bank (EIB)	
African Development Bank (AfDB)	Inter-American Development Bank (IDB)
	Asian Development Bank (ADB)

10.9. PROBLEMS

1. For each of the following import purchases, (a) calculate the annual cost of the cash discount foregone, and (b) determine the date and amount paid if the discount is taken. Assume that the invoice date is March 10 and that there are 30 days in a month.

   (1) $500, 2/10, net 30
   (2) $3,500, 4/20, net 60
   (3) $1,500, 3/30, net 40
   (4) $4,400, 2/10, net 70

2. An exporter has a $20,000 bankers' acceptance for six months, the acceptance fee is 2 percent per year, and the discount rate on this bankers' acceptance is 10 percent per year.

   a. How much cash will the exporter receive if it holds the bankers' acceptance until maturity?

   b. How much cash will the exporter receive if it sells the bankers' acceptance at a 10 percent discount rate?

   c. The exporter's opportunity cost of funds is 10.2 percent per year. If the exporter wishes to maximize the present value of her bankers' acceptance, should she discount the bankers' acceptance or hold it until maturity?

3. An exporter has recently factored its accounts receivable at a rate of $10,000 a month. The factor advances 80 percent of the receivables, charges 1 percent interest per month on advances, and charges a 3 percent factoring fee. The interest and fee are paid on a discount basis.

   a. Determine the net proceeds to the exporter.

   b. Determine the effective annual cost of this financing arrangement.

4. There are three alternatives to increase a net working capital of $10,000. Calculate the effective annual cost of each alternative.

   a. Forego cash discounts with the terms of 2/10, net 40.

   b. Borrow the money at 7 percent from the bank. This bank loan requires a minimum compensating balance of 20 percent and interest on the loan is paid at maturity.

   c. Sell commercial paper at 8 percent. The underwriting fees of the issue are 2 percent of the face value.

   d. Which alternative should be chosen and why?

5. A $10,000 bank loan has a coupon rate of 10 percent.

   a. Calculate the effective interest cost if the loan is on a discount basis.

   b. Calculate the effective interest cost if the loan requires a minimum compensating balance of 20 percent and it is on a discount basis.

   c. Calculate the effective interest cost if the loan requires a 25 percent compensating balance but it is on a collect basis.

6. A US company borrows Japanese yen for one year at 5 percent. During the year, the yen appreciated from $0.010 to $0.012 against the US dollar.

   a. Determine the percentage appreciation of the yen.

   b. Compute the effective interest rate of the loan in dollar terms.

7. A Mexican subsidiary of a US company needs a peso (local) loan. The Mexican loan rate is 15 percent per year, while a foreign loan rate is 7 percent per year. By how much must the foreign currency appreciate to make the cost of the foreign loan equal to that of the local loan?

8. A US company is considering three financing plans for 1 year: a dollar loan at 6 percent; a Swiss franc loan at 3 percent; and a euro loan at 4 percent. The company has forecasted

that the franc will appreciate by 2 percent for the next year and that the euro will appreciate by 3 percent for the same period.

a. Compute the expected effective interest rate for each of the three plans.

b. Which plan appears to be most feasible?

c. Why might the company not necessarily choose the plan with the lost interest rate?

Closing Case 10: The World Bank

Representatives of 44 governments founded the World Bank on July 1, 1944, during their conference in Bretton Woods, New Hampshire. The Bank is a sister institution to the International Monetary Fund (IMF) but has a separate distinct objective. The Bank was largely the brainchild of the economist John Maynard Keynes, who envisioned an institution that would initially focus on postwar reconstruction in Europe and Asia and then shift to focusing on development of poor countries. As such, the Bank's overriding modern purpose is to spur development worldwide through loans and grants to underdeveloped countries. To help stress this goal, the mission statement of the Bank is the elegant and simple sentence: "Our dream is a world free from poverty."

With 189 member countries, staff from more than 170 countries, and offices in over 130 locations, the World Bank Group is a unique global partnership: five institutions working for sustainable solutions that reduce poverty and build shared prosperity in developing countries. Membership in the Bank is only allowed for countries that are first members of the IMF. Typically, countries join both organizations. Member countries are shareholders who carry ultimate decision-making power in the World Bank. Each member nation appoints a Governor and an Alternate Governor to carry out these responsibilities. The Board of Governors, who are usually officials such as Ministers of Finance or Planning, meets annually at the Bank's Meetings each fall. The chairperson of the Board of Governors is the President of the World Bank. The governors decide on key Bank policy issues, admit, or suspend country members, decide on changes in the authorized capital stock, determine the distribution of income, and endorse financial statements and budgets.

Specifically, their policy discussions during the annual meetings cover a variety of issues, such as poverty reduction, international economic development, and global development finance. This annual gathering provides a forum for international cooperation and enables the Bank to better serve its member countries. The meetings are traditionally held in Washington two years out of three and, in order to reflect the international character of the two institutions (the World Bank and the IMF), every third year in a different member country.

Because these ministers meet only once a year, the bulk of the Governors' powers are delegated throughout the year to the Board of Executive Directors. Every member government of the World Bank Group is represented at the Bank's headquarters in Washington, D.C. by an Executive Director. The five largest shareholders — France,

Germany, Japan, the United Kingdom, and the United States — each appoint an Executive Director, while the other member countries are represented by 19 Executive Directors who are elected by groups of countries (constituents). Some countries — China, Russia, and Saudi Arabia — have formed single-country constituencies, while others have joined together in multi-country constituencies. The 24 Executive Directors normally meet twice a week to oversee the Bank's business, such as loan applications and guarantees, new policies, the administrative budget, country assistance strategies, and borrowing and financial decisions.

The World Bank is part of a larger organization, the World Bank Group. The World Bank Group consists of five closely associated institutions, all owned by member countries, that carry ultimate decision-making power. As explained below, each institution plays a distinct role in the mission to fight poverty and improve living standards for people in the developing world. The term "World Bank Group" encompasses all five institutions. The term "World Bank" refers specifically to two of the five, the International Bank for Reconstruction and Development (IBRD) and the International Development Association (IDA). Table 10.1 shows a brief summary of each organization that makes up the World Bank Group.

The Bank has taken some specific actions that it rightly boasts about. It has become the world's largest external funder of education. Since its education funding began in

Table 10.1   The World Bank Group organization.

Title	Start Date	Mission
The International Bank for Reconstruction and Development (IBRD) (184 Members)	1945	The IBRD aims to reduce poverty in middle-income and creditworthy poorer countries by promoting sustainable development, through loans, guarantees, and analytical and advisory services.
The International Development Association (IDA) (162 Members)	1960	The IDA provides interest-free credits to the world's poorest countries. These countries have little or no capacity to borrow on market terms. Each year the cutoff to qualify for IDA credits is determined. In 2002, the operational cutoff for eligibility was a 2000 GNI per capita of $885.
The International Finance Corporation (IFC) (175 Members)	1956	The IFC's mandate is to promote economic development through the private sector. Working with business partners, it invests in sustainable private enterprises in developing countries and provides long-term loans, guarantees, and risk management/advisory services.
The Multilateral Investment Guarantee Agency (MIGA) (157 Members)	1988	The MIGA helps encourage foreign investment in developing countries by providing guarantees to foreign investors against losses caused by noncommercial risks, such as expropriation, currency inconvertibility and transfer restrictions, and war and civil disturbances.
The International Center for Settlement of Investment Disputes (ICSID) (134 Members)	1966	The ICSID helps to encourage foreign investment by providing international facilities for conciliation and arbitration of investment disputes; in this way, it helps to foster an atmosphere of mutual confidence between states and foreign investors.

1963, the World Bank has provided some $31 billion in loans and credits, and it currently finances 158 education projects in 83 countries. It is also the largest external funder of the fight against AIDS/HIV. As a co-sponsor of UNAIDS, which coordinates the global response to the epidemic, the Bank has committed more than $1.7 billion to combating the spread of HIV/AIDS around the world. The Bank has pledged that no country with an effective HIV/AIDS strategy will go without funding and, in partnership with African governments, launched the Multi-Country HIV/AIDS Program (MAP), which makes significant resources available to civil society organizations and communities.

Case Questions

1. Table 10.1 summarized the five organizations of the World Bank Group, and this chapter discussed the Asian Financial Crisis. How might each part of the World Bank Group have helped after the crisis started?
2. Many critics claim that the World Bank Group is too large and attempts to do too much. Additionally, they claim that many of their activities overlap with the work of the World Trade Organization, the International Monetary Fund, and the United Nations. How valid do you find this criticism?
3. Imagine that you are the President of the World Bank. Who are your most powerful constituents? How much power do you have? Would you want this job?
4. What are the major differences between the IMF and the World Bank?
5. Visit the World Bank's website, www.worldbank.org. to find its current projects.

Source: The World Bank's website, www.worldbank.org, accessed August 30, 2022.

PART FOUR
THE GLOBAL INVESTMENT STRATEGY

Part Four (Chapters 11–15) covers the management of assets, or the efficient allocation of funds among various assets. This part describes the management of current assets, financial assets, capital budgeting, and political risks associated with foreign investment. The objective of current asset management is to protect the purchasing power of assets and to maximize the return on investment. The management of current assets is extremely important for the multinational company. Thus, the complicating international factors and approaches for resolving them should be analyzed carefully. National capital markets have recently changed to an integrated global capital market, oftentimes followed by widespread international multiple listings of securities. Consequently, investors are starting to realize the enormous potential of international portfolio investment. As a result, relatively sophisticated techniques exist to analyze how foreign investment decisions are made. Investment decisions affect the value of a company's stock by influencing both the size of the earnings stream and the riskiness of the company. This risk factor in foreign operations takes on a new dimension of importance because it is rarely encountered in domestic business operations.

Chapter 11

INTERNATIONAL WORKING CAPITAL MANAGEMENT

Opening Case 11: Transfer Pricing — Federal Regulations and International Guidelines

Transfer pricing is a mechanism for determining arm's length pricing in related-party transactions, often in cross-border related-party transactions. The US transfer pricing regulations under §482 seek to ensure that appropriate amounts of income of a multinational company are subject to US taxation. The Organization for Economic Cooperation and Development (OECD) also maintains its own guidelines related to transfer pricing. Collectively these guidelines aim to prevent profit-shifting lower jurisdictions and avoid international double taxation.

Some examples of transfer pricing disputes?

High-profile disputes between three major companies and the IRS made recent headlines: Coca-Cola, Altera, Facebook, and Medtronic.

Coca-Cola: A US Tax Court ruled that Coca-Cola Co. must pay most of a $3.4 billion additional tab ordered by the IRS for attributing too much profit to foreign affiliates.

On November 20, 2020, The Tax Court's decision upheld the IRS's method for reallocating profits between Coca-Cola and affiliates that made and sold ingredients for the company's soft drinks. The ruling pertained to the company's taxable income between 2007 and 2009.

Altera: In 2020, the US Supreme Court announced that it would not review the Ninth Circuit 2019 decision in the semiconductor manufacturer *Altera Corp. case.* That decision required the cost of employee stock-based compensation ("SBC") to be included in the pool of intangible development costs ("IDC") under cost-sharing arrangements ("CSA"). This decision has had important implications for companies where their SBC costs were excluded from IDC under a CSA.

Medtronic: The Medtronic case centers on the company's allocation of profits for tax purposes between its US parent company, US distributor, and Puerto Rican device manufacturer. While the IRS argued that the company owed nearly $1.4 billion in taxes, the US Tax Court found in a 2016 opinion that it had underpaid by just about $14 million. In 2018, though, the US Court of Appeals for the Eighth Circuit sent the case back, ordering the Tax Court to make numerous additional findings.

Facebook: The tech giant is challenging a $1.73 million tax bill for 2010 that hinges on the value of intangible assets, such as trademarks and copyrights, that it transferred to an Irish subsidiary. The IRS claims that these assets are worth $13.8 billion — more than twice as much as Facebook's $6.5 billion valuation. The company said in a January 10-K filing that as much as $9 billion plus interest and penalties could be on the line because the IRS's position could apply to its subsequent tax years.[1]

The management of current assets and current liabilities constitutes **working capital management**. The efficient allocation of funds among various current assets and the acquisition of short-term funds on favorable terms are conceptually the same for both multinational companies (MNCs) and domestic companies. However, these two types of companies are different because they do business in different environments. These differences include the impact of currency fluctuations, potential exchange controls, and multiple regulatory and tax jurisdictions on working capital decisions. In addition, MNCs enjoy a wide variety of short-term financing and investment opportunities.

This chapter emphasizes current asset management, which can be viewed as either a dynamic (flow) process or a static (stock) responsibility. The first part of this chapter — the dynamic approach — focuses on the denomination of liquid funds by currency and the placement of such holdings by country. This flow process places a heavy emphasis on transfers of liquid funds from one geographic location or currency to another. The second part — the static approach — focuses on individual processes such as the composition of various current assets. The important aspect of this approach is how to determine appropriate levels of cash, accounts receivable, and inventories.

11.1. BASIC CONCEPTS OF WORKING CAPITAL MANAGEMENT

The basic objective of working capital management is to determine the optimal amount of investment in various current asset accounts. This optimal amount of investment in current assets is the level of current asset holdings that maximizes the overall profitability of a firm. However, there are a variety of economic constraints which make it difficult for MNCs to achieve the objective of working capital management.

11.1.1. *Importance of Working Capital Management*

Current asset management is important not only because it involves the largest portion of a financial manager's time but also because current assets represent more than half the total

---

[1]Bloomberg Tax, https://pro.bloombergtax.com/brief/what-is-transfer-pricing/?trackingcode=BTXI2210 8865&utm_medium=paidsearch&utm_source=google&gclsrc=aw.ds&gclid=Cj0KCQiA45qdBhD-ARIsAOH bVdFtC87jO1Cii2QmqHwCVwb_02Qo-I_e-ONM_1PP3NXXCY8ay3XiwAEaAkqiEALw_wcB&gclsrc=aw. dsTr, August 23, 2022.

assets of most companies. In addition, there is a close relationship between sales growth and the level of current assets. For example, increases in credit sales require more accounts receivable and inventories. Finally, companies may minimize their investments in fixed assets through leases, but it is practically impossible to avoid an investment in current assets.

Despite the importance of international working capital management, literature on this topic is rather limited for a number of reasons. First, decisions on working capital are relatively routine and frequent. Second, unlike capital investment decisions, these routine decisions on working capital are easily reversible. Third, working capital management requires cash flow projections; however, cash flows cannot be forecasted by the financial manager alone. In other words, financial aspects of a decision are sometimes concealed by marketing (credit policy) and production (inventory management) which have a major impact on a company's cash flows.

11.1.2. *Net Working Capital Funding*

The higher level of sales by an MNC necessitates more accounts receivable and higher inventory levels. On the liability side, accounts payable are expected to increase with increases in sales. Accounts payable would automatically finance part of sales increases. These three components make up net working capital. It is important to note that we do not include cash and short-term debt as part of net working capital because they are not spontaneous.

In principle, MNCs attempt to minimize their net working capital. Aggressive selling techniques and more lenient credit terms may immediately lower the time required to convert inventories into accounts receivable. Greater cash discounts and tighter collection policies may considerably reduce the time required to convert accounts receivable into cash. All such policy changes require additional costs. Thus, MNCs should reduce the cycle until the marginal revenue generated equals the marginal cost; at this point, they maximize their profits.

A common method of benchmarking working capital management practice is to compute the net working capital of a company on a "days sales" basis. To do this, we must first calculate the following three values: (1) days receivables (accounts receivable divided by the average daily sales), (2) days inventory (inventory divided by the average daily sales), and (3) days payables (accounts payable divided by the average daily sales). By combining these three items, we obtain days working capital as follows:

$$\text{Days working capital} = \text{Days receivables} + \text{Days inventory} - \text{Days payables}$$

11.1.3. *Economic Constraints of Current Asset Management*

Because MNCs operate across national borders, they face regulatory, tax, foreign exchange, and other economic constraints. To achieve a predetermined objective of current assets, the financial manager must give special consideration to these constraints.

11.1.3.1. *Foreign exchange constraints*

Foreign exchange constraints are an important limiting factor on fund flows from one country to another. International fund flows involve foreign exchange transaction costs and exchange rate fluctuations.

11.1.3.2. *Regulatory constraints*

Regulatory constraints can block dividend repatriation or other forms of fund remittances. This blockage occurs because of restrictions on the international movement of funds and other exchange controls.

11.1.3.3. *Tax constraints*

Tax constraints limit the free flow of affiliate funds to a parent or to sister affiliates. These may occur because higher taxes on all corporate earnings or extra taxes on dividends may be imposed to curb inflation.

11.1.3.4. *Summary of constraints*

Other economic factors such as inflation and interest rates also have an important impact on the international mobility of corporate funds.

There are many elements and issues in international current asset management. Here, we assume that the major tasks of current asset management consist of (1) the ability to transfer funds, (2) the positioning of funds within a multinational firm, (3) arbitrage opportunities, and (4) different channels to move funds.

11.1.4. *The Ability to Transfer Funds*

An MNC has the ability to adjust intracompany fund flows and profits on a global basis. This ability is one of the most important advantages that MNCs enjoy. Financial transactions within an MNC stem from the internal transfer of goods, services, technology, and capital. Such intracompany flows range from finished goods to intangible items such as management skills, trademarks, and patents. Furthermore, capital investments and direct loans give rise to future flows of dividends, interest, and principal payments. On the other hand, many of the gains achieved through intracompany fund flows derive from some questionable business practices. For example, the amount of gains could depend on a company's ability to take advantage of soft spots in tax laws and regulatory barriers. Consequently, conflicts between MNCs and their host governments are quite likely.

11.1.5. *Positioning of Funds*

Another main task of current asset management is to position working cash balances or excess liquidity within an MNC. The division of funds among various affiliates involves the choice of country and the selection of currency denomination for all liquid funds. In domestic businesses, fund flows among units of a large company confer little or no advantage to the company because tax rates and regulations are uniform throughout the country.

The value of intracompany fund flows for MNCs lies precisely in the fact that there are wide variations in national tax systems and regulatory barriers. In other words, many different types of market imperfections increase the value of internal fund flows among units of an MNC. These market imperfections include foreign exchange markets, financial markets, and commodity markets.

11.1.6. *Arbitrage Opportunities*

The ability to relocate working cash balances and profits on a global basis provides MNCs with three different types of arbitrage opportunities: (1) tax arbitrage, (2) financial market arbitrage, and (3) regulatory system arbitrage.

First, MNCs can reduce their overall tax burden by shifting profits from subsidiaries in high-tax countries to subsidiaries in low-tax countries. Second, internal fund transfers may enable MNCs to circumvent exchange controls, earn higher yields on excess funds, and tap domestically unavailable capital sources. Third, if affiliate profits depend on government regulations or union pressure, MNCs can disguise true profits through transfer pricing and other intracompany adjustments.

11.1.7. *Different Channels to Move Funds*

Multinational business operations require a steady flow of funds from parent to subsidiary, from subsidiary to parent, and between subsidiaries. Because these fund flows are unique, we will consider one at a time.

11.1.7.1. *Fund flows from parent to subsidiary*

The largest flow of funds from parent to subsidiary is the initial investment. The subsidiary may also receive additional funds in the form of loans or added investments. The purchase of goods from the parent offers another form of fund flows from parent to subsidiary. This form of fund flows involves transfer pricing, the price on goods sold between related entities.

11.1.7.2. *Fund flows from subsidiary to parent*

The major components of fund flows from subsidiary to parent consist of dividends, interest on loans, principal reduction payments, royalty payments, license fees, technical service fees, management fees, export commissions, and payments for goods received from the parent. The parent does not have total control over the size of the flow of funds because of various external factors, such as foreign exchange controls and tax constraints. For example, many governments impose a withholding tax when dividends are remitted to foreign owners.

11.1.7.3. *Fund flows from subsidiary to subsidiary*

Funds flow from one subsidiary to another when they lend funds to each other or buy goods from each other. Funds from one subsidiary may also be used to establish another subsidiary. When such investments are made, all dividends and principal payments may go directly to the home office. However, it is possible for these two subsidiaries to have cash flows similar to parent company cash flows.

Many factors, such as exchange controls and domestic political pressures, can block dividend repatriation or other forms of fund remittances. If funds are blocked in perpetuity, the value of a foreign project to the parent company is zero. However, MNCs have secretive methods to remove blocked funds, including (1) multilateral netting, (2) leading and lagging, (3) transfer pricing, (4) reinvoicing centers, (5) intracompany loans, and (6) payment adjustments.

11.1.7.4. *Multilateral netting*

Large MNCs often require a highly coordinated interchange of material, parts, work-in-process, and finished goods among various units because they must handle a large volume of intracorporate fund flows. These crossborder fund transfers involve the foreign exchange spread, the opportunity cost of the float, and other transaction costs such as cable charges. Netting has been frequently suggested as one method of minimizing the total volume of interaffiliate fund flows.

Netting is a method designed to reduce the foreign exchange transaction cost through the consolidation of accounts payables and accounts receivable. Multilateral netting is an extension of bilateral netting. For example, if subsidiary A purchases $10 million worth of goods from subsidiary B and B in turn buys $11 million worth of parts from A, the combined flows are $21 million. On a net basis, however, subsidiary A would pay subsidiary B only $1 million. Bilateral netting would be useless where internal sales are more complex. Think of a situation where subsidiary A sells $10 million worth of goods to subsidiary B, subsidiary B sells $10 million worth of goods to subsidiary C, and subsidiary C sells $10 million worth of goods to subsidiary A. In this case, bilateral netting would be of no use, but multilateral netting would eliminate interaffiliate fund transfers completely.

Example 11.1

Table 11.1 shows a more complex multilateral netting system. Without netting, total payments add up to $5,500. If the cost of foreign exchange transactions and transfer fees were 1.5 percent, the total cost of settlement would be $82.50.

Multilateral netting enables the subsidiaries to transmit information about their obligations to a single center, which combines them in the form shown in Table 11.2. Netting reduces total foreign exchange transfers from $5,500 to $600 and transaction costs from $82.50 to $9. As a result, this netting reduces both foreign exchange transfers and transaction costs by 89 percent.

An accelerated globalization of production, distribution, and finance in recent years has created an unusually large volume of intracompany fund flows. By netting intra-affiliate payments, MNCs can realize significant cost savings. It is no wonder why so many MNCs use netting procedures to reduce transaction costs. As with all other transfer mechanisms, however, many governments impose controls on netting. Certainly, this will limit the degree to which the multilateral netting system can reduce foreign exchange transfers and transaction costs.

Table 11.1 International payments matrix.

Receiving Subsidiary	Paying Subsidiary				Total Receipts
	United States	Japan	Germany	Canada	
United States	—	$500	$600	$700	$1,800
Japan	$200	—	400	500	1,100
Germany	600	500	—	300	1,400
Canada	600	400	200	—	1,200
Total payments	$1,400	$1,400	$1,200	$1,500	$5,500

Table 11.2 Multilateral netting schedule.

Subsidiary	Total Receipt	Total Payment	Net Receipt	Net Payment
United States	$1,800	$1,400	$400	—
Japan	1,100	1,400	—	$300
Germany	1,400	1,200	200	—
Canada	1,200	1,500	—	300

11.1.7.5. *Leads and lags*

MNCs can accelerate (**lead**) or delay (**lag**) the timing of foreign-currency payments in order to reduce foreign exchange exposure or to increase working capital available. These leads and lags can be achieved by modifying the credit terms extended by one unit to another. In order to reduce foreign exchange exposure, companies should accelerate the payment of hard-currency payables and delay the payment of soft-currency payables. If subsidiary X buys goods worth $10 million monthly from subsidiary Y on 60-day credit terms, Y is, in effect, financing $20 million of working capital for X. The extension of the terms to 120 days would enable subsidiary X to have an additional $20 million of working capital.

Most US and non-US MNCs use leads and lags to minimize foreign exchange exposure and to shift the burden of financing from one unit to another. This technique has a number of advantages over direct loans. First, leading and lagging do not require a note that officially recognizes an obligation to the seller. Moreover, the amount of credit can be adjusted up or down by shortening or lengthening the credit terms. Second, indications are that governments interfere less with payments on intracompany accounts than on intracompany loans. Third, under Section 482 of the US tax code, US firms do not have to pay interest on intracompany accounts up to 6 months, but they have to pay interest on all intracompany loans.

11.1.7.6. *Transfer pricing*

Transfer prices are prices of goods and services sold between related parties such as a parent and its subsidiary. There are increasing transfers of goods and services between related units in different countries as MNCs have become larger and more diversified. Because transfer prices are frequently different from arm's length prices (fair market prices), there is obviously room for manipulation. Governments usually assume that MNCs use transfer prices to reduce or avoid their taxes. For this reason, most governments have set up policing mechanisms to review the transfer pricing policies of MNCs. MNCs are also concerned with transfer prices because they affect direct cash flows for payments of goods and taxes, for cost structures, and for the evaluation of management performance. Thus, Section 482 of the US Tax Code authorizes the Internal Review Service to adjust the income, deductions, credits, or allowances of commonly controlled taxpayers to prevent evasion of taxes or to clearly reflect their income

Transfer prices can avoid financial problems or improve financial conditions. For example, some countries restrict the amount of profits that can leave that country. In this case, a parent company can remove funds from this particular foreign country by charging higher prices on goods sold to its subsidiary in that country. Transfer prices also channel funds into a subsidiary to bolster its financial condition by charging lower prices on goods sold to that subsidiary.

Example 11.2

To illustrate the effects of a change in transfer prices on the flow of funds, assume the following: (1) Affiliates A and B have the same tax rate at 50 percent, (2) Affiliate A produces 100 radios for $5 per unit and sells them to affiliate B, and (3) Affiliate B sells these radios for $20 per unit to an unrelated customer. Table 11.3 shows the effects of low vs. high transfer price on flow of funds.

A consolidated gross profit of $1,500 is the same under both conditions. If both affiliates have the same tax rate at 50 percent, a consolidated net income of $450 is also the same under both conditions. The policy of the low transfer price results in a cash transfer of $1,000 from B to A, whereas the policy of the high transfer price causes an additional $500 of cash to move from B to A. If it were desirable to transfer funds out of affiliate B, the high transfer-price policy would achieve this purpose. The use of the low transfer price ($1,000) allows B to make a net income of $300, whereas the use of the high transfer price ($1,500) permits B to earn only $50. Hence, if it were desirable to bolster B's financial condition, the low transfer-price policy would achieve this end.

A major consideration in setting a transfer price is the income tax effect. For example, those countries with high tax rates are likely to induce higher transfer prices on flows from the parent and lower transfer prices on flows to the parent. On the other hand, those countries with lower tax rates would induce lower transfer prices on flows from the parent and higher transfer prices on flows to the parent. These transfer pricing policies shift profits from a country with a higher tax rate to a country with a lower tax rate so that worldwide corporate profits may be maximized.

Table 11.3   Effects of low vs. high transfer price on flow of funds.

	A	B	Combined A + B
Low Transfer Price			
Sales price	$1,000	$2,000	$2,000
Cost of goods sold	$500	$1,000	$500
Gross profit	$500	$1,000	$1,500
Operating expenses	$200	$400	$600
Earnings before taxes	$300	$600	$900
Taxes (50%)	$150	$300	$450
Net income	$150	$300	$450
High Transfer Price			
Sales price	$1,500	$2,000	$2,000
Cost of goods sold	$500	$1,500	$500
Gross profit	$1,000	$500	$1,500
Operating expense	$200	$400	$600
Earnings before taxes	$800	$100	$900
Taxes (50%)	$400	$50	$450
Net income	$400	$50	$450

Example 11.3

To illustrate the tax effects of a change in transfer prices on corporate earnings, assume the following: (1) Affiliate C is in a low tax country (20 percent tax rate) and affiliate D is in a high tax country (50 percent tax rate). (2) Affiliate C produces 150 calculators for $5 per unit and sells them to affiliate D. (3) Affiliate D sells these calculators for $20 per unit to an unrelated customer. Table 11.4 shows the tax effects of low vs. high transfer price on company earnings.

Under the low transfer price, C pays taxes of $90 and D pays taxes of $450 for a total tax bill of $540 and a consolidated net income of $810. Under the high transfer price, C pays taxes of $240 and D pays taxes of $75 for a total tax bill of $315 and a consolidated net income of $1,035. Earnings before taxes are the same at $1,350 despite the different prices at which the calculators transfer from C to D. Still, the higher transfer price reduces total taxes by $225 ($540 – $315) and increases consolidated net income by the same amount ($1,035 – $810).

Multinational business executives are reluctant to discuss policies for transfer pricing. But in multinational cases, transfer pricing has been used to minimize income taxes and tariffs, to adjust for currency fluctuations, to avoid economic restrictions, and to present a favorable financial picture of a foreign affiliate. In the early 1990s, President Clinton made a proposal to extract billions of dollars from foreign companies in the United States. By cracking down on foreign companies that manipulate transfer prices, Clinton argued that the US government could collect $45 billion over 4 years from foreign companies.

11.1.7.7. *Reinvoicing centers*

Some MNCs circumvent or bypass governments' restrictions and regulations by setting up reinvoicing centers in tax haven countries. Tax haven countries are those nations which provide foreign companies with permanent tax inducements. It is possible for a reinvoicing center in the Bahamas to issue invoices for all goods sold by a US parent to its subsidiaries

Table 11.4   Tax effect of low vs. high transfer price.

	Low Tax C	High Tax D	Combined C + D
Low Transfer Price			
Sales price	$1,500	$3,000	$3,000
Cost of goods sold	$750	$1, 500	$750
Gross profit	$750	$1,500	$2,250
Operating expenses	$300	$600	$900
Earnings before taxes	$450	$900	$1,350
Taxes (20%/50%)	$90	$450	$540
Net income	$360	$450	$810
High Transfer Price			
Sales price	$2,250	$3,000	$3,000
Cost of goods sold	$750	$2,250	$750
Gross profit	$1,500	$750	$2,250
Operating expense	$300	$600	$900
Earnings before taxes	$1,200	$150	$1,350
Taxes (20%/50%)	$240	$75	$315
Net income	$960	$75	$1,035

or independent customers in different countries. In this case, the reinvoicing center takes titles of all goods sold by one corporate unit to its customers, even though the goods move directly from the seller in the United States to the buyer in Japan. The Bahamas center pays the US seller and is paid by the Japanese buyer to complete the transaction.

In June 2000, the Organization for Economic Cooperation and Development (OECD) named Monaco, the US Virgin Islands, and the British Gibraltar among 35 jurisdictions whose status as tax havens poses potentially harmful tax competition. The OECD asked the 35 jurisdictions to specify how and when they would bring their tax regimes into line with international standards. At the London G20 summit on April 2, 2009, G20 countries agreed to define a blacklist for tax havens, to be segmented according to a four-tier system, based on compliance with an "internationally agreed tax standard. The list, drawn up by the OECD, was updated on April 2, 2009 in connection with the G20 meeting in London. In May 2009, the OECD decided to remove all three remaining jurisdictions (Andorra, the Principality of Liechtenstein and the Principality of Monaco) from the list of uncooperative tax havens. Those actions by G20 countries and the OECD were successful in compelling all former tax haven countries to comply with the standard by 2010. As a result, no jurisdiction is currently listed as an uncooperative tax haven by the OECD. The four tiers used by the OECD are as follows: (1) those that have substantially implemented the standard; (2) tax havens that have committed to — but not yet fully implemented standard; (3) Financial centers that have committed to — but not yet fully implemented; and (4) Those that have not committed to the standard.

Reinvoicing centers are often used to cope with foreign exchange exposures. Subsidiaries buy and sell goods in multiple currencies and must manage the resulting currency exposures. Mechanisms such as the reinvoicing center are necessary so that subsidiaries operate their business exclusively on a local currency basis without the active management of foreign exchange exposures. To see how the reinvoicing center works to minimize currency exposures, assume that the Canadian subsidiary purchases equipment from a Japanese firm and that payment should be made in Japanese yen. In this case, the reinvoicing center would buy the equipment in the name of the Canadian firm, pay the seller in Japanese yen, bill the Canadian firm in Canadian dollars, and receive Canadian dollars from the buyer. Thus, the objective of foreign exchange management based on the reinvoicing center is to centralize foreign exchange exposures in one unit — the reinvoicing center in a single country. To achieve this goal, the reinvoicing center buys on behalf of all related companies in various foreign currencies and then rebills those purchases to the buying units in their local currencies.

11.1.7.8. *Intracompany loans*

There are many different types of intracompany loans, but direct loans, credit swaps, and parallel loans are the most important. Direct loans involve straight dealings between the lending unit and the borrowing unit, but credit swaps and parallel loans normally involve an intermediary.

A **credit swap** is a simultaneous spot-and-forward loan transaction between a private company and a bank of a foreign country. For example, a US company deposits a given amount of dollars in the Chicago office of a Mexican bank. In return for this deposit, the bank lends a given amount of pesos to the company's subsidiary in Mexico. The same contract provides that the bank returns the initial amount of dollars to the company at a specified date and that the subsidiary returns the original amount of pesos to the bank at a specified date.

Credit swaps are, in fact, intracompany loans hedged and channeled through banks. These loans are also risk free from a bank's point of view because the parent's deposit fully collateralizes them. Credit swaps have several advantages over direct intracompany loans. First, credit swaps are free of foreign exchange exposures because the parent recovers the amount of its deposit in the original parent currency from the bank. Second, cost savings may be available with credit swaps because certain countries apply different tax rates to interest paid to the foreign parent and to interest paid to the local bank.

Parallel loans consist of two related but separate borrowings and typically involve four parties in two different countries. For example, a US parent lends an agreed amount in dollars to the American subsidiary of a Mexican parent. In return for this loan, the Mexican parent lends the same amount of money in pesos to the Mexican subsidiary of the US parent. These loan arrangements involve the same amount for both loans and the same loan maturity. Certainly, each loan is paid in the subsidiary's currency.

Parallel loans are frequently used to effectively repatriate blocked funds by circumventing exchange control restrictions. To see how the back-to-back loan can be used to repatriate blocked funds, suppose that the Mexican subsidiary of IBM is unable to repatriate its peso profits. It may lend the money to the Mexican subsidiary of AT&T; AT&T would, in turn, lend dollars to IBM in the United States. As a result, IBM would have the use of dollars in the United States while AT&T would obtain pesos in Mexico.

11.1.7.9. *Payment adjustments*

There are many different forms of payments by foreign subsidiaries to the parent company. These payments can be adjusted to remove blocked funds. Dividend payments are by far the most important form of fund flows from foreign subsidiaries to the parent company, accounting for approximately 50 percent of all remittances to US companies. Money-market countries recognize dividend payments as a method by which the earnings of a business firm can be distributed to the stockholders of the firm. Not all nations, however, allow dividends of local companies to be paid in hard currencies to the foreign parent companies. Countries characterized by balance-of-payments problems and foreign exchange shortages frequently place restrictions on the payment of dividends to foreign companies.

Two methods to adjust dividend payments in the case of these restrictions have become increasingly popular. These two methods artificially inflate the value of the local investment base because the level of dividend payments depends on the company's capital. First, the parent company can magnify its subsidiary's registered capital by investing in used equipment whose value has been artificially inflated. Second, the parent company may acquire a bankrupt local firm at a large discount from book value and then merge it with its subsidiary on the basis of the failed firm's book value. Of course, this action would raise the subsidiary's equity base.

In addition to dividends, royalties and fees are also important components of fund flows from foreign subsidiaries to the parent company. Royalties are paid to use certain technologies, patents, and trademarks. Fees are compensations for managerial services and technical assistance. Such royalties and fees are unique and thus do not have a reference in market value. Most host governments look with more favor on payments for royalties and fees than on payments for profit remittances. Hence, it is easier for MNCs to repatriate blocked funds through inflated royalty and fee payments rather than through any other form of payment.

11.1.7.10. *Unbundling fund transfers*

MNCs frequently unbundle remittances into separate flows for such purposes as royalties and management fees rather than lump all flows under the heading of profit (dividend). Host countries are then more likely to perceive the so-called "remittance of profits" as essential purchases of specific services that would benefit the host country. Unbundling makes it possible for MNCs to recover funds from their affiliates without irritating host country sensitivities with large dividend drains. This form of fund transfers is particularly useful for business operations in socialist and Islamic countries where interest and dividend payments are regarded unfavorably.

MNCs can also unbundle remittances into separate cash flows to reduce their overall income taxes. Royalties and management fees have certain tax advantages over dividends when the host country tax rate is higher than the parent country rate. Obviously, this tax advantage arises because royalties and management fees are usually tax deductible locally. Under the foreign tax credit system, countries relinquish tax on profits earned abroad up to the amount of the foreign tax. Because local income taxes are paid before the dividend distribution, the parent company can take a tax credit for the local income taxes paid. If the local income tax rate is higher than the parent country rate, part of the benefit may be lost, but the entire benefit is obtained when the payment is for royalties and management fees.

Example 11.4

Assume that the foreign subsidiary of a US parent company earns $1,000 before any taxes. The parent company wants to receive $400 before US taxes. The local tax rate is 50 percent and the US tax rate is 30 percent.

Table 11.5 shows how the US parent company can unbundle remittances into separate cash flows to reduce its worldwide taxes. In the case of a "bundled situation," the parent company receives $400 in cash dividends. In the case of an "unbundled situation," the parent company receives a royalty of $300 and a dividend of $100 for a total of $400 in cash. Under the bundled situation, the subsidiary pays taxes of $500 and the parent company pays no taxes for a total tax bill of $500 and a consolidated net income of $500. Under the unbundled situation, the subsidiary pays taxes of $350 and the parent company pays taxes of $90 for a total tax bill of $440 and a consolidated net income of $560. Earnings before any taxes are the same at $1,000. Still, the unbundled situation reduces total taxes by $60 and increases consolidated net income by $60.

11.2. CASH MANAGEMENT

Cash gives an MNC the ability to pay bills as they come due, but it is not an earning asset. Thus, it is very important to determine an optimal level of investment in cash. The

Table 11.5 Bundled vs. unbundled contribution to consolidated income.

	Bundled $400 Dividend	Unbundled $100 Dividend
Subsidiary Statement		
Earnings before taxes	$1,000	$1,000
Less: royalties and fees	—	$300
Taxable income	$1,000	$700
Less: local tax at 50% (A)	$500	$350
Available for dividends	$500	$350
Cash dividend to parent	$400	$100
Reinvested locally	$100	$250
Parent Statement		
Royalty received	—	$300
Less: US tax at 30% (B)	—	$90
Net royalty received	—	$210
Net cash dividend	$400	$100
Total cash received in the US	$400	$310
Worldwide Income		
Original earnings before any taxes	$1,000	$1,000
Less: total taxes paid (A + B)	$500	$440
Contribution to worldwide income	$500	$560

major sources of cash inflows are dividends, royalties and fees, cash sales and collections on accounts receivable, depreciation, sales of new securities, loans from banks or nonbank financial institutions, and advance cash payments on contracts. In contrast, cash outflows are necessary for interest and dividend payments, retirement of debt and other securities, income tax payments, payments on accounts payable, wages and salaries, and purchases of fixed assets. The term cash management is used here to mean optimization of cash flows and investment of excess cash.

Companies prefer to hold cash rather than other forms of assets for three main reasons: the transaction motive, the precautionary motive, and the speculative motive. The **transaction motive** holds that cash balances are held partly in anticipation of day-to-day cash disbursements. The **precautionary motive** suggests that cash balances are held partly as protection against deviations from budgeted cash flows. The **speculative motive** relates to the holding of cash in order to take advantage of profit-making opportunities.

11.2.1. *Objectives of cash management*

General principles that apply to cash management on an international basis are frequently similar to those utilized by many companies domestically. The overall cash management objective of any corporation is to minimize the cash balance within the company with the goal of optimizing corporate fund utilization. However, the parameters within which MNCs operate are broader and more complex than those of purely domestic companies are. Furthermore, the relationships among these parameters are constantly changing. Hence, those responsible for cash management on an international basis must consider new variables such as tax concepts, governmental restrictions on intracompany fund flows, differences in cultures, and foreign exchange rates.

More specifically, international cash managers try to attain the traditional objectives of domestic cash management on a global basis: (1) to minimize the cost of funds, (2) to improve liquidity, (3) to reduce risks, and (4) to improve the return on investment.

First, with interest rates of more than 10 percent in many countries, considerable savings are possible when the cost of funds is lowered. MNCs should attempt to reduce their overall cost of funds by increasing internal funds and reducing borrowings.

Second, international cash managers must attempt to improve liquidity on a global basis. Certainly, it is difficult to improve liquidity on a worldwide basis because government regulations prohibit the free transfer of funds. But MNCs can use centralized cash management and electronic fund transfers to improve their overall liquidity.

Third, international cash management involves a variety of risks such as political, economic, and exchange risks. Insurance, careful negotiations, forward contracts, and currency options may be used to reduce these risks.

Fourth, a variety of ratios, such as return on investment and return on net worth, are often used to measure performance. The improvement of financial performance is perhaps the most important aspect of treasury management.

11.2.2. *Floats*

To carry out its operations, an MNC causes a steady flow of funds to take place among its family members. These fund flows cannot avoid the problem of float. **Float** refers to the status of funds in the process of collection. Float, from a domestic point of view, represents only the temporary loss of income on funds that are tied up in the process of collection. In international operations, however, the problem of float is twofold: (1) the loss of income on the funds tied up during the longer transfer process and (2) their exposure to foreign exchange risk during the transfer period. Nearly all aspects of both international and domestic cash management are associated with the concept of float. Thus, we ought to understand float to effectively evaluate the collection and disbursement procedures of any cash management system. For purposes of measurement and analysis, we can break down float into five categories:

1. Invoicing float refers to funds tied up in the process of preparing invoices. Because this float is largely under the direct control of the company, it can be reduced through more efficient clerical procedures.
2. Mail float includes funds tied up from the time customers mail their remittance checks until the company receives them.
3. Processing float consists of funds tied up in the process of sorting and recording remittance checks until they can be deposited in the bank. Like invoicing float, this float is under the company's internal control and thus can be reduced through more efficient clerical procedures.
4. Transit float involves funds tied up from the time remittance checks are deposited until these funds become usable to the company. This float occurs because it takes several days for deposited checks to clear through the commercial banking system.
5. Disbursing float refers to funds available in a company's bank account until these funds are actually disbursed by the company.

11.2.3. *Collection and disbursement of funds*

The overall efficiency of international cash management depends on various collection and disbursement policies. To maximize available cash, an MNC must accelerate its collection process and delay its payments. Hence, it must consider these two policies simultaneously to improve its overall cash management efficiency. Significant benefits exist because long delays are possible in collecting accounts receivable and in paying accounts payable. Delays of seven to ten business days are common to allow for transit and other floats across national borders. Effective collection and disbursement policies have become even more important in recent years because of high interest rates, wide fluctuations in foreign exchange rates, and widespread credit restrictions.

11.2.3.1. *Acceleration of collections*

International cash managers should use every means in their power to gain control over incoming funds as quickly as possible after the collection process starts. The principal goals of speeding the collection process are to reduce floats, to minimize the investment in accounts receivable, and to reduce banking and other transaction fees.

An MNC can use a number of useful techniques to speed the collection process: lock boxes, cable remittances, electronic fund transfers, and the use of wire transfers. There are not significant differences between domestic and international lock-box operations. In international lock-box arrangements, MNCs simply use banks in foreign countries to speed up the collection process of their international accounts receivable. With respect to payment instructions to customers and banks, the use of cable remittances is a crucial means for MNCs to minimize delays in receipt of payments and in conversion of payments into cash.

MNCs use electronic fund transfers (EFTs) to move several trillion dollars throughout the world every day. EFTs move funds faster and more efficiently than checks. Moreover, EFTs are completed at a relatively low cost.

There are three computerized systems designed to process international wire transfers: the Clearinghouse Interbank Payment System (CHIPS), the Clearinghouse Payment Assistance System (CHPAS), and the Society for Worldwide Interbank Financial Telecommunications (SWIFT). These and other computerized systems are widely used today to facilitate the wire transfer process of funds around the globe. The SWIFT is an interbank communication network founded in 1973 to move messages for financial transactions. Chapter 9 discussed these three Interbank Clearing House Systems in detail.

11.2.3.2. *Cryptocurrency*

A **cryptocurrency** (or **crypto currency**) is a digital asset designed to work as a medium of exchange that uses strong cryptography to secure financial transactions, control the creation of additional units, and verify the transfer of assets. Cryptocurrencies use decentralized control as opposed to centralized digital currency and central banking systems. The decentralized control of each cryptocurrency works through distributed ledgertechnology, typically a blockchain, that serves as a public financial transaction database. Bitcoin, first released as open-source software in 2009, is generally considered the first decentralized cryptocurrency. Since the release of bitcoin, over 17,000 altcoins (alternative variants of bitcoin, or other cryptocurrencies) have been created. The rise in the popularity of cryptocurrencies and their adoption by financial institutions have led some governments to adopt regulation in order to protect users.

11.2.3.3. *Delay of payments*

In addition to accelerating collections, international cash managers can produce a faster turnover of cash by controlling disbursements efficiently. By delaying disbursements, a company keeps cash on hand for longer periods. When the firm purchases goods on credit, it must delay its payments until the last day in order to have the additional funds for the extra time. An MNC can delay its payments in a number of ways: (1) mail, (2) more frequent requisitions, and (3) floats.

First, in spite of the widespread availability of electronic fund transfer networks, a surprisingly large number of cross-border payments are still made by mail. It is not unusual for regular airmail to take seven days or more to reach its ultimate destination.

Second, a parent can use large sums of money on a temporary basis because of frequent requisitions of funds by foreign subsidiaries from the parent's central office and the centralized disbursements. For example, if a firm switches its requisition policy from monthly requisitions to weekly requisitions, it can keep cash on hand as much as three weeks longer.

Third, the use of float is yet another method used to maximize the availability of cash. At any given time checks written by a firm have yet to be cleared through the banking system because that process takes a number of days. Thus, it is possible for a firm to have a negative balance on its checkbook but a positive balance on its bankbook for a number of days.

11.2.3.4. *The cost of cash management*

An MNC company may use various collection and disbursement procedures to improve the efficiency of its cash management. Because these two types of procedures constitute two sides of the same coin, they have a joint effect on the overall efficiency of cash management. Accelerating collections and delaying disbursements involve additional costs. Hence, a company must determine how far it should go to make its cash operations more efficient. In theory, a company should adopt various collection and disbursement methods as long as their marginal returns exceed their marginal expenses.

The value of careful cash management depends on the opportunity cost of funds invested in cash. The opportunity cost of these funds in turn depends on the company's required rate of return on short-term investments. For example, assume that the adoption of a lock-box system is expected to reduce the investment in cash by $100,000. If a company earns 11 percent on short-term investments, the opportunity cost of the current system is $11,000. Hence, if the cost of the lock-box system is less than $11,000, it can be adopted to improve earnings performance.

11.2.4. *Cash Centers*

Cash management can be centralized, regionalized, or decentralized on a company level. Decentralization permits subsidiaries to use excess cash in any way they see fit. While this is popular among subsidiary managers, decentralization does not allow an MNC to utilize its most liquid asset on a widespread basis. Effective cash management requires that executives predetermine cash flow centers. For example, an MNC should not choose to hold cash in a country which has violent political upheavals and rampant inflation. Rather, it should transfer idle local cash balances as quickly as possible to a stable environment.

Centralized cash management or cash pooling calls for each local subsidiary to hold at the local level the minimum cash balance for transaction purposes. All funds not needed for transaction purposes are channeled to a central cash center. This cash center is responsible for placing a central pool of funds in those currencies and money market instruments which will best serve the needs of the MNC on a worldwide basis.

11.2.4.1. *Advantages of cash pooling*

Centralized cash management has a number of advantages over decentralized cash management:

1. The central cash center can collect information more quickly and make better decisions on the relative strengths and weaknesses of various currencies. Such information and decisions are necessary if one wishes to invest a central pool of funds most profitably.
2. Funds held in a cash center can quickly be returned to a subsidiary with cash shortages by wire transfer or by providing a worldwide banking system with full collateral in hard currency. The central pool of funds eliminates the possibility that one subsidiary will borrow at higher rates while another holds surplus funds idle or invests them at lower rates.
3. By holding all precautionary balances in a central cash center, an MNC can reduce the total pool without any loss in the level of production. This is due to a synergistic effect which is said to exist when the whole is worth more than the mere sum of its parts. This effect has frequently been defined as "$2 + 2 = 5$."

Before any cash is remitted to a central cash center, local cash needs must be properly assessed. The proper assessment of local cash needs in relation to the cash center involves the following steps:

1. Cash budgets should be prepared to know anticipated cash outflows and inflows at key future dates.
2. Each subsidiary must have effective cash collection procedures which will speed cash flows into the company.
3. Each subsidiary must also have systematic cash disbursement procedures which will delay cash flows out of the company.
4. Each subsidiary should estimate when and how much surplus cash it will have.
5. Each subsidiary should also estimate when and how much shortages it will have.
6. The MNC must develop necessary steps for cash mobilization such as a management information system and a cash transfer system; it should have the clear responsibility for making cash transfer decisions.

11.2.4.2. *Factors affecting the location of cash centers*

Many factors affect the location of cash centers. From an economic point of view, idle funds should move toward those locations which provide the highest profitability and safety. These funds are accumulated in cash centers for temporary investment prior to reassignment elsewhere. Thus, an MNC should choose those locations from which funds can again be readily assigned to other places in the world.

Perhaps the most important factor affecting the location of cash centers is the local government's political stability and its attitude toward foreign-based companies. Local laws may require partial ownership of alien companies by nationals of the host country or by the government itself. Hostility of the courts toward foreign business claims and disclosure requirements may all work against a subsidiary operating as a cash center. Aggregate tax levels and penalty rates on excessive dividend remittances also play an important role in the selection of cash centers.

An MNC must also consider several economic factors when selecting cash centers. These cash centers should be located in countries whose currencies are stable in value and readily convertible into other currencies. It is extremely difficult for financial managers to predict the exact timing of a change in the exchange rate. Most governments take all possible measures to avoid speculation against their currencies. It is critical, therefore, to engage in hedging operations to assure that foreign exchange losses can be minimized. Thus, the existence of an active forward market and the availability of suitable money market instruments for the deployment of temporary excess resources are important.

Cash centers are usually located in the major financial centers of the world such as New York and London. Brussels has become popular as a cash center for companies operating in Europe. Other popular locations for cash centers are tax haven countries, such as Luxembourg, the Bahamas, Bermuda, and the Netherlands. These countries offer most of the prerequisites for a corporate cash center: political and economic stability, freely convertible currency, access to international communications, and well-defined legal procedures.

11.2.5. *Investing Excess Funds*

Along with optimization of cash flows, the other key function of international cash management is to make certain that excess funds are wisely invested. This section discusses three types of portfolio management and portfolio guidelines.

11.2.5.1. *Portfolio management*

There are at least three types of portfolio management available to international cash managers. First, MNCs can optimize cash flows worldwide with a zero portfolio. All excess funds of subsidiaries are remitted to the parent and then used to pay the parent's short-term debts. Second, they can centralize cash management in third countries such as tax heaven countries and invest funds in marketable securities. Third, they can centralize cash management at headquarters with subsidiaries holding only minimum amounts of cash for transaction purposes.

11.2.5.2. *Portfolio guidelines*

Most surplus funds are temporary. If MNCs invest funds in marketable securities such as Treasury bills, they should follow sound portfolio guidelines. First, instruments in the short-term investment portfolio should be diversified to maximize the yield for a given amount of risk or to minimize the risk for a given amount of return. Second, for companies that hold marketable securities for near-future needs of liquidity, marketability considerations are of major importance. Third, the maturity of the investment should be tailored to the company's projected cash needs. Fourth, the securities chosen should be limited to those with a minimum risk of default. Fifth, the portfolio should be reviewed daily to decide what new investments will be made and which securities will be liquidated.

Global Finance in Practice 11: Money Rates

Table 11.6 shows money rates and/or money-market instruments and they can be used as both borrowing and investing benchmarks.

Inflation is the rate of increase in prices over a given period of time.

The US consumer price index is a measure of the average change over time in the prices paid by urban consumers for a market basket of consumer goods and services.

Prime rate is the interest rate that banks use as a basis to set rates for different types of loans, credit cards and lines of credit.

Policy rate is a short-term, often overnight, rate that banks charge one another to borrow funds.

Overnight purchase is a type of trading in which you can purchase assets or securities after markets close and through the night before the markets reopen the next morning.

Discount rate refers to the interest rate charged to commercial banks and other financial institutions for short-term loans they take from the Federal Reserve Bank.

Federal fund rate refers to the target interest rate set by the Federal Open Market Committee (FOMC). This target is the rate at which commercial banks borrow and lend their excess reserves to each other overnight.

Treasury bills are short-term debt obligations backed by the US Treasury Department with a maturity of 1 year or less.

Fannie Mae is a government-sponsored enterprise (GSE) that purchases mortgage loans from smaller banks or credit unions and guarantees, or backs, these loans on the mortgage market for borrowers.

Call money is the benchmark interest rate that banks charge brokers who are borrowing the money to fund margin loans.

Commercial papers are short-term unsecured primary notes issued by companies.

Table 11.6 Money rates and money market instruments.

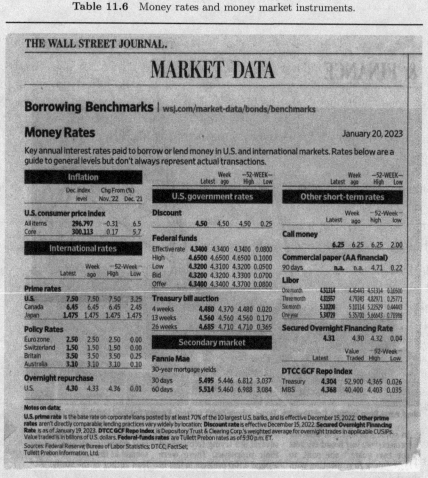

Source: *The Wall Street Journal*, January 20, 2023.

Secured overnight financing rate broad measure of the cost of borrowing cash overnight collateralized by Treasury securities.

Repo index is the only index that tracks the average daily interest rate paid for the most-traded GCF Repo contracts for US Treasury and mortgage-backed securities issued by Fannie Mae. GCF stands for a greatest common factor. For example, 12, 20, and 24 have two common factors: 2 and 4. The largest is 4, so we say that the GCF of 12, 20, and 24 is 4.

11.3. ACCOUNTS RECEIVABLE MANAGEMENT

The level of accounts receivable depends upon the volume of credit sales and the average collection period. These two variables, in turn, depend upon credit standards, credit terms, and collection policy. As management moves from customers who are more likely to pay their bills to customers who are less likely to pay their bills, sales tend to increase. However, a lenient credit policy is also likely to increase bad debt losses and investments in accounts receivable. In theory, a company should liberalize its credit policy to the point where the marginal profit on its increased sales equals the marginal cost of credit.

Because money has a time value, accounts receivable have a cost in terms of foregone interest. Nevertheless, many MNCs frequently decide to sell for credit in order to expand sales volume and profits. If sales are made on the basis of drafts on importers, trade acceptances or bankers' acceptances are created, and these may be discounted at banks or sold in the money market. In addition, in many countries the accumulation of accounts receivable is even highly desirable because government agencies extend export credit at preferential interest rates.

11.3.1. *Currency Value Problems*

One truly unique problem area of multinational accounts receivable management has to do with the risk of currency value changes. The accounts receivable manager should understand this risk and take all necessary actions to minimize it. Multinational accounts receivable are created by two separate types of transactions, sales to customers outside the corporate group and intracompany sales. We must consider these two types of transactions separately because their economic consequences are different.

11.3.1.1. *Sales to independent customers*

Management of accounts receivable from independent buyers involves two types of decision, the denomination of currency to be used for payment and the terms of payment. Domestic sales are always denominated in the local currency. In contrast, export sales can be denominated in the currency of the exporter, the currency of the importer, or a third country currency. The exporter would prefer to price and to invoice in the strongest currency, while the importer would prefer to pay in the weakest currency. Competition or custom will frequently resolve the problem, but the usual result is a tradeoff between the terms of payment and the denomination of currency. For example, an exporter may grant a longer credit period in exchange for an importer's promise to pay for its purchase in a hard currency.

Many factors affect the terms of payment, but perhaps one of the most important is the strength of the currency denominated in a transaction. If payments are to be made in a soft currency, accounts receivable should be collected as quickly as possible in order to minimize the possibility of exchange losses between the sale date and the collection date. Sales made in a hard currency may be permitted to remain outstanding somewhat longer. If the devaluation of its home currency is imminent, an exporter might want to encourage slow payment of its hard currency receivables.

There are at least two ways that the accounts receivable manager can alleviate currency value problems: currency denomination and the use of factors. A seller may require that all payments are to be made in hard currencies. This requirement assures the seller that payments are to be made in currencies likely to face little or no devaluation on the foreign exchange market. In certain instances, an MNC refuses credit sales denominated in foreign currencies altogether. MNCs may buy currency credit insurance. For example, American exporters can purchase protection from the Foreign Credit Insurance Association or the Export–Import Bank described.

Accounts-receivable managers also use factors to minimize accounts-receivable risks from changes in exchange rates between the sale date and the collection date. **Factoring** is a process whereby a company sells its accounts receivable on a nonrecourse basis. Nonrecourse means that the factor takes the loss if the customers of its client do not pay their accounts. In addition to risk bearing, the factor performs a number of additional services such as credit checking, bookkeeping, and the collection of accounts.

11.3.1.2. *Intracompany sales*

Intracompany sales differ from sales to independent customers in that little concern is given to credit standing and that the timing of the payments may depend upon a company's desire to allocate resources rather than normal payment schedules. Such sales are necessary for many reasons. Subsidiaries produce different products and often sell to each other. Like the location of cash balances, the location of intracompany receivables and their amounts are a policy consideration of the MNC when it allocates its resources on a global basis. If a parent company desires to transfer funds to its affiliate, it may do so by having the affiliate delay the payment for intracompany purchases.

Because international credit sales usually cross national boundaries, companies are concerned about currency values. Changes in exchange rates between the sales date and the collection date create accounts-receivable risks. Leading and lagging can be used to alleviate currency-value problems of intracompany credit sales. If subsidiaries are located in countries whose currencies are likely to devalue or to float downward, a parent company may instruct its subsidiaries to pay for their purchases more quickly (leading). In contrast, if subsidiaries are located in countries whose currencies are expected to upvalue or to float upward, the parent company may instruct its subsidiaries to delay payments (lagging). It is important to note that early payments and later payments in conjunction with intracompany sales are feasible only when the parent company owns 100 percent of its various affiliates.

11.4. INVENTORY MANAGEMENT

The overall efficiency of inventory management is extremely important for two reasons. First, inventories represent a significant segment of total assets for most MNCs. Second, they are the least liquid of current assets; thus, errors in inventory management are not quickly remedied. Hence, for the last few decades the greatest improvements within the area of current asset management have been made in inventory control and investment. The size of inventories in relation to sales has been greatly reduced with the application of computers and new inventory management systems.

Many US and European MNCs have recently adopted a Japanese inventory management system known as the "just-in-time" inventory system. The **just-in-time inventory system** requires that when orders are placed, specific goods are ordered along with an exact delivery date. The goal on the part of the company is to reduce inventory balances to practically zero. Under such an arrangement, it is not uncommon for suppliers to build facilities close to their major customers in order to ensure a ready supply of inventory. For example, many Japanese automotive suppliers have established their production facilities close to Japanese car assembly transplants in the United States and Canada. In essence, the customer is passing the inventory balance problem back to the supplier.

11.4.1. *Determining the Amount of Inventory*

The level of sales, the length of the production cycle, and the durability of the product are major determinants of investment in inventory. In domestic or one-country operations, companies attempt to balance their inventory level in such a way that both carrying costs and stockout costs are minimized. However, differentials in the costs of production and storage in different countries allow the MNC to maintain more flexible inventory policies. For instance, an MNC can take advantage of lower costs in a particular country by shifting its production or storage function to that country. These advantages are offset by such disadvantages as tariff levels and other forms of import restrictions used by governments.

Given the fact that many foreign affiliates operate under inflationary conditions, an MNC must determine whether to buy inventory in advance or to delay purchase until the inventory is actually needed. Advance purchases involve such carrying costs as interest on funds tied up in inventory, insurance premiums, storage costs, and taxes. Later purchases increase the possibility of higher costs either through inflation or devaluation. Inflation increases the costs of locally purchased items, and devaluation increases the costs of imported items.

Despite the desire for optimizing inventory levels, many companies which rely on imported inventories maintain over-stocked inventory accounts. The fears of continued inflation, raw materials shortages, and other environmental constraints induce companies to maintain high overseas inventory levels rather than risk curtailment of their overseas operations. Additional environmental constraints include anticipated import bans in foreign countries, anticipated delivery delays caused by dock strikes and slowdowns, the lack of sophisticated production and inventory control systems, and increased difficulty in obtaining foreign exchange for inventory purchases.

11.4.2. *Protective Measures Against Inflation and Devaluation*

Many foreign affiliates operate under inflationary economic conditions. Thus, it is important for MNCs to determine the effects of an increasing local price level or devaluation on their inventory management policies. The type of inventory normally stocked by subsidiaries is of importance in this decision. Some subsidiaries rely heavily on imported inventories, while other subsidiaries depend heavily upon locally acquired inventories. Some other subsidiaries may rely almost equally on imported and locally acquired inventories.

If a subsidiary relies heavily on imported goods, it should seek to build its inventory of supplies, equipment, and components in advance of an expected devaluation because devaluation at a later date effectively increases the costs of imported goods. For example, if a host country declares a 10 percent devaluation of its currency in relation to the dollar, a subsidiary should pay 10 percent more local currency for the same amount of imported goods from the United States.

On the other hand, if a subsidiary depends heavily upon locally purchased goods, it should seek to minimize its inventory of supplies, equipment, and components because devaluation at a later date effectively reduces the dollar value of inventories acquired locally. If inventories are translated at current rather than at historical exchange rates, a 10 percent devaluation of the local currency against the dollar would reduce the dollar value of its inventory by 10 percent.

Finally, if a subsidiary relies almost equally on imported inventories and locally purchased inventories, it should seek to reduce its locally acquired inventories and to increase its imported inventories in advance of an expected devaluation. However, if accurate forecasts of devaluation are not possible, a company should maintain the same amount of imported goods and locally purchased goods to avoid foreign exchange risks because a devaluation would affect both types of inventories equally, and thus the subsidiary would experience neither a gain nor a loss.

11.4.2.1. *Pricing*

Up to this point, our discussion has centered on preventive measures that MNCs can take to reduce risks associated with devaluation. Additional action can be taken in pricing to reduce these risks.

Example 11.5

Assume that 10 American-made radios have been imported into Korea which has subsequently devalued its currency by 50 percent. The original exchange rate was ₩500 per $1, the original cost was ₩1,000 per radio, and the original selling price was ₩1,500 per radio.

The Korean subsidiary has a choice of two basic policies with respect to price: (1) it can maintain the original price of its inventory in an effort to undercut competition, or (2) it can increase the price of its inventory in order to earn all or part of the original dollar profit expected. Table 11.7 shows the effects of both policies on the Korean subsidiary. Maintenance of the old price will result in a dollar loss of $5 on the sale of the 10 radios even if local figures indicate a profit of ₩5,000. If the subsidiary increases its selling price to the dollar equivalent of the original selling price, it will earn a profit of $10. However, it is important to note that this assumes the Korean government does not maintain price controls. Although there are no price controls imposed by the Korean government, a price increase of the magnitude indicated in policy (2) would perhaps discourage some sales. If the price elasticity of demand for the merchandise is extremely high, the local market may not bear the higher price. Nevertheless, a certain level of price increase is required to prevent a deterioration of converted earnings.

Another important question is whether a subsidiary should continue to import that type of merchandise. If local sales prices can be raised to cover the current higher dollar import prices, imports should continue. If not, imports could cease. Although the decision not to

Table 11.7 Effect of pricing on profits.

| Exchange Rate | (1) Maintain Old Price | | (2) Adjust Price | |
	Korean Currency	US Dollars	Korean Currency	US Dollars
₩1,000 (now) sold for	₩15,000	$15	₩30,000	$30
₩500 (old) Cost	₩10,000	$20	₩10,000	$20
Profit	₩5,000	−$5	₩20,000	$10

import merchandise does not cause any transaction loss, it may result in idle production and an eventual operating loss due to the surrender of that particular foreign market. If possible, MNCs should price their inventory goods in such a way that sales revenues include the sum of the increase in replacement cost of the inventory sold, the loss in real value of the monetary profit expected, and increased income taxes.

11.5. SUMMARY

Techniques of international working capital management are essentially similar to those employed domestically, but additional variables are involved. In domestic operations, all transactions are subject to the same rules of movement, accumulation, and reinvestment, but these rules vary when these transactions occur across national boundaries. These additional variables include political, tax, foreign exchange, and other economic constraints.

This chapter discussed cash, accounts-receivable, and inventory management. Cash management can be centralized or decentralized on a company level. Although decentralization is popular among subsidiary managers, it does not permit the MNCs to use its most liquid asset on a widespread basis. Multinational accounts receivable are created by two separate types of transactions: sales to independent customers and intracompany sales. Management of accounts receivable from independent customers involve the denomination of currency to be used for payments and the terms of payment. Intracompany sales differ from sales to independent customers in that little concern is given to credit standing and that the timing of the payments may depend upon a company's desire to allocate resources rather than normal payment schedules. The overall efficiency of inventory management is extremely important for two reasons. First, inventories represent a significant segment of total assets for most MNCs. Second, they are the least liquid of current assets and thus errors in inventory management are not quickly remedied.

11.6. KEY TERMS

working capital management	foreign exchange constraints
regulatory constraints	tax constraints
netting	lead
lag	transfer price
credit swap	transaction motive
precautionary motive	speculative motive
float	cryptocurrency
inflation	US consumer price index
prime rate	policy rate
overnight purchase	discount rate
federal fund rate	treasury bills
Fannie Mae	call money
commercial papers	secured overnight financing rate
repo index	factoring
just-in-time inventory system	

11.7. PROBLEMS

1. Assume that the netting center uses a matrix of payables and receivables to determine the net payer or creditor position of each subsidiary at the date of clearing. The following table shows an example of such a matrix.

Intersubsidiary Payment Matrix

Receiving Subsidiary	Paying Subsidiary				
	United States	Japan	Germany	Canada	Total Receipts
United States	—	$800	$700	$400	$1,900
Japan	$600	—	$400	$200	$1,200
Germany	$200	$0	—	$300	$500
Canada	$100	$200	$500	—	$800
Total payments	$900	$1,000	$1,600	$900	$4,400

a. Prepare a multilateral netting schedule, such as Table 11.2.
b. Determine the amount of total payments to be reduced by netting.
c. Determine the percentage reduction in total payments by netting.

2. A multinational company has a subsidiary in country A that produces auto parts and sells them to another subsidiary in country B, where the production process is completed. Country A has a tax rate of 50 percent, while country B has a tax rate of 20 percent. The income statements of these two subsidiaries are shown in the following table. Assume that the multinational company reduces its transfer price from $4,000 to $3,200. Determine the tax effect of this low transfer price on the company's consolidated net income.

Pro Forma Income Statements for Two Subsidiaries

	High Tax A	Low Tax B	Combined A + B
High transfer price			
Sales price	$4,000	$7,000	$7,000
Cost of goods sold	$2,200	$4,000	$2,200
Gross profit	$1,800	$3,000	$4,800
Operating expenses	$800	$1,000	$1,800
Earnings before taxes	$1,000	$2,000	$3,000
Taxes (50%/20%)	$500	$400	$900
Net income	$500	$1,600	$2,100

3. The foreign subsidiary of a US parent company earns $1,000 before any taxes. The parent company wants to receive $400 before US taxes. The local tax rate is 50 percent and the US tax rate is 30 percent. The US company is considering two options: option X: $400 in cash dividends and option Y: $160 in cash dividends plus $240 in royalty fees for a total of $400 in cash. Which option should the company select to maximize its consolidated income?

4. A US company has $10,000 in cash available for 45 days. It can earn 1 percent on a 45-day investment in the United States. Alternatively, if it converts the dollars to Swiss francs, it can earn 1.5 percent on a Swiss deposit for 45 days. The spot rate of the Swiss franc is $0.50. The spot rate 45 days from now is expected to be $0.40. Should this company invest its cash in the United States or in Switzerland?

Closing Case 11: Navistar International's Netting System

Navistar International Corp. was formed in a reorganization of International Harvester in 1987, the farm and equipment manufacturer. Today Navistar manufactures and markets medium-and heavy-duty trucks, school buses, and mid-range diesel engines in North America and selected export markets. The company's products, parts, and services are sold through nine distribution centers, 16 used truck centers, and a network of 1,000 dealer outlets in the United States, Canada, Brazil, Mexico, and 75 other countries. Navistar also provides financing for its customers and distributors principally through its wholly owned subsidiary, Navistar Financial Corporation.

During a dismal stretch from the late 1980s through the early 1990s, Navistar was the industry's underachiever. In 1995, however, new Navistar CEO Horne had created a "culture of entitlement" that made the company a sluggish competitor. As part of his effort to energize Navistar, he has introduced a number of top-level managers from other companies into the truck maker's historically insular executive suite. With the new management team in place and a solid stream of cash from strengthening industry conditions, Navistar has achieved significant productivity increases at its existing plants, built new facilities, and revitalized the once-stable product line. These actions along with its unique netting system have enabled Navistar to improve its financial performance significantly in recent years.

Navistar, Inc. ("Navistar") is reimagining how to create more cohesive relationships, build higher-performing teams and find solutions where others don't. Based in Lisle, Illinois, Navistar or its subsidiaries and affiliates produce International® brand commercial trucks and engines, IC Bus® brand school and commercial buses, all-makes On Command® Connection advanced connectivity services, and Fleetrite®, ReNEWeD® and Diamond Advantage® brands aftermarket parts. With a history of innovation dating back to 1831, Navistar has more than 14,500 employees worldwide and is a member of TRATON SE, a global champion of the truck and transport services industry.

Navistar's netting system depends on a currency-clearing center located in Switzerland. The netting system works on a monthly cycle. By the 15th day of each month, all participating subsidiaries send information to the currency clearing center on payables and receivables existing at that time in local currencies. The clearing center converts all amounts into dollar terms at the current spot exchange rate and sends information to those subsidiaries with net payables on how much they owe and to whom. These paying subsidiaries are responsible for informing the net receivers of funds and for obtaining and delivering the foreign exchange. Settlement is on the 25th day of the month and the funds are purchased two days in advance so that they are received on the designated day. Any difference between the exchange rate used by the Swiss center on the 15th and the rate prevailing for settlement on the 25th gives rise to foreign exchange gains or losses, and these are attributed to the subsidiary.

Navistar used this original clearing system for intracompany transactions and did not use the system for its transactions with independent companies. After a decade with this system, the company introduced a scheme for foreign exchange settlements for payments to outside companies. There are two different dates, the 10th and 25th, on which all foreign exchange is purchased by and transferred from the Swiss center. The payment needs are sent electronically to the center from the subsidiary more than two days before the settlement date. Then the center nets the amounts of each currency in order to make the minimum number of foreign exchange transactions. The subsidiary, which owes the foreign exchange, settles with the clearing center by the appropriate settlement date. This netting system can cut the total number of transactions with outsider companies in half.

The use of interdivisional leading and lagging makes the cash management system even more flexible. If a subsidiary is a net payer, it may delay or drag payment for up to 2 months while compensating the net receiver at the prevailing interest rate. Net receivers of funds may, at their discretion, make funds available to other subsidiaries at an appropriate interest rate. In this way, the Swiss clearing center serves to bring different subsidiaries together so that they can reduce outside borrowing. The netting with leading and lagging has allowed the company to eliminate intracompany floats and reduce the number of transactions by 80 percent.

Case Questions

1. Why did Navistar choose Switzerland as its clearing center for the company's netting system?
2. What are the direct cost savings of Navistar's netting system?
3. What are the benefits derived from Navistar's netting system in addition to the direct cost savings discussed in Question 2?
4. Assume that Navistar hired you as a consultant for its working capital management. How would you advise the company when it faces the following conditions: absence of forward markets, high transaction costs, high political risk, liquidity needs by subsidiaries, and high taxes.
5. Major international banks provide a variety of working capital and cash management services for multinational companies. Use the website of the Bank of America — www.bankamerica.com/ — and the website of the Bank of Montreal — www.bmo.com/ — to assess their multinational cash management services.

Sources: *Navistar International Annual Report*, various issues; Levi, M. D., *International Finance*, New York: McGraw-Hill, 1996, pp. 427–428; Miller, J. P., "Navistar Gains Spotlight Amid Volvo's Rumored Interest," *The Wall Street Journal*, March 10, 1999, p. B4; and https://www.navistar.com/about-us/our-company, March 23, 2023.

Chapter 12

INTERNATIONAL PORTFOLIO INVESTMENT

Opening Case 12: What Beta Means When Considering a Stock Risk

How should investors assess risk in the stocks that they buy or sell? While the concept of risk is hard to factor in stock analysis and valuation, one of the most popular indicators is a statistical measure called beta. Analysts use it often when they want to determine a stock's risk profile. However, while beta does say something about price risk, it has its limits for investors looking to determine fundamental risk factors.

What is Beta?

Beta is a measure of a stock's volatility in relation to the overall market. By definition, the market, such as the S&P 500 Index, has a beta of 1.0, and individual stocks are ranked according to how much they deviate from the market. A stock that swings more than the market over time has a beta above 1.0. If a stock moves less than the market, the stock's beta is less than 1.0. High-beta stocks are supposed to be riskier but provide higher return potential; low-beta stocks pose less risk but also lower returns.

Key Points

- Beta is a concept that measures the expected move in a stock relative to movements in the overall market.
- A beta greater than 1.0 suggests that the stock is more volatile than the broader market, and a beta less than 1.0 indicates a stock with lower volatility.
- Beta is a component of the Capital Asset Pricing Model, which calculates the cost of equity funding and can help determine the rate of return to expect relative to perceived risk.
- Critics argue that beta does not give enough information about the fundamentals of a company and is of limited value when making stock selections.
- Beta is probably a better indicator of short-term rather than long-term risk.

Table 12.1 Low beta industry and high beta industry.

Low Beta Industry	Number of Firms	Beta	High Beta Industry	Number of Firms	Beta
Banks	563	0.70	Air Transport	21	1.58
Beverage-Alcohol	21	0.82	Auto Parts	38	1.40
Cable TV	11	0.93	Broadcasting	28	1.35
Food Processing	92	0.75	Green and Renewal Energy	20	1.59
Healthcare Products	131	0.94	Home Building	29	1.69
Insurance — Props/Cas.	52	0.86	Hotel and Gaming	66	1.79
Retail (grocery and food)	15	0.30	Oil Field Service/Equipment	100	1.50
Transportation	17	0.79	Publishing & Newspapers	21	1.69
Utility — Water	15	0.77	Trucking	34	1.44
Total Market	7,229	1.09	Total Market	7,229	1.09

Table 12.1 shows a sample of betas for 18 industries: nine defensive stocks and nine aggressive stocks. Beta may be used to classify stocks into two broad categories: defensive and aggressive. As far as these 18 industries are concerned, defensive stocks are those stocks that have beta less than 1.09. Their returns fluctuate less than the market index. Aggressive stocks are those stocks that have betas greater than 1.09. Their returns fluctuate rise (fall) more than the market index rise (fall). Food Processing Industry and Retail Industry (Grocery and Food) have stable earnings stream because they are necessities. Swings in the earnings and stock returns of these two industries are modest relative to the earnings and returns of most industries in the economy. Thus, the food processing industry and the retail industry (grocery and food) have a very low level of risk and low beta.

At the other extreme, revenues of industries in Home Building, Hotel and Gaming, and Publishing & Newspapers are overly sensitive to changes in economic activity. This basic variability in revenues is amplified by high operating and financial leverages. These factors cause earnings and returns of those industries to produce wide variations relative to swings in the earnings and returns of most industries in the economy.[1]

In 1990, two American finance professors — Harry Markowitz and William Sharpe — received the Nobel Prize in economic science because of their contribution to portfolio theory. A highly respectable mean-variance model developed by Markowitz (1959) and Sharpe (1964) employs two basic measures: an index of expected return (mean) and an index of risk (variance or standard deviation). The expected value for a portfolio of securities is simply the sum of the individual returns for the securities that make up the portfolio. The standard deviation as a measure of risk for the portfolio is not easily measured. In many

---

[1]Catlano, T. J., "What Beta Means When Considering a Stock's Risk," May 4, 2021, https://www. investopedia.com/investing/beta-know-risk/; and *Source*: https://pages.stern.nyu.edu/~adamodar/New_Home_Page/datafile/Betas.html, October 13, 2022.

business situations, risks of individual securities tend to offset each other. Thus, with successful diversification, the investor may select a portfolio having less risk than the sum of the risks of individual securities.

There was a time when investment opportunities stopped at national borders. However, today we assume a unified and integrated world capital market when analyzing international finance and macroeconomics. Indeed, recent national policy discussions rely on this premise stimulated by global integration of capital markets. Thus, many countries have internationalized their capital markets since 1980. National capital markets have changed to an integrated global capital market, often followed by widespread international multiple listings of securities. An economic revolution is taking place in many parts of the world as countries deregulate financial markets.

Diversification among risky securities in a particular country reduces risk. Yet, this potential is rather limited because most companies usually earn more during booms and less during recessions, which suggests that international portfolio diversification reduces additional risk. In fact, gains from such diversification have become so commonplace in recent years that additional empirical studies are not needed to confirm the benefits of international diversification. Still this chapter describes key diversification terminologies, the gains from international diversification, and methods of international diversification.

12.1. KEY TERMINOLOGIES

In the real world, no company or individual invests everything in a single asset. Accordingly, it is useful to consider the risk and return of a particular asset in conjunction with its counterparts in existing assets or new investment opportunities. Portfolio theory deals with selecting investment projects that minimize risk for a given rate of return or that maximize the rate of return for a given degree of risk.

12.1.1. *Risk Analysis: Standard Deviation*

Two conflicts from investment in assets are that: (1) very few financial variables are known with certainty and (2) investors are basically risk averters. Risk is variability in the return generated by investment in an asset. For example, investors buy common stock hoping to receive growing dividends and an appreciating stock price. However, neither the dividend stream nor price appreciation is certain or guaranteed. Thus, investors evaluate risk before they invest in common stock.

Risk may be measured by the dispersion of alternative returns around the average return. **Standard deviation**, being a measure of dispersion, fits nicely as a technique for measuring risk. To determine the standard deviation of, say, monthly returns for an asset, we may use the following formula:

$$\sigma = \sqrt{\frac{\sum (R - \bar{R})^2}{n - 1}} \tag{12.1}$$

where σ = standard deviation; R = monthly returns; and $\bar{R}$ = average monthly return. To illustrate, assume that the monthly returns of a common stock are 0.40, 0.50, and 0.60 for 3 months. The average monthly return is 0.50, and the standard deviation is 0.10.

Standard deviation is an absolute measure of dispersion. If returns are expressed in dollars, the standard deviation shows the amount of risk per dollar of average return. A relative measure of dispersion is the **coefficient of variation**, which is the standard deviation divided by the average return. In general, the coefficient of variation measures risk better than the standard deviation for assets whose returns are stated in dollars. Standard deviation should be used to measure risk only for those assets whose returns are stated as percentages.

12.1.2. *Capital Asset Pricing Model*

The **capital asset pricing model** (CAPM) assumes that the total risk of a security consists of systematic (undiversifiable) risk and unsystematic (diversifiable) risk. **Systematic risk** reflects overall market risk — risk that is common to all securities. Common causes of systematic risk include changes in the overall economy, tax reform by Congress, and change in national energy supply. Because it is common to all stocks, systematic risk cannot be eliminated by diversification.

Unsystematic risk is unique to a particular company. Some causes of unsystematic risk include wildcat strikes affecting only that company, new competitors producing essentially the same product, and technological breakthroughs making an existing product obsolete. Because it is unique to a particular stock, unsystematic risk can be eliminated by diversification.

Within an international context, systematic risk relates to such global events as worldwide recessions, world wars, and changes in world energy supply. Unsystematic risk relates to such national events as expropriation, currency controls, inflation, and exchange rate changes.

If a market is in equilibrium, the expected rate of return on an individual security (j) is stated as follows:

$$R_j = R_f + (R_m - R_f)\beta_j \qquad (12.2)$$

where R_j = expected rate of return on security j, R_f = riskless rate of interest, R_m = expected rate of return on the **market portfolio**, which is a group of risky securities such as Standard & Poor's 500 Stocks or London Financial Times 100 Stocks, and β_j = systematic risk of security j. This equation, known as the security market line, consists of the riskless rate of interest (R_f) and a risk premium $[(R_m - R_f)\beta_j]$. It is important to understand that **beta** — $\beta_j = [(R_j - R_f)/(R_m - R_f)]$ — is an index of volatility in the excess return of one security relative to that of a market portfolio.

12.1.2.1. *Aggressive vs. defensive stocks*

Because beta reflects the systematic risk of a stock or a mutual fund relative to that of the market as a whole, the market index is assigned a beta of 1. Beta may be used to classify stocks into two broad categories: aggressive and defensive. Aggressive stocks are those stocks which have betas greater than 1. Their returns rise (fall) more than the market index rises (falls). Defensive stocks are those stocks which have betas less than 1. Their returns fluctuate less than the market index. Those stocks with betas equal to 1 are frequently called neutral stocks.

Food processing companies, such as Nabisco and Kellogg's, have very stable earnings streams because their products are necessities. Swings in the earnings and stock returns of food processing companies are modest relative to the earnings and returns of most companies in the economy. Thus, food processing companies have a very low level of systematic risk and low betas.

At the other extreme, revenues of airline companies, such as Delta Airlines and British Airways, are closely tied to passenger miles, which are in turn very sensitive to changes in economic activity. This basic variability in revenues is amplified by high operating and financial leverage. These factors cause airline earnings and returns to produce wide variations relative to swings in the earnings and returns of most firms in the economy. Hence, airline companies have high betas.

In a portfolio context, the security market line constitutes various portfolios which combine a riskless security and a portfolio of risky securities. The general decision rule for accepting a risky project (j), can be stated as follows:

$$R_j > R_f + (R_m - R_f)\beta_j \qquad (12.3)$$

This decision rule implies that to accept security j, its expected return must exceed the investor's hurdle rate, which is the sum of the riskless rate of interest plus a risk premium for the riskiness of the security. Figure 12.1 shows the decision rule in general terms: accept

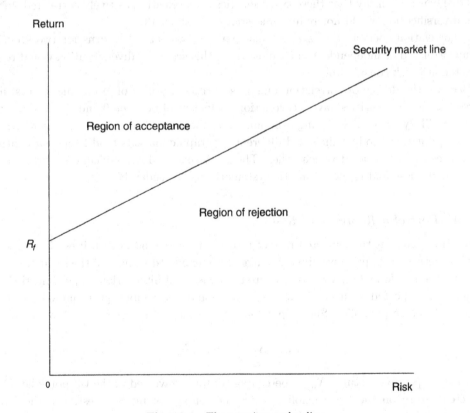

Fig. 12.1   The security market line.

all securities that plot above the security market line and reject all securities that plot below the security market line.

12.1.3. *Correlation Coefficients*

Portfolio effect is defined as the extent to which unsystematic risks of individual securities tend to offset each other. Portfolio effect or portfolio standard deviation depends not only on the standard deviation of each security but also on the degree of correlation between two or more securities. The **correlation coefficient** measures the degree of correlation between two securities and varies from zero (no correlation, or independence) to +1.0 (perfect correlation).

A correlation coefficient of −1.0 means that the two sets of returns for two securities tend to move in exactly opposite directions. Assume that a boom occurs. Security A is expected to earn $100, while security B is expected to earn nothing. In contrast, if a recession occurs, security A would earn nothing, whereas security B would earn $100. Consequently, these two securities are perfectly negatively correlated. Diversification can totally eliminate unsystematic risk when two securities are perfectly negatively correlated.

A correlation coefficient of +1.0 means that two sets of returns for two securities tend to move in exactly the same direction. Suppose that a boom occurs. Securities X and Y would earn an equal amount of $200. But if a recession occurs, they would yield an equal amount of $50. Then we can say that these two securities are perfectly positively correlated. In this case, diversification would not reduce unsystematic risk at all.

A correlation coefficient of zero means that the two sets of returns for two securities are uncorrelated or independent of each other. In this scenario, diversification would reduce unsystematic risk considerably.

Because the degree of correlation among securities depends on economic factors, most pairs of domestic securities have a correlation coefficient of between 0 and +1.0. Most stock prices are likely to be high during a boom, while they are likely to be low during a recession. But different product lines and different geographic markets tend to have a relatively low degree of correlation to each other. Thus, international diversification may eliminate unsystematic risk and reduce domestic systematic risk considerably.

12.1.4. *Portfolio Return and Risk*

Portfolio return is the expected rate of return on a portfolio of securities. The expected portfolio return is simply a weighted average of the expected returns of the securities which make up the portfolio. One way to measure the benefits of international diversification is to consider the expected return and standard deviation of return for a portfolio which consists of US and foreign portfolios. Such a portfolio return may be computed as follows:

$$R_{\mathrm{p}} = X_{\mathrm{us}}R_{\mathrm{us}} + X_{\mathrm{fn}}R_{\mathrm{fn}} \qquad (12.4)$$

where R_{p} = portfolio return, X_{us} = percentage of funds invested in the US portfolio, R_{us} = expected return on the US portfolio, X_{fn} = percentage of funds invested in the foreign portfolio, and R_{fn} = expected return on the foreign portfolio.

The standard deviation of a portfolio measures the riskiness of the portfolio. The standard deviation of a two-security portfolio can be calculated as follows:

$$\sigma_p = \sqrt{X_{us}^2\sigma_{us}^2 + X_{fn}^2\sigma_{fn}^2 + 2X_{us}X_{fn}\sigma_{us,fn}\sigma_{us}\sigma_{fn}} \tag{12.5}$$

where σ_p = portfolio standard deviation, σ_{us} = standard deviation of the US portfolio, σ_{fn} = standard deviation of the foreign portfolio, and $\sigma_{us,fn}$ = correlation coefficient between the returns on the US and foreign portfolios.

Example 12.1

Assume that an international portfolio consisting of a US portfolio and a foreign portfolio calls for a total investment of $10 million. The US portfolio requires an investment of $4 million and the foreign portfolio requires an investment of $6 million. The expected returns are 8 percent on the US portfolio and 12 percent on the foreign portfolio. The standard deviations are 3.17 percent for the US portfolio and 3.17 percent for the foreign portfolio.

Because the percentage of the international portfolio invested in the US portfolio is 40 percent and that of the foreign portfolio is 60 percent, we can use Eq. (12.4) to compute the return on the international portfolio:

$$R_p = (0.4)0.08 + (0.6)0.12 = 10.4\%$$

It is important to recognize that the return on the international portfolio is the same regardless of correlation of returns for US and foreign portfolios. However, the degree of the international portfolio risk varies according to interportfolio or intersecurity return behavior. Intersecurity returns can be perfectly negatively correlated, statistically independent, and perfectly positively correlated.

12.1.4.1. *Case A: Perfectly negative correlation*

If US and foreign portfolios are perfectly negatively correlated, their correlation coefficient becomes -1. The return on the international portfolio and its standard deviation (use Eq. (12.5)) are

$$R_p = 10.4\%$$

$$\sigma_p = [(0.4)^2(0.0317)^2 + (0.6)^2(0.0317)^2 + 2(0.4)(0.6)(-1)(0.0317)(0.0317)]^{1/2}$$

$$= 0.63\%$$

Because the standard deviation of US and foreign portfolios are 3.17 percent each, their weighted average is 3.17 percent ($0.0317 \times 0.40 + 0.0317 \times 0.60$). Thus, the standard deviation of the international portfolio is only 20 percent of the weighted average of the two individual standard deviations ($0.0063/0.0317$). If a considerable number of perfectly negatively correlated projects are available, risk can be almost entirely diversified away. However, perfect negative correlation is seldom found in the real world.

12.1.4.2. *Case B: Statistical independence*

If these two portfolios are statistically independent, the correlation coefficient between the two is 0. The return of the international portfolio and its standard deviation are:

$$R_p = 10.4\%$$
$$\sigma_p = [(0.4)^2(0.0317)^2 + (0.6)^2(0.0317)^2 + 2(0.4)(0.6)(0)(0.0317)(0.0317)]^{1/2}$$
$$= 2.29\%$$

In this case, the standard deviation of the international portfolio is 72 percent of this weighted average $(0.0229/0.0317)$. This means that international diversification can reduce risk significantly if a considerable number of statistically independent securities are available.

12.1.4.3. *Case C: Perfectly positive correlation*

If the two portfolios are perfectly positively correlated with each other, their correlation coefficient becomes 1. The portfolio return and its standard deviation are

$$R_p = 10.4\%$$
$$\sigma_p = [(0.4)^2(0.0317)^2 + (0.6)^2(0.0317)^2 + 2(0.4)(0.6)(1)(0.0317)(0.0317)]^{1/2}$$
$$= 3.17\%$$

The standard deviation of the international portfolio equals the weighted average of the two individual standard deviations. Thus, if all alternative investments are perfectly positively correlated, diversification would not reduce risk at all.

12.1.5. *Efficient Frontier*

An **efficient portfolio** is a portfolio that incurs the smallest risk for a given level of return and/or provides the highest rate of return for a given level of risk. Suppose that A, B, and C are three exclusive portfolios which require the same amount of investment, say, $10 million. They have an equal rate of return, but their respective standard deviations are different. Figure 12.2 shows that A incurs the smallest risk for a given level of return; A is called the efficient portfolio. By the same token, assume that W, X, and Y are three exclusive portfolios which require the same amount of money, say, $10 million. They have the same amount of risk, but their rates of return are different. As shown in Fig. 12.2, we notice that W provides the highest rate of return for a given level of risk; W is also called the efficient portfolio. If we compute more points such as A and W, we may obtain curve AW by connecting such points. This curve is known as the **efficient frontier**. Portfolios B, C, X, and Y are inefficient because some other portfolios could give either a lower risk for the same rate of return or a higher return for the same degree of risk.

There are numerous efficient portfolios along the efficient frontier. An efficient frontier does not tell us which portfolio to select but shows a collection of portfolios that minimize risk for any expected return or that maximize the expected return for any degree of risk. The objective of the investor is to choose the optimal portfolio among those on the efficient frontier. Thus, the efficient frontier is necessary but not sufficient for selecting the optimal portfolio. Given an efficient frontier, the choice of the optimal portfolio depends on the security market line.

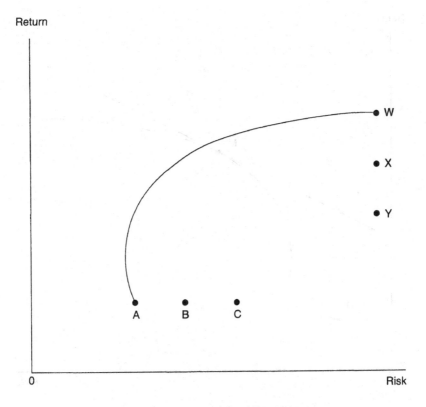

Fig. 12.2   An efficient frontier.

If investors want to select the optimal portfolio from portfolios on a particular efficient frontier, they should land on the highest security market line. This **optimal portfolio** is found at the tangency point between the efficient frontier and the security market line. Tangency point M in Fig. 12.3 marks the highest security market line that investors can obtain with funds available for investment. An optimum portfolio is the portfolio which has, among all possible portfolios, the largest ratio of expected return to risk. Once investors identify the optimal portfolio, they will allocate funds between risky assets and risk-free assets to achieve a desired combination of risk and return.

12.2. BENEFITS OF INTERNATIONAL DIVERSIFICATION

A rather convincing body of literature holds that internationally diversified portfolios are better than domestically diversified portfolios because they provide higher risk-adjusted returns to their holders.[2] This section, based on several empirical studies, discusses:

---

[2]For details, see Eaker, M. R. and D. M. Grant, "Currency Hedging Strategies for Internationally Diversified Equity Portfolios," *The Journal of Portfolio Management*, Fall 1990, pp. 30–32; Levy, H. and Z. Lerman, "The Benefits of International Diversification in Bonds," *Financial Analysts Journal*, September/October 1988, pp. 56–64; Sill, K., "The Gains from International Risk Sharing," *Business Review*, Federal Reserve Bank of Philadelphia, 3rd Quarter 2001, pp. 23–31; and Thomas, L. R., "The Performance of Currency-Hedged Foreign Bonds," *Financial Analysts Journal*, May/June 1989, pp. 25–31.

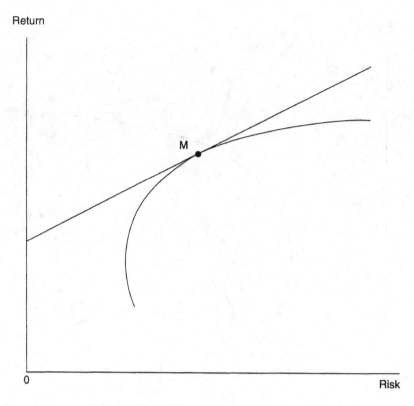

Fig. 12.3 An optimal portfolio.

(1) arguments for international diversification, (2) risk–return characteristics of national capital markets, and (3) selection of optimal international portfolios.

12.2.1. *Risk Diversification Through International Investment*

Table 12.2 provides correlations of stock market returns for ten major countries known from 1980 to 2001. First, the intracountry correlation is one for every country. On the other hand, the intercountry correlation is much less than one for every pair of any two countries. In other words, stock market returns have lower positive correlations across countries than within a country. Second, member countries of the European Union — France, Italy, Germany, the Netherlands, and the United Kingdom — have relatively high correlations because their currencies and economies are highly interrelated. Third, the intercountry correlation for the United States ranges from as high as 0.74 with Canada to as low as 0.29 with Japan. The extremely high correlation between the United States and Canada comes as no surprise because these two neighboring countries have close business linkages in terms of trade, investment, and other financial activities. The United States and Japan have the extremely low correlation because they are situated in different continents and their economic policies are different. It is important to understand that the inclusion of the latest data would have a little impact on correlations of stock market returns in Table 12.2.[3]

---

[3]Robin, J. A., *International Corporate Finance*, New York: McGraw-Hill/Irwin, 2010, p. 393.

Table 12.2 Correlations of major stock market returns from 1980 to 2001.

	AU	CA	FR	GE	IT	JA	NE	SW	UK	US
Australia	1.00									
Canada	0.60	1.00								
France	0.37	0.46	1.00							
Germany	0.34	0.42	0.69	1.00						
Italy	0.25	0.35	0.50	0.43	1.00					
Japan	0.33	0.33	0.41	0.33	0.37	1.00				
Netherlands	0.44	0.58	0.66	0.71	0.44	0.42	1.00			
Sweden	0.44	0.49	0.49	0.57	0.44	0.39	0.54	1.00		
UK	0.54	0.57	0.57	0.50	0.38	0.42	0.70	0.51	1.00	
US	0.47	0.74	0.50	0.45	0.31	0.29	0.62	0.49	0.58	1.00

Source: Monthly issues of Morgan Stanley's *Capital International Perspectives*.

Of course, a reason for low intercountry correlations is that much of the stock market risk in an individual country is unsystematic and so can be eliminated by international diversification. Low international correlations may reflect different geographic locations, independent economic policies, different endowments of natural resources, and cultural differences. In summary, these results imply that international diversification into geographically and economically divergent countries may significantly reduce the risk of portfolio returns. According to Fig. 12.4 drawn by Solnik and McLavey, that is indeed the case.[4]

Figure 12.4 shows the total risk of domestically and internationally diversified portfolios as a function of the number of securities held. In this figure, 100 percent of risk as measured by standard deviation represents the typical risk of a single US security. As an investor increases the number of securities in a portfolio, the portfolio's risk declines rapidly at first, then slowly approaches the systematic risk of the market expressed in the broken line. However, the addition of more securities beyond 15 or 20 reduces risk very little. The remaining risk — the part not affected by holding more US stocks — is called market risk, which is also known as systematic risk. Is there a way to lower portfolio risk even further? Only if we can lower the market risk. One way to lower the market risk is to hold stocks not traded on US stock exchanges.

Figure 12.4 illustrates a number of striking facts. First, the risk of a well-diversified US portfolio is only 27 percent of the typical risk of a single security. This relationship indicates that 73 percent of the risk associated with investing in a single security is diversifiable in a fully diversified portfolio. Second, the addition of foreign stocks to a purely domestic portfolio reduces risk faster, as shown in the bottom curve. Third, a fully diversified international portfolio is less than half as risky as a fully diversified US portfolio. The addition of foreign stocks to a US portfolio reduces the US market risk even further because foreign economies generally do not move one-for-one with the US economy. When the US economy is in a recession, foreign economies might be in expansion and vice-versa. This and other studies have established that security returns are less highly correlated internationally than domestically. This makes a strong case for international diversification as a means of risk diversification.

---

[4]Solnik, B. and D. W. McLavey, *International Investments*, Reading, Mass.: Addison-Wesley Publishing Company, 2003, p. 129.

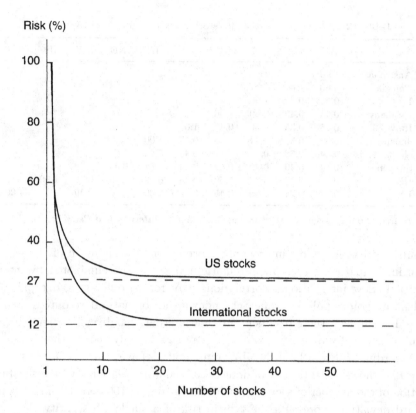

Fig. 12.4 Gains from international diversification.
Source: Solnik, B. and D.W. McLavey, *International Investments*, Reading, MA: Addison-Wesley, 2003, p. 129.

It is important to note that a fully diversified portfolio or an efficient portfolio is one that has zero, or very little, unsystematic risk. As illustrated in Fig. 12.4, an efficient international portfolio cuts the systematic risk of an efficient domestic portfolio in half. Domestic systematic risk declines because international diversification offsets US-specific reactions to worldwide events.

12.2.2. *Risk–Return Characteristics of Capital Markets*

In the previous section, we discussed the benefits from diversifying international portfolios in terms of risk reduction, but we ignored return, another important aspect of investment. Certainly, investors simultaneously consider both risk and return in making investment decisions. In other words, they want to maximize expected return for a given amount of risk and to minimize the amount of risk for a given level of return. Consequently, we ought to examine risk–return characteristics of stock markets.

To ascertain the gains from international diversification, Morgan Stanley constructed portfolios that began with a 100 percent US portfolio and then they made it increasingly more international in increments of 10 percent. Switching from domestic to foreign investments was implemented by acquiring equally weighted portfolios of the 20 foreign indexes in Europe, Australia, and the Far East using quarterly data for 71 years from 1926 to 1997. Figure 12.5 shows the performance of these portfolios in terms of risk–return tradeoffs.

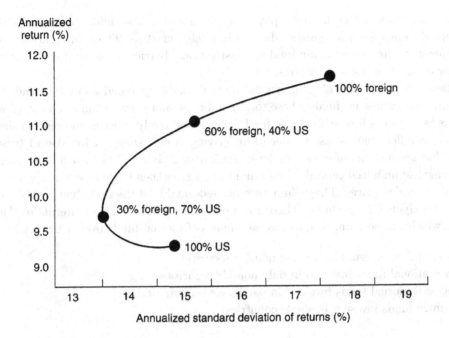

Fig. 12.5 Risk–return trade-offs of international portfolios, 1926–1997.
Source: Morgan Stanley Capital Investment.

As the proportion of the portfolio invested abroad increased, the return increased; in addition, the risk decreased until the proportion of foreign equities reached 50 percent of the portfolio. In other words, American investors could have enjoyed higher returns and less risk if they held a portfolio that contains up to 50 percent invested in foreign stocks. The inclusion of the data for the last 25 years or so has had almost no impact on the performance of the above portfolios in terms of risk–return tradeoffs.

12.3. METHODS OF INTERNATIONAL DIVERSIFICATION

US investors try to obtain international diversification through one of the following methods: (1) international mutual funds; (2) purchases of American depository receipts (ADRs), (3) direct purchases of foreign securities; (4) hedge funds, and (5) investment in US multinational companies.

12.3.1. *International Mutual Funds*

Investors may purchase shares of an international mutual fund with a small minimum investment, such as $1,000. Large brokerage firms around the world, such as Vanguard (the US), Interactive Brokers (The EU), and Nomura (Japan) create and manage many families of international mutual funds. Mutual funds are perhaps the most important by-product of the portfolio theory developed by Markowitz and Sharpe. **Mutual funds** are financial institutions that accept money from savers and then use these funds to buy a variety of securities. **International mutual funds** are portfolios of securities from various countries.

International mutual funds have several advantages over individual foreign securities. First, international mutual funds pool funds and thus reduce risk by diversification.

Second, investors would have to pay extra transaction and information costs if they attempted to buy foreign securities directly in foreign markets. Third, international mutual fund investors circumvent many legal and institutional barriers associated with direct portfolio investments in foreign markets.

There are two classes of international mutual funds: open-end and closed-end. **Open-end mutual funds** are funds whose total number of shares under management grows and shrinks as investors buy and sell the fund. They stand ready to issue and redeem shares at prices that reflect the net-asset value of underlying foreign shares. **Closed-end funds** are funds that the amount of money under management is fixed. They issue a fixed number of shares against an initial capital offering and these shares then trade in secondary markets at prevailing market prices. These shares are not redeemable at the underlying net asset value of the underlying foreign shares. There are approximately 300 US-based international mutual funds, which can be grouped into several families of mutual funds from a US perspective:

1. Global funds invested in US and non-US securities.
2. International funds invested in only non-US securities.
3. Regional mutual funds invested in particular geographic areas.
4. Country funds invested in single countries.

12.3.2. *American Depository Receipts (ADRs)*

Investors may purchase ADRs which are traded on organized exchanges and/or in the over-the-counter markets. ADRs are securities distributed in the United States backed by foreign stock. Exchanges around the world have listing requirements before they accept a firm's shares for trading. Rules for listing vary markedly from country to country, with US requirements being among the most restrictive. Banks have created ADRs so that foreign companies can avoid these restrictions on trading in the United States.

American depository receipts represent the ownership of underlying foreign stocks which are held in custody by the bank that issues them. In other words, the bank holds the foreign shares and trades ADRs that represent title to those shares held on deposit. In effect, the bank owns the shares and trades claims against those shares. ADR investors are entitled to all the privileges of stock ownership including dividend payments. The bank, the issuer of ADRs, usually collects the dividends in local currency and transfers the dollar-equivalent to the ADR investors. Today, ADRs have become so popular that companies have begun to issue global depository receipts. **Global depository receipts** are similar instruments to ADRs, but can be simultaneously issued on stock exchanges all over the world.

12.3.3. *Direct Purchases of Foreign Securities*

Investors may buy foreign securities listed on foreign exchanges through stockbrokers for inclusion in their portfolios. This method of international diversification, however, is not recommended for small investors because of market imperfections such as insufficient information, transaction costs, tax differentials among countries, and different exchange-rate risks.

Alternatively, investors may invest in foreign securities listed on US exchanges in the same way they can buy any US stock listed on a US exchange. Because the number of foreign securities listed on US exchanges is limited, this route by itself may be inadequate to obtain full international diversification benefits.

12.3.4. *Hedge Funds*

Hedge funds are private partnerships with a general manager and a number of limited partners. Unlike other investment tools such as stocks and mutual funds, these hedge funds are largely unregulated investment pools open to only wealthy investors. Many hedge funds use short positions, or bets that prices will fall, to offset their securities holdings. Some bet on cross-border mergers and acquisitions, convertible securities, or foreign currencies. They frequently use borrowed money in an effort to boost returns. Hedge funds have grown in popularity in recent years, both because of their oversized returns and their aura of exclusivity.

Estimates of industry size vary widely due to the lack of central statistics, the lack of a single definition of hedge funds and the rapid growth of the industry. As a general indicator of scale, the industry had managed around $2.5 trillion at its peak in the summer of 2008. However, the Credit Crunch of the 2009–2010 had caused the size of hedge funds to fall sharply through a combination of trading losses and the withdrawal of assets from funds by investors.[5] However, since 2011, they have grown again to be a substantial fraction of asset management, with assets totaling around $3.235 trillion in 2018.[6]

Hedge funds have recently become the target of frequent criticism in the financial press because of the lucrative compensation packages paid to management, the fact that they are unregulated, and the huge speculative positions taken by some hedge funds For these reasons, experts suggest that an investor should ask the following questions before putting money into a hedge fund: First, how does the investment strategy work? Second, what are the risks? Third, what market conditions favor the manager's strategy — and which ones work against it? Fourth, what is the manager's experience and track record? Fifth, how long do I have to wait before I can withdraw my money? Sixth, how are the manager and the consultant helping select the hedge fund compensated?

Global Finance in Practice 12: Investment in US Multinational Companies

It used to be that if you wanted to invest globally, you bought foreign stocks. But the recent wave of cross-border mergers and acquisitions along with accelerated globalization by US companies have turned many US shareholders into global investors, whether they like it or not. Thus, investors may choose securities of US-based multinational companies (MNCs) for their international portfolio diversification. An MNC represents a portfolio of international operations, thus its performance is somewhat insulated from US market downturns. An MNC can reduce risk by diversifying sales not only among industries, but also among countries. This means that the MNC as a single firm can achieve stability similar to that of an internationally diversified portfolio.

---

[5] http://en.wikipedia.org/wiki/Hedge_fund, March 10, 2010.
[6] https://www.hedgefundresearch.com/news/hedge-fund-assets-eclipse-record-level-for-eighth-consecutive-quarter-despite-mixed-capital, May 20, 2019.

12.3.5. *Global Investing*

Empirical studies conclude that international diversification pushes out the efficient frontier, thus allowing investors simultaneously to reduce risk and increase return. This benefit exists for a number of reasons. First, more profitable investments are possible in an enlarged universe because faster-growing economies create higher returns or investors may see another advantage from currency gains. Second, the advantages of international diversification may occur because companies in different countries are subject to divergent cyclical economic fluctuations.[7] Some experts think that investors would be better off patterning their asset allocations much closer to total world capitalizations. Of course, opportunity varies region by region, country by country. And some regions and countries come with greater risk — liquidity, political, or currency risk.

The manager of a US stock fund has just one way to beat the competition, by making better stock picks. But an international stock fund manager has three different ways to add value: by picking countries, by picking currencies, and by picking stocks.

How can US investors best select a global fund? Some helpful hints may cut down on the potential for loss.[8] They are: (1) stick with large players in the global market; (2) combine funds to minimize the effect of the failure of one fund on the total portfolio; (3) select regional rather than totally global funds; (4) consider combining regional funds with stock or bond index funds; and (5) try publicly traded funds. These suggestions will not assure success, but can reduce the likelihood of failure.

12.4. SUMMARY

Political and economic events since the 1990s underscored the growing importance of free flows of finance, trade, and investment among countries. These changes, along with improved ability to collect and analyze data, give us low-cost information about foreign securities. As a result, investors are realizing substantial benefits from international investment. In this chapter, we saw that international stock and bond diversification can yield higher returns with less risk than investment in a single market.

In the last 20 years or so, researchers have convincingly argued in, terms of the mean-variance model, the case for international portfolio investments, as opposed to purely domestic diversification. A major reason for such a case is that international investment offers a broader range of opportunities than domestic investment even in a market as large as the United States or Europe. Studies have stressed the following two points: (1) adding foreign securities to a purely domestic portfolio reduces the total risk of the portfolio because of a low correlation between foreign securities and the domestic market; (2) in the past, international portfolios could have yielded both a higher return and a lower volatility than purely domestic portfolios.

---

[7]Simmons, K., "Should US Investors Invest Overseas?" *New England Economic Review*, Federal Reserve Bank of Boston, November/December 1999, pp. 29–40.
[8]Clements, J., "Choosing the Best Global Fund for You: Experts Offer Some Winning Strategies," *The Wall Street Journal*, March 4, 1992, p. C1 and p. 14.

Even though investors are increasingly interested in foreign securities, investment in foreign securities represents a small portion of their total investment in stocks and bonds. Most commonly expressed barriers to international investment include: (1) excessive information and transaction costs, (2) double taxation of foreign investment profits, (3) foreign exchange regulations and currency risk, (4) greater rate-of-return volatility, (5) unfamiliarity with operating procedures of foreign stock exchanges, (6) unavailability of high-quality financial data for foreign companies, and (7) significant delays of transactions and settlements associated with foreign securities.

12.5. KEY TERMS

standard deviation	coefficient of variation
capital asset pricing model (CAPM)	systematic risk
unsystematic risk	market portfolio
beta	portfolio effect
correlation coefficient	portfolio return
efficient portfolio	efficient frontier
optimal portfolio	mutual funds
international mutual funds	open-end mutual funds
closed-end funds	American depository receipts
global depository receipts	hedge funds

12.6. PROBLEMS

1. The expected rate of return on the market portfolio is 20 percent. The riskless rate of interest is 10 percent. The beta of a multinational company is 0.5. What is the cost of this company's common equity?
2. At present, the riskless rate of return is 10 percent and the expected rate of return on the market portfolio is 15 percent. The expected returns for five stocks are listed below, together with their expected betas.

Stock	Expected Return	Expected Beta
A	0.22	1.5
B	0.30	1.3
C	0.12	0.8
D	0.15	0.7
E	0.14	1.1

On the basis of these expectations, which stocks are overvalued? Which stocks are undervalued?
3. The prices of a common stock were $40, $50, and $60 for the last three days. Compute the average stock price and the standard deviation.

4. A portfolio manager wishes to invest a total of $10 million in US and British portfolios. The expected returns are 15 percent on the US portfolio and 12 percent on the British portfolio. The standard deviations are 10 percent for the US portfolio and 9 percent for the British portfolio. Their correlation coefficient is 0.33. What is the expected return and standard deviation of an international portfolio with 25 percent invested in the US portfolio and 75 percent in the British portfolio?

5. An international portfolio with a total investment of $10 million consists of a US portfolio and a foreign portfolio. The US portfolio requires an investment of $5 million and the foreign portfolio requires an investment of $5 million. The standard deviations are 4 percent for the US portfolio and 4 percent for the foreign portfolio.

   a. If these two portfolio are perfectly positively correlated, what is the standard deviation of the international portfolio?

   b. If the two portfolios have a correlation coefficient of 0.2, what is the standard deviation of the international portfolio?

   c. If the two portfolios are perfectly negatively correlated, what is the standard deviation of the international portfolio?

Closing Case 12: Investing in Toyota Stock in the USA

Largely thanks to the rise of American depository receipts (ADRs), these days US investors can trade many foreign shares, such as non-US, foreign-based foreign companies — Toyota Motor Corp. (Japan) and Shinhan Financial Group Co. (South Korea). There are currently 455 ADRs that trade on US stock exchanges. These days, Americans can buy Toyota stock with no more difficulty than it takes to buy domestic shares. Created in 1927 by financier J.P. Morgan as a way of facilitating US investment abroad, an ADR is a negotiable certificate issued by a US bank in the USA to represent the underlying shares of foreign stock, which are held in a custodian bank. ADRs are sold, registered, and transferred in the same way as any share of domestic stock. Fueled by Americans' interest in foreign markets, ADRs now account for more than 15 percent of all trading volume on the major US exchanges.

ADRs are one type of depositary receipt (DR), which are any negotiable securities that represent securities of companies that are foreign to the market on which the DR trades. DRs enable domestic investors to buy securities of foreign companies without the accompanying risks or inconveniences of cross-border and cross-currency transactions.

Each ADR is issued by a domestic custodian bank when the underlying shares are deposited in a foreign depositary bank, usually by a broker who has purchased the shares in the open market local to the foreign company. An ADR can represent a fraction of a share, a single share, or multiple shares of a foreign security. The holder of a DR has the right to obtain the underlying foreign security that the DR represents, but investors usually find it more convenient to own the DR. The price of a DR generally tracks the price of the foreign security in its home market, adjusted for the ratio of DRs to foreign company shares. In the case of companies domiciled in the United Kingdom, creation of ADRs attracts a 1.5 percent stamp duty reserve tax (SDRT) charge by the UK government. Depositary banks have various responsibilities to DR holders and to the issuing foreign company the DR represents.

When a company establishes an ADR program, it must decide what exactly it wants out of the program, and how much time, effort, and other resources they are willing to commit. For this reason, there are different types of programs, or facilities, that a company can choose.

Unsponsored ADRs

Unsponsored shares trade on the over-the-counter (OTC) market. These shares are issued in accordance with market demand, and the foreign company has no formal agreement with a depositary bank. Unsponsored ADRs are often issued by more than one depositary bank. Each depositary services only the ADRs it has issued.

As a result of an SEC rule change effective October 2008, hundreds of new ADRs have been issued, both sponsored and unsponsored. The majority of these were unsponsored Level I ADRs, and now approximately half of all ADR programs in existence are unsponsored.

Sponsored Level I ADRs ("OTC" Facility)

Level 1 depositary receipts are the lowest level of sponsored ADRs that can be issued. When a company issues sponsored ADRs, it has one designated depositary who also acts as its transfer agent. A majority of American depositary receipt programs currently trading are issued through a Level 1 program. This is the most convenient way for a foreign company to have its equity traded in the United States. Level 1 shares can only be traded on the OTC market and the company has minimal reporting requirements with the US Securities and Exchange Commission (SEC). The company is not required to issue quarterly or annual reports in compliance with Generally Accepted Accounting Principle (GAAP). However, the company must have a security listed on one or more stock exchange in a foreign jurisdiction and must publish in English on its website its annual report in the form required by the laws of the country of incorporation, organization or domicile. Companies with shares trading under a Level 1 program may decide to upgrade their program to a Level 2 or Level 3 program for better exposure in the United States markets.

Sponsored Level II ADRs ("Listing" Facility)

Level 2 depositary receipt programs are more complicated for a foreign company. When a foreign company wants to set up a Level 2 program, it must file a registration statement with the US SEC and is under SEC regulation. In addition, the company is required to file a Form 20-F annually. Form 20-F is the basic equivalent of an annual report (Form 10-K) for a US company. In their filings, the company is required to follow US GAAP standards. The advantage that the company has by upgrading their program to Level 2 is that the shares can be listed on a US stock exchange.

These exchanges include the New York Stock Exchange (NYSE), NASDAQ, and the American Stock Exchange (AMEX). While listed on these exchanges, the company must meet the exchange's listing requirements. If it fails to do so, it may be delisted and forced to downgrade its ADR program.

Sponsored Level III ADRs ("Offering" Facility)

A Level 3 American Depositary Receipt program is the highest level a foreign company can sponsor. Because of this distinction, the company is required to adhere to stricter rules that are similar to those followed by US companies. Setting up a Level 3 program means that the foreign company is not only taking steps to permit shares from its home market to be deposited into an ADR program and traded in the US; it is actually issuing shares to raise capital. In accordance with this offering, the company is required to file a Form F-1, which is the format for an Offering Prospectus for the shares. They also must file a Form 20-F annually and must adhere to US GAAP standards or IFRS as published by the IASB. In addition, any material information given to shareholders in the home market, must be filed with the SEC through Form 6K. Foreign companies with Level 3 programs will often issue materials that are more informative and are more accommodating to their US shareholders because they rely on them for capital. Overall, foreign companies with a Level 3 program set up are the easiest on which to find information. Examples include the British telecommunications company Vodafone (VOD), the Brazilian oil company Petrobras (PBR), and the Chinese technology company China Information Technology, Inc. (CNIT).

Case Questions

1. Describe American depository receipts in some detail.
2. Why Did Toyota and other foreign companies decide to list their ADRs on the NYSE?
3. Briefly describe how to choose ADRs.
4. What is the downside of ADR investment?
5. To list their stocks on the New York Stock Exchange, foreign companies have to comply with the registration and disclosure requirements established by the US Securities and Exchange Commission (SEC). Use the website of the SEC — www.sec.gov — to review disclosure requirements in SEC final rules related to foreign investment and trade.

Sources: http://en.wikipedia.org/wiki/American_depositary_receipt, August 10, 2022; and https://stockmarketmba.com/listofadrs.php, August 20, 2022.

Chapter 13

THE COST OF CAPITAL FOR FOREIGN PROJECTS

Opening Case 13: Cost of Capital — What it is, Why it Matters, and Example

Importance of Cost of Capital — Businesses and financial analysts use the cost of capital to determine if funds are being invested effectively. If the return on an investment is greater than the cost of capital, that investment will end up being a net benefit to the company's balance sheets. Conversely, an investment whose returns are equal to or lower than the cost of capital indicates that the money is not being spent wisely. The cost of capital can also determine a company's valuation. Since a company with a high cost of capital can expect lower proceeds in the long run, investors are likely to see less value in owning a share of that company's equity.

Real-World Examples — Every industry has its own prevailing average cost of capital. The numbers vary widely. Homebuilding has a relatively high cost of capital, at 6.35 percent, according to a compilation from New York University's Stern School of Business. The retail grocery business is relatively low, at 1.98 percent. The cost of capital is also high among both biotech and pharmaceutical drug companies, steel manufacturers, internet software companies, and integrated oil and gas companies. Those industries tend to require significant capital investment in research, development, equipment, and factories. Among the industries with lower capital costs are money center banks, power companies, real estate investment trusts (REITs), and utilities (both general and water). Such companies may require less equipment or may benefit from very steady cash flows.

Why is Cost of Capital Important? — Most businesses strive to grow and expand. There may be many options: expand a factory, buy out a rival, build a new, bigger factory. Before the company decides on any of these options, it determines the cost of capital for each proposed project. This indicates how long it will take for the project to repay what it cost, and how much it will return in the future. Such projections are always estimates, of course. But the company must follow a reasonable methodology to choose between its options.[1]

---

[1]Hayes, A., "Cost of Capital: What It Is, Why It Matters, Formula, and Example," *Investopedia*, https://www.investopedia.com/terms/c/costofcapital.asp#toc-real-world-examples, June 13, 2022.

In this chapter, we consider four major topics. First, we discuss the weighted average cost of capital and its component costs of capital (the cost of debt and the cost of equity). In addition, this section explains how corporate and country characteristics influence the cost of capital for multinational cases. Second, we analyze a firm's capital structure, which consists of long-term debt and common equity. In doing so, we explain how an MNC considers corporate and country characteristics when it establishes its capital structure. Third, we describe the relationship between the marginal cost of capital and foreign investment analysis. The marginal cost of capital refers to the cost of additional funds which the firm wishes to raise. Fourth, we compare the cost of capital and the capital structure across countries.

13.1. THE WEIGHTED AVERAGE COST OF CAPITAL

The **weighted average cost of capital** (WACC) is a weighted average of the component costs: the cost of debt, the cost of preferred stock, and the cost of equity. The WACC is normally used as the firm's cost of capital for a number of reasons. First, if a single component cost is used as a criterion for acceptance, projects with a low rate of return may be accepted while projects with a high rate of return may be rejected. Some low-return projects would be accepted because they could be financed with a cheaper source of capital, such as debt. Some high-return projects would be rejected because they have to be financed with an expensive source of capital, such as equity. Second, if a firm accepts projects that yield more than its WACC, it can increase the market value of its common stock. In this situation, the market value of the common stock increases because these projects are expected to earn more on their equity-financed portion than the cost of equity.

The WACC is the cost for each type of capital multiplied by its proportion of the total amount of all capital issued by the firm:

$$k = \frac{S}{B+S}(k_e) + \frac{B}{B+S}(k_t) \qquad (13.1)$$

where k = weighted average cost of capital, k_e = cost of equity, k_t = after-tax cost of debt, B = market value of the firm's debt, and S = market value of firm's equity.

13.1.1. *Cost of Equity*

Interest and preferred dividends are directly measurable components of debt and preferred stocks, but we do not have such a measurable element for the cost of common equity. The reason is apparent once we realize that dividend declarations on common stock are made at the discretion of a firm's board of directors. Consequently, the cost of common equity is the most difficult concept to measure.

The **cost of equity** for a firm is the minimum rate of return necessary to attract investors to buy or hold a firm's common stock. This required rate of return is the discount rate that equates the present value of all expected future dividends per share with the current price per share. If dividends per share are expected to grow at a constant growth rate indefinitely, we can measure the cost of equity by the following formula:

$$k_e = \frac{D_1}{P} + g \tag{13.2}$$

where D_1 = expected dividends per share to be paid at the end of 1 year, P = current market price per share, and g = annual dividend growth rate.

An alternative approach to the above dividend valuation model for the cost of capital is the capital asset pricing model (CAPM) described in Chapter 12. If a market is in equilibrium, the expected rate of return on an individual security (j) is stated as follows:

$$R_j = R_f + (R_m - R_f)\beta_j \tag{13.3}$$

where R_j = expected rate of return on security j; R_f = riskless rate of interest; R_m = expected rate of return on the market portfolio, which is a group of risky securities such as Standard & Poor's 500 Stocks; and β_j = systematic risk of security j. This equation is known as the **security market line**, which consists of the riskless rate of interest (R_f) and a risk premium [$(R_m - R_f)\beta_j$] for a particular firm j; the term $(R_m - R_f)$ is known as the **market risk premium**.

CAPM is based on the assumption that intelligent risk-averse investors seek to diversify their risks. As a result, the only risk that is rewarded with a risk premium is systematic or undiversifiable risk. This theory suggests that the cost of capital for MNCs is generally lower than the cost of capital for domestic companies. In Chapter 12, we saw that a well-diversified MNC company can significantly cut the systematic risk of a well-diversified domestic company. Within the international context, systematic risk relates to such global events as worldwide recessions, world wars, and changes in the world energy supply. Unsystematic risk relates to such national events as expropriation, currency controls, inflation, and exchange rate changes.

One potential problem with using CAPM is how to compute beta (β). Beta may be estimated solely on the basis of subjective probability distributions. But it is a common practice to use past data to estimate future betas. If the beta computed from historical data is a reliable surrogate for a future beta, financial managers have an important tool in formulating profitable investment decisions. Some empirical surveys indicate that past betas are useful in predicting future betas. Betas tend to have greater stability when the number of securities in a portfolio is larger and when the time intervals being studied are longer.

Another approach to measuring the cost of equity is the **price–earnings (P–E) ratio**, which is the price per share divided by the earnings per share. More accurately, the price-earnings ratio can be used to determine the rate of return demanded by shareholders. If we denote the price–earnings ratio by P–E ratio, we can calculate the cost of equity by the following formula:

$$k_e = \frac{1}{\text{P–E ratio}} \tag{13.4}$$

As shown in Eq. (13.4), the cost of equity is one (1) divided by the P–E ratio. Thus, a high P–E ratio suggests a low cost of capital. This model assumes a zero growth rate in profits and a 100-percent dividend payout ratio so that Eq. (13.4) is identical with Eq. (13.2).

The main difference between the three approaches to estimate the cost of equity is that the dividend valuation model and the P–E ratio emphasize the total risk of expected returns while CAPM emphasizes only the systematic risk of expected returns. In any case, the cost of equity is some function of the market's preference for return and risk.

13.1.2. *Cost of Debt*

The **explicit cost of debt** for a firm may be defined as the discount rate that equates the net proceeds of the debt issue with the present value of interest and principal payments. If we want to express all cost-of-capital rates on an after-tax basis, we must adjust this explicit cost of debt for taxes because interest charges are usually tax deductible. We denote the after-tax cost of debt by k_t and determine it by the following equation:

$$k_t = k_i(1 - t) \tag{13.5}$$

where k_i = before-tax cost of debt and t = tax rate.

MNCs must account for a number of complicated factors to measure the cost of debt. First, MNCs can borrow in Eurocurrency markets, international bond markets, or national capital markets. Hence, they must — in order to measure the before-tax cost of debt — estimate interest rates and the proportion of debt to be raised in each market. Second, MNCs must — in order to measure the after-tax cost of debt — estimate tax rates in each market in which they intend to borrow and determine the deductibility of interest by each national tax authority. Third, the nominal cost of principal and interest in foreign currency must be adjusted for foreign exchange gains or losses when MNCs issue debt denominated in a foreign currency.

For example, the before-tax cost of foreign currency-denominated debt equals the before-tax cost of repaying the principal and interest in terms of the parent's own currency. This before-tax cost of capital includes the nominal cost of principal and interest in foreign currency terms, adjusted for any foreign exchange gains or losses:

$$k_i = (k_f \times k_a) + k_p \tag{13.6}$$

where k_f = before-tax interest in foreign currency terms; k_a = additional interest due to exchange rate change; and k_p = additional principal due to exchange rate change.

Example 13.1

A US company borrows euros for 1 year at 7 percent. During the year, the euro appreciates 9 percent relative to the dollar. The US tax rate is 35 percent. What is the after-tax cost of this debt in US dollar terms?

The before-tax cost of this debt is computed as follows:

$$k_i = (k_f \times k_a) + k_p$$

$$= (0.07 \times 1.09) + 0.09$$

$$= 16.63\%$$

The added 9.63 percent cost of this debt in terms of US dollars is reported as a foreign exchange transaction loss. The nominal interest rate of 7 percent and the added cost of 9.63 percent are deductible for tax purposes. Thus, the after-tax cost of this debt would be:

$$k_t = k_i(1 - t)$$
$$= 0.1663(1 - 0.35)$$
$$= 10.81\%$$

13.1.3. *The Appropriate Cost of Capital*

If MNCs make separate allowance for different levels of risk in foreign projects, they must use the WACC as an appropriate cost of capital. They have three choices in deciding their subsidiary cost of capital: (1) cost of capital to the parent company, (2) cost of capital to the subsidiary, and (3) some weighted average of the two.

If a parent company finances the entire cost of its foreign project by itself, the cost of capital to the parent company may be used as the appropriate cost of capital. If its foreign subsidiary obtains all of the capital for the project overseas, the foreign cost of capital may be used as the appropriate cost of capital. In most cases, however, the MNC uses the whole world as a combined source of funds. Thus, the appropriate cost of capital is usually an overall weighted average of the two.

The inflation-adjusted discount rate may have to be used as an appropriate cost of capital if the analyst wishes to reflect local inflation for local projects. However, inflation tends to be built into the cost of debt and equity for a company because the WACC reflects such anticipated price changes. When lenders and equity holders anticipate price increases, they will demand a rate of return higher than in ordinary cases so that the WACC reflects inflation. Thus, the MNC should not add an increase to the discount rate derived from the cost of capital in order to adjust for inflation.

13.2. OPTIMUM CAPITAL STRUCTURE

The **optimum capital structure** is defined as the combination of debt and equity that yields the lowest cost of capital. In this situation, the amount of capital to be obtained is fixed, but the debt ratio is changed to determine the optimum capital structure. For example, the capital structure of companies in the same industry varies widely from country to country because of different environmental variables.

13.2.1. *Book-Value vs. Market-Value Weights*

To measure the WACC, we first calculate the cost of each component of the capital structure. Once we have computed the costs of individual components of the capital structure, we need to weigh them according to some standard. Two alternative ways to specify the proportions of the capital structure are practiced: book-value weights and market-value weights.

13.2.1.1. *Book-value weights*

Book-value weights are derived from the stated values of individual components of the capital structure on the firm's current balance sheet. There are two major advantages to book-value weights. First, the proportions of the capital structure are stable over time because book-value weights do not depend on market prices. Second, book-value weights are easy to determine because they are derived from stated values on the firm's balance sheet. However, book-value weights may misstate the WACC because the market values of bonds and stocks change over time and thus do not reflect the desired capital structure.

13.2.1.2. *Market-value weights*

Market-value weights are based on the current market prices of bonds and stocks. Because the primary goal of a firm is to maximize its market value, market-value weights are consistent with the company's objective. The market values of a business's existing securities depend on the expected earnings of the company and the risk of the securities as perceived by investors. In other words, market values reflect assessments of current buyers and sellers of future earnings and risk. Thus, the WACC with market-value weights should be the valid average rate of return required by investors in the firm's securities.

13.2.2. *Implications*

The traditional approach to valuation and leverage assumes that an optimum capital structure exists. This model implies that the varying effects on the market capitalization rates for debt and equity allow the firm to lower its cost of capital by the intelligent use of leverage (debt). Debt has two types of cost: explicit cost and implicit or bankruptcy cost. The explicit cost is the interest rate, whereas the implicit cost refers to added debt which increases the cost of equity and debt.

If we start with an all-equity capital structure, the introduction of debt enables a firm to lower its cost of capital. The WACC falls with increases in leverage because the increase in the cost of equity does not completely offset the use of low-cost debt. Therefore, the traditional approach implies that beyond some point both the cost of equity and the cost of debt increase at an increasing rate. With the heavy use of leverage, the increase in the cost of equity more than offsets the use of low-cost debt. Thus, at a critical point, such as a 40-percent debt ratio in Fig. 13.1, the subsequent introduction of additional leverage increases the overall cost of capital. The optimum capital structure is the point at which the WACC bottoms out.

Example 13.2

A company is planning to raise $200 million for foreign investments. It wishes to keep the amount of capital constant and to change only the combination of financing sources. As given in Table 13.1, there are three different financial structures under consideration by the company: A, B, and C.

The company initially reduces the cost of capital with leverage, but beyond plan B the continued use of debt increases the cost of capital. Most theorists believe that there is a U-shaped capital-cost curve in relation to debt-equity mixes for the company. Figure 13.1 shows that the optimum capital structure occurs at a 40-percent debt ratio.

Most companies use 30–50 percent debt in their capital structure without exceeding norms acceptable to creditors and investors. This rather broad flat area with a wide range of debt ratios, 30–50 percent in Fig. 13.1, is usually called an optimal or target debt range,

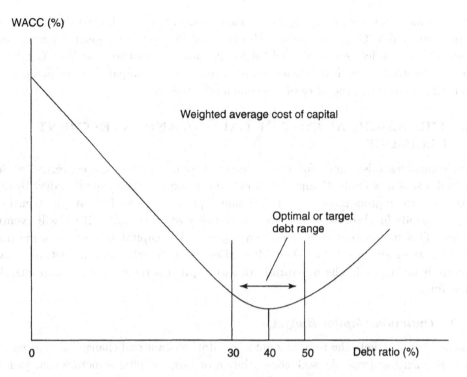

Fig. 13.1 Debt ratio and the cost of capital.

Table 13.1 Three different financial plans.

Financial Plan	After-Tax Cost	Weight	Weighted Average Cost
Plan A			
Debt	6.5%	20%	1.3%
Equity	12.0	80	9.6
WACC			10.9%
Plan B			
Debt	7.0%	40	2.8%
Equity	12.5	60	7.5
WACC			10.3%
Plan C			
Debt	9.0%	60	5.4%
Equity	15.0	40	6.0
WACC			11.4%

where little difference exists in the cost of capital. The optimal range of the flat area and the location of a particular company's debt ratio within that range are determined by a variety of noncost variables, such as availability of capital and financial risk. International availability of capital to an MNC and its lower financial risk permit it to maintain its desired debt ratio, even if significant amounts of new funds must be raised. In other words, the marginal cost of capital for an MNC is constant for a broad range of its capital budget.

In summary, the company's optimum capital structure simultaneously (a) minimizes the company's WACC, (b) maximizes the value of the company, and (c) maximizes the company's share price. As debt is added to the capital structure, the WACC falls. This increases the value of the firm. Because this increase in the company's value accrues to the owners of the company, the price of the company's stock rises.

13.3. THE MARGINAL COST OF CAPITAL AND INVESTMENT DECISIONS

When companies raise funds for new investment projects, they are concerned with the marginal cost of new funds. Companies should always expand their capital budget by raising funds in the same proportion as their optimum capital structure. However, as their capital budget expands in absolute terms, their marginal cost of capital (MCC) will eventually increase. This means that companies can tap only the capital market for some limited amount in the short run before their MCC rises, even though the same optimum capital structure is maintained. The **marginal cost of capital** is the cost of an additional dollar of new funds.

13.3.1. *Optimum Capital Budget*

In one analysis, we hold the total amount of capital constant and change only the combination of financing sources. We seek the optimum or target capital structure that yields the lowest cost of capital. In a second analysis, we attempt to determine the size of the capital budget in relation to the levels of the MCC so that the optimum capital budget can be determined. The **optimum capital budget** is defined as the amount of investment that maximizes the value of the company. It is obtained at the intersection between the internal rate of return (IRR) and the MCC; at this point total profit is maximized.

A variety of factors affect a company's cost of capital: its size, access to capital markets, diversification, tax concessions, exchange rate risk, and political risk. The first four factors favor the MNC, whereas the last two factors appear to favor the purely domestic company. As shown in Fig. 13.2, MNCs usually enjoy a lower cost of capital than purely domestic companies for a number of reasons. First, MNCs may borrow money at lower rates of interest because they are bigger. Second, they may raise funds in a number of capital markets such as the Euromarkets, local capital markets, and foreign capital markets. Third, their overall cost of capital may be lower than that of purely domestic companies because they are more diversified. Fourth, they may lower their overall taxes because they can use tax heaven countries, tax-saving holding companies, and transfer pricing.

It seems reasonable to assume that investments outside the United States are, for a US company, riskier than investment in US assets. However, this is not necessarily true because returns on foreign investments are not perfectly positively correlated with returns on US investments. In other words, MNCs may be less risky than companies which operate strictly within the boundaries of any one country. Consequently, to minimize risk companies should diversify not only across domestic investment projects but also across countries. The lower overall risk of MNCs tends to reduce their overall cost of capital.

Figure 13.2 shows that the optimum capital budget (M) of a typical MNC is higher than the optimum capital budget (D) of a purely domestic company. MNCs can tap foreign

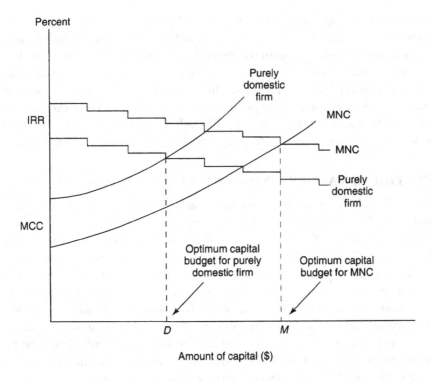

Fig. 13.2 Optimum capital budget: Domestic firm versus multinational firm.

capital markets when domestic capital markets are saturated, and their risk is lower than that of domestic companies. International capital availability and lower risk permit MNCs to lower their cost of capital and to maintain a constant MCC for a broad range of their capital budget. They have more investment opportunities than purely domestic companies. These two factors — the lower cost of capital and better investment opportunities — give MNCs higher optimum capital budgets than the optimum capital budgets of domestic companies.

Many analysts believe that some countries, such as Germany and Japan enjoy capital cost advantage mainly due to their high leverage. As the debt ratio increases, the weighted average cost of capital decreases because of the heavier weight of low-cost debt compared to high-cost equity. The low cost of debt is, of course, due to the tax deductibility of interest.

Example 13.3

Assume that there are two countries: X and Y. The cost of debt (10 percent), the cost of equity (15 percent), and the tax rate (50 percent) are the same for these two countries. However, X's capital structure is 20 percent debt and 80 percent equity, while Y's capital structure is 50 percent debt and 50 percent equity. Compare the cost of capital in the two countries. The WACC for country X is 13 percent $[0.20 \times 0.10)(1 - 0.50) + (0.80 \times 0.15)]$. If we apply the same costs of debt and equity to the more leveraged country, it will have a WACC of 10 percent $[(0.50 \times 0.10)(1 - 0.50) + (0.50 \times 0.15)]$. Hence, the more leveraged country (Y) has a lower cost of capital than the less leveraged country (X).

Companies in Germany and Japan have greater borrowing capacity because their creditors tolerate a high degree of financial leverage. Traditionally, banks in both countries have played a much more important role in corporate financing than capital markets. Companies in both countries could carry a high degree of financial leverage because banks frequently hold bonds and stocks of these companies. Finally, German and Japanese companies have close working relationships with their government. Hence, it may be in the best interest of the government to rescue failing companies through direct subsidies and long-term loans, which have enabled these companies to carry a high degree of financial leverage.

13.4. CULTURAL VALUES AND CAPITAL STRUCTURE

Can cultural values be used to predict capital structure across countries? A study by Chui, Lloyd, and Kwok found that differences in institutional backgrounds provide only a partial answer to the question of why countries have differences in capital structure.[2] Researchers from different disciplines have investigated the effects of culture on various business practices, such as the study of management functions, organization design, business performance, compensation practices, cross-border acquisition performance, and managerial attitudes, perceived importance of job outcomes and job satisfaction, and investor stock trading decisions. Alternatively, other researchers analyzed the relationship between economic variables and international differences in capital structure, but their test results indicated no significant relationship between the two. These two groups of researchers found the role of culture active in differences in the capital structure (debt ratio) across countries.

Empirical studies found that capital structure norms for companies vary widely from one country to another, but they cluster together for companies domiciled in the same industry. For example, Sekely and Collins compared debt ratios for 677 companies in nine industries from 23 countries. The researchers concluded that cultural factors, such as political, legal, social, institutional, and tax environments cause debt ratios to cluster by country rather than by industry or size. They classified these 23 countries into several cultural "realms" with similarities in capital structure norms[3]:

Anglo-American:	Australia, Canada, South Africa, the US, and the UK
Latin American:	Argentina, Brazil, Chile, and Mexico
West Central Europe:	Benelux, Switzerland, and Germany
Mediterranean Europe:	France, Italy, and Spain
Scandinavian:	Denmark, Finland, Norway, Sweden
Indian Peninsula:	India and Pakistan
South East Asia:	Malaysia and Singapore

Table 13.2 shows mean debt ratios for these seven regions. They found low debt ratios in the Southeast Asia, Latin American, and Anglo-American groups of countries. They found

[2]Chui, A., A. E. Lloyd, and C. Kwok, "The Determination of Capital Structure: Is National Culture a Missing Piece to the Puzzle?" *The Journal of International Business Studies*, First Quarter, 2002, pp. 99–126.

[3]Sekely, W. S. and J. M. Collins, "Cultural Influences on International Capital Structure," *Journal of International Business Studies*, Spring 1988, pp. 87–100.

Table 13.2 Debt ratios for seven regions.

Region	Sekely & Collins (1988)	Chui, Lloyd & Kwok (2002)
Anglo-American	0.53	0.46
Latin American	0.46	0.51
West Central Europe	0.59	0.65
Mediterranean Europe	0.70	0.60
Scandinavian	0.69	0.56
Indian Peninsula	0.67	—
Southeast Asia	0.35	0.48

high debt ratios in the Scandinavian, Mediterranean Europe, and Indian Peninsula groups. The West Central European counties had debt ratios in the middle of the seven groups.

Have these debt ratio norms of different regions changed since 1988? Yes, but not much, according to a study by Chui, Lloyd, and Kwok. Like the 1988 study, this 2002 study found low debt ratios in the Southeast Asia, Latin Anglo-American, and Latin American groups of countries; it found high ratios in the Mediterranean Europe and Scandinavia groups. One major exception is West Central Europe whose mean debt ratio has changed from the middle group to the high group. The increase in the high debt ratio of the West Central Europe has almost exclusively to do with the increased debt ratios of German companies. The high cost of German unification may be partly blamed for this increase in its overall debt ratio. Chui, Lloyd, and Kwok compared debt ratios for 5,591 companies in four different industries across 22 countries to determine the impact of cultural factors on national corporate debt ratios. To achieve this objective, they tested two hypotheses: (1) the corporate debt ratio of a country is negatively related to the country's level of conservatism, and (2) the corporate debt ratio of a country is negatively related to the country's level of mastery. Conservatism includes values that are important in close-knit harmonious relationships, in which the interests of the individual are not viewed as distinct from those of the group. These values are primarily concerned with security, conformity, and tradition. Mastery accentuates active mastery of the social environment through self-assertion by placing more emphasis on control and individual success. Such values promote their surroundings and get ahead of others.

Their empirical findings support these two hypotheses at both the national and firm levels, which mean that countries with high scores on the cultural dimensions of "conservatism" and "mastery" tend to have low corporate debt ratios. The results are robust even after controlling for the industry effect, the differences in economic performance, legal systems, financial institution development, and other well-known determinants of debt ratios in each country (such as assets tangibility, agency cost, firm size, and profitability).

Global Finance in Practice 13: Real-World Examples of the Cost of Capital

Every industry has its own prevailing average cost of capital. The numbers vary widely. Homebuilding has a relatively high cost of capital, at 6.35 percent, according to a compilation from New York University's Stern School of Business. The retail grocery business is relatively low, at 1.98 percent.

The cost of capital is also high among both biotech and pharmaceutical drug companies, steel manufacturers, internet software companies, and integrated oil and gas companies. Those industries tend to require significant capital investment in research, development, equipment, and factories.

Among the industries with lower capital costs are money center banks, power companies, real estate investment trusts (REITs), and utilities (both general and water). Such companies may require less equipment or may benefit from very steady cash flows.[4]

13.5. SUMMARY

The cost of capital, the optimum capital structure, and the optimum capital budget have a major impact on an MNC's value. The cost of capital is used to evaluate foreign investment projects. The optimum capital structure is a particular debt ratio that simultaneously (a) minimizes the company's WACC, (b) maximizes the value of the company, and (c) maximizes its share price. The optimum capital budget is the amount of investment that will maximize an MNC's total profits.

Although the main issues used to analyze the cost of capital in the domestic case provide the foundation for the multinational case, it is necessary to analyze the unique impact of foreign exchange risks, institutional variables, and cultural values. International capital availability, lower risks, and more investment opportunities permit MNCs to lower their cost of capital and to earn more profits.

13.6. KEY TERMS

weighted average cost of capital (WACC) cost of equity
security market line   market risk premium
price–earnings ratio   explicit cost of debt
optimum capital structure   book-value weights
market-value weights   marginal cost of capital
optimum capital budget

13.7. PROBLEMS

1. A foreign project has a beta of 0.50, a risk-free interest rate of 8 percent, and the expected rate of return on the market portfolio is 15 percent. What is the cost of capital for the project?
2. A US company borrows Japanese yen for 1 year at 8 percent. During the year, the yen appreciates 10 percent relative to the dollar. The US tax rate is 50 percent. What is the after-tax cost of this debt in US dollar terms?

---

[4]Hayes, A., "Cost of Capital: What It Is, Why It Matters, Formula, and Example," *Investopedia*, https://www.investopedia.com/termGl/c/costofcapital.asp#:~:text=The%20firm's%20overall%20cost%20of,cost%20of%20debt%20is%207%25, June 13, 2022.

3. The cost of debt (10 percent), the cost of equity (15 percent), and the tax rate (50 percent) are the same for countries A and B. However, A's capital structure is zero percent debt and 100 percent equity, while B's capital structure is 50 percent debt and 50 percent equity. Compare the cost of capital in the two countries.

4. A company earns $300 per year after taxes and is expected to earn the same amount of profits per year in the future. The company considers three financial plans: A with a debt ratio of 20 percent and a WACC of 15 percent; B with a debt ratio of 40 percent and a WACC of 10 percent; and C with a debt ratio of 80 percent and a WACC of 20 percent. Which debt ratio will maximize the value of the company?

5. Assume that a company wishes to sell $6 million worth of bonds and $14 million worth of common stock. The bonds have 13 percent before-tax interest and the stock is expected to pay $1.4 million in dividends. The growth rate of dividends has been 8 percent and is expected to continue at the same rate. Determine the weighted average cost of capital if the tax rate on income is 50 percent.

Closing Case 13: Do Multinational Firms Have Lower Debt Ratios than Domestic Firms?

Authors of international finance textbooks have suggested a number of practical concepts. First, MNCs should support more debt in their capital structure than purely domestic companies. They point out that an MNC should have a higher target debt ratio than its domestic counterpart because of its size, access to capital markets, diversification, and tax concessions. The target debt ratio is the optimum capital structure, which is defined as the combination of debt and common equity that yields the lowest cost of capital. Second, MNCs should have lower business risk than purely domestic companies. Business risk, such as the cost of financial distress and expected bankruptcy cost, refers to the variability of operating profits or the possibility that the firm will not be able to cover its fixed costs. An MNC operates in many different countries and thus this diversification should translate into lower earnings volatility.

Some financial analysts argue that there is an inverse relationship between business risk and the optimum debt level. Companies with less business risk are supposed to assume more debt without added risk. Debt has two types of cost: explicit cost and implicit or bankruptcy cost. The explicit cost is the interest rate, whereas the implicit cost refers to added debt, which increases the possibility of liquidating a business. Thus, given the traditional paradigm of a trade-off between the tax shelter of debt and the expected bankruptcy cost, MNCs should have lower expected bankruptcy costs and hence higher leverage ratios. In other words, MNCs should be able to carry higher debt loads because they are able to diversify their business risk across national economies.

Third, an MNC is more sensitive to exchange rate fluctuations than a purely domestic company. A purely domestic company may not face economic exchange rate risk because it operates in just one country. Finally, an MNC should have higher agency costs than a purely domestic company because the MNC faces higher auditing costs, language differences, sovereign uncertainty, divergent political and economic systems, and varying accounting systems.

To ascertain these four concepts, Burgman (1996) has conducted an extensive empirical study of 251 domestic firms and 236 MNCs. His findings are as follows: First, the mean leverage ratio for the multinational sample is significantly less than that for the domestic sample at the 1 percent level. Second, operating profits of the multinational sample are more volatile than the domestic sample, though the statistical significance of the difference is weak. Third, domestic companies are significantly more sensitive to exchange rate risk than MNCs at the 5 percent level. Finally, MNCs have significantly higher agency costs than their domestic counterparts at the 1 percent level. Thus, Burgman's study confirmed only the 4th concept and rejected the other three concepts.

Case Questions

1. What is the agency problem? What are agency costs? Why do multinational companies incur higher agency costs than domestic companies?
2. Contrary to common expectations, the 1996 study by Burgmann has found that multinational companies have lower debt ratios and higher business risks than purely domestic companies. What are possible explanations for this finding?
3. What is the economic exchange rate risk? Is it easy to hedge this risk? Contrary to common expectations, the 1996 study by Burgmann has concluded that multinational companies have lower economic exchange rate risk than domestic companies. What are possible explanations for this finding?
4. Use the web site of Bloomberg — http://biz.yahoo.com/funds — to compare yield rates of government securities for several countries.

Source: Burgmann, T. A., "An Empirical Examination of Multinational Corporate Capital Structure," *Journal of International Business Studies*, Third Quarter, 1996, pp. 553–570. For agency theory, see Kim, K. and S. Kim, *Global Corporate Finance: A Focused Approach*, 3rd Edition, New Jersey: World Scientific, 2020, pp. 16–17.

Chapter 14

FOREIGN DIRECT INVESTMENT ANALYSIS

Opening Case 14: How Can Companies Get the Most Out of Their Foreign Investment?

We can classify the benefits of foreign direct investment into two broad categories: tangible and intangible. Some benefits, such as reductions in labor, capital, and logistics costs, are tangible and easy to measure; others, such as new ideas from foreign research centers, customers, and suppliers, are intangible and difficult to measure. If foreign manufacturing operations play a negligible strategic role, the tangible benefits usually dominate the decision to manufacture abroad. As a company upgrades the strategic role of its foreign manufacturing operations, however, it stresses the intangible benefits more.

Many multinational companies (MNCs) establish and manage their own foreign plants only for the benefits of tax concessions, cheap labor, and capital subsidies. However, Ferdows (1997) argues that higher market share and greater profits can only be achieved if both tangible and intangible benefits are realized. When an MNC employs a foreign plant to produce intangible benefits, the plant will have a better chance to be innovative, to be productive, to achieve low costs, and to provide exemplary service to customers throughout the world. To get more out of its foreign factories, therefore, the MNC should use them to get closer to their customers and suppliers, to attract skilled and talented employees, and to create centers of expertise for the entire company.

Some companies indeed invest abroad to seek technology, managerial expertise, and other intangible benefits. For example, German, Japanese, and Korean companies have purchased US-based electronics firms for their technology. Take a look at LG's acquisition of Zenith as an example. On July 17, 1995, LG Electronics of Korea acquired Zenith, the last remaining TV manufacturer in the United States, to obtain its HDTV and multimedia technologies. This is because changes in international competitiveness had compelled LG to engage its own aggressive research and development.[1]

---

[1]K. Ferdows, "Making the Most of Foreign Factories," *Harvard Business Review*, March/April 1997, p. 82.

Direct investments are equity investments such as the purchase of common stock, the acquisition of entire firms, or the establishment of new subsidiaries. The US Department of Commerce defines **foreign direct investment** (FDI) as investment in either real capital assets or financial assets with a minimum of 10 percent equity ownership in a foreign firm. These days companies look for and need to explore growth opportunities on a global basis. In principle, growth of the foreign presence in any national economy could take place in either of two ways. Companies could grow primarily through the construction of new production facilities in a foreign country, financed either through the establishment of new subsidiaries or through investment by their existing facilities in the foreign country. Alternatively, companies could grow through acquisition of existing foreign firms.

Obviously, both kinds of growth have recently taken place in the US and other countries. For example, such ventures as the establishment of Japanese automobile plants in the United States have occurred simultaneously with such events as Chinese acquisitions of US companies. In quantitative terms, however, acquisitions (external growth) are much larger than the construction of new production facilities abroad (internal growth). Although internal growth is usually natural and economical, the process of growth may be very slow. In recent years, a company's growth through a merger with the existing business activities of a foreign firm has received substantial attention as an alternative to internal growth.

We consider the purchase of an individual asset as a capital budgeting decision. When a company is buying another company, it is making an investment. Thus, the basic principles of capital investment decisions apply. But mergers are often more difficult to evaluate. First, the financial manager must be careful to define benefits. Second, the financial manager needs to understand why mergers occur and who gains or loses as a result of them. Third, the acquisition of a company is more complicated than the purchase of a new machine because special tax, legal, and accounting issues must often be addressed. Finally, the integration of an entire company is much more complex than the installation of a single new machine.

The basic principles of capital budgeting analysis are the same for foreign and domestic investment projects. However, a foreign investment decision results from a complex process, which differs in many aspects from the domestic investment decision. Relevant cash flows are the dividends and royalties that would be repatriated by each subsidiary to a parent firm. Because these net cash flows must be converted into the currency of a parent company, they are subject to future exchange-rate changes. Moreover, foreign investment projects are subject to political risks such as exchange controls and discrimination. Normally, the cost of capital for a foreign project is higher than that for a similar domestic project. Certainly, this higher risk comes from two major sources, political risk and exchange risk.

This chapter is composed of six major sections. Section 14.1 discusses modes of foreign investment. Section 14.2 describes the entire process of planning capital expenditures in foreign countries beyond 1 year. Section 14.3 examines how international diversification can reduce the overall riskiness of a company. Section 14.4 compares capital budgeting theory with capital budgeting practice. Section 14.5 considers motives for cross-border mergers and acquisitions. Section 14.6 covers political risk analysis.

14.1. HOW TO INVEST ABROAD: MODES OF FOREIGN INVESTMENT

When a company decides to invest its money abroad, it has seven distinct alternatives available: construction of new plants, mergers and acquisitions, joint ventures, equity alliances, licensing agreements, franchising agreements, and contract manufacturing.

14.1.1. *Construction of New Plants (Internal Growth)*

Companies can penetrate foreign markets by establishing new operations in foreign countries to produce and sell new products. Some companies may prefer this internal growth because they can tailor their foreign operations to their exact needs. For example, General Motors had spent several years to determine the market size for its cars in China before the company decided to build a \$1 billion auto assembly plant in the country. Such a demand forecast or potential market size depends on many factors, such as competition, income, population, economic conditions, and the feasibility of serving nearby foreign markets. However, it would take some time for MNCs to reap any rewards from internal growth because they have to build a plant and establish a customer base first. We discuss this type of foreign investment in detail later in this chapter.

14.1.2. *Mergers and Acquisitions (External Growth)*

Although internal growth is usually natural and economical, the process of growth may be too slow. These days many MNCs acquire other firms in foreign countries to penetrate foreign markets rather than to build factories that may take years to complete. Some companies purchase parts of foreign firms to obtain a stake in foreign operations. In many cases, MNCs acquire foreign firms to obtain instant access to the market they serve and to reduce their competitors. For example, in December 1998, British Petroleum purchased Amoco of the United States to expand their US market share and to reduce one of its major US competitors. Some \$171.8 billion of cross-border merger and acquisition deals between US and European companies had been made to offset sluggish growth.[2] We discuss motives of cross-border mergers and acquisitions in detail later in this chapter.

14.1.3. *Joint Venture*

A joint venture is a venture that is owned by two or more firms. Sometimes the owners of a joint venture are from several different countries. Many MNCs penetrate foreign markets by forming a joint venture with companies that reside in those markets. Most joint ventures permit two companies to use their respective comparative advantages in a given project. For example, General Mills of the United States and Nestle of Switzerland formed a joint venture so that the cereals produced by General Mills could be sold through the huge global distribution network established by Nestle.

The basic advantage of a joint venture is that it enables a company to generate incremental revenue or cost savings. A joint venture, however, normally faces many complex

---

[2]https://www.reuters.com/article/us-europe-usa-deals-idUSKBN18I1M6, February 28, 2019.

problems. Because representatives of both companies sit on the board of directors, it is difficult to forge a consensus, especially when an MNC and host-country firms form a joint venture. Nevertheless, these days international joint ventures crop up everywhere. The rush of new technology, the expense of staying on the leading edge, the demands of customers, and worldwide competition have required many MNCs to form a wide range of joint ventures and partnerships.

14.1.4. *Equity Alliances*

An **equity alliance** is an alliance where one company takes an equity position in another company. In some cases, each party takes an ownership in the other. The purpose of the equity ownership is to solidify a collaborative contract so that it is difficult to break, particularly if the ownership is large enough to secure a board membership for the investing company. The airline industry epitomizes the use of equity alliances. IBM maintains more than 500 equity alliances around the world.

14.1.5. *Licensing Agreement*

A **licensing agreement** is an agreement where an MNC (the licensor) allows a foreign company (the licensee) to produce its products in a foreign country in exchange for royalties, fees, and other forms of compensation. MNCs can set up their own production facilities abroad or license a local firm to manufacture their products in return for royalties. AT&T has a licensing agreement to build and operate part of India's telephone system. Sprint Corp. has a licensing agreement to develop telecommunications services in England.

Advantages to a licensor include: (1) a relatively small amount of investment, (2) an opportunity to penetrate foreign markets, (3) lower political and financial risks, and (4) an easy way to circumvent foreign-market entry restrictions. Benefits to a licensee include: (1) a cheap way to obtain new technology, (2) an easy way to diversify into other product lines, and (3) an opportunity to capitalize on its unique positions, such as the channels of distribution, the financial resources, and the marketing know-how.

Like all aspects of good business, successful licensing requires management and planning. Because there is no global clearing house for technology, the matching process stretches around the world with a wide variety of intermediaries. The process is further complicated because of politics, international laws, different cultures, and global secrecy. Consequently, a continuous stream of profitable licensing agreements comes from hard thinking, good planning, and large outlays for research and development.

14.1.6. *Franchising Agreement*

A **franchising agreement** is an agreement where an MNC (franchiser) allows a foreign company (franchisee) to sell products or services under a highly publicized brand name and a well-proven set of procedures. Under this arrangement, the franchiser allows the franchisee not only to sell products or services but also assists on a continuing basis in the operation of the business.

The United States is a leader in franchising, a position it has held since the 1930s when it used the approach for fast-food restaurants, food inns and, slightly later, motels at the time of the Great Depression. Fast-food operations, such as McDonald's, Kentucky Fried Chicken, and Dunkin Donuts, are the most numerous. Other types of franchisers are hotels (Hilton), soft drinks (Coca Cola), clerical services (Kelly Services), automotive products (Midas), and family marts (7-Eleven). Such US household-name franchisors have expanded globally through franchising, giving this mode of market entry a distinct American flavor.[3]

Global Finance in Practice 14: What Foreign Franchises Coming to the US should Know

Although many Americans may not realize it, the US is not the only mother of invention. Companies worldwide are giving birth to their own franchised concepts and, with increasing frequency, are crossing borders and offering franchises all over the world.

Because of its size, the US market is extremely attractive to many foreign franchisors. Americans also have a deep-rooted fascination with franchising, relatively high disposable income, and enthusiastically embrace new products and services. We are also the consummate consumers — just check out our credit card debt!

The biggest problem for foreign franchisors is fear. They fear being sued because of the US's reputation for litigation. Furthermore, foreign franchisors know that playing the game in the US requires investing a lot of money because of the regulatory environment and are often daunted by the size and diversity of the market.

Foreign franchisors often offer master franchises or set up joint ventures when entering the US. That's not surprising because they have seen US franchisors using master franchising in their home countries. But this likely is *not* the most productive way to expand in the US because master franchising is rarely used by US franchisors at home.

Foreign companies entering the US need to understand the US market and answer the same key questions we posed for US franchisors going overseas. Even if foreign franchisors are convinced that their concept will work in the US, they could drain their financial resources if they miss the mark.

Working far from home presents challenges that foreign franchisors must be ready for in the US. These include the following:

- Will you adapt the concept to the local market? Who will control the adaptations? Who is your local consumer and competition? Remember: Unlike many foreign countries, the US is not a homogeneous market. It also is a very sophisticated market and readily adopts foreign concepts. Care should be taken, therefore, in changing a brand offering based on some perception that Americans shop in any unified way.

---

[3]Laurent J. Jacque, *International Corporate Finance*, Hoboken, New Jersey: Wiley & Sons, 2020, p. 559.

- Are inventory and equipment available locally? If you must import them, what are the duties, shipping costs, and time constraints?
- Will you store inventory locally to make up for potentially longer delivery times to your franchisees of the products and supplies they will need?
- Does your brand have enough name recognition to demand a higher price — especially compared with local competition — to cover any increased costs?
- What happens if things don't work out?
- What are your termination provisions and dispute resolution procedures?
- What is your corporate culture like? Do you have open communication? How will you communicate with franchisees who speak a different language from that spoken by everyone else in the system?
- How will you get paid? Are you required to pay taxes and, if so, to whom?
- Can you enforce your core rights related to payments, termination, and intellectual property?[4]

14.1.7. *Contract Manufacturing*

Contract manufacturing occurs when MNCs contract with a foreign manufacturer to produce products for them according to their specifications. The contract manufacturer does not market the products it produces. Instead, these MNCs market the products under their own brand name, just like Wal-Mart sells a variety of products made by contract manufacturers under its own brand name. Thus, the buying public normally does not know the fact that the selling company did not actually produce the product. Sometimes, MNCs subcontract assembly work or the production of parts to independent companies overseas.

14.1.8. *Global Trend in Foreign Direct Investment (FDI)*

As shown in Fig. 14.1, the OECD (Organization for Economic Cooperation and Development) estimate that global FDI flows for 2013 finished around $1.3 trillion, a decline of 6 percent from 2012. This would be the second consecutive annual decline, following a 21 percent decline between 2011 and 2012. The sluggish performance would seem to owe to several sources of uncertainty that discouraged multinational companies from FDI. These sources included persistent Eurozone sluggishness, slowing growth in China, and fears about the financial stability of emerging markets in general. China became the first FDI destination in 2013 and the United States maintained its position as the leading investing economy. In 2013, 47 percent of global FDI inflows were hosted by only six countries. China attracted the lion's share by $220 billion followed by the Unites States ($151 billion), Canada ($68 billion), Russia ($65 billion), Brazil ($58 billion), and the United Kingdom ($53 billion). Global FDI flows have been around $1.2 trillion since 2013.[5]

---

[4]Mazero, J. and M. Seit, "What Foreign Franchises Coming to the US should Know," https://www. franchising.com/articles/what_foreign_franchises_coming_to_the_us_should_know.html.
[5]https://unctad.org/en/pages/newsdetails.aspx?OriginalVersionID=1980, March 20, 2019.

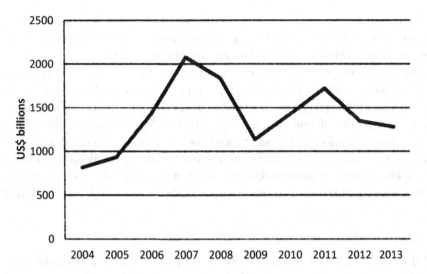

Fig. 14.1   Global foreign direct investment inflows: 2004–2013.

Source: OECD International Direct Investment Statistics Database. Data for 2013 are estimated based upon a linear projection of first three quarters of 2013, http://www.oecd.org/industry/inv/FDI-in-Figures-April-2014.pdf, accessed May 5, 2014.

14.2. THE FOREIGN INVESTMENT DECISION PROCESS

The foreign investment decision process (internal growth) involves the entire process of planning capital expenditures in foreign countries beyond 1 year. The 1-year time frame is arbitrary, but a 1-year boundary is rather widely accepted. There are many steps and elements in this process. Each element is a subsystem of the capital budgeting system. Thus, the foreign investment decision process may be viewed as an integral unit of many elements which are interrelated. Here we assume that the entire foreign investment decision process consists of 11 phases: (1) the decision to search for foreign investment, (2) an assessment of the political climate in the host country, (3) an examination of the company's overall strategy, (4) cash flow analysis, (5) the required rate of return, (6) economic evaluation, (7) selection, (8) risk analysis, (9) implementation, (10) expenditure control, and (11) post audit.

14.2.1. *Search for Foreign Investment*

The availability of good investment opportunities sets the foundation for a successful investment program. Hence, a system should be established to stimulate ideas for capital expenditures abroad and to identify good investment opportunities. Moreover, good investment opportunities come from hard thinking, careful planning, and frequently, large outlays for research and development.

The first phase in the foreign investment decision process is an analysis of the forces that lead some company officials to focus on the possibilities of foreign investment. If a company recognizes foreign investment as a legitimate program, its search for foreign investment opportunities will start. The economic and political forces in the host countries are largely responsible for the expansion of foreign investment. Many companies also desire foreign investment to seek new markets, raw materials, and production efficiency. Chapter 2 described these and other motives for foreign investment in detail.

It is not easy to pinpoint one motive for a decision to invest abroad in any particular case or to find out exactly who initiated a foreign project. The decision to search for foreign investment comes at the end of a series of events, and it is a combination of several motivating forces and activities of different people. Typically, the decision to look abroad depends on the interaction of many forces. Considerations such as profit opportunities, tax policy, and diversification strategies are economic variables which may affect a decision to look overseas. In addition, environmental forces, organizational factors, and a drive by some high-ranking officials inside a company could be major forces leading a company to look abroad.

14.2.2. *Political Climate*

Political risks may exist for domestic investment. Price controls may be established or lifted, some regulated industries may be deregulated, or quotas and tariffs on cheap imported components may be imposed. Certainly, there are more political risks in foreign investment. For one thing, at least two national governments have become involved in a foreign investment project — the home country of the parent company and the host country of the subsidiary. The goals of the two countries may differ; laws may change; rights to repatriate capital may be modified; and in an extreme situation, assets may be seized by a host government without adequate compensation.

One major concern of MNCs is the possibility that the political climate of a host country may deteriorate. The multinational financial manager must analyze the political environment of the proposed host country and determine whether the economic environment would be receptive to the proposed project. In general, projects designed to reduce the country's need for imports and thus save foreign exchange are given the highest priority by the host government.

Political actions, such as exchange controls and discrimination, adversely affect company operations. Thus, the analyst should emphasize such factors as the host government's attitudes toward foreign investment, the desire of the host country for national rather than foreign control, and its political stability. The analyst should also determine whether adequate and prompt compensation is guaranteed if a host country nationalizes alien assets in the public interest.

14.2.3. *Company's Overall Strategy*

If the initial screening of the political climate is favorable, the MNCs can move on to the next stage of the decision process. The analyst then assesses the usefulness of each alternative within the company's overall strategy to determine how foreign operations may perpetuate current strengths or offset weaknesses. This approach allows a company to reduce alternatives to a manageable number. At this stage, the company must check whether the project conflicts with company goals, policies, and resources. The analyst must also evaluate whether the company has the experience to handle the project and how the project could be integrated into existing projects.

The company's overall strategy consists of objectives, policies, and resources. In capital expenditure analysis, there are objectives to be attained and policies designed to achieve these objectives. If a particular set of policies is not consistent with the stated objectives, either the policies or the objectives should be revised. The company must also have resources necessary to carry out its policies. If resources are not available, they must be acquired, or the policies and/or the objectives must be revised.

14.2.3.1. *Company goal*

The primary goal of the MNC is to maximize its stock price. The market price of the firm's stock reflects the market's evaluation of its prospective earnings stream over time and the riskiness of this stream. Thus, the company must attempt to accept projects whose profits are higher and whose risks are lower.

14.2.3.2. *Company policy*

If the company has carefully established policies to achieve its goal, it can overcome the threat of competitors and use its oligopolistic advantages. The company should systematically evaluate individual entry strategies in foreign markets, continuously audit the effectiveness of current entry modes, and use appropriate evaluation criteria.

14.2.3.3. *Company resources*

Resources are assets that enable the company to carry out its objectives and policies; they include marketing skills, management time and expertise, capital resources, technological capabilities, and strong brand names.

14.2.4. *Cash Flow Analysis*

The fourth stage of the screening process involves a standard cash flow analysis. The after-tax cash outflows and inflows directly associated with each project must be estimated to evaluate capital investment alternatives. An MNC must forecast its expected expenditures for the proposed project. Ordinarily, it obtains these forecasts from data of similar ventures. A company may also make forecasts by such techniques as the percent-of-sale method or a linear regression analysis. An important difference in the application of cash flow analysis for foreign investment is that a company must make two sets of cash flow analysis, one for the project itself and one for the parent company.

14.2.4.1. *Demand forecast*

The first step in analyzing cash flows for any investment proposal is a forecast of demand. These estimates of usage are highly correlated with historical demand, population, income, alternative sources of products, competition, the feasibility of serving nearby markets, and general economic conditions.

There are a number of reasons for emphasizing market size in the investment decision process. First, the expected market size can be used as an indication of profit possibilities for the proposed investment project. Second, small markets tend to have high uncertainty. If a market is small, the MNC has little or no leeway in case of an erroneous estimate. Third, small markets are not worth the effort. Because management is one of scarce resources in a company, the proposed project should be large enough to support management time on project analysis.

14.2.4.2. *Duties and taxes*

Because foreign investment cuts across national boundaries, a unique set of tax laws and import duties may be applicable. An MNC must review the tax structure of the host country. In this analysis, the evaluator would include the definition of a taxable entity, statutory tax rates, tax treaties, treatment of dual taxation, and tax incentive programs. The MNC should also know whether the host government imposes customs duties on imported production equipment and materials not obtainable from local sources.

14.2.4.3. *Foreign exchange rates and restrictions*

Another important feature of foreign investment analysis is that project inflows available to the investor are subject to foreign exchange rates and restrictions. When the host country has a stable exchange rate, no problems are presented. However, if the exchange rate is expected to change or allowed to float, cash flow analysis becomes more complicated because the analyst must forecast the exchange rate which may be applicable to convert cash flows into hard currencies.

It is equally important to recognize that many host governments have various exchange control regulations. Under these regulations, permission may be required to buy foreign exchange with local currency for payment of loan interest, management fees, royalties, and most other billings for services provided by foreign suppliers. Processing applications for permission to purchase foreign exchange may take a long time. Moreover, granting of permission to buy foreign exchange does not guarantee that a related foreign exchange will be available in time because commercial banks can allocate only such amounts as are made available by a central bank.

Many factors affect the blockage of funds to non-residents. They include an expected shortage of foreign exchange, a long-run deficiency of the foreign exchange, and certain types of domestic political pressures. If all funds are blocked in perpetuity, the value of a project is zero to the parent company. However, in actuality funds are likely to be only partially blocked because MNCs have many ways to remove blocked funds. These methods include transfer price adjustments, loan repayments, royalty adjustments, and fee adjustments. Furthermore, most host countries limit the amount of fund transfers to nonresidents or block the transfer of funds only on a temporary basis. Nevertheless, MNCs must analyze the effect of blocked funds on project return. It is critical that an analyst determines the amount of blocked funds, their reinvestment return, and ways in which funds can be transferred under the host country's law.

14.2.4.4. *Project vs. parent cash flows*

To determine after-tax profits from a proposed project, the MNC must develop a demand forecast, forecast its expected expenditures, and review the tax structure of the host country.

The estimated sales, less estimated expenses plus non-cash outlays such as depreciation, gives the cash inflows from operations.

Typically, an MNC desires to maximize the utility of project cash flows on a worldwide basis. The MNC must value only those cash flows which can be repatriated because only these funds can be used for investment in new ventures, for payment of dividends and debt obligations, and for reinvestment in other subsidiaries. Project cash flows would have little value if they could not be used for these alternatives.

Project cash flows and parent cash flows can be substantially different due to tax regulations and exchange controls. Moreover, some project expenses, such as management fees and royalties, are returns to the parent company. In general, incremental cash flows to the parent company are worldwide parent cash flows after investment minus worldwide parent cash flows before investment. These differences raise the question of which cash flows should be used as the relevant cash flows in project evaluation. Because the value of a project is determined by the net present value of future cash flows to an investor, a foreign investment analyst should use cash flows available for repatriation as the relevant cash flows. Hence, the MNC must analyze the impact of taxation, exchange controls, and other operational restrictions on cash flows to the parent company.

14.2.4.5. *Capital budgeting and transfer pricing*

Cash flow analysis of a foreign investment project involves many unique environmental variables. They include (1) different tax systems, (2) foreign exchange risk, (3) project vs. parent cash flows, (4) restrictions on remittance of funds, and (5) political, financial, and business risks. In these five environmental variables, a transfer pricing policy is an integral part of each of the following three issues: First, MNCs should know the amount of funds they can withdraw from their foreign investment. Transfer price adjustments, dividends, royalties, and management fees are the only techniques to withdraw funds where there are restrictions on fund flow movements. Second, transfer-pricing policies are regarded as one of the best ways to reduce a variety of taxes, such as income taxes, tariffs, and other taxes. Third, transfer-pricing policies are one of the better means to minimize foreign exchange losses from currency fluctuations because they enable MNCs to shift funds from one country to another. However, it is important to understand that use of market-based transfer prices may lead to the better investment decision because transfer price adjustments may significantly distort the profitability of a foreign project.

14.2.5. *The Cost of Capital*

The **cost of capital** is the minimum rate of return that a project must yield in order to be accepted by a company. This minimum rate of return is sometimes called the discount rate or the required rate of return. The cost of capital is an extremely important financial concept. It acts as a major link between the firm's foreign investment decision and the wealth of the owners as determined by investors in the global marketplace. It is in effect the "magic number" used to decide whether a proposed foreign investment will increase or decrease the firm's stock price. Clearly, only those projects expected to increase stock price would be accepted. Because it plays a key role in international capital expenditure analysis, Chapter 13 discussed the cost of capital for foreign investment projects in detail.

14.2.6. *Economic Evaluation*

Once cash flows and the required rate of return have been determined, the company begins the formal process of evaluating investment projects. Many techniques have been developed for evaluating projects under conditions of certainty. They range from simple rules of thumb to sophisticated mathematical programming methods. The most commonly used methods for an economic evaluation of individual projects are divided into two board categories: unsophisticated methods and discounted cash flow approaches, also known as sophisticated methods.

Literature on capital expenditure analysis favors the net-present-value and internal-rate-of-return methods, which are sometimes called the **discounted cash-flow approaches**. The two discounted cash-flow approaches provide a more sophisticated basis for ranking and selecting investment projects because the payback and average-rate-of return methods have various limitations. These two methods clearly recognize that money has a time value and that money in the near future is more valuable than money in the distant future. They also use the cash flows of a project over its entire lifespan. Analysts can avoid difficult problems underlying the measurement of income by using cash flows, thus eliminating such irrelevant influences as depreciation methods and inventory valuation.

The **net present value** of a project is the present value of its expected cash inflows minus the present value of its expected cash outflows. The **internal rate of return** is the discount rate that equates the present value of the net cash flows to the present value of the net cash investment, or the rate that provides a zero net present value. The decision rule tells us to (1) accept a project if its net present value is positive and (2) accept a project if its internal rate of return is greater than a firm's cost of capital.

The net-present-value and internal-rate-of-return methods lead to the same decision in many situations. These two rules lead to the same decision if the following conditions hold:

1. Investment proposals under consideration are mutually independent and they are free of capital rationing constraints.
2. All projects are equally risky so that the acceptance or rejection of any project does not affect the cost of capital.
3. A meaningful cost of capital exists to the extent that a company has access to capital at that cost.
4. A unique internal rate of return exists; every project has just one internal rate of return.

In the absence of these assumptions, the two discounted cash-flow approaches may lead to different decisions, thus making the capital budgeting decision much more complex.

When the net-present-value and internal-rate-of-return methods produce different answers, net present value is better for a number of reasons:

1. The net present value is easier to compute than the internal rate of return.
2. If the primary goal of a firm is to maximize the value of the firm, the net-present-value method leads to the correct decision, while the internal-rate-of-return method may lead to an incorrect decision.
3. A single project may have more than one internal rate of return under certain conditions, whereas the same project has just one net present value at a particular discount rate.

4. Once computed, the internal rate of return remains constant over the entire life of the project. This assumption about static conditions is hardly realistic during a period of rising interest rates and inflation. Uneven discount rates present no problems when the net-present-value method is used.

5. In the net-present-value method, the implied reinvestment rate approximates the opportunity cost for reinvestment. However, with the internal-rate-of-return method, the implied reinvestment assumption does not approximate the opportunity cost for reinvestment at all.

Although the net-present-value method is theoretically superior, the internal-rate-of-return method has certain advantages. First, internal rate of return is easier to visualize and interpret because it is identical with the yield to the maturity of bonds or other securities. Second, we do not need to specify a required rate of return in the computation. In other words, it does not require the prior computation of the cost of capital. Third, business executives are more comfortable with internal rate of return because it is directly comparable to the firm's cost of capital.

14.2.7. *Selection*

Each of the capital budgeting techniques described in the previous section measures the rate of return on a uniform basis for all projects under consideration. A project or a set of projects will be chosen at this stage if the following three assumptions hold: first, the company has a definite cutoff point which all projects must meet; second, all cash outflows and inflows from each project are known with absolute certainty; third, the company's investment programs are not constrained by any lack of funds. The final selection of projects depends on three kinds of capital budgeting decisions: the accept–reject decision, the mutually exclusive choice decision, and the capital rationing decision.

The selected project must successfully pass the accept–reject decision. If projects under consideration are mutually independent and not subject to capital rationing constraints, the company must accept all projects whose expected rate of return exceeds its hurdle rate in order to maximize stockholder wealth. The **hurdle rate** may be based on the cost of capital, the opportunity cost, or some other arbitrary standard. However, it is important to recognize the possibility that (1) certain projects may compete with each other and (2) available projects may exceed available funds. Mutual exclusiveness and capital rationing constraints are two cases where otherwise profitable projects are rejected. Investment proposals are said to be mutually exclusive if the acceptance of one project means the rejection of all the other projects. Capital rationing refers to an upper ceiling on the size of capital expenditures during a given period of time.

14.2.8. *Risk Analysis*

Up to this point, we have assumed that the dollar cash flows will certainly occur. In reality, all foreign investment projects are subject to various risks — business and financial risks, inflation and currency risks, and political risks. A change in some of these risks may have a decisive impact on the financial consequences of a particular project. Furthermore, the risks vary widely from country to country.

Only a few of the financial variables are normally known with a fair degree of accuracy in advance. Investors are basically risk averters. If investors do not know in advance exactly which future events will occur, they will have to determine the risk–return tradeoff in order to choose attractive projects.

Many MNCs use the risk-adjusted discount rate and the certainty equivalent approach to adjust for project estimates. The **risk-adjusted discount rate** is a rate that consists of the riskless rate of return plus a risk premium. Assume that the cost of capital for a firm is 10 percent when the riskless rate of return is 7 percent. This 3 percent difference between the cost of capital and the riskless rate of return reflects the degree of risk for the company. The company may increase its discount rate by 2 percent to a total of 12 percent for a mildly risky project, by 5 percent to a total of 15 percent for a more risky project, and so on. Hence, the risk-adjusted discount rate accounts for the time value of money and the relative risk of the project in terms of a risk premium.

The **certainty equivalent approach** is a method used to adjust for project risk in the numerator of the net present value formula. In other words, while the risk-adjusted discount rate adjusts for risk in the denominator of the net-present-value formula, the certainty equivalent approach adjusts for risk in the numerator of the same equation.

When an analyst uses the certainty equivalent approach, the annual cash flows are multiplied by a certainty equivalent coefficient, which is a certain cash flow divided by an uncertain cash flow. If the analyst is indifferent between a certain $140 and an uncertain $200, its coefficient is 0.70 ($140 ÷ $200). The coefficient assumes a value of between 0 and 1. It varies inversely with risk. If a firm perceives greater risk, it uses a lower coefficient which would deflate the dollar return value. Once all the risky cash flows are adjusted downward to reflect uncertainty through the use of the coefficient, the analyst then discounts these certain cash flows at the risk-free rate of interest to determine the certain net present value.

14.2.9. *Implementation, Control, and Post Audits*

The last three steps of the capital budgeting system consist of implementation, expenditure control, and post audits.

14.2.9.1. *Implementation*

Authorization to expend funds for the accepted projects may be obtained by submission of individual capital expenditure requests in accordance with formal procedures set forth by the budget director. These procedures typically cover the use of standard forms, the channels for submission and review, and the authority requirements and limits for approval.

14.2.9.2. *Control*

There is a specific phase of the capital budgeting process during which the practical cost control of a foreign project becomes important. This is the time between the approval of the project and its completion. The expenditure control of a foreign project in process is designed to increase the probability that it is completed within the established guidelines. This phase is particularly important for foreign investment projects because operations are typically supervised from a distance.

14.2.9.3. *Post audit*

Because multinational capital budgeting decisions are made on the basis of assumptions in foreign countries, estimates and actual results may differ. Thus, when a foreign project is completed, the firm should perform a post-audit on the entire project to determine its success or failure. The results of post-audits enable the firm to compare the actual performance of a foreign project with established standards. If the capital budgeting process used by an MNC has been successful, the system is likely to be reinforced. If the system has been unsatisfactory, it is likely to be revised or replaced for future foreign projects.

Example 14.1

In September 2018, the government of Jordan requested that the International TV Corporation establish a plant in Jordan to assemble television sets. The company wishes to invest 1,500 Jordanian dinars in the proposed plant in return for an increase in tariffs against other companies in the industry. The JD1,500 will be financed with only common stock, all of which will be owned by the parent company. The plant is to be depreciated over a 5-year period on a straight-line basis for tax purposes. It is expected to have a salvage value of JD750 at the end of 5 years. The company will pay income taxes at 20 percent on net income earned in Jordan and no withholding taxes on dividends repatriated. In this case, the United States also has a 50 percent tax rate with direct credit for Jordanian taxes. This means that net income earned in Jordan by US companies will be subject to a total of 50 percent tax. Expected revenues, operating costs, and applicable exchange rates are given in Tables 14.1–14.3. There is no restriction on dividend repatriation, but depreciation cash flows may not be repatriated until the company is liquidated. These cash flows can be reinvested in Jordanian government bonds to earn tax-exempt interest at the rate of 8 percent. The company's cost of capital is 15 percent.

Table 14.1 shows the projected cash flows for the proposed plant. It is important to recognize that for the first year a total tax of 50 percent (JD225) will be levied: 20 percent in Jordanian tax (JD90) and 30 percent in US tax (JD135).

Table 14.2 shows the depreciation cash flows and interest-compounded depreciation cash flows at the termination of the project at the end of 5 years. Thus, a total of JD880 will be repatriated to the United States along with the plant's fifth-year earnings of JD375 at the end of 5 years.

The last two steps in the analysis are: (1) to convert the cash flows from dinars to dollars and (2) to determine the net present value of the plant. Table 14.3 shows these two computation steps. It should be noted that the fifth-year cash flow of JD2,005 consists

Table 14.1   Projected earnings after taxes for the proposed project.

	Year 1	Year 2	Year 3	Year 4	Year 5
Revenues	JD1,500	JD1,650	JD1,800	JD1,950	JD2,100
Operating costs	900	900	1,050	1,050	1,200
Depreciation	150	150	150	150	150
Taxable income	JD450	JD600	JD600	JD750	JD750
Total tax at 50%	225	300	300	375	375
Earnings after tax	JD225	JD300	JD300	JD375	JD375

Table 14.2   Depreciation cash flows.

Year	Depreciation	Interest Factor at 8%	Terminal Value Year 5
1	JD150	1.360	JD204
2	150	1.260	189
3	150	1.166	175
4	150	1.080	162
5	150	1.000	150
			JD880

Table 14.3   The parent's net present value.

Year	Cash Flows	Exchange Rate	Cash Flows	Present Value at 15%	Cum. Net Pres. Value
0	−JD1,500	5.00	−$300	−$300	−$300
1	225	5.00	45	39	−261
2	300	5.25	57	43	−218
3	300	5.51	54	36	−182
4	375	5.79	65	37	−145
5	2,005	6.08	330	164	19

of dividends (JD375), the estimated salvage value of the plant (JD750), and the interest-accumulated depreciation cash flows (JD880).

The current exchange rate of five dinars to the dollar is expected to hold during the first year. However, the dinar is expected to depreciate at a rate of 5 percent per year after the first year. The expected cash flows in dollars are obtained by dividing the cash flows in dinars by the exchange rates. The dollar cash flows are then discounted at the firm's cost of capital (15 percent) to arrive at a present value figure for each year. Cumulative net present values are the final amounts given in Table 14.3. We see that from the parent's point of view, the plant would break even on a discounted cash flow basis during the fifth year. Because the net present value of the project is positive ($19), the International TV Corporation should accept the proposed plant in order to maximize the market value of the company. The project's internal rate of return is approximately 17 percent. Because the internal rate of return (17 percent) is greater than the cost of capital (15 percent), the internal rate of return criterion also indicates acceptance.

14.2.10. *Real Option Analysis*

The literature on capital investment analysis pays insufficient attention to the possibility of future options over an investment project. Ordinarily, an investment project is evaluated as though a company were committed to the project over its entire economic life. However, it may be more profitable to expand or retire an investment project before the end of its estimated economic life rather than continue its operation. When investment proposals are originally considered, key financial variables are identified and assumptions are made in order to arrive at a choice. As time passes, some unforeseen problems can occur and they could affect these key variables. Initial assumptions may turn out to be incorrect, or perhaps some additional investment opportunities may arise.

Real option analysis is the application of option pricing models to the evaluation of investment options in real projects. Option pricing models work best for simple options on financial assets, such as stocks, interest rates, currencies or commodities, but they are also useful for foreign investment analysis because a key variable faced by every foreign project is uncertainty. Currency, political, and cultural risks are the most prominent additional risks in foreign investment. Additionally, business risk on foreign projects is higher than that of domestic projects. When uncertainty is high, an MNC's investment opportunities can be viewed as real options. Real options include: (1) options to expand or contract; (2) options to accelerate or delay; (3) options to continue or retire.[6]

14.3. PORTFOLIO THEORY

In the real world, practically no company or individual invests everything in a single project. Thus, it is useful to consider the risk and return of a particular project in conjunction with its counterparts in existing assets or new investment opportunities. **Portfolio theory** deals with the selection of investment projects that would minimize risk for a given rate of return or that would maximize the rate of return for a given degree of risk. Such a portfolio is sometimes called the optimum portfolio.

Markowitz and Sharpe developed a powerful technique for a simultaneous risk–return analysis of multiple projects. Although the technique was applied first for the selection of portfolios of common stocks, it is also applicable to the evaluation of capital investment projects. This approach employs two basic measures: an index of expected value and an index of risk. The expected value for a portfolio of investments is simply the sum of the individual present values for the projects that make up the portfolio. The standard deviation as a measure of risk for the portfolio, however, is not so easily measured. There are many business situations where the risks of individual projects tend to offset each other. Thus, successful diversification makes it possible for the company to have the risk of a portfolio less than the sum of the risks of the individual projects.

Example 14.2

A company has two proposed projects in an isolated Caribbean island whose major industry is tourism: (A) build a suntan lotion factory and (B) build a disposable umbrella factory. Project A's sales, earnings, and cash flows are highest in sunny years. Contrary to Project A, Project B's sales, earnings, and cash flows are highest in rainy years. Project A has a cost of $800, while Project B has a cost of $1,000. These two projects are mutually independent and their possible net cash flows at the end of 1 year are given in Table 14.4. Assume that the cost of capital is 5 percent.

---

[6]Butler, K. C., *Multinational Finance,* 3rd Edition, Mason, Ohio: Thomson/South-Western, 2016, Chapter 18.

Table 14.4   Net cash flows under different weather conditions.

		Net Cash Flows	
Weather Condition	Probability	Project A	Project B
Sunny year	0.50	$2,000	$0
Rainy year	0.50	0	2,000

Because the expected net cash flow for each project is $1,000 ($2,000 × 0.5 + $0 × 0.5), their net present values (NPVs) are computed as follows:

$$\text{NPV}_\text{A} = \frac{\$1,000}{(1.05)^1}\$800 = \$152$$

$$\text{NPV}_\text{B} = \frac{\$1,000}{(1.05)^1} - \$1,000 = -\$48$$

The standard deviation of a project (σ) is computed as follows:

$$\sigma = \sqrt{\sum_{i=1}^{n}(R_i - R)^2 P_i} \tag{14.1}$$

where R_i = net cash flow associated with the ith event (i.e., a particular weather condition such as a sunny summer or a rainy summer), R = expected net cash flow, and P_i = probability of the ith event. Thus, the standard deviations of Projects A and B can be obtained as follows:

$$\sigma_\text{A} = \sqrt{(\$2,000 - \$1,000)^2(0.50) + (\$0 - \$1,000)^2(0.50)} = \$1,000$$

$$\sigma_\text{B} = \sqrt{(\$0 - \$1,000)^2(0.50) + (\$2,000 - \$1,000)^2(0.50)} = \$1,000$$

Project A has a net present value of $152 and Project B has a net present value of −$48. Both projects have an equal standard deviation of $1,000. Project B would have no chance to be accepted because its expected net present value is negative. Project A has a positive net present value of $152, but most investors are likely to reject the project because its risk is too high.

We can completely eliminate unsystematic risk by combining these two projects, because the unsystematic risks of individual projects tend to offset each other. Whether you have a sunny year or a rainy year, the expected net cash flow of this combination is $2,000 and their combined net present value is $104 ($152 – $48). The standard deviation of this two-project portfolio is zero (0) because the portfolio always produces a net present value of $104. When we consider Projects A and B separately, both projects are clearly undesirable. However, when we treat them as a portfolio, we find the portfolio acceptable.

Total risk elimination is possible in Example 14.2 because there is a perfect negative relation between the returns on Projects A and B. In practice, such a perfect relation is rare. The returns on most domestic projects are highly interrelated with each other because they depend on the same state of economy. However, the returns on foreign projects and domestic projects are less interrelated with each other because they depend on different states of economy. As a result, international diversification is more effective than domestic diversification.

14.4. CAPITAL BUDGETING THEORY AND PRACTICE

14.4.1. *Project Evaluation Techniques*

Many methods have been developed to guide management in acceptance or rejection of proposed investment projects. The five most commonly used methods are payback period, average rate of return, net present value, profitability index, and internal rate of return. Because the first two methods do not consider the time value of money, they are frequently called unsophisticated methods. The last three methods are termed discounted cash-flow approaches, which consider the time value of money. Each of these five methods is defined as follows:

1. **Payback.** The payback period is the number of years required to recover the original cost (present value of the net investment) of a project by its net cash flows.
2. **Average rate of return.** This rate is the ratio of the average annual net cash flows to the average net investment.
3. **Net present value.** This value is the present value of the net cash flows minus the present value of the net investment.
4. **Profitability index.** This index is the present value of the net cash flows divided by the present value of the net investment.
5. **Internal rate of return.** This rate is the discount rate that equates the present value of the net cash flows to the present value of the net investment.

The literature on foreign capital investment theory reveals that business firms should use discounted cash-flow techniques for ranking and selecting overseas projects because these methods recognize the time value of money and employ cash flows of a project over its life span. These empirical studies revealed two important points: first, discounted cash-flow approaches are more popular than rules of thumb; second, internal rate of return is more popular than net present value. Thus, most MNCs use discounted cash-flow approaches for ranking and selecting overseas projects.[7]

14.4.2. *Company Goals*

Most leading finance textbooks now agree with Anthony and Donaldson that a firm, first of all, should maximize the wealth of stockholders.[8] The best measure of stockholder wealth is the market value of a firm's stock because the market value reflects the effects of all financial decisions. The financial decisions made by the managers of a firm determine the level of its stock price by affecting the riskiness and size of its earnings. In other words, the maximization of stockholder wealth depends on the tradeoff between risk and return. These relationships are diagrammed in Fig. 14.2. Although practically all financial decisions involve such risk–return tradeoffs, this model is particularly important for capital budgeting

---

[7]Kim, S. H. and G. Ulferts, "A Summary of Multinational Capital Budgeting Practices," *Managerial Finance*, Spring 1996, pp. 75–85.

[8]Anthony, R. N., "The Trouble with Profit Maximization," *Harvard Business Review*, November–December 1960, pp. 126–134; and Donaldson, G., "Financial Goals: Management vs. Stockholders," *Harvard Business Review*, May–June, 1963, pp. 116–129.

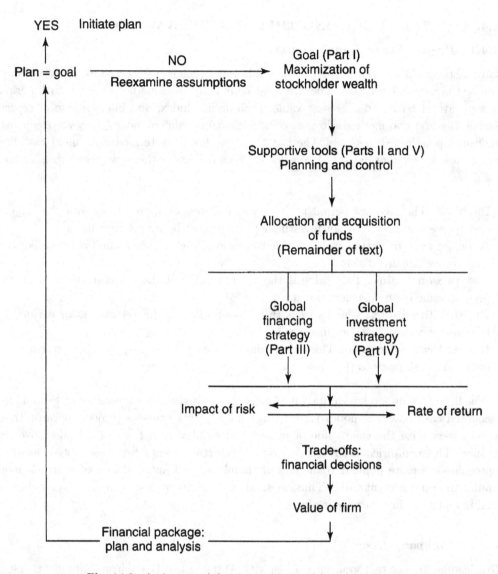

Fig. 14.2 An integrated decision-making model in global finance.

decisions because capital investments are profitable, but they are subject to a variety of risks.

Investments decisions — usually requiring very large sums of money — are made in expectation of benefits over an extended period. Once capital budgeting decisions have been made, they are extremely costly to reverse. Most used plant and equipment have a limited market. In certain areas, production methods are rapidly outmoded by increasingly higher levels of technology. Moreover, most financial variables used in the analysis of capital expenditures are not accurately known in advance. Because investors and business executives are risk averters, efficient management of capital expenditures has become essential for healthy company growth.

In other words, more sophisticated capital budgeting techniques may be economically justified only if they increase the total value of a firm. Academic writers favor "sophisticated" capital budgeting techniques (e.g., the net present value method) over rules of thumb (e.g., the payback method). They argue that use of sophisticated methods will lead to higher earnings and less risk, thereby increasing the market price of the common stock. Thus, it seems reasonable to suspect that a significant relationship exists between stock prices and capital budgeting practices. The hypothesis may be stated in the following way: firms using a more sophisticated capital budgeting system enjoy higher stock prices than do firms using a less sophisticated capital budgeting system.

Risk and performance measures based on the firm's common stock market values are better than risk and performance measures based on any other criterion. However, most writers on capital budgeting reject this view on the grounds that shareholders know little about corporate capital budgeting practices. Therefore, previous research studies have determined firm risk and performance measures from accounting data. To investigate the changes and effects of capital budgeting practices on risk and return, we can examine the results of capital budgeting studies to test the following two hypotheses:

1. Firms using a more sophisticated capital budgeting system have greater profitability than firms using a less sophisticated system.
2. Firm using a more sophisticated capital budgeting system are less risky than firms using a less sophisticated system.

Our literature review indicated that only a handful of empirical studies had tested these two hypotheses. Some tested these two hypotheses for domestic investment projects, but these studies found no significant relationship between budgeting practices and risk or return. We found only one such study for foreign investment projects. The study of the 121 respondents by Stanley and Block revealed a strong interest in stockholder wealth maximization as the primary goal of the firm.[9] In explaining why firms in their study might choose one capital budgeting method over another, the factors of firm size, corporate goals, beta coefficients (systematic risk), and foreign sales as percent of total sales were used to test for significant relationships. However, their study failed to establish any significant relationship between capital budgeting practices and earnings performance (stockholder wealth maximization) or risk (beta coefficients). Stanley and Block, like other researchers, narrowly defined capital budgeting practices as the use or non-use of specific capital budgeting methods, such as payback or internal rate of return.

14.5. MOTIVES FOR CROSS-BORDER MERGERS AND ACQUISITIONS

A company's acquisition of another firm is economically justified only if it increases the total value of a firm. The traditional approach to the valuation of the firm consists of four basic steps:

---

[9]Stanley, M. T. and S. B. Block, "A Survey of Multinational Capital Budgeting," *Financial Review*, Spring 1984, pp. 38–43.

1. Determine the earnings after taxes the company expects to produce over the years or earnings before taxes multiplied by (1 − tax rate).
2. Determine the capitalization rate (discount rate) for these earnings.
3. Determine the extent to which the company may be leveraged or the adequate amount of debt.
4. Compute the total value of the firm from the following formula:

$$\text{Value of firm} = \frac{\text{Earnings before taxes } (1 - \text{tax rate})}{\text{Capitalization rate}} \tag{14.2}$$

One can examine the effect of a merger on each of the factors that affect the total value of the firm.

14.5.1. *Earnings Before Taxes*

A merger itself creates a larger physical size and opportunities for a synergistic effect. The **synergistic effects** of business mergers are certain economies of scale from the firm's lower overhead. The merger allows the firm to acquire necessary management skills and to spread existing management skills over a larger operation. There are also opportunities to eliminate duplicate facilities and to consolidate the functions of production, marketing, and purchasing. Finally, the merger enables the firm to enjoy greater access to financial markets and thus to raise debt and equity at a lower cost of capital. These types of better management, operating economies, and financial economies can increase the profit margin and reduce risks as well.

Example 14.3

Assume that Buyco Corporation with a 10 percent cost of capital is analyzing the acquisition of the Sellco Corporation for $1 million. Sellco has expected net cash flows (earnings after taxes plus depreciation) of $100,000 per year indefinitely. Furthermore, the synergistic effect of the merger (in this case, combining production facilities) will add $20,000 per year to net cash flow indefinitely.

The present value of net cash flows from this merger is $1.2 million [($100,000 + $20,000)/0.10]. As a result, the acquisition appears to represent a desirable alternative for the expenditure of cash with a positive value of $200,000 ($1,200,000 − $1,000,000).

A company is often able to improve its risk–return performance through international acquisition rather than through domestic acquisition. The key element here is the correlation coefficient between acquired firms and an acquiring firm. When firms with low degrees of correlation are combined with each other, the acquiring firm is able to reduce its risk of expected return. Companies from different countries tend to be less correlated with each other than domestic companies are. For example, the economic cycles of different countries do not tend to be totally synchronized. On the other hand, most domestic companies tend to be highly correlated with each other because they depend on the same state of economy.

14.5.2. *Tax Considerations*

The tax benefit for mergers comes from the fact that the tax loss carryforward expires at the end of a certain number of years unless the firm makes sufficient profits to offset it completely.

Table 14.5 Effects of tax loss carryforward.

	Year 1	Year 2	Year 3	Total Values
Company A without Merger				
Earnings before taxes	$100,000	$100,000	$100,000	$300,000
Taxes (40%)	$40,000	$40,000	$40,000	$120,000
Earnings after taxes	$60,000	$60,000	$60,000	$180,000
Company A with Merger				
Earnings before taxes	$100,000	$100,000	$100,000	$300,000
Tax loss carryforward	$100,000	$100,000	$20,000	$220,000
Earnings before tax	0	0	$80,000	$80,000
Taxes (40%)	0	0	$32,000	$32,000
Earnings after taxes	$100,000	$100,000	$68,000	$268,000

There are two situations where mergers could actually avoid corporate income taxes. First, when a profitable company acquires companies with a large tax loss carryforward, it can reduce its effective tax rate and consequently increase its net operating income after taxes. Second, a company with a tax loss carryforward may acquire profitable companies in order to use its carryforward.

Example 14.4

In this example, we assume all losses can be carried forward. Company A acquires company B, which has a $220,000 tax loss-carry forward. Company A with a tax rate of 40 percent expects to earn $100,000 a year for the next 3 years.

As shown in Table 14.5, the tax shield value of a carryforward is equal to the loss involved times the tax rate ($220,000 × 0.40 = $88,000). Based on the carryforward, company A can reduce its total taxes from $120,000 to $32,000 and thus it could pay $88,000 for the carryforward alone (this is on a nondiscount basis). Earnings after taxes also have gone up by $88,000 ($268,000 − $180,000). Obviously, company B's anticipated operating gains and losses for future years must also be considered in analyzing the deal.

Accounting and tax laws may create even more competitive advantages for acquiring firms in some countries. If the acquiring company pays more than the net worth of the acquired company, the excess is treated as goodwill. Goodwill write-offs are not deductible for federal income taxes in some countries. This accounting treatment results in lower reported earnings for several years. However, in most industrialized countries, goodwill does not affect the acquiring company's earnings. Thus, foreign companies with more favorable accounting and tax laws may be able to bid higher prices for target companies.

Example 14.5

Suppose that company C and firm D try to acquire Echo Corporation with a $4 million book value (net worth) for $6 million. Company C is located in a country where goodwill write-offs are not deductible for income taxes, but firm D is located in a country where companies are allowed to deduct goodwill amortization for tax purposes. The tax rate of 40 percent is the same for company C and firm D.

Because a company can acquire a firm with $4 million book value for $6 million, $2 million of goodwill is created on the books of the acquiring company. If it must be written off over a maximum period of 10 years, this would cause a $200,000-per-year reduction in reported earnings ($2 million/10 years). Because the write-offs of goodwill are not tax deductible expenses for company C, the company suffers the full amount of the deduction without any tax relief. On the other hand, firm D would realize $800,000 in real cash savings ($2,000,000 × 0.40) over 10 years because firm D is allowed to deduct goodwill amortization for tax purposes. Hence, the firm could pay $800,000 more due to this goodwill tax advantage alone.

14.5.3. *Capitalization Rate*

An important advantage of mergers is the fact that earnings of larger companies are capitalized at lower rates. The securities of larger companies have better marketability than those of smaller companies. Larger companies are also better known among investors. An acquiring company can develop these factors, which lead to lower required rates of return and higher price-earnings ratios. Consequently, the value of the acquiring firm exceeds the values of the companies operating separately.

A potential benefit of international acquisition is the lower required rate of return for the acquiring company. The required rate of return varies among countries because the cost of capital is different from country to country. As a result, companies in some countries may find acquisitions more attractive than companies in other countries.

14.5.4. *Debt Capacity*

The appropriate mix of debt and equity reduces the overall cost of capital and thus raises the market value of the firm. There are two situations where a merger can raise the debt capacity for the acquiring company above the sum of debt capacities for the individual firms prior to the merger. First, there are companies that fail to make optimum use of debt. Second, it is frequently possible for the acquiring company to borrow more than the companies were able to borrow individually.

Companies normally finance a portion of international acquisitions with borrowed funds. Companies in some countries have more flexibility to borrow, because investors and creditors in these countries are more receptive to higher debt ratios. The debt ratio for most companies in Denmark, Finland, Norway, and Sweden, for example, is higher than the comparable debt ratio for American companies. In other words, companies in Scandinavian countries have more flexibility to borrow than US companies. Thus, US companies may be more successful in international acquisitions because they can borrow in countries where higher degrees of financial leverage are tolerated than in the United States.

Example 14.6

Suppose that the cost of debt (6 percent), the cost of equity (10 percent), the tax rate (50 percent), and annual earnings after taxes ($10,000) are the same for company X and firm Y. Company X's optimal capital structure is 20 percent debt and 80 percent equity. Firm Y is a multinational company and thus enjoys a higher debt ratio of 60 percent without additional risk. Compare the cost of capital for these two companies and their market value.

The weighted average costs of capital are 8.6 percent $[(0.20 \times 0.06)(1 - 0.50) + (0.80 \times 0.10)]$ for company X and 5.8 percent $[(0.60 \times 0.06)(1 - 0.50) + (0.40 \times 0.10)]$ for firm Y. Market values are $116,279 for company X ($10,000/0.086) and $172,414 for firm Y

($10,000/0.058). The multinational firm enjoys a lower cost of capital, a higher market value, and a higher share price because it has greater borrowing capacity. As cheaper debt is added to the capital structure, the cost of capital falls. This increases the value of the firm. Because this increase in the firm's value accrues to the owners of the firm, the price of the firm's stock rises.

14.5.5. *Other Considerations*

A variety of other factors affect international acquisitions: exchange rate movements, country barriers, and strategic choices, among others.

The ideal time for Japanese investors to buy a US company is when the spot rate of the US dollar is perceived to be very low and is expected to appreciate over time. Several studies confirmed that international acquisitions, in fact, are influenced by exchange rate movements. A study by Rohatyn, for example, found that the combination of a relatively weak dollar and a strong Japanese stock market in the late 1980s encouraged Japanese acquisitions of US firms.[10,11]

Many country governments impose explicit and implicit barriers to foreign acquisitions of their domestic companies. These barriers prevent or discourage international acquisitions rather than offer advantages to specific acquiring companies. All countries have one or more agencies that monitor mergers and acquisitions, but they vary among countries. International acquisitions are tolerated more in the United States than in Japan. Consequently, it is much easier for Japanese investors to purchase a US firm than for US investors to purchase a Japanese firm.

To achieve corporate growth, companies these days view the world as a total business community. They consider international acquisitions as a viable alternative for achieving a corporate growth strategy. Newman suggested that a growth-oriented company can globally close four types of growth gaps between its sales potential and its current actual performance. A product-line gap can be closed by introducing improved or new products.[12,13] A distribution gap may be reduced by expanding an existing distribution network. A usage gap is reduced by inducing current nonusers. A competitive gap can be closed by making inroads into the market position of direct competitors. These strategic choices encourage companies to engage in international acquisitions.

14.6. POLITICAL RISK MANAGEMENT

Foreign investment decisions must be made today based on the likely political climate for many years to come. **Political risk** is an assessment of economic opportunity against political odds. Thus, political risk assessment requires that MNCs evaluate both economic and

---

[10]Kelly, M. E. and G. Philippatos, "Comparative Analysis of the Foreign Investment Evaluation Practices by US-Based Manufacturing Multinational Companies," *Journal of International Business Studies*, Winter 1982, pp. 19–42.

[11]Rohatyn, F., "American Economic Dependence," *Foreign Affairs*, Winter 1989, pp. 53–65.

[12]Goddard, S., "Political Risk in International Capital Budgeting," in *The International Financial Reader*, ed. Robert W. Kolb, Boulder, CO: Kolb Publishing Co., 1991, pp. 357–362.

[13]Newman, L. H., in BenDaniel, D. J. eds., *The Handbook of International Mergers and Acquisitions*, Englewood Cliffs, N.J: Prentice Hall, 1990, pp. 1–24.

political indicators. Political risk management refers to steps taken by companies to protect against economic losses from unexpected political events.

When the goals of MNCs and their host countries conflict, MNCs face a variety of political risks. The primary goal of an MNC is to maximize the wealth of its stockholders. On the other hand, most host countries desire to develop their economy through greater utilization of local factors of production in order to maintain more control over key industries through less reliance on foreign capital and know-how, and to strengthen their international position through less imports and more exports.

Multinational investors should understand the forces at work when political uncertainty occurs, so that they can forecast future business climates, establish appropriate objectives, and take precautionary measures when necessary. In this chapter, we discuss the nature of political risks, types of political risks, political risk forecasting, and responses to political risks.

14.6.1. *Nature of Political Risks*

Traditionally, conflicts between MNCs and host countries have occurred over such issues as conversion of an economy to the style of a specific political system, joint ventures, control of key industries, contribution to balance of payments, national sovereignty, and economic development. Such conflicts are not limited to developing countries. More subtle, yet very real, conflicts exist between MNCs and developed countries.

It is frequently difficult to separate political and economic risks. While government decisions are political by definition, underlying forces behind the decisions may be purely economic. For example, funds to nonresidents may be blocked because of an unexpected shortage of foreign exchange or a long-run deficiency of the foreign exchange instead of certain types of domestic political pressures. Some government decisions are partly political and partly economic. The United Nations imposed economic sanctions against Iraq in the Fall of 1990 because of Iraq's invasion of Kuwait. The Organization of American States imposed economic sanctions against Haiti in 1994 because of Haiti's human rights violations. Finally, the United States and several Western countries have imposed a variety of economic sanctions against Afghanistan, Cuba, Iran, Libya, and North Korea for many years.

Countrywide political risks depend on three broad groups of variables: political climate, economic climate, and foreign relations. The political climate may be measured by tendencies toward subversion, rebellion, or political turmoil. Multinational investors should consider such factors as levels of political violence, the existence of extreme tendencies among political parties, and recurring governmental crises.

Investment analysts should make an overall assessment of the economic climate to protect foreign investment from political risks. Relevant economic factors include the likelihood of government intervention in the economy, levels of interest and inflation rates, persistent balance-of-payments deficits, levels of foreign debts, and worsening monetary reserves.

Finally, multinational investors should determine the extent to which host countries manifest hostility toward other countries. Important factors here are incidence of conflict with their neighbors, evidence of an arms race, and sizes of defense budgets.

Table 14.6 Types of political risk and their importance.

United States		United Kingdom	
Rank	Variable	Rank	Variable
1	Restrictions on remittances	1	Expropriation or nationalization
2	Operational restrictions on ownership, employment, and market shares	2	Political stability within the country
3	Expropriation or nationalization	3	Restrictions on remittances of dividends and royalties
4	Discrimination	4	Currency stability
5	Breaches in agreements	5	Tax changes
6	Others	6	Exchange controls

Source: Goddard, "Political Risk in International Capital Budgeting," in Kolb, R. K. ed., *The International Financial Reader*, Miami: Kolb Publishing Co., 1991, p. 360.

14.6.2. *Types of Political Risks*

Empirical studies have revealed some interesting findings about the attitudes of US and UK MNCs toward political risk. Kelly and Philippatos surveyed 67 US companies to obtain the perceived importance of five variables in political risk.[10] Goddard surveyed 51 UK companies to determine the importance of six variables in political risk.[12] Ranked in the descending order of importance, their findings appear in Table 14.6. Although there are several different types of political risk, these risks can be divided into two broad categories for all practical purposes: actions that restrict the freedom of a foreign company to operate in a given host environment, and actions that result in the takeover of alien assets.

14.6.2.1. *Operational restrictions*

Actions that restrict the freedom of a foreign company include operational restrictions such as employment policies; locally shared ownership; loss of transfer freedom; exchange controls; financial, personal, or ownership rights; breaches or unilateral revisions in contracts and agreements; discrimination through taxes or compulsory joint ventures; and damage to property or personnel from riots, revolutions, and wars.

Funds are usually blocked in the host country when operational restrictions are imposed. There are a number of ways to remove blocked funds. The most obvious way is to arrange swaps between corporations. Here each corporation lends to the other in the country where its own funds are restricted. Other methods include transfer price adjustments and other adjustments such as fees, royalties, and loan repayments. Of course, most of these methods raise some serious ethical and legal questions. Moreover, black market operations may not be available for relatively large transfers of money and highly visible transactions, such as an attempt to terminate company operations in a small, developing country.

14.6.2.2. *Expropriation*

Expropriation includes sales of business assets to local shareholders, compulsory sales of business assets to local and federal government units, and confiscation of business assets with or without compensation.

Ball and McCulloch say that many governments nationalize both foreign and domestic companies and may do so for a number of reasons[14]:

1. The government believes that it could run the business more efficiently.
2. The government believes that the company is concealing its profits.
3. Left-wing governments, oftentimes after being elected, nationalize business firms.
4. Politicians wish to win popular support as they save jobs by putting dying industries on a life support system.
5. The government can control a company or industry by pumping money into the company or industry.

Business operations in foreign countries are subject to the power of host countries. It is customary to seize foreign assets for a public purpose without discrimination and with adequate compensation. Although these three rules are in accordance with traditional principles of international law, they have often been ignored by some developing countries.

Kennedy analyzed 79 countries in terms of political regimes and their expropriation policies. This study revealed that during the 1960–1987 period, these 79 developing countries nationalized 1,118 foreign companies in 599 separate actions. The overwhelming majority of expropriations were politically motivated acts that had been undertaken by only a few governments. In fact, only 28 governments out of more than the 300 total accounted for two-thirds of all acts of expropriation.[15]

Figure 14.3 shows expropriation trends from 1960 to 1987. We could divide relations between MNCs and host governments into three eras: MNC domination (1945–early 1960s), MNC-host government confrontation (mid-1960–1980), and MNC-host government realignment (1980s). The history of expropriation activity by less developed countries tracks these three periods quite well. By the mid-1960s, the number of expropriation acts rose significantly, but the forced divestment of foreign direct investment was most pronounced in the 1970–1979 period. In the 1980s, the number of expropriation acts dropped dramatically.

14.6.3. *Forecasting Political Risks*

Once a manager has examined political risks and their implications, the manager shifts her attention to forecasting these risks in foreign countries where her company has business interests. As MNCs have become more experienced and more diversified, they maintain political forecasting staffs on the same level as economic forecasting staffs.

In political risk analysis, a manager gives special attention to the "nationalism" of a host country. Nationalism represents loyalty to one's country and pride in it based on shared common features such as race, language, religion, or ideology. In other words, it is an emotion that can hinder or prevent rational dealings with foreigners. Some effects of nationalism on MNCs are: (1) requirements for minimum local ownership, (2) reservation of certain

---

[14]Ball, D. A. and W. H. McCulloch, *International Business*, Homewood, IL.: McGraw-Hill, 1999, pp. 306–307.
[15]Kennedy, C. R., "Multinational Corporations and Expropriation Risk," *Multinational Business Review*, Spring 1993, pp. 44–55.

Frequency of expropriations

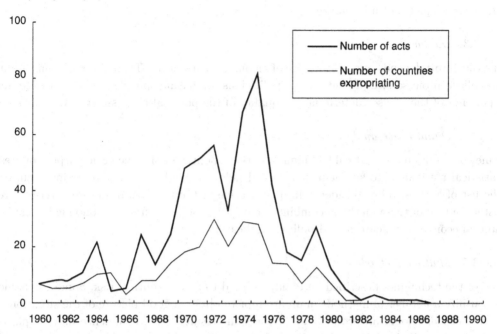

Fig. 14.3 Expropriation acts, by year.

Source: C.R. Kennedy, "Multinational Corporations and Expropriation Risk", *Multinational Business Review*, Spring 1993, p. 45.

industries for local companies, (3) preference of local suppliers for government contracts, (4) limitations on number and type of foreign employees, (5) protectionism based on quotas and tariffs, and (6) expropriation or confiscation of assets.

A number of political-risk assessment techniques are available to MNCs. Some popular techniques include the Delphi technique, the grand tour, the old hand, and quantitative analysis.

14.6.3.1. *Delphi technique*

The **Delphi technique** combines the views of independent experts in order to obtain the degree of political risk on a given foreign project or a particular foreign country. The opinions of these experts about political risk are collected and averaged. One advantage of this method is that political-risk assessment is made easily and quickly. However, its major disadvantage is that it is completely based on opinions rather than facts and analyses.

14.6.3.2. *Grand tour*

The **grand tour** relies on the opinions of company executives visiting the country where investment is being considered. Their visit usually involves a series of meetings with government officials, local businesspeople, and potential customers. This method places responsibility for political-risk assessment in the hands of those who must carry out the proposed investment project. But the results of such a visit can be very superficial and may produce only selected pieces of information.

14.6.3.3. *Old hand*

The **old hand** depends upon the advice of an outside consultant. Typically, such consultants are college professors, diplomats, local politicians, or businesspeople. The knowledge and experience of the advisor determine the quality of the political-risk assessment.

14.6.3.4. *Quantitative analysis*

Some companies use statistical techniques to assess political risk. The basic purpose of these statistical methods is to supplement personal judgment and increase forecasting accuracy. The list of factors to be considered in quantitative methods varies from forecaster to fore-caster. But all of these methods combine three major factors: external economic indicators, internal economic indicators, and political indicators.

14.6.3.5. *Multiple methods*

Any of the techniques described here may be used to assess political risk. Some companies may utilize a number of methods in an attempt to obtain a good picture of the situation. If these methods should all produce about the same results, more confidence may be placed in the findings. If they give widely divergent results, a more careful investigation is needed. Because political-risk assessment is extremely important for success or failure of a project, the multiple-method approach appears to be a sound policy.

14.6.4. *Responses to Political Risks*

Forecasting political risk is critical to an MNC in deciding on a particular project. The MNC can protect itself against political risks with government insurance policies and guarantee programs.

14.6.4.1. *Defensive measures before investment*

There are three types of defensive measures before investment: concession agreements, planned divestment, and adaptation to host-country goals.

Many host countries have recently increased their surveillance of foreign operations within their borders. An MNC ought to negotiate concession agreements to minimize subsequent political risks. The concession agreement spells out contractual obligations of the foreign investor and the host government. Careful negotiations may result in contracts that address such critical issues as provision for arbitration of disputes, funds remittances, transfer prices, local equity participation, method of taxation, price controls, the right to exports, and limitations on nationality of personnel.

Planned divestment has been frequently suggested as one of the most important preinvestment strategies in order to avoid subsequent operational restrictions and expropriations. **Planned divestment** provides for the sale of majority ownership in foreign affiliates to local nationals during a previously agreed-upon period of time. Planned divestment is often a necessary condition for entry into foreign markets, or it may be imposed on already existing companies.

The concession agreement specifies rights and responsibilities of both the foreign company and the host country, but it is often revised to adapt to changing host-country priorities. When the foreign company sticks to the legal interpretation of its concession agreement, the host-country government uses pressures in areas not covered by the agreement. If these pressures do not work, the host-country government reinterprets the agreement to obtain changes from the foreign company. Thus, it is advisable for MNCs to voluntarily adapt to changing host-country priorities whenever possible.

14.6.4.2. *Defensive measures after investment*

Once managers decide to invest and take preinvestment defensive measures, they can use several operating strategies to cope with political risks. We grouped them for convenience into two categories: strategies which are necessary to be a good citizen of the host country and strategies to alleviate political risks. In addition, joint ventures can be used to diffuse political risks.

Many foreign affiliates attempt to harmonize their policies with their host-country priorities and goals. They may hire an increasing number of local persons for positions initially held by representatives of the parent company management. They may share ownership with host-country private or public companies. They may develop and use local sources of supply for their raw materials and component requirements. They may try to export their products to bolster host-country reserves of foreign exchange.

Many operational policies and organizational approaches can be used to alleviate political risks. MNCs may maintain technological superiority over local companies and other competing foreign firms. The challenge here is to introduce into the host country technological improvements on a continuing basis. An MNC may integrate individual subsidiaries into a worldwide production and logistical system through highly interrelated international operations. Under such an integration, a subsidiary alone cannot operate or compete successfully, as is the case in the petroleum industry. Control of key patents and processes, joint-venture arrangements, capitalization with a thin equity base and a large local debt proportion, and control of key export markets for a subsidiary's products are examples of policy actions which can alleviate political risks.

Joint ventures with local partners have been frequently suggested as one answer to national demands for an ownership share in certain industries. A joint venture can improve the public image of a subsidiary, provide more capital, and deter operational restrictions. Joint ventures with investors from a number of different countries, such as the United States, Italy, and England, can make operational restrictions extremely costly because they could distress private investors in all three countries and thus impair good economic relations with these national groups of business executives.

14.7. SUMMARY

Once companies decide to enter new foreign markets, their next concern is how to enter the foreign market. Theory views the construction of new plants, mergers and acquisitions, joint ventures, equity alliances, licensing agreements, franchising agreements, and contract manufacturing as foreign-entry alternatives through investment. This chapter focused on two major foreign entry modes: the construction of new plants and the acquisition of foreign firms.

Although we broke down the entire decision-making process for foreign investment projects into components and relationships for a detailed inspection, these stages should not be used mechanically. Some steps may be combined, some may be subdivided, and others may be skipped altogether without jeopardizing the quality of the capital budgeting system. It is likely, however, that several of these steps will be in progress simultaneously for any project under consideration. For example, if expenditure controls and post-audits are not planned until the economic evaluation of a project is completed, the capital budgeting process will hardly be realistic. Decisions for expenditure controls and post audits affect plans, just as planning decisions affect controlling decisions. Thus, the capital budgeting process consists of several related activities that overlap continuously rather than following an ideally prescribed order. Because all steps in the capital investment decision-making process are interwoven, their relationships should not permanently place any one stage first or last in a sequence.

A company's acquisition of another firm is economically justified only if it increases the total value of a firm. Cross-border mergers and acquisitions tend to increase the total value of a firm because they enjoy higher earnings before taxes, lower overall taxes, lower capitalization rate, and larger debt capacity. Foreign investment projects involve many complex variables, which do not exist in domestic projects. Two major risks for foreign investment projects are political risk and foreign exchange risk. In Part II, we considered the nature of foreign exchange risk and some methods to reduce it. In the last part of this chapter, we described the nature of political risk and some techniques to minimize it. A company may incur losses from political risks because of governmental action, which interferes with the completion of contractual obligations between the foreign company and its host government. Political risks cannot be predicted in the same way as credit losses and thus cannot be offset precisely in measurable ways. Thus, MNCs must understand the types of political risks which they can expect to encounter, assess the likelihood of the encounter, and take various protective measures to minimize the risks.

14.8. KEY TERMS

foreign direct investment (FDI)	equity alliance
licensing agreement	franchising agreement
contract manufacturing	cost of capital
discounted cash-flow approaches	net present value
internal rate of return	hurdle rate
risk-adjusted discount rate	certainty equivalent approach
real option analysis	portfolio theory
payback	average rate of return
net present value	profitability index
internal rate of return	synergistic effects
political risk	expropriation
Delphi technique	grand tour
old hand	planned divestment

14.9. PROBLEMS

1. Assume that the American Electrical Corporation (AEC) is considering the establishment of a freezer manufacturing plant in Spain. AEC wants to invest a total of 10,000 Spanish pesetas in the proposed plant. The Pts10,000 will be financed with only common stock, all of which will be owned by the parent company. The plant is to be depreciated over a 5-year period on a straight-line basis for tax purposes. It is expected to have a salvage value of Pts5,000 at the end of 5 years. Spain has 35 percent corporate income tax and no withholding taxes on dividends paid. The United States has 50 percent corporate income tax with direct credit for Spanish taxes. Spain does not impose any restrictions on dividend repatriation, but it does not allow the parent company to repatriate depreciation cash flows until the plant is liquidated. These depreciation cash flows may be reinvested in Spanish government bonds to earn 8 percent tax-exempt interest. The cost of capital used to analyze the project is 15 percent. The current exchange rate of Pts5.00 per US dollar is expected to hold during year one, but the Spanish peseta is expected to depreciate thereafter at a rate of 5 percent a year. Assume the following revenues and operating costs in terms of Spanish pesetas:

	Year 1	Year 2	Year 3	Year 4	Year 5
Revenues	10,000	11,000	12,000	13,000	14,000
Operating costs	6,000	6,000	7,000	7,000	8,000

(a) Determine the projected earnings after taxes for the proposed plant.
(b) Determine the interest-compounded depreciation cash flows at the end of 5 years.
(c) Determine the net present value of the plant, the profitability index, and the internal rate of return for the plant in terms of the US dollar.

2. The Wayne Company currently exports 500 calculators per month to Jordan at a price of $60 and the variable cost per calculator is $40. In May 1990, the company was approached by the government of Jordan with a request that it establish a small manufacturing plant in Jordan. After a careful analysis, the company decided to make an equity investment of $1 million, half of which would represent working capital and the other half-fixed assets. The company would sell the plant to a local investor for the sum of $1 at the end of 5 years and the central bank of Jordan would repay the company for the working capital of $500,000. In return for an increase in tariffs against other companies, the Wayne Company is willing to sell its calculators in Jordan for $50 per unit. In addition, the company will have to buy certain raw materials from local suppliers and will have to use local managers. Total costs of local managers and materials would be $15 per calculator. Other materials would be purchased from the parent at $10 per unit and the parent would receive a direct contribution to overhead after variable costs of $5 per unit sold. Under this arrangement, the company expects that it can sell 1,000 calculators per month. The fixed assets are to be depreciated on a straight-line basis over a 5-year period. The company will have to pay income taxes at 50 percent on profits earned in Jordan. The United States also has a 50 percent tax rate with direct credit for Jordanian taxes. The current exchange rate is ten Jordanian dinars per dollar

and it is expected to stay the same for the next 5 years. There is no restriction on cash flow repatriation.

a. Determine the net present value of the project at 10 percent.

b. The Wayne Company has been informed that, if it decides to reject the project, it would lose its entire export sales. How does this affect the decision by the Wayne Company?

3. Problems 1 and 2 highlight the complexities involved in foreign investment decisions. Identify these problems.

4. A project with an initial cost of $15,000 is expected to produce net cash flows of $8,000, $9,000, $10,000, and $11,000 for each of the next 4 years. The firm's cost of capital is 12 percent, but the financial manager perceives the risk of this particular project to be much higher than 12 percent. The financial manager feels that a 20 percent discount rate would be appropriate for the project.

a. Compute the net present value of the project at the firm's cost of capital.

b. Compute the risk-adjusted net present value of the project.

5. A project has a cost of $1,400. Its net cash flows are expected to be $900, $1,000, and $1,400 for each of the next 3 years. The respective certainty equivalent coefficients are estimated to be 0.75, 0.55, and 0.35. With a six percent risk-free discount rate, determine the certain net present value.

6. Project F has a cost of $3,000 and Project G has a cost of $4,000. These two projects are mutually independent and their possible net cash flows are given below. Assume the cost of capital is 10 percent.

		Net Cash Flows	
Economic Condition	Probability	Project F	Project G
Boom	0.50	$8,000	0
Recession	0.50	0	8,000

a. Determine the net present value of Projects F and G.

b. Determine the standard deviation of Projects F and G.

c. Determine the portfolio net present value and the portfolio standard deviation.

d. Discuss the significance of the portfolio effect in terms of international context.

7. GM is analyzing the acquisition of a British company for $1 million. The British company has expected cash flows of $90,000 per year. The synergistic benefits of the merger will add $10,000 per year to cash flow. Finally, the British company has a $50,000 tax loss carryforward that can be used immediately by GM. GM is subject to a 40 percent tax rate and has a 10 percent cost of capital. Should GM acquire this British company?

8. The cost of debt (10 percent), the cost of equity (15 percent), the tax rate (50 percent), and annual earnings after taxes ($10,000) are the same for a domestic firm and a multinational company. The firm's target debt ratio (optimum capital structure) is 20 percent, while the company's target debt ratio is 50 percent.

a. Determine the weighted average costs of capital for these two enterprises.

b. Determine the market values of the two enterprises.

9. Assume that the worldwide profit breakdown for Ford is 85 percent in the United States, 5 percent in Japan, and 10 percent in the rest of the world. On the other hand, the worldwide profit breakdown for Toyota is 40 percent in Japan, 35 percent in the United States, and 25 percent in the rest of the world. Earnings per share are $5 in the United States, $8 in Japan, and $10 in the rest of the world for both companies.

   a. What are the weighted average earnings per share of Ford and Toyota?
   b. Which company is likely to have the international competitive advantage?

10. We assume that IBM is analyzing the acquisition of a privately held French company. The French company is more similar to Low Tech (LT) than any other company whose stock is traded in the public market. To establish a fair market price for the French company, IBM has compiled the statistics presented in the following table. Estimate the market value of the French company (FM) in the following three ways: (a) price-earnings ratio, (b) market value/book value, and (c) dividend growth model.

Variables	French Company	Low Tech
Earnings per share	$2.00	$4.00
Dividend per share in year 1	$1.50	$2.00
Annual dividend growth rate	0.04	0.04
Price per share	?	$40.00
Book value per share	$16.00	$20.00
Cost of equity	?	0.14
Number of shares outstanding	1 million	1.2 million

Closing Case 14: Multinational Capital Budgeting Practices

The literature on foreign capital investment theory reveals that business firms should use discounted cash-flow techniques for ranking and selecting overseas projects because these methods recognize the time value of money and employ cash flows of a project over its life span. Table 14.7 illustrates the extent to which discounted cash-flow methods were used by companies which were surveyed from 1980 to 1994. These empirical studies revealed two important points: first, discounted cash-flow approaches are more popular than rules of thumb; second, internal rate of return is more popular than net present value.

Table 14.7   Use of primary project evaluation techniques.

Method	(1980)	(1982)	(1984)	(1984)	(1994)
Payback (percent)	10	18	5	12	25
ARR	14	27	11	14	14
IRR	60	36	65	62	40
NPV	10	14	16	9	17
Others	6	5	3	3	4
Total (percent)	100	100	100	100	100

Thus, most MNCs use discounted cash-flow approaches for ranking and selecting overseas projects. The five studies cited in Table 14.7 show that at least half of the respondents used discounted cash-flow approaches, ranging from 50 percent according to Kelly's study to 81 percent in Stanley's study. Although findings vary in these surveys, their overriding implication suggests that discounted cash-flow approaches are unmistakably more popular than rules of thumb. In fact, the use of those techniques favored by academicians has become so commonplace in recent years that we do not need more empirical studies to confirm the adoption of discounted cash-flow techniques by most MNCs.

Results are not strictly comparable because terms like "exclusive", "most important", and "primary" used by these surveys are not synonymous. On the other hand, key characteristics for most of these surveys are so similar that our inferences are valid. The firms surveyed were drawn mostly from large industrial categories; sample sizes were relatively large; respondents and sample groups were surveyed by mail; and research methods were carefully adhered to. The respondents revealed that most companies use discounted cash flow approaches for foreign investment projects. With this fact established, it is reasonable to expect that firms using such sophisticated techniques as internal rate of return should make better investment decisions and thus perform better than firms using such unsophisticated techniques as payback.

Case Questions

1. What are the disadvantages of the payback method and the average-rate-of-return method?
2. What are the conditions under which the net-present-value and internal-rate-of-return methods will lead to the same capital-budgeting decision?
3. Why is the net-present-value method theoretically better than the internal-rate-of-return method?
4. Why is internal rate of return more popular than net present value in practice?
5. The web site of the Bank for International Settlements–www.bis.org/cbanks.htm–and the web site of the US State Department–www.state.gov–give economic information on most countries around the world. Access these web sites to obtain economic information, which can be used to assess the feasibility of projects in a developing country.

Source: Kim, S. H. and G. Ulferts, "A Summary of Multinational Capital Budgeting Practices," *Managerial Finance*, Spring 1996, pp. 75–85.

Chapter 15

CORPORATE PERFORMANCE OF FOREIGN OPERATIONS

Opening Case 15: SEC Enforcement Actions — FCPA Cases

Enforcement of the Foreign Corrupt Practices Act (FCPA) continues to be a high priority area for the Securities and Exchange Commission (SEC). In 2010, the SEC's Enforcement Division created a specialized unit to further enhance its enforcement of the FCPA, which prohibits companies issuing stock in the US from bribing foreign officials for government contracts and other business. Consequently, the SEC enforcement has increased the prominence of the FCPA from 2010 onwards. The SEC website shows a complete list of enforcement cases since 1978. Notable cases of the application of FCPA for 2022 and 2021 are as follows:

2022
- **ABB** — Switzerland-based global electrification and automation company was ordered to pay more than $147 million to resolve charges that it violated the anti-bribery, books and records, and internal accounting controls provisions of the FCPA in connection with a bribery scheme in South Africa; specifically, $75 million in a civil monetary penalty, $58 million in disgorgement and over $14.5 million in prejudgment interest. Payment of the penalty and prejudgment interest were deemed satisfied by an earlier payment of ill-gotten gain to the government of South Africa. (12/3/22)
- **Oracle Corporation** — The company agreed to pay more than $23 million to settle charges that it violated the anti-bribery, books and records, and internal accounting controls provisions of the FCPA in connection with violations at its subsidiaries in Turkey, the United Arab Emirates, and India. (9/27/22)
- **Gol Intelligent Airlines Inc.** — The second largest carrier in Brazil agreed to pay more than $160 million to the SEC, DOJ, and Brazilian authorities to resolve anti-bribery, books and records, internal accounting controls, and other related charges, for its involvement in a bribery scheme that a senior executive orchestrated. The US authorities waived all but $41.5 million due to its inability to pay. (9/15/22)
- **Tenaris** — A Luxembourg-based global manufacturer and supplier of steel pipe products, agreed to pay more than $78 million to resolve charges that it violated the anti-bribery, books and records, and internal accounting controls provisions of the FCPA in connection with a bribery scheme involving its Brazilian subsidiary. (6/2/22)

- **Stericycle, Inc.** — A leading provider of medical waste and other services agreed to pay more than $28 million to settle SEC charges that it violated the anti-bribery, books and records, and internal accounting controls provisions of the FCPA in connection with violations at its subsidiaries in Argentina, Brazil, and Mexico. (4/20/22)
- **KT Corporation** — The largest South Korean Telecommunications company agreed to pay more than $6.3 million to settle charges that it violated the books and records and internal accounting controls provisions of the FCPA in connection with improper payments for the benefit of government officials in Korea and Vietnam. (2/17/2022)

2021
- **Credit Suisse** — The firm agreed to pay nearly $100 million in disgorgement, PJI and penalty to settle charges that it violated the anti-fraud provisions of the federal securities laws and the books and records and internal accounting controls provisions of the FCPA in connection with its role in three financial transactions on behalf of Mozambican state-owned entities. (10/19/21)
- **WPP plc** — The world's largest advertising group agreed to pay more than $19 million to settle charges that it violated the anti-bribery, books and records, and internal accounting controls provisions of the FCPA in connection with violations at its subsidiaries in India, Brazil, China, and Peru. (9/24/21)
- **Amec Foster Wheeler Ltd.** — The company agreed to pay $22.7 million to settle SEC charges that it violated the anti-bribery, books and records, and internal accounting controls provisions of the FCPA in connection with a scheme to obtain an oil and gas engineering and design contract from the Brazilian state-owned oil company, Petroleo Brasileiro S.A. (6/25/21)
- **Asante Berko** — SEC charged a former executive of a financial services company with orchestrating a bribery scheme to help a client to win a government contract to build and operate an electrical power plant in the Republic of Ghana. (6/23/21)
- **Deutsche Bank AG** — The firm agreed to pay more than $43 million in disgorgement and PJI to settle charges that it violated the books and records and internal accounting controls provisions of the FCPA in connection with improper payments to intermediaries in China, the UAE, Italy, and Saudi Arabia.[1] (1/8/21)

Chapter 1 presented hard evidence that companies earn more money as they boost their presence in foreign markets. Furthermore, the first chapter discussed seven principles of global finance which help MNCs perform better than domestic companies. In fact, the entire text of this fourth edition attempted to cover those financial concepts and techniques that would boost corporate performance of foreign operations. We conclude this book by discussing how MNCs can use international accounting, taxation, and transfer pricing to improve their overall performance even further.

This chapter consists of three major sections. The first section examines the global control system and performance evaluation of foreign operations. Accurate financial data and an

---

[1] https://www.sec.gov/enforce/sec-enforcement-actions-fcpa-cases, April 2, 2023.

effective control system are especially important in international business where operations are typically supervised from a distance. The second section considers the significance of national tax systems on international business operations. Perhaps multinational taxation has the most pervasive effect on all aspects of multinational operations. Where to invest, how to finance, and where to remit liquid funds are just a few examples of management actions affected by multinational taxation. The third section covers international transfer pricing. Because transfers between business entities account for approximately one-third of total world trade, the multinational company must try to satisfy a number of objectives. This chapter examines some of these objectives, such as taxes, tariffs, competition, inflation rates, exchange rates, and restrictions on fund transfers.

15.1. GLOBAL CONTROL SYSTEM AND PERFORMANCE EVALUATION

In order to achieve the firm's primary goal of maximizing stockholder wealth, the financial manager performs three major functions: (1) financial planning and control, (2) investment decisions, and (3) financing decisions. These financial functions cannot be performed effectively without adequate, timely accounting information. The two fundamental financial statements of any company are the balance sheet and the income statement. The **balance sheet** measures the assets, liabilities, and owners' equity of a business at a particular time. The **income statement** matches expenses to revenues in order to determine the net income or net loss for a period of time. In addition to these two financial statements, a control system is used to relate actual performance to some predetermined goal.

The actual and potential flows of assets across national boundaries complicate the accounting functions of an MNC. The MNC must learn to deal with environmental differences such as different rates of inflation and changes in exchange rates. If an MNC is to function in a coordinated manner, it must also measure the performance of its foreign affiliates. Equally important, managers of the affiliates must run operations with clearly defined objectives in mind.

An MNC consists of the parent and its subsidiaries in foreign countries. To operate the MNC as a system, the parent and its subsidiaries need continuing flows of data. Hence, the key element in the control system is the company's system for collection and dissemination of data on a worldwide basis. The company's information system between the parent and its subsidiaries generally consists of: (1) impersonal communications such as budgets, plans, programs, electronic messages, and regular reports; and (2) personal communications such as meetings, visits, and telephone conversations.

Communications essential to evaluating the performance of an enterprise usually follow established organizational channels. An effective communication system requires an efficient reporting system for collecting information on the results of actual operations and for disclosing deviations from predetermined standards. The more efficient the system, the more quickly managers may take corrective action.

Financial results of profits have traditionally provided a standard to evaluate the performance of business operations. However, as MNCs expand their operations across national boundaries, the standard itself is affected by the environment in which they operate. Inflation and foreign exchange fluctuations affect all the financial measures of performance for MNCs. To compare the results of various affiliates of an MNC, multinational financial managers must understand the various ways in which inflation and exchange fluctuations affect operations as measured by traditional financial statements.

15.1.1. *Inflation and Exchange-Rate Fluctuations*

Every control system establishes a standard of performance and compares actual performance with the standard. The most widely used standards are budgeted financial statements. The preparation of the statements is a planning function, but their administration is a controlling function. We will compare budgeted financial statements with actual financial statements to determine the impact of inflation and exchange rate fluctuations on financial statements. Budgeted statements are prepared without anticipated inflation or exchange rate fluctuations, but the actual statements are prepared after these phenomena have occurred.

15.1.1.1. *The impact of inflation on financial statements*

Table 15.1 presents the effects of a 10 percent and a 20 percent rate of inflation on the major accounts of the balance sheet and the income statement. If we assume that one unit is sold every month and that prices increase at an even rate throughout the year, the annual inflation rates reflected on sales would be 5 percent and 10 percent instead of 10 percent and 20 percent.

If we follow the results of a case having a total annual inflation rate of 10 percent or 0.83 percent per month, annual sales increase to 2,100 — a 5 percent increase over the budgeted price. The cost of goods sold increases by only 4 percent from the budgeted cost of 1,500 to the actual cost of 1,560 because the cost of goods sold is based on historical costs. We assumed that interest expenses remain constant. The budgeted depreciation charges are based on historical costs. The combination of higher prices in sales and the use of historical costs in the two major accounts will increase the profits after taxes by 20 percent from 100 to 120.

The effects of inflation on the balance sheet accounts depend on the date when assets were acquired or liabilities incurred. Fixed assets and inventory are carried at cost, but accounts receivable and accounts payable are carried at the prices prevailing at the time of the transactions. The budgeted cash of 400 consists of profits after taxes (100), taxes payable (100), and depreciation (200).

15.1.1.2. *Impact of exchange-rate fluctuation on financial statements*

Let us assume that a subsidiary purchases its raw materials from country A and sells its finished products to country B. Thus, both exports and imports are denominated in foreign currencies. In this case, exchange-rate fluctuations affect the level of both revenues and costs measured in terms of the domestic currency. Table 15.2 shows that an appreciation in the revenue currency (Country B's currency) raises profits, assuming that costs remain constant. In contrast, an appreciation in the cost currency (Country A's currency) reduces profits after taxes unless selling prices are adjusted to reflect the increase in costs.

There are similarities between the effect of inflation and the effect of exchange-rate fluctuations on reported profits. If prices in the local currencies are increased by the same

Table 15.1 The impact of inflation on financial statements.

Income Statement (In Foreign Currency)	Budget	Actual with Annual Inflation Rate of: 10%	Actual with Annual Inflation Rate of: 20%
Sales	2,000	2,100	2,200
Cost of goods sold	1,500	1,560	1,620
Gross margin	500	540	580
Depreciation	200	200	200
Operating income	300	340	380
Interest expense	100	100	100
Profit before taxes	200	240	280
Taxes (50%)	100	120	140
Profit after taxes	100	120	140

Balance Sheet (In Foreign Currency)	Initial	Budget	Actual with Annual Inflation Rate of: 10%	Actual with Annual Inflation Rate of: 20%
Cash	0	400	440	480
Accounts receivable	200	200	220	240
Inventory	100	100	110	120
Total current assets	300	700	770	840
Plant and equipment	350	350	350	350
Less: Depreciation	—	(200)	(200)	(200)
Total assets	650	850	920	990
Accounts payable	300	300	330	360
Notes payable	300	300	300	300
Taxes payable	—	100	120	140
Total current liabilities	600	700	750	800
Equity	50	50	50	50
Retained earnings	—	100	120	140
Total liabilities & equity	650	850	920	990

Table 15.2 Impact of currency fluctuations on profits.

	Budget	B's Currency Appreciate 10%	A's Currency Appreciate 10%	Both Currencies Appreciate 10%
Sales	2,000	2,100	2,000	2,100
Cost of goods sold	1,500	1,500	1,560	1,560
Gross margin	500	600	440	540
Depreciation	200	200	200	200
Operating income	300	400	240	340
Interest expense	100	100	100	100
Profit before tax	200	300	140	240
Taxes (50%)	100	150	70	120
Profit after tax	100	150	70	120

percentage as the increase in the cost of imports, the effect of exchange-rate fluctuations on profits is identical with the effect of a comparable local inflation rate. A 10 percent increase in export prices, accompanied by a proportional increase in import prices, produces profits of 120; this is identical to the profit obtained when the local inflation rate was 10 percent in the example from Table 15.1.

We cannot determine the true impact of exchange-rate fluctuations on foreign operations unless a parent's accounts and those of its subsidiaries are expressed in terms of a homogeneous currency unit. Any changes in the value of the local currency relative to the parent currency will affect the reported profits when financial statements expressed in the local currency are translated into the currency of the parent company. The translation procedure, already discussed in Chapter 8, is regulated by the accounting profession.

15.1.2. *Performance Evaluation*

Performance evaluation is a central feature of an effective management information system. A management information system is a comprehensive system to provide all levels of management in a firm with information so that production, marketing, and financial functions can be effectively performed to achieve the objectives of the firm. Management must plan its economic activities in advance, carry out its plans, and make sure that deviations are properly evaluated and handled. Thus, performance evaluation based on the concept of the management information system relates to the fundamentals of the management process: planning, execution, and control.

Because every subsidiary is unique in many respects, each subsidiary should be evaluated based on specific targets and individual objectives set for each. A survey of 125 MNCs by Person and Lessig identified four purposes of an internal evaluation system: (1) to ensure adequate profitability; (2) to have an early warning system if something goes wrong; (3) to have a basis for the allocation of resources; and (4) to evaluate individual managers.[2] The study also revealed that MNCs always use more than one criterion to evaluate the results of their foreign subsidiaries. Of course, the performance evaluation system is designed to measure actual performance against budgeted objectives as well as prior year's results. In the best of situations, the evaluation system should monitor and control performance on a year-to-date and regular basis.

15.1.2.1. *Performance criteria*

MNCs use multiple performance evaluation criteria because no single criterion can capture all facets of performance that interest management at the main headquarters. Moreover, no single basis of measurement is equally appropriate for all units of an MNC. For example, companies can appropriately evaluate their production unit based on such measures as cost reduction, quality control, and meeting shipment targets. For a sales unit, however, cost reduction and quality control may be less appropriate than such measures as market share and number of new customers. Thus, it is highly desirable for companies to use multiple

---

[2]Persen, W. and V. Lessig, *Evaluating the Performance of Overseas Operations*, New York: Financial Executive Institute, 1979.

bases for performance measurement; that is, different ones for different kinds of operations in different countries.

Two broad groups of performance evaluation criteria — financial criteria and non-financial criteria — are used most widely by companies for evaluating their overseas operations. The **return on investment** relates enterprise income to some specified investment base such as total assets. Many companies compare their actual operating performance with their budgeted performance; budgets are pre-established standards against which operations are evaluated, compared, and adjusted by the exercise of control. Abdallah and Keller surveyed 64 MNCs to identify the financial criteria that they used to evaluate the performance of foreign subsidiaries. According to Abdallah and Keller, the four most important criteria were: (1) return on investment (ROI), (2) profits, (3) budgeted ROI compared to actual ROI, and (4) budgeted profit compared to actual profit.[3]

Many MNCs do not define their performance criteria to mere financial considerations. Non-financial criteria complement financial measures because they account for actions that may not contribute directly to profits in the short run but may contribute significantly to profits in the long run. The market share is measured by sales or orders received as a percentage of total sales in a market. The sales growth is measured by unit volume gains, selling price increases, and exchange variations. Other important non-financial criteria include quality control, productivity improvement, relationship with the host country's government, cooperation with the parent company, employment development, employee safety, and community service.

Once questions of performance criteria have been resolved, companies should ascertain whether their criteria could be useful in comparing a foreign unit's performance against its competitors' performance, either in the same country or across different borders. However, there are many pitfalls in such comparisons. For example, it is almost impossible to determine the transfer pricing of competitors as well as their accounting principles. Certainly, cross-border comparisons would compound the problem even further. Companies with many affiliates — at home or abroad — must also take caution whenever questions of comparability arise. Differences in subsidiaries would automatically distort performance comparisons unless they are directly accounted for. Even if subsidiary objectives are the same, differences in country risk profiles, such as exchange controls and export subsidies, could distort performance comparisons.

15.1.2.2. *Performance measurement issues*

There are many crucial yet perplexing elements in the performance evaluation process. As described earlier, two measurement problems unique to MNCs are exchange rates and inflation.

Perhaps the most critical element in the evaluation process is how to deal with results that are denominated in currencies other than that of the parent company. The financial performance of overseas operations can be measured in terms of local currency, home country currency, or both. The choice of currency can have a significant effect on the assessment

---

[3]Abdallah, W. M. and D. E. Kelley, "Measuring the Multinationals' Performance," *Management Accounting*, October 1985, pp. 25–30.

of a foreign subsidiary's performance if major changes occur in the exchange rates. For example, a subsidiary could make a profit in local currency but could incur a loss in the parent company's currency. Most US companies analyze the operating results of their foreign operations in dollar terms. However, several of these companies also use different rates for budgeting and performance tracking because they recognize variations between actual and expected results, which arise purely from exchange rate changes.

Fluctuating exchange rates may pose the most significant obstacle to proper evaluation, but this is certainly not the only environmental factor. Wide variations and rapid changes in inflation rates from country to country also complicate the evaluation process. Generally, accepted accounting principles in the United States are based on the assumption of price stability. However, other countries have runaway inflation, thus making it essential to adjust local asset values for changing prices. Such restatements directly affect the measurement of various ROI components and performance statistics for budgeting purposes. Because failure to account for inflation may result in an overstatement of return on investment, company resources may not be channeled to their most promising use. Unfortunately, solutions to these problems are not readily formulated. Furthermore, MNCs must consider two sets of laws, two competitive markets, and two governments. As a result, pricing considerations in international business are more numerous, more complex, and riskier than those in purely domestic business.

15.1.3. *Organizational Structure*

Many internal and external pressures strain a firm's existing organizational structure as strictly domestic companies evolve into MNCs. Some responsibilities are changed, new ones are created, and some existing ones are eliminated. Furthermore, control and finance functions change over time as changes occur in countries' socioeconomic environments. Companies must constantly adjust their organizational structure to deal with new opportunities and challenges as they grow, diversify, and internationalize.

How should the financial staff of a company with foreign operations organize itself to carry out tasks that require the specialized expertise of multinational finance? There are three basic forms of organizational structure: centralization, decentralization, and hybrid structure.

A centralized financial function has a strong staff at the parent company level, which controls virtually all treasury decisions. The subsidiary financial staff only implements the decisions of its parent company. In a decentralized financial function, parent company executives issue a few guidelines, but most financial decisions are made at the subsidiary level. Many companies split responsibilities for international financial management between the corporate level and the regional level. The corporate level typically determines policy and grants ultimate approval on major financial decisions. However, day-to-day decisions to implement policy are made at regional headquarters.

Both centralization and decentralization carry advantages. The advantages of a centralized financial function include close control of financial issues at headquarters, attention of top management to key issues, and an emphasis on parent company goals. A decentralized company may argue that these advantages could be disadvantages. Data collection costs may be enormous, centralized decision-making may stifle flexibility, and many opportunities may be lost because of slow actions.

15.1.3.1. *Decision variables*

The ultimate choice of a particular organizational structure depends largely upon the types of decisions one must make: (1) transfer pricing and performance evaluation, (2) tax planning, (3) exchange exposure management, (4) acquisition of funds, and (5) positioning of funds.

First, transfer-pricing decisions made to minimize taxes may ruin the performance evaluation system for foreign subsidiaries. This problem sometimes forces a company to keep a second set of books for evaluation purposes. Many MNCs may, in fact, keep three or more sets of books: one for taxes, one for financial reporting, and one for evaluation purposes. There may be a need for two transfer prices: one for tax purposes made at headquarters and one for evaluation purposes decided by direct negotiations between affiliates.

Second, the centralized organization usually works well to minimize worldwide taxes. When tax planning is centralized, it is easier to use tax haven countries, tax-saving holding companies, and transfer pricing. Thus, it is more efficient for MNCs to centralize their tax planning function rather than allow each region to create its own layer of tax havens and holding companies.

Third, most companies centralize their foreign exchange exposure management because it is difficult for regional or country managers to know how their foreign exchange exposure relates to other affiliates.

Fourth, many MNCs borrow money from local sources for their working capital. On the other hand, cheap sources of funds depend upon alternatives in all capital markets and the cost of exchange gains or losses. Regional managers can hardly know all alternative sources of funds outside a local market.

Fifth, positioning funds involves paying dividends and making intracompany loans, thereby reducing consideration of total corporate tax liabilities, foreign exchange exposure, and availability of capital. Consequently, most companies tend to control positioning of funds from a centralized vantagepoint rather than from a regional viewpoint.

15.1.4. *Foreign Corrupt Practices Act*

The US Securities and Exchange Commission (SEC) first investigated illegal foreign payments in 1974 with its probe of questionable contributions by US companies to the reelection campaign of former President Nixon. Subsequent inquiries by the SEC, the Department of Justice, and the Senate Foreign Relations Committee disclosed questionable payments of $300 million by 450 companies. Revelations of such dubious payments by US firms to foreign officials rocked governments in Japan and the Netherlands.

Congress felt that the US corporate bribery (1) tarnished the credibility of American business operations, (2) caused embarrassment with allies and foes alike, (3) created foreign policy difficulties, and (4) generally tarnished the world's image of the United States. Consequently, they passed and signed the **Foreign Corrupt Practices Act (FCPA)** on December 19, 1977, as an amendment to the Securities Exchange Act of 1934. In 1988, the

FACPA was modified in an effort to address its perceived deficiencies. In December 1997, members of the Organization for Economic Development and Cooperation (OECD) with five other nations signed a binding convention to outlaw bribery in international business dealings. Since 1998, they also apply to foreign firms and persons who take any act in furtherance of such a corrupt payment while in the United States.[4]

15.1.4.1. *Content of the FCPA*

The FCPA consists of two separate sections, antibribery and accounting. The antibribery section was the first piece of legislation in US history making it a criminal offense for US companies to corruptly influence foreign officials or to make payments to any person when they have "reason to know" that part of these payments will go to a foreign official. In other words, the FCPA applies only to US companies and not to their agents or subsidiaries. US companies or citizens could, however, be held in violation of the law if they had "reason to know" that their subsidiaries or agents would pay bribes on their behalf.[5]

The accounting section establishes two interrelated accounting requirements. First, public companies must "keep books, records and accounts, which, in reasonable detail, accurately and fairly reflect the transactions and dispositions" of their assets. Second, corporations are also required to "devise and maintain a system of internal accounting controls sufficient to provide reasonable assurance" that transactions have been executed in accordance with management's authorized procedures or policies.

Congress concluded that the antibribery and accounting sections would effectively prevent payments of foreign bribes and off-the-book slush funds. Penalties for violations include fines and jail time. Thus, both the antibribery section and the accounting section are enforced through civil and criminal liabilities.

15.1.4.2. *Modifying the FCPA*

President Reagan signed the FCPA amendment of 1988 into law as part of an omnibus trade bill. Most proponents of its changes affirmed the original purposes of the FCPA. They found that the FCPA had been effective in curtailing bribes, kickbacks, and other unethical activities by US companies. Still, the 1988 amendment removed one of the statute's strongest export disincentives: the threat of statutory criminal liability based on accidental or unknowing negligence in the retention of certain accounting records. So, only corporate employees who "knowingly" circumvent corporate accounting controls or falsify records of corporate payments are now subject to criminal liability. In fact, the old law and the new law differ in notable ways:

1. The old law assessed both civil and criminal sanctions against both deliberate and negligent violators of the accounting section. The new law assesses only civil (no criminal) penalties against negligent or unintentional violators of the accounting section. Violators convicted of intent to deceive still face criminal penalties.

---

[4]http://en.wikipedia.org/wiki/Foreign_Corrupt_Practices_Act, March 29, 2010.
[5]Kim, S. H., "On Repealing the Foreign Corrupt Practices Act," *Columbia Journal of World Business*, Fall 1981, pp. 75–80.

2. The old law did not define "reasonable detail" in the accounting section and "reason to know" in the antibribery section. The new law defines them as those which would satisfy a "prudent individual" under similar circumstances.

3. The old law did not define "grease payments" and virtually precluded all forms of grease payments to foreign officials. In fact, grease payments were enforced via both civil and criminal sanctions. The new law specifically permits such grease payments if: (1) they help expedite routine governmental action; (2) they are legal in that foreign country; or (3) they demonstrate gratitude or reimbursement for expenses incurred in connection with a contract.

4. The old law had been severely criticized from its inception on the ground that it was vague and difficult to interpret. Still, no government agency issued interpretative guidelines. The new law specifies that the government will issue a set of clear guidelines if the business community wants further clarification of the new law.

5. The old law did not require any government agency to give its opinion on the legality of a contemplated transaction. The new law requires the Department of Justice to give its opinion on the legality of a planned transaction within 30 days after receiving the necessary information.

6. Penalties for violations increased from $1 million to $2 million for corporations and from $10,000 to $100,000 and/or 5 years in jail for individuals. The Internal Revenue Service will not allow a firm to treat a foreign bribe as a business expense for tax purposes: such bribes are treated as profits currently subject to US taxation. A company is not allowed to reimburse individuals for fines paid as a consequence of violating the FCPA.

7. Enforcement of the antibribery provisions for all jurisdictions has been consolidated within the Justice Department. The SEC retains the responsibility to enforce the provisions of the accounting section.

15.2. INTERNATIONAL TAXATION

Usually, one of the most important variables in multinational operations is taxation. Perhaps no environmental variable, with the possible exception of foreign exchange, has such a pervasive influence on all aspects of multinational operations as taxation: (1) the choice of location in the investment decision, (2) the form of the new enterprise, (3) the method of finance, and (4) the method of transfer pricing.

International taxation is complicated because tax laws differ among countries and are constantly changing. Hence, it is not accidental that international taxation still remains somewhat of a mystery for many international executives. For example, multinational financial managers need to understand the following:

1. Shareholders of foreign and domestic corporations are subject to different rules.
2. Accounting for foreign taxes on foreign operations is not identical to that on domestic operations.
3. Bilateral tax treaties and foreign tax credits exist to avoid double taxation of income.
4. Many countries offer a number of tax incentives to attract foreign capital and know-how.
5. Tax savings realized in low-tax countries may be offset by taxes on undistributed earnings.

There are many such added complexities because governments have failed to come to any general agreement on tax policies. Each country has its own tax philosophies, tax incentives, transfer-pricing policies, and the like. Multinational financial managers must sort them out in order to maximize profitability and cash flow. To attain this end, they must acquaint themselves with the overall tax environment.

15.2.1. *Types of Taxes*

MNCs face a variety of direct and indirect taxes. **Direct taxes** include corporate income taxes and capital gains taxes. **Indirect taxes** include value-added taxes, tariffs, and withholding taxes. In addition to these direct and indirect taxes, MNCs may have to pay property taxes, payroll taxes, stamp and registration taxes, taxes on registrations of agreements of various types, sales and excise taxes (excluding value-added taxes), and taxes on undistributed earnings.

15.2.1.1. *Income and capital gains*

As with individual income taxes, corporate income taxes are an important source of revenue for many countries. Because most developing countries have low per-capita income, individual income taxes or sales taxes are not very appropriate. Thus, developing countries obtain a larger share of government revenues from corporate income taxes than industrial countries.

Gains and losses on sales of capital assets are called **capital gains and losses**. Capital assets are those assets that are not primarily for resale and not acquired in the ordinary course of business. These assets include stocks and bonds. If capital assets are held longer than a specified period of time, gains on sales of these assets may be subject to preferential tax treatment.

15.2.1.2. *Value-added taxes*

Value-added taxes are a special type of sales taxes. Sales taxes are those taxes assessed at one or more stages in the production process. In Canada, sales taxes are levied when production is complete; in England, when products are wholesaled; in the United States, when products are retailed; and in some European countries, at all stages in the production cycle. Many European countries have adopted the value-added tax as the major source of revenue to avoid the compounding effect of sales taxes. For example, if a car dealer purchased a car for $10,000 from a car manufacturing company and then sold it for $15,000, the value added would be $5,000 and the tax would be levied on this $5,000 increment.

15.2.1.3. *Tariffs*

Tariffs are simply taxes assessed on imported goods, which parallel excise and other indirect taxes paid by domestic producers of similar goods. They may be imposed for purposes of revenue or protection. When tariffs are employed to increase revenues, they are usually modest. However, when tariffs are used to protect domestic companies from foreign competition, they are typically high. Although protective tariffs do not eliminate the importation of foreign products completely, they clearly put foreign sellers at a comparative disadvantage. In this instance, consumers must pay more for foreign goods, which in turn would reduce their consumption of imported commodities.

15.2.1.4. *Withholding taxes*

Withholding taxes are those taxes imposed by host governments on dividend and interest payments to foreign investors and debt holders. These taxes are collected before receipt of the income. In other words, they are usually withheld at the source by the paying corporation. For example, a 20 percent withholding tax on $10,000 interest payments to foreigners means that the tax proceeds of $2,000 are deducted from the interest payment made to the lender and collected by the borrower on behalf of the government. Hence, the purchaser of the bonds would receive only $8,000, or 80 percent of the $10,000 interest payment. Withholding taxes are generally modified by bilateral tax treaties because they frequently restrict the international movement of long-term investment capital.

15.2.2. *Tax Morality*

The issue at stake is the conflict between economics (profits) and ethics (corporate morality). Some business executives think that profits are one thing and corporate morality is another; thus, they conclude that they have to make a choice. It is well known that in many countries both corporate and individual taxpayers are not completely honest with their tax authorities. MNCs must decide whether to comply with the tax laws voluntarily. Although most MNCs comply fully with the tax laws, some companies feel that they should evade taxes to the same extent as their competitors in order to protect their competitive position. Ethical standards vary greatly among people, companies, and societies because business ethics are partly a function of cultural patterns and historical development. Therefore, there is obviously no universally accepted answer to the problem.

Host governments also have a similar moral problem. Two basic tax principles are that taxes should be equitable and neutral. In other words, taxes should be fair to everyone, and they should not affect decisions in the economic system. Nevertheless, many countries have imposed some arbitrary tax penalties on MNCs for presumed violations of local tax laws. Many developing countries have various tax incentive programs for private foreign investments. These tax incentive programs abandon the principle of an economically neutral system. Under a neutral tax system, supply and demand should be left alone to determine prices and economic activity if we want the most efficient economic system.

15.2.3. *Tax Burdens*

Because different countries have varying statutory rates of income tax, differences in overall tax burdens are another natural feature of international business operations. The corporate tax rate ranges from zero in such tax haven countries as the Bahamas to 60 percent in such countries as Libya.

Differences in definitions of taxable corporate income create greater disparities than differences in nominal corporate tax rates. Thus, differential tax rates tell us only part of the story. In one country, taxable income may be computed on a cash basis while in another country it may be determined on an accrual basis. Investment allowances and credits, reserves, the timing of depreciation deductions, and asset valuations vary greatly from country to country. Some countries provide companies with full credit for taxes on the income paid in other countries.

Tax systems also affect relative tax burdens internationally. In general, there are three classes of systems: single tax, double tax, and partial double tax. Under the single tax system, income is taxed only once. If corporations pay no taxes, their stockholders pay taxes on dividends. Under the double tax system, corporations pay taxes on profits at a given rate and dividends are then taxed as income to stockholders at their personal income tax rates. Under the partial double tax system, taxes are levied on corporate income, but dividends are taxed at a lower rate than other forms of personal income, or distributed corporate earnings are taxed at a lower rate than undistributed earnings (retained earnings).

15.2.3.1. *Carrybacks and carryforwards*

An operating loss is the excess of deductible expenses over gross income. Operating losses can often be carried back or forward to offset earnings in other years. Tax provisions for carrybacks and carryforwards vary among countries. Most countries do not permit operating losses to be carried back. However, virtually all countries allow companies to carry their losses forward for a limited number of years.

US companies may carry their excess foreign tax credit back 3 years and carry it forward 15 years to offset US tax on foreign source income. The choice depends largely upon whether a company has had foreign source income in the 2 years immediately prior to the excess foreign tax credit. If this is the case, the company must carry the excess foreign tax credit back in order to expedite the refund of tax payment.

The purpose of this provision is to allow corporations to average their operating results, which fluctuate widely from year to year. However, some profitable MNCs have used the carryback and carryforward feature as a means of reducing their taxable income by merging with other firms that have considerable operating losses or excess foreign-tax credits.

15.2.4. *Parent Country Taxation of Multinational Operations*

Countries differ with respect to their tax treatment of foreign source income earned by their MNCs. Major differences include varying interpretations of tax neutrality, the method of granting credit for foreign-income taxes already paid, and concessions gained in bilateral tax treaties.

15.2.4.1. *Tax neutrality*

A **neutral tax** is one that would not affect the location of the investment or the nationality of the investor. Tax neutrality is justified on the ground that world welfare would be increased if capital were free to move from countries whose rate of return is low to those whose rate of return is high.

Tax neutrality consists of domestic neutrality and foreign neutrality. Domestic neutrality means the equal treatment of Americans who invest at home and Americans who invest abroad. This neutrality involves equalization of all taxes on profits.

Foreign neutrality indicates that the tax burden imposed on each foreign subsidiary of a US company should equal the tax burden placed on its competitors in the same country. The firm owned by residents of the host country and the foreign subsidiary of a non-US company are the two basic types of competitors faced by the foreign subsidiary of a US firm.

Tax neutrality is designed to achieve a status of equality within the tax system. In practice, however, it is difficult to define and measure tax neutrality. The issue of tax equality is also difficult to define and measure. Many governments claim that they tax foreign income at the same rate as domestic income. However, most countries in the world have many important departures from the theoretical norm of tax neutrality.

15.2.4.2. *Tax treaties*

Countries enter into bilateral tax treaties to avoid double taxation and thus to encourage the free flow of investments internationally. Treaty countries agree on how taxes will be imposed, shared, or otherwise eliminated on business income earned in one taxing jurisdiction by nationals of another.

Tax treaties are designed to serve the following four purposes:

1. To prevent double taxation on the same income.
2. To prevent national tax discrimination against foreign nationals of the other treaty country.
3. To increase predictability for the nationals of the treaty nations by specifying taxable obligations. Predictability also tends to reduce opportunities for tax evasion or tax fraud.
4. To specify the type of tax subsidies that will be mutually acceptable to both treaty nations.

The provisions of most tax treaties override the provisions of national income tax laws. For example, Section 8894 of the US Internal Revenue Code states that "income of any kind, to the extent required by any treaty obligation of the United States, shall not be included in gross income and shall be exempt from taxation under this subtitle." Thus, US tax treaties provide that profits earned by US companies in a foreign country are exempt from taxation unless they have permanent establishment in the foreign country. Tax treaties also reduce withholding taxes on dividends, interest, and royalties.

15.2.4.3. *Foreign tax credit*

The purpose of the foreign tax credit is to avoid international double taxation when profits earned abroad become subject to the full tax levies of two or more countries. Under the **foreign tax credit** system, the United States relinquishes tax on profits earned abroad up to the amount of the foreign tax. Thus, the foreign government takes the first bite of profits earned in its jurisdiction. In addition, taxes subject to these credit provisions include withholding taxes on dividends, interest, and other income.

Example 15.1

Assume that a US corporation has $1,000 of foreign income earned in the United Kingdom. the US tax rate is 35 percent and the U.K tax rate is 30 percent. The net US tax of $50 is computed as follows:

Foreign income	$1,000
Foreign tax (30%)	$300
Net income after tax	$700
US taxable income	$1,000
US tax (35%)	$350
Foreign tax credit	$300
US tax payable	$50
Total foreign and US taxes	$350
Effective tax rate	$35%

As this example illustrates, the purpose of the foreign tax credit is to limit the total tax on foreign income to the higher tax rate of the two countries. If the foreign tax on income earned abroad and remitted to the United States is less than or equal to the US tax rate, that income will be subject to a total tax of 35 percent. Thus, if the foreign tax rate is lower than the US rate, the US government receives some tax revenues on the foreign income. If the foreign tax rate is higher than the US rate, the US government receives no tax revenues on the foreign income.

As an alternative to the foreign tax credit, US companies can treat any foreign tax paid directly as a deductible expense. Because both a credit and deduction cannot be claimed in the same year, the US company must decide whether to claim the credit or deduction for foreign income taxes. In general, it is advantageous to claim a credit against federal income tax rather than a deduction.

Example 15.2

Assume that a US corporation has $1,000 of foreign income earned in Spain. Spain and the United States have an identical tax rate of 35 percent. The following computation shows that the credit is better than the deduction:

	Foreign Tax Credit	Foreign Tax Deduction
Foreign income	$1,000	$1,000
Foreign tax (35%)	$350	$350
Net income after tax	$650	$650
US taxable income	$1,000	$650
US tax (35%)	$350	$227
Foreign tax credit	$350	0
US tax payable	0	$227
Total foreign and US taxes	$350	$577
Effective tax rate	35%	57.7%

15.2.5. *Tax Incentives for Foreign Investment*

The location of foreign investment is influenced by three major tax factors: tax incentives, tax rates, and tax treaties. The existence of tax incentives can significantly reduce the cash outflow required for an investment project, which will increase the net present value of the project. It is important to be familiar with local tax laws because the determination of revenues and expenses for tax purposes is a function of tax laws in most countries. Tax treaties are essential in terms of how they affect the cash flows related to withholding taxes on dividends, interest, and royalties. Paying close attention to tax treaties can help investors choose wisely the location of their legal operations.

Many countries, especially developing countries, offer tax incentives to attract foreign capital and know-how to their countries. The four basic forms of tax incentive programs are government concessions, tax havens, foreign trade zones, and other tax incentives.

15.2.5.1. *Government concessions*

Developing countries offer many concessions to attract MNCs. Most concessions are in the form of a complete tax exemption for the first few years, known as "tax holidays." Some other forms of temporary tax concessions include reduced income tax rates, tax credits on new investments, tax deferrals, and reduction or elimination of various indirect taxes. These concessions, along with lower labor costs in relation to developed countries, have made many developing countries attractive for assembly and manufacturing operations.

15.2.5.2. *Tax havens*

Tax havens are those countries that offer strict bank-secrecy laws and zero or low taxation in order to attract foreign investors and depositors. These nations have few natural resources. In addition to low tax rates, tax havens must have (1) a stable government, (2) good communication facilities, (3) freedom of currency movements, and (4) the availability of financial services. Tax havens may be classified into four broad categories:

1. Countries with no income taxes, such as the Bahamas, Bermuda, and the Cayman Islands.
2. Countries with very low taxes, such as Switzerland, Liechtenstein, and the Channel Islands.
3. Countries which tax income from domestic sources but exempt income from foreign sources, such as Liberia and Panama.
4. Countries which allow special privileges to make them suitable as tax havens for very limited purposes.

A large number of MNCs have foreign affiliates which act as tax havens for corporate funds. These corporate funds are held in the tax havens until they are reinvested or repatriated elsewhere. Tax haven affiliates are the outgrowth of tax deferral features on foreign earnings allowed by some parent countries to their MNCs. Normally, parent companies could defer taxes on their foreign earnings until these earnings are received as dividends.

Increasing capital flows across countries have many benefits, but they pose policy challenges, such as tax avoidance and tax evasion. The vast increase in global capital flows has made it tougher for countries to monitor their taxpayers for compliance. Nobody really knows how much tax revenue is lost to offshore schemes, but everybody agrees it is huge. The Tax Justice Network estimated that global tax revenue lost in 2012 to tax havens is between USD $190 billion and $255 billion per year. Thus, industrialized countries have recently pressured tax havens to adopt international standards for banking regulation and safeguards against money laundering activities.

15.2.5.3. *Foreign trade zone*

A **foreign trade zone** (FTZ) is an enclosed area where domestic and imported merchandise can be stored, inspected, and manufactured without being subject to formal customs procedures until the goods leave the zone. There are thousands of these areas in most countries around the world. Most FTZs are located in developing countries: Brazil, China, the Philippines, Malaysia, Pakistan, Mexico, Costa Rica, Honduras, and Madagascar have FTZ programs. In 1997, 93 countries had set up FTZs employing 22.5 million people, and 5 years later, in 2003, FTZs in 116 countries employed 43 million people.[6]

FTZs have operated in the United States since the passage of the Foreign Trade Zone Act of 1934. This law also created the Foreign Trade Zone Board, which authorizes and regulates activities within the FTZs. Over the years, the law and administration have been liberalized to permit more activities within the FTZs and more flexibility in the location

---

[6]John, S. and M. Linda, "China vs. Mexico in the Global EPZ Industry: Maquiladoras, FDI Quality and Plant Mortality," University of Texas Pan America. http://ea.panam.edu/cbes/pdf/WorkingPaper1-06.pdf, March 20, 2010.

of FTZs. The number of FTZs has increased from less than a dozen before 1970 to about 300 today throughout the 50 states.

Goods in FTZs have not entered the country so far as import documentation, collection of customs duties, and the allocation of quotas or other import restrictions are concerned. Federal and local excise taxes are not levied on goods while they are located in FTZs. Except for customs and excise taxes, products and firms in FTZs are subject to the same local and federal laws and regulations, such as immigration laws, safety laws, and regulation of carriers.

FTZs must be located adjacent to US customs "port of entry," but these are no longer located adjacent to "inland ports of entry." Within FTZs, companies may store and assemble imported goods. They may also use imported parts and raw materials to conduct manufacturing operations in FTZs.

Although the advantages of the FTZ to importers are well known, its benefits to exporters appear to have been overlooked. FTZs can provide accelerated export status for purposes of excise tax rebates and customs drawbacks. Manufacturers of such items as tires, trucks, and tobacco products are required to pay federal excise taxes when these items are produced, but the taxes are rebated if the items are exported. Companies must pay duty on the imports, but this duty is returned when the product is exported (custom drawback). Because the recovery of this money takes time, the exporter can have considerable capital tied up in excise taxes and import duties. The use of FTZs resolves this problem. A product is considered exported as soon as it enters an FTZ and thus the exporter can immediately apply for a rebate or a drawback while waiting to make an export sale.

Global Finance in Practice 15: The Power of Foreign Trade Zones

More and more US companies are using FTZs to better manage their global supply chain costs. Here are seven advantages that showcase FTZ as a competitive alternative to a domestic distribution center.

Duty Deferral: Duties are only paid when imported merchandise enters US Customs territory. Goods may be held without payment of duty in an FTZ until sold, allowing for improved cash flow.

Duty Avoidance: There are no duties on FTZ merchandise that is exported, transferred to another zone, or destroyed. This eliminates the need to manage costly and time-consuming duty drawback programs.

Duty Inversion: The user may elect to pay the duty rate applicable to the component materials or the finished goods produced from raw materials, depending on which is lower.

No Duty on Value Added: There are no duties on labor, overhead, or profit to operations performed within an FTZ.

Save with One Weekly Entry: Customs allows for weekly entry processing, which benefits importers because they pay a single entry fee and may realize significant MPF savings.

Inventory Tax Incentives: Companies that hold goods in an FTZ may be exempt from inventory taxes.

Enhanced Security: By using an FTZ, the internal controls requirements of the Sarbanes-Oxley Act (Section 404) are met. FTZ and Customs Trade Partnership Against Terrorism (CTPAT) are complementary programs. Participating in both results in increased internal and external security enhancements.[7]

15.3. TRANSFER PRICING AND TAX PLANNING

Transfer prices are prices of goods and services bought and sold between parent companies and subsidiaries. Internal transfers include raw materials, semifinished goods, finished goods, allocation of fixed costs, loans, fees, royalties for use of trademarks, and copyrights. International transfer pricing policies become increasingly complex as companies increase their involvement in international transactions through foreign subsidiaries, joint ventures, and parent-owned distribution systems. Discrepancies between transfer pricing methods used by companies and those allowed by taxing agencies take place because taxing agencies and companies have different objectives. For example, MNCs try to maximize profits and improve performance evaluation by manipulating internal transfer prices. Taxing authorities, on the other hand, try to allocate through fair market prices the profit of a sale between their country and other countries. Thus, multinational financial managers must understand transfer pricing objectives and their impact on transfer prices.

15.3.1. *Transfer Pricing Objectives*

Transfer pricing strategies are sensitive internal corporate issues, because successful pricing is a key element in achieving profits. Transfer pricing also helps MNCs determine how company profits are allocated across divisions. Governments show interest in transfer pricing because these prices will decide tax revenues and other benefits. So, many host governments have policing mechanisms to review the transfer pricing policies of MNCs.

Transfer pricing has the following objectives:

1. Income tax minimization.
2. Import duty minimization.
3. Avoidance of financial problems.
4. Adjustment for currency fluctuations.

---

[7]Mohawk Global, "Foreign Trade Zones: The Power of Foreign Trade Zones," https://mohawkglobal.com/, April 2, 2023.

Table 15.3 Tax effect of low vs. high transfer price.

	Low Tax A	High Tax B	Combined A + B
Low Transfer Price			
Sales price	$1,000	$2,000	$2,000
Cost of goods sold	$500	$1,000	$500
Gross profit	$500	$1,000	$1,500
Operating expenses	$200	$400	$600
Earnings before taxes	$300	$600	$900
Taxes (20%/50%)	$60	$300	$360
Net income	$240	$300	$540
High Transfer Price			
Sales price	$1,500	$2,000	$2,000
Cost of goods sold	$500	$1,500	$500
Gross profit	$1,000	$500	$1,500
Operating expense	$200	$400	$600
Earnings before taxes	$800	$100	$900
Taxes (20%/50%)	$160	$50	$210
Net income	$640	$50	$690

15.3.1.1. *Income tax minimization*

Many researchers singled out tax minimization as an important variable influencing international transfer pricing decisions. Their finding is not surprising because transfers between related business entities account for approximately 35 percent of total world trade. Economic benefits are immediate if transfer prices can shift profits from a country with a higher tax rate to a country with a lower tax rate. After an economic bailout in which the US government lent, spent or guaranteed as much as $12.8 trillion, the Obama administration faced a projected budget deficit of $1.5 trillion in 2010. In February 2010, the administration said it would **target** some of the techniques companies use to shift profits offshore — part of a package intended to raise $12 billion a year over the coming decade. But that was only about a fifth of the $60 billion in annual US tax revenue lost to thousands of companies' income shifting.[8] Yet, a company using transfer pricing for maximizing profits must balance this approach by having prices consistent with regulations of taxing authorities.

Example 15.3

To illustrate the tax effects of a change in transfer prices on corporate earnings, assume the following: (1) Affiliate A is in a low tax country (20 percent tax rate) and affiliate B is in a high tax country (50 percent tax rate). (2) Affiliate A produces 100 radios for $5 per unit and sells them to affiliate B. (3) Affiliate B sells these radios for $20 per unit to an unrelated customer. Table 15.3 shows the tax effects of low ($10 per unit) vs. high ($15 per unit) transfer price on company earnings.

Under the low transfer price, A pays taxes of $60 and B pays taxes of $300 for a total tax bill of $360 and a consolidated net income of $540. Under the high transfer price,

---

[8]http://www.bloomberg.com/news/2010-05-13/american-companies-dodge-60-billion-in-taxes-even-tea-party-would-condemn.html, May 6, 2014.

A pays taxes of $160 and B pays taxes of $50 for a total tax bill of $210 and a consolidated net income of $690. Earnings before taxes are the same at $900 despite the different prices at which the radios transfer from A to B. Still, the higher transfer price reduces total taxes by $150 ($360 – $210) and increases consolidated net income by the same amount ($690 – $540).

15.3.1.2. *Import duty minimization*

Affiliate A sells goods to affiliate B. The rule of thumb for income tax minimization is: (1) set the transfer price as high as possible if A's tax rate is lower than B's tax rate and (2) set the transfer price as low as possible if A's tax rate is higher than B's tax rate. The introduction of import duties complicates this rule because multiple objectives could conflict. For example, a lower transfer price reduces import duties, but it increases income taxes. A higher transfer price reduces income taxes, but it increases import duties. Suppose that B must pay import duties at the rate of 10 percent. Import duties are normally levied on the invoice (transfer) price. The higher transfer price raises tariffs by $50 ($1,500 × 0.10 –$1,000 × 0.10), thus offsetting tax effects of $50 in terms of increased tariffs.

Import duty minimization is easy, but tax reductions, which have offsetting effects, may complicate it. Also, a country with low import duties may have high income taxes, while a country with high import duties may have low income taxes. If MNCs use low or high transfer prices in certain countries, they have to balance import duties and income taxes to maximize a combined benefit from tariff and income tax reductions.

15.3.1.3. *Avoidance of financial problems*

Transfer prices can be used to avoid financial problems or to improve financial conditions. Transfer pricing often avoids economic restrictions and exchange controls that host countries place on MNCs. For example, some developing countries restrict the amount of profits that can leave the country. An obvious way around this restriction is to charge high prices for imports. So, countries with such restrictions watch import and export prices closely.

Some countries do not allow MNCs to charge certain expenses against taxable income. For instance, they do not permit expenses for research and development done elsewhere. Royalty fees a parent company charges against its subsidiary income are often not allowed. Because the host country does not allow them, they can be recaptured by increasing the transfer price of goods shipped into the country.

Transfer prices can also channel profits into an affiliate to bolster its financial condition, thus presenting a favorable profit picture to satisfy earnings criteria set by foreign lenders. So, the parent company does not need to commit much capital to its foreign subsidiary even though the subsidiary may be required to secure the loan. Besides, low transfer prices give the subsidiary a competitive edge that it might need when starting a new venture or when reacting to an economic downturn.

15.3.1.4. *Adjustment for currency fluctuations*

A wide range of currency fluctuations may influence the performance reports of foreign subsidiaries. Many US MNCs evaluate the performance of foreign subsidiaries with reports stated in US dollars. If currency exchange rates fluctuate, it may be difficult to evaluate the performance of the subsidiary. Management of the subsidiary often prefers to evaluate its performance with reports stated in local currency rather than US dollars. Adjusting transfer prices for currency fluctuations can solve this performance evaluation problem. Performance evaluation, however, is difficult when the objective is tax minimization or when currency fluctuates. One subsidiary's profit in one country may be greater than another subsidiary's profit in another country, not because of better management but because of the transfer price. One way to solve this problem is to maintain two sets of books: one for foreign authorities and another set for performance evaluation purposes.

15.4. SUMMARY

Multinational accounting has become increasingly important in recent years because of a great increase in foreign investment, capital flows, and trade. Accurate financial reports on operations must be prepared for stockholders and creditors to make decisions about the value of existing operations. They are especially important in international business where operations are typically supervised from a distance. This chapter discussed major issues in multinational accounting, control system and performance evaluation, and the Foreign Corrupt Practice Act of 1977. Financial control systems must fit international circumstances to check performance against standards on a worldwide basis. The Foreign Corrupt Practices Act of 1977 intended to stop the erosion of international confidence in US business and institutions. The FCPA made it unlawful for US companies to influence foreign officials through payments and required these firms to maintain strict accounting controls over their assets. Many US business executives had regarded the FCPA as one of the statute's strongest export disincentives for many years. Thus, Congress amended the FCPA in 1988 to make US companies more competitive in the world market. In addition, by the end of 1998, countries around the world adopted tough laws of their own to crack down companies that bribe to win foreign contracts.

For multinational operations, taxation has a significant impact on the choice of location in the initial investment decision, form of the new enterprise, method of finance, and many other international financial decisions. Tax planning for multinational operations involves complex problems such as national tax environments, double taxation, and various tax incentive programs. Thus, it is highly desirable that MNCs seek the inputs of experienced tax and legal counsel in both parent and host countries. Nevertheless, to preserve profit opportunities abroad and to receive special tax incentives, it is important for the financial manager of an MNC to be acquainted with the national tax environments and other tax problems in the host countries in which the company operates.

Transfer prices are prices of goods and services bought and sold between parent companies and subsidiaries. Internal transfers include raw materials, semifinished goods, finished goods, allocation of fixed costs, loans, fees, royalties for use of trademarks, and copyrights. International transfer pricing policies become increasingly complex as companies increase their involvement in international transactions through foreign subsidiaries, joint ventures, and parent-owned distribution systems. Discrepancies between transfer pricing methods used by companies and those allowed by taxing agencies take place because taxing agencies and companies have different objectives. For example, multinational companies try to maximize profits and improve performance evaluation by manipulating internal transfer prices. Taxing authorities, on the other hand, try to allocate through fair market prices the profit of a sale between their country and other countries. Thus, multinational financial managers must understand transfer pricing objectives and their impact on transfer prices.

15.5. KEY TERMS

balance sheet	income statement
return on investment	Foreign Corrupt Practices Act (FCPA)
direct taxes	indirect taxes
capital gains and losses	value-added taxes
tariffs	withholding taxes
neutral tax	foreign tax credit
tax havens	foreign trade zone (FTZ)
transfer prices	

15.6. PROBLEMS

1. AT&T purchases its raw materials from Germany and sells its finished products to Japan. Both exports and imports with terms "net 60 days" are denominated in foreign currencies (yen and euro), but the levels of both revenues and costs are measured in the US dollar. AT&T has: sales = $4,000; cost of goods sold = $3,000; depreciation = $400; interest expenses = $200, and tax rate = 50 percent. Assume that the euro mark and the Japanese yen appreciate by 10 percent before these credit transactions are settled.

   a. Use the above information to prepare an income statement such as Table 15.2.
   b. Under what condition will a 10-percent appreciation in the yen raise AT&T's profits?
   c. Under what condition will a 10-percent appreciation in the mark reduce AT&T's profits?
   d. What will happen to AT&T's profits if selling prices and costs are adjusted to reflect the 10-percent appreciation in both the yen and the euro?

2. The following selected amounts are from the separate financial statements of a US parent company and its foreign subsidiary:

	Parent	Subsidiary
Cash	$180	$80
Accounts receivable	$380	$200
Accounts payable	$245	$110
Retained earnings	$790	$680
Revenues	$4,980	$3,520
Rent income	0	$200
Dividend income	$250	0
Expenses	$4,160	$2,960

Additional assumptions are: (1) the parent owes the subsidiary $70; (2) the parent owns 100 percent of the subsidiary. (3) during the year, the subsidiary paid the parent a dividend of $250; (4) the subsidiary owns the building that the parent rents for $200; and

(5) during the year, the parent sold some inventory to the subsidiary for $2,200, whose cost was $1,500 to the parent, in turn, the subsidiary sold the inventory to an unrelated party for $3,200.

  a. What is the parent's unconsolidated net income?
  b. What is the subsidiary's net income?
  c. What is the consolidated profit on the inventory that the parent originally sold to the subsidiary?
  d. What are the amounts of the following items, on a consolidated basis?
     cash; accounts receivables; accounts payable; revenues; expenses; dividend income; rent income; and retained earnings.

3. Assume: (1) a multinational corporation has $1,000 of foreign income; (2) the foreign country's tax rate is 40 percent; and (3) the domestic tax rate is 50 percent. What is the domestic tax liability?

4. Assume: (1) a multinational corporation has $1,000 of foreign income; (2) the foreign country's tax rate is 50 percent; and (3) the domestic tax rate is 50 percent. The multinational company can treat any foreign tax paid directly as a deductible expense or as a tax credit. What are the effective tax rates of the multinational corporation under the credit and the deduction?

5. Assume a value-added tax of 10 percent. What would be the selling price and taxes at each stage if the following were the values added?

Seller	Value Added by Seller
Extractor	$300
Processor	$500
Wholesaler	$75
Retailer	$75

6. Eurowide Corporation has two foreign affiliates : A is in a low tax country (30 percent tax rate) and B is in a high tax country (50 percent tax rate). Affiliate A produces partially finished products and sells them to affiliate B, where the production process is completed. The proforma income statements of these two affiliates are shown in the following table. Assume that the company increases its transfer price from $3,000 to $3,600. Determine the tax effect of this high transfer price on the company's consolidated net income.

Proforma Income Statements for Two Affiliates

	Low Tax A	High Tax B	Combined A+B
Low transfer prices			
Sales price	$3,000	$4,400	$4,400
Cost of goods sold	$2,000	$3,000	$2,000
Gross profit	$1,000	$1,400	$2,400
Operating expenses	$200	$200	$400
Earnings before taxes	$800	$1,200	$2,000
Taxes (30%/50%)	$240	$600	$840
Net income	$560	$600	$1,160

7. Eurowide Corporation has two foreign affiliates: A is in a low tax country (30 percent tax rate) and B is in a high tax country (50 percent tax rate). Affiliate A produces partially finished products and sells them to affiliate B, where the production process is completed. Affiliate B must pay import duties at the rate of 10 percent — 10 percent of the value of the imported goods. These tariffs are tax deductible. The proforma income statements of these two affiliates are shown in the following table. Assume that the company increases its transfer price from $3,000 to $3,600. Determine the tax-plus-tariff effect of this high transfer price on the company's consolidated net income.

Proforma Income Statements for Two Affiliates

	Low Tax A	High Tax B	Combined A + B
Low transfer prices			
Sales price	$3,000	$4,400	$4,400
Cost of goods sold	$2,000	$3,000	$2,000
Import duty (10%)	—	$300	$300
Gross profit	$1,000	$1,100	$2,100
Operating expenses	$200	$200	$400
Earnings before taxes	$800	$900	$1,700
Taxes (30%/50%)	$240	$450	$690
Net income	$560	$450	$1,010

8. Assume that IBM's Canadian subsidiary sells 1,500 personal computers per month to the German affiliate at a transfer price of $2,700 per unit. The tax rates are 45 percent for Canada and 50 percent for Germany. The transfer price can be set at any level between $2,500 and $3,000.

   a. At what transfer price will IBM taxes be minimized? Explain.

   b. If the German government imposes an import duty of 15 percent on imported personal computers, at what transfer price will IBM tariffs be minimized? Explain.

9. Suppose that Ford Motor sells 100 trucks per month to its Mexican subsidiary at a transfer price of $27,000 per unit. Ford Motor is allowed to set its transfer price at any level between $25,000 and $30,000.

   a. At what transfer price will Ford Motor move the maximum amount of funds from Mexico? Explain.

   b. At what transfer price will Ford Motor bolster the subsidiary's financial condition most? Explain.

Closing Case 15: Advanced Technology's Ethical Dilemma

The Executive Committee of Advanced Technology (AT) — Robert Smith, President; Linda Humphrey, Vice President of Finance; Sam Miller, Vice President of Marketing; and Susan Crum, Vice President of Production — scheduled a luncheon meeting on September 1, 1996 to discuss two major problems for the welfare of the company: (1) how to finance the rapid expansion of its production facilities and (2) how to cope with a growing competition in its major overseas markets. In addition, the Department of Justice requested AT to answer several questions about bribes, gifts, slush funds, and grease payments in relation to its foreign sales. This inquiry began in response to a 100-page complaint by its overseas competitor, which alleged that AT violated the Foreign Corrupt Practices Act of 1977.

AT has recently enjoyed a rapid growth in business. The company anticipated substantial increases in sales for the next few years. However, it must solve two major problems — capacity and strong competition in foreign operations — if it is to maintain fast sales growth for years to come.

AT produces office automation systems and equipment. In addition to introducing a newly designed mainframe computer, the company aggressively increased research in mini-computers and word processors. These products are in high growth markets, and the firm's expenditures for these projects have more than proved their worth. In fact, the company's major problem has been to increase production fast enough to meet demand of its Asian customers. The company's capacity has expanded steadily since 1980, but it has often lost sales because of insufficient production.

The industry recognizes AT as one of the fastest growing companies in the market. Experts in the high-tech industry have projected for the next 10 years a potential bonanza for minicomputers and word processors. Thus, the company plans to invest heavily in research and development for the next 5 years. It also plans to increase production quickly by acquiring existing computer manufacturing firms and by establishing new production facilities.

AT is a multinational company with headquarters in Los Angeles, California. The company has five manufacturing locations in the United States and three abroad, with offices in 13 countries. Approximately 40 percent of its sales came from foreign operations in 1995 — primarily South America and Asia where the company had recently faced stiff competition from its larger rivals, such as IBM, Digital Equipment, and Olivetti. The company depended on distributors for most of its overseas sales.

Conflict of Interest in Financial Affairs

Thomas Nickerson is a Special Assistant to the Vice President of Finance, Linda Humphrey. He graduated from a major university in St. Louis, Missouri with an MBA in Finance. After 2 years of experience with Ernst & Young, a major CPA firm in St. Louis, he joined the accounting staff and served in a variety of accounting and finance positions for 5 years. He was appointed 2 years ago Special Assistant to Ms. Humphrey at an unusually high salary mainly because of his outstanding financial

Table 15.4   Key statistics for computer engineering and high tech.

Variables	Computer Engineering	High Tech
Earnings per share	$1.00	$2.00
Dividend per share in year 1	$0.75	$1.00
Annual dividend growth rate	0.04	0.09
Price per share	?	$20.00
Book value per share	$8.00	$10.00
Cost of equity	?	0.14
Number of shares outstanding	1 million	1.2 million

and communication talents. Thomas Nickerson has a large family and a home with a $450,000 mortgage. His deep debt and huge financial needs hardly matter to him because he has a promising future at the company.

Ms. Humphrey approached Thomas with a special task on August 1, 1996. She informed him that she met with other vice presidents and decided to purchase Computer Engineering to alleviate the capacity problem. She further stated that the acquisition will be highly advantageous for AT, but she needed to convince two members of the Board of Directors. Then she instructed him to prepare a report justifying the acquisition of the company. Under the terms, AT will offer Computer Engineering two million shares of its stock. The market price of the stock was $20 per share.

Normally Thomas would have welcomed the assignment, but this one made him uneasy. Computer Engineering's financial statements indicated poor performance as compared with comparable companies in the field. He knew that Ms. Humphrey and other vice presidents helped current top executives of Computer Engineering set up their company. He suspected that vice presidents of AT owned sizable blocks of Computer Engineering stock which was not publicly traded. To establish a fair market price for Computer Engineering, he has compiled the statistics presented in Table 15.4. High Tech is more similar to Computer Engineering than any other company whose stock is traded in the public market.

Ethics vs. Profits in Global Business

The Foreign Corrupt Practices Act of 1977 (FCPA) has encouraged US companies to introduce policies against corrupt foreign payments and to improve internal controls. The FCPA bans illegal payments to foreign officials, monitors accounting procedures, and levies heavy penalties for violations. The FCPA forced AT to think about its way of doing business overseas. The company had expanded its foreign operations very quickly. In the 1960s, less than 2 percent of its sales came from foreign operations, but by the late 1970s its foreign operations accounted for 30 percent of total sales.

Just like many other companies, AT had undertaken positive steps to prevent illegal payments to foreign officials and to improve internal control. In 1980, the company published its first corporate code, along with two separate area codes: one for the US and another one for the foreign area. The code of business conduct for overseas employees reflected most provisions of the FCPA so that the company would not have any trouble with the law.

Marketing Vice President Miller has been under heavy pressure from President Smith to increase the company's foreign sales by 30 percent per year for the next 5 years. Mr. Miller thought that when in Rome, some do as the Romans do. In other words, he did not hesitate to call the FCPA "bad business" and "unnecessary." Miller felt that the FCPA should be repealed for several reasons. First, it forced US companies to increase audit costs substantially. Second, the Department of Justice and the SEC failed to establish clear guidelines. Third, it put US companies at a competitive disadvantage. Fourth, in many countries, foreign payments are not outlawed, but they are encouraged. Fifth, the FCPA was unnecessary because US law enforcement agencies already had many statutes to prevent illegal foreign payments by US companies.

Mr. Miller reflected on the report he would present to the Executive Committee. The purpose of this report was to make certain that AT was complying with its corporate code of conduct. There was, however, one situation that required a tough decision. This particular situation was considered an acceptable practice in the countries where they occurred, but he did not know how he would handle specific questions if they should come up.

Kevin Hart is the exclusive distributor for Advanced Technology products in South American countries. He had a reputation for reliability and efficiency. However, the most recent audit suggested that he had corruptly influenced customs officials to obtain lower duty rates for AT's products. In doing so, he violated both the FCPA and the company's code of conduct.

AT had asked Kevin to agree in writing to abide by the code, but he refused to do so. He argued that these "grease payments" were customary in these countries. He insisted that he could not compete effectively without them. Kevin had represented AT for many years and generated approximately $10 million worth of business per year for the company. His exclusive dealership contract would be up for renewal in a few months. AT had suggested that it might refuse to renew its contract unless he agreed to abide by the code. Mr. Miller knew that it would be difficult to resolve this problem while he was under heavy pressure to increase the company's overseas sales by 30 percent per year.

Case Questions

1. Use the data in Table 15.4 to estimate the market value of Computer Engineering in the following three ways: (1) price-earnings ratio, (2) market value/book value, and (3) dividend growth model.
2. List and discuss options available to Thomas Nickerson.
3. Discuss the two major sections of the FCPA — antibribery and accounting.
4. List and discuss pros and cons concerning corporate codes of conduct.
5. If you were Sam Miller, what would you do about the situation in these South American countries?

6. The Internet Center for Corruption Research provides the transparency international perceptions index and a comprehensive assessment of country's integrity performance. Use the website of this organization — www.gwdg.de/~uwvw/icr.htm — to identify the five most corrupt countries and the five least corrupt countries.

Source: Aronoff, A. "Complying the Foreign Corrupt Practices Act," *Business America*, 1991, pp. 10–11; Kim, S.H. "On Repealing the Foreign Corrupt Practices Act: Survey and Assessment," *Columbia Journal of World Business*, Fall 1981, pp. 16–21; "Is the Foreign Corrupt Practices Act a Success or Failure?" *The Journal of International Business Studies*, Winter 1981, pp. 123–126; Langlois, C. C. and B. B. Schlegelmilch, "Do Corporate codes of Ethics Reflect National Character?" *Journal of International Business Studies*, Fourth Quarter 1990, pp. 519–540; Velasquez, M., "Unicomp, Inc.," St. Charles, Illinois: Center for Professional Education, Arthur Anderson & Co., 1990; and Whiteside, D. and K. E. Goodpaster, "Dow Corning Corporation: Business Conduct and Global Values," in *Managerial Decision Making and Ethical Values*, eds. Kenneth E. Goodpaster and Thomas R. Piper, Boston: Publishing Division/Marketing Department, Harvard Business School, 1991.

ANSWERS TO SELECTED END-OF-CHAPTER PROBLEMS

Chapter 2

1. 1 food = 3 units of clothing.
2. 1 food = 4 units of clothing.
3. The USA in food, while Taiwan in clothing.

Chapter 3

1b. A balance-of-payments deficit of $10,000.
2a. A balance-of-payment surplus of $2,000.
3. Service trade balance = −$12,000.
4. Reserve account = $5,000.

Chapter 4

1. Franc-yen cross rate = ¥0.0137 per franc.
   Yen-franc cross rate = SKr72.9610 per yen.
2. (a) Percentage change = −9%.
   (b) Percentage change = 11%.
3. 3.03%
4. Canadian Dollar: −1.0%; Swiss franc 5.7%.
6. Pound future spot rate = $2.095.
7. (a) ¥129.63 per dollar.
   (b) Undervalued.
8a. Premium = 16%.
8b. A profit of $400; require $4,000 of capital.
8c. A profit of $231; requires no investment.
9a. Premium = 40%; Interest Differential = 5% in favor of the US; Yes, there is an incentive
   for arbitrage transaction.
9b. Net profit = $360.
9c. Yes, because the net profit ($360) is greater than the transaction costs ($100).
9e. The forward-market approach: $4,400.
   The money market approach: $4,048.74.

10a. Invest in the United States: $102,000.
    Investment in the UK: $101,360.
10b. Equilibrium forward rate = 1.7910.
10c. Equilibrium interest rate = 12.44%.
11b. ¥0.001.

Chapter 5

1a. $15,000.
1c. $6,000.
2a. 151.51%.
2b. −$5,156.25.
2c. 98.48%.
3c. A windfall gain of $2,625.
3d. The exchange loss = $28,750.
4a. Net profit = $5,000.
4b. Net loss = $5,000.
 5. $2,500.
 6. No hedge: $103,750. Hedge: $102,500.
 7. Hedge: $58,750. No Hedge: $57,500.
    Hedge: $58,750. No Hedge: $63,750.
 8. $5,000.
 9. $1,250.
10a. Out of money.
10b. Intrinsic value = 0.
10c. Return on investment = 50%.
11a. In the money.
11b. $0.05.
11c. Return on investment = 100%.

Chapter 6

1. $10,000.
2. $100,000.
3. An annual net cash flow of 2%.

Chapter 7

 1. The cost of forward-market hedging = $140,000.
    The cost of unhedging = $144,000.
    The real cost of hedging = −$4,000.
2a. Potential exchange gain = $200,000.
2b. Potential exchange loss = $360,000.
3a. Potential exchange gain: $5 million.
3b. Total gain = $15 million.
 5. Potential exchange loss: −$800,000.

6. No hedging position: maximum expected cost = $520.
   Lowest expected cost = $460.
   Forward market hedge = $510.
   Money market hedge = $509.66.
8a. Exchange rate = 2.20.
8b. Either direct loan or credit swap.
8c. Credit swap.
8d. Exchange rate = 2.095238.

Chapter 8

1a. Net exposure = ¥300 million.
1b. Potential exchange loss = –$1 million.
1c. Potential exchange gain = $0.5 million.
2a. Net exposed assets = £2.0 million.
2b. Potential exchange loss = –$0.4 million.
3b. Dollar net income is $100.
3c. FASB No. 8 would produce a translation gain of $75, and FASB No. 52 would produce a translation loss of $150.
3d. FASB No. 8 should be used. The company's net income would increase by $75 and thus its total net income would be $175 ($100 + $75).
3e.

	French Francs	FASB No. 8	FASB No. 52
DR	4000/7000 = 57.14%	800/1625 = 49.23%	800/1400 = 57.14%
ROI	225/7000 = 3.21%	175/1625 = 10.77%	100/1400 = 7.14%
LE	3000/3000 = 1.00x	600/800 = 0.75x	600/600 = 1.00x

4b. $878 million.
4c. $615 million.

Chapter 9

2a. $400.
2b. $400.
2d. $2,000.
2f. $38,000.
 3. $108.
4a. $386.
4b. $463.
4c. $322.
 5. $30.

Chapter 10

1a. (1) 36.73%.
    (2) 37.50%.
    (3) 111.34%.
    (4) 12.24%.

1b. (1) March 20: $490.
   (2) March 30: $3,360.
   (3) April 10: $1,455.
   (4) March 20: $4,312.
2a. $19,600.
2b. $18,600.
2c. Hold the bankers' acceptance until maturity.
3a. $7,623.
3b. 16.06%.
4a. 24.5%.
4b. 8.8%.
4c. 8.9%.
4d. The bank loan.
5a. 11.1%.
5b. 14.3%.
5c. 13.3%.
6a. 20%.
6b. 26%.
 7. 7.5%.
8a. Dollar loan: 6.00%; Euro loan: 5.06%; Mark loan: 7.12%.

Chapter 11

1b. $3,200.
1c. 73%.
 2. The total tax payments have been reduced from $900 to $660.
 3. The unbundled situation reduces taxes by $48 and increases net income by $48.
 4. US investment: $10,100.
   Swiss investment: $8120.

Chapter 12

 1. 15%.
 2. A, undervalued; B, undervalued; C, overvalued; D, undervalued; E, overvalued.
 3. Average stock price = $50; Standard deviation = $10.
 4. Portfolio return = 12.75%; Portfolio standard deviation = 7.93%.
5a. 4%.
5b. 3.1%.
5c. 0%.

Chapter 13

 1. 11.5%.
 2. 9.4%.
 3. Cost of capital for A: 15%. Cost for capital for B: 10%.
 4. 40%.
 5. 14.55%.

Chapter 14

1a. Year 1 = 1,500; year 2 = 2,000; year 3 = 2,000; year 4 = 2,500; year 5 = 2,500.

1b. 5,866.

1c. NPV = $127.

Profitability index = 1.0635.

Internal rate of return = 17%.

2a. NPV = −$45,200.

2b. NPV = $182,200.

4a. $13,433.

4b. $9,002.

5. $138.

6a. F = $636; G = $364.

6b. F = $4,000; G = $4,000.

6c. Portfolio Return = $272.

The portfolio standard deviation = $0.

7. Yes.

8a. The WACC for the domestic firm is 13%; The WACC for the multinational company is 10%.

8b. Market values are $76,923 for the domestic firm and $100,000 for the multinational company.

9a. EPS of Ford = $5.65.

EPS of Toyota = $7.45.

9b. Toyota.

10. Using price-earnings ratio: $20. Using market value/book value: $32. Using dividend growth model: $15.

Chapter 15

2a. $760.

2b. $1,070.

2c. $1,700.

2d. Cash = $260; accounts receivable = $510; accounts payable = $285; retained earnings = $1,720; revenues = $6,300; rent income = $0; dividend income = $0; expenses = $4,720.

3. $100.

4. Tax rate under the credit: 50%. Tax rate under the deduction = 75%.

5.

Seller	Value Added	Tax	Purchase Price	Selling Price
Extractor	$300	$30	$0	$330
Processor	$500	$50	$330	$880
Wholesaler	$75	$7.5	$880	$962.5
Retailer	$75	$7.5	$962.5	$1,045

6. Higher transfer price reduces total taxes by $120 and increases net income by $120.

7. The higher transfer price is still desirable, but its benefits have been reduced by $30 to $90.
8a. $3,000.
8b. $2,500.
9a. $35,000.
9b. $25,000.

GLOSSARY

Accommodating (Compensating) Transactions: Those transactions necessary to account or compensate for differences between international payments and receipts. These transactions are used to eliminate international disequilibrium.

Accounting (Translation) Exposure: Measures the impact of exchange-rate changes on published financial-statement items of a firm.

Acquisition: The purchase of one company by another company.

Advising Bank: A bank which notifies the beneficiary of a letter of credit without adding its own commitment to that of the issuing bank.

Affiliate: A foreign operation formed as either a branch or a subsidiary.

African Development Bank (AfDB): A regional development bank for Africa established in 1964 and located in Abidjan, Ivory Coast.

Agency: An office established by a foreign bank to offer a limited range of banking services such as loans in that area.

Agency for International Development (AID): An office within the US State Department established in 1961 to carry out non-military US foreign assistance programs.

Agency Theory: A theory that deals with a conflict of interest between managers and stockholders.

Agreement Corporation: A bank chartered by a state to operate in international banking under an agreement with the Board of Governors of the Federal Reserve System.

American Depository Receipts (ADRs): Negotiable certificates that represent underlying shares of a foreign company other than the United States.

American Option: An option that can be exercised at any time before its maturity date.

American Terms: Foreign exchange quotations for the US dollar, expressed as the number of US dollars per unit of non-US currency.

Antidumping Duty: A custom duty imposed on an imported product whose price is lower than that of the same product in the home market.

Arab League: A political organization of 22 North African and Middle Eastern Arab countries.

Arm's Length Price: The price that would take place between unrelated parties.

Appreciation: A rise in the value of a currency against other currencies.

Arbitrage: The purchase of something in one market and its sale in another market to take advantage of price differential.

Asian Development Bank (ADB): A regional development bank for Asia formed in 1966 by several Asian countries in partnership with the United States, Canada, and a number of European countries.

Asian Dollar Market: Market in Asia where banks accept deposits and make loans denominated in US dollars.

Ask Price: Price at which a trader of foreign exchange is willing to sell a particular currency.

Association of South East Asian Nations (ASEAN): An economic integration agreement among a group of Asian countries.

At the Money: Descriptive term implying that the strike price of any currency call or put option equals the current spot rate.

Average Rate of Return: The ratio of the average annual profit after taxes to the average net investment.

Back-to-Back Loan: A loan which involves an exchange of currencies between two parties, with a promise to re-exchange the currencies at a specified exchange rate on a specified future date.

Balance of Payments: A financial statement that records all transactions between a given country and the rest of the world during a specified period of time.

Balance Sheet Hedge: A method designed to protect the value of a company's exposed assets. It involves the selection of the currency in which monetary assets and liabilities are denominated so that an exchange rate change would make exposed assets equal to exposed liabilities.

Bank for International Settlements (BIS): A bank in Switzerland which facilitates transactions among central banks.

Bankers' Acceptance: A draft accepted by a bank. When a bank accepts a draft, it promises to honor the draft at maturity.

Barter: An exchange of goods and services between two countries without the involvement of finance.

Basis Point: One-hundredth of one percent or 0.0001.

Bearer: The person who holds an instrument.

Benelux Countries: The countries of Belgium, the Netherlands, and Luxembourg.

Best Method Rule: The method that provides the most accurate measure of an arm's-length result under the facts and circumstances of the transaction under review.

Beta: Second letter of Greek alphabet, used as a statistical measure of systematic risk in the capital asset pricing model.

Bid Price: The price at which a trader is willing to buy a given item such as foreign exchange.

Bilateral Netting: Netting method used for transactions between two related units.

Bill of Exchange (Draft): An order written by an exporter that requires an importer to pay a specified amount of money at a specified time.

Bill of Lading: A shipping document issued to the exporting firm or its bank by a common carrier that transports the goods.

Bitcoin: A peer-to-peer payment system introduced as open-source software in 2009 by developer Satoshi Nakamoto. The bitcoin system has no central repository and no single administrator, which has led the US Treasury to call bitcoin a decentralized virtual currency.

Black Market: An illegal foreign exchange market.

Bloc: A group of countries tied by treaty or agreement for mutual support or interest.

Blocked Funds: Financial assets which cannot be repatriated because the local monetary authorities forbid their conversion into foreign exchange.

Book Value: The asset value recorded at historical cost.

Brady Bonds: Loans converted into collateralized bonds with a reduced interest rate devised to resolve the international debt crisis in the late 1980s. Named after the US Treasury Secretary Charles Brady.

Branch: A foreign bank that provides a full range of banking services under the name and guarantee of the parent bank.

Bretton Woods Agreement: An agreement signed by the representatives of 44 countries at Bretton Woods, New Hampshire, in 1944 to establish a system of fixed exchange rates.

Brexit is the name given to the United Kingdom's departure from the European Union. It is a combination of Britain and exit.

BRICS is the acronym for an association of five major emerging national economies: Brazil, Russia, India, China and South Africa.

Broker: An intermediary in the foreign exchange market.

Buy-American Policy: A policy that requires the recipients of American aids to buy goods and services from American companies.

Call: An option to buy a foreign currency or other financial assets.

A Call Swaption: The right to receive fixed-interest payments.

Capital Account: In the balance of payments, the section that records the net changes in capital transfers and the acquisition or disposal of nonproduced, nonfinancial assets.

Capital Asset Pricing Model (CAPM): A theoretical model implying that the total risk of a security consists of systematic (undiversifiable) risk and unsystematic (diversifiable) risk.

Capital Budgeting: The entire process of planning expenditures whose benefits are expected to extend beyond 1 year.

Capital Gains and Losses: Gains and losses on sales of capital assets such as stocks and property.

Capital Market: The market for long-term funds such as bonds, common stock, and preferred stock.

Capital Structure: The combination of long-term debt, preferred stock, common stock, paid-in surplus, and retained earnings.

Cartel: A formal written or oral agreement among firms or countries to set the price of the product and the outputs of individual cartel members or divide the market for the product geographically.

Cash Center: A geographic location where all idle funds from the subsidiaries of a multi-national company are maintained until they are needed.

Cashier's Check: A bill of exchange (draft) issued by the cashier of a bank, for the bank, upon the bank.

CBD: Cash before delivery.

Central Bank: The official bank of a government, such as the Federal Reserve Bank in the United States or the Bank of Japan.

CEO: The chief executive officer of a company.

Certainty Equivalent Approach: A method used to adjust for project risk. It adjusts for risk in the numerator of the net-present-value formula.

Certificate of Deposits (CDs): A time deposit with a specific future maturity date.

CHPAS: Clearing House Payments Assistance System. It is used to move funds between the London offices of most financial institutions.

CHIPS: Clearing House Interbank Payments System. A computerized clearing system used by banks in New York to settle interbank foreign exchange obligations.

Clearing House: An institution through which financial obligations are cleared by the process of netting obligations of various members.

COD: Cash on delivery.

Coefficient of Variation: The standard deviation divided by the average return.

Collecting Bank: Any bank that handles an item for collection.

Common Market: A form of regional economic integration in which countries abolish internal tariffs among themselves, levy common external tariffs, and eliminate restrictions on the flow of factors of production.

Comparable Profits Method: The method allowed by the US Internal Revenue Service to determine the arm's-length Price of intracompany transactions. Under this method, comparable companies' performance results are used to compute pro forma or benchmark operating income results for the taxpayer.

Comparable Uncontrolled Price Method: The method allowed by the US Internal Revenue Service to determine the arm's-length price of intracompany transactions. Under this method, uncontrolled sales are comparable to controlled sales if their physical property and circumstances are identical with the physical property and circumstances of controlled sales.

Comparative Advantage: The relative advantage of a country in producing goods or services.

Compensation (Buy-Back) Agreement: A form of countertrade. Under this form of countertrade, the initial seller receives compensation in products that arise out of the original sale.

Competitive Trade: A practice whereby two countries buy from each other similar goods which both can produce.

Confirmed Letter of Credit: The letter of credit confirmed by a bank other than the opening bank. Thus, the confirmed letter of credit is a firm obligation of two banks.

Confirming Bank: A bank that confirms a letter of credit issued by another bank.

Consignment: The delivery of goods into the possession of another for the purpose of sale.

Consolidation: An accounting process in which financial statements of related entities are added together to produce a unified set of financial statements.

Consortium Bank: A bank formed by a group of banks from different countries to handle larger international loans.

Contract Manufacturing: Occurs when multinational companies contract with a foreign manufacturer to produce products for them according to their specifications.

Controlled Corporation: A foreign corporation in which more than 50 percent of the voting shares are owned by US shareholders.

Convertibility: The ability to exchange one currency for another currency.

Convertible Currency: The currency which may be converted into other currencies without government restrictions.

Corporate Governance: The way in which major stakeholders exert control over operations of a company. However, it is often narrowly defined as the prudent exercise of ownership rights.

Correlation Coefficient: Measures the degree of correlation between two securities.

Correspondent Bank: A bank located in any other city, state, or country that provides a service for another bank.

Cost of Capital: The required rate of return that the company must earn on its projects for the market value of its common stock to remain unchanged.

Cost and Freight (C&F): The FOB (free on board) value and the cost of transportation to the named point of destination.

Cost, Insurance and Freight (CIF): The FOB (free on board) value, the cost of transportation, insurance premium, and other costs incurred in connection with the shipment from the time of loading in the export country to its arrival at the named port of destination.

Cost Method: The method used in consolidating the financial statements of affiliates into those of a US parent when the parent owns less than 20 percent of the affiliate. Under this method, the parent carries its affiliates at the initial investment plus its dividends received.

Cost Plus Method: The method allowed by the Internal Revenue Service to determine the arm's-length price of intracompany transactions. Under this method, an arm's-length price is obtained by adding an appropriate markup to the seller's cost.

Counterpurchase: A form of countertrade that involves a standard hard-currency export but the seller agrees to a return purchase with a minimum quantity of specified goods from the buyer.

Countertrade: International trade arrangements that are variations on the idea of barter.

Countervailing Duty: An import charge used to offset an export subsidy by another country.

Covered-Interest Arbitrage: Portfolio investment in a foreign country "covered" by forward sale of the foreign currency to eliminate foreign exchange risk.

Covering: The purchase or sale of foreign exchange forward to protect a foreign exchange loss in the conversion from one currency to another.

COVID-19 Recession, also referred to as the Great Lockdown, is a global economic recession caused by the government responses to the COVID-19 pandemic.

Crawling Band: A combination of crawling peg and a trading band.

Crawling Peg: A proposal for regular change in the par value according to an agreed upon formula.

Credit Swap: A hedging device that involves a simultaneous spot and forward loan transaction between a private company and a bank of a foreign country.

Credit Tranche: The amount that a member country of the International Monetary Fund can borrow from the IMF above the gold tranche.

Crosslisting: The listing of shares of common stock on two or more stock exchanges.

Cross Rate: The exchange rate between two currencies when it is obtained from the rates of these two currencies in terms of a third currency.

Cross Hedging: A technique designed to hedge exposure in one currency by the use of futures or other contracts on another currency that is correlated with the first currency.

Cryptocurrency (or Crypto Currency): A digital asset designed to work as a medium of exchange that uses strong cryptography to secure financial transactions, control the creation of additional units, and verify the transfer of assets.

Culture Shock: A generalized trauma one experiences in a new or different culture.

Currency Board: A monetary institution that only issues currency to the extent it is fully backed by foreign reserves.

Currency Cocktail Bond: Bond denominated in a basket of currencies.

Currency Futures: An obligation to buy and sell a specified amount of a foreign currency for delivery at a specified date.

Currency Futures Options: The right, but not the obligation, to buy or sell a futures contract of a foreign currency at any time through a specified period.

Currency Options: The right, but not the obligation, to buy or sell a specified amount of a foreign currency at a specified price through a specified date.

Currency Swap: An agreement made between parties to exchange one currency with another for a specified period of time and then exchange the latter currency with the former currency.

Current Account: In the balance of payments, the section which includes merchandise exports and imports, earnings, and expenditures for invisible trade items (services), income on investments, and current transfers.

Current/Noncurrent Method: A method that translates the financial statements of a foreign affiliate into the parent reporting currency. All current items are translated at the current exchange rate, and all noncurrent items are translated at their historical exchange rates.

Current Rate Method: A method that translates the financial statements of a foreign affiliate into the parent reporting currency. All assets and liabilities are translated at the currency exchange rate.

Customs Union: A form of regional economic integration which eliminates tariffs among member countries and establishes common external tariffs.

Debit: In the balance of payments, the part of an international transaction that increases assets of a country and reduces liabilities or net worth of the country.

Debt-Equity Swap: An exchange of foreign debt for equity in local companies.

Delphi Technique: A technique which combines the views of independent experts in order to obtain the degree of political risk on a given foreign project or a particular foreign country.

Depreciation: A decrease in the foreign exchange market value of a currency.

Devaluation: An official reduction in the par value of a currency by the government of that currency.

Development Bank: A bank established to support the economic development of under-developed areas through long-term loans.

Direct Investment: Equity investment such as the purchase of stock, the acquisition of an entire firm, or the establishment of a new subsidiary. The US Department of Commerce defines direct investment as investment in either real capital assets or financial assets with a minimum of 10 percent equity ownership in a foreign firm.

Direct Quote: A home currency price per unit of a foreign currency, such as $1.65 per British pound for a US resident.

Dirty (Managed) Floating System: A system in which exchange rates are allowed to change according to market forces but governments intervene to prevent undesired fluctuations. The monetary system since 1973 is sometimes called a dirty floating system because most industrial countries have permitted their currencies to fluctuate with frequent government intervention in the foreign exchange market.

Discounted-Cash-Flow Approaches: Net-present-value and internal-rate-of-return methods which take into account the time value of money.

Diversification Strategy: A term used in international business to mean that a company produces or sells in many countries.

Divestment: Reduction in the amount of investment.

Division of Labor: An economic theory which allows each person or nation to utilize any peculiar differences in skills and resources in the most economic manner. Division of labor is frequently called specialization of function.

Documentary Draft: A draft which accompanies such documents as bills of lading, commercial invoices, and other documents.

Double-Entry Accounting: An accounting principle that requires each transaction to be recorded as debits and credits of an equal amount.

Draft (Bill of Exchange): An order written by a seller that requires a buyer to pay a specified amount of money at a specified time.

Drawee Bank: A bank upon which a draft is drawn and which thus must pay. Such a bank is often called paying bank.

Drawer Bank: A bank which draws (writes) a draft offering payment.

Dumping: A practice of selling a product in a foreign market at a price lower than that of the same product in the home market.

Duty: A government tax (tariff) levied on goods shipped internationally.

Eclectic Theory: A theory that tries to combine both trade and investment theories.

Economic Exposure: Expected future cash flows whose real values may be changed because of exchange rate changes.

Economic Integration: Cooperation among different countries: the elimination of trade barriers among member countries and bringing separate economies together to form one large market.

Economic Union: A form of regional economic integration which combines common-market characteristics with harmonization of economic policy.

Economies of Scale: A reduction in average cost per unit as sales volume or output increases.

Edge Act Corporation: A subsidiary of a US commercial bank created under the Edge Act of 1916.

Efficient Exchange Market: The exchange market where exchange rates reflect available information and market prices adjust quickly to new information. In the efficient exchange market, market participants buy and sell foreign currencies in a way that eliminates all profits in excess of the minimum required to sustain their continued participation.

Efficient Frontier: The locus of all efficient portfolios.

Efficient Portfolio: A portfolio that provides the highest return for a given level of risk or the smallest amount of risk for a given level of return.

Elasticity: The degree of responsiveness in one variable to changes in another. For example, in international trade the price elasticity measures the degree of responsiveness in exports or imports to changes in prices.

Embargo: A practice that prohibits all trade.

Equilibrium Exchange Rate: The exchange rate at the intersection of the demand curve for and the supply curve of foreign exchange.

Equity Alliance: An alliance where one company takes an equity position in another company.

Equity Method: The method used in consolidating the financial statements of affiliates into those of a US parent when the parent owns between 20 and 50 percent of the affiliate. Under this method, the parent carries its affiliates at the initial cost of the investment plus its proportionate share of profits or losses.

Euro: A new currency unit designed to replace the individual currencies of European Union countries.

Eurobond: A bond that is sold in a currency other than that of the country of issue.

Euro-Commercial Paper: Unsecured short-term promissory notes sold in the Eurocurrency market by multinational companies.

Eurocurrency: A currency deposited in a bank located in a country other than the country issuing the currency.

Eurodollar: Dollar-denominated deposits in banks outside the United States. These banks may be foreign banks or foreign branches of a US bank.

Euro-Medium-Term Note: A medium-term note guaranteed by financial institutions with the short-term commitment by investors. These notes are issued outside the country in whose currency they are denominated.

Euronote: Short- to medium-term debt instruments sold in the Eurocurrency market.

European Bank for Reconstruction and Development (EBRD): A regional development bank established in 1990 by 42 countries for emerging democracies in Eastern Europe.

European Community (EC) or European Economic Community (EEC): An organization formed in 1957 by France, Germany, Italy, Belgium, the Netherlands, and Luxembourg to remove trade barriers among the member countries. The United Kingdom, Ireland, Denmark, Greece, and Portugal, and Spain joined later.

European Currency Unit (ECU): A weighted average value of a basket of 12 EC currencies.

European Free Trade Association (EFTA): A form of regional economic integration involving a group of central European countries which are not the members of the EC.

European Investment Bank (EIB): A regional development bank established in 1958 by members of the EC.

European Monetary System: A complex exchange rate and intervention system adopted in 1978 by EC countries to replace the snake.

European Option: An option that can be exercised only on the day on which it expires.

European Terms: Foreign exchange quotations for the US dollar, expressed at the number of non-US currency units per US dollar.

European Union (EU): The official name of the former European Economic Community (EEC) as of January 1, 1994.

Eurosclerosis is a term coined in the 1970s and the early 1980s to describe a European economic pattern of high unemployment and slow job creation in spite of overall economic growth.

Excise Tax: A tax on various commodities within a country, such as tobacco and alcoholic beverages.

Exchange Rate: The price of one currency expressed in terms of another currency.

Exchange Rate Risk: The variability of a company's earnings that may occur due to uncertain exchange rate changes.

Exercise Price (Strike Price): The price at which the owner of a currency call option is allowed to buy a foreign currency or the price at which the owner of a currency put option is allowed to sell a foreign currency.

Expatriates: Noncitizens of the country where they are working.

Export–Import Bank (Exim Bank): A US government agency established to promote US exports.

Export Trading Company: A trading company sanctioned by law to become involved in international trade as an agent or a direct outlet. The US Trading Company Act of 1982 relaxed the anti-trust law and the bank holding company act.

External Debt: Public debt owed to foreign citizens, firms, and institutions.

Factor: A financial institution which buys a company's accounts receivable on a nonrecourse basis.

Factors of Production: Those things necessary for producing finished goods. Factors of production consist of land, capital, labor, and technology.

FASB No. 8: Under this rule, monetary items of a foreign affiliate are translated at the current exchange rate, and nonmonetary items are translated at the historical exchange rate.

FASB No. 52: Under this rule, the current exchange rate is used in translating foreign-currency financial statements into US dollars.

FASB No. 133: Under this rule issued in 1998, companies are required to report the fair market value of their derivatives in their balance sheets and to include derivative gains and losses in their income statements.

Filter Rule: One form of technical analysis suggesting that investors buy a currency when it rises more than a given percentage above its recent lowest value and sell the currency when it falls more than a given percentage below its highest recent value.

Financial Account: In the balance of payments, the section that records the net change in foreign direct investments, foreign portfolio investments, and other investments.

Financial Accounting Standards Board (FASB): The private-sector organization in the United States that sets financial accounting standards.

Financial Assets: Claims on such wealth as stocks, bonds, and other securities.

Financial Market: The market that deals in financial assets.

Financial Risks: In international finance, those risks which may occur because of varying exchange rates, divergent tax laws, different interest and inflation rates, and balance-of-payments problems.

Fisher Effect: This theory assumes that the nominal interest rate consists of a real interest rate and an expected rate of inflation.

Fixed Exchange Rate: An exchange rate which does not fluctuate or which changes within a predetermined band.

Flexible (Floating or Fluctuating) Exchange Rate: An exchange rate which fluctuates according to market forces.

Foreign Base Company: A corporation whose base or registration is in a country in which it does not conduct active operations.

Foreign Bond: Bond sold outside the borrowing country but in the country of the currency in which the bond is denominated.

Foreign Corrupt Practices Act: US law that makes it illegal for American companies and managers to make payments to foreign government officials for the purpose of obtaining business.

Foreign Credit Insurance Association (FCIA): An association of insurance companies in the United States which provide credit insurance to export sales.

Foreign Currency Swap: An agreement between two parties to exchange local currency for hard currency at a specified future date.

Foreign Currency Translation: The expression of balance-sheet items denominated in a foreign currency into a local currency.

Foreign Direct Investment: The acquisition of physical assets in a foreign country to be managed by the parent company.

Foreign Exchange: Any currency other than the currency used internally in a given country.

Foreign Exchange Exposure: The possibility that a firm will gain or lose due to changes in exchange rates.

Foreign Tax Credit: The amount by which a domestic company may reduce domestic income taxes for income tax payments to a foreign government. This credit is used to avoid international double taxation.

Foreign-Trade Zones (FTZ) are secure areas under US Customs and Border Protection (CBP) supervision that are generally considered outside CBP territory upon activation. Located in or near CBP ports of entry, they are the United States' version of what are known internationally as free-trade zones.

Forfaiting: The purchase of financial obligations such as promissory notes with no recourse to the exporters. This technique is used to finance medium-term export financing.

Forward Discount or Premium: An annualized percentage by which the forward exchange rate is less or more than the spot rate.

Forward Exchange Rate: An exchange rate for a currency to be delivered at a future date.

Fourth Industrial Revolution: The digital revolution that has been occurring since the middle of the last century. It is characterized by a fusion of technologies that is blurring the lines between the physical, digital, and biological spheres.

Franchising Agreement: An agreement where a multinational company (franchiser) allows a foreign company (franchise) to sell products or services under a highly published brand name and a well-proven set of procedures.

Free Alongside (F.A.S.): A price that includes the delivery of the goods along side overseas vessel within reach of its loading tackle.

Free Float: An exchange rate system characterized by the absence of government intervention.

Free on Board (FOB): The price of the goods to the foreign buyer which includes all costs, charges, profits, and expenses accruing up to the point where the goods are deposited on board the exporting vessel or aircraft.

Free Trade: The absence of artificial barriers to trade among individuals and firms in different countries.

Free Trade Area: A form of regional economic integration which eliminates tariffs among member countries and establishes common external tariffs.

Free Trade Zone: An area within a country into which foreign goods may be brought duty free for purposes of additional manufacture, inventory storage, or packaging.

Freely Floating Exchange Rate System: A system which allows exchange rates to move on the basis of market forces without government intervention.

Functional Currency: The currency of the primary economic environment in which the entity operates.

Fundamental Analysis: A forecast based on fundamental relationships between economic variables and exchange rates.

Futures Contract: A contract that specifies an exchange rate in advance of the future exchange of the currency.

Futures Options: The right to buy or sell the futures contract of a specified currency at a specified price by a specified expiration date.

Gap Analysis: A tool used to estimate why a market potential for a given product is less than a company's sales in a country.

General Agreement on Tariffs and Trade (GATT): An agreement signed in 1947 by 23 countries to liberalize world trade.

Generalized System of Preferences: Arrangements through which industrialized countries grant preferential import duty rates to products from developing countries.

Geographic Arbitrage: A practice which buys a currency in a market where its price is lower and then sells the currency in another market where its price is higher.

Global Bond: A bond sold inside as well as outside the country in whose currency they are denominated.

Global Company: A generic term used to describe an organization that attempts to standardize and integrate operations worldwide in all functional areas.

Global Fund: A mutual fund that can invest anywhere in the world, including the country of issuer.

Gold Standard: A system where a country uses gold as a medium of exchange and a store of value.

Gold Tranche: The amount that each IMF member country contributes in gold or dollars as a part of its membership quota in the IMF. The gold tranche is usually 25 percent of a country's quota.

Grand Tour: A political-risk forecasting technique which relies on the opinions of company executives visiting the country where investment is considered.

Grandchild Subsidiary: A so-called second-tier subsidiary, which is under a tax-haven subsidiary.

Great Recession (also referred to as the global recession of 2009) was a US economic decline for 18 months from June 2007 to December 2009. We call this recession "great recession" because it was the deepest and longest downturn since the Great Depression of the 1930s.

Gross National Product (GNP): The total market value of all final goods and services produced in the economy during a year.

Group of Five: Five industrial countries: France, Germany, Japan, the United Kingdom, and the United States.

Group of Seven: Group-of-five countries plus Canada and Italy.

Group of Ten: Ten major industrial countries which pledged in 1962 to lend their currencies to the IMF under the so-called General Agreement to Borrow. These ten countries are the Group of Seven countries plus Belgium, the Netherlands, and Sweden.

Hedge Funds: Private partnerships with a general manager and a number of limited partners. Unlike other investment pools such as stocks and mutual funds, these hedge funds are largely unregulated investment pools open to only the wealthy investors.

Hard Currency: Currency that may be used in international trade.

Hedging Device: An approach designed to reduce or offset a possible loss. For example, the multinational company may sell forward exchange or use other means such as credit swap to offset or reduce possible losses from exchange rate fluctuations that affect values of assets and liabilities.

Horizontal Expansion: A combination of firms engaged in the same line of business.

Host Country: The non headquartered country in which an international firm operates.

Fourth Industrial Revolution: This revolution describes a world where individuals move between digital domains and offline reality with the use of connected technology to enable and manage their lives.

Import Quota: The maximum amount of a given product to be imported during a specified period of time.

Import Substitution: An industrialization policy whereby new industrial developments emphasize products that would otherwise be imported.

Indexing: The practice of adjusting assets, liabilities, or payments by some measure of inflation to preserve the purchasing power of the original amounts.

Indirect Quote: A foreign currency price per unit of a home currency, such as SFr1.35 per US dollar for a US resident.

Inflation: The overall rate of increase in prices for a group of goods and services in a given country.

International Monetary Reserves: Assets held by central banks or governments which can be used to settle international payments.

Initial Margin: Amount futures-market participants must deposit at the time they enter into a futures contract.

Inter-American Development Bank (IDB): A regional development bank founded in 1959 by the United States and 19 Latin American countries to further the economic development of its member countries.

Interbank Market: The foreign exchange market among banks.

Interbank Transactions: Foreign exchange transactions that take place between banks as opposed to those between banks and nonbank clients.

Interest Arbitrage: A practice of lending or investing in another currency to take advantage of higher interest rates.

Interest Parity Line: A line that describes the equilibrium position for the relationship between interest differentials and forward premium or discount. Every point on the line represents a situation in which the interest differential equals the forward premium or discount.

Interest Parity Theory: A theory stating that the difference between the spot rate and the forward rate equals the difference between the domestic interest rate and the foreign interest rate.

Interest Rate Cap: A maximum rate on floating rate interest payments.

Interest Rate Collar: A combination of an interest rate cap and an interest rate floor.

Interest Rate Floor: A minimum rate on floating rate interest payments.

Internal Rate of Return: The discount rate that equates the present value of expected net cash flows to the present value of the net investment.

Interest Rate Swap: Under this swap, companies exchange cash flows of a floating rate for cash flows of a fixed rate or exchange cash flows of a fixed rate for cash flows of a flexible rate.

International Accounting Standards Committee: The international private-sector organization established to set financial accounting standards that can be used worldwide.

International Bank for Reconstruction and Development (IBRD): The World Bank which is a companion institution to the IMF.

International Banking Facilities (IBFs): Vehicles that enable bank offices in the United States to accept time deposits in either dollars or foreign currency from foreign customers, free of reserve requirements and of other limitations.

International Bonds: Those bonds that are initially sold outside the country of the borrower.

International Development Association (IDA): An affiliate of the IBRD established to make long-term "soft" loans for development.

International Finance Corporation (IFC): An affiliate of the IBRD established to make development loans in forms which could be sold to other investors and converted into equity.

International Fisher Effect: A theory that the spot exchange rate should change by an amount equal to the difference in interest rates between two countries.

International Investment Position is a stock concept because it summarizes a country's assets and liabilities on a given date.

International Monetary Fund (IMF): An international monetary organization created at the Bretton Woods conference to make the new monetary system feasible and workable.

International Monetary System: A system of such elements as laws, rules, institutions, instruments, and procedures which include international money.

International Mutual Fund: A mutual fund that contains securities of foreign companies.

Intervention: The buying and selling of currencies by central banks to influence the exchange rate.

In the Money: Descriptive term implying that the current spot rate exceeds (is less than) the strike price on a currency call (put) option.

Intrinsic Value: The difference between the exchange rate of the underlying currency and the strike price of a currency option.

Irrevocable Letter of Credit: A letter of credit that can not be changed without consent of all parties involved in the letter.

Issuing Bank: The bank which issues a letter of credit, usually the importer's bank.

Joint Venture: A business venture in which two or more parties, for example, a foreign firm and a local firm, have equity interest.

J Curve: J curve is the term most commonly used by economists to describe the relationship between the trade balance and currency devaluation.

Just-in-Time (JIT) Inventory System: A manufacturing system that reduces inventories by having components and parts delivered as they need to be used in production.

Keiretsu: A Japanese word which stands for large, financially linked groups of companies that play a significant role in the country's economy.

Kennedy Round: The trade negotiations concluded in 1967 to reduce trade barriers between the United States and the EC countries.

Law of One Price: A law stating that all goods sell for the same price worldwide when converted to a common currency.

Leads and Lags: Payment of a financial obligation earlier (leads) or later (lags) than is expected or required.

Less Developed Countries (LDCs): Countries characterized by relatively low levels of economic output and income per capita, limited industrial activity, and lack of adequate health, educational, and other social services.

Letter of Credit: A document issued by a bank at the request of the importer. In the document, the bank agrees to honor a draft drawn on the importer if the draft accompanies specified documents.

Leveraged Buy-Outs (LBO): A large amount of loan to buy a controlling interest of a company.

Life-Time Employment: A customary Japanese situation in which workers are effectively guaranteed employment with the company for their working lifetime.

Licensing Agreement: An agreement whereby one firm gives rights to another for the use of such assets as trademarks, patents, or copyrights.

Link Financing: An arrangement that commercial banks in strong-currency countries help subsidiaries in weak-currency countries obtain loans by guaranteeing repayment on the loans.

Local Currency: The currency of the country to which reference is made.

London Interbank Offered Rate (LIBOR): The arithmetic average of the interest rates offered by 16 major banks in London on six-month Eurodollar time deposits at a certain time during the morning. This is the reference rate in London for interbank Eurocurrency deposits.

Long Position: An agreement to buy a futures contract.

Mail Float: Mailing time involved in payments sent by mail.

Maintenance Margin: A set minimum margin futures-market participants must always maintain in their account.

Managed Float: Also known as dirty float, a system that floats exchange rates with central bank intervention to reduce currency fluctuations.

Margin: Money deposited with a broker to finance futures trading.

Margin Call: A broker's request for additional deposit when funds in his client's account fall below the minimum amount.

Marginal Cost of Capital: The cost of the last dollar of funds raised. It is assumed that each dollar is financed in proportion to the firm's optimum capital structure.

Market-Based Forecast: A forecast based on market indicators, such as forward rates or spot rates.

Market Economy: An economic philosophy in which resources are allocated and controlled by consumers who "vote" by buying goods.

Market Portfolio: A well-diversified group of risky securities with little or no unsystematic risk.

Marshall Plan: The European Economic Recovery Program established by the United States in 1948 to restore the productive capacity of European industry and agriculture destroyed during World War II.

Merchandise Trade Balance: The net of merchandise imports and exports within a country's balance of payments.

Merger: A situation where two companies combine their operations to form a new company.

Monetary/Nonmonetary Method: Under this method of translation, all monetary accounts are translated at the current exchange rate, and all nonmonetary accounts are translated at the historical exchange rate.

Money Market: Financial market where short-term securities such as commercial paper and bankers' acceptances are sold and bought.

Money Market Hedge: A hedging device which involves a contract and a source of funds to carry out that contract. If an American firm has a British pound import payable in 60 days, it may borrow in dollars, convert the proceeds into pounds, buy a 60-day British Treasury bill, and pay the import bill with the funds derived from the sale of the Treasury bill.

Most-Favored Nation (MFN): A nation which receives the most favored treatment in application of duties from another country. The MFN clause requires that if a member country of the World Trade Organization grants a tariff reduction to one country, it must grant the same concession to all other WTO member countries.

Multicurrency Clause: A clause that gives a Eurocurrency borrower the right to switch from one currency to another when the loan is rolled over.

Multinational (Transnational) Corporations: Companies that conduct business operations in several countries. They usually consist of a parent firm and a number of affiliates.

Multiple Exchange Rate System: Under this system, a government sets different exchange rates for different transactions.

Mutual Funds: Corporations which accept money from savers and then use these funds to buy a variety of securities issued by businesses or government units.

Negotiating Bank: A bank which negotiates such things as discounts or purchases of drafts drawn by exporters.

Net Exposure: The difference between exposed assets and liabilities.

Net Present Value: The present value of future net cash flows minus the present value of the net investment for a project.

Netting: A method designed to reduce the foreign exchange transaction cost through the consolidation of accounts payable and accounts receivable. For example, if subsidiary A buys $1 million worth of goods from subsidiary B and B in turns buys $3 million worth of parts from A, the combined flows are $4 million. But on a net basis, subsidiary A would pay subsidiary B only $2 million.

Newly Industrialized Countries (NICs): Third world countries in which the cultural and economic climate has led to a rapid rate of industrialization and growth since the 1960s.

Nikkei Index: A measure of the level of stock prices on the Tokyo Stock Exchange, based on the prices of a group of Japanese securities.

Nominal Interest Rate: The rate of interest that consists of a real interest rate and an expected rate of inflation.

Nonmarket Economy: An economy in which resources are allocated and controlled by government decision.

Nontariff Barriers: Restrictive practices in trade other than custom duties used by governments or by private firms. Nontariff barriers used by governments include import quotas, voluntary restrictions, exceptional customs valuation procedures, and health regulations. Nontariff barriers used by private firms include price control, division of markets, restriction of supplies, patent agreements, or control of technology.

United States-Mexico-Canada Agreement (USMCA): In November 2018, the US, Canada, and Mexico reached a new trade agreement to update the North American Trade Agreement. The new deal will be known as the United States-Mexico-Canada Agreement, or USMCA.

Notifying (Advising Bank): A bank which notifies the beneficiary of the opening of a letter of credit.

Offer Price: The price at which a trader is willing to sell a given item.

Offset Agreement: Trade demanded by a foreign buyer to produce parts, source parts, or assemble the product in the importing country.

Official Reserves: Government-owned assets which consist of gold, SDRs, and convertible foreign exchange.

Offshore Banking: Banking activities that accept deposits and make loans in foreign currency — the Eurocurrency market.

Offshore Funds: Funds which use the currency of a country but are located outside that country for tax and other purposes.

Oligopoly Model: This model assumes that business firms make foreign investments to exploit their quasi-monopoly advantages.

Opening Bank: A bank which opens a letter of credit.

Opportunity Cost: The rate of return that funds could earn if they were invested in the best available alternative project.

Optimal Portfolio: A portfolio found at the tangency point between the efficient frontier and the security market line. This is the portfolio which has, among all possible portfolios, the largest ratio of expected return to risk.

Optimum Capital Budget: The amount of investment that will maximize a company's total profits.

Optimum Capital Structure: The combination of debt and equity that yields the lowest cost of capital or maximizes the overall value of the company.

Option: The right to buy or sell a given amount of foreign exchange or other financial asset at a fixed price for a specified time period.

Option Premium (Price): The price the option buyer must pay the option seller.

Organization for Economic Cooperation and Development (OECD): An organization of 29 countries, most of which are industrialized countries.

Organization of Petroleum Exporting Countries (OPEC): An organization established by a number of oil exporting countries to formulate uniform policies such as selling prices on their oil export sales. Full members with vote and veto include Algeria, Ecuador, Indonesia, Iran, Iraq, Kuwait, Libya, Nigeria, Qatar, Saudi Arabia, the United Arab Emirates, and Venezuela.

Out of the Money: Descriptive term implying that the current exchange rate is less than (exceeds) the strike price on a currency call (put) option.

Outright Forward Rate: A forward exchange rate expressed in terms of the amount of one currency required to buy a unit of another currency.

Outsourcing: A situation in which a domestic company uses foreign suppliers for components or finished products.

Over-The-Counter Market (OTC): A market in which participants privately trade securities, options, foreign exchange, or other financial contracts with each other, often using a bank as an intermediary. The OTC market has no physical location and thus is differentiated from organized exchanges with a physical location where trading takes place.

Overdraft: A line of credit which permits the customer to write checks beyond deposits.

Overseas Private Investment Corporation (OPIC): A US government agency established in 1969 to insure American overseas investors against political risks.

Par (Mint) Value: The value of a currency specified by the government of the currency.

Parallel Loan: A loan which involves an exchange of currencies between four parties, with a promise to re-exchange the currencies at a specified exchange rate and future date.

Parent: A company that controls another (its subsidiary).

Payback Period: The number of years required for the net cash flows of a project to return its cost.

Payee: The party to whom payment is made. The drawer may also be a payee of a draft.

Paying Bank: The drawee bank on which a draft is drawn.

Peg: To fix the value of a currency to some benchmark such as the US dollar.

Petrodollars: OPEC deposits of dollars in the Eurocurrency market.

Piracy: The unauthorized use of property rights protected by patents, trademarks, or copyrights.

PIIGS is an acronym for five weak EU economies (Greece, Italy, Portugal, Spain, and Irelands) — the weak sisters of Europe with high structural deficits which have created the so-called "Euro Debt Crisis" in the late 2000s.

Plain Vanilla Swap: The basic form of a swap — the simplest kind.

Political Risk: Potential changes in political conditions that may cause company operating positions to deteriorate.

Pooling-of-Interest Method: A method in case of a merger under which the items on the balance sheets of the two companies are added together so that the merger would not create goodwill.

Portfolio Effect: The extent to which the variations or risks of individual assets tend to offset each other.

Portfolio Investment: Investment in foreign financial assets without significant management control of the real assets.

Portfolio Theory: A theory that indicates a company is often able to improve its risk-return performance by holding an internationally diversified portfolio of assets as opposed to a domestically diversified portfolio.

Possessions Corporation: A US firm engaged in business within US possessions such as Guam and American Samoa. The possessions corporation obtains tax advantages if it meets certain requirements.

Premium: The excess of the forward exchange rate over the spot exchange rate.

Private Export Funding Corporation (PEFCO): A corporation established in 1970 at the initiation of the Bankers' Association for Foreign Trade to mobilize private capital in order to finance US exports of big-ticket items.

Privatization: A situation in which government-owned assets are sold to private individuals or groups.

Product Differentiation: Development of a product that is different from those produced by competitors to maintain or improve market share.

Product Life Cycle Theory: A theory that attempts to explain both world trade and foreign investment patterns on the basis of stages in a product's life. Product life cycle is the time it takes to bring new and improved products to markets.

Production Efficiency: The production of goods in the least costly way.

Profit Split Method: A new transfer pricing method adopted by the US Internal Revenue Service in 1994. This method consists of two steps to estimate an arm's-length return: (1) by comparing the relative economic contributions that the parties make to the success of a venture; and (2) by dividing the returns from that venture between them on the basis of the relative value of such contributions.

Project Finance: A way for a project sponsor to raise non-recourse financing for a specific project. Most often, a separate legal entity is formed to operate the project.

Protectionism: A political attitude or policy intended to prohibit the import of foreign goods and services.

Proxy: The assignment of the voting right to management or a group of outsiders.

Public Law 480: The US law that permits less developed countries to purchase surplus American agricultural products and to pay for them with their own currencies rather than with dollars.

Purchase-of-Assets Method: A method in case of a merger under which the acquired assets or companies are usually recorded in the accounts of the acquiring company at the market value of assets given in exchange.

Purchasing-Power-Parity Theory: An economic theory that in the long-run exchange rates reflect the relative purchasing power of currencies.

Put: An option to sell foreign exchange or financial contracts.

Put Swaption: The right to make fixed interest payments.

Quality Control Circle: A production system that small groups of workers meet regularly to detect and solve problems in their area.

Quota: A limit set on the import of a product.

Real Interest Rate: Nominal (quoted) interest rate minus the inflation rate.

Recourse: A right of an intermediary to claim reimbursement from a drawer of a draft if the drawee fails to pay.

Regional Development Bank: A development bank that makes loans only to countries in particular regions.

Reinvoicing Center: A subsidiary that takes title to all goods sold by one corporate unit to other affiliates or independent customers. The center pays the seller and in turn is paid by the buyer.

Resale Price Method: The method allowed by the US Internal Revenue Service to determine the arm's-length price of intracompany transactions. Under this method, an arm's-length price is obtained by subtracting an appropriate markup from the applicable sale price.

Reporting Currency: The currency in which the parent firm prepares its own financial statements.

Required Rate of Return: The minimum rate of return required by the investors.

Reserve or Official Reserve Account: In the balance of payments, the section that represents the changes in official reserves such as SDRs and convertible foreign exchange.

Reserve Country: A country whose currency is held as a reserve asset by central banks or governments of other countries.

Reserve Currency: A currency held as a reserve asset by central banks or governments of countries other than the country of the currency.

Return on Investment (ROI): Profits divided by the amount of investment, usually total assets.

Revaluation: Either an upvaluation or a devaluation.

Revocable Letter of Credit: A letter of credit that can be canceled at any time without prior notification to the beneficiary.

Risk: The variability of return associated with a project.

Risk-Adjusted Discount Rate: A rate which consists of the riskless rate of return plus a risk premium.

Risk Analysis: An analysis of the different outcomes under different assumptions that each of these outcomes will occur.

Royalties: The payment for use of assets abroad.

Safe Harbor: A rule set in legislation which guarantees favorable treatment to the party.

Safeguard Clause: A clause for conditions under which tariffs and nontariff barriers may be reintroduced.

Section 482: A provision of the US Internal Revenue Code regulating transfer pricing practices.

Secured Overnight Financing Rate (SOFR): SOFR is an influential interest rate that banks use to price US dollar denominated derivatives and loans. The SOFR is based on transactions in the US Treasury repurchase market, where investors offer banks overnight loans backed by their bond asset.

Securities and Exchange Commission (SEC): A US government agency that regulates securities brokers, dealers, and markets.

Semistrong-Form Efficiency: When related to foreign exchange markets, this theory implies that current exchange rates reflect all publicly available information, thereby making such information useless for forecasting exchange-rate movements.

Short Position: An agreement to sell a futures contract.

Short Selling: Short selling involves borrowing a security whose price you think is going to fall from your brokerage and selling it on the open market. Your plan is to then buy the same stock back later, hopefully for a lower price than you initially sold it for, and pocket the difference after repaying the initial loan.

Sight Draft: A draft payable on demand (at sight).

Smithsonian Agreement: An agreement reached in December 1971 to widen the band up to 2.25 percent on either side of the par value.

Snake Within Tunnel: A system that EC countries agreed to allow their currencies to fluctuate a maximum of 2.25 percent against one another and permitted a 4.5 percent band against other countries. The tunnel disappeared in 1973 and the snake ended in 1978.

Society for Worldwide Interbank Financial Telecommunications (SWIFT): An interbank communication network that carries messages for financial transactions.

Sovereign Risk: The risk of a country that will impose foreign exchange regulations or the risk of government default on a loan made to it or guaranteed by it.

Sovereignty: The power of a country to act as it wishes within its own borders.

Specific Duty: A duty imposed as a fixed charge per unit, such as $2 per ton.

Special Drawing Rights (SDRs): A reserve asset created in 1967 by the IMF. SDRs are rights to draw on the IMF.

Spot Rate: A foreign exchange rate paid for delivery of a currency within two days from the date of the trade.

Spread: The difference between the bid and ask prices in a price quote, or the difference between the spot rate and the forward rate.

Strategic Alliance: A formal relationship between two companies to obtain economies of scale.

Strike Price: The price at which a currency can be sold or bought in an option contract.

Strong-Form Efficiency: When related to foreign exchange markets, this theory suggests that current exchange rates reflect all pertinent information, whether publicly available or privately held.

Subpart F: Foreign-source "unearned income" taxed by the Internal Revenue Service whether or not it is remitted to the United States.

Subsidiary: A foreign-based affiliate which is separately incorporated under the host country's law.

Subsidies: Direct or indirect governmental assistance to companies, thereby making them more competitive with imports.

Swap: An agreement between two parties who exchange sets of cash flows over a period of time in the future.

Swap Loan: A loan made by a local bank based on deposit of funds in offices of that bank in another country.

Swaption: An option to enter into a plain vanilla interest-rate swap.

Switch Trading: A practice where payments for exports to the East-bloc and nonmarket countries are made through clearing units whereby sales are balanced with purchases from other countries.

Syndicated Loan: A credit in which a group of banks makes funds available on common terms and conditions to a particular borrower.

Synergistic Effect: A situation where the combined company is worth more than the sum of its parts.

Systematic Risk: The risk common to all assets or all countries, which cannot be diversified away.

A Tender Offer: An offer to buy a certain number of shares at a specific price and on a specific date for cash, stock, or a combination of both.

Tariff: A duty or tax imposed on imported commodities.

Tariff Harmonization: The process of making tariffs more homogeneous by eliminating disparities in tariff rates on the same commodity.

Tax Haven: A country which promises permanent tax inducements to attract multinational companies.

Tax Holidays: The form of a complete tax exemption for the first few years given by a country when multinational firms invest their money in that country.

Technical Analysis: A currency forecasting technique that uses historical prices or trends.

Temporal Method: A method that translates the financial statements of a foreign affiliate into the parent reporting currency. Monetary assets and liabilities are translated at current exchange rates; nonmonetary assets, nonmonetary liabilities, and owners' equity are translated at historical exchange rates.

Third World: A term used to mean those countries other than the industrial countries and the centrally planned economies.

Time Draft: A draft payable a specified number of days after presentation to the drawee.

Trade Acceptance: A draft accepted by an importer or a business enterprise.

Trademark: A name or logo which distinguishes a company or product.

Translation Exposure: Exchange gains or losses that will occur when a company translates its foreign-currency operations into its home currency.

Transaction Exposure: The possibility that gains or losses may result from the settlement of transactions whose terms are stated in foreign currency.

Transfer Price: The price of goods and services sold between related parties such as parent and subsidiary.

Triangular Arbitrage: The process of buying and selling foreign exchange at a profit due to price discrepancies where three different currencies are involved.

Unilateral Transfer: In the balance of payments, the account which covers gifts by domestic residents to foreign residents, or gifts by the domestic government to foreign governments.

Unit of Account: A benchmark on which to base the value of payments.

Unitary Tax: A method of taxing a company's worldwide profits rather than on profits in the area where the taxing authorities are located.

Unsystematic Risk: The risk unique to a particular company or country, which can be diversified away.

Upvaluation: An official increase in the par value of a currency by the government.

United States-Mexico-Canada Agreement: The United States-Mexico-Canada Agreement (USMCA) entered into force on July 1, 2020. The **USMCA** substituted the North America Free Trade Agreement (NAFTA).

Value-Added Tax (VAT): A sales tax assessed at one or more stages in the production process but only on the value added during that production stage.

Vertical Integration: The integration of different stages in which the special drawing rights of a product move from the earliest production to the final distribution.

Weak-Form Efficiency: This theory implies that all information contained in past exchange-rate movements is fully reflected in current exchange rates.

Withholding Tax: A tax collected from income to employees, stockholders, and others; it is collected before receipt of the income.

World Bank: A multinational financial institution established in 1944 to enhance economic development.

World Trade Organization (WTO): The new organization which has replaced the General Agreement on Tariffs and Trade (GATT) since the Uruguay Round accord became effective on January 1, 1995.

Yankee Bonds: Dollar-denominated bonds issued within the United States by a foreign borrower.

Yield: The actual rate of return on a financial asset. It depends on the price paid for the security and the stated rate of interest or dividend.

Zero-Coupon Bond: A bond that pays no coupon interest and simply returns the face value at maturity.

INDEX